PERFORMANCE APPRAISAL

Published in Cooperation with the
A. G. Bush Library of Management, Organization and Industrial Relations
The University of Chicago

PERFORMANCE APPRAISAL

RESEARCH AND PRACTICE

EDITED BY

Thomas L. Whisler and Shirley F. Harper

THE UNIVERSITY OF CHICAGO

HOLT, RINEHART AND WINSTON

NEW YORK

Library of Congress Catalog Card Number: 62-9749
29348-0112

Printed in the United States of America

PREFACE

For centuries the world over, men who manage have sought more effective and systematic ways of appraising the performance of those whom they manage. In the United States these efforts have, over the past ninety years, produced an enormous literature of widely varying quality and content. Throughout this literature are scattered a number of good research reports as well as thoughtful analyses and criticisms of formal appraisal systems.

The literature of performance appraisal is found in a wide range of journals, books, and other publications. It covers a number of fields—industrial psychology, personnel administration, social psychology, and sociology—with contributions coming also from military psychology, industrial engineering, accounting, and public administration. Some of the materials are out of print or in journals dating back several decades, and are therefore accessible only in fairly large or specialized libraries.

We have visualized this volume as one solution to the problems posed by this vast and scattered literature. The book is designed to contain representative reports of theory, research, and practice in sufficient quantity and detail that it might serve as reference for researchers and administrators alike. We hope, also, that the organization of the material and the editorial comment will help make the interested student reader a well-informed one—aware of the controversial issues, the empirical evidence, and the interrelation of individual and organization problems centering around the appraisal of performance.

There are, of course, a variety of opinions on various aspects of performance appraisal and its use. The book begins with some statements defining appraisal and the general problems and questions in the field, and includes, in the first part, several empirical studies of the effect of various environmental factors on rating of individuals. The second part is devoted to the many formal techniques of appraisal.

In the first two parts, the grouping of readings and the order of their presentation differ little from the headings that would appear in the chapter on rating in an industrial psychology or personnel management textbook. The particular readings selected have been chosen on the basis of several criteria: how well they represent the total contributions on the specific topic, how well they are written, and how comprehensive and well thought out they are. In many cases, of course, the choice was difficult.

Part Three is a summary and evaluation of performance appraisal. Here the editors present their views of the place of this activity in the modern organization, taking into consideration contemporary social and economic factors affecting the job of the manager. A summary of technical developments, suggestions for making appraisal more effective, and some thoughts on research needs complete this section.

The final section of the volume is made up of case studies. One group of cases is described and analyzed by a single observer. This is followed by an interesting study of a cooperative rating plan run jointly by management and a union, and by several reports on executive appraisal in different companies.

We have been highly selective in compiling this material, but not solely because of the usual space limitations. With the proliferation of management literature today, we believe that carefully screening out what is worth preserving and building upon, becomes *in itself* an important contribution. Where appropriate, suggestions for further reading are included with the introductions to sections of the book. We have been sparing in these suggestions, mentioning only those publications we might have included in the book, had space not been so limited. A few general bibliographies are included with the introduction to Part One.

The one best way in performance appraisal still eludes us. However, the administrator may discover a useful pattern among the profusion of evaluations, counterevaluations, and reappraisals of technique and philosophy in the readings presented here. It is hoped that the same readings may provide the researcher with a clearer appreciation of the gaps in our knowledge in this area.

T. L. W.
S. F. H.

Chicago, Illinois
April 1962

ACKNOWLEDGMENTS

We extend sincere thanks to the authors whose works are a part of this book, and to the many publishers who so cordially responded to our requests for use of their material. We are especially grateful to two major sources, *Personnel* and other publications of the American Management Association, and *Personnel Psychology*.

Our helpers have been many, though we can mention but a few. The staff of the Bush Library deserve special thanks—for their forbearance during periods of intensive work on this volume, as well as for the assistance given by individuals. The wisdom and thoroughness of Mrs. Nancy Rennick, who worked with us during the initial selection of materials, are gratefully remembered. Other important contributions were made by Effie M. Phipps, Mrs. Lisa Freund, and Charles T. Payne of the Library, and by Mrs. Julie Swano of the Graduate School of Business.

We wish also to acknowledge the help of the Industrial Relations Center's member companies, who came through with a record 65 percent response to our inquiry about the potential usefulness of this book. And, finally, we thank our colleagues in the Industrial Relations Center and the Graduate School of Business, who have evaluated portions of the material for us and have otherwise helped along the way.

CONTENTS

PART ONE • THE NATURE OF PERFORMANCE APPRAISAL

The appraisal of individual performance is a fundamental human act. Long before the emergence of the great bureaucracies which dominate so much of our lives today, each man watched other men, appraising their behavior in terms of his own goals and needs and modifying his own behavior in accordance with his interpretation of what he saw. Relationships were initiated, strengthened, or severed on the basis of personal appraisals of others.

Even though we now live in a world of organizations, each of us still makes many of these personal appraisals—and subsequent choices. We choose doctors, hairdressers, business advisors, and others largely on the basis of our judgments of their effectiveness, the problem always being that of estimating future performance on the basis of past behavior. Eventually we work out rules of thumb to guide our choice—rules which cause us to search only for the certain restricted kinds of evidence we believe to be significant in making judgments. We differ in our ability as judges, probably largely because of differences in our rules of evidence and judgment (biases). Such differences in ability to judge are familiar to all of us.

Not only do we judge one another, but we are sensitive to the fact that others are always judging us. We are aware that our acceptability to others can be strongly affected by our ability to sense correctly what others think of us. Most of us want to know how others judge us, yet often, at the same time, resent a critical judgment.

This fundamental human experience of appraisal, action, feedback, reappraisal, also conditions the behavior of individuals within the organization. The problems inherent in interpersonal relations must be anticipated in organizational life as well as in general social experience.

But organizations—especially large, formal organizations—pose some additional problems. These organizations have goals apart from those of the people who make them up. Limited kinds of behavior are expected of the individual for limited periods. These limited activities are expected, in the aggregate, to contribute to the achievement of organization goals. In practice the impersonal mechanistic model of an organization underlying these expectations inevitably falls short of perfection for a number of reasons, reasons analyzed well by students of bureaucratic behavior.

Even if the model works rather well, it needs policing—control, if you prefer—and the police are usually people. They are people who appraise and reprimand or reward. Further, they are people with whom one usually has to continue to associate. The problems of interpersonal relations bulk large. Organizational goals are sometimes compromised for personal reasons.

Yet, organizations are here to stay. They have tremendous advantages, even when they work less than perfectly. And, if the organization is to function moderately well in the bureaucratic tradition, with formally defined roles and replaceable personnel, information—good information—must be available about the performance and capacities of its members. Where certain members are designated as executives and are given the power of decision, this kind of information becomes vital to their decisions and, hence, to their own success. So, appraisal is inevitable.

All these matters—the needs of individuals and their varying abilities (including the ability to judge), the needs of the organization for accurate information, and the difficult problems of judgment and transmission of information growing out of a highly personalized appraisal process—set the problem of performance appraisal in the organization.

Many able analysts have written about the matters just discussed. In this section are readings which give one perspective on these problems and, occasionally, some tentative solutions.

A. Appraisal of the Individual in the Organization

INDUSTRIAL MERIT RATING

JOSEPH TIFFIN AND ERNEST J. MCCORMICK

WHAT ARE RATING SCALES GOOD FOR?

ARTHUR W. KORNHAUSER

CURRENT TRENDS IN APPRAISAL AND DEVELOPMENT

GEORGE E. BROWN, JR. AND ALLAN F. LARSON

This section deals with the reasons that organizations seek a mechanism for formal appraisal of individuals, and with the needs—both organizational and individual—that formalized systems endeavor to meet. The brief excerpt from Tiffin and McCormick is an introductory statement. Note that Kornhauser's article antedates this by thirty-two years. While his optimism about the inevitability of great gains from rating seems old-fashioned, his statement of the purposes of rating makes it clear that we have known why if not how to appraise for a long time.

Brown and Larson state concisely some recent trends in appraisal, notably the strong emphasis upon its relation to development or training.

FURTHER READING

Halsey, George D., *Making and Using Industrial Service Ratings.* New York, Harper, 1944.

Jurgenson, Clifford E., Felix M. Lopez, Jr., and Kenneth E. Richards, *Employee Performance Appraisal Re-Examined,* (Personnel Report no. 613). Chicago, Public Personnel Association, 1961.

Mahler, Walter R., *Twenty Years of Merit Rating, 1926–1946.* New York, Psychological Corporation, 1947.

Selected, annotated, and classified references from industry, business, government, and education.

New York State Teachers Association, *Teacher Merit and Teacher Salary:* Report of Special Committee on Merit Payments, 1957. Albany, New York, 1957.

INDUSTRIAL MERIT RATING*

Joseph Tiffin

and Ernest J. McCormick

Merit rating is a systematic evaluation of an employee by his supervisor or by some other qualified person who is familiar with the employee's performance on the job. Merit ratings are usually made by means of a standardized form that is adapted to the needs of the particular industry. Usually the ratings are made at periodic intervals. A merit rating thus becomes a permanent part of an employee's record with a given company, and, at least in theory, is a part of the record that may be used by management in subsequent promotion, transfer, or layoff.

• THE GROWTH OF MERIT RATINGS

A survey of 400 companies carried out by the National Industrial Conference Board[1] indicated that about one half had employee merit rating plans. Although this is not a majority of the companies surveyed, it represents a significant proportion. Despite certain criticisms that have been made regarding merit rating systems, it seems probable that merit rating will remain an important part of personnel administration programs of many companies. Such an assumption justifies a rather careful discussion of this topic.

One point should be made clear immediately: although the term "merit rating" is new, the rating of men by supervisors is by no means a new development. Supervisors have *always* rated men, and it is no doubt true that the ratings made in a random, slipshod, and unsystematic fashion, unrecorded and undefended, whether valid or not, have in the past been just as important in determining whether a given employee should hold his job as any rating made by means of a modern merit rating chart. The changes that came with systematic merit rating, then, did not involve making ratings where none had existed before; rather they involved the transfer of ratings from haphazard, random, and frequently irresponsible judgments of supervisors, made perhaps during the heat of a quarrel, to ratings made calmly, deliberately, systematically, and in a manner that made the ratings, if not completely comparable from one employee to another, at least much more comparable than were the older, haphazard evaluations of employees by supervisors. The question, then, is not whether supervisors should rate their employees—this always has been and probably always will be done—but whether the use of a formal merit rating system will increase the value of such ratings both to management and to employees.

• PURPOSES OF MERIT RATING

Various reasons have been given by company executives for using merit rating systems. In a survey reported in *The*

[1] "Personnel Practices in Factory and Office," *Studies in Personnel Policy*, No. 145, National Industrial Conference Board, 1954.

Management Record,[2] fifteen different uses of merit ratings were listed. In general, however, these purposes seem to fall into two major categories: "administrative" and "self-improvement" (or clinical). In the second category, the emphasis is upon helping employees to understand their strengths and shortcomings, so that they can have some basis for self-improvement.

A summary of the uses of merit ratings suggests that the following are the most important.

Administrative Uses of Merit Ratings

Promotion. It is probable that this is the most important administrative use of merit ratings. It is to the common interests of both management and employees to promote employees into positions where they can most effectively utilize their abilities. It is a disservice to both parties to promote employees into positions where they cannot perform effectively at the time in question. A properly developed and administered merit rating system can aid in determining whether individuals should be considered for promotions. There is, however, an important distinction to be made in using merit ratings for this purpose. Such ratings should differentiate between the *performance* of the individual *on his present job,* and his *potentiality* for performance on a *higher level job.* The ability to perform effectively on one job does not necessarily give assurance of an employee's potentialities for greater responsibilities. These potentialities need to be evaluated separately.

Other Personnel Actions. There are occasions in most companies when it is necessary to consider various types of personnel actions such as *transfers, layoffs,* and *discharges.* In some cases such actions may be necessary because of unsatisfactory performance on a present job. In other cases the actions may be necessary because of economic conditions over which the company has no control, or because of changes in the production processes.

Although most companies like to avoid taking such actions as layoffs, discharges, and transfers necessitated by inadequate performance, when they become necessary such actions must be faced squarely. If the employees in question, as well as others, realize that fairness and consideration serve as the keynote of personnel policy, such actions may cause less criticism than if they are based on whim or expediency. When properly used, merit ratings can serve as the basis for fairness and consideration in taking such actions.

Wage and Salary Administration. In some companies, merit ratings are used as a basis for granting increases in wages or salaries. In some cases both merit and seniority are used in combination in granting wage or salary increases.

Training. An appropriate merit rating system can be useful for training purposes in two ways. In the first place, it can aid in identifying areas of skills or knowledges in which numerous employees are not up to par, thus pointing up general training deficiencies which presumably should be corrected by additional training. In the second place, ratings can help to identify individuals who may need additional, special training.

Criteria for Personnel Research. As indicated in Chapter 2, merit ratings fre-

[2] Summarized in "Appraisal of Job Performance," *Studies in Personnel Policy,* No. 211, National Industrial Conference Board, 1951.

quently are used as criteria for personnel research purposes such as in test validation.

Employee Self-Improvement. For a merit rating system to serve this purpose, it is necessary that each employee know where he stands with his supervisor. This involves an interview between a supervisor or some other company representative and the employee in question. It is very difficult for some supervisors to bring themselves to talk with their employees, especially with employees whose work is unsatisfactory. An improperly conducted interview can do more harm than good. The objectives of employee self-improvement are laudable, but a company needs to consider carefully the desirability of inaugurating a program that will fail or succeed depending upon the abilities of supervisors (or others) to conduct interviews with the employees in question.

A very strong case can be made out to provide for *someone* to discuss the ratings of employees with them, in order, as Davis[3] has pointed out, to avoid misinterpretation. Moore[4] has remarked that one of the most valuable uses of a rating program is to identify the weaknesses of employees that may be corrected. Knowles[5] also has emphasized that employees should be informed of their ratings and encouraged to overcome their shortcomings. Armstrong[6] has outlined several principles that may be advantageously followed in discussing ratings with employees, namely:

1. Criticism and reprimand should be based upon facts and should avoid personalities.
2. Public criticism is rarely justified.
3. Private reprimands should be preceded by a statement of some of the more desirable traits of the employee.

The experience of many industries has been that employees should be informed of their ratings by some production man—either the foreman himself or the departmental head. Production men, however, often require special training before they are able to do this smoothly and effectively. Many supervisors who are good production men are not very skillful in discussing a man's weak points face to face with him. To do so successfully calls for tact, objectivity, and a sincere interest in helping the man as well as the business. Many companies have found it wise to devote an extended series of training conferences to teaching supervisors how to inform their men of weak spots without offending the men. When this result has been accomplished and when a supervisor is able to talk face to face with his men about their weak as well as their strong points, a long step has been taken toward solidarity in the working group and toward the upgrading of men who otherwise might, for lack of information, either remain exactly where they are or actually regress.

If an employee, either for lack of experience or lack of information, continually performs his job in the wrong way, the supervisor will be doing both the employee and the company, as well as himself, a favor by bringing this matter to the employee's attention in the proper manner. Unless a supervisor is required periodically to evaluate all of his employees with regard to their ability in

[3] H. A. Davis, "Inefficient Efficiency Rating," *Personnel Journal,* 1944, 22, 268–270.

[4] H. Moore, "Real Use for Rating Scales," *Personnel Journal,* 1942, 21, 165–170.

[5] A. S. Knowles, "Merit Rating and Labor Management," *Personnel,* 1940, 17, 29–42.

[6] T. O. Armstrong, "Talking Your Ratings," *Personnel,* 1943, 20, 112–115.

various directions, it is quite likely that many aspects of an employee's performance that could easily be improved and that the employee himself would like to improve if he were made aware of his shortcomings, will go on from day to day without correction on his part. To inform an employee of his strong and weak points is not only a reasonable and fair thing to do but is also good business for any management that is sincerely interested in having its employees perform their jobs in the best possible way.

• CONSIDERATIONS OF MERIT VS. SENIORITY

Although the attitudes of unions toward merit ratings vary a great deal, by and large they tend to take a dim view of merit ratings when used for administrative purposes such as promotions, layoffs, and wage increases. Historically, unions place primary emphasis on seniority as the basis for such actions. Seniority, of course, can be objectively determined, whereas merit ratings, by their nature, are based on subjective judgments.

The provisions of union contracts regarding the use of seniority and merit ratings for personnel actions vary. Although some such contracts provide that most personnel actions will be based exclusively on seniority, most of them include provisions such as the following: "Promotions within the bargaining unit will be made on the basis of merit, other things being equal,"[7] or that seniority shall govern promotions when the "ability, skills, and job performance of applicants are equal." Usually the burden of proof for characterizing relative merit of employees in such cases lies with management.

The extent to which seniority is a factor in various types of personnel actions in non-union companies is summarized in Table 1, which is based on a survey among 130 companies.[8] It can be seen that even non-union companies place a great deal of emphasis on seniority in taking various personnel actions. However, of a total of 110 of these companies (with less than 400 employees each), only four used seniority as a *sole* basis for granting promotions. More typically, various personnel actions were based in part on other considerations. Eighty-two per cent of the companies, for example, considered merit or ability in conjunction with seniority. Other factors that were taken into account by some companies included marital or family status, physical fitness, hardship, attendance, and cooperativeness.

Table 1

THE SENIORITY FACTOR IN DIFFERENT SITUATIONS

SITUATION WHERE SENIORITY IS A FACTOR	COMPANIES NO.	PER CENT
Layoffs	116	89
Promotion	107	82
Rehiring after layoff	96	74
Transfer	69	53
Others	7	5

Source: Adapted from "Seniority Systems in Non-union Companies," *op. cit.*

[7] "Appraisal of Job Performance," *Studies in Personnel Policy,* No. 121, National Industrial Conference Board, 1951.

[8] "Seniority Systems in Non-union Companies," *Studies in Personnel Policy,* No. 110, National Industrial Conference Board, 1950.

WHAT ARE RATING SCALES GOOD FOR?*

Arthur W. Kornhauser

Few personnel procedures have conclusively justified their existence. The sceptic can retain his honest doubts in the face of all the objective evidence we can spread before him. What we have, at best, are certain bits of valid evidence which we find helpful in forming our judgment about this or that device. Usually, in decisions regarding personnel policies and procedures, the directly relevant data are woefully inadequate—though they are far from worthless. Decisions are made largely on the basis of our impressions and feelings—the results of our unanalyzed previous experience. What we need to do is to improve these decisions, even in the absence of scientific bodies of knowledge. That means, above all else, that we must think analytically, that we must see the whole range of varied considerations which each problem involves. The fragments of evidence that are available can then be fitted into the total picture and seen in true perspective.

Rating scales, like other personnel devices, are in need of continual reexamination—critical and analytical. What is demanded is not only more factual evidence, valuable as that will be, but also a view of the entire array of evidence that is relevant—indirect, intangible, and impressionistic evidence as well as direct statistical measurements. The present paper attempts to suggest the main directions in which that evidence may be looked for.

* From *Journal of Personnel Research,* Vol. 5, no. 5, September 1926, pp. 189–193. Copyright 1926 by *The Journal of Personnel Research* (now called *Personnel Journal*). Reprinted by permission of *Personnel Journal*.

• DIRECT AND INDIRECT EFFECTS OF RATING SYSTEMS[1]

Rating scales are simply convenient forms for securing more adequate personal estimates of people than are obtained by less formal methods. The ratings are typically estimates given periodically by executives, supervisors, or teachers concerning the workers or students under them. The judgments may, however, be made by acquaintances, by interviewers, by subordinates rather than by those superior in rank; or they may be ratings by the person himself. The estimates are usually of such qualities as intelligence, initiative, industry, and so on. A variety of rating procedures are in use. The methods range from the simple labeling of people as "Very Good," "Good," "Average," etc., and the arranging of individuals in rank order from highest to lowest, to more refined devices such as the Scott "man-to-man comparison rating scale" and the "graphic rating scale."[2]

[1] The discussion which follows is stated in terms meant to apply both to industry and to educational institutions. The uses of rating scales and the ends served by them in the two fields appear sufficiently similar to justify this common treatment. Slight adaptations of wording and illustration, and certain shifts of emphasis, will make the points fit one or the other field a little more specifically and concretely.

[2] Descriptions of the rating forms and discussions of the several methods may be found in the following: W. D. Scott and R. C.

The most obvious purpose of any rating system is the securing of personal information that will be useful to administrative officers engaged in personnel activities. In addition, however, important results are achieved by the rating process in the effects it has on the people rated and on those doing the rating. The procedure may also have distinct value in disseminating the personnel viewpoint and in supplying data for personnel research. The educational and inspirational effects of rating systems may, indeed, be as important as the obtaining of information about the individuals judged. It certainly is true that these less obvious results deserve careful consideration when we seek to evaluate the use of rating scales. A brief sketch of the several points follows:

1. Personal estimates are an aid to administrative officers. The estimates furnish useful information about characteristics and abilities over and above what is supplied in other records. Attention is called to individuals who are exceptionally strong or exceptionally weak in certain traits and also to cases where the person is rated markedly high or low by particular raters. Furthermore, successive ratings lead to a recognition of marked improvement or retrogression. As a result of these facts:

a. Better guidance and training are made possible. The selection of occupation and of courses of study can be more adequately adapted to the needs and characteristics of the individual. In general, the efforts to adjust the person to his opportunities and limitations are made more effective.

b. Better judgments are made possible in administrative decisions concerning the individual—in matters of promotion, transfer, dismissal, granting of special privileges, wage adjustments, and so on.

c. Better recommendations and reference reports are made possible (especially true in the case of students who are seeking employment).

2. The use of the personal estimates has an educational and stimulating effect on the persons who are rated. This influence arises in two ways:

a. The knowledge that his abilities and characteristics are being studied and recorded leads the individual to strive to make a good impression. He is likely, moreover, to be favorably affected by the thought that his personal points of excellence are appreciated and that they (as well as his deficiencies) will be used in all decisions regarding him—including recommendations to future prospective employers. He recognizes as never before that the management (or school administration) is really interested in him.

b. When the estimates are made known to the person in a tactful and sane manner, he can gain some useful views of himself. The material is likely to make him do some real thinking about himself and his possibilities. This self-analysis in some cases will lead to serious consideration of vocational aptitudes and plans. It will also suggest the whole problem of developing a more effective personality and may lead to efforts in that direction.

Clothier: *Personnel Management,* Chap. XIII; D. G. Paterson: Methods of Rating Human Qualities, *The Annals,* November, 1923, pp. 81–93; M. Freyd: "The Graphic Rating Scale," *J. Educ. Psychol.,* 1923, Vol. 14, pp. 83–102; R. W. Kelly: *Training the Industrial Worker;* H. D. Kitson: *The Psychology of Vocational Adjustment,* Chap. XII.

3. *The making of these personal judgments has a beneficial effect on the persons doing the rating.* The procedure brings prominently to the attention of faculty members, supervisors, or executives the importance of knowing their students and workers *as individuals.* The necessity of giving estimates on personal characteristics leads the rater to a thoughtful analysis of the people rated and tends to make him more alive to his opportunities and responsibilities in developing men.

4. *The rating activities help to introduce, reenforce, and keep alive, the "personnel spirit."* Specific personnel devices and bits of technique are less important than a pervasive personnel spirit and an appreciation of personnel objectives by everyone within an organization. The use of rating scales helps significantly in this larger aim. The rating scale concerns everyone—those rated, those rating, and those using the ratings. It constitutes a natural and useful link between personnel officers and other members of the organization, leading readily to discussions of the use of rating scales in dealing with people individually and personally—and thence to the whole personnel "philosophy."[3]

5. *The ratings furnish useful material for personnel research.* Problems of selection and turnover continually call for study of the personal qualities of men as determinants of their success. Rating scales aid in ascertaining the personal traits which differentiate poor workers from good workers. They are useful in checking the results of mental tests and other selective devices. Ratings may likewise be valuable as a technique for studying such psychological problems as the existence of "personality types," the interrelatedness of traits, the influence of various factors in determining our estimates of people, and so on.

• SPECIAL ADVANTAGES OF THE RATING SCALE METHOD

The effects of rating systems which have been outlined are true in some degree of any procedure for obtaining estimates of individuals' characteristics. The standardized rating scale is ordinarily believed to possess certain special merits as compared with informal and unstandardized personal estimates. Some of the more important points usually adduced in support of the rating scale procedure are as follows:

1. The rating scale is analytic; it calls for judgments on a variety of distinct and defined character traits. These traits have been carefully chosen as the essential ones for the purpose. The analytic nature of the scale prevents the rater's seeing only one or two striking characteristics and omitting others. It makes the rater stop and think instead of using merely his first off-hand opinion. It also tends to keep him from letting a single general impression blind him to specific strong and weak points in the person rated.

2. The ratings are explicit and unambiguous, and they are recorded. This means that the estimates can be studied, compared, checked over. The person

[3] It is enlightening to note that the personnel system entered the Army in 1917 by the rating scale route. In a number of colleges and business establishments rating procedures have likewise been prime influences in establishing and maintaining the personnel point of view.

doing the rating is likely to be more careful when he recognizes that inaccurate ratings will reflect on him. More important, the ratings can be clearly interpreted; they are not vague statements which can mean almost anything that one pleases to read into them.

3. The ratings are uniform and standardized. Estimates given by different raters and estimates made at different times are directly comparable. These ratings can be readily compiled and summarized for use.

4. The ratings are quantitative. This makes especially feasible the recording, combination, and statistical treatment of the data. Judgments of different raters are easily compared with one another, averaged, or checked against independent facts concerning the person rated. Bad rating tendencies can be detected and, in some measure, corrected. It becomes possible to find out quantitatively how reliable and usable the personal ratings are.

Moreover, those rated can be directly compared with one another and the relative position of each can be stated. This is to be contrasted with the results from a nonquantitative plan of estimates. With the rating scale, such statements as this are made possible: "In intelligence, this man is in the top ten per cent of his group, according to the average rating of three supervisors." Without the quantitative scale, we would be able to say: "One judge states that the man is 'exceptionally alert and keen.' Another says he is a 'brilliant fellow,' etc." The trouble is that we do not know how these various phrases are related to one another.

5. Ratings are given periodically and systematically. Where this is not the case, judgments are likely to be too much colored by some recent striking achievement or failure on the part of the person rated.

6. Finally, some rating scales (particularly the graphic scale) are extremely easy to use. The rater does not have to rack his brain for appropriate adjectives nor to hunt for something to say.

It should be added that the actual value of all these points is not beyond dispute. The evidence in support of some of the contentions is meager. They are *a priori* arguments which have to be accepted or rejected largely on the basis of personal opinion.

In opposition to these points it may well be argued, for example, that nonquantitative expressions of opinion about people are more personal and realistic. Specific facts can be given about the person rated and his special peculiarities can be reported in a way that it is not possible in a formal quantitative rating. There is a great amount of truth in this view. Frequently one appropriate remark concerning an individual tells us more about him than would a long string of numerical ratings.

The practical conclusion is obvious. Quantitative and nonquantitative reports are not alternatives; they are supplementary. We need to use both.

THE NEED FOR • QUANTITATIVE STUDIES OF RATINGS

If the foregoing paragraphs are even approximately correct, they mean that the task of evaluating rating scales is exceedingly complex. The evidence to be weighed in any given situation ranges from detailed statistical studies of the actual uniformity of the ratings, to vague impressions about the effects on morale or the growth of personnel spirit among executives. Technical statistical studies alone can never give a final judgment as to the value of the effects produced by rating scales.

But statistical analysis of rating scale results is highly useful even though we recognize the intangible and unmeasured effects of ratings which are not appraised statistically. After all, the ratings must have some degree of reliability if they are to be useful in the directions indicated. By studying the ratings quantitatively we can learn whether they do actually show that some individuals are high and others low in the several traits. We can also see how much the estimates vary with the rater and the activities on which the ratings are based. To the extent that ratings do not show reliable differences among the people rated, to that extent their direct administrative usefulness is reduced and, indirectly, their beneficial effects on those rated and those doing the rating are also diminished.

Analytical study of the rating results is needed, then, to help throw light on how well the rating procedure works. Such study, in addition, shows some of the causes for poor results and thus makes possible corrective and remedial measures for improving the rating methods. It is this possibility of finding how well ratings are working and of ascertaining where the trouble lies, that constitutes one of the great advantages of the formal quantitative rating scale.

CURRENT TRENDS IN APPRAISAL AND DEVELOPMENT*

George E. Brown, Jr. and Allan F. Larson

The increasing attention paid by management to the systematic appraisal of an employee's performance by his supervisor, and the development of his capacity to perform more effectively on the job, has resulted largely from the findings of human relations research on the functioning of human beings in group or organizational settings. Research has shown that the quality of leadership displayed by the supervisor is a key factor in effective group functioning. Formal appraisal and development practices provide an opportunity for the use of effective leadership, as well as for meeting employee's needs in such areas as security in work relationships, aid in self-development, and recognition of achievements. Thus Lawrence Appley described management as "the development of people and not the direction of things."[1]

With the aim of exploring current trends in appraisal and development practices, the authors recently surveyed 23 governmental and industrial organizations in California. Included in the study were seven government agencies (with a total of 150,000 employees), six utilities (with 55,000), three aircraft companies (with 85,000), three oil companies (with 15,000), and six companies engaged in manufacturing and other miscellaneous activities (with 35,000). Information was obtained from interviews with personnel and industrial relations staff members, and from manuals, policy statements, forms, and other material where possible.

Before discussing individual company programs it may be helpful to note some of the more general trends observed.

The separation of performance appraisal from salary administration was virtually complete. While almost all the companies claimed some form of "merit" pay system, particularly at the supervisory and executive levels, the procedures for administering salaries on a merit basis were almost completely divorced from the procedures for performance appraisal. Only a few of the government agencies showed vestiges of a direct relationship between the two, mainly in the form of requiring a "satisfactory" rating for salary raises.

• EMPHASIS ON DEVELOPMENT

The use of the term "merit rating" to denote performance appraisal is also declining. Instead, "merit" is now used to describe pay plans based on regular review of individual rates, with advances recommended by supervisors after considering such factors as performance, time since last increase, budgetary allotments, pay range for the job, profit picture of the enterprise, seniority, and morale of the work group. Appraisal

[1] L. A. Appley, "Management The Simple Way," *Personnel*, January, 1943, pp. 595–603.

* From *Personnel*, Vol. 34, no. 4, January–February 1958, pp. 51–58.

plans were designated by such titles as Job Performance Review, Progress Review Guide, Employee Progress Report, Report of Performance, Appraisal and Development Guide, Employee Counseling Program, Performance Evaluation, Employee Appraisal and Development Plan, and so forth. The emphasis is on such key words as "performance," "progress," "development," and "appraisal." Titles implying that the program relates to the employee's personal characteristics, rather than his performance, or that it includes an exact or mathematical measurement, are not in favor.

Within the past few years a marked change in attitude toward performance appraisal has taken place in the government agencies studied. Formerly, merit rating was considered as a method used by the supervisor to discipline the employees under his direction. This approach was frequently incorporated in the law or regulations governing the merit rating program, and the ratings were used to withhold salary raises and to influence other personnel transactions. As a result of the attitudes of both employee and supervisor, the rating systems tended to become perfunctory and of no real value. Thus the second Hoover Commission found that in the federal government, performance ratings "were not in fact a means of measuring the relative merit of employees," and that approximately 98 per cent of those rated were lumped together in the "satisfactory" category while the remaining 2 per cent fell into the "outstanding" or "unsatisfactory" category.[2] "The processing of papers to achieve this Olympian judgment," the Commission noted, was "a burden far beyond any benefits it produced." The rating systems used by the State of California, City of Los Angeles, and County of Los Angeles were also subject to this type of criticism.

At the present time the major emphasis is on the development of both the employee and the supervisor in the effective performance of their jobs. The periodic appraisal is merely one of several related activities aimed at the improvement of work performance. These activities may include:

1. Securing a clear-cut understanding of the duties of the position by the employee, through discussion with the supervisor and other means.
2. Establishing agreement between employee and supervisor on reasonable performance standards for the job.
3. Continuous observation and discussion with the employee of his work, with particular attention to activities demonstrating either unusual accomplishment or the need for assistance or training.
4. Preparation and review of the periodic performance appraisal report.
5. Discussion of the appraisal report with the employee.
6. Developing plans for employee improvement and progress which are mutually agreed upon.
7. Following up the appraisal and employee development plans with specific action.

• SOME AGENCY PROGRAMS

The County of Los Angeles has taken the lead in this type of program. Its program is centrally coordinated by the

[2] Task Force Report on Personnel and Civil Service, Commission on Organization of the Executive Branch of the Government, U. S. Government Printing Office, Washington, D. C., February, 1955, p. 91.

Employee Development Division of the Civil Service Department, with support from the Civil Service Commission, the Board of Supervisors, and the Chief Administrative Officer, along with the County Personnel Council, representing department management. The division helps operating departments make performance evaluation "their" program.[3] While only one staff member is used for this activity, his work is closely coordinated with supervisory improvement programs and other training activities carried on by the division.

The County has also gone further than the other agencies in the area in using departmental ratings of employees for promotional purposes. While not directly related to the periodic performance evaluations, these appraisals of promotability are undoubtedly aided by them. The supervisory ratings of promotability, made only in connection with promotional examinations, are given a weight of 20 per cent on the final grade. Thus their influence may be substantial.

The cities of Burbank and Glendale are using similar performance appraisal plans which appear to be working effectively. The State of California is developing an extensive training program in what it calls a "constructive approach" to performance evaluation, with emphasis on improving supervisor-employee relationships and developing more effective employees. The Los Angeles City Board of Education, which has rated employees for many years, is currently analyzing its programs for both teachers and other employees to determine if improvements can be made, particularly in supervisory training in the value of performance appraisal. The East Bay Municipal Utility District evaluates the performance of all nonsupervisory employees and considers this a key aspect of its personnel program.

Each of the four major utilities studied has a well-developed program of employee appraisal. In three, the program applies to all the employees, while in the fourth it is used primarily for the management group only—about 20 per cent of the employees. However, the fourth utility plans to extend its program to cover more employees as soon as possible.

• BETTER JOB PERFORMANCE

The major emphasis is on the development of both the employee and his supervisor in better performance of their work. The important contribution of improved human relations skills to this goal is recognized. The relationship between performance appraisal and the selection and training of supervisory and administrative personnel is more highly developed than in the government agencies, undoubtedly because of the greater freedom of private utilities in managing personnel.

Three utilities have ratings made by several persons. In two companies the rating is made jointly at a conference; in the third, ratings are made individually and combined into a composite by the Industrial Relations Department. The fourth utility uses a "field review" type of rating, with a staff member from the Employee Relations office assisting the supervisor in making his rating.

[3] Los Angeles County Civil Service Commission: 43rd Annual Report, 1956, p. 18 ff.

A conference between the supervisor and the employee to discuss the performance appraisal is used by the four concerns as the primary means of effecting changes in attitude and performance. Coordinated training programs for supervisory development are also used in all four companies.

Among the eleven other companies surveyed, one has no formal employee-appraisal program and one is currently developing a new program after discarding a previously used plan. The other nine have plans varying in comprehensiveness. There seems to be a close relationship between a company's reputation for progressive management and the development of its employee appraisal program.

All the plans are aimed primarily at improved employee performance. The majority provide for rating by the immediate supervisor only, but several provide for committee ratings for higher level jobs. Review of the ratings by a high-level supervisor is common. All the plans include provision for some form of discussion with the employee of his evaluation.

The better plans place more emphasis upon the appraisal interview, with training of supervisors in counseling and a follow-up of the interview. Some of the companies use the continuous recording of specific examples of good and poor work performance (critical incidents) and center the appraisal interviews on them rather than on general factors such as "adaptability" or "initiative." All the companies consider that the details of the rating forms are of secondary importance, and that the forms should be developed with the cooperation of the persons who will use them.

MANAGEMENT • DEVELOPMENT PROGRAMS

Many of the organizations have formal management-development plans based upon and closely related to their performance-appraisal plans. As we have noted, in most cases the primary goal of the appraisal plan is closely related to employee or management development. Formal management-development plans are being adopted with increasing frequency, most recently by the larger utilities. Public agencies appear to be lagging in this area, probably because of the legal restrictions on the placement and promotion of employees. No public agency has a formal management-development program comparable to those in progressive private companies, although in some cases informal efforts are being made.

Three of the four utilities are devoting major efforts to the systematic development of management personnel. At least half of the other firms surveyed also have programs of various degrees of formality. Standard Oil of California and Crown Zellerbach both have programs widely recognized as outstanding.

It may be helpful to discuss in detail four of the better programs so that similarities in approach may be noted.

Company A. While this company, as a matter of policy, delegates substantial authority for personnel management to its geographical divisions, the importance of securing capable replacements for the present management group has resulted in the assignment of the top-level general management staff to this activity. On a company-wide basis the management development program includes:

1. Estimating future needs for management personnel for a period of several years based upon retirements, resignations, death, company growth, and requirements of increased technology and growing complexity of management positions.
2. Estimating personnel available to fill projected needs.
3. Appraisal of existing personnel on a systematic basis as to their potential for management jobs.
4. Planning of individual development programs.
5. Training of management personnel through on-the-job coaching, job rotation, special courses, and so forth.

Ninety existing jobs of various kinds have been earmarked as rotational positions for training purposes. Personnel are assigned to these jobs for not over two years as part of their development program. Ten additional jobs have been allocated to the program to be established as needed. District managers and other key field personnel are also brought in to the main offices for six months to a year as part of a general orientation program.

The existing rate of promotion into and within management positions, which is now about 500 per year, is expected to increase for at least the next 10 years. Data obtained from analysis of projected retirements, available replacements, and performance appraisals has been used to prepare replacement tables and color-coded organization charts to aid in visualizing the problem. Organizational units which have no available replacements are thus highlighted, as well as promotional ladders, dead-end jobs, and so forth. The close relationship between organization planning and management development is also emphasized.

A comprehensive manual sets forth the basic philosophy of the program—that the company's most valuable asset is its employees and that good supervisors are concerned with training and developing employees to the greatest extent possible. The ultimate objective of the program is to insure qualified candidates for positions at all levels of management. At the same time, this provides opportunities for capable men to progress to successively higher levels, as well as a method of planning for their development. By analyzing the need for candidates for all types of positions, the program can concentrate training and development efforts in the area where they are most needed.

Need for Management Replacements

Company B. This company has initiated a comprehensive management development program within the past year. In reviewing the content of the program, as presented in company manuals, its similarity to the program of Company A is evident. While this is due in part to collaboration in the development of the two programs, it also reflects the growth of an agreed-upon body of principle and practice. The company's "Management Development Manual" states that its need for the program is intensified by the uniformity of age among the three or four top-management levels, and that this could mean a crippling loss to the company unless properly qualified replacements become available in the relatively short span of years during which most of these men will leave the company. The major aims of the program are:

1. To insure that each employee has the opportunity to use his talents as completely as possible, both for his own satisfaction and for the good of the organization.
2. To motivate and encourage each employee to develop himself.
3. To provide a formal method for appraising and recording the company's manpower assets in terms of both current and future needs.
4. To foster among management a full appreciation of the obligation to appraise, select, train, place, and use key personnel on a company-wide, rather than a purely departmental basis.
5. To build up a roster of qualified people to fill management positions.

The over-all direction of the program is the function of a management development committee. Department heads are responsible for applying the program within their own divisions. The key man in the operation is the line supervisor. The job of coordinating and administering the program rests with a management development coordinator.

Company C. This company has an outstanding program which has served as a model, in part or in whole, for many other companies. It was established on a formalized, company-wide basis in 1946, with these aims:

1. To provide adequate reserves of qualified, seasoned candidates to fill executive, supervisory, and key staff positions as needs occur throughout the company and its subsidiaries.
2. To assure promising people the opportunity to develop and use their capabilities to the mutual advantage of individual and company.
3. As replacements occur, to assure that key positions are filled by individuals fully qualified to meet all requirements.
4. To develop management's appreciation of the obligation to select, train, appraise, place, and use key personnel on a company-wide rather than a departmental basis.

The program provides for the maintenance of essential records such as organization charts, job descriptions, personnel inventories, appraisals of performance, and present and future replacement schedules. Organization charts and job descriptions are prepared by the department on organization. The personnel inventory, or personal experience record, is prepared by the employee and is supplemented by appraisal records of his performance and potentiality. Replacement schedules, in the form of organization charts, show incumbents and replacement candidates who are or will be qualified.

The program is administered by an office of executive development, a staff agency which advises and assists management. It receives all job requests and after careful screening prepares a list of available candidates. The list is then discussed with the line department, which makes the final selection.

The mutual advantage of the program to the company and to its employees is stressed throughout. From the company standpoint, the purpose is to provide adequate reserves to fill all key positions. From the employee standpoint, the purpose is to assure that each employee's potential will be considered in filling relevant jobs.

Development of Management Potential

Company D. This company has a well worked-out program, whose details are set forth in its "Management Development Manual," which covers such matters as appraisal procedures, preparation of replacement tables, training, and promotion. Appraisals are made by committees of three to five persons, including the immediate supervisor, and include a narrative account of the employee's job performance, his personal qualifications, his placement, plans for his development, and general remarks. Appraisals must be unanimously agreed upon by the committee. There is no numerical or graphic rating. A "management potential" form is prepared separately which estimates the employee's readiness for promotion and the direction of the promotion. Appraisals are generally made every one or two years. While discussion of the appraisal with the employee is not required, it usually takes place on an informal basis. Of prime importance is the preparation and carrying out of the development plans for the employee. This generally involves personal study, on-the-job training, job rotation, participation in conferences and institutes, and so forth. The company may create managerial training jobs, either line or staff, as needed.

Central files are maintained and used for filling management vacancies wherever they occur. The program is closely coordinated with organzation planning to insure flexibility and maximum opportunity for development.

The major goal is to maintain a climate favorable to the development of employees and with particular emphasis on those with management potential. Basically the program is considered a line responsibility, but there is a central staff of three persons. The organization planning unit is about the same size.

• TENTATIVE CONCLUSIONS

On the basis of the various findings discussed, the authors offer these tentative conclusions. In our opinion these programs represent more than a new set of techniques to get more production from employees, or to improve the management of an enterprise, important as these goals may be. They indicate the development of a mature philosophy governing the relations of people working together in formal organizations—one based on the relatively new science of human relations. The basic concern for the growth and development of people, which is the core of our education and government, is becoming respectable as a principle of management. A business enterprise or government agency, which fosters the development of people and what Erich Fromm calls the "productive personality," will get a full return from its manpower resources.

As has been said, performance appraisal and development practices provide an opportunity for using the skills and attitudes of effective leadership. The supervisor who uses these skills and attitudes, and the organization which encourages their use, are contributing to the goal of a full and satisfying life in the framework of our industrial society.

B. Issues and Problems in Appraisal

1. PROBLEMS RELATED TO HUMAN JUDGMENT

THE NATURE AND INTERPRETATION OF EMPLOYEE RATINGS

HAWTHORNE WORKS, WESTERN ELECTRIC COMPANY

THE ABILITY TO JUDGE PEOPLE

RONALD TAFT

The first reading in this section is a sensible statement, by the personnel department in a large company, about the problem of appraising others in an organizational context. This statement was issued some twenty years ago in a company which had already had much experience with formal appraisal. In the second reading, Taft summarizes the wide range of research on the varying abilities of individuals to judge. This complete review of the literature includes an extensive bibliography, which has been retained here as an aid to those interested in further study of the subject.

FURTHER READING

Flanagan, John C., "The Evaluation of Methods in Applied Psychology and the Problem of Criteria," *Occupational Psychology,* Vol. 30, no. 1, January, 1956, pp. 1–9.

Mandell, Milton M., "Supervisory Characteristics and Ratings: A Summary of Recent Research," *Personnel,* Vol. 32, no. 5, March, 1956, pp. 435–440.

U. S. Office of Strategic Services, *Assessment of Men,* by the OSS Assessment Staff. New York, Holt, Rinehart and Winston, 1948.

Vernon, P. E., *The Assessment of Psychological Qualities by Verbal Methods: A Survey of Attitudes Tests, Rating Scales and Personality Questionnaires.* Part IV, "Assessment of Human Traits by Ratings," pp. 43–66. (Industrial Health Research Board, Great Britain, Report no. 83) London, His Majesty's Stationery Office, 1938.

THE NATURE AND INTERPRETATION OF EMPLOYEE MERIT RATINGS*

Hawthorne Works, Western Electric Company

The system of employee merit ratings as discussed in the following manuscript was devised at Western Electric's Hawthorne Works, Chicago, and has been used at Hawthorne. Other Western Electric plant locations may use different systems of merit ratings.

• THE NATURE OF EMPLOYEE RATINGS

First of all, it is necessary to keep in mind that a rating is a *record of opinion* about an employee. Much misunderstanding of the use and interpretation of ratings has grown out of failure to recognize this principle.

Interest in employee ratings involves, fundamentally, a recognition of the fact that most of our important decisions about employees are based, in part, on "intangible" factors—that is, on considerations which cannot be "measured" in the sense in which the number of piece parts in a pan can be counted. We know, for example, that, assuming that a man's output is up to standard, his versatility and dependability might weigh more heavily in his supervisor's estimate than would unusually high output. His ability to cooperate, to get along with people, to "fit" into the organization, will also count. Such factors as these receive consideration in all personnel adjustments, such as lay-off, transfer, promotion, and rate revisions.

These intangible factors are not measured as piece parts are counted, but this must not be interpreted as meaning that they are not "real." We are constantly making judgments, such as that Jones is more dependable than Smith, that he has more initiative, that he makes a better impression on people, that on the whole he is doing a better job. We have some confidence in these judgments, and we act on the basis of them.

That these judgments of intangible factors are not a figment of our own imagination is evidenced by the fact that *other persons who are in a position to judge Jones and Smith will agree with us reasonably well.* If this were not true, no group of supervisors could ever reach an argeement that Jones should be promoted, given a raise, or retained on the pay roll instead of Smith, whenever such a decision is required.

The fact that various competent judges will agree reasonably well in their judgments of intangible factors bears on the statement sometimes made, that "ratings are really a rating of the rater rather than of the person presumably being rated." Of course, such factors as personal prejudice and imperfect opportunity to observe a person color our ratings of him. However, we could not agree reasonably well with other persons, either in rating people or in making personnel changes,

* From Training Department, Personnel Service Branch, Chicago. Used by permission of the Company.

if these purely personal peculiarities were the dominant factor in our judgments.

It is sometimes said that "it is wrong to pigeonhole people. People vary in such complicated ways, and the whole thing is so 'intangible' that we should not try to sum it all up and put them in fixed pigeonholes."

Actually, it is *inevitable* that people are pigeonholed. Their rates of pay pigeonhole them with respect to each other. Their level in the Company pigeonholes them. All the machinery for "maintenance of pay differentials" and for providing labor grades and supervisory levels points to the necessity of classifying, or "pigeonholing," people in a few broad ways.

It is management's concern simply to insure that the classification of people shall be done wisely rather than by chance, and that the classification shall be subject to frequent and careful revision. Ratings should be viewed, then, as a tool for use in the *revision of classifications,* rather than as a device which of itself tends to "pigeonhole" persons who otherwise would not or should not be pigeonholed.

The above presents some thoughts with regard to the nature of ratings. It is based on recognition of the fact that human judgment plays an important part in our classification of people; that judgment is dependable in that various qualified judges will agree reasonably well in their judgments of people; and that ratings must be interpreted as a *record of judgments or opinions.*

We may now turn to some precautions with regard to the use of ratings, keeping in mind the nature of ratings. Two precautions are of particular importance. These are:

1. A rating should always be interpreted as having a "zone of uncertainty."
2. No rating should be expected to tell the whole story with regard to an individual.

These two points are discussed in the following paragraphs.

• THE "ZONE OF UNCERTAINTY" IN RATING

We have so far focused attention on the fact that in our judgments of the intangible factors affecting the value of employees we agree reasonably well, so that records of judgment, or personnel adjustments based on judgment, will not be a matter of whim or chance. It will be obvious, however, that these judgments cannot be perfect, and that in consequence, no record of them can be expected to be 100% correct. For example, if there are 25 punch press operators in a department, a rating will show that one of them ranks 12th, another 13th. The "zone of uncertainty" is certainly wide enough that no important differential treatment should be accorded these two men on the assumption that one was really better than the other. On the other hand, the man who ranks first in such a group, and the one who ranks last, are almost certainly different. The "zone of uncertainty" would not be this broad.

The "zone of uncertainty" is affected by many factors. If we keep in mind that ratings are *records of a man's opinions,* it will be clear that we cannot expect the rating assigned by a man to provide direct comparisons of a type which the man himself is not in a position to make. His rating cannot tell you something which he himself does not even know.

For example, a man's highest ranking punch press operator is very likely better than his 25th operator. But is his best operator better than some *other* supervisor's 25th operator in some other organization? The rater himself does not know. We may say that in all probability the two organizations are reasonably comparable, so that the best man in one is likely to be better than the lowest man in the other. But our "zone of uncertainty" is greater than when the men being compared are both in the same organization.

It may be useful to list some of the major factors which affect the "zone of uncertainty."

1. The smaller the number of raters, the greater the zone of uncertainty.
2. The smaller the number of employees in similar work in the organization, the greater the zone of uncertainty. A rating of departmental stenographers, for example, where a rater may know the work of no other stenographers, has a wider zone of uncertainty than a rating of punch press operators in organizations employing a large number of people on such work.
3. Comparisons among men in different organizations have a wider zone of uncertainty than among men in the same organization.
4. Comparisons of men in somewhat different occupations have a wider zone of uncertainty than among men doing exactly the same work.
5. The longer the time since the rating was made, the greater the zone of uncertainty that it is true at the present time.

All these data are available on the individual personnel merit-rating record form and are kept in mind by the personnel organization in interpreting ratings.

• RATINGS DO NOT TELL THE WHOLE STORY

Disregarding the zone of uncertainty, it must be kept in mind that our judgment of a man's general effectiveness, for example, is not the only factor involved when he is being considered for transfer, upgrading, rate revision, lay-off, or other change in status. The promotion of the most "meritorious" individual is not always the most equitable or the most sensible action to take at a given moment. Some other individual may be peculiarly fitted for the particular job which is to be filled. Or some other individual may have broader Company experience which fits him for an immediate promotion over another who is, in one sense, doing a more effective job.

Ratings may thus be thought of as providing a *guide* or a *basis for discussion,* rather than as providing a cut-and-dried answer to all problems of personnel adjustment.

• RATINGS AS A CONTROL MECHANISM

The use of employee ratings as a guide in effecting personnel adjustments may be thought of as a control mechanism, much as labor grades and rate ranges are used as control mechanisms. Ratings in this sense may be used by *higher level supervisors* and by the personnel organizations. Here are some questions which a supervisor might ask, to which ratings would provide relevant information.

1. When promotions are recommended, are the men chosen generally those who have received high ratings? When this is

not the case, has it been agreed that other factors justify this choice?

2. Have we had an opportunity to look at outstanding men in other organizations before filling our promotional jobs? Have we reasonable assurance that the men we have looked at in other organizations are really outstanding?

3. At times of lay-off, are we tending to lose our best people, or are we improving the organization, consistent with proper consideration for service?

4. In taking people from other organizations which are reducing their force, have we obtained a reasonable cross-section of their people, or have we been asked to take more than our share of the employees receiving low ratings?

5. In determining pay increases, are we giving proper attention to our most effective people, consistent with their service and their type of work? If pay increases are recommended for employees who have received low ratings, has it been agreed that other factors in the situation justify this action?

6. In rehiring, are we giving proper preference to those whom we had previously considered to be most effective?

From the standpoint of the Personnel Placement organization, ratings might be involved in answering the same questions as those listed above, with emphasis on coordinating the personnel activities of the various organizations. Placement people could assure themselves, for example:

1. That outstanding people in each organization are not overlooked in considering promotions, either in that organization or elsewhere in the Works.

2. That in large-scale transfers from one organization to another, a fair cross-section of people are transferred.

3. That in lay-off and rehiring, improvement of the personnel is brought about to as great an extent as possible.

It should be clearly understood that this control function of ratings, like most control mechanisms, rests on the needs of a reasonably large company. It is not possible for the immediate supervisor of an operating unit, for example, to know what outstanding persons there are in other parts of the Works, who might be well fitted for work in his unit. Nor is it possible for him to locate opportunities for his own outstanding people, which may be better than any position available in his own unit. In a large organization, it cannot be expected that outstanding people will be placed to their own and the Company's best advantage simply as a result of the routine contacts among hundreds of supervisors. Systematic procedures for locating these outstanding people may be expected to improve placement from the over-all Company standpoint.

• DO RATINGS HELP OR HAMPER THE IMMEDIATE SUPERVISOR?

Still viewing ratings as a control mechanism, chiefly used as information for supervisors and for personnel organizations, does this mechanism help or hamper the personnel activities of the immediate supervisor? There is undoubtedly some hesitancy on the part of some supervisors to put down in black and white their opinions of their people, for fear that this record may upset some personnel change which they may later wish to recommend.

This is a crucial point in the evaluation of the usefulness of employee rating procedures. Two observations occur in connection with it.

If ratings are *rightly used,* they do not

tend to hamper the supervisor in any action which is to the best interest of the Works *as a whole.*

If he wishes to transfer an employee with a low rating, he will be hampered in doing so by virtue of the rating which shows that the man has a low rating. However, another supervisor who might have that man "wished" on him may be grateful for the record. The proper placement of this employee then becomes, as it should, a matter of serving best the interests of the employee and the Company as a whole, rather than a matter of immediate advantage to any one organization.

If a supervisor wishes to hold on to an outstanding man for whom better opportunities exist elsewhere in the Works, he will be hampered by the record, which may mark that man for special attention. However, if a supervisor has a spot for an outstanding man, his work will be facilitated by the existence of records which provide him with candidates throughout the Works who were not put forth simply by organizations having someone to "sell."

Of course, it is not meant to imply that supervisors customarily follow selfish or unfair tactics in giving information for a particular purpose to other organizations. It is only meant that *unless* a purely selfish action is contemplated, which is not in line with over-all Company interests, ratings, if properly used, should tend to facilitate the action rather than hamper it.

If ratings are *improperly used*—that is, without regard for the cautions outlined—then a supervisor may be hampered in taking an action which, everything considered, is reasonable. If higher supervisors or personnel people should require all personnel changes to be strictly in accordance with ratings, without proper regard for other factors in the individual situation, then it is not to be expected that the action thus required will be necessarily correct, and the individual supervisor may feel that ratings have hampered him rather than helped him in carrying on his work.

It is thus essential that those who maintain controls on personnel changes, in part through the use of ratings, must recognize:

1. The "zone of uncertainty" in ratings.
2. That ratings do not tell the whole story and should be used only as a guide or a basis for discussion in determining proper personnel adjustments.

Assume, for example, that a supervisor wishes to promote or upgrade an employee. He will prepare the necessary forms and requisitions, and will state, probably in written form, the basis upon which he is recommending this particular action.

These forms will then go to the proper line executives and personnel organizations for approval. These persons have been given the responsibility, as a part of their job, of taking a broad look at all personnel readjustments in their territory, and of assuring themselves, before approval, that the action is in line with Company policies and practices and that it will serve the best interests of the Company and the employee.

If the person being recommended differs radically *in any respect* from the type of person who would normally be chosen for upgrading, this difference will flag the attention of those who are responsible for approvals. If he has unusually short service, for example, they may wish to be informed, in some detail, as to whether longer service employees with similar experience were given consideration, and as to the reasons why such employees were not chosen.

Assume that the person being recommended has a very low rating. Neither this, nor any other single consideration, should be used as a basis for disapproval of the proposed action. It should simply give rise to discussion along these lines:

1. Have we looked at Jones, who received the highest rating in this line of work in our organization? What were our reasons for not upgrading him?
2. What of the others who were rated considerably above the man who has been chosen in our organization?
3. Have we looked at men with similar experience in other organizations who rated higher than this man? What were our reasons for rejecting them?
4. Can we give some evidence, in spite of this man's low rating, for our belief that he can handle the work to which we are recommending his promotion?

If the answers to such questions as these indicate that the action being recommended has been given proper thought and that no important considerations have been overlooked, then the unusual factors, such as a low rating, would not be expected to stand in the way of approval of the recommendation.

• POSSIBLE ADVANTAGES OF EMPLOYEE RATINGS OTHER THAN AS A CONTROL MECHANISM

Certain arguments are sometimes advanced in favor of employee ratings, which may be listed here.

1. That employees would prefer to be rated, since it gives them a feeling that the Company is trying systematically to provide opportunities and recognition for them. There is less chance of being "lost in the shuffle."

The extent to which rating procedures are being suggested by labor organizations, and appear in labor contracts, would seem to bear this out. Doubtless, outstanding employees would welcome rating procedures more than less competent ones. It is difficult to evaluate the extent to which employees are concerned about the matter. In some cases, they may not even know that they are being rated.

2. That it is desirable for supervisors to be impressed by this evidence that the Company considers employee recognition and mobility to be important and worth attention. The extent to which ratings do foster this feeling among supervisors is unknown.

3. That supervisors benefit, in handling their people, from having taken the time to think over and evaluate their employees as is necessary in rating them. This appears reasonable, although the extent to which ratings improve the supervisor's thinking in this way is, of course, difficult to evaluate. Comments from a number of supervisors indicate that the time they have devoted to rating their people has been helpful.

4. That the ratings themselves give the supervisor *new information* about his people—tell him something he did not know before.

This is quite improbable, if we recall that the ratings are records of his opinions about his people. It does not appear likely that the immediate supervisor will find much need for consulting the ratings in determining the standing of his own people.

5. That there is an educative value in ratings for the person being rated, since it is possible, on the basis of ratings, for the supervisor to point out an employee's strong and weak points to him and thus assist him in developing himself. This is possibly a very real point, as far as a detailed analytical rating of a man is concerned.

The procedures to be used in getting a good rating for control purposes are quite different from those which should be used if the educational value to the employee is to be emphasized. It is confusing if these two objectives are mixed. Present emphasis at Hawthorne is on obtaining good ratings for over-all control purposes.

6. The ratings may also be used to counsel and aid the employee in his personal development.

• USE OF RATINGS AT HAWTHORNE

As stated above, ratings at Hawthorne are now serving largely as a control mechanism. Continuous and systematic use of them is being made by the personnel organization. Instances could be given of the use of ratings as a basis for discussion in connection with practically every question listed earlier in this report under the heading Ratings as a Control Mechanism.

Use of ratings by the line organizations, on the other hand, has been increasing. As a result of their experience in making ratings and in using them, supervisors have indicated their confidence in the ratings and the need for them when considering personnel changes. Some organizations feel the importance of ratings so strongly that they would carry on rating programs for their own use even if the Works as a whole were not doing so. Other organizations use the ratings chiefly when the matter is brought up in their dealings with personnel people.

• SUMMARY

The chief points covered in this statement are:

1. That ratings must be recognized as *records of opinion.*

2. That ratings should be interpreted with two particular precautions in mind. These are:

(a) A rating should always be interpreted as having a "zone of uncertainty."

(b) No rating should be expected to tell the whole story with regard to any personnel adjustment. Ratings should be used rather as a basis for discussion of proposed personnel changes.

3. That the use of employee ratings as a guide in effecting personnel adjustments may be thought of as a control mechanism, much as labor grades and rate ranges are used as control mechanisms. In this sense, ratings are chiefly used by higher level supervisors and by personnel organizations in connection with their responsibilities for approval of personnel adjustments.

4. That this use of ratings as a control mechanism, if properly administered, should not tend to hamper a supervisor in making any personnel adjustment which is to the best interest of the Works as a whole.

5. That there are certain possible advantages of employee ratings other than as a control mechanism. These points have been discussed briefly.

THE ABILITY TO JUDGE PEOPLE*

Ronald Taft

What are the factors related to the ability to judge accurately such behavioral characteristics as the abilities, traits, action tendencies, motives, and emotions of other people?[1] Are there some persons who consistently demonstrate good ability to judge others accurately and, if so, what are the correlates of such ability? These are the general questions to which this review is addressed. The practical importance of the above questions in psychology is obvious, especially when we consider the role of the psychologist's personality in determining the validity of the observations and inferences with which he works.

METHODS OF MEASURING ABILITY TO JUDGE OTHERS

The number of differing methods of measuring ability to judge others that have been used in the experiments in this area may partly account for the varied and sometimes conflicting results found. The distinction between analytic and nonanalytic judgments (Wallin, *75*) appears to be a particularly important one. In analytic judgments, the judge (*J*) is required to conceptualize, and often to quantify, specific characteristics of the subject (*S*) in terms of a given frame of reference.[2] This mainly involves the process of inference, typical performances of *J* being rating traits, writing personality descriptions, and predicting the percentage of a group making a given response. In nonanalytic judgments, *J* responds in a global fashion, as in matching persons with personality descriptions and in making predictions of behavior. An empathetic process is usually involved in nonanalytic judgments.

A Classification of Tests of Ability to Judge Others

The classification that follows is based on that suggested by Notcutt and Silva's review of the experimental approaches (*54*).

1. *Perception of emotional expressions in photographs, drawings, models, and movies.* This method has been used to study ability to judge in a number of studies (*2* [ch. 8–10], *3, 13, 18, 25, 26, 30, 33, 37, 38, 39, 73, 76, 78*). The required response may be a multiple-choice, a one-word free response, or a completely free response. The criteria are usually *S*'s intention, or the judgment of psychologists. Less controversial criteria were used by Coleman (*18*), where *J* had to select from a check list the situation to which S was responding.

[1] The review is confined to judgments about the emotional, personality, and behavioral characteristics of others, not their physical or sociological characteristics.

NOTE: The major part of this review was prepared by the writer while he was a research assistant at the Institute of Personality Assessment at the University of California. He wishes to thank Professors D. W. MacKinnon and T. R. Sarbin for their advice and assistance which have been given unstintingly.

* From *Psychological Bulletin*, Vol. 52, no. 1, January 1955, pp. 1–23. Copyright 1955 by the American Psychological Association, Inc. Reprinted by permission.

[2] *J* stands for judge and S for subject. Throughout this review, the term "subject" refers to the person being judged.

This type of test usually evokes a nonanalytic judgment, although, as F. H. Allport (*2*) has demonstrated, these judgments can be made analytically. The method has the advantage of being neat, but the expressions tend to be culturally stereotyped. In real-life situations the expression of emotions may be idiosyncratic (*38, 42*) and thus their recognition may require a different type of ability from the recognition of stereotyped responses.

2. *Rating and ranking of traits.* This is an analytic method, and has the advantage of clear-cut quantification. It also has the virtue of requiring a performance which is frequently used in psychological work. It suffers from all the drawbacks of ratings in general, particularly the lack of consensus about the meaning of terms and the quantitative standards to be used.

A further difficulty with this method of measuring ability to judge others is the establishment of criteria. Two different approaches to these criteria may be distinguished: (a) Peer judgments, i.e., pooled judgments made by the Ss themselves, which may or may not include the self-ratings (*1, 6, 17, 24, 27, 32, 60, 67, 73, 81*). The use of this type of criterion suffers from the doubt whether we are measuring ability to judge or simply the degree to which *J* conforms to the criterion group; the nonconformist would score poorly, but might in fact be a good judge. (b) External criteria—these may be judgments made by other observers who may or may not be well acquainted with the Ss; or they may be derived from test results (*3, 17, 23, 40, 52, 53, 67, 71, 73, 78*). (Only Cogan *et al.* [*17*], Estes [*23*], and Vernon [*73*] used tests as well as ratings to provide the criteria.) Taft (*67*) obtained an intercorrelation of .72 between ratings using each of the two types of judgmental criteria, peer judgments and external judgments.

3. *Personality descriptions.* The *J* is provided with some data about S and required to write a description of his personality. The data provided might be a brief interview with S, and observation of S in some standard situation, or some descriptive material concerning him. This method, in general, involves analytic judgments, but suffers from the vagueness of *J*'s task; also the criterion lacks precision, and is usually based on the opinions of persons who are arbitrarily regarded as "expert judges" (*9, 12, 55*).

4. *Personality matchings.* In this method, *J* is required to match some data concerning S with some other data concerning him. Where the Ss are known personally to *J*, the task may be to match S with the relevant data. The method lends itself readily to nonanalytic judgments, but some *J*s may use analytic modes of inference to assist them to make the matchings. The matching method (*23, 67, 73, 81*) has the great advantage over the previously described methods of studying the ability to judge others in that its criterion is completely objective, but it has the weakness that it constitutes an artificial situation not paralleled in everyday life or in psychological practice.

5. *Prediction of behavior or life-history data.* The *J* has some acquaintance with S or is given data about him, and his task is to predict S's performance on various test items or his responses to personality and attitude inventories, or to predict specified aspects of his life history. These are the so-called "empathy" tests (*20*) and are probably pri-

marily nonanalytic. A related test is the "mass-empathy" test (*72*) in which *J* predicts the combined responses of a group of people. It is suggested that the mass-empathy test of prediction is more likely to be tackled analytically than is the empathy test, as it does not lend itself so readily to empathizing with any particular person. Thus the empathy test will be regarded as nonanalytic, and the mass-empathy test as analytic, wherever such a distinction is cogent to our argument. It is perhaps significant in this reference that a mass-empathy test (Kerr) and an empathy test (Dymond) were found to be uncorrelated for 87 subjects (*8*). The empathy method was used in fifteen other studies analyzed (*9, 10, 20, 21, 28, 34, 40* [ch. IIIC], *44, 54, 56, 57, 59, 73, 78, 79*) and the mass-empathy method in ten (*16, 40, 41, 66, 67, 68, 69, 70, 72, 74*).

The method of behavioral prediction, like the matching method, has the advantage of possessing an objective criterion. The reliability of the predictions on any one item tends to be low, and, therefore, the test should preferably consist of a number of items or behavioral events to be predicted. One weakness of the empathy method, demonstrated by Hastorf and Bender (*11, 35*), is the spurious effect of projection; the predictions made by *J* are often partly the result of projection of his own personality, and, consequently, an accidental resemblance between *J* and *S* will render the predictions more accurate than they otherwise would be. Hastorf and Bender suggest the use of an index separating the effect of projection, similarity, and empathy. A further weakness of the "empathy" method is the possibility that judgments may often be made correctly by using cultural stereotype responses without attempting to predict the responses of the particular S. Gage (*28*) has demonstrated how accuracy of stereotype predictions can be kept separate from accuracy of individual predictions.

6. A few miscellaneous techniques should also be mentioned, although studies based on them, in general, fall outside the scope of this review. Most of these techniques employ indices that attempt to measure the ability to judge others in an indirect manner, *e.g.*, Dymond's empathy index on the TAT (*17*), Walton's generalized empathy test (*76*), and McClelland's "role-playing ability" scale (*46*). Even more remote are the tests devised by Chapin (*15*), Moreno and Moreno (*49*), Sherriffs (*61*), Moss Social Intelligence Test (*50* used in *73*). Most of these measures are either assumed to possess face validity or have been validated against one of the first five methods of testing ability to judge others.

• IS THERE A GENERAL ABILITY TO JUDGE OTHERS?

Is there sufficient consistency in the ability to judge others for persons to be characterized as good or poor judges? We are here concerned with the generality and specificity of the ability to judge others and with test-retest reliability of the measures used. G. W. Allport suggests that the ability to judge others is analogous to artistic ability in that it is neither entirely general nor entirely specific. "It would be unreasonable, therefore, to expect a judge of people to be uniformly successful in estimating every quality of every person. . . . It seems more of an error, however, to consider the ability entirely specific than to consider it entirely general" (*5*, p. 512 and footnote). Let us now look at the experimental evidence which, on the whole, supports Allport's contention.

Consistency Between Different Types of Tests

Some persons may be better at judging others on analytical tests, while others may be better on nonanalytic tests. F. H. Allport (*2*) found that, in judging emotional expression (Rudolph poses), some *J*s were superior at judging the intended emotion when using a naive type of intuitive method, while other *J*s were superior after receiving a training in the use of analytic methods of making the same judgments. Using 44 measures of ability to judge, Vernon (*73*) obtained significant correlations of over .30 for S's ability to rate strangers (analytic) and his performance on subtests of the Moss Social Situations Test involving nonanalytic judgments about people (Social Situations and Observation of Human Behavior). Wedeck (*78*) obtained significant positive correlations ranging from .18 to .56 (mean .31) between a test of ability to rate the personality traits of verbally described persons and seven other tests of ability to judge emotions and personal qualities of persons depicted in various ways, both pictorial and verbal. The Ss consisted of 203 adolescent school girls. A factor analysis revealed a "psychological factor" with a high saturation in the judgment of emotions tests (nonanalytic) but a negligible one in the trait-rating tests (analytic). Wolf and Murray (*81*) using four *J*s found a "fairly consistent" rank order between the accuracy of *J*'s predictions of the 15 Ss' rank order on three objective tests and *J*'s ability to match the Ss with their Dramatic Production Test records. Taft (*67*) obtained a significant correlation of .36 between the ability to rate others on traits and the abiltiy to predict group responses on an inventory. On the other hand, a test of ability to match the Ss with their mosaic productions did not correlate significantly with these two analytic tests. Neither did an empathy test with a mass-empathy test (see p. 30). In general then, significant but low consistency has usually been found between one test of ability to judge others and another, but some studies suggest that analytic and nonanalytic tests tend to differ in their results. We shall therefore need to note in our review the type of test used in the particular experiments reported.

Reliability of Tests

Adams (*1*) reports an average test-retest reliability of .55 for the accuracy of sorority girls in ranking nine of their "sisters" on 63 personality traits, the interval between the two tests being approximately three weeks. The criteria were the pooled rankings. This index of reliability indicates that there is some consistency for a particular judge in making specific judgments, but that the consistency is not high. If this is typical, the influence of attenuation on correlation coefficients using such data would be considerable. In fact, only a few of the studies report even moderately high reliabilities. Dymond (*21*) reports a split-half reliability for her empathy test (predictions of S's ratings of himself and of *J* on six characteristics) of .82 and a test-retest reliability after six weeks of .60 (*20*). Travers (*69*) asked his Ss to predict the percentage of a specified population who would answer "true" or "false" to each of 25 items, and the split-half reliability of the accuracy scores for this test was .64.

Taft (*67*) obtained a test-retest reliability coefficient of .82 for a 30-item prediction test similar to that of Travers but this contrasted with a split-half reliability of only .20. Correlations between single items tend to be even lower than .20 (*67, 69, 74*), a further indication of the low reliability of any one item. We thus see the necessity for tests of this nature to include a large number of items in order to ensure reliability.

Consistency in Accuracy Between Traits and Between Subjects

Travers, in a further experiment (*70*), found correlations of .44 and .47 respectively for two groups of students (*N*, 26 and 31) between ability to judge the word knowledge of S's own group and ability to judge that of the general population. "The evidence then indicates that some subjects are generally good at judging what various groups of men know, while others are poor" (*70*, p. 98). Taft's study yielded a corresponding correlation of .31 for 40 Ss on tests analogous to those of Travers.

Vernon (*73*) did not compute the reliabilities of the tests which he used, but, on the basis of "logically related aggregates," *i.e.*, clusters, he suggests that his data show four independent dimensions—ability to judge self, to judge acquaintances, to rate strangers, and to judge character sketches of strangers. Kelly and Fiske (*40*, ch. IIIC) attempted to devise a test of the ability of psychologists to predict inventory responses of two patients whom the latter had diagnosed. The respective accuracies achieved in judging each patient intercorrelated .23 for 100 *J*s. In contrast to this low consistency, Estes (*23*) reports that his ten best judges in a test of ability to rate the traits of persons depicted in short movies were consistently more accurate than the ten poorest judges on all 23 variables and for all eight Ss. The criteria of accuracy were the ratings assigned by clinical psychologists.

Gage (*28*) also reports high generality in the ability of his *J*s to judge the responses of six strangers on the Kuder Preference Inventory after they had directly observed S's expressive behavior for a short time. He found high consistency in *J*'s ability to judge, irrespective of the specific items or Ss on which he was being tested. Consistency (correlation of .71) was also shown between ability to predict the responses of the six strangers and those of three randomly selected classmates. Similar findings, with regard to consistency in *J*'s accuracy between different Ss are reported by Bender and Hastorf (*11*).

Luft (*45*) suggests that there might be individual differences in consistency among *J*s. In one of his experiments using 74 *J*s, all persons with various degrees of training in psychology, he found that 27 per cent of the *J*s were able to predict the personal inventory responses of both of two Ss with above chance accuracy. The predictions were made on the basis of case-record material. However, the accuracy scores of the total sample of 74 *J*s did not correlate significantly from one S to the other. These findings may be taken in conjunction with those of Dymond (*20*) in her experiment referred to above. She found that the capable judges tended to show less variation in the accuracy with which they could judge the S's self-ratings on each of six traits than did poorer judges. Thus, good judges, at least, seem to show some consistency in ability to judge, irrespective of the type of S or the type of qualities being judged. We could not expect, however, that even a capable judge would be able to judge members of another culture as well as he can judge members of his own; there is evidence that judgments are more accurate when *J* and S are similar in cultural backgrounds, also in age and sex (*34, 36, 67, 71, 81*). Nor could even a good judge be expected to judge all areas of the personality or use different kinds of "clinical evidence" equally well. (Space does not permit the inclusion of a systematic review of the experiments that have been performed on these specific factors in judging [*67*, pp. 12–23]).

Conclusion. Allport's dictum at the beginning of this section seems to be justified by the data. A reasonable conclusion might be stated as follows: The degree to which a person can make accurate judgments about others is a function of his general ability to judge and of specific situational and interactional factors, but the greater his general ability to judge, the less will be the relative influence of the specific factors. The specific factors concerned are the type of S, the relationship between *J* and S, the type of judgment demanded, the traits being judged, and the material available to *J*. In addition, the consistency in the performance of any individual *J* is limited by the low reliability that characterizes many of the tests used to measure ability to judge. In view of the effect of specific factors we must be cautious in drawing general conclusions from studies that do not require *J* to make a variety of judgments about a variety of Ss.

• THE CHARACTERISTICS OF GOOD JUDGES OF OTHERS

In consequence of the above conclusions, some of the findings quoted in the review that follows should be limited to the actual Ss, judging situations, traits, or modes used in the particular experiments. Wherever similar findings are obtained over several situations, we may expect that the individual characteristics of the good judges concerned can be generalized, but where contradictory findings are obtained between one study and another the variation may merely be due to the specific factors involved in the experiments. Our plan has been to report findings as conclusions where the weight of the evidence clearly supports them, even though some contradictory findings may raise doubts.

Age

Gates (*30*) found a progressive increase from the ages of 3 to 14 years in the ability to judge the intended emotional expressions in six of the Ruckmick poses. Walton (*76*), using various tests of empathy with emotional expression, obtained similar results for *J*s ranging from kindergarten to university age. His published tables seem to suggest that the greatest improvements occur between 9 and 11, and between 14 and adulthood. Further support for the development of empathy in children is provided by Dymond *et al.* (*22*), where a marked increase in signs of empathy is reported between 7 and 11 years. The test consisted of predictions by the *J*s of whether their classmates liked or disliked them.

On the other hand a number of studies using adults as *J*s failed to find any increase with age in ability to judge others (*16, 23, 41, 56, 64, 67*). These studies employed *J*s ranging from 18 to at least the late thirties, but the tests mostly tested their ability to predict the responses of college age Ss. Consequently, the older *J*s would be less similar to their Ss than would the younger *J*s, and the former may therefore have been under a handicap.

Conclusions. While ability to judge emotional expressions increases with age in children—probably through experience—no increase with age has been found in adults on various tests of ability to judge others. This latter finding, however, is subject to the limitation that the subjects being judged have mostly been closer in age to the younger judges.

Sex

It has been contended that "Experimental studies, so far as they go, establish only a slight margin in favor of women" (*5*, p. 517). This seems to be a reasonable summary of the many studies that have been conducted on sex differences in ability to judge people. One study (*37*) reports a significant superiority for women students in judging the emotional expressions in the Rudolph poses, but in the other studies of judging emotional expressions in photographs, models, and movies, no significant or consistent sex differences are reported. In five studies (*2, 18, 25, 30, 33*) the authors report no differences; in three (*13, 26, 39*) a slight, but apparently insignificant, superiority for women; and in one (*38*) a slight superiority for men. The results are not related to the sex of the person whose emotions were being judged.

Similar results have been found in other tests of judging ability. Dymond (*20*) reports no sex differences at first in the ability of students to predict how other members of their group rated themselves and *J*; however, in a second administration, six weeks later, the female *J*s were significantly better than the males. In a further experiment (*21*), she found female students significantly superior to males in making judgments similar to those in her first experiment. These two studies differed from most of the other ones on sex differences in that the *J*s were well acquainted with the Ss. However, where husbands and wives predicted each other's responses to an inventory (*54*), sex differences in accuracy were not significant; if anything, the males were the more accurate.

None of the other five reported experiments (*46, 56, 64, 69, 71*) which compare the ability of males and females either to rate their S's traits or to predict their responses found significant differences. It is also interesting to note that no relationship was found between the ability of males on these types of tests of judging and their scores on inventory and projective tests of femininity (*67*).

Conclusions. The weight of evidence is in favor of no sex difference in ability to judge, or perhaps a slightly superior ability in women. The reported studies do not suggest any convincing explanations for this possible superiority of women, and until further evidence suggests a changed view, it would be wise to conclude that there are no differences.

Family Background and Sibling Rank

In a study of ability to predict how other boys would answer personal inventory questions (mass-empathy), Sweet (*66*) found a positive relationship between judging ability and the socioeconomic status of the *J*s. These results, however, could have been due to the influence of intelligence. The only other study reported on this topic, Taft (*67*), found no correlation among graduate students between ability to judge and socioeconomic status, where the test required *J* to rate S on six traits, and to predict their personal inventory responses. The criteria for the ratings were both peer and psychological assessments.

Regarding size of family and order of birth, an earlier suggestion by F. H. Allport (*2*) that *J*s from larger families are better at judging emotional expression has not been supported. (Allport used only 26 *J*s and does not report significance.) Estes (*23*) found no relation between "sibling status" and ability to judge on a trait-rating test, and in Taft's study (*67*) there was actually a negative correlation between ability to judge and number of siblings. In this latter study it was also found that the best *J*s were only children; then came eldest, middle, and youngest children in that order. The explanation given is that the fewer the older siblings, the more likely is a child to be brought into contact early with adult modes of judging others.

Taft also found that those *J*s who had a rural background were poorer at judging than the urban ones but this might be explicable again in terms of sibling status. Minority group status showed an interesting pattern in this study: Negroes and foreign students were poorer and Jewish students better than the average in judging (see above for the details of the test used). The explanation given is that the former groups are too isolated and dissimilar from the others to judge them accurately, but the Jewish group possesses a marginal position in the American culture as a whole which provides both the opportunity and the stimulus for making accurate judgments.

Conclusions. The findings reported on the influences of background factors on ability to judge are derived from very few studies, and almost entirely from one. Thus no consistencies can be educed until we have more evidence.

Intelligence and Perception

G. W. Allport sums up the studies up to 1937 on the relationship between ability to judge others and intelligence as follows:

> Experimental studies have found repeatedly that some relationship exists between superior intelligence and the ability to judge others . . . even within a high and narrow range of intelligence. . . . Understanding people is largely a matter of perceiving relations between past and present activities, between expressive behavior and inner traits, between cause and effect, and intelligence *is* the ability to perceive just such relations as these (*5*, p. 514).

In an early study, Cogan *et al.* (*17*) found a significant correlation between *J*'s intelligence and his ability to rate the intelligence of others, and also to rate sense of humor. The criteria were pooled ratings. The correlations between intelligence and ability to rate seven other personality traits were not significant. Adams' study (*1*) was similar but more complex. He studied 80 female students living together in groups of 10. They ranked themselves and each other on 63 traits, including seven related to intellectual functioning; the pooled rankings acted as the criterion both for measuring the accuracy of the judgments and for measuring the characteristics of the *J*s. The seven intellectual characteristics had an average correlation of only .12 with ability to judge others, the highest correlations being .21 for "observation" and for "mentally bright" (significant at 5 per cent level). We should note, however, the possibility that the use of peer ratings as the criterion may have provided a measure of *J*'s conformity to his group, rather than of his ability to judge his peers.

Where some independent measure of the criterion was used (*21, 55, 67, 73*), the accuracy of analytic judgments of personality traits showed significant positive correlations with intelligence fairly generally. Vernon obtained significant correlations of approximately .30 between intelligence and various analytic measures of ability to judge strangers. For other judgments, however, involving nonanalytic modes, the correlations obtained with intelligence were approximately zero.

Taft (*67*) scored the intelligence of his 40 *J*s according to their best performance in any of a number of various cognitive tests. This index of intelligence correlated .37 with their ability to judge the traits of their peers and to predict their peers' responses to an inventory (analytic). Academic ability also showed low positive correlations with these tests of ability to judge others but the sample was highly selected in this regard (senior graduate students). Wedeck (*78*), using 203 girls, reported saturations of *g* factor ranging from .18 to .34 for his seven varied tests of ability to judge others. There were no consistent differences in this respect between the analytic and the nonanalytic tests.

The results of other studies correlating intelligence and ability on nonanalytic modes of judging are contradictory. In Sweet's study (*66*), 12- to 14-year-old boys at a YMCA camp predicted how their peers would respond to a questionnaire on 22 different activities. There was a "high relationship" between their accuracy and their CAVI scores. The assessees in the OSS procedures (*55*) wrote personality sketches of their peers and these were rated by the assessment staff for accuracy. Despite the admitted unreliability of the criteria, the assessees' ability to judge correlated significantly with various verbal intelligence tests (.32 to .48) and .54 with the final staff rating on Effective Intelligence. The latter rating, however, was continted both with the scoring of the judging test and with the intelligence test results.

The only other study found that reported a significant positive correlation between judging ability and verbal intelligence (.21) was that of Kanner (*38*), which correlated the ability of students to judge the intended emotions in the Feleky poses and their Thorndike intelligence scores. Dymond (*21*) reports a positive correlation between her *J*s' ability to predict the *S*'s self and other ratings on six traits and *J*s' scores on the Wechsler Performance Scale. However, a further study repeating the same technique (*43*) found no correlation with the ACE Group Test. Similarly Kelly and Fiske (*40*) found a significant correlation between ability to predict inventory responses and score on the fluency subtest of the PMA but not with any of the other subtests or with the Miller Analogies test.

All the other studies correlating nonanalytic modes of judging with intelligence found no correlation, for example, between (a) the accuracy of predictions of the questionnaire responses of eight psychology students and the *Js*' ACE scores (*9*), (b) ability to "throw" scores on a masculinity-femininity test and Thorndike "intelligence score" or grade point ratio (*41*), (c) Army Alpha scores and the ability of *Js* to match correctly a short behavior record with personality sketches (*23*), (d) ability to predict group responses and the Otis, Cooperative General Culture Test, or Thorndike Reading Test scores of the *Js* (*69, 70*), (e) various intelligence tests and the ability of graduate students to match mosaic productions with acquaintances (*67*), and (f) various group intelligence tests and ability to predict inventory responses on the basis of a brief observation of *S*'s expressive behavior (*28*).

Conclusions. There seems to be a positive relationship between intelligence and ability to judge others analytically. The highest correlation reported is .55 but the use of intellectually homogeneous groups in most of the studies would have reduced the correlations obtained. The superiority of more intelligent *Js* is probably the most pronounced in ability to rate the intelligence of others. The results for analytic modes do not appear surprising, as such modes require a precise understanding of the meaning and application of abstract terms (traits).

Nonanalytic modes of judging tend to manifest lower correlations between intelligence and accuracy of judgment. It is possible that accurate nonanalytic judgments of others are more a function of good perceptual and judgmental attitudes than of the use of abstract intelligence, provided the mode of making the judgments is clearly within the level of comprehension of *J*.

Training in Psychology

It is often assumed that qualified psychologists are more capable than laymen of making unbiased judgments, since they receive training in the dynamics of personality and also in the correct manner of making judgments, *e.g.*, using fixed standards, considering only relevant evidence, avoiding projection, combining probabilities in their correct weight, etc. On the other hand, some writers argue the opposite. For example, Murray (*51*) claims that the use of analytic perception and induction together with the repression of emotion and feeling leads to poor ability to judge others.

Let us now turn to the experimental evidence on the question. Are those who have taken courses in psychology more accurate judges than those who have not? In a test of judging emotional expressions in the Boring-Titchener models on an adjective check-list, students who had completed at least one course in psychology were, if anything, less accurate than students just taking their first course (*13*). Hanks (*34*) found no relationship between training in psychology and the ability to predict *S*'s answers to inventory questions from biographical and other inventory data. Polansky (*56*), on the other hand, found graduate students in psychology to be better judges than those without psychological training when judging Ss who were friends of the author. Whether the Ss, as well as the *J*s, were also trained in psychology is not stated. The tests required *J*s to make specific behavioral predictions about three Ss whose actual behavior was known.

Studies comparing the ability of professional psychologists with nonpsychologists do not, in general, suggest that those trained in psychology are better judges. If anything, the contrary seems to be the case. In Estes' experiment (*23*) psychologists were significantly poorer than the average of a wide variety of *J*s (professional and nonprofessional persons) in judging others on ratings, check lists, and matching tests. The material presented consisted of brief samples of S's expressive behavior recorded in a movie. These findings are supported by Wedell and Smith (*79*), who compared qualified, experienced clinicians with untrained, inexperienced interviewers on their ability to predict the responses of 200 interviewees to an attitude questionnaire. The untrained *J*s made the more accurate predictions.

Luft (*44, 45*) compared the ability of clinicians (psychiatrists, psychologists, and social workers), graduate psychology students, and physical science students on a series of tests in which they were required to predict the responses of individuals to objective and projective test items. The physical scientists were superior to all the other groups of *J*s on the tasks taken as a whole. On the other hand, Taft (*67*) found psychologists to be superior to graduate students in various other disciplines. In a study of ability to rate traits and to predict the inventory responses of graduate students participating in an assessment program, judgments made by the assessment staff (psychologists) were more accurate than similar judgments made by the assessees themselves (both staff and peer ratings being used as criteria for the ratings). The assessees did not include psychology graduate students, but the assessment psychologists were "definitely" superior to social science students and "probably" superior to physical science students in judging. In this latter respect, the results appear to contradict those of Luft, but there was some evidence (not reported by Taft [*67*]) that the superiority of the psychologists in Taft's study was due primarily to the accuracy of the experimental psychologists rather than the clinical. In Luft's study the psychologists were clinicians.

Let us now consider some studies in which *J*s with different degrees of training in psychology are compared. Kelly and Fiske (*40*) did not find advanced graduate students of clinical psychology any more accurate at predicting the personality inventory responses of patients whom they had diagnosed through normal psychological techniques than similar students with one year less training. Kelly and Fiske were also able to compare the validity of the assessments of the professional promise of clinical psychology trainees made by other graduate students in clinical psychology with similar assessments made by professional psychologists and psychiatrists. The judgments were made on the basis of test protocols and interview reports and the Ss were actually unknown to the

Js. The validity of the assessments was determined by S's later performance as a clinical psychologist. The authors conclude that the students "utilized the materials as effectively as the more mature 1947 staff [psychologists]" (*40*, p. 175). However, the students had certain advantages over the psychologists—they had greater similarity to the Ss and had themselves undergone the experience of assessment; also, being in training themselves, they had a more appropriate frame of reference for interpreting the criterion (as the authors point out). These factors are less likely to explain Soskin's finding (*62*) that experienced clinical psychologists were not more accurate than graduate students in predicting the inventory responses of a 26-year-old mother from her projective test protocols.

Professional psychologists were more successful than psychology students in correctly diagnosing the psychiatric patients depicted in the Szondi Test (*57*). The superiority, however, could well be due to the psychologists' greater familiarity with the diagnostic categories used in the test. Technical knowledge could also account for the clinicians' superiority in Luft's experiment referred to above. Luft found that the clinicians were significantly superior to psychology students in predicting two Ss' responses to a projective test (but not to an objective test) after they had been provided with written interview data about the Ss.

Conclusions. The results on the comparative ability of nonpsychologists, psychology students, and professional psychologists to judge other people are partly obscured by the effect of similarity in age and academic status between *J* and S. Attempting to allow for this effect in the reported results, physical scientists, and possibly other nonpsychologists, *e.g.*, personnel workers, appear to be more capable of judging others accurately than are either psychology students or clinical psychologists. There is a suggestion that experimental psychologists may be superior as judges to clinical psychologists, but this conclusion must await further evidence.

There is also evidence that suggests that courses in psychology do not improve ability to judge others and there is considerable doubt whether professional psychologists show better ability to judge than do graduate students in psychology.[3] Do these findings necessarily lead to the conclusion that training in psychology blunts a judge's ability? Actually, the results could be wholly attributed to selective factors operating (a) in the accreditation of graduate students as psychologists and (b) in the selection of psychology as a career. On this latter point, there are some interesting but unanswered questions. Perhaps those taking up psychology, especially clinical psychology, are too concerned about social relations (see below, "Attitude Toward Social Relations") to be good judges, or perhaps they have had insufficient experience with a wide range of people. Watson (*77*) has pointed out that many professors and clinicians tend to live in isolation from the general life experiences of the people whom they are endeavoring to understand.

---

[3] In spite of this finding there is reason to believe that ability to judge others can be improved by specific training in judging and repeated specific practice, except where the person already has good ability to judge others (*3, 4, 14, 20, 33, 37, 47*).

Esthetic Ability and Sensitivity

G. W. Allport claims that of all the characteristics of a good judge of others "esthetic" ability stands above the others, and can even compensate for such things as lack of intelligence and experience (5, p. 538).

Allport and Allport (3) reported that the only correlation found for "susceptibility to social stimuli" (ability to judge emotional expression—Rudolph poses?) was with artistic ability. Of the nine best judges on the test, seven had literary productions to their credit. Unfortunately, no comparable figures are given for those low on the test. Vernon (73) found that the more accurate raters of strangers and of acquaintances (analytic) tended to be more artistic according to their scores on various musical and art judgment tests and were rated high on esthetic values by their peers. Ability to match character sketches with case history material did not correlate with esthetic judgments. Bender (9) reports on a test of ability to write accurate descriptions of the *Ss* on the basis of test profiles. The author acted as a referee for accuracy. He states that all the good judges were interested in literary or dramatic activity, but again no statement is furnished regarding the poor judges in this respect. On another test by Bender in which *J* was required to rate *S*'s standing on various opinion scales, ability to judge did not correlate significantly with the Meier-Seashore Art judgment test. Estes (23), however, found clear evidence that good ability to match character sketches was related to painting and dramatic avocations but not to musical.

Taft (67) concluded that the ability to rate traits accurately and to predict the *Ss*' inventory responses (analytic) correlates positively with "simple, traditional, artistic sensitivity." This was measured by art judgment tests similar to those used by Vernon and Bender in which high scores are allotted for ability to follow traditional artistic rules. On the other hand, the same *Js*' scores, on a test in which their preferences for various patterns were compared with the preferences of actual artists,[4] correlated negatively with analytic judging ability. None of the artistic tests correlated with performance on a nonanalytic test (matching). There was also zero correlation between all the tests of ability to judge others and an index of dramatic ability, *i.e.*, ratings of the *Js*' ability to empathize with roles in a role-playing test.

Conclusions. The ability to judge others seems to be higher in those persons who have dramatic and artistic *interests*, but the relationship is not as clear-cut in the case of dramatic and artistic *ability*.

The evidence on dramatic ability is too limited as yet, but in view of role-playing theory, this would seem to be an important area for study, particularly in its relationship to the ability to make accurate nonanalytic judgments of others.

The conclusion on artistic ability must turn on the definition of such ability; while there may be a positive correlation between ability to judge others on analytic modes and ability to endorse traditionally accepted esthetic rules, this may possibly be a function of intelligence and interest. The above relationship is not found where the sophisticated

[4] The distinction between these two types of esthetic judgment corresponds roughly with the symmetrical and asymmetrical types described by Barron (7).

standards of professional artists are used, and it might well be that professional artists, if tested, would perform poorly on tests of ability to judge others. The accuracy of nonanalytic judgments seems to be even less dependent on artistic ability—with the possible exception of literary ability—than are analytic judgments. (This is explicit in Taft and implicit in Vernon.)

Emotional Stability and Character Integration

It may be argued that the well-adjusted person is less subject to projecting himself into others than a poorly adjusted person and therefore he is able to judge them better. However, it is also possible to argue that a poorly adjusted person, who at the same time is aware of his emotional difficulties, is more sensitive to similar difficulties in others. Most of the findings in this area indicate that the first argument is the more correct, but the evidence is not unequivocal.

Where the tests of ability to judge are analytic in nature, the studies have reported a significant positive relationship between accuracy and emotional adjustment. The only possible exception is that of Adams (*1*), who reports that his good raters of personality traits tend to be rated high by their peers on the following: touchy, lack courage, work for present, independent, talkative, egotistic. These are signs of poor superficial adjustment, but do not necessarily point to a fundamental maladjustment. The other experiments reveal a positive relationship between analytic tests of judging and (a) the Bell Adjustment Inventory (*69, 70*), (b) the Character Education Test (*66*), (c) teacher's ratings that children need psychological help (*32*), (d) steel-workers' accident-proneness (*63*), (e) the California Authoritarian Scale (*59*), and (f) ratings of graduate students by their faculty on "personal soundness" (*67*). The latter study also reported a positive correlation between ability to make accurate analytic judgments and the "psychotic" scales on the MMPI (*Pa, Pt, Sc*).

The relationship between various measures of adjustment and nonanalytic tests of judging are more equivocal. Studies using the MMPI support the results quoted above: the ability of clinical psychologists to predict the inventory responses of their patients correlated negatively with their scores on the *Pt* scale (*41*); good judges (undergraduates) on Dymond's empathy test (*43*) tended to be low on *Pd, Pa, Pt,* and *Sc*, and psychology graduate students who were rated high by their peers on "role-playing ability" (nonanalytic?) also were low on these latter scales and on the *D* scale (*46*).

Emotional adjustment as measured by the Bell Scale correlated positively with ability to match the Ruckmick and Frois-Wittman emotional expression pictures (*26*) but not with ability to predict inventory responses after observing *S*'s expressive behavior (*28*). A test of matching a short film of expressive behavior with character sketches showed zero correlation with the Bernreuter (*23*), whereas matching mosaic productions with the acquaintances who produced them showed a significant *negative* correlation with ratings on "personal soundness" (*67*).

Conclusion. Ability to judge others on analytic modes correlates positively with emotional adjustment; presumably the more psychologically significant aspect of this correlation is that poor judges tend to be poorly adjusted, and, therefore, probably more likely to allow personal biases to affect their judgments. Studies are still needed in this area, using Ss who are more heterogeneous on emotional adjustment than the highly selected groups used in most of the experiments reported. Such studies would perhaps throw light on the connection between poor adjustment and poor ability to judge. The need for further studies is even more evident in the case of nonanalytic modes of judging in which the evidence is more contradictory. There is, however, a clear trend for the MMPI on both analytic and nonanalytic judgments—the poorer judges tend to be elevated on the psychotic scales, in particular, "psychasthenia."

Self-Insight

Is there any relationship between having a good knowledge of oneself and being an accurate judge of others? The inference that there is such a relationship seems reasonable if we accept the theory that we learn to know ourselves by our acceptance of the attitudes of others toward ourselves, and that we learn to know others by observations and inferences deriving from our introjection of the behavior of others. According to this formulation the acquiring of self-knowledge and knowledge of others are indispensable to each other. Writers who have stressed this viewpoint include Mead (*48*), Sullivan (*65*), and Cottrell (*19*).

Before looking at the experimental evidence on this question, we should refer briefly to a difficulty involved in handling the concept of insight experimentally. For experimental purposes self-insight is usually defined operationally as the ability of *J* to judge himself accurately, using as the criteria of accuracy judgments made by some other persons. However, it is possible, especially in the case of persons with complex, recondite personalities, that the self-judgments may be more veridical than those made by others. The use of tests, objective and projective, as the criteria can somewhat ameliorate this difficulty (*e.g., 73*). Other steps that might be taken are: (a) to use, as criteria, judgments made by "experts" (*e.g., 53*) defined either as persons who know the person well or as professional psychologists – although, as we have seen, there is considerable doubt whether these latter *J*s are, in fact, more expert than lay *J*s; (b) to require *S* to judge himself as he predicts he will be judged by the other Ss, and then to use these latter judgments as the criteria (*e.g., 20*)—this method has the disadvantage of contaminating judgments of self with judgments of others; and (c) to use over-all clinical judgments of the person's "self-insight" (*e.g., 73, 80*).

In many studies it has been found that the *J*s tend to rate themselves high on admirable traits and low on reprehensible ones (*3, 17, 32, 60, 67*). Consequently, those who are *actually* high on admirable or low on reprehensible traits will tend to be scored higher than others on self-insight. This artifact operates in all studies of self-insight, no matter how measured, and could affect the relationship found between self-insight and ability to judge others.

Let us now look at the results of experiments in this area:

1. Do good judges of self possess the same personality characteristics as good

judges of others? Adams tested the ability of girls to rank themselves and acquaintances on 63 traits, using the pooled rankings as the criterion (*1*). He concluded that good judges of self and good judges of others possess quite different personality syndromes—strangely enough, the former were oriented towards society, whereas the latter were more egotistic. Compared with the good judge of others, the good self-judge is more intelligent, possesses the more desirable emotional attributes, and is much more socially minded. Vernon (*73*) obtained substantially the same findings as Adams, using ratings by the *J*s of themselves, friends, and strangers. He used both pooled judgments and tests as criteria, but note the weakness that these tests were mainly of the inventory, *i.e.*, self-rating, type. When he grouped the intercorrelations between his data into "logically related aggregates," self-ratings formed a different cluster from ratings of others. The good self-raters tended to have a good sense of humor and good abstract intelligence and were sociable, whereas the good judges of others were less sociable and intelligent, but more artistic than good self-raters.

The Ss (graduate students taking part in a "living-in" assessment procedure) in Taft's experiment (*67*) predicted their sociometric standing, their relative status in the group on inventory item responses, and also how their peers would rate them on six traits. Good judges of self were taken as those assessees who were accurate in making these predictions. The assessees were rated by the staff on the Gough check list of 279 descriptive adjectives, and the characteristics of good judges of self were thus compared with the characteristics of those assessees who were good judges of the traits and the inventory responses of their fellow assessees. Sixteen of the adjectives distinguished good judges of self from good judges of others, at the 1 per cent level of confidence. Similarly, ten adjectives distinguished the poor judges of self from the poor judges of others. The qualitative differences confirmed Adams' and Vernon's finding that good judges of self tend to be more sociable than good judges of others.

2. What relationship has been found between self-insight and ability to judge others? In the most simplified instance, where the correlations are based on *J*'s ability to judge himself and his peers on single traits, a high positive relationship has been found consistently. Traits on which this relationship has been established include both socially approved and socially disapproved characteristics as follows: beauty (*58*), leadership (*32*), empathy (*19*), obstinacy and disorderliness (*60*). Evidence has also been presented demonstrating that *J*s possessing disapproved traits but lacking insight into them tend to project these traits into persons whom they are judging more than do other *J*s who possess the same traits but do not lack insight (*60, 80*). Where self-insight has been measured over a number of traits, or in a "global" fashion, the results quoted are conflicting. For example, in a further experiment, Vernon used peer ratings of his *J*s' self-insight as the measure; this measure correlated significantly with the objective measure of ability to rate self accurately described above, and correspondingly these peer-ratings showed no correlation with various measures of ability to judge (ability to rate traits, to make predictions about the behavior of friends and strangers,

and to match character sketches with case study material). Similarly, Frenkel-Brunswik (*27*) found "no consistent relationship" between three psychologists' self-insight and their accuracy in rating adolescents on the Murray needs. The criteria for measuring accuracy of both self and other ratings were the judgments made by the other two psychologists. Taft (*67*) also failed to find a significant correlation between *J*s' scores on the over-all index of ability to judge others (rating the Ss on six traits and predicting their responses to inventory items) and the index of ability to judge self, described above. On the other hand, Norman (*53*) did obtain significant correlations in a very similar study, using as Ss 72 graduate students in psychology who were taking part in an assessment program. Their over-all ability to judge themselves on 31 personality traits correlated positively with their ability to judge their peers on the same traits, both when peer ratings and when staff ratings were used as the criteria.

The reason for the clear-cut differences in the results of the above experiments is not obvious. One difference between Norman's study and the others is that, in his experiment, ability to judge self and others is measured by *J*'s accuracy in rating himself and his peers on the same list of traits. In Vernon's and Taft's studies the measure of ability to judge included more than tests of ability to rate self and others on a list of traits. Frenkel-Brunswik's study differs in that the *J*s were not rating their peers.

Taft's results also suggest one subtlety not mentioned by Norman; a chi-square analysis revealed a significant relationship that would not show up in either a linear or a curvilinear correlation: dividing the *J*s into three groups on the basis of their accuracy, it was found that whereas good judges of others tended to be average on ability to judge self and average judges of others tended to be good judges of self, poor judges of others tended to be either good or poor judges of self (rather than average).

Conclusion. Persons who show insight into their own status with respect to their peers on individual traits tend also to rate their peers accurately on those traits. However, when over-all indices are obtained of the subject's self-insight and of ability to judge others, using a variety of tests of these abilities, the relationship is not so clear-cut.

Good judges of self have been shown to possess a number of traits that differentiate them from good judges of others: in particular, greater social orientation. A more mature consideration is required in future work on this topic of the extent to which motivational forces that cause *J* to be accurate in his judgments of himself also cause him to distort his judgments of others.

Social Relations

Social Skill and Popularity. Common sense would suggest that a person who possesses good ability to judge people is able to use this ability to advantage in situations requiring social skill, *e.g.*, in leadership or salesmanship. It may be argued that ability to empathize with others and to play their roles, particularly in their relationships to oneself, is positively related to social skill. While there is some evidence to support this viewpoint, there is sufficient evidence to the contrary to force us to seek a more sophisticated attitude. In a study related to the area of role playing and social judgment, Moreno and Moreno (*49*) found that those children who were able to perceive social roles more accurately than others (according to the psychologist's judgment) were not necessarily those who could enact them best.

Vernon (*73*) found that the ability to judge strangers is related positively and significantly to scores on the Social Situations and the Memory for Names and Faces subtests of the George Washington Test of Social Intelligence, and negatively to scores on the Observation of Human Behavior subtest. In the OSS study (*55*), however, scores on the Judgment of Others Test (ability to write accurate personality descriptions of one's peers) had such a low correlation with the staff ratings of the candidates on Social Relations that it was discarded as a measure of this trait. Taft (*67*) used several tests and ratings to measure the social skills of his subjects; in a role-playing test the good judges of others were rated significantly lower on "ingenuity" than were the poor judges; there were no differences between good and poor judges in the ratings made by the assessment staff on "persuasiveness" in discussion nor on "likeability" as defined by peer sociometric choices. Both analytic and non-analytic judgments showed the same pattern.

Norman, in the Clinical Psychologist Assessment Study described above, also failed to obtain a linear correlation between ability to judge and a sociometric measure of the acceptability of his *J*s as professional co-workers. There was, however, a curvilinear relationship; those who received a medium score on acceptability were significantly better at judging than those who received a low score on acceptability. There is a hint here that a study which included more socially maladjusted persons than are usually found among *J*s in these types of investigation would reveal the expected positive correlation between social skill and ability to judge others.

Studies of the ability to predict group responses have found almost without exception a positive relationship between ability to judge and popularity; also good leaders and salesmen tend to be good judges. The study by Chowdhry and Newcomb (*16*) finds that those chosen as leaders in a sociometric test are good judges of group opinion only on topics relevant to the group. Ability on the "mass empathy" test (Psychometric Affiliates) correlates positively with various measures of the popularity and efficiency of union officials (*72*), with the ability of new car salesmen to sell (*68*), with the sociometric scores of steel workers as working companions (*63*), and with sociometric ratings of students on leadership after a half-hour discussion (*8*). In this latter study the Dymond test also correlated significantly with these ratings on leadership. Gage (*29*) reviews several studies (by Gage and Suci, Wood, and Sprunger) that confirm the positive relationship between the degree to which a group accepts *J* and his ability to predict the responses of this group to various opinion items. The one exception quoted is a Naval Leadership Project study which failed to find a correlation between the popularity of leaders on a ship and their ability to predict their crew's opinions on an attitude scale. Gage also found a positive correlation with popularity among high school students when the item responses were predicted by the *J*s for each individual S separately instead of for the group as a whole (*28*).

Conclusions. The ability to predict how Ss will respond to opinion items shows a consistent positive relationship with measures of social skill, such as leadership, salesmanship, and popularity. This relationship would follow logically from the probability that these types of social skill are aided by the ability to predict how people will behave. Unfortunately, this relationship could also be due simply to a combination of *J*'s tendency to project his own responses onto his S and his being in fact similar to S in his responses. Until these factors have been more carefully isolated, it is impossible to know which explanation is the correct one. Recently a method has been proposed (*11*) for separating the effects of projection, similarity, and empathy in such tests of judging ability. Other tests of ability to judge others, *e.g.*, rating traits or matching expressive behavior, do not show this same consistent relationship with social skills.

ATTITUDE TOWARD SOCIAL RELATIONS. In addition to considering the ability to judge others as a social "capacity," it should also be considered as an "attitude." An interest in social relations does not, however, mean good ability to judge the personality of others.

Adams working with the judgment of traits (see above) found that the good judges were independent but "talkative." "The good judge tends towards the egotistic . . . is cold-blooded towards others and not interested in them . . . he develops a shrewd ability to measure others, not as human beings, but as tools" (*1,* p. 181). This is consistent with the findings already mentioned that good judges of others tend to be less sociable than good judges of self (*1, 67, 73*).

Dymond (*21*) reports characteristics for her "high empathy" group that were more comparable to Adams' good self-raters than his good raters of others. On the basis of a TAT analysis, they are described as "outgoing, optimistic, warm, emotional people, who have a strong interest in others," while those low in empathy are "either self-centered and demanding in their emotional contacts or else lone wolves who prefer to get along without strong ties to other people" (*21,* p. 349). Possibly this finding results from Dymond's method of measuring "empathy" which includes in the score the ability to predict how the Ss will rate *J* as well as how they will rate themselves. This former measure is close to what we have called ability to judge self.

Taft asked his *J*s to check their own traits on the Gough Adjective Check List; the poor judges selected socially relevant traits almost exclusively, *e.g., egotistical, noisy,* whereas the good judges put far more stress on traits concerned with executing tasks, *e.g., industrious, patient.* In the tests of judging, the poor judges were significantly more likely to make their errors in the direction of generosity to their Ss than were the good judges. These and other data lead to the conclusion that the poor judges were more socially oriented than the good judges, while the latter were more task oriented. The social dependence of the poor judges makes them unwilling—or, perhaps, unable—to judge their Ss in a "hard-headed," extraceptive manner.

Conclusion. The evidence supports the contention that social detachment is a necessary prerequisite for making accurate judgments of others. This social detachment of the good judge of others could well account for the superior ability in this respect of physical scientists, referred to previously (*45, 67*), since this group might be thought to be less concerned with social matters than psychologists or social scientists.

JUDGABILITY. Are good judges those who are themselves more difficult to judge? On two grounds it might be expected that this would be the case: first, "As a rule people cannot comprehend others who are more complex and subtle than they" (5, p. 515), and, second, good judges are less socially expressive than poor judges, as we have just seen. Actually, Bender states that the better judges in his study were, in his opinion, persons whom others would have found more difficult to judge (9). His test required the *Js* to predict, on the basis of character sketches of eight Ss, their scores on seven opinion scales. Taft also found that his good judges were less accurately judged by their peers than were the poor judges.

Dymond found the contrary in her study, but since her good judges were *more* sociable than the poor ones, this suggests that the judgability of good and poor judges is possibly a function of their respective sociability. The validity of this explanation is borne out by the fact that, in an unreported part of Taft's experiment, the sociability of the Ss was positively correlated with the accuracy with which they were judged by both the assessment staff and their peers.

• OVER-ALL SUMMARY AND CONCLUSIONS

The ability to judge others has been considered as a personality trait, and its correlates have been discussed. Five different methods of measuring this ability have been described, and it was suggested that the results of the studies quoted may vary according to the operational definition used. This would seem to apply particularly to the distinction between analytic and nonanalytic techniques, although when we review the findings on the correlates of the ability to judge, we find few that reveal a definite difference between these two types of techniques.

The contradictions found between studies may be due partly to the low reliability of the measures used, and partly to the effect of specific factors such as the type of judgment required, the traits being judged, and the Ss used. This problem of specificity arises with all traits, but it seems to be particularly marked in the case of the ability to judge others; nevertheless, there does seem to be sufficient generality on this ability to justify describing at least some judges as "good" or "poor."

A great deal of carefully designed investigation is obviously required in the area of judging ability, both with respect to this ability as a general trait, and with respect to differences in the ability under specific conditions. Further experiments should employ longer, more reliable tests of the ability to judge the characteristics of others, and should systematically vary the types of tests used, the types of Ss being judged, and the range of *Js*. Studies are also required in which the effect of motivational factors can be observed.

Our review of the literature suggests that the following characteristics are fairly consistently found to be positively correlated with the ability to judge the personality characteristics of others: (a) age (children), (b) high intelligence and academic ability (with analytic judgments especially), (c) specialization in the physical sciences, (d) esthetic and dramatic interests, (e) insight into one's status with respect to one's peers on specific traits, (f) good emotional adjustment and integration (analytic tests only), and (g) social skill (only with tests of ability to predict S's behavior). The ability to judge correlates negatively with J's social dependence and his "psychasthenic" score on the MMPI. Characteristics showing fairly consistent lack of correlation are age (in adults), sex, and training in psychology. Some possible relationships on which more evidence is still required before we can substantiate the possible correlation with ability to judge mentioned in parentheses are number of older siblings (negative), literary ability (positive with analytic judgments), and being a clinical psychologist (negative). Two characteristics that may hold for especially poor judges only are poor social adjustment and either good or poor (not average) ability to judge self.

The main attributes of the ability to judge others seem to lie in three areas: possessing appropriate judgmental norms, judging ability, and motivation. Where J is similar in background to S, he has the advantage of being readily able to use appropriate *norms* for making his judgment. The relevant *judging ability* seems to be a combination of general intelligence and social intelligence, with the possibility of an additional specific factor for nonanalytic judgments ("intuition")—so far only Wedeck has distinguished such a factor. But probably the most important area of all is that of *motivation*: if the judge is motivated to make accurate judgments about his subject and if he feels himself free to be objective, then he has a good chance of achieving his aim, provided of course that he has the requisite ability and can use the appropriate judgmental norms. The act of judging one's fellows is a purposive piece of behavior that involves not only conscious motivation but also ingrained attitudes toward social relationships, including the relationships inherent in the act of judging itself.

REFERENCES

1. Adams, H. F. The good judge of personality. *J. abnorm. soc. Psychol.*, 1927, 22, 172–181.
2. Allport, F. H. *Social psychology*. Cambridge: Riverside Press, 1924.
3. Allport, F. H., & Allport, G. W. Personality traits: their classification and measurement. *J. abnorm. soc. Psychol.*, 1921, 16, 6–40.
4. Allport, F. H., & Musgrave, R. S. Teleonomic description in the study of behavior. *Charact. & Pers.*, 1941, 9, 326–343.
5. Allport, G. W. *Personality: a psychological interpretation*. New York: Henry Holt, 1937.
6. Argelander, Annalies. The personal factor in judging human character. *Charact. & Pers.*, 1937, 5, 285–296.
7. Barron, F. Personality style and perceptual choice. *J. Pers.*, 1952, 20, 385–401.
8. Bell, G. B., & Hall, H. E., Jr. The relationship between leadership and empathy. *J. abnorm. soc. Psychol.*, 1954, 49, 156–157.

9. Bender, I. E. A study in integrations of personalities by prediction and matching. Unpublished doctor's dissertation, Univer. of Syracuse, 1935.
10. Bender, I. E., & Hastorf, A. H. The perception of persons: forecasting another person's responses on three personality scales. *J. abnorm. soc. Psychol.*, 1950, 45, 556–561.
11. Bender, I. E., & Hastorf, A. H. On measuring generalized empathic ability (social sensitivity). *J. abnorm. soc. Psychol.*, 1953, 48, 503–506.
12. Bracken von, H. Persönlichkeitsfassung auf Grund von Persönlichkeitsbeschreibungen. *Jenaer. Beit. Z. Jugend und Erzihungspsychologie*, 1925, 1, 1–50. Reported in reference 5, 459–460.
13. Buzby, D. E. The interpretation of facial expression. *Amer. J. Psychol.*, 1924, 35, 602–604.
14. Cantor, R. R. An experimental study of a human relations training program. Unpublished doctor's dissertation. The Ohio State Univer., 1949.
15. Chapin, F. S. Preliminary standardization of a social insight scale. *Amer. soc. Rev.*, 1942, 7, 214–225.
16. Chowdhry, K., & Newcomb, T. M. The relative abilities of leaders and non-leaders to estimate opinions of their own group. *J. abnorm. soc. Psychol.*, 1952, 47, 51–57.
17. Cogan, L. G., Conklin, R. M., & Hollingworth, H. L. An experimental study of self-analysis, estimates of associates and the results of tests. *Sch. & Soc.*, 1915, 2, 171–179.
18. Coleman, J. C. Facial expressions of emotion. *Psychol. Monogr.*, 1949, 63, No. 1 (Whole No. 296).
19. Dymond, Rosalind F. A preliminary investigation of the relationship of insight and empathy. *J. consult. Psychol.*, 1948, 12, 228–233.
20. Dymond, Rosalind F. A scale for the measurement of empathic ability. *J. consult. Psychol.*, 1949, 13, 127–133.
21. Dymond, Rosalind, F. Personality and empathy. *J. consult. Psychol.*, 1950, 14, 343–350.
22. Dymond, Rosalind F., Hughes, Anne S., & Rabbe, Virginia L. Measurable changes in empathy with age. *J. consult. Psychol.*, 1952, 16, 202–206.
23. Estes, S. G. Judging personality from expressive behavior. *J. abnorm. soc. Psychol.*, 1938, 33, 217–236.
24. Ferguson, L. W. The value of acquaintance ratings in criteria research. *Personnel Psychol.*, 1949, 2, 93–102.
25. Fernberger, S. W. False suggestion and the Piderit model. *Amer. J. Psychol.*, 1928, 40, 562–568.
26. Fields, S. J. Discrimination of facial expression and its relation to personal adjustment. *J. soc. Psychol.*, 1953, 38, 63–71.
27. Frenkel-Brunswik, Else. Motivation and behavior. *Genet. Psychol. Monogr.*, 1942, 26, 121–265.
28. Gage, N. L. Judging interests from expressive behavior. *Psychol. Monogr.*, 1952, 66, No. 18 (Whole No. 350).

29. Gage, N. L. Explorations in the understanding of others. *Educ. psychol. Measmt,* 1953, 13, 14–26.
30. Gates, G. S. An experimental study of the growth of social perception. *J. educ. Psychol.,* 1923, 14, 449–462.
31. Goodenough, Florence L. Sex differences in judging the sex of handwriting. *J. soc. Psychol.,* 1945, 22, 61–68.
32. Green, G. H. Insight and group adjustment. *J. abnorm. soc. Psychol.,* 1948, 43, 49–61.
33. Guilford, J. P. An experiment in learning to read facial expression. *J. abnorm. soc. Psychol.,* 1929, 24, 191–202.
34. Hanks, L. M., Jr. Prediction from case material to personality data. *Arch. Psychol., N.Y.,* 1936, 29, No. 207.
35. Hastorf, A. H., & Bender, I. E. A caution respecting the measurement of empathic ability. *J. abnorm. soc. Psychol.,* 1952, 47, 574–576.
36. Heymans, G., & Wiersma, E. Beitrage zur speziellen Psychologie auf Grund einer Massenuntersuchung. *Z. Psychol.,* 1906, 42. Reported in reference 6.
37. Jenness, A. The recognition of facial expressions of emotions. *Psychol. Bull.,* 1932, 29, 324–350.
38. Kanner, L. Judging emotions from facial expressions. *Psychol. Monogr.,* 1931, 41, No. 3 (Whole No. 186).
39. Kellogg, W. N., & Eagleson, B. M. The growth of social perception in different racial groups. *J. educ. Psychol.,* 1931, 22, 367–375.
40. Kelly, E. L., & Fiske, D. W. *The prediction of performance in clinical psychology.* Ann Arbor: Univer. of Michigan Press, 1951.
41. Kelly, E. L., Miles, C. C., & Terman, L. Ability to influence one's score on a typical pencil and paper test of personality. *Charact. & Pers.,* 1936, 4, 206–215.
42. Landis, C. The interpretation of facial expression in emotion. *J. gen. Psychol.,* 1929, 2, 59–72.
43. Lindgren, H. C., & Robinson, Jacqueline. The evaluation of Dymond's test of insight and empathy. *J. consult. Psychol.,* 1953, 17, 172–176.
44. Luft, J. Some relationships between clinical specialization and the understanding and prediction of an individual's behavior. Unpublished doctor's dissertation, Univer. of California, Los Angeles, 1949.
45. Luft, J. Implicit hypotheses and clinical predictions. *J. abnorm. soc. Psychol.,* 1950, 45, 756–760.
46. McClelland, W. A preliminary test of role-playing ability. *J. consult. Psychol.,* 1951, 15, 102–108.
47. Martin, H. W. Effects of practice on judging various traits of individuals. *Psychol. Bull.,* 1938, 35, 690. (Abstract)
48. Mead, G. H. *Mind, self and society.* Chicago: Univer. of Chicago Press, 1934.
49. Moreno, J. L., & Moreno, Florence B. Role tests and role diagrams of children. In J. L. Moreno (Ed.), *Group psychotherapy.* New York: Beacon House, 1945. Pp. 188–203.
50. Moss, F. A., Hunt, T., Omwake, K. T., & Bonning, M. M. *Social intelligence test.* Washington: Center for Psychological Service, 1927.

51. Murray, H. A. *Explorations in personality.* New York: Oxford Univer. Press, 1938.
52. Newcomb, T. M. An experiment designed to test the validity of a rating technique. *J. educ. Psychol.,* 1931, 22, 279–289.
53. Norman, R. D. The interrelationships among acceptance-rejection, self-other identity, insight into self, and realistic perception of others. *J. soc. Psychol.,* 1953, 37, 205–235.
54. Notcutt, B., & Silva, A. L. M. Knowledge of other people. *J. abnorm. soc. Psychol.,* 1951, 46, 30–37.
55. OSS Assessment Staff. *Assessment of men.* New York: Rinehart, 1948.
56. Polansky, N. A. How shall a life history be written? *Charact. & Pers.,* 1941, 9, 188–207.
57. Rabin, A. I. Szondi's pictures: identification of diagnoses. *J. abnorm. soc. Psychol.,* 1950, 45, 392–395.
58. Rokeach, M. Studies in beauty. II. Some determiners of the perception of beauty in women. *J. soc. Psychol.,* 1945, 22, 155–169.
59. Scodell, A., & Mussen, P. Social perceptions of authoritarians and nonauthoritarians. *J. abnorm. soc. Psychol.,* 1953, 43, 181–184.
60. Sears, R. R. Experimental studies of projection. I. Attribution of traits. *J. soc. Psychol.,* 1936, 7, 151–163.
61. Sherriffs, A. C. The "intuition questionnaire." A new projective test. *J. abnorm. soc. Psychol.,* 1948, 43, 326–337.
62. Soskin, W. F. Bias in postdiction from projective tests. *J. abnorm. soc. Psychol.,* 1954, 49, 69–74.
63. Speroff, B. J. Empathic ability and accident rate among steel workers. *Personnel Psychol.,* 1953, 6, 297–300.
64. Steinmetz, H. C. A study of the ability to predict test responses. Unpublished doctor's dissertation, Purdue Univer., 1947.
65. Sullivan, H. S. Conceptions of modern psychiatry. *Psychiatry,* 1940, 3, 1–117.
66. Sweet, Lennig. *The measurement of personal attitudes in younger boys.* New York: Association Press, 1929.
67. Taft, R. Some correlates of the ability to make accurate social judgments. Unpublished doctor's dissertation, Univer. of California, 1950.
68. Tobolski, F. P., & Kerr, W. A. Predictive value of the empathy test in automobile salesmanship. *J. appl. Psychol.,* 1952, 36, 310–311.
69. Travers, R. M. W. A study in judging the opinions of groups. *Arch. Psychol., N.Y.,* 1941, No. 266, 1–73.
70. Travers, R. M. W. A study of the ability to judge group-knowledge. *Amer. J. Psychol.,* 1943, 56, 54–65.
71. Valentine, C. W. The relative reliability of men and women in intuitive judgments of character. *Brit. J. Psychol.,* 1929, 19, 213–238.
72. Van Zelst, R. H. Empathy test scores of union leaders. *J. appl. Psychol.,* 1952, 36, 293–295.
73. Vernon, P. E. Some characteristics of the good judge of personality. *J. soc. Psychol.,* 1933, 4, 42–57.

74. Wallen, R. Individual's estimates of group opinions. *J. soc. Psychol.*, 1943, 17, 269–274.
75. Wallin, P. The prediction of individual behavior from case studies. *Soc. Sci. Res. Coun. Bull.*, 1941, No. 48, 181–250.
76. Walton, W. E. Empathic responses in children. *Psychol. Monogr.*, 1936, 48, No. 1 (Whole No. 213), 40–67.
77. Watson, D. L. On the role of insight in the study of mankind. *Psychoanal. Rev.*, 1938, 25, 358–371.
78. Wedeck, J. The relationship between personality and "psychological ability." *Brit. J. Psychol.*, 1947, 37, 133–151.
79. Wedell, C., & Smith, K. U. Consistency of interview methods in appraisal of attitudes. *J. appl. Psychol.*, 1951, 35, 392–396.
80. Weingarten, Erica M. A study of selective perception in clinical judgment. *J. Pers.*, 1949, 17, 396–406.
81. Wolf, R., & Murray, H. A. An experiment in judging personality. *J. Psychol.*, 1937, 3, 345–365.

B. Issues and Problems in Appraisal

2. THE CASE FOR QUANTITATIVE MEASURES OF PERFORMANCE

SENIORITY AND MERIT RATING IN LABOR RELATIONS

GUY W. WADSWORTH, JR.

HOW TO APPRAISE EXECUTIVE PERFORMANCE

ARCH PATTON

PROFIT PERFORMANCE MEASUREMENT OF DIVISION MANAGERS

JOEL DEAN

A common criticism of performance rating systems is that while appraisals are thus made systematic, they remain subjective in nature. Men have exercised considerable ingenuity in trying to devise ways of minimizing the subjective character of human judgment. One way, discussed in later readings, has been the substitution of group judgment for that of the individual. Another way—one that has been explored for a long time—is that of applying direct (and preferably quantitative) measures of performance. Such measures, ideally, would require no further interpretation, but would be like the readings taken from a recording thermometer. Judgment is not completely obviated, of course. But it is exercised only in the setting of standards, the later performance ratings being automatically determined.

The production output records used for incentive pay purposes in the factory are quantitative measures comparable to those sought for over-all performance. The literature of wage administration includes a wealth of material on incentive pay systems and output records. These topics are excluded here to provide space for the readings on efforts being made to develop more general quantitative or objective measures of individual performance.

The most pervasive of the objective measures is seniority. Perhaps it sounds strange to call seniority a performance record. In fact, many have argued the existence of an inverse correlation between performance quality and seniority. Strictly speaking, it is true that performance and seniority are alternative measures of merit. But it is generally conceded, by managers as well as others, that it is reasonable to infer quality of performance from length of service to some degree. American labor unions, in general, have behaved as though the relationship were clear and linear. But managers, too, have relied heavily upon seniority in their devotion to promotion from within and in the high value they place upon experience or tenure. In his article Wadsworth analyzes the relationship between performance ratings and seniority in one company.

Serious effort is currently being devoted to seeking quantitative performance measures for effective assessment of managers. Most attention has been given to profit performance measurement, although some people have tried to develop specific activity measurement where achievement is rated against quantitative standards. The readings in this section set forth the philosophy of the individuals who advocate use of objective performance measures. Further readings in Part Two–E describe the methods being developed.

FURTHER READING

Baumback, Clifford M., *Merit And Seniority As Factors In Promotion And In-Grade Progression.* Iowa State University, Bureau of Labor and Management, 1956 (Research Series No. 11).

A discussion of worker efficiency and production cost as influenced by opportunities for increased earnings and for advancement in accordance with individual merit and/or seniority.

Gaylord, Richard H., and others, "The Relation of Ratings to Production Records: An Empirical Study," *Personnel Psychology,* Vol. 4, no. 4, Winter 1951, pp. 363–371.

Rothe, Harold F., "The Relations of Merit Ratings to Length of Service," *Personnel Psychology,* Vol. 2, no. 2, Summer 1949, pp. 237–242.

SENIORITY AND MERIT RATING IN LABOR RELATIONS*

Guy W. Wadsworth, Jr.

Considering the difficulties inherent in union-management relationships in reaching really workable understandings on seniority versus merit in promotions and layoffs, the title of this discussion might well be "Seniority and/or Merit." The merit issue, as I shall discuss it, is somewhat more basic than the question of whether or not merit rating systems, as such, can be made acceptable to unions and managements alike. Therefore this is not essentially a treatise on rating methods, though they will receive some attention. Certainly I have no super-rating system to suggest.

Another point that should be made clear at the outset is that the discussion in its entirety relates to the operation of seniority formulae in promotions and layoffs only as applied to rank-and-file jobs—those distinctly below the supervisory level. It is assumed out of hand that except for borderline instances where minor supervisory functions are vested in what might be termed "upper case" rank-and-file jobs, there is no occasion for a management to accept application of hard-and-fast seniority formulae to supervisory or executive positions.

Industry in general is confronted, first, by the fact that the average rank-and-file worker, expressing himself collectively, is likely to demand some form of seniority protection. We are confronted, further, by the fact that the average employer feels that seniority formulae in general operate in disregard of valid differences in individual ability and merit. Are these viewpoints irreconcilable, or can they be adjusted upon some reasonably satisfactory basis?

Why Employers Fear Straight Seniority

A seniority formula that must be applied in promotions and layoffs can result in a number of the unhappy consequences generally visualized by employers, particularly if its advent is taken as a calamity, on the assumption that it amounts to just one more interference with the management's right to run the business. It can prove equally disappointing to the individual worker. Depending upon the accident, or series of accidents, that may have placed him in a given spot at a given time, the chances are no better that a seniority formula will really improve the individual worker's prospects than they are that it will bury him alive in a dead-end job. He may find that he has bought a semblance of "job security" at the expense of his right to compete and his right to aspire. Even the protection of seniority in layoffs does not forestall layoffs or insure continuing employment to any given number of people. It merely establishes an order in which people affected by shortages of work are to be laid off.

These negative considerations could be expanded if there were any profit in doing it. It may be that there is no completely satisfactory answer to some

* From *Advances in Methods of Personnel Evaluation,* pp. 22–32. American Management Association, Personnel Series No. 107, 1947.

of the contentions raised both by employers and by workers with respect to seniority. On the other hand, a great many of us do our thinking on this subject in a very bad frame of mind. It is hard to deal intelligently with an issue when you start off convinced that it offers no workable solution. We make the problem worse when we convey our own misgivings to other people, particularly supervisors and others who must get results from workers subject to the operation of a seniority formula. Therefore I do not propose to dwell at length upon all the harm that a seniority formula can do; nor will I admit that even strict observance of a seniority formula in promotions and layoffs is invariably incompatible with considerations involving merit.

• TWO BASIC ISSUES

The general problem of seniority versus merit in promotions and layoffs appears to divide itself into two basic issues. The first is whether or not the employer can or should maintain the traditional practice of singling out exceptional employees, promoting them more or less at will without reference to their seniority, and retaining such employees on the payroll when other employees in comparable jobs, but with greater length of service, must be laid off. The second issue is whether or not application of a seniority formula in promotions means that people who do not merit promotions must be promoted anyway, and whether observance of seniority in layoffs means that satisfactory employees must be laid off while nonproducers are kept on the payroll.

It is important to maintain the distinction between these two issues. In the first, the principal concern is with the right of the employer to pick and choose as he sees best in making promotions, and in designating who shall be laid off in face of a shortage of work. In the second, the point in question is the practical authority of the employer, in face of a seniority formula, to forestall unmerited promotions and distinguish between workers who perform adequately and those who do not, in cases of layoff.

Why Do Workers Want Seniority?

The first issue is most easily considered by trying to understand why the workers want seniority, or think they want it, or can be made to think they want it. Seniority in promotions has a fairly obvious and direct appeal to any worker who has been passed up for a promotion for which he had some reason to feel that he was in line. It has a somewhat less direct but almost as effective an appeal to his fellow workers. They see someone they like, or at least regard as deserving, lose out on a chance to get ahead. They visualize themselves in his shoes, and conclude that they, as individuals, may expect to fare no better. Placing workers, or allowing them to drift, into locations where they are apparently in line for promotions for which they will not actually receive serious consideration provides the basis not only for the most ancient of all individual grievances, but for the demand that all promotions be governed entirely by length of service, either on the job or with the company.

Pressure for observance of seniority in layoffs, on the thesis that the man last hired should be the first fired, is attributable at least in part to incidents alleged to have happened in periods of reduced business activity. Necessary lay-offs, it is charged, have been used indiscriminately by employers to "weed out dead timber"; supervisors who did not have the courage forthrightly to remove employees who were not producing on the job in good times, lay in wait, so to speak, and caught the offenders at the crossroads during periods of retrenchment. Probably in comparatively few instances, but certainly in enough cases to attract attention, workers of advanced age were laid off on this basis, and more promising newcomers kept, in apparent disregard of term of service. Some of this happened in the 1930's, when attention was generally focused on unemployment, the problems of the senior citizen, and so on. The "job security" thesis may have hatched from eggs laid by thoughtless employers during this period.

From the Employer's Viewpoint

If we, as employers, look open-mindedly at the proposition of maintaining the right to pick and choose as we see best in making promotions, I think we will have to conclude that if successful in standing our ground, we would gain one point at the sacrifice of another, almost as important. Our position in this regard, of course, would have to be reinforced by a valid assumption that we have the means at hand with which to distinguish between a meritorious and exceptional employee and one who is not, but more of that later. The immediate point is whether or not we gain more by exercising a free hand in promotions than we lose by giving the average satisfactory employee reason to feel that his chances for even a minor promotion can be foreclosed at any time if his supervisor, or perhaps some other supervisor, elects to promote someone else who is regarded as superior.

If normal expectancy operates in the distribution of exceptional employees in the total working force, some 20 to 25 per cent might validly be tabbed exceptional or superior, and thus have a prior claim on promotions. How can we preserve the incentive of the remaining three quarters of the rank and file, if one quarter are given the inside track on the promotions to which the average rank-and-file worker can look forward?

I think there is considerable basis for feeling that both the employer and the employee are well served when the average satisfactory worker is convinced that he can expect actual consideration in promotions. Possibly that is what we had in mind when we coined the phrase "promotion from within." What we probably meant was that when some relatively attractive opening occurred, we were disposed to look over the existing force for possible candidates rather than hire an outsider out of hand. On this basis, many companies can point to the fact that their top management people have risen from the ranks as a result of promotion-from-within policies. This is good as far as it goes, but carries with it no real assurance that the principle of promotion from within will figure in the majority of promotions, or especially in the relatively minor ones in which the rank and file has the most immediate interest. What the average employee wants to know is: (a) whether he can point toward some particular job in a line of promotion that is fairly well ordered and recognized, and (b) whether, if he does good work in his current job, he can expect a shot at the next job ahead. We cannot convey either point to him if, in practice, we reserve at all times the right to cut him out in favor of someone who in our opinion can perform the next job up somewhat better.

ACTUAL PRACTICE IN PROMOTIONS

Of almost equal importance in considering promotional practices in general is the fact that the average supervisor who exercises a free hand in upgrading does not tend to handle promotional moves in a manner that suggests that each employee who might reasonably expect consideration for a given promotion will necessarily receive it.

Almost any shop superintendent or office manager who is asked about promotional opportunities and particularly lines of promotion in his bailiwick will quickly sketch out a traditional multi-jointed spider-leg organization chart that shows the beginning jobs in various sections of his shop or office, and the line-up of jobs above that level in perhaps several working units. Such a chart will usually identify the key jobs and the understudy jobs in each line of work. You can readily conclude that this chart shows how the supervisor actually operates in making promotions, but do not set this down in the book until you get the answers to a few more questions. Ask him, for example, where the occupant of the third position in a vertical line of five or six jobs came from. Did the employee work up from the bottom, or was he sandwiched in there ahead of several people down the line? Is the employee in the next job below one of the foremen actually an acceptable understudy for his boss, or, if the foreman should move up or out, would the supervisor have to get someone else to fill the bill? You want to know whether the supervisor, left to his own devices, applies the promotion-from-within policies of the company in a manner which suggests order in the general scheme of promotions, or whether he merely gives a general look around and picks whom he chooses (from his own group to be sure).

Typing Employees

I can tell you that an initial discussion with the average supervisor on this subject usually reveals that, unless definite lines of promotion have been established in his shop or office, the history of individual promotions leaves little to suggest that given jobs really lead to other jobs in actual practice. I can tell you, further, that when the promotional possibilities of his people are discussed with the supervisor, employee by employee, throughout the whole of his working group, the discussion bears all the earmarks of being the first time that he has given any number of his workers a thought in this regard. It appears, rather, that he tends to "type" individuals early in the course of their employment, to tab them either as people who might fit into some promotional spot later on, or not, as the case may be. Ordinarily he does not plan promotions either in terms of one job leading to another, or in a manner that necessarily insures individual consideration to each worker.

How a Seniority Formula Operates

How does a seniority formula operate in this situation? Well, it establishes an order in which employees must be considered for promotions, and the condition that an individual worker can be by-passed on a promotion for which he is in line only on some definite showing that he cannot satisfactorily perform the duties of the better job.

A typical union seniority clause provides that "where ability and qualifications are equal, seniority"—either "job seniority" or "company seniority"—"shall decide promotions." After some years of wrestling with the "equal ability and qualifications" feature of this clause, unions currently demand clauses that require seniority to operate in promotions "where ability and qualifications are sufficient." They argue that the expression "equal ability" tends to be shaded too finely by many supervisors, and that it is used as justification for skipping down the seniority list. Make no mistake on this score—no company with a union seniority clause will continuously evade the basic purpose of the clause itself—namely, that an employee who is in line for a promotion, and who can perform the work required on the next job up, shall be entitled to really serious consideration for it. He is not to be passed up unless there are sound reasons to believe that he cannot deliver on the promotional job.

This, of course, hits at the primary conception of merit promotions in the sense of picking and choosing employees for promotion at will. Under this conception, an average worker would be considered for a promotion only when no superior worker is a candidate. The arguments for a stand-and-die attitude on this score on the part of employers would be a little stronger than they are if we knew more than we actually know about determining and evaluating merit.

What Ratings Really Show

Probably anyone who directs a group of workers of such size that he can observe their performance daily and intimately can spot outstanding individuals as distinguished from employees who merely do enough to get by. That is, he can do so if he really takes the trouble to follow up each worker and make a continuing study of his performance on the job. However, anyone who is thoroughly familiar with rating procedure in its current state of development knows that the average supervisor does no such thing. He works on his rating reports with about the same delight that he takes in filling out his personal income tax return—usually in about the same proximity to the deadline. This is wholly unbecoming a true champion of merit. The most horrible example I can think of was in Federal Civil Service, where something over 80 per cent of the employees in one of the largest governmental agencies received superior ratings almost continuously during World War II. There is an explanation for this quaint situation, but in general one of the last things I would necessarily believe is that a given worker is actually superior merely because he was so rated on an efficiency report—whether in public service or private enterprise. This is to say that if we are to stand and die on the merit principle, I, for one, would want a bit more substantial basis for my martyrdom than the distinctions between "satisfactory" and "superior" tossed off by the average supervisor in rating workers.

In some 15 years of working with rating systems, and particularly of trying to find out what prompts "superior" as opposed to "average" or less than average ratings, I have become convinced that, except where they are based on recorded performance of measured work, the vast majority of supervisors' ratings are essentially negatively diagnostic. This is to say that even where considerable effort is devoted to developing facts in support of any opinion or judgment-type rating—and most ratings are of that type—the average supervisor is on sounder ground when he describes failure on the job than when he distinguishes between "satisfactory" and "superior" performance.

An Illustration. An example, one drawn from a large number of similar examples, illustrates this point. Two years before the war, supervisors in one of our collection departments asked me what the chances were of getting merit raises for some portion of a group of about 100 collectors. I inquired whether they could give me a list of their 25 best collectors, the top performers in the group. A list of 25 names was in my hands in about 15 minutes, along with enthusiastic questions about "How much?" and "When do we tell the men?"

I asked the supervisors if they had specific criteria of excellence in collecting, and they said they certainly had. The first of these was the amount of average daily collections per man, which was reasonable because the bills involved averaged about the same in amount, and the number of collection calls assigned to each collector was about the same. The second criterion was the percentage of collection assignments completed in relation to the number assigned. Since the bills were carefully routed for time and distance involved per collection, this too seemed fair enough. The third criterion was the proportion of instances in which the collector got the money as opposed to turning off the gas. There is a delicate point here. Out West in the golden sunshine of California, a turned-off gas meter does not mean that anyone will freeze to death, but the Gas Company does not pay dividends from the proceeds of shut-off meters.

Now these supervisors had kept very accurate records of the performance of all of the collectors against these criteria, and, indeed, some others that I have not mentioned. Just by way of making a check, therefore, I asked not only for the records in the case of each "superior" collector, but for the records of the rest of the collectors, including those who were considered saisfactory (but not superior), and those who were considered less than satisfactory or frankly unsatisfactory.

Well, the records of the 25 superior collectors as named by the supervisors did not show up any better on any individual criterion than those of 25 other collectors in the same group who had not been named for a raise. There was no combination of the criteria in which the recorded performance of the selected 25 was any better than that of a like number of collectors who had not been named. To be sure, all the favored candidates had good records—but almost an equal number of others had equally good records.

The really striking feature of this comparison was that, even in face of this showing, the supervisors stoutly held to the point that they had named the 25 best men. Perhaps, in addition to being good performers, the collectors involved were also pleasant and obliging—perhaps they appealed on some other basis—frankly, I do not know. However, in these days when we carefully endeavor to describe and evaluate job duties, and to price jobs in accordance with the value of the work itself, we can hardly turn to less tangible criteria in deciding merit. If the merit is there it should show up clearly in line with the values with which we price the job.

A collateral finding in this study, however, was of great value. When I asked the supervisors to name the poorest 25 collectors in the group, the collectors they included showed up poorly in one or more, if not all of the criteria on which records had been kept. There was no basis for applying the question mark to unsatisfactory or barely satisfactory ratings, at least so far as the criteria were concerned. I have found such negative diagnosis, as we might call it, uniformly better supported by facts than are distinctions between satisfactory and better than satisfactory employees in every study of this kind that we have made. To my mind, this places grave doubt on the advisability of being nailed to the cross in support of the "superior" or "exceptional" employee, as named in the average supervisory rating, in relation to either promotions or layoffs.

On Balance

All in all, it is difficult to build a convincing case for complete freedom to pick and choose, with only nominal consideration of length of service, either in promotions or layoffs. Probably there is some loss of incentive in regimentation of promotions—but quite possibly also there is potentially as much loss of incentive where the average satisfactory employee who has worked the longest for a promotion can be by-passed at will. This applies, whether the by-passing occurs in favor of someone else regarded as superior, or whether it happens under conditions in which the supervisor is under no real compunction to give each worker truly individual consideration. The key point to my mind, however, is the great uncertainty that attaches to supervisory judgment as exercised in making distinctions between "satisfactory" and "superior." All too often such distinctions are made without the ghost of substantial supporting fact.

Having dealt intimately with large numbers of supervisors for many years, I am fully aware that they greatly resent any abridgement of the right to assign and promote employees as they please. They are terribly put out, at least initially, when management requires them to develop and follow fixed lines of promotion, and they abhor requirements in which workers must be considered for promotion in a fixed order. Yet both conditions have been required in our companies as regards all promotions in the area of rank-and-file jobs. I am not half so much worried about the merit issue in relation to the promotion of superior individuals in the ranks, as I am about whether or not the supervisor exacts performance of an adequate day's work from each employee who reports to him. The superior or exceptional individual, if a factual basis for characterizing him as such can be established, undergoes little harm by serving an apprenticeship on equal terms with other employees in the rank and file. He can be lifted in due time into a supervisory position, or he can be placed in some other lower or middle management capacity where seniority does not operate. We have plenty of room there for superior people. Otherwise, so long as we retain the right to veto or turn back rank-and-file promotions that should not occur, and so long as we actually remove nonproducers from the job as we go along rather than wait for a slump to provide the occasion for getting rid of them, it makes little practical difference to us whether the order in which an employee must be considered for a promotion or layoff is determined by his seniority, by the alphabet, or by the signs on his horoscope.

• PRACTICAL QUALITY CONTROLS

This brings us up to the second issue involved in considering the problem of seniority versus merit. What practical quality controls can be exercised within a hard-and-fast seniority formula to see to it that employees are promoted only when their performance merits it, and what can be done about nonproducers who should not be on the job, and who certainly deserve no special protection, irrespective of term of service, when layoffs occur? I believe that our companies have developed satisfactory answers to both questions.

Selection with Promotion in View

First, because we have established lines of promotion, we know when we hire someone for a beginning job just what possible promotions are in store for him. We try so far as possible to see to it that the newcomer has the capacity to handle the top rank-and-file job in the work for which he is being considered. To accomplish this we use psychological tests which have been applied first to successful workers in the top job. The showing made by the candidate in the tests must compare favorably with that of employees of known success at the top of the line. This has served us well for so many years that I shall not digress to discuss "How good is testing?" Tests have done a good job for us, and if you can make them do a good job for you, you ought to use them.

Second, we reinforce our initial employee selection job with a rigid follow-up during our probationary period of six months. The supervisor is required to observe the newcomer at work, and to recommend that he be kept on or dropped, well before expiration of the six months. An affirmative recommendation must state in detail what the employee does in relation to the requirements of his job that warrants his becoming a regular employee. We do not permit the probationary period to go by default, nor does the mere fact that the new employee proves to be inoffensive assure him regular employment. Upward of 12 per cent of all newcomers are dropped for failure to show positive promise under actual job conditions during the probationary period.

The Field Review Method

Third, we use what we call a "Field Review Method" of employee evaluation in which, in lieu of a check-item rating device, we discuss in ordinary cross-table conversation the performance of each employee with his supervisor. These reviews are conducted on a system-wide basis twice a year. Discussion covers each employee's good points, his weaknesses, if any, his suitability for the next job up, and so on. Good points and weaknesses are taken up in some detail with the supervisor in order to develop specific supporting facts, drawn from his direct observation of the employee at work. This is accomplished by a standard questioning procedure. Its ultimate purpose is to prompt the superior to plan a specific action, whenever one is called for.

For example, if the employee is obviously making good and merits promotion to the next job up, the supervisor "okays" him for promotion. If the employee appears exceptional, he is tabbed for further follow-up. If the employee is not making good, and it is clear (a) that he has been warned of the fact, and (b) that the supervisor has made a reasonable effort to bring the employee's performance up to standard, a demotion or discharge is scheduled. If the employee appears unsuitable for promotion, possible correctives are considered, or, failing that, a specific basis for denying any promotion in the immediate offing is developed. This includes a bill of particulars setting forth the facts that prompt and support denial of the promotion, which is used initially in discussing the matter with the employee. It also has its uses in any resultant grievance action, and, in very rare instances, in arbitrations. In some hundreds of instances in which our supervisors have denied promotions on the foregoing basis, we have backed up in grievance procedure less than a dozen times. Denials of promotion have gone to arbitration only twice in the last six years. The supervisor was sustained in both instances.

"Yardstick of Fair Play"

A collateral feature of this Field Review Method, which is used in all demotions, discharges, and denials of promotion, is application of a four-point test of the fairness of the proposed action which we call a "Yardstick of Fair Play." After all the facts have been assembled and reviewed, the action under consideration is finally checked against the following questions:

1. Is the alleged job failure or inadequacy so clearly established by facts and so supported by related information as to time, place, and surrounding circumstances, as to leave no doubt that work failures have actually occurred, or that inadequacies have been definitely demonstrated?
2. Are the job failures or inadequacies typical and representative of the employee's work as a whole, or do they merely represent minor lapses in a generally good record of performance?
3. Would the proposed action assess a penalty against this employee for failures or inadequacies which other employees in the same group are allowed to get by with?
4. Has the employee been told about his weaknesses and been given a real chance to improve?

Space does not permit further elaboration of the Yardstick of Fair Play, except to indicate that after considerable experience with grievance procedure in demotions, discharges, and denials of promotion, we know that each of the four points or questions represents a possible loophole that should be plugged with facts, or a condition that should be met, before the supervisor acts. I should like to add, also, that while the Field Review Method sounds formidable, and appears to place a great many exactions upon the supervisors and the personnel department staff, it is actually a relatively uninvolved procedure. Essentially the supervisor is prompted periodically to review the whole of his working force, and at the same time to plan a course of action where needed in individual cases. He is questioned rather searchingly, but any action that results is his own. In practice, the discussion brings out many points on which the supervisors will not commit themselves in written rating reports, and certainly it prompts many an action that would not be taken otherwise.

On the whole the interest that the supervisors take in the Field Review discussions and in planning their own personnel moves, plus the working knowledge of the personnel situation throughout the company that representatives of our personnel department gain in the process, amply repays the working time involved. If anything, the Field Review Method requires less of the supervisors' working time and less personnel department staff than did our former practice of preparing rating forms and schedules, training supervisors in how to rate, recording and studying their ratings, and then making the necessary follow-up inquiries to find out why some employees with mediocre ratings were nonetheless promoted, why some with very high ratings were consistently held back, and why in the world a supervisor would continuously rate an employee as obviously incompetent, but do nothing about it.

What Has the Plan Accomplished?

Have we achieved a workable solution to the problem of seniority versus merit in promotions and layoffs? Well, that is a question of viewpoint. By hindsight, I believe that if we had voluntarily established order in the general scheme of promotions in our companies before the unions demanded it, and if we had voluntarily taken steps to see to it that every employee who was logically in line for a promotion would actually receive specific consideration for it, irrespective of the outcome, we would have placed no improper exactions on ourselves. I am sure that the average rank-and-file worker is better off under our present seniority system than he was before we had it. We, on our part, pay more detailed attention to what goes on in promotions and layoffs because we have that system. The fact that our piety on this score was somewhat belated and that we were converted under pressure has not added particularly to our standing with the employees. However, I am satisfied that the average promotion in our companies goes to a good man, and that more incompetents have been removed because of the exactions of our seniority formula than would have been removed without it.

A Better Personnel Job

In the main, the emphasis placed by unions on seniority means that you have to do a better personnel job. You have to know what you are doing when you place an applicant for employment in a given assignment. You have to prompt your supervisors really to study their people and to plan logically for a better working force. You have to develop standards of fairness, and see to it that they are applied in promotions and layoffs. As a personnel man, what else are you there for?

HOW TO APPRAISE EXECUTIVE PERFORMANCE*

Arch Patton

What makes an executive successful? Why does one man forge his way to the top, while another, equally trained, fails to live up to company expectations? How can we better understand the process by which executives develop?

In hopes of finding answers to these important questions, one of the country's largest corporations made a survey, a few years ago, of the educational, economic, and social backgrounds of more than 100 top-echelon executives. The objective of the study was to discover if the early life experiences of this demonstrably successful group of men had common elements that could be used to improve the corporation's executive selection and development process.

• AS DIVERSE AS AMERICA

The research team carefully studied the early family life of each top-management executive, including his family's financial and social status, the extent of his formal education, subjects studied, marks received, and his early work experience. When the results of the survey were reviewed, it was found that the environment of the company's key executives during their formative years tended to be as diverse as America itself. These highly successful executives came from poor as well as wealthy families, some had Master's degrees while others failed to finish high school, and outstanding and average students were found in equal numbers.

Only one common historic relationship was discovered: *within two years after joining the company, the compensation of each executive topped the average for his age group, and this pay differential above the average widened at an accelerating rate throughout his career.*

The results of this study underscore the dangers inherent in a recruiting process that slavishly follows preconceived ideas of what it takes to make an outstanding executive. The results indicate, furthermore, that intelligence, courage, aggressiveness, and other qualities making for business success are incubated in virtually every conceivable early environment.

The most significant contribution of the survey may turn out to be a better understanding of the executive development process. For if we cannot prejudge the *capacity* of the individual with any certainty, it follows that we must assign critical importance to the ability to judge on-the-job *performance.* This performance appraisal is a never-ending process, for individuals reach the peak of their ability, or willingness, to accept responsibility at different stages in their careers. As every top executive knows, many apparently well-endowed individuals reach "plateaus" of arrested development early in their careers, while others seem able to draw indefinitely on hidden reserves of strength to take on ever larger responsibilities.

* From *Harvard Business Review,* January–February 1960, Vol. 38, no. 1, pp. 63–70.

In effect, this means that the soundest basis for judging an individual's ability to handle a higher-level job is how well he is dealing with similar problems in his present job. Or, to put it another way, an executive's past and present performance is the most reliable key to his future performance. This being the case, the ability of management to judge an individual's performance is basic to the continuing success of the enterprise.

• EARLY APPRAISAL EFFORTS

The need for sound appraisals of executive performance has been recognized in industry for many years. The first efforts in this direction tended to have psychological overtones and usually consisted of appraisals of traits that were deemed important to a successful executive. Thus, these early approaches did not appraise performance in terms of the results stemming from decisions made or influenced by an individual, but rather in terms of preconceived characteristics that management personnel were presumed to have. Particularly in the years following World War II, performance appraisal was often looked on as an integral part of an executive development program.

Subjective Approach

Unfortunately, the executive characteristics appraised in development programs—leadership, initiative, dependability, judgment, getting along with people, ambition, and so on—do not necessarily measure a man's *effectiveness* on the job. Indeed, all too often judgments of performance under such plans reflect what is *thought* of the man rather than what he *does*.

The great weakness in this approach has proved to be the lack of performance criteria that are related to job responsibilities. Such concentration on personality traits ignores the more objective measures of on-the-job performance that are developed from budgets and accounting reports. This highly subjective approach, in turn, has made it difficult for management to communicate its judgment of an executive's performance to the man who has been evaluated. It is the rare individual who will concede that he does not display executive characteristics, and an even rarer boss who can comfortably explain shortcomings of so personal a nature to his subordinate. By contrast, the more objective criteria—rising or falling sales, profit margins, scrap losses, employee turnover, absenteeism, machine down time, and the like—are more readily understood by the subordinate and easier to explain because they are in quantitative terms which are part of the operating language of the business.

Another factor that tends to obsolete trait-oriented appraisals in recent years has been the increasing use of executive incentive plans in industry. More and more companies have found their bonus plans "in trouble" because eligible executives do not believe that incentive payments based on subjective appraisals reflect their individual efforts. This belief apparently results from an instinctive revulsion among executives to having their compensation largely dependent on what senior executives *think* of them. First, they suspect favoritism, and second, they exhibit a subconscious desire to have their performance measured by yardsticks that are based on more tangible, quantitative targets they have learned to understand and trust.

Mathematical Approach

Some companies have taken steps to overcome the "popularity contest" aspects of subjective appraisals and to meet the growing need for judging performance in terms of individual targets. Often, however, such procedures have swung to the other extreme in bonus plan administration: setting individual goals for the year in quantitative terms (*e.g.*, increase sales 10% or cut scrap losses 7%) and paying off on "performance" directly keyed to those goals. This approach has the great advantage of eliminating subjective judgment as the determinant of an individual's bonus. Furthermore, it does measure performance, and in terms that are understandable to the individual.

But the experience of many companies which have adopted this mathematical approach indicates that it, too, has serious shortcomings. The most important weakness revolves around the fact that once the individual targets have been established, mathematics takes over the basic responsibility of management to manage. If the individual goals set at the beginning of the year are not consistent between divisions, or between functions within divisions, the mathematically derived payoff at the year's end, undoubtedly, will be unfair. Some executives will be overpaid and others underpaid as a result of forces beyond the control of the individual. An unexpected price war, for instance, may seriously reduce profit margins in one division, while margins in another division benefit from the liquidation of a competitor. With mathematics deciding who gets what bonus, such basic economic shifts go unrecognized.

Then, too, the mathematically derived payoff that results from preset goals permits no adjustment in rewards for the *difficulty* of accomplishment. A manufacturing department, for example, may have surmounted major problems in fulfilling commitments that were easily attained by the sales department, or vice versa. But unless the program permits the *judgment* of management to reflect the difficulty of accomplishment, great incentive values are lost to the inflexibility of mathematics.

Because unfavorable results frequently stem from these relatively extreme approaches to performance appraisal—the wholly subjective and the mathematically determined evaluations—a number of leading companies have blended the best of the two into what appears destined to become a formidable management tool. The remainder of this article will examine in some detail the philosophy underlying the new concept, the administrative problems encountered, and the benefits derived from its use. (See Part Two—E—Eds.)

PROFIT PERFORMANCE MEASUREMENT OF DIVISION MANAGERS*

Joel Dean

• INTRODUCTION

In introduction, we shall touch on (A) the importance, (B) the difficulty, and (C) the role of profit centers in measuring executive performance.

Importance

Measuring executive performance is important in five ways:

1. It directs top management's supervision and assistance to where it is most needed and where it will be most productive.
2. It shapes the future executive team by indicating whom to promote, whom to retain, and whom to remove.
3. It directs the activity of executives toward high scores on the aspects of performance on which they are measured and judged.
4. It gives job satisfaction directly by letting the executive know how he is doing.
5. It provides the objective, factual foundation for sound incentive compensation.

Difficulty

Measuring executive performance in a big company is difficult. The performance you want to measure is achievement of the company's goals. Measuring the executive's contribution to this achievement is made complex by the fact that the corporation usually has several objectives which overlap and in some degree conflict: profits, growth, market share, and eternal life.

Profits should be the corporation's dominant goal in view of its obligation to stockholders and to a free-enterprise society, but other objectives contribute in diffuse ways to long-run profits and thus cannot be ignored in measuring executive performance. Hence, the main executive performance you want to measure is contribution to the corporation's profits today and tomorrow.

The problem is made more difficult by the fact that facets of executive activity are numerous and contribute to profits in complex ways. There are few profit-determining activities that are absolutely good or bad in themselves. To make the most money often requires foregoing a high score in one activity in order to push another (*e.g.*, high quality product vs. low cost of making it).

To combine performance measures of separate activities requires proper weights which are hard to determine and change continuously. For example, a textile mill manager is scored on (1) quality control, (2) cost compared with standards, (3) safety, (4) equipment modernity, (5) production volume, (6) meeting delivery deadlines. How should these facets of performance be weighted?

---

* From *The Controller,* Vol. 25, no. 9, September 1957.

Thus, responsibility for profits in a big company is in danger of being diffused. This makes measurement hard and cuts economic efficiency of the firm. Decentralization, *i.e.*, setting up profit centers, is a promising way to overcome this diffusion of profit responsibility.

Role of Profit Center Decentralization

For measuring performance, executives can be put in two groups: (1) Staff specialists, (2) businessmen, *i.e.*, profit center (*i.e.*, division) managers.

Complex problems of measuring and weighting executives' contributions to profits are best solved by dividing the corporation into semiautonomous profit centers whose management is measured by the contributions his center makes to corporation's overhead and profits.

A big, integrated multiple-product company functions best if made into a miniature of the competitive free-enterprise economy. You can do this by dividing firms into independent operating units which act like economic entities free to trade outside as well as inside the company.

Powered with the right incentives, each profit center in maximizing its own contribution profits will do what will also maximize the profits of the entire company. It works the same way that selfish profit-seeking by individual firms in a private-enterprise society generates the high productivity and automatic economic adjustments of a competitive economy. (The remainder of this article, "Requirements for Profit Center Performance Measurement," is presented in Part Two–E–Eds.)

B. Issues and Problems in Appraisal

3. PROBLEMS RELATED TO ORGANIZATIONAL CHARACTERISTICS AND MANAGERIAL PHILOSOPHY

AN UNEASY LOOK AT PERFORMANCE APPRAISAL

DOUGLAS MCGREGOR

PERFORMANCE APPRAISAL AND THE ORGANIZATION MAN

THOMAS L. WHISLER

NEW ANGLES IN APPRAISAL

MARION S. KELLOGG

These three articles examine the problems of interpersonal relations between the judge and the man being judged within the organization. All agree that the problems are persistent and serious. Kellogg dramatizes the pervasive character of these difficulties in her description of repeated workshop "experiments" on appraisal. Each writer has a somewhat different suggestion for improving the appraisal process, with McGregor and Kellogg focusing on the interaction between superior and subordinate, and Whisler on the organization structure.

FURTHER READING

Foundation for Research on Human Behavior, *Performance Appraisal and Review.* Ann Arbor, Michigan, 1958.

Harrington, Alan, *Life in the Crystal Palace.* New York, Alfred A. Knopf, 1959.
An intriguing view of the manager's life in the corporation. Chapter nine takes a hard look at management development and performance appraisal from the perspective of the insider—the manager being appraised and developed.

AN UNEASY LOOK AT PERFORMANCE APPRAISAL*

Douglas McGregor

Performance appraisal within management ranks has become standard practice in many companies during the past twenty years, and is currently being adopted by many others, often as an important feature of management development programs. The more the method is used, the more uneasy I grow over the unstated assumptions which lie behind it. Moreover, with some searching, I find that a number of people both in education and in industry share my misgivings. This article, therefore, has two purposes:

1. To examine the conventional performance appraisal plan which requires the manager to pass judgment on the personal worth of subordinates.
2. To describe an alternative which places on the subordinate the primary responsibility for establishing performance goals and appraising progress toward them.

• CURRENT PROGRAMS

Formal performance appraisal plans are designed to meet three needs, one for the organization and two for the individual:

1. They provide systematic judgments to back up salary increases, promotions, transfers, and sometimes demotions or terminations.
2. They are a means of telling a subordinate how he is doing, and suggesting needed changes in his behavior, attitudes, skills, or job knowledge; they let him know "where he stands" with the boss.
3. They also are being increasingly used as a basis for the coaching and counseling of the individual by the superior.

Problem of Resistance

Personnel administrators are aware that appraisal programs tend to run into resistance from the managers who are expected to administer them. Even managers who admit the necessity of such programs frequently balk at the process —especially the interview part. As a result, some companies do not communicate appraisal results to the individual, despite the general conviction that the subordinate has a right to know his superior's opinion so he can correct his weaknesses.

The boss's resistance is usually attributed to the following causes:

A normal dislike of criticizing a subordinate (and perhaps having to argue about it).

Lack of skill needed to handle the interviews.

Dislike of a new procedure with its accompanying changes in ways of operating.

Mistrust of the validity of the appraisal instrument.

To meet this problem, formal controls —scheduling, reminders, and so on—are often instituted. It is common experience that without them fewer than half the appraisal interviews are actually held. But even controls do not necessarily work. Thus:

In one company with a well-planned and carefully administered appraisal program,

* From *Harvard Business Review,* Vol. 35, no. 3, May–June 1957, pp. 89–94. Copyright 1957 by the President and Fellows of Harvard College. Reprinted by permission.

an opinion poll included two questions regarding appraisals. More than 90% of those answering the questionnaire approved the idea of appraisals. They wanted to know how they stood. Some 40% went on to say that they had never had the experience of being told—yet the files showed that over four-fifths of them had signed a form testifying that they had been through an appraisal interview, some of them several times!

The respondents had no reason to lie, nor was there the slightest supposition that their superiors had committed forgery. The probable explanation is that the superiors, being basically resistant to the plan, had conducted the interviews in such a perfunctory manner that many subordinates did not recognize what was going on.

Training programs designed to teach the skills of appraising and interviewing do help, but they seldom eliminate managerial resistance entirely. The difficulties connected with "negative appraisals" remain a source of genuine concern. There is always some discomfort involved in telling a subordinate he is not doing well. The individual who is "coasting" during the few years prior to retirement after serving his company competently for many years presents a special dilemma to the boss who is preparing to interview him.

Nor does a shift to a form of group appraisal solve the problem. Though the group method tends to have greater validity and, properly administered, can equalize varying standards of judgment, it does not ease the difficulty inherent in the interview. In fact, the superior's discomfort is often intensified when he must base his interview on the results of a *group* discussion of the subordinate's worth. Even if the final judgments have been his, he is not free to discuss the things said by others which may have influenced him.

The Underlying Cause

What should we think about a method —however valuable for meeting organizational needs—which produces such results in a wide range of companies with a variety of appraisal plans? The problem is one that cannot be dismissed lightly.

Perhaps this intuitive managerial reaction to conventional performance appraisal plans shows a deep but unrecognized wisdom. In my view, it does not reflect anything so simple as resistance to change, or dislike for personnel technique, or lack of skill, or mistrust for rating scales. Rather, managers seem to be expressing very real misgivings, which they find difficult to put into words. This could be the underlying cause:

> The conventional approach, unless handled with consummate skill and delicacy, constitutes something dangerously close to a violation of the integrity of the personality. Managers are uncomfortable when they are put in the position of "playing God." The respect we hold for the inherent value of the individual leaves us distressed when we must take responsibility for judging the personal worth of a fellow man. Yet the conventional approach to performance appraisal forces us, not only to make such judgments and to see them acted upon, but also to communicate them to those we have judged. Small wonder we resist!

The modern emphasis upon the manager as a leader who strives to *help* his subordinates achieve both their own and the company's objectives is hardly consistent with the judicial role demanded by most appraisal plans. If the manager must put on his judicial hat occasionally, he does it reluctantly and with understandable qualms. Under such conditions it is unlikely that the subordinate will be any happier with the results than will the boss. It will not be surprising, either, if he fails to recognize that he has been told where he stands.

Of course, managers cannot escape making judgments about subordinates. Without such evaluations, salary and promotion policies canont be administered sensibly. But are subordinates like products on an assembly line, to be accepted or rejected as a result of an inspection process? The inspection process may be made more objective or more accurate through research on the appraisal instrument, through training of the "inspectors," or through introducing group appraisal; the subordinate may be "reworked" by coaching or counseling before the final decision to accept or reject him; but as far as the assumptions of the conventional appraisal process are concerned, we still have what is practically identical with a program for product inspection.

On this interpretation, then, resistance to conventional appraisal programs is eminently sound. It reflects an unwillingness to treat human beings like physical objects. The needs of the organization are obviously important, but when they come into conflict with our convictions about the worth and the dignity of the human personality, one or the other must give.

Indeed, by the fact of their resistance, managers are saying that the organization must yield in the face of his fundamental human value. And they are thus being more sensitive than are personnel administrators and social scientists whose business it is to be concerned with the human problems of industry!

• A NEW APPROACH

If this analysis is correct, the task before us is clear. We must find a new plan —not a compromise to hide the dilemma, but a bold move to resolve the issue.

A number of writers are beginning to approach the whole subject of management from the point of view of basic social values. Peter Drucker's concept of "management by objectives"[1] offers an unusually promising framework within which we can seek a solution. Several companies, notably General Mills, Incorporated, and General Electric Company, have been exploring different methods of appraisal which rest upon assumptions consistent with Drucker's philosophy.

Responsibility on Subordinate

This approach calls on the subordinate to establish short-term performance goals *for himself*. The superior enters the process actively only *after* the subordinate has (a) done a good deal of thinking about his job, (b) made a careful assessment of his own strengths and weaknesses, and (c) formulated some specific plans to accomplish his goals. The superior's role is to help the man relate his self-appraisal, his "targets," and his plans for the ensuing period to the realities of the organization.

The first step in this process is to

[1] See Peter Drucker, *The Practice of Management* (New York, Harper & Brothers, 1954).

arrive at a clear statement of the major features of the job. Rather than a formal job description, this is a document drawn up *by the subordinate* after studying the company-approved statement. It defines the broad areas of his responsibility as they actually work out in practice. The boss and employee discuss the draft jointly and modify it as may be necessary until both of them agree that it is adequate.

Working from this statement of responsibilities, the subordinate then establishes his goals or "targets" for a period of, say, six months. These targets are *specific* actions which the man proposes to take, *i.e.*, setting up regular staff meetings to improve communication, reorganizing the office, completing or undertaking a certain study. Thus, they are explicitly stated and accompanied by a detailed account of the actions he proposes to take to reach them. This document is, in turn, discussed with the superior and modified until both are satisfied with it.

At the conclusion of the six-month period, the subordinate makes *his own* appraisal of what he has accomplished relative to the targets he had set earlier. He substantiates it with factual data wherever possible. The "interview" is an examination by superior and subordinate together of the subordinate's self-appraisal, and it culminates in a resetting of targets for the next six months.

Of course, the superior has veto power at each step of this process; in an organizational hierarchy anything else would be unacceptable. However, in practice he rarely needs to exercise it. Most subordinates tend to underestimate both their potentialities and their achievements. Moreover, subordinates normally have an understandable wish to satisfy their boss, and are quite willing to adjust their targets or appraisals if the superior feels they are unrealistic. Actually, a much more common problem is to resist the subordinates' tendency to want the boss to tell them what to write down.

Analysis vs. *Appraisal*

This approach to performance appraisal differs profoundly from the conventional one, for it shifts the emphasis from *appraisal* to *analysis*. This implies a more positive approach. No longer is the subordinate being examined by the superior so that his weaknesses may be determined; rather, he is examining himself; in order to define not only his weaknesses but also his strengths and potentials. The importance of this shift of emphasis should not be underestimated. It is basic to each of the specific differences which distinguish this approach from the conventional one.

The first of these differences arises from the subordinate's new role in the process. He becomes an active agent, not a passive "object." He is no longer a pawn in a chess game called management development.

Effective development of managers does not include coercing them (no matter how benevolently) into acceptance of the goals of the enterprise, nor does it mean manipulating their behavior to suit organizational needs. Rather, it calls for creating a relationship within which a man can take responsibility for developing his own potentialities, plan for himself, and learn from putting his plans into action. In the process he can gain a genuine sense of satisfaction, for he is utilizing his own capabilities to achieve simultaneously both his objectives and those of the organization. Unless this is the nature of the relationship, "development" becomes a euphemism.

Who Knows Best?

One of the main differences of this approach is that it rests on the assumption that the individual knows—or can learn—more than anyone else about his own capabilities, needs, strengths and weaknesses, and goals. In the end, only he can determine what is best for his development. The conventional approach, on the other hand, makes the assumption that the superior can know enough about the subordinate to decide what is best for him.

No available methods can provide the superior with the knowledge he needs to make such decisions. Ratings, aptitude and personality tests, and the superior's necessarily limited knowledge of the man's performance yield at best an imperfect picture. Even the most extensive psychological counseling (assuming the superior possesses the competence for it) would not solve the problem because the product of counseling is self-insight on the part of the *counselee.*

(Psychological tests are not being condemned by this statement. On the contrary, they have genuine value in competent hands. Their use by professionals as part of the process of screening applicants for employment does not raise the same questions as their use to "diagnose" the personal worth of accepted members of a management team. Even in the latter instance the problem we are discussing would not arise if test results and interpretations were given *to the individual himself,* to be shared with superiors at his discretion.)

The proper role for the superior, then, is the one that falls naturally to him under the suggested plan: helping the subordinate relate his career planning to the needs and realities of the organization. In the discussions the boss can use his knowledge of the organization to help the subordinate establish targets and methods for achieving them which will (a) lead to increased knowledge and skill, (b) contribute to organizational objectives, and (c) test the subordinate's appraisal of himself.

This is help which the subordinate wants. He knows well that the rewards and satisfactions he seeks from his career as a manager depend on his contribution to organizational objectives. He is also aware that the superior knows more completely than he what is required for success in this organization and *under this boss.* The superior, then, is the person who can help him test the soundness of his goals and his plans for achieving them. Quite clearly the knowledge and active participation of *both* superior and subordinate are necessary components of this approach.

If the superior accepts this role, he need not become a judge of the subordinate's personal worth. He is not telling, deciding, criticizing, or praising—not "playing God." He finds himself listening, using his own knowledge of the organization as a basis for advising, guiding, encouraging his subordinates to develop their own potentialities. Incidentally, this often leads the superior to important insights about himself and his impact on others.

Looking to the Future

Another significant difference is that the emphasis is on the future rather than the past. The purpose of the plan is to establish realistic targets and to seek the most effective ways of reaching them. Appraisal thus becomes a means to a *constructive* end. The 60-year-old "coaster" can be encouraged to set performance goals for himself and to make a fair appraisal of his progress toward them. Even the subordinate who has failed can be helped to consider what moves will be best for himself. The superior rarely finds himself facing the uncomfortable prospect of denying a subordinate's personal worth. A transfer or even a demotion can be worked out without the connotation of a "sentence by the judge."

Performance vs. *Personality*

Finally, the accent is on *performance,* on actions relative to goals. There is less tendency for the personality of the subordinate to become an issue. The superior, instead of finding himself in the position of a psychologist or a therapist, can become a coach helping the subordinate to reach his own decisions on the specific steps that will enable him to reach his targets. Such counseling as may be required demands no deep analysis of the personal motivations or basic adjustment of the subordinate. To illustrate:

> Consider a subordinate who is hostile, short-tempered, uncooperative, insecure. The superior need not make any psychological diagnosis. The "target setting" approach naturally directs the subordinate's attention to ways and means of obtaining better interdepartmental collaboration, reducing complaints, winning the confidence of the men under him. Rather than facing the troublesome prospect of forcing his own psychological diagnosis on the subordinate, the superior can, for example, help the individual plan ways of getting "feedback" concerning his impact on his associates and subordinates as a basis for self-appraisal and self-improvement.

There is little chance that a man who is involved in a process like this will be in the dark about where he stands, or that he will forget he is the principal participant in his own development and responsible for it.

• A NEW ATTITUDE

As a consequence of these differences we may expect the growth of a different attitude toward appraisal on the part of superior and subordinate alike.

The superior will gain real satisfaction as he learns to help his subordinates integrate their personal goals with the needs of the organization so that both are served. Once the subordinate has worked out a mutually satisfactory plan of action, the superior can delegate to him the responsibility for putting it into effect. He will see himself in a consistent managerial role rather than being forced to adopt the basically incompatible role of either the judge or the psychologist.

Unless there is a basic personal antagonism between the two men (in which case the relationship should be terminated), the superior can conduct these interviews so that both are actively involved in seeking the right basis for constructive action. The organization, the boss, and the subordinate all stand to gain. Under such circumstances the opportunities for learning and for genuine development of both parties are maximal.

The particular mechanics are of secondary importance. The needs of the organization in the administration of salary and promotion policies can easily be met within the framework of the analysis process. The machinery of the program can be adjusted to the situation. No universal list of rating categories is required. The complications of subjective or prejudiced judgment, of varying standards, of attempts to quantify qualitative data, all can be minimized. In fact, *no* formal machinery is required.

Problems of Judgment

I have deliberately slighted the many problems of judgment involved in administering promotions and salaries. These are by no means minor, and this approach will not automatically solve them. However, I believe that if we are prepared to recognize the fundamental problem inherent in the conventional approach, ways can be found to temper our present administrative methods.

And if this approach is accepted, the traditional ingenuity of management will lead to the invention of a variety of methods for its implementation. The mechanics of some conventional plans can be adjusted to be consistent with this point of view. Obviously, a program utilizing ratings of the personal characteristics of subordinates would not be suitable, but one which emphasizes *behavior* might be.

Of course, managerial skill is required. No method will eliminate that. This method can fail as readily as any other in the clumsy hands of insensitive or indifferent or power-seeking managers. But even the limited experience of a few companies with this approach indicates that managerial *resistance* is substantially reduced. As a consequence, it is easier to gain the collaboration of managers in developing the necessary skills.

Cost in Time

There is one unavoidable cost: the manager must spend considerably more time in implementing a program of this kind. It is not unusual to take a couple of days to work through the initial establishment of responsibilities and goals with each individual. And a periodic appraisal may require several hours rather than the typical 20 minutes.

Reaction to this cost will undoubtedly vary. The management that considers the development of its human resources to be the primary means of achieving the economic objectives of the organization will not be disturbed. It will regard the necessary guidance and coaching as among the most important functions of every superior.

• CONCLUSION

I have sought to show that the conventional approach to performance appraisal stands condemned as a personnel method. It places the manager in the untenable position of judging the personal worth of his subordinates, and of acting on these judgments. No manager possesses, nor could he acquire, the skill necessary to carry out this responsibility effectively. Few would even be willing to accept it if they were fully aware of the implications involved.

It is this unrecognized aspect of conventional appraisal programs which produces the widespread uneasiness and even open resistance of management to appraisals and especially to the appraisal interview.

A sounder approach, which places the major responsibility on the subordinate for establishing performance goals and appraising progress toward them, avoids the major weaknesses of the old plan and benefits the organization by stimulating the development of the subordinate. It is true that more managerial skill and the investment of a considerable amount of time are required, but the greater motivation and the more effective development of subordinates can justify these added costs.

PERFORMANCE APPRAISAL AND THE ORGANIZATION MAN*

Thomas L. Whisler

This article argues that, except for the very smallest business organizations, appraisal and development of managers is least effectively done if carried out within the same organizational structure as that used for supervising operations. It follows that if the chief executive of the business firm seeks to improve such appraisal and development appreciably, he must expect to introduce some structural modification. The basic purpose of such modification is to alter the power relationships of the individuals involved. Questions of ethics as well as efficiency are involved. The argument presented here is that a proper change in structure resolves matters so that ethics and efficiency reinforce each other rather than conflict.

Such an argument has some novel elements, the usual approach to appraisal and development coming from the personnel-management man and involving the use of appraisal forms, boss-subordinate conferences, organizational development charts, etc.[1] This personnel-management approach usually relies upon the individual boss to furnish appraisal information, with the personnel department frequently playing a decisive role in planning the "development" of the individual.

An interesting protest against this way of doing things has been voiced by McGregor.[2] He argues that the traditional techniques of appraisal place the superior in the position of "playing God" in judging his subordinates, that most men find this role intolerable, and that they will reject it. This, he believes, explains the failure of most management appraisal schemes. As a substitute, McGregor suggests shifting responsibility to the subordinate for setting goals and appraising his own progress toward them. The boss ceases to play God and becomes a counselor, advising the subordinate on the validity of his goals and his appraisals in terms of the facts of organization life *as the superior sees them.*

McGregor makes two useful points—first, that the appraisal and development of managers are activities so closely related as to be nearly inseparable and, second, that it is important and timely to seek the cause of failure of traditional appraisal plans.[3]

But, like the personnel man, McGregor does not question the feasibility

[1] See, *e.g.*, M. J. Dooher (ed.), *The Development of Executive Talent* (New York: American Management Association, 1952), pp. 378–418.

* From *Journal of Business,* Vol. 31, no. 1, January 1958, pp. 19–27. Copyright 1958 by the University of Chicago. Reprinted by permission.

[2] Douglas McGregor, "An Uneasy Look at Performance Appraisal," *Harvard Business Review,* XXXV, No. 3 (May–June, 1957), 89–94.

[3] About seventy-five years ago, a formal appraisal plan instituted in the new civil service system of New York City was abandoned because it was ineffective. This experience has been repeated continuously in American management practice since then—a truly appalling record.

of using the hierarchical command structure as a mechanism for appraisal. He recommends only that the nature of the man-boss relationship be voluntarily altered. This proposal strikes me as revolutionary—and unrealistic.

These three points of view as to the most effective way to appraise managerial performance—the traditional personnel-management approach of imposing a formal rating plan upon managers; McGregor's suggestion for consultative rating sessions; and, finally, the proposition that modification of the organization structure is necessary—differ radically. The remainder of this article is devoted to the case for structural modification and the case against the other two approaches.

MAN AND BOSS IN • THE HIERARCHICAL ORGANIZATION

McGregor's position that overtly "playing God" is repellent to many men is a defensible one. Such a role is certainly at odds with the traditional American ethic—the spirit of freedom, independence, and equality. But the God-playing role is not simply the invention of the personnel experts. It is, I believe, an unavoidable feature of the hierarchical organization.

Hierarchical organizations, by definition, are built up from man-boss units. These units are the organizational molecules. They are endowed with certain identifiable dimensions in structure by the total logic of such organizations—by organization theory, if you prefer. The whole business of delegation of authority and responsibility, of accountability and control, and the rest is accomplished through a series of man-boss units—through the "line." This logic translates into a pretty clear prescription for the nature of the man-boss relationship and for such things as performance appraisal.

The molecules are necessarily "Godman" units, units in which a man's worth is communicated to the organization power center via his boss and the succeeding series of man-boss links, thus building in a high degree of personal dependence of man upon boss. These are the units in which the boss and the subsystem he runs are evaluated together by *his boss* as much as possible in reference to goals set by the power center of the organization. Thus the freedom of either man or boss to devise his own goals in performance norms is severely limited. Such arrangements tend, naturally, not to generate free and easy discussion but an atmosphere of obsessive attention of the man to the expectations of his boss. The power and dependence relationship is unmistakable and unalterable in any permanent sense, without a change in the supportive organization logic.

McGregor proposes changing the molecule. But it seems unlikely that we can change molecular structure in the organization without a concomitant change in the basic character of the organization. There is research evidence, for example, that attitudes can be changed in supervisory development programs but that they tend to change back if the working environment creating the original attitudes remains unchanged.[4] What appear to be the only real innovations in man-boss relation-

[4] E. A. Fleishman, E. F. Harris, and H. E. Burtt, *Leadership and Supervision in Industry* (Bureau of Educational Research Monographs, No. 33 [Columbus: Ohio State University, 1955], pp. 90–95).

ships have occurred where organization structure has been significantly altered —in divisionalization schemes at a high organization level and in the Scanlon Plan at the nonmanagerial level.

It seems to me that traditional appraisal plans have failed in the past and will continue to fail in the future for reasons more basic than the one suggested by McGregor. One part of the problem is the perpetual conflict between the demands of personal and organizational needs upon the time and effort of the man in the organization. The individual seeks his own goals; the organization tries to devise ways of assuring that his goal-seeking behavior also serves organizational needs. But the results, historically, have fallen short of perfection, and diversity of interest exists. This is admirably illustrated in the performance-appraisal area. Performance appraisal is intended to serve at least two important organization needs—providing information for deciding how to allocate individuals to positions in the organization and providing information to individuals which will aid them in becoming more effective performers. The first demands a constant flow of information, since decisions must be made frequently. Here the boss must have an answer always ready—an adequate answer—or pay the penalty. This activity, in other words, yields a payoff to the individual. Measurement of the effectiveness and promptness of such information is possible—and is made.

The second aspect—development of subordinates—does not often pay off to the superior. Clearly, he must insure that his subordinates are adequate to their present jobs, but investment in developing men—an investment which one would think to be quite important to the organization—is a costly activity which he will rationally avoid. Perhaps one reason why the organization does not pay off to the superior for development of subordinates is the freedom of the individual to leave the organization. There is always a substantial probability that any investment will be lost. By making development an ancillary activity, such as sending men to training programs, its cost is known and the activity easily terminable. If it were possible to make development an ingrained part of the supervisor's behavior, both these advantages would be lost. Another reason is the almost complete inability (at present) to trace the effectiveness of development efforts. Reinforcing both these reasons is a cultural factor—it is part of the American ethic that each man is responsible for his own development. Actually, the notion that a superior has responsibilities for development of subordinates has definite overtones of paternalism. So the lack of well-counseled and "developed" subordinates (which seems to be a common complaint in organizations) is not likely to result in a penalty against the superior.

With just so much time and effort available, the superior will be inclined to do that which enhances his own standing in the organization and ignore that which does not. He will evaluate individuals (as informally as possible to save time) and not coach and counsel them. No amount of urging by staff specialists and social scientists is likely to change him on this. One unpublished study made within a gigantic corporation indicated that those who had reached the highest positions were not remembered by anyone in the company as having done anything significant in developing men, while those who had achieved a reputation of being wise and effective counselors invariably reached only modest levels.[5] Hence, in my opinion, the very limited effectiveness of formal appraisal systems. There is little in it for the supervisor. Nor is there in McGregor's proposal. Some supervisors may find counseling enjoyable in itself. If they are prepared to pay the penalty, they should study McGregor's suggestions carefully, for they are useful. Such a supervisor will not, however, succeed in abdicating the role of God. He will cease to be a jealous God and become a benevolent, consultative one.

• EVALUATING THE ORGANIZATION MAN

Criticism of the McGregor proposal should not obscure the fact that he was aiming directly at the heart of the problem of evaluating men in organizations—the power and dependence dimensions of the man-boss relationship. William H. Whyte, Jr., has something to say on the same point:

> No one likes to be played checkers with, and the man The Organization needs most is precisely the man who is most sensitive on this point. To control one's destiny and not be controlled by it; to know which way the path will fork and to make the turning oneself; to have some index of achievement that no one can dispute—concrete and tangible for all to see—not dependent on the attitudes of others. It is an independence he will never have in full measure but he must forever seek it.[6]

Whyte must be thinking largely of the organization's need for top-level executives—that part of the organization where the power of the boss begins to pay off, where results more than men become the master, where a somewhat different form of organization molecule must exist. The organization has the problem of finding and developing men to fill posts here—men of independence and imagination—using as a source the power and dependence hierarchy below. It is not clear from this quoted fragment whether Whyte thinks it essential to have men in lower-level jobs who value independence highly. Such men might find life intolerable. The man with a substantial desire for dependence could well be a far happier organization man. Whyte's exhortation to subordinates to fight the system seems to face the same obstacles as McGregor's exhortation to the boss to become a counselor.

Since organizations, including larger ones, do survive and flourish in the face of the indifference of superiors to the development of subordinates, it must mean that some subordinates do fight the system, and successfully. But even if current organization structure cannot be said to have destroyed the independent man, most chief executives and many outside observers believe that the organization needs better evaluation information than it usually gets. The decision to place an individual in one of the important top-level jobs is a momentous one—one of appreciable risk for the organization. It is one which must be made by men who realize, by the time that they must make such a decision, that the organization has no

---

[5] See also Fleishman *et al., op cit.*, pp. 100–101. This reference describes the inverse relationship found between ratings given production foremen by their superiors and the consideration shown by these foremen to their subordinates, as rated by subordinates.

[6] McGregor, *op. cit.*, p. 94; quoted from William H. Whyte, Jr., *The Organization Man* (New York: Simon & Schuster, 1956), pp. 166–67.

automatic device for developing the kind of man needed at the top; who realize that the individual superior's judgments of his subordinates have been and will continue to be made in terms of how effectively these subordinates' efforts support the department or section rather than in terms of how the subordinate is likely to contribute to the organization in other and higher jobs. It must be made in face of the fact that specialization tends to make appraisals incommunicable: It is hard to translate reported excellence in special skills into potentialities for top-level operation; those specialists who, as superiors, are called upon to help make such judgments may well find themselves unable to formulate any conception of what the organization as a whole needs. There is, in other words, an organization need, which the organization has no built-in mechanism to serve (except, perhaps, very small organizations).

It seems to me that any attempt to remedy this organizational defect must meet two conditions: (1) It must involve a change in organization structure and supportive organizational logic. Appeals to the individual—either boss or man—to alter his behavior are likely to have no substantial effect when they run counter to the payoff rules of the organization. (2) It must free the individual from being evaluated chiefly by his boss. Only in this way can we solve the ethical problem of the relationship of man to organization in a manner consistent with American ideals, as well as the practical and important organization problem of getting objective and communicable appraisals of members of the organization. The second condition, at first glance, seems unrealistic enough to preclude further action of any kind. Conceding this as a possible outcome, let us explore it a little further.

• APPRAISAL AND INDEPENDENCE

Since that point in history when Western civilization largely abandoned the practice of appealing to the infinite, through the priesthood or the king, for an appraisal of the activities of men, it has been necessary to evolve some way for men to appraise men. Two different techniques have become institutionalized. One, characteristic of hierarchical organizations, is the evaluation of man by another in authority over him. The other, consonant with the creeds of individualism and democracy, is the evaluation of man by many others standing largely in a peer relationship to him. It is the method characteristic of the professions and is the essence of the economic market. In a society valuing achievement rather than status, the individual is presumably evaluated under either system in terms of what he contributes rather than who he is. But the two systems differ substantially.

Peer evaluation, as in the professions, frees a man from the whims and biases of a superior. But it tends to be a cold, hard, competitive process. From the verdict rendered, there is no appeal to another authority. The system is more impersonal and objective than is evaluation by the superior; it provides no mechanism of consolation, no satisfactory excuse for failure. Since it squares with the ideals of a pragmatic and democratic society, it provides those who succeed with the highest degree of fame. The man who chooses to take his chances in this system and succeeds is regarded as independent, competent, and a most useful citizen.

Evaluation by superiors retains many of the features of the rejected religious-authoritarian system. It is a highly personalized arrangement. And, unfortunately, when man was substituted for God in the evaluation process, doubt was built in. Man is fallible—the evaluaations are open to question. Further, the evaluation process does not fit the general social ethic. Questions of relation of man to boss, of man to organization, arise. What are the limits to which the authority (boss and organization) can go in peering into the man's soul? In the old established hierarchical organizations, such as the church and the military, the question has been resolved. The man belongs to the organization; there are no limits. Business organization tends toward anomaly—needing independent men who can guide it in competing openly and freely with other organizations for survival; trying to grow them in an environment of protectionism and dependence within the firm.

Men, drawn into these organizations and seeing the contradiction, take action. Engineers, trained in schools where the traditions of professionalism are strong, seem, in their early years in the management hierarchy, to have a painful time adjusting to a work role which lacks a peer evaluation system. On their own, they endeavor to evolve some analogous system of evaluation by superiors. Most engineering supervisors are aware of strong pressures from engineering subordinates on this point. Even men with no professional traditions sense the value of the market. Many join associations and societies, make speeches, seek to offset their invisibility and dependence within the organization. But other men become "politicians" and Machiavellian manipulators, diverting much time and effort to exploitation of the self-doubt and inarticulateness of the hierarchical evaluation system, with the goal of levering themselves upward. Whether this cleverness will translate into the sort of competence necessary to guide the competitive organization is a question that the organization is still unable to answer clearly when such individuals become eligible for top office.

The contradiction of the hierarchical, status-ridden organization within the equalitarian, pragmatic society has become a source of worry to many with the arrival of the "age of business." What was once an anomalous role for a few may resolve into a way of life for many. The possibility of a dominant institution's changing cultural norms is a real one. The specter of the Organization Man *should* chill the spine.

• THE PROBLEM: ACHIEVING VISIBILITY

Resolution of the dilemma—the way out of the failure noted by McGregor and the restriction feared by Whyte—must, it seems to me, come through partially altering the structure of the hierarchical organization in some way which will automatically and unalterably move performance appraisal toward the total-visibility ideal. (The very small firm, *e.g.*, one with fewer than five managers, can scarcely avoid such visibility.) The individual and the organization must have the benefit of the appraisals of a number of people of the achievements of each man. To aid further in breathing the clean air of independence into organizations, primary responsibility for initiating "management development" should be left where it has always belonged—with the individual.

Achieving this without doing fatal damage to the operating efficiency and speed of hierarchical, internally specialized organizations is the whole problem. One promising step forward has been decentralization and divisionalization, particularly as combined with the tangible performance index of profitability.[7] This structural change can be utilized in many more places than it has been; transition from the monolith to the federation is difficult—a sort of organizational adolescence.

But decentralization of this kind can go only so far. Many man-boss units will remain largely unaltered in the process. To attack these directly, some arrangement will have to be made which will provide for the individual the opportunity to engage in organizationally useful work in full view of a number of other people. Rotation into and out of a series of man-boss relationships is not enough; appraisers need the opportunity to examine, interpret, and evaluate together the same performance incidents. Furthermore, the work assigned for this purpose should be the kind spanning departments, the kind requiring application of knowledge to the persistent and important problems of the whole enterprise, the kind requiring commitment to and defense of a position.

Although logic is against successfully using the same organization structure for both command and evaluation, I see no practicable way totally to divorce the two, so that the leader leads and some other functionary evaluates both how well he has led and how well his subordinates have performed.[8] For appraisal of current job performance, we shall probably continue to rely upon the superior. For appraisal of career potential, together with doing some real management development, we must provide an escape, on a voluntary basis, from the man-boss bondage. The escape must be into a real world, not a modified clinic.

Some possibilities exist. Some companies have experimented with junior advisory boards.[9] Their weakness is that they usually tend not to be risky enough assignments. Too little rides on what is said and done by participants. Bluntly stated, what is required is that a man can make or break himself on such assignments. Perhaps these should be full-time assignments. Certainly, they must require accomplishment—demonstration of the ability to achieve results. Organization departments, product-development committees, capital-budgeting committees, corporate planning committees—all wrestle with difficult and important problems. Perhaps a staff of juniors working full time on temporary assignment to such committees with the task of studying these problems, getting information, and making recommenda-

[7] See, *e.g.*, Peter Drucker, *The Practice of Management* (New York: Harper & Bros., 1954), pp. 202–18; and Joel Dean, *Managerial Economics* (Englewood Cliffs, N.J.: Prentice-Hall, Inc., 1951), pp. 39–43.

[8] This is not impossible, of course, the assistant to the president (or to the vice president) can do this, and apparently frequently does (see Thomas L. Whisler, "The Assistant To: The Man in Motley," *Journal of Business*, XXIX, No. 4 [October, 1956], 274–79). My colleague, Jack Hirshleifer, cites another case—the inspector-general in the military. The inspector-general has undoubtedly increased internal visibility, but, at the same time, the organization seems to have devised powerful informal defenses against him.

[9] See Dooher, *op. cit.*, pp. 109–21.

tions is a possibility. There must be a chance for individual assignments. There must also be opportunity for team operations, for demonstration of leadership ability. There must be evaluation of the results not only by the senior committee members but also by the juniors themselves. The juniors' evaluations must be evaluated. There must be a chance for juniors (anonymously?) to indicate those of their colleagues whom they judge to show superior intelligence, ability to accomplish, leadership, etc. There must be, of course, no opportunity to make a career of working on such committee assignments.[10]

Suggestions of this kind imply that control over an individual's future in the organization will be removed from immediate superiors in the line, that the formal decision will be made elsewhere upon the basis of a wide range of evidence which will include the superior's recommendation. An additional organization change would then have to be made because of the now explicitly recognized separateness of interest between the immediate departmental operational needs and the long-run, organization-wide needs. Supervisors would retain command, which includes the right to apply sanctions. The boss would have to be free to fire the subordinate—back to the organization as a whole. Such a firing could indicate any number of things; it is the company's task to reach a conclusion. The decision would, in most cases, probably await the results of a new assignment and further observation.

Requiring a new kind of duty as prerequisite to top-level assignment and thus removing control of a man's future from superiors would consume substantial time and resources. Whether dropping the whole maze of training and development devices and performance-appraisal sessions, which this plan would replace, would offset the additional cost is doubtful. Programs like that suggested here would be most economical, of course, where needed most—in the big corporations. They would be more clearly advantageous, the more rigorously they were conceived. They would incorporate voluntarism; if they also incorporated serious and substantial performance expectations, volunteers would not appear in excessive numbers. If such a program were compared with one of those so common at present which "develop" one and all with marvelous indiscrimination, it should be a hands-down choice, economically.

The suggestions made in the preceding paragraphs could be put into effect only after solving some difficult problems of transition. Even if we were to assume them to be immediately workable, they fall short of dealing with those things which most worry McGregor and Whyte. Programs of the sort mentioned might provide a mechanism for doing a better evaluation job from the point of view of the organization and of those men of ambitious and independent cut. But they do not wash paternalism and au-

---

[10] Professor Harold J. Leavitt makes an interesting observation at this point. He says that the recommendations in this paragraph say, in effect, that the salvation of the independence and integrity of the *individual* lies in creation of special evaluation *groups*. As he points out, this is in distinct contrast to those who see committees as part of the general conspiracy to destroy the individual. Certainly, it is more than sheer accident that committees have developed historically at the top levels of management—levels at which there is great awareness and support of individualism. At another level the virtues of that famous group incentive plan, the Scanlon Plan, in giving visibility to a man's ability have seldom been stressed.

thoritarianism out of hierarchical organizations. And they are not therapeutic. They would not make over timorous, dependent, conformist men. The God role would still be there to be played.

But an avenue would be opened and an escape provided. Top and bottom management, young and old, could meet together and work together on serious problems in the relatively unprotected environment near the surface of the organization. Those who wished to do so could escape the absolute monarchy of middle management. This alone would be worthwhile. And we could hope that such a mechanism would replace the "crown princes" and the "boy" system of the modern corporation with an objective testing of the professional competence of the young manager.

NEW ANGLES IN APPRAISAL*

Marion S. Kellogg

I'm a part of the headquarters organization of the General Electric Company, specifically charged with finding out more about growth and development of people—what is the process by which growth occurs—what stimulates it—what inhibits it—and then working with managers to improve their development practices.

About a year ago, I set myself the task of developing a short workshop aimed particularly at the development aspect of the appraisal discussion, and I started around the country giving this workshop to groups of our managers, about twenty at a time. In doing this, I discovered some things about their understanding and application of fundamental principles which rather startled me. And because I feel they are probably common to managers generally, I'd like to tell you a little about them.

Let me begin by describing the workshop itself.

I stress for the workshop participants the important role of the work assignment in the development process and then go on to outline the usual, standard criteria for a sound development plan. I'm sure you are familiar with them, but so that we all have the same items in mind, let's take a quick look at them.

1. Make plans specific and concrete; where possible, show desirable timing.
2. Emphasize strengths on which the individual can build or which he can use more effectively, rather than stress weaknesses to be overcome.
3. Avoid suggestions involving the changing of personal characteristics and traits; instead, describe behavior which has hurt the individual in certain situations and suggest alternate, more acceptable ways of acting.
4. Concentrate on the opportunities for growth which exist within the framework of the individual's present position, recognizing that advancement generally stems from outstanding contribution on assigned responsibilities.
5. Limit plans for growth to a few important items which are possible of accomplishment within a reasonable time period.
6. Focus the plans on an objective—*e.g.* to increase effectiveness as a communications specialist or as a cost accountant, etc. —rather than general improvement.

During most of this presentation, which takes about fifteen minutes, I find that managers sit, looking slightly bored and nodding occasionally (some to indicate agreement, others just dozing, I think). Finally, I give them something to do in order to involve them. The group is divided in two and is given a case history of a mythical individual named John Jones. One half is instructed to pretend that it is John Jones' manager, that it is the evening before a discussion with John to help him make a plan for his development. To help the manager group, it is given the kinds of materials that managers usually have available about their employees—personal data about John (age, education, work history, etc.), a summary of John's past performance appraisals, a few re-

* Speech given at American Management Association personnel meeting at Chicago, February 15, 1961. Used by permission of the author.

sults of tests taken when he was first hired, a description of the way the manager feels about him, and a little sketch of the manager himself (age, education, work history, and career goals).

The other half is asked to put themselves in the place of John himself, faced the next day with a discussion of his development needs and plans. The John Jones group is given materials that an employee would usually know about himself or have available—personal history data, a summary of past performance appraisals, and a little description of how John feels about his manager, his job, and his career.

Both groups are given as well a position description for John's present job, a list of his major goals for the year, and a summary of his major accomplishments throughout his career. They also both have the list of criteria for a sound development plan which I showed you earlier.

The workshop participants really work on this problem. They enjoy the case, usually accuse me of borrowing true incidents, and, in general, there is a great deal of involvement. Voice level rises and there are arguments and disagreements. When the groups have made their recommended plans, a spokesman from each presents them to the total class, describing first the situation as his group sees it and the reasons for the selected plans. In doing this, all the old wives' tales, the misconceptions, and the confusions become obvious and some of the basic problems in the relationship between a man and his manager are illuminated.

Let me quickly summarize the case for you. John Jones is a young man in his thirties, with a liberal arts degree and a law degree. He was in the top fifth of his class in arts, but only in the top half in law. He was originally hired on a relations rotating program and was placed in union relations for his first job. After about a year there, he went into salary and wage administration and has been in this field for about three years. He is bright, quick, outgoing; he is quite a leader; he is persuasive both orally and in writing. He is not very detail minded, dislikes routine and records very much. He wants to be eventually at least a relations manager and possibly a general manager. He had had some assignments in manufacturing and he liked them very much, so that he is torn between relations and manufacturing and really would welcome advice on this point. John's manager is about fifty years old. He has been in the salary and wage field all his life. He would like to be promoted but has been passed over twice, so that he feels it is not very likely. He is personally very methodical, detail minded, and a little withdrawn and reserved. He feels that John's records are not as accurate as they could be and that John does not spend enough time at his desk doing his paper work. He does recognize some excellent results—John has won the confidence of managers, his advice on pay levels and rates is frequently asked, and better understanding about pay administration has been achieved. You get the picture.

Now what are some of the things that startled me?

The first striking point was how differently the manager and John Jones groups viewed the situation and each other. Now, of course, we know this happens every day, but I had not appreciated the extent of the difference. I have given this workshop eleven times and to over two hundred participants. In every case, the manager group saw John as, at best, performing at a minimum level, in spite of the fact that his appraisals all rated him "average" or better. And John saw his manager as blocking his advancement, almost impossible to work for, and failing to give reward for good work even though he had been given some very substantial salary increases. The groups deliberately selected the material they wished to support their position and deliberately rejected or overlooked other information. So strongly did one group feel that when a John Jones' group member accused a member of the manager group of underestimating John's performance, the manager insisted he could find the quotes in the material to prove that John was only a marginal performer. And when he couldn't find it, his cohorts started to help him look. They were truly startled when they could not find this information. They were impossible to convince. This deliberate selectivity in the use of material is not, I am sure, confined to the "pretend" situation. Managers and individuals to a greater or lesser extent view things through their own set of filters, and screen the facts they use. This points up a dangerous feature of appraisal and development discussions and makes two things important: (1) that managers and individuals alike recognize and are aware of this tendency in themselves so that they can try to minimize it, and (2) that in so far as possible objective standards and data are used as a basis for appraisal. Since we lack these for so many kinds of work, we in personnel relations have a long development job ahead of us.

The next startling thing that happened was that as each side described its plans, it became apparent that there was a wide discrepancy in objective. In every case, the man's objective was to get out of this job which he disliked and out from under this manager, with whom he felt incompatible, and he had to do it in a way that would not offend or upset the manager, thereby making him, in effect, his enemy.

The manager in well over half the cases (not always, but better than half) had as his sole objective to get the man to be more exact, keep his records better, and exhibit more evident self-discipline. Now, whether we want to admit it or not, this difference in objective probably usually exists. The focus for the individual is apt to be some sort of appeasement of the manager so that he can get what he wants for himself in the future. The focus for the manager is apt to be on the work he wants the man to do and is probably much more immediately oriented. This difference in objective makes for a communication problem in the discussion. A manager and his subordinate may be using the same words to describe actions but actually may have quite different results in mind. The implication is that the discussion will be far more productive if this discrepancy in objective is recognized and time is taken to set some mutually agreeable or, at least compatible, objectives which the development plans are designed to achieve.

The third point that came out clearly was the effect of the difference in objective and the selectivity with which material was used. This was a variation of the old halo effect. If John was described in the written material as *somewhat* less able to work with numbers than with words, the manager group saw him as positively *poor* in dealing with numbers, whereas John saw himself as reasonably good with numbers. If John was described as outgoing, persuasive, and disliking routine, the manager group saw him as overly talkative, given to wasting time, inefficient, and lacking in self-discipline. John saw himself as a leader-manager type and not as a bookkeeper, etc. In other words, the "gray" areas were black in the eyes of the manager but white in John's eyes. This difference in view would make it very difficult for John to accept his manager's criticisms and unlikely that he would do anything about them.

The implication gives renewed emphasis to the point that a manager's discussion of an employee's characteristics or traits is usually a waste of effort. We recognized this generally in the Company when we changed from appraisals of traits to performance-type appraisals. But for some reason the old personality characteristics reared their ugly heads in the so-called development discussion. My workshop experiences make me believe that they are no more appropriate there than they were in the old rating sheets.

The next point that startled me was that in spite of the apparent acceptance of the criterion that a sound development plan should be built on an individual's strengths and not his weaknesses, in *every* case, without exception, the managers' first plan to recommend to John was based on doing something detailed, numerical, routine—the very areas in which John was described as being weaker than other qualities. In over half the cases the John Joneses came up with similar plans. This point was thoroughly hashed out, and it became obvious that neither group really believed that one should build on strengths. And yet if you agree that one should make development plans on which an individual will work, and if you build plans based on weaknesses, you find yourself faced with the horrifying picture of everyone in a company working very hard at the things he does poorly. Profits would surely flow down the drain! Now I certainly grant that there are some things which we do not do well simply because we have never had enough practice in doing them, and these will improve with practice. And there are other things which we do not do well because we are careless or disinterested or think no one cares, and these will respond to effort. But there are other things which we do not do well simply because we have no talent for them and effort here is largely wasted or a plan focused on them looks like punishment, and most individuals will not work on them. Besides, surely we are not so hamstrung in our work—and I am speaking now of professional and managerial people—that there is only one way to accomplish a result! The thing to do is to decide on the results that are needed in a job and then ask ourselves how we can achieve them, using our greatest strengths, our greatest talents.

Next, I found two areas of confusion. Managers tend to equate appraisal with development. Appraisal is one tool used in the development cycle but it is not the whole development cycle. When a manager appraises an individual's performance, he tells him (or gets the man to tell him) of certain things which are going well and of other things which need improvement. Preferably these are discussed in terms of the results to be achieved. The development process goes on, however, to ask what can be done to add to the capacity of the individual to obtain results—greater results, faster, perhaps. I'll have more to say about this later.

Managers also equate development with career planning. Development, once more, means adding to the individual's capacity, giving him greater knowledge and skill, extending his talents. If a person is able to do this, he may apply this to his present job or to a next job or to the job he ultimately wants to have. When we talk about career planning, we are talking about ways and means of achieving a certain career goal. Some of this may involve development of the individual, but more often involves recognizing the kind of work experience and strategy needed in order to progress to a given job.

Finally, I was amazed at the inflexibility of both managers and individuals. If a person had done a job, or even if he had never done it, he apparently had formed a stereotype of *how* the job should be done—not the results, mind you, but the *means* for obtaining results. He found it very hard to think of any other way of doing it. Now the essence of development is giving the individual some freedom to choose how he will do his job. In this way he can see how to get a thing done best in the particular situation in which he finds himself and do it by using his best talents. To the groups I worked with, a salary and wage man just had to keep records. Only after they finally asked themselves the fundamental questions: "What does John need the records for and what are all the ways in which John might have readily available, accurate position level and pay rate information?" did they begin to think creatively. Then some suggested that John's clerk or steno might do the posting work, or the records might be kept by the payroll organization which really kept them anyway, or the records might be mechanized so that the computers could take over much of the detail, etc., etc.

The point which must be made to our managers, I think, is that there are many, many ways to do a job and for best results, the individual, with or without his manager's help, must ask himself: "What is the best way for me to tackle this job in order to get the best possible results in the shortest possible time?" If we look around us at successful managers, it is almost always apparent that they have done this. Yet managers who themselves have taken this approach all their working lives may, in dealing with their subordinates, insist that there is only one way to do a piece of work. This is not good for the work and certainly does not contribute to the development of either the subordinate or the manager.

With all these problems confronting managers and individuals alike, it seemed to me that there must be some better solution to the development of an employee than using the tail end of a performance appraisal to discuss a man's strengths and weaknesses and recommend ways for him to improve.

Besides, the strengths-weaknesses route is a hazardous one at best. When is a strength a strength and when is it a weakness, and vice versa? To John's manager, John's outgoing nature and ability to work with the broad picture represented a weakness in that it did not make him a good record keeper. In union relations, these same characteristics might well have represented strengths. I once listened to a discussion between a manager of marketing and a sales manager, in which the marketing manager said to the sales manager: "You build excellent relationships. People like you. Your customers are glad to see you and many of your large orders are the direct result of these fine relationships," and later on, "You are too soft with your subordinates. You don't demand enough of them." And I asked myself whether it was not the same basic quality that he was praising on the one hand and criticizing on the other. Perhaps the sales manager in going to work to correct his softness with subordinates might be reducing the very quality which made his customers like him so much. For a manager to work with an employee, using the strengths-weaknesses approach takes more than I think we can expect of our managers and may well be one of the reasons that some managers feel that appraisal discussions ruin relationships with subordinates or, at least, make them more difficult.

I have an alternate approach to suggest and one that I believe is more in line with a manager's usual work, is easier for him to carry out, will be more acceptable to the employee, and will have greater pay-off in terms of development of the individual.

Let's go back a minute to the concept of development. By the development process we mean the process by which we add to the knowledge and skill of the individual, extend his talents, add to his capabilities. Development goes on all the time whether managers do anything or not. In industry, our special problem is to accelerate the development and give it a focus which is useful to us. Whether this usefulness is directed toward present job or later job is a matter of choice and may well be both. But in any event, the work that the person is assigned to do *now* represents the greatest opportunity for him to develop himself.

There are several reasons for this:

1. He is rewarded for his work in terms of pay, recognition, and advancement.
2. He identifies himself and at least part of his personal worth with the extent to which he accomplishes what is expected of him.
3. He is "a risk" in his job. Failure to accomplish results may lead to termination, demotion, loss of face, etc. In other words, something hangs in the balance. It *matters* whether or not he does his job.

The work, then, has built-in motivational values.

For purposes of our thinking about development then, let's view the total work cycle as one large learning process which, of course, it really is. Usually the first step in the work cycle is the reaching of agreement between a man and his manager of what is to be done or accomplished. *I see this discussion as the fundamental development discussion,* because it is at this time that goals can be set or work assignments given which will demand that the individual add to his knowledge, skill, and capability. How is this done? Well, we know that we do not grow by doing the same old thing in the same old way. So the odds will be increased that the individual will grow faster and in a needed direction if a carefully selected element of "newness" is put into the work program. The conservatives among you are probably thinking that that is a ridiculous thought —we cannot always be doing something new; sometimes we have to do old things. True, but not *all* old things. I believe that every work program can afford and should have some new thing in it—it may be a new, higher objective or goal, a new piece of work, a new or higher standard for work, a new application, a new customer, etc.

Now something new just for the sake of newness isn't enough. It may "develop" a person but the development may not be in a useful way. In order to give useful direction, in order to give the manager a solid motive for encouraging and helping the man, and in order to give the man himself an incentive, the new element should have the probability of adding to the over-all result of the component, helping the component make a larger contribution to the business.

In order to increase the odds that the man will succeed and will grow and develop in the course of doing it, the new work element should make increased demands on the man's greatest talents and should require him to add to his knowledge in certain areas and develop certain skills which perhaps have not been needed to date.

Let me summarize very briefly what I've just said. In the course of planning the work an individual will do, man and manager agree on some new things which will demand that the individual add to his capability in order to accomplish them, and they select these new elements so that if accomplished they will bring about an improved contribution to the business.

Through the year, then, as the man goes about his job, his development moves forward in a very normal way; he learns; he grows as he does his job.

What about performance appraisal, then? What is its role in this work-oriented development process? Well, we know that for learning to occur efficiently, feedback is necessary. The role of appraisal is one of feedback. The man and the manager review what has been done well and not so well. They review this in work terms and emphasize the translation of this information into ways and means of improving performance in the future. Like all feedback, this is best done close to actual performance so that it should desirably appear in the day-to-day coaching as well as in periodic work-progress reviews and formal appraisals. But with appraisal viewed as feedback, at no time is it necessary for the manager to describe to the individual his strengths and weaknesses as he sees them, nor work out plans for correcting the individual's weaknesses. They work on what was done and not done, and they discuss reasons why something was not done, how it can be accomplished in the future, and set new goals for themselves based on what they learned during the first attempt at doing it. The approach is very specific to the tasks at hand, and, of course, this specificity increases understanding.

Let me emphasize, however, that if this work approach to development is used, the amount and direction of the development are controlled by the quality of the work goals that were set at the time the work was agreed upon. (Naturally the man's ability and willingness to respond are vital, too, but this is true in all concepts of development.)

Now, this process sounds fairly simple.

The best managers have probably operated in this way for a long time. But you will find that the majority will need help in translating the ideas into practice. It takes considerable insight and imagination to select new elements to put into the work program which will really have the desirable payoff of benefit to the business and development for the man. Managers need help, too, in giving their employees more freedom to choose how to go about achieving a specific result. In fact, they often need help in formulating work in terms of results or goals.

So there is still something left for manpower development people to do, and for many it is work they have not done before. Perhaps it will be the "new element" which they can add to their work to ensure their own development.

B. Issues and Problems in Appraisal

4. EMPIRICAL STUDIES

CHANGING ATTITUDES TOWARD A MERIT RATING SYSTEM

ALVIN ZANDER AND JOHN GYR

VALIDITY OF RATINGS AS RELATED TO RATING TECHNIQUES AND CONDITIONS

A. G. BAYROFF, HELEN R. HAGGERTY, AND E. A. RUNDQUIST

INFLUENCES ON MERIT RATINGS

AARON J. SPECTOR

THE VALIDITY OF RATINGS OF SEVERAL LEVELS OF SUPERVISORS

DEAN K. WHITLA AND JOHN E. TIRRELL

THE IMPACT OF INTERPERSONAL RELATIONS ON RATINGS OF PERFORMANCE

VERNE KALLEJIAN, PAULA BROWN, AND IRVING R. WESCHLER

In this section we turn from general discussion of problems to five empirical studies of the effect of various environmental factors on ratings of individuals in an organization. The effects of organizational distance, of status differences, of varying degrees of knowledge and acquaintance, and of variations in the rating procedure are examined. Information from these and other studies may help the administrator understand why he may be having difficulty with performance appraisal in his own organization. The student is given a chance to examine the methodology of applied research illustrated in these and other studies in the book.

FURTHER READING

Bass, Bernard M., "Reducing Leniency in Merit Ratings," *Personnel Psychology,* Vol. 9, no. 3, Autumn 1956, pp. 359–369.

Ferguson, Leonard W., "The Effect upon Appraisal Scores of Individual Differences in the Ability of Superiors to Appraise Subordinates," *Personnel Psychology,* Vol. 2, no. 3, Autumn 1949, pp. 377–382.

Ferguson, Leonard W., "The Value of Acquaintance Ratings in Criterion Research," *Personnel Psychology,* Vol. 2, no. 1, Spring 1949, pp. 93–102.

Glaser, Robert, Paul A. Schwarz, and John C. Flanagan, "The Contribution of Interview and Situational Performance Procedures to the Selection of Supervisory Personnel," *Journal of Applied Psychology,* Vol. 42, no. 2, April 1958, pp. 69–73.

Glickman, Albert S., "Effects of Negatively Skewed Ratings on Motivations of the Rated," *Personnel Psychology,* Vol. 8, no. 1, Spring 1955, pp. 39–47.

Harrison, Roger L., "Workers' Perceptions and Job Success," *Personnel Psychology,* Vol. 12, no. 4, Winter 1959, pp. 619–625.

Hausman, Howard J., and Strupp, Hans H. "Non-Technical Factors In Supervisors' Ratings of Job Performance," *Personnel Psychology,* Vol. 8, no. 2, Summer 1955, pp. 201–217.

Massarik, Fred, and others, "Evaluating Efficiency Rating Systems Through Experiment," *Personnel Administration,* Vol. 14, no. 1, January 1951, pp. 42–47. (Institute of Industrial Relations, University of California, Los Angeles, Reprint no. 20.)

Another article based on the same study is:

Weschler, Irving R., and others, "Experimenting with Federal Efficiency Ratings: A Case Study," *Journal of Social Psychology,* Vol. 36, 1952, pp. 205–222. (Institute of Industrial Relations, University of California, Los Angeles, Reprint no. 26.)

Ricciuti, Henry N., "Ratings of Leadership Potential at the U. S. Naval Academy and Subsequent Officer Performance," *Journal of Applied Psychology,* Vol. 39, no. 3, June 1955, pp. 194–199.

Rundquist, Edward A., and Bittner, Reign H. "Using Ratings to Validate Personnel Instruments: A Study in Method," *Personnel Psychology,* Vol. 1, no. 2, Summer 1948, pp. 163–184.

Stockford, Lee, and H. W. Bissell, "Factors Involved in Establishing a Merit-Rating Scale," *Personnel,* September 1949, pp. 94–115.

Taylor, Erwin K., and others. "Supervisory Climate and Performance Ratings: An Exploratory Study," *Personnel Psychology,* Vol. 12, no. 3, Autumn 1959, pp. 453–468.

Underwood, Willis O., "Executive Appraisals for Inventory and Promotion," *Personnel Administration,* Vol. 23, no. 2, March–April 1960, pp. 26–32.

CHANGING ATTITUDES TOWARD A MERIT RATING SYSTEM*

Alvin Zander and John Gyr

• SUMMARY

An effort was made to change the attitudes of 400 men in a favorable direction concerning a merit appraisal procedure used in one department of a large company. Two experimental methods were used, one in which the members of 12 crews counselled their supervisor on the practices that he should use in order that he might be equally fair to all persons in making his judgments, and another in which 12 foremen explained to their crews the method each follows so that he might be impartial in his ratings. These supervisors were trained in the procedures necessary for conducting permissive and stimulating meetings and also in standard techniques of reporting appraisal results to each individual workman. The merit evaluations were made monthly instead of the usual practice of twice a year. A number of supervisors, who were also trained in reporting methods, described the appraisal results to the men monthly but held no prior group meetings with them. These were controls on the effect of the increase in frequency of feedback. Another set of crews provided an over-all control by making no change from the usual practices. Attitude measures were made at the beginning and end of the experimental period. Measures concerning the crew meetings were also obtained.

The difference between the average changes in attitude toward the appraisal plan in the two experimental methods is not statistically significant and the attitude change in the two procedures is not significantly different from the over-all control group. The over-all control group did not change at all.

The effectiveness of the meetings in both treatments were alike in creating positive attitudes toward the appraisal plan if the foreman was seen to have the best interests of the men in mind, knew what he was talking about, and the men agreed with his beliefs about the evaluation methods during the meeting. Where these features were absent, the attitudes of the men concerning the evaluation methods did not change.

The workmen in the *consultation* procedure made a significant favorable change in attitude toward the appraisal methods if they felt that the meeting outcome was satisfactory, the men were skilled in discussion procedures, and there was difference in opinion during the session prior to arriving at a group decision. Those who were given an *explanation* of his practices by the boss made a significant positive change in attitude concerning the evaluation meth-

* From *Personnel Psychology,* Winter 1955, Vol. 8, no. 4, pp. 429–448. Copyright 1955 by Personnel Psychology, Inc. Reprinted by permission.

ods only if they felt that higher management was sincere and that there was a high degree of similarity in the opinions of the crew members and with their boss.

The men in the feedback-frequency control groups made the greatest average favorable change in attitude toward the appraisal procedures and also developed a strong perception of control over their own fate. It was suggested that these men viewed their foreman as greatly interested in them—even more than those supervisors who held prior meetings with crews—and willing to provide means for improvement of the men.

Average attitudes concerning the liking of the foreman and the company, or the power of the supervisor, were not changed during the study in either experimental treatment, nor did the changes where they occurred appear to affect feelings toward the evaluation methods.

Positive attitudes toward a potential source of reward or punishment are a function of the probability that one's needs will be satisfied by that source. In the consultation method the group members' feelings about the practices used by a powerful person depend upon how effective they themselves are as a group in determining his behavior. In the explanation treatment the attitudes depend upon how sincere higher management is perceived to be in sanctioning the superior's behavior. Finally, monthly appraisal reports seem to generate a perception that supervisors will help the subordinate to improve his performance and thus to have control over his own need gratification; therefore, attitudes improve when appraisal feedback interviews are frequent.

• PURPOSE AND METHOD

This study concerns the effort of persons occupying supervisory positions to change negative attitudes of subordinates to positive ones. The attitudes concern the company's appraisal procedures —a visible symbol of the superior's use of his greater power. The results show that several different procedures may be used to influence feelings, each of which require certain conditions in order to be maximally effective.

A number of recent studies indicate that a person with high power within a hierarchical social structure can be a source of either tension or comfort for his subordinates depending upon whether he uses his power in a need satisfying or in a frustrating manner (*3*, *5*, *6*). As a result, much of the behavior of subordinates toward superiors in a hierarchy (other than that intended to accomplish the work of the organization) are either symptoms of the degree of tension felt, or are efforts to minimize tension. In these investigations *power* is defined as an individual's ability, sanctioned by at least some part of the organization, to determine the behavior or fate of others whenever he desires to do so. Low tension is a function of the degree to which a person feels he may satisfy the needs he aspires to gratify in a specific social relationship.

Other research has shown that the attitudes and behaviors developed by subordinates in order to minimize tension may create strain, misunderstanding, or negative feelings among the persons within the social structure (*2*, *7*). Because superiors are usually responsible for the health of the organization, it is typical for them to take action in order to change any such feelings among those at lower levels. To do so they attempt to reduce the potential threat inherent in their behavior by assuring subordinates that the superiors' behavior can be trusted to consider the needs of the less powerful persons. That this can be done is suggested by the findings in several studies.

Ross (*6*) reduced the possibility that industrial supervisors could exert any punishing power by eliminating all functions such as quality control or determination of assignments from their role, leaving only the potentially rewarding function of coaching on job skills. When the behavior of the employees toward the supervisors prior to this modification was compared to that shown afterwards, it was apparent that the workers were considerably more positive in their feelings about superiors following the change. Biddle (*1*) found that practice teachers were more at ease with, and positive toward, a supervisor who had no right to give them a course grade than with one who had freedom to judge them as well as criticize their work. In a study of the interrole relations among members of professional groups it was observed that persons in ancillary professions were more secure, and had more favorable attitudes about superiors, the more that the higher status person turned to them for help, or advice.

Other means for affecting the tension of subordinates, by direct statements from superiors, and by requesting the participation of subordinates in decisions concerning appropriate superior behavior will be reported here. The two methods are: (a) superiors seek criticism and advice from subordinates, and (b) superiors explain the nature and reasons for their behavior to subordinates. In the former method (called *consultation*) the superior gives the members the right to influence the superior's behavior. The members, therefore, determine how he will influence their own fate. The effectiveness of this method in changing negative attitudes about powerful persons will depend upon how well the subordinates are able to devise practices for the superior to follow which are seen as gratifying to themselves. They become the potential source of their own need gratification.

In the *explanation* procedure the supervisor describes the nature and intentions of his behavior toward subordinates. This increases the accuracy of the subordinate's perception of his relations with superiors and enables them to understand management's point of view. It in no way increases the power of the superior over the subordinate.

Since all concerned are members of a hierarchy, higher authority retains the usual right to sanction the immediate superior's behavior. Pelz (*4*) has reported that a worker's acceptance of a supervisor, and of the latter's influence attempts, is strongly affected by the degree to which the employee believes that higher executives will support the position taken by the supervisor. The efficiency of the explanation procedure in changing attitudes will, therefore, depend upon the trust the subordinates have in the intentions of higher authority —the major source of need satisfaction via the supervisor.

In summary, the favorableness of the subordinate's attitudes toward the superiors depends in part upon the degree to which they feel that the agents who sanction the superior's behavior will gratify the needs of those on the subordinate level.

An opportunity to develop and test the validity of such notions arose in a large utility.[1] Within one department of the company workers were skeptical of management's fairness in making and using appraisal ratings. In two attitude surveys separated by several years it was found that almost 50% of the employees felt that the bi-annual judgments had little to do with obtaining promotions or salary increases and that the evaluation method was used unfairly. Many believed that the foreman and those at higher levels of management selected men for advancement who were favorites or who had "pull" of some sort.

The management were ready to admit that the appraisal procedure was not a perfect measuring instrument either in its makeup or execution, but they believed that there was little basis in fact for suspicion concerning favoritism in the ratings or in choosing persons for increases in status. They reasoned that the doubts were due to the fact that the workers were not sufficiently informed about, and had no means of control over, the way in which judgments were made and used by their supervisor. The appraisal procedure was seen as threatening by the men, management believed, since the evaluations had such a large share in determining the employee's fate. It was decided to see if the attitudes toward the evaluation methods would change if the workers were convened in groups to discuss the appraisal procedures so that they might be assured that they were given just ratings. The decision was made to compare the effectiveness of consultation and explanation procedures.

Experimental Plan

In preparation for this field experiment 48 supervisors were selected on a random basis. Twenty-four of these were given several days' training in how to lead a group meeting as well as instruction concerning a standard method for reporting to individuals the results of the appraisal judgments. The latter step was taken since the regular procedure required the foreman to tell each employee about his ratings and to encourage discussion concerning how he might remove any apparent weakness. It was assumed that many supervisors were not skilled in describing and discussing these ratings and that they should be made alike as possible in this respect by teaching them a standard good practice. Prior to the experiment all men in the department were given an attitude questionnaire as a base line measure.

The group *consultation* treatment required that each of 12 foremen conduct a two-hour meeting with his crew. He first described the nature of the evaluation procedures and then told them that he would abide by their advice, reached as a group decision, on three broad questions. These three issues were: (a) "What is the best method for me to follow in order to insure that I am being fair in appraising you?" (b) "What is the most effective method for reporting to you the results of the appraisal I make?" and (c) "How can I best help you to improve your skills in areas in which they are weak?"

These three questions do not cover all

[1] This study was sponsored and financed by the Michigan Bell Telephone Company.

the doubts about the appraisal procedure; however, it was felt wise to select issues which were obviously important to the men and to keep this list short enough to be thoroughly discussed within time limitations.

In the *explanation* method each of 12 different supervisors also held a two-hour meeting with his crew. After he had described the evaluation method he uses, the changes he intends to make in the future, and what he does in order to be equally fair and instructive for each man, he answered any questions raised by the members of the group. The description of the rating procedure, which he promised to follow thereafter in making his judgments and reports, was the same as the one proposed by a matched crew in the consultation method. Each explanation-treatment foreman was instructed in the decisions reached by a paired consultation crew. As nearly as possible the crews were also matched for similarity in crew-size, skill, and relations between foreman and workers. The pairing of crews was to ensure that any attitude changes could not be attributed to causes other than the experimental treatments.

In order that the existence of the appraisal procedures might have maximum visibility within a reasonable period of time, each foreman made his ratings monthly for a total of six months and reported these results to the individuals concerned at the time the ratings were made. Since this increase in the frequency of feedback is in itself a variable which can influence the attitudes of the men toward the evaluation procedures, it was necessary to devise a *monthly-feedback control* treatment. This was done by training 12 other supervisors in the previously mentioned standard procedures for describing evaluation results. These foremen then made and reported monthly appraisals but did not have a group meeting with the men prior to the beginning of this practice. Finally, an *over-all control* was created in which 12 more supervisors were directed to continue the appraisal procedure once every six months just as they had always done. These latter supervisors were given no training prior to the outset of the study and held no meeting with the men. Six months after the meetings the attitude questionnaire was again administered to all men in the 48 crews.

The assumptions and predictions concerning the effectiveness of these attitude-change procedures may be reviewed in the light of this design. The general assumption was that the meetings would create perceptions concerning the evaluation methods which, along with subsequent interactions with the foreman and other parts of the company, would affect their attitudes toward the appraisal method—the relevant instrument of management's power. If they perceived a likelihood that the practices followed by the supervisor would probably gratify, among others the crucial need for fair and unprejudiced ratings, these feelings would be favorable; if not, the attitudes would be negative.

In the *consultation* treatment the men are given the right to influence the practices of the foreman, and the superior has pledged himself to adhere to the group decision. Therefore, attitudes will shift in a positive direction if the men feel that they have made the most of this opportunity and have developed good suggestions for the foreman to follow. If, in contrast, they perceive that the crew did not perform in a capable fashion and thus there is little likelihood that their needs will be satisfied, the attitudes will be less likely to change or they may even become more negative.

In the *explanation* condition, if the workers believe that higher authority is sincere in its intention to allow the foreman to follow the new and fairer practices, and to be impartial themselves; and if, in fact, the foreman's plan appears to them to be fairer, the employees will perceive a greater likelihood that needs will be satisfied henceforth and they will view the evaluation plan favorably. In contrast, if they suspect that the officials will not permit the supervisor to practice what he is teaching or if they do not have the impression that the foreman's plans are better than the old ones, the men's cynicism about appraisal ratings will continue.

One other matter may influence the nature of the worker's feelings about the appraisal plan. The skill of the foreman in conducting individual feedback sessions should make a difference since these are relevant indicators of the foreman's intentions. A workman who feels that his supervisor does well in individual report sessions will develop favorable attitudes concerning the evaluation procedure, while one who perceives that the boss does poorly will remain unchanged. On the basis of the same reasoning about possibility of need gratification, the increase in the frequency of appraisal discussions should be well received by the men and have a positive effect upon their attitudes. Finally, since the meetings are concerned primarily with the evaluation practices, it is likely that attitudes concerning other aspects of the company will tend to remain relatively unchanged.

Measurements Made

Two different instruments were used to obtain the data necessary for testing these predictions: (a) an attitude questionnaire and (b) a post-meeting reaction form.

(a) The attitude measuring device contained 55 questions organized into six pretested Guttman-type scales. The computation of scale scores was done by the Minimum Error Technique, which is a method based on finding the relationship between the obtained reproducibility of an item and the minimum reproducibility which it has as a result of its response frequencies. The replies on the scales during the study were found to lead to similar reproducibility indices as those in a test prior to the experiment. The six scales concerned attitude toward the appraisal plan, liking of the company, liking of the foreman, attributed power of the higher management over the fate of the workers, and attributed power of the foreman. This form was completed by all workers in each of the 48 crews (about 400 men) in June just prior to the crew meetings and again in December.

(b) The post-meeting reaction questionnaire was given to the men in the consultation and explanation treatments immediately after their crew meetings. It contained 53 questions again organized into scales. These were intended to measure their feelings about the effectiveness of the meeting, the foreman's apparent interest in the needs of the men (sincerity), the sincerity of higher management, the quality of the foreman's performance as a chairman, the caliber of the men's skill in the dis-

Table 1

MEAN CHANGE IN ATTITUDE TOWARD THE EVALUATION METHOD DURING PERIOD JUNE-DECEMBER

TREATMENT TYPE	*N*	MEAN CHANGE IN ATTITUDE	MEAN DIFF. FROM OVER-ALL CONTROL	*p* VALUE OF DIFF. FROM OVER-ALL CONTROL
Consultation	108	.75	.67	.10
Explanation	90	.63	.55	.18
Control, monthly feedback	97	.82	.74	.05
Control, over-all	96	.08	—	—

cussions, and the worker's perception of the attitudes held by the rest of his crew concerning the appraisal methods. These scales could not be pre-tested since answers to the questions were unique to the meeting experience and it was not practical to obtain a population of responses large enough for prior reliability evaluation.

All questionnaires were anonymous and were mailed directly to the authors by a worker in the crew selected by the members.

• RESULTS

Each of the scales in the attitude questionnaire were scored in such a way that the resultant describes the amount of change in feelings which occurred during the experimental period. The degree of shift may vary from zero to about −7 for an unfavorable change or to +7 for a positive shift. The mean changes in feelings toward the appraisal plan in the two experimental treatments and the control methods from June to December are summarized in Table 1.

It may be seen that the over-all control crews had almost no change in average attitude toward the appraisal procedure by the end of the experimental period. We may reasonably assume, therefore, that no unexpected influences arose during this time which were important in changing the feelings of the men toward the evaluation procedure. The average shift of those in the consultation condition was greater than that made by the workers who were given explanations; however, the difference is not great and neither group made a statistically significant change when compared to the control groups. The greatest positive changes in both experimental treatments were in reply to two questions included within the appraisal attitude scale: "How fair do you feel the appraisal plan is in showing the company how well you are doing?" (p of difference from control, consultation = .04; explanation = .03); and, "How familiar are you with the appraisal plan?" ($p = .05$ in both conditions).

Note that the members of the crews in the monthly feedback control made the greatest mean shift in a positive direction and that this is significantly different from that made by the over-all control crews ($p = .05$). Most of this change is contributed by an increase in awareness that the foreman is "familiar" with the plan (p of difference from control = .03). This will be discussed later.

Three types of conditions within each

Table 2

PROPORTION OF PERSONS PERCEIVING CERTAIN CHARACTERISTICS IN FOREMAN'S MEETING BEHAVIOR

	CONSULTATION CREWS		EXPLANATION CREWS	
CHARACTERISTIC PERCEIVED IN MEETING	N	% OF TOTAL N (108)	N	% OF TOTAL N (90)
Foreman sincere	53	49%	32	36%
Foreman not sincere	55	51	58	64
Foreman knew appraisal plan and issues	59	55	44	49
Foreman did not know appraisal plan and issues	49	45	46	51
Foreman and men's opinions agree	53	49	48	53
Foreman's and men's opinions disagree	55	51	42	47
Foreman skilled as chairman	59	55	37	41
Foreman not skilled as chairman	47	45	53	59

treatment can affect its efficiency in changing attitudes: (a) conditions within the crew meetings, (b) influences stemming from concomitant feelings about the company or foreman which are outside and subsequent to the crew meetings, and (c) the frequency of appraisal ratings.

The Effect of the Crew Meetings

Immediately after the crew meetings a larger proportion of the participants in the consultation treatment than in the explanation method expressed approval concerning their supervisor's behavior during the session. These data are shown in Table 2. A greater per cent of the men in the consultation meetings thought that the supervisor was sincere, knew what he was talking about, expressed opinions which were acceptable to the men, and was a skilled chairman. The differences between the proportions in the two treatments are all significant at the .05 level or better. It is noteworthy that a significantly larger proportion of men within the explanation condition felt that their foreman was not sincere and that he was not skilled as a chairman during the meeting.

These attributes of foreman behavior during the meeting are related to favorable shifts in attitude during the subsequent six months in both types of experimental treatments. The results are shown in Table 3.

When the men in both treatments stated that their foreman was either sincere in his intentions, knew the facts about the appraisal procedure, or had opinions which were generally similar to those of the crew during the meeting, the attitudes changed in a favorable direction concerning the appraisal methods (significant levels ranging from .02 to .05). If, in contrast, the supervisor did not have these attributes, the workers' feelings about the appraisal plan did not appreciably change. The discussion skill of the chairman in both treatments was less important in stimulating attitude change since the positive attitude shifts related to that attribute are marginal in significance.

We may conclude that the possession

Table 3

CHARACTERISTICS OF CREW MEETINGS DIRECTLY RELATED TO SUBSEQUENT CHANGES IN ATTITUDE TOWARD EVALUATION METHODS IN BOTH EXPERIMENTAL TREATMENTS

	CONSULTATION CREWS				EXPLANATION CREWS			
CHARACTERISTIC ATTRIBUTED TO MEETING	*N*	*M* ATTITUDE CHANGE	*M* DIFF. FROM CONTROL	*p* VALUE OF DIFF. FROM CONTROL[a]	*N*	*M* ATTITUDE CHANGE	*M* DIFF. FROM CONTROL	*p* VALUE OF DIFF. FROM CONTROL[a]
Foreman sincere	53	1.42	1.34	.02	32	1.66	1.58	.02
Foreman not sincere	55	.10	.02	—	58	.06	−.02	—
Foreman knew appraisal plan and issues	59	1.12	1.04	.05	44	1.52	1.44	.02
Foreman did not know appraisal plan and issues	49	.31	.23	—	46	−.26	−.34	—
Foreman's and men's opinions agree	53	1.42	1.34	.02	48	1.38	1.30	.02
Foreman's and men's opinions disagree	55	.11	.03	—	42	−.21	−.29	—
Foreman skilled as chairman	59	1.12	1.04	.06	37	1.14	1.06	.09
Foreman unskilled as chairman	49	.31	.23	—	53	.30	.22	—

[a] An empty cell indicates that the value of *p* is greater than .10 and therefore considered not significant.

of characteristics such as these determines the success of his efforts when an authority figure meets with his subordinates in an attempt to change their feelings about his own behavior, regardless of which method he uses. Furthermore, a larger proportion of lower status persons are likely to attribute these characteristics to the superior in the consultation method than in the explanation treatment; except for the per cent of members accepting the foreman's opinions, which was equal in both methods.

In respect to other attributes of these meetings, it may be seen in Table 4 that a larger per cent of those in the consultation crews, compared to the explanation groups, were satisfied with the meeting outcome and perceived themselves as skilled in group discussion. Among the men in the explanation treatment a greater proportion perceived agreement among themselves and attributed sincerity to higher management. The differences between these percentages in the two treatments are all significant at the .01 level or better.[2]

These meeting characteristics had dif-

[2] At the end of the post-meeting questionnaire 79% of the men in the consultation groups spontaneously added favorable remarks, while 69% did so after the explanation meetings (p of diff. is .05). Among the consultation crews 23% liked them because they were "democratic," "open forum," "good discussion," while in the explanation groups 13% gave such reasons. That the meetings were "informative," and "educational," was said by 10% of the consultation crew members and 26% of the explanation groups.

Table 4

Proportion of Persons Perceiving Certain Characteristcs in Meeting

Characteristic Perceived in Meeting	Consultation Crews N	Consultation Crews % of Total N (108)	Explanation Crews N	Explanation Crews % of Total N (90)
Satisfied with meeting outcome	63	58%	30	34%
Dissatisfied with meeting outcome	45	42	60	66
Men skilled in group discussion	51	47	29	32
Men unskilled in group discussion	57	53	61	68
Perceive agreement in crew on issue	25	24	52	58
Perceive disagreement in crew on issue	83	76	38	42
Company is sincere in allowing session	50	48	64	71
Company is insincere in allowing session	58	52	36	29

Table 5

Characteristics of Crew Meetings Related to Changes in Attitude toward Evaluation Methods

	Consultation Crews				Explanation Crews			
Characteristic Attributed to Meeting	N	M Attitude Change	M Diff. from Control	p Value of Diff. from Control[a]	N	M Attitude Change	M Diff. from Control	p Value of Diff. from Control[a]
Satisfied with meeting outcome	63	1.19	1.11	.02	30	1.10	1.02	–
Dissatisfied with meeting outcome	45	.13	.05	–	60	.40	.32	–
Men skilled in group discussion	51	1.18	1.10	.05	29	.65	.53	–
Men unskilled in group discussion	57	.42	.36	–	61	.62	.54	–
Perceive agreement in crew on issue	25	–.32	–.40	–	52	1.17	1.09	.05
Perceive disagreement in crew on issue	83	1.07	.99	.03	38	–.11	–.19	–
Company is sincere in allowing session	50	.96	.88	.11	64	1.14	1.06	.04
Company is insincere in allowing session	58	.57	.49	–	36	–.62	–.70	–

[a] An empty cell indicates that the value of p is greater than .10 and therefore considered not significant.

ferential importance in creating attitude shifts in the two treatments, see Table 5. In the consultation groups a mean positive change occurred if the men were satisfied with the product of their group effort, if they perceived that the members were skilled in group discussion, and if lively differences of opinion arose out of which they developed their group decision. Contrariwise, no significant change in feelings about the evaluation method developed in the men who were dissatisfied with the meeting outcome, who felt that the members were inept in group discussion, or who perceived that everyone readily agreed. The results suggest that the men changed most when they felt that they were able to make the fullest use of their opportunity to influence the behavior of an authority figure, were forced to create common agreements out of disparate opinions, and were pleased with the nature of the plans they had developed.

In the explanation groups the attitudes changed most if the men believed that the company was sincere in their intention to allow the foreman freedom, and if the employees perceived constant unanimity of opinion among themselves. It is noteworthy that a separate analysis indicated that 70% of the employees in the explanation condition who perceived that the men agreed as a group also felt that the workers and the foreman were in agreement. Thus, perceived commonality of opinion among the men strongly implies acceptance of the superior's beliefs as well. This perception of agreement among the workers in the explanation crews may indicate the presence of group pressures toward accepting the superior's statements, which, in the absence of any contrary group discussion, primarily served to determine the feelings of the men.

The consultation treatment, in short, aroused reactions in terms of the group's effectiveness in handling its own fate, while the explanation method invoked reactions concerning the motives of power persons. Favorable attitude changes were made if either of these matters were perceived to be potentially need gratifying. A perception of differences in opinion among the members was helpful in changing attitudes in the consultation treatment but hindered attitude changes in the explanation procedure.

The Effects of Company Conditions External to the Meetings

(a) Did attitudes, other than those concerning the appraisal procedure, change during the study period? The questionnaire given in June and again in December measured the degree of attraction that the company and his supervisor had for each workman. It furthermore provided an indication of the amount of power that higher management and the boss had over each employee as seen by the workman. During the six months intervening between the pre- and post-measurements there were no significant average changes in these four attitudes in either of the two treatments, nor were there any significant differences between the experimental and control groups either at the beginning or end of the period studied.

(b) Was a positive or negative change on the above attitudes related to a shift in feelings toward the appraisal plan? The average change in feeling toward the evaluation procedure was examined for those men who made positive changes in attitude on any of the four above-mentioned scales as compared to those who did not shift on these four. In only one case was there a significant relationship. Men who perceived that they had developed greater control over their own fate in relation to the management above their own supervisor tended to develop more favorable feelings about the evaluation method, whereas those who saw no change in their own influence did not change. In the consultation groups the mean change by those who perceived an improvement in their own power was 1.34 and in the explanation crews it was 1.64. The value of p concerning the difference of these changes from those made by the over-all control groups is .04 and .01, respectively.

(c) Did the foreman's skill in individually reporting appraisal results affect feelings toward the evaluation procedure? In the final attitude questionnaire the men were asked to rate their satisfaction with the method used by the boss in the individual evaluation conferences. In both the consultation and explanation crews a significant positive shift in attitude toward the entire evaluation method was associated with satisfaction concerning the foreman's procedure during the individual conferences. The workers who were gratified by the supervisor's feedback skill had a mean positive shift of 1.69 in the consultation treatment, and 1.06 in the explanation groups. The former value is different from the control groups at a confidence level of .003, while the latter has a p value of .04. In contrast, when they did not approve of the foreman's feedback methods, the change in attitude toward the appraisal procedure for the consultation and explanation groups was −.19 and −.37, respectively. We may conclude that the worker's reaction to the foreman's aptitude in the appraisal individual-conferences had an important bearing on the feelings toward the evaluation procedure.

The Effect of Frequent Appraisals

In Table 1 it was observed that the monthly feedback control groups had the most significant positive change during the study. Thus, we must conclude that the more frequent reporting of evaluations accounted for an important part of the average change in attitude toward the appraisal plan made by the consultation and explanation crews. Indeed, more frequent individual appraisal discussions may be more effective than the group procedures. The supervisors in the monthly feedback control crews were trained in giving appraisal reports to the men, as were the supervisors in the two experimental treatments. However, the amount of satisfaction or dissatisfaction with the feedback methods used by the supervisor in the monthly-feedback control groups did not affect the attitudes toward the appraisal plan. Men who were pleased with the foreman's skill showed no more or less change than those who were displeased with the evaluation reporting methods used by the boss.

The men in the monthly-feedback control crews developed a positive perception of an increase in their own autonomy (i.e., a relative decrease in the power of the supervisor), which is statistically significant at the .01 level of confidence. There was no significant increase in liking of the foreman, no important change in the liking of the company or in a perception of own power in relation to higher management; nor did the mean attitudes toward the appraisal procedure differ when those who are high in the above scales are compared to the individuals low on these dimensions.

In summary, the more frequent appraisals had the effect of improving attitudes toward the evaluation procedures, and in causing the worker to believe that control over his own fate had been increased.

Discussion of the Results

It is apparent that power persons in a hierarchical social structure can create positive changes in the attitudes of subordinates concerning the practices of the superiors. The results indicate that this may be done by several different procedures each of which requires certain conditions to be maximally effective.

The consultation groups, we believe, felt that an improvement of the evaluation methods was up to themselves and subsequent attitude change was therefore a function of the degree to which they were satisfied by their own efforts in setting practices which the supervisor was to follow. In this instance the crew itself was the means whereby the needs of the workers might or might not be fulfilled and they therefore held themselves accountable. In the explanation groups, on the other hand, the sessions were viewed as informational meetings. The men believed the statement made by the foreman if they felt that the management as a whole were sincere and if it was believed that the rest of the crew (including the foreman) shared this and other opinions. The explanation of, and assurances about, the appraisal procedures by a representative of higher authority is judged on the basis of the sincerity of the power figures and not on the satisfactoriness of the meeting outcome or the ability of the men to carry on a good discussion.

It may be concluded that the two experimental methods were effective in changing attitudes toward the merit appraisal plan (wherever this occurred) for somewhat different reasons because the two procedures put the workers in unlike fields of forces. In the consultation method they were given responsibility over themselves, whereas in the explanation procedure they were asked to trust authority. We may derive from this the hypothesis that a positive attitude change will be most likely if the consultation procedure is used where the members are confident of their ability to make wise decisions, while the explanation method has an effect if it is used in a situation where the higher authorities are trusted and where the views of the men are fairly consistent with those of management.

Why did the two experimental methods change attitudes less, on the whole, than in the crews in the monthly-feedback control method? The special control groups did not hold meetings and therefore measures of the conditions which were found to be most crucial in inducing attitude changes in the experimental conditions were not obtainable. (It should be added in this respect that when the consultation and explanation sessions were characterized by the most appropriate features, the shifts toward approval of the evaluation methods were always larger than the increase in positive feelings produced in the monthly-feedback control groups.)

The fact that the monthly-feedback

control groups had no meetings suggests a reason for the greater average success of this control treatment. The men in the feedback control crews were suddenly given, without any preparation, monthly reports on their merit ratings. It is most likely that the men interpreted these more frequent conversations with the boss as an indication that the foreman is interested in helping them to improve, since they had no prior meeting to ready them for his increase in attention to them. Because no other feelings, such as those created among the men in the crew meetings, were thus aroused to interfere or aid in the development of positive attitudes about the evaluation method, their change was largely affected by frequent relations with the foreman. Since the more frequent appraisals were interpreted by the men as indicating greater interest on the part of the foreman, they were effective in creating positive attitudes, we believe, because the supervisor was viewed as likely to gratify the worker's needs as a direct result of his increased attention to the men and his readiness to help them improve and control their own fate.

REFERENCES

1. Biddle, B. An application of social expectation theory to the initial interview. Unpublished doctor's dissertation, Univer. of Michigan, 1954.
2. Cohen, A. R. The effects of individual self-esteem and situational structure on threat-oriented reactions to power. Unpublished doctor's dissertation, Univer. of Michigan, 1953.
3. Jambor, Helen. Discrepancies in role expectations for the supervisory position—a concern of social work administration. Unpublished doctor's dissertation, Univer. of Minnesota, 1954.
4. Pelz, D. *Power and leadership in the first-line supervisor.* Ann Arbor, Mich.: Survey Research Center, 1951.
5. Pepitone, A. Motivational effects in social perception. *Human Relat.*, 1950, **3**, 57–75.
6. Ross, I. Role specialization in supervision. Unpublished doctor's dissertation, Columbia Univer., 1955.
7. Stotland, E. Peer groups and reactions to power figures. Unpublished doctor's dissertation, Univer. of Michigan, 1953.

VALIDITY OF RATINGS AS RELATED TO RATING TECHNIQUES AND CONDITIONS*

A. G. Bayroff, Helen R. Haggerty, and E. A. Rundquist

• SUMMARY

The widespread use of ratings as management and psychometric devices has focussed attention upon problems of their soundness and effectiveness and has led to numerous research efforts to improve their adequacy. This paper summarizes a comprehensive study of officer rating methodology conducted in 1950 by the Personnel Research Branch (PRB) of the Department of the Army and is reported in detail in the 13 PRB reports listed in the references.

The study was the outgrowth of previous studies of procedures used for officer efficiency reporting in the Army, and of the use of ratings as criteria for the validation of various psychometric instruments. The findings, although based on an Army officer population, will be of interest to those concerned with rating problems in other populations.[1]

• INTRODUCTION

Generally speaking, ratings on the performance of individuals may be considered as serving three purposes: (a) they may provide a basis for personnel actions; (b) they may be used as criteria for validating personnel instruments and procedures; or (c) they may furnish diagnostic information for use in counseling. In this paper, ratings for counseling purposes are not considered. In any event, a rating represents a recorded judgment by one individual regarding the behavior of another individual. Whether such a judgment is useful is a function of many factors. One such group of factors relates to the obvious need for sufficient opportunity to observe the individual in a sufficient number of pertinent situations, to evaluate the behavior, and to record the judg-

NOTE. The opinions expressed in this article are those of the authors and do not necessarily express the official views of the Department of the Army. Acknowledgment is made of the participation of various staff members of the Personnel Research Branch, particularly Gloria H. Falk, E. Kenneth Karcher, Jr., Dorothy E. Schneider. Acknowledgment is also made of the generous assistance of the Commandant, Command and General Staff College, Fort Leavenworth, Kansas, and his staff, and the officer students in attendance during the gathering of the field data basic to the study.

* From *Personnel Psychology,* Vol. 7, no. 1, Spring 1954, pp. 93–113. Copyright 1954 by Personnel Psychology, Inc. Reprinted by permission.

[1] Personnel Research Branch Reports are available for general distribution only through the American Documentation Institute. Copies may be obtained by ordering the appropriate document by number from the American Documentation Institute, c/o Library of Congress, Washington 25, D. C., remitting the correct price for microfilm (images 1 inch high on Standard 35 mm. motion picture film) or for photostat readable without optical aid. Document numbers and prices are listed in the references.

ment. A second group of factors is concerned with the motivation of the rater to do a careful and accurate job. It is particularly important in obtaining comparable ratings of individuals that the motivation to rate accurately be strong and uniform for all raters and toward all ratees.

Other factors which may condition the effectiveness of ratings are such matters as:

1. The rater's knowledge of the use to be made of the rating score.
2. The administrative conditions surrounding the rating session: How many ratings are to be made at one time? Does the rater have time to do a careful job?
3. The type of rating technique: Is the rater to use one scale or several? forced choice or graphic scale? ranking, paired comparisons, nominations, etc.?
4. The characteristics of the individual rater: Is he hard or easy? How competent is he in various aspects of his own job?

The multiplicity of factors involved makes it necessary in research on rating methodology to hold certain factors constant in order to explore the effect of varying others. Because of the overriding importance of opportunity to observe, evaluate, and record, and of rater motivation, it was decided in this study to try to control these aspects of the rating situation and to vary others in order to obtain some information about the following problems: Does the use to be made of a rating affect its validity? How many ratings should be made during a single rating session? Do some rating techniques, e.g., graphic or forced-choice, yield more valid ratings than others? Can validity of ratings be increased by combining ratings made by a number of raters? What kind of individuals make more valid ratings? Are "hard" raters more accurate than "easy" raters?

• PLAN OF THE STUDY

Selection of the Population

This study was conducted at the Command and General Staff College at Fort Leavenworth, Kansas, in March, 1950. Approximately 400 officer students (primarily majors and lieutenant colonels) who had been in attendance since the previous September served as a rater-ratee population. Selection of these officers as the experimental population was based on several considerations.

The first of these was concerned with the school program at the Command and General Staff College. Prior to their attendance at Command and General Staff College, the officers were for the most part strangers to each other. After admission and for several months prior to this study, they had been organized into 12 comparatively stable study groups or classes. Each such class consisted of approximately 40 officers who had had opportunity to observe each other perform in tasks which were comparable to duty assignments. The course work was to a large extent concerned with the type of problems that would confront division commanders and general staff officers. Solution of these problems required the cooperative efforts of various members of a group. The students, furthermore, were all highly competent individuals, selected for the courses at Command and General Staff College because of their experience in and potentialities for positions which require high-level command and staff qualities. Thus the two requirements were met—opportunity to observe and evaluate and high constant motivation on the part of the rater.

A second consideration for the selection of Command and General Staff College students for this study was that a stable criterion score could be obtained for each rated officer by averaging rankings made by his classmates. The procedure used to obtain this criterion will be described later in this paper.

A third consideration related to the need for conducting rating research in operating rather than experimental situations. The results of this study were intended in part for use in developing a new officer efficiency report. The officers attending the Command and General Staff College were familiar with and greatly concerned with operating problems in efficiency reporting.

Variables

Two types of graphic rating scales and two modifications of the forced choice technique were studied. One type of graphic rating form consisted of a single eight-step scale on over-all value to the Army. The two highest steps on this scale were: (a) the most outstanding officer I know, and (b) one of the few highly outstanding officers I know. The two lowest steps were: (a) an officer who performs acceptably in a limited range of assignments, but who could easily be replaced, and (b) an officer who does not have the calibre that one should reasonably expect in an officer.

The other graphic forms, of which there were four, were similar in pattern to each other in that each form consisted of seven five-step graphic scales. Two types of characteristics were to be rated: (a) personal traits, of which there were seven (e.g., "resourcefulness," "ability to present views in a concise, clear manner") and (b) fitness for various types of duty assignment, of which there were seven (e.g., "represent your viewpoint and make decisions in your name at a higher headquarters," "command a unit immediately subordinate to you on a combat mission"). Each of these types of characteristics were rated using two different types of scale-step definitions: (a) degree of rater's preference for having the ratee serve under him, and (b) degree of competence of ratee.

Each of the two forced choice forms contained 48 descriptive phrases which had been used previously in the officer Efficiency Report, WD AGO Form 67–1. In one form (Forced Choice Pairs) the phrases were arranged in 24 pairs. The rater was to select the phrase in each pair which was the more descriptive of the ratee. Two pairs are shown below as examples:

1a. Willing to accept responsibility
1b. Follows closely directions of higher echelons
2a. Can take over in an emergency
2b. Fair and just in his dealings

In the other forced choice form (Controlled Check List), the same 48 phrases were arranged in two lists of 24 each. The rater was to select the 12 phrases in each list which were most descriptive of the ratee.

The primary criterion in this study was the average of anonymous rankings on value to the Army made by approximately 20 associates (a random half of the group) for all 40 officers in a class.

The raters were informed that these rankings would not be available for official use. In making his ranking each rater sorted cards containing the names of his associate officers into three equal groups representing high, middle, and low thirds of each rating group. Officers in the high, middle, and low thirds were scored 1, 2, and 3, respectively.

Two auxiliary criteria were used for certain of the analyses in this study: scores on the official Efficiency Report, WD AGO Form 67–1, and class standing in courses at the Command and General Staff College.

The Efficiency Report scores were obtained from reports rendered on periods of duty just prior to the officers' attendance at the Command and General Staff College. These efficiency report ratings suffered from two limitations which precluded their use as the primary criterion. There were too few ratings per rated officer to provide a stable criterion measure and the types of duty covered differed in various respects from the duties covered by the ratings in this study.

Experimental Design

The study was designed to provide data on the relation to validity of different types of rating techniques, of a number of characteristics of raters, and of several aspects of the conditions under which both administrative and criterion ratings are collected and used. The general features of the design are shown in Figure 1. Examination of the figure will make it apparent that certain findings will need to be stated and interpreted with due regard for the complexity and interrelations of the experimental design. These considerations will be taken into account in the subsequent discussions.

All ratings were obtained at the close of the common period of instruction, seven months after the beginning of the course. It was expected that after such long and close contact, ratings would be based less on reputation, more on direct observation.

Each officer in the total population of 400 students served both as a rater and as a ratee. Rater-ratee assignments were kept within classes, i.e., no rater evaluated any other officer in a class other than his own. Each class was divided in random halves: A raters and B raters. In the treatment of the data, A raters of all classes ($N = 200$) were combined, as were the B raters ($N = 200$). In Figure 1, these rater groups are shown as Group A and Group B.

Ratings were made on six different days, as indicated: Day 1, Day 9, and Days 20 through 23 (three weeks after the first rating). On Days 1 and 9, ratees were assigned to raters by a procedure which approximated random selection. On the last four days, ratees assigned to each rater were selected so as to provide all raters with approximately the same ranges of ratee talent, as indicated by the criterion evaluations.

On the first day of the experiment, each rater rated approximately half of his class, using the eight-step graphic scale on over-all value. Group B raters signed their ratings; Group A raters did not. Group A raters also made the criterion rankings. On Day 9, each rater in each group made a forced choice rating, followed by the eight-step graphic rating, on the first two officers he had rated on Day 1. On the last four days, the groups were combined and each

Total Population

12 Classes, $N = 400$

GROUP A RATERS	GROUP B RATERS
Random half of each class, $N = 200$	Random half of each class, $N = 200$

Ratees

Total Population: $N = 400$

Day 1

GROUP A RATERS	GROUP B RATERS
Unidentified ratings as follows	Identified ratings
1. Each rater rated 20 officers on over-all scale	1. Each rater rated 20 officers on over-all scale
2. Each rater ranked 40 officers to provide a criterion	

Each Ratee Received

Criterion ranking by half of class unidentified

Over-all ratings by 10 identified raters and by 10 unidentified raters

Day 9

GROUP A RATERS	GROUP B RATERS
Identified ratings	Identified ratings
Each rater rated two officers rated on Day 1 with Controlled Check List followed by over-all scale	Each rater rated two officers rated on Day 1 with Forced Choice Pairs followed by over-all scale

Each Ratee Received

One Controlled Check List rating and one over-all rating.

One Forced Choice Pairs rating and one over-all rating.

Days 20 to 23

ALL RATERS

Identified ratings

Each rater rated four other officers, one on each of four consecutive days, using a different form each day. Each form was used an equal number of times. Range of proficiency of ratees was same for all raters. Four forms of five-step scales.

Desirability of Ratee for Seven Types of Duty Assignment
Competence of Ratee on Seven Traits
Competence of Ratee for Seven Types of Duty Assignment
Desirability of Ratee on Seven Traits

Each Ratee Received

One rating on each of four forms

Fig. 1. General plan of study methodology, Army Command and General Staff College, 1950.

rater rated four other officers, one each day, using a different form each day. Conditions were arranged so that each ratee received ratings from four different raters on four different forms. The forms were used in four different orders, with the same number of forms in each order completed each day.

It will be noted that in this design two major limiting conditions are present: (a) for some of the analyses, the same raters were involved ("rater contamination"), and (b) there was a relatively short time between the criterion rankings and the other ratings.

At the end of the study each of the 400 ratees had received the following ratings:

1. Criterion scores completed by all Group A raters (unidentified and not available for official use).
2. Ten ratings (eight-step scale) completed by ten raters of Group A (unidentified).
3. Ten ratings (eight-step scale) completed by ten raters of Group B (identified and available for official use).
4. One rating with the Controlled Check List followed by a graphic rating (eight-step over-all scale) completed by one rater in Group A (identified).
5. One rating with Forced Choice Pairs followed by a graphic rating (eight-step over-all scale) completed by one rater in Group B (identified).
6. One rating on each of the four types of five-step scales on traits and duty assignments, completed by four raters from the total rater population (identified).

For certain analyses, other information was obtained about the officers: class standing at Command and General Staff College, scores on the Efficiency Report, prior to attendance at the College, and score on the Officer Classification Test, a high-level test of mental ability.

• RESULTS

The average of a number of ratings per ratee was more valid than was a single rating per ratee (6). An important consideration in evaluating personnel performance and in validating personnel instruments and procedures is the number of ratings needed to obtain an accurate measure of an individual's ability. Frequently in the Armed Forces, as well as in industry, a single rating of an individual is all that is available as a basis for administrative decisions. Because ratings are known to be subject to bias, various means have been proposed to minimize such bias or to allow for it. Some of these were evaluated in this study, e.g., the use of different types of rating techniques, selection of raters according to certain rater characteristics, modifying the conditions under which ratings were made, comparison of ratings from identified and from unidentified raters, and averaging ratings made by a number of raters for each ratee.

In general, the findings of this study were in line with those of other studies, both in the Army and elsewhere, namely, that the one most effective means of increasing the validity of the ratings was by increasing the number of raters of comparable competence for each ratee. In this study the raters had relatively equal opportunity to observe, over an extended period of time, on activities which were essentially the same.

Furthermore, it will be remembered, raters were assigned to ratees at random. It is therefore assumed that each ratee was rated by some more competent raters, by some moderately competent raters, and by some less competent raters. (See below for discussion of relationship between rater characteristics and validity.) The validities of averages of the ratings by ten raters per ratee on the eight-step graphic scale was, for Group A, $r = .89$; and for Group B, $r = .84$. These validities were considerably higher than the corresponding validities for a single rating per ratee, $r = .52$ and $r = .53$, respectively. The administrative implications of this finding are clear. The additional faith which can be placed in an average of several ratings obtained from equally competent raters is probably sufficient to warrant the extra trouble and expense involved in getting and using them, particularly when the rating is to be used as the basis for personnel actions. While this principle cannot be applied where the ratee's performance is not observable by several equally competent people, it can at least be applied by cumulating successive ratings by single supervisors.

In passing, it may be remarked that the more ratings per ratee which are collected, the more difficult and complex becomes the process. This problem is particularly important in obtaining criterion ratings. If fewer ratings could be used with little loss in stability, the resultant economy in criterion studies would be worthwhile. In this study, where all the ratings per ratee were collected simultaneously and were rendered relatively independent of one another, it was appropriate to apply the Spearman-Brown formula to the validity of a single rating to estimate the validity of an average of ten ratings. The estimated validity coefficient ($r = .86$) agreed closely with the coefficient obtained empirically ($r = .84$). From this it would seem that in certain research studies, when the Spearman-Brown Prophecy Formula holds, a single criterion rating for each individual might be used. However, the decision to do so should be made in terms of the factors and requirements of the particular situation. It might be remarked further that although single ratings per ratee might possibly be suitable for criterion purposes in particular cases, their usual lack of reliability makes them very unsafe as a basis for administrative action involving individuals.

Ratings by identified raters were as valid as were ratings by unidentified raters (3). A problem arises when ratings are obtained for administrative use. This problem is related to the fact that the raters know both the official nature of the ratings, and that they themselves are identified as making them. It has long been supposed that ratings obtained specifically for administrative purposes were likely to have lower validity than ratings which were made anonymously and which were known to be unavailable for examination by superiors, peers, or subordinates, or for any personnel action.

The findings of this study were not in accord with this belief. For a rating by one identified rater per ratee which was known to be available for official use, the validity coefficient was $r = .53$; for a rating by one unidentified rater per ratee which was known to be unavailable for official use, the validity coefficient was $r = .52$. For an average of ratings by ten raters per ratee, the validity coefficients were .84 and .89, respectively.

One fact which must be kept in mind is the possibility that the validity of the unidentified ratings were inflated because of rater contamination. The raters who provided the unidentified graphic ratings, it will be remembered, (see Figure 1) also made the associate rankings used as the criterion measure.

From these facts, it would seem that the identified raters produced ratings which were at least as valid as the ratings produced by the unidentified raters. This finding implies that identified ratings obtained for administrative use can be used as criterion measures under some circumstances with as much confidence as though the ratings had been obtained anonymously. Furthermore, if confirmed, the findings could be of value in the use of ratings for criterion purposes where the practice has been to stress the anonymity of the ratings collected. Frequently the attempt to collect such ratings has involved complicated procedures to preserve their anonymity. It has also resulted in the loss of data which were desirable for studying important relationships.

Ratings earlier in a series were more valid than were those at the end of a series (4). Frequently, raters are required to fill out a number of ratings at one session. It is important to know whether the later ratings in a temporal series are more valid or less valid than ratings made earlier. The data used to provide this information were the ratings made by the 200 identified raters (Group B) who completed the eight-step graphic rating on twenty of their associates at a single one-half hour session on Day 1. Validity coefficients were determined for all the 200 raters' first ratings, all their second ratings, and so on through their last ratings. When the validity coefficients were computed for each of the twenty order positions separately, there was considerable irregularity in their magnitude. However, when the validity coefficients were averaged in quarters (first five ratings, second five ratings, third five ratings, last five ratings) a trend appears, as indicated. The validity coefficients for the successive ratings showed a slight initial rise and were higher in the first half of the ratings than in the second. The average of the coefficients for the first five ratings was $r = .50$; for the second five, $r = .55$; for the third five, $r = .46$; and for the fourth five, $r = .47$. Although these differences were not as marked, they were in line with those of an earlier study carried on at the U. S. Military Academy (1) in which cadets completed ratings on four fellow cadets, using the Efficiency Report. There was a drop in validity coefficients from first rating to fourth rating ($r = .60$ to $r = .48$) with Aptitude for Service Rating as the criterion measure (a composite of associates' and superiors' ratings).

The finding that the later ratings appeared to be less valid than those in the first half has obvious practical significance. It is not possible to generalize the course of the rise and fall in validity of successive ratings, but it does seem likely that there is a limit to the number of ratings which can be made at any one time without reducing their validity.

Ratings using different types of rating techniques were not markedly different in validity (8, 9). Various types of rating techniques have been used singly and in combination to obtain more adequate ratings. This study afforded the opportunity to compare the validity of several different graphic rating scales and forced choice forms. The data used were: (a) the first graphic ratings made on Day 1 by the Group B raters; (b) the

Table 1

VALIDITY COEFFICIENTS FOR GRAPHIC RATING SCALES AND FORCED CHOICE SECTIONS FOR VARIOUS CRITERIA

PREDICTOR RATINGS (ALL RATINGS IDENTIFIED)	VALIDITY COEFFICIENTS: CRITERION SCORE, RANK BY ASSOCIATES	CLASS STANDING, COMMAND AND GENERAL STAFF COLLEGE	EFFICIENCY REPORT SCORE
Graphic Scales			
Eight-step scale on over-all value	.53	.35	.19
Five-step scale: Desirability of ratee for duty assignment	.44	.26	.16
Five-step scale: Competence of ratee for duty assignment	.43	.25	.10
Five-step scale: Desirability of ratee on traits	.44	.30	.19
Five-step scale: Competence of ratee on traits	.39	.25	.15
Forced Choice Sections			
Forced choice pairs	.41	.25	.19
Controlled check list	.44	.31	.26

forced choice ratings made by both Groups A and B on Day 9; and (c) the four graphic ratings made on Days 20 through 23. All raters were identified.

For ratings by one rater per ratee the validity coefficients for the various types of techniques ranged from .53 to .39. They are shown in Table 1. The most valid rating was the eight-step graphic rating on over-all value made on Day 1 ($r = .53$). Validity coefficients for the two forced choice forms were .44 and .41, and for the four different forms involving the groups of five-step graphic scales, the validity coefficients were .44, .43, .44, and .39.

Additional information on the effectiveness of the different forms was provided by using the rating on the Efficiency Report rendered prior to attendance at Command and General Staff College, and class standing at Command and General Staff College as auxiliary criteria. With both Efficiency Report score and class standing, the validity of the eight-step graphic scale was similar to the validity of the two forced choice forms and the four five-step graphic forms.

Generalization of the findings on the relative effectiveness of the different types of rating techniques is limited because of certain features of the over-all design of the study. The fact that it was necessary to use the same raters for more than one type of rating technique raises the possibility that differences in the effectiveness of the various rating techniques studied may be masked. This complication may result from the persistence of the set established by raters so that subsequent ratings of the same ratees by the raters are in substantial agreement with the first rating, regardless of the fact that different rating techniques may be employed.

A second complicating factor in the design is perhaps more apparent than real in its effect upon the validity of the different types of scales. The most valid technique was a graphic rating scale which was rendered at approximately the same time as the criterion ranking. The forced choice ratings rendered eight days later were less valid. However, there was little difference between the forced choice ratings and the later graphic ratings made 20 days after the criterion ratings. It would thus seem that it is not the time factor alone which accounted for the small difference in validity between the first graphic ratings and the forced choice ratings.

Ratings by hard raters and by easy raters were not markedly different in validity (*10*). One of the most persistent problems in rating methodology is the difference in leniency among raters. Considerable attention has been given in the past to methods intended to correct for such differences. In this study, another approach to the problem was taken, namely, are there differences in the validity of ratings by hard raters and by easy raters?

To provide the necessary data, raters were divided into equal thirds of hard, average, and easy raters according to the mean ratings they gave. In addition to the precaution of assigning ratees to raters at random, a further step was taken to minimize the possibility that the rater differences were not attributable to differences in the performance of the ratees. This step consisted of eliminating those raters whose ratees had extremely high or extremely low criterion scores. It is believed, therefore, that the grouping of the raters represented differences in their leniency rather than differences in the quality of their ratees.

The findings indicated that there was little difference in the validity of the ratings made by the three groups of raters. The slight differences in the validity coefficients for ratings by one identified rater per ratee ($r = .55$ for hard raters, $r = .57$ for average raters, and $r = .50$ for easy raters) are illustrative of the differences obtained. A similar finding occurred when the Efficiency Report score was used as an auxiliary criterion instead of the associate rankings (e.g., $r = .22$ for hard raters, $r = .22$ for average raters, and $r = .19$ for easy raters). In a subsequent study on a different officer population, groups of raters were identified on the basis of ratings they made on a graphic rating scale. The criterion was the average of scores received by the ratees on the official Efficiency Report, WD AGO Form 67–1. Validity coefficients for groups of hard, average, and easy raters were .39, .39, and .33, respectively (13).

The implications of this finding are far-reaching and further study is needed. It is significant that raters in the three groups placed the ratees in approximately the same order even though different parts of the scale were used. However, this finding does not mean that the problem of differences in raters' standards has been solved. Differences in raters' standards remain the most serious problem in the use of single ratings.

Raters who scored high on certain variables made more valid ratings than did raters who scored low on those variables (*11*). Since raters differ in the accuracy with which they can appraise the performance of their ratees, it would obviously be of value if the more accu-

Table 2

VALIDITY OF RATINGS BY RATERS OF DIFFERENT CHARACTERISTICS. CRITERION: RANK BY ASSOCIATES

RATERS DIVIDED INTO HIGH (H), MIDDLE (M), AND LOW (L) THIRDS ON		EIGHT-STEP GRAPHIC RATING	CONTROLLED CHECK LIST	FORCED CHOICE PAIRS
Officer classification test	H	.50	.45	.46
	M	.51	.43	.48
	L	.48	.44	.30
Final class standing	H	.54	.50	.50
	M	.49	.46	.31
	L	.44	.37	.40
Criterion ranking	H	.55	.48	.49
	M	.51	.48	.30
	L	.45	.31	.43

rate raters could be identified. In this study, three rater characteristics: Officer Classification Test score, class standing, and mean criterion ranking by associates, were related to the validity of ratings given by the raters. When the raters were divided into high, middle, and low thirds of their class on each of these characteristics, the raters in the high third in every case gave more valid ratings than did raters in the low third, both on the eight-step graphic rating scale and on the two forced choice forms. The validity coefficients are given in Table 2. For example, with final class standing as the rater characteristic, the validity coefficients for the high third and the low third raters for the Forced Choice Pairs were .50 and .40, and for the Controlled Check List .50 and .37, respectively.

It appears, therefore, that in this study it was possible to distinguish between the more accurate and the less accurate raters according to certain characteristics. Further research may indicate that other rater characteristics are appropriate for identifying the more accurate raters in other rater populations and types of ratings. This finding has importance for possible improvements in criterion ratings and also for administrative ratings where superiors have options in designating raters.

There was no difference in the validity of graphic ratings made at the beginning of the study and those made after a lapse of time and an interpolated forced choice rating (5). The design of this study provided an opportunity to compare the validity of two sets of ratings made by the same raters on the same ratees using the same rating scale but under different rating conditions. As indicated earlier in this report, the eight-step graphic rating on over-all value to the Army was made on Day 1 by each rater, identified and unidentified, on twenty of his associates. Eight days later, each rater re-rated the first two officers he had rated previously, using first, one of the two forced choice techniques, and, second, the same graphic scale as was used on Day 1.

There was no difference in the validity of the two sets of graphic ratings. For the Day 1 graphic ratings the validity coefficients were .53 and .50 for ratings by one identified rater per ratee and for ratings by one unidentified rater per ratee, respectively. For the Day 9 graphic ratings, the corresponding coefficients were .49 and .48.

The validity coefficients are remarkably similar considering that a number of factors both in the situation and in the experience of raters intervened and might have resulted in changes in the ability of the rater to make accurate appraisals. The findings indicate that the lapse of time and the making of another rating using a different technique did not affect the validities of the graphic ratings. This finding suggests that an interpolated rating and the passage of a brief interval of time will not alter the rater's original set toward the ratee and that such conditions are therefore not likely to affect the validity of ratings. No conclusion can be drawn concerning the value of the interpolated material. Because of the possible influence of the rater's set, a separate control group design is necessary to evaluate any interpolated material, rather than the design of utilizing the rater as his own control that was used in this study.

Use of the same raters resulted in greater agreement between two sets of ratings than did use of the same techniques (7). It is an axiom of validation research that the criterion measures should be obtained by procedures which are independent of the procedures for obtaining the predictor measures. For a long time, it has been realized that when the two ratings are provided by the same individual there is a high degree of agreement because of the fact that it is the same person making the two evaluations (rater contamination). When ratings are used as criterion measures to validate various types of predictor ratings, there is the additional question of the extent to which the validity coefficients are artificially inflated because of the resemblance in technique (technique contamination). This study provided an opportunity to estimate the relative importance of the two types of contamination.

The findings indicated that two sets of ratings agreed more with each other when the same raters were employed than when the same techniques were employed. The design did not permit comparison among all possible combinations of raters and techniques. However, the findings were internally consistent. The highest correlation occurred between two sets of ratings made by the same raters using the same technique (graphic rating scale, $r = .82$). The lowest correlations occurred when both raters and techniques were different (graphic rating scale and forced choice rating, $r = .29$), and when the raters were different but the techniques were the same (graphic rating scale, $r = .30$). When the raters were the same but the techniques were different, the coefficient was of intermediate magnitude (graphic rating scale and forced choice rating, $r = .60$). Thus, whenever the two sets of ratings were made by the same raters, regardless of whether the same or different techniques were used, the coefficients were higher than when the two sets of ratings were made by different raters. In other words, rater contamination was far more serious than was technique contamination.

• CONCLUSIONS

The investigation reported here may be considered to have made three major contributions to the study and use of ratings.

1. It pointed directly to the fruitfulness of research in a relatively untapped area of rating methodology, namely, the study of characteristics of raters which are related to the validity of the ratings they give. The finding that raters who scored high on certain variables produced more valid ratings than did ratees who scored low on those variables suggests that further study in this area would be profitable.

2. The results indicated that the more effective method for increasing validity of ratings remains the averaging of ratings by a number of equally competent raters for each ratee rather than the use of a particular technique of rating. The validity of a rating using one technique was essentially similar to the validity of a rating using another technique. If it becomes possible to select raters according to those characteristics found to be associated with the more valid raters, the use of a number of raters per ratee may increase validity even more. Stated broadly, the rater is more important than the rating technique, and the larger the number of competent raters employed, the greater is the resulting validity.

3. The study emphasized certain considerations that need to be taken into account in conducting research on rating problems. One of these is the fact that independent control groups are needed in order to determine the relative effectiveness of rating procedures. The evidence for the greater seriousness of rater contamination over technique contamination and the possible influence of rater set in the lack of change in the ratings following an interpolated rating and over an interval of time indicates that raters should not serve as controls on themselves. A second consideration is the possibility that under certain circumstances criterion ratings need not be anonymous and rendered in confidence. The finding that the validity of ratings by unidentified raters did not differ from the validity of the ratings by identified raters, points in the direction of greater economy in obtaining criterion ratings. A third consideration is the undesirability of requiring the rating of too many ratees from a rater at one sitting, on the grounds that the later ratings may be less valid than the earlier ones.

A final word may be in order regarding certain difficulties in applying concepts of reliability and particularly that of validity to studies of rating methodology. The internal consistency concept of reliability of test items is not applicable to rating scale items because of the well-known phenomenon of halo which affects such items and which prevents their being independent measures. Similarly, the concept of test-retest reliability is of doubtful applicability, since raters tend to give the same ratings on the re-rating as on the first rating. Perhaps the concept of reliability is most applicable to the case of agreement among raters, especially where it is known that the raters made independent observations and ratings.

Considerable doubt has existed as to the soundness of validating ratings against other ratings used as criteria. The fact that both predictor and criterion ratings are obviously judgmental measures in which rater biases and capabilities must operate raises the question as to the independence of these measures. One answer has been to define validity in such cases as agreement among raters, especially the agreement of one rating with a consensus of ratings. Validity thus interpreted becomes similar to reliability.

With ratings as with tests, the terms *reliability* and *validity* need precise definition in terms of the operations involved. Where, as in this study, the criterion must reflect effectiveness in interpersonal relationships, use of associate ratings as a criterion has maximum justification. Under such circumstances, any increase in the "validity" of predictor ratings which could be obtained by reducing bias, selection of raters, etc., appears especially worthwhile.

REFERENCES

Reports of the Personnel Research Branch (formerly, Personnel Research Section, Personnel Research and Procedures Branch), The Adjutant General's Office, Department of the Army.

1. PRS Report 817. Analysis of an Officer Efficiency Report (WD AGO Form 67–1) Using Multiple Raters. 13 April 1952. ADI Document No. 3936, microfilm $2.00, photostat $3.75.
2. PRS Report 900. A Study of Officer Rating Methodology. I. The Over-all Design of the Study. 30 July 1951. ADI Document No. 3864, microfilm $1.75, photostat $2.50.
3. PRS Report 901. A Study of Officer Rating Methodology. II. Ratings Made by Identified and Anonymous Raters. 17 April 1952. ADI Document No. 3854, microfilm $2.00, photostat $3.75.
4. PRS Report 902. A Study of Officer Rating Methodology. III. Order of Rating and Validity of Rating. 17 April 1952. ADI Document No. 3855, microfilm $1.75, photostat $2.50.
5. PRS Report 903. A Study of Officer Rating Methodology. IV. Effect of Forced Choice Items on Validity of Rating Scales. 17 April 1952. ADI Document No. 3856, microfilm $1.75, photostat $2.50.
6. PRS Report 904. A Study of Officer Rating Methodology. V. Validity and Reliability of Ratings by Single Raters and Multiple Raters. 17 April 1952. ADI Document No. 3865, microfilm $1.75, photostat $2.50.
7. PRS Report 905. A Study of Officer Rating Methodology. VI. Independence of Criterion Measures from Predictor Variables. 17 April 1952. ADI Document No. 3866, microfilm $1.75, photostat $2.50. (Also, Falk, Gloria H., and Bayroff, A. G. Rater and technique contamination in criterion ratings. *J. Appl. Psychol.*, 1954, 38, 100–102.
8. PRS Report 906. A Study of Officer Rating Methodology. VII. Validities of Four Types of Five-step Rating Scales. 17 April 1952. ADI Document No. 3867, microfilm $1.75, photostat $2.50.
9. PRS Report 907. A Study of Officer Rating Methodology. VIII. Validity of Two Types of Rating Techniques: Forced Choice Items and Rating Scales. 17 April 1952. ADI Document No. 3868, microfilm $2.00, photostat $3.75.
10. PRS Report 908. A Study of Officer Rating Methodology. IX. Validity of Ratings by Hard and Easy Raters. 17 April 1952. ADI Document No. 3869, microfilm $1.75, photostat $2.50.

11. PRS Report 909. A Study of Officer Rating Methodology. X. Effect of Selected Rater Characteristics on Validity of Ratings. ADI Document No. 3870, microfilm $1.75, photostat $2.50. (Also, Schneider, Dorothy E. and Bayroff, A. G. Relationship between rater characteristics and validity of ratings. *J. Appl. Psychol.*, 1953, **37**, 278–280.)
12. PRS Report 910. A Study of Officer Rating Methodology. XI. Summary of Major Findings. December 1952. ADI Document No. 4025, microfilm $2.00, photostat $3.75.
13. PRS Report 971. A Comparison of the Validity of Officer Ratings Rendered by Hard and Easy Raters. 25 August 1952. ADI Document No. 3878, microfilm $1.75, photostat $2.50.

INFLUENCES ON MERIT RATINGS*

Aaron J. Spector

Many sources of errors in merit ratings are well known to users of these devices. Laboratory and field investigations have identified errors which may be classified as: (a) characteristic biases of classes of raters, e.g., men, women, peers, etc.; and (b) universal errors, e.g., halo effect, error of central tendency, etc.[1] Somewhat neglected is the fact that the stimulus, the ratee's behavior, may contribute errors which are not ordinarily considered. His total behavior is complex and includes some behaviors which are pertinent and some which aren't pertinent to the factors on which he is being rated. Evaluation of the pertinent behaviors independently of all others may require special training of the raters. This may be especially true when the factors being evaluated are in themselves complex and subjectively loaded, e.g., potentialities of the ratee, cooperativeness, quality of work, etc. Irrelevant characteristics may be so influential as to seriously bias the evaluations on the desired characteristics. The research presented here has been designed to investigate the effects of irrelevant ratee behaviors on ratings assigned to him.

A ratee characteristic, which is irrelevant to the others being evaluated, has been experimentally varied in order to measure its effects on the pertinent characteristics. The variable being manipulated is that of amenability to suggestions. This variable was selected because of the prevalence in industry of situations where suggestions may be accepted or rejected by the ratee and may, therefore, influence the rater's evaluation of other characteristics. In order to complete the experimental design, a second variable, the rater's opportunity to make suggestions to the ratee, was also manipulated.

• PROCEDURES

In five sections of a General Psychology course[2] a guest lecturer was introduced to the class as a student who was interested in becoming a college teacher. The classes, ranging in size from 19 to 30 students, were advised that they would be asked to evaluate his teaching ability after he had lectured. In all classes he delivered the day's lecture in exceedingly poor fashion, making several glaring pedagogical errors, although the material itself was adapted from a well-known textbook.[3] After the first 15-minute period, the experimental variable was introduced according to the plan

---

[1] For a summary of the major studies, see (*1*). Mahler's (*2*) review is more comprehensive and recent.

NOTE. The author was a member of the faculty at the University of Massachusetts when this study was conducted. He wishes to express his gratitude to his colleagues who contributed their class time to this research, and to Mr. Churchill Morgan for the preliminary analyses of the data.

* From *Journal of Applied Psychology,* Vol. 38, no. 6, December 1954, pp. 393–396. Copyright 1954 by the American Psychological Association, Inc. Reprinted by permission.

[2] The subjects were sophomore students at the University of Massachusetts. Sections of this course were randomly assigned to the experimental treatments.

[3] The guest lecturer was trained for approximately seven hours in order to insure that his delivery would be comparable in all classes.

shown in Table 1. Three of the groups (A, B, and C) wrote notes to the lecturer after the first 15 minutes, suggesting improvements to be made in his techniques. A second 15-minute lecture followed, which was as poor as the first. At the conclusion of this lecture the students evaluated the lecturer using a rating scale described below.

Table 1

EXPERIMENTAL DESIGN

TREATMENT	15 MINUTES	10 MINUTES	15 MINUTES	10 MINUTES
A	lecture	suggestions written and *accepted*	lecture	rating
B	lecture	suggestions written and *not accepted*	lecture	rating
C	lecture	suggestions written but *not submitted*	lecture	rating
D	lecture	*no suggestions;* announcement read instead	lecture	rating
E	lecture	*no suggestions;* ratings made		

After looking over the notes in Group A the lecturer *accepted* the suggestions by thanking the students for them and expressing his intention of modifying his techniques, as per their suggestions. In Group B he *rejected* their suggestions by telling them he had his own ideas on improvement. Although the students in Group C also wrote notes, they were *not submitted* until the conclusion of the second 15-minute period of lecture. At this time they made their evaluations and then submitted their suggestions.

Groups D and E were not given the opportunity to suggest any changes to the ratee. Instead of writing suggestions Group D listened to an announcement read by the officially assigned instructor; the amount of time required for the announcement was roughly equivalent to the time other groups used in writing suggestions.

Group E made *no suggestions* and evaluated the lecturer after the first 15-minute period.

The lecturer was evaluated on a rating scale containing five questions measuring: (1) manner; (2) ability; (3) knowledge; (4) potential; and (5) poise. For each question the individual subjects checked one of seven boxes which were ordered on a continuum, as illustrated by question 1, which read, "Compared to others, this lecturer's *manner* while lecturing was: As poor as any I've seen; Considerably worse than most; Not quite as good as most; As good as most; Somewhat better than most; Considerably better than most; As good as any I've seen." The responses on each factor were weighted 0–6, higher scores being assigned to the more favorable responses.

• RESULTS

The most favorable ratings on all five factors were recorded by the *acceptance* group (A), as shown in Table 2. The poorest ratings were given by Group E, which made no suggestions and had only 15 minutes of lecture. The other *no-suggestion* group (D) also rated the lecturer relatively unfavorably.

Table 2

MEANS AND STANDARD DEVIATIONS OF RATINGS ON EACH CHARACTERISTIC FOR EACH TREATMENT

		QUESTIONS							
		1	2	3	4	5			
TREATMENT		MANNER	ABILITY	KNOWL-EDGE	POTEN-TIAL	POISE	N	$MEAN_M$	SD_{row}
A	M	2.11	2.16	2.95	3.47	2.37	19	2.61	.86
	SD	.45	.59	.51	.88	.87			
B	M	1.28	1.52	2.64	2.60	1.36	25	1.88	1.19
	SD	.77	.94	.93	1.10	1.30			
C	M	1.30	1.64	2.25	2.57	2.04	28	1.88	.99
	SD	.70	.98	.95	1.01	.64			
D	M	1.53	1.69	2.29	2.06	1.43	35	1.76	.92
	SD	.89	.69	.81	.89	.87			
E	M	1.50	1.13	2.07	1.93	1.50	30	1.55	1.34
	SD	1.51	.85	1.18	1.26	1.54			
	SD_{col}	1.02	.91	.98	1.12	1.15			

The mean ratings of B and C groups were equal, but higher than either D or E. It appears that expression of criticism of the lecturer, via written suggestions, resulted in raters giving higher evaluations than when the raters had no opportunity for this expression. These results obtained when the rater's suggestions were not submitted to the ratee, as well as when they were submitted and accepted or rejected.

The most favorable ratings, however, were consistently made by the group whose suggestions were accepted by the ratee. Apparently, amenability to suggestions or expressed intention of compliance with the suggestions, operated to bias the raters' evaluations of the lecturer.

The data were analyzed further by analysis of variance.[4] An F ratio, obtained with *total scores*[5] of all subjects in each treatment, indicated that the mean total scores were significantly influenced by the treatments accorded the groups (Table 3).

Table 3

ANALYSIS OF VARIANCE OF TOTAL MERIT RATING SCORES OF ALL SUBJECTS IN FIVE EXPERIMENTAL TREATMENTS

SOURCE OF VARIATION	*df*	M.S.	F	p
Between treatments	4	2123.66	5.49	.01
Within treatments	132	386.51		

The ratings on each characteristic were then examined. F ratios indicated

[4] The variances were found to be homogeneous by Bartlett's test.

[5] An average intercorrelation of .18 was obtained between items on the rating sheet, using Peters and Van Voorhis' formula (*4*, pp. 196–200).

Table 4

ANALYSIS OF VARIANCE OF RATINGS ON EACH QUESTION FOR ALL TREATMENTS SIMULTANEOUSLY

QUESTION	BETWEEN TREATMENTS / WITHIN TREATMENTS	df	F	p
1	2.902 / 1.052	4 / 132	2.76	.05
2	.025 / .801	4 / 132	.03	
3	2.882 / 1.109	4 / 132	2.60	.05
4	8.516 / 1.310	4 / 132	6.50	.01
5	3.534 / 1.356	4 / 132	2.61	.05

that the responses on four of the questions varied significantly between groups (Table 4). That is, the experimental treatments accorded to the groups differentially affected their ratings on four out of the five characteristics.

The only Between Groups variance which was not significantly different from chance was on evaluation of the lecturer's ability. If the students measured the lecturer's ability by the amount they had learned or by the quantity of notes they could take, it is understandable that their evaluations would agree, since neither learning nor note taking came easily from his lecture.

However, no such simple criteria existed for rating his manner, knowledge, poise, or particularly his potential. These ratings may reflect personal frames of reference and hence are more readily influenced by extraneous factors such as acceptance or rejection of suggestions. Similarly, the factors of promotability and quality of work, which are frequently found on industrial merit-rating scales, may be especially prone to the influence of irrelevant behaviors of the ratee.

• DISCUSSION

The cathartic effects of expression of criticism via written messages, noted above, are consistent with the findings of Thibaut and Coules (5). Their data indicated that persons who were insulted and then allowed to express their hostility toward the instigator, via written notes, later made a greater number of friendly remarks about the instigator than did other insulted persons who had no opportunity to express their hostility. The present data suggest that poor impressions, like ill feelings, may be altered or reduced, by their expression.[6] Low ratings may reflect a barrier in communications between the supervisor and his subordinates, rather than true deficiencies of the ratees. Therefore, a likely hypothesis is that merit ratings in industry may be influenced by the degree to which the rater feels free to criticize or make suggestions to ratees.

The practical importance of the finding that irrelevant characteristics of ratees may bias raters' judgments is difficult to evaluate without more knowledge of: (a) the kinds of ratee behaviors which act in this way; and (b) the amount of bias these behaviors induce. At any rate, it is clear that amenability to suggestions induces sufficient bias to significantly affect ratings on several factors.

---

[6] The dynamics of this phenomenon are described by Newcomb (3) in his discussion of "autistic hostility."

• SUMMARY

Students in five sections of a general psychology course listened to a lecture which was intentionally delivered in poor fashion. They were then asked to rate the lecturer on five characteristics, using a seven-point scale. Before they rated him, three of the groups suggested methods by which the lecturer might improve his techniques. One of these groups *did not submit* their suggestions to the lecturer; in another group the lecturer *rejected* the suggestions, while in the third he *accepted* them. In two other groups the subjects did *not write* suggestions. In no case did the lecturer actually implement the suggestions or improve his delivery.

The ratings were: (a) consistently most favorable in the *acceptance* group; (b) more favorable in the *suggestion* than the *no-suggestion* group; (c) significantly different on the characteristics of manner, poise, potential and knowledge.

It has been suggested that poor ratings may reflect barriers in communications between the rater and the ratee, rather than true deficiencies in the ratees.

REFERENCES

1. Guilford, J. P. *Psychometric methods.* N. Y.: McGraw-Hill, 1936.
2. Mahler, W. R. *Twenty years of merit rating, 1926–1946.* N. Y.: The Psychological Corp., 1947.
3. Newcomb, T. Autistic hostility and social reality. *Hum. Rel.,* 1947, 1, 69–86.
4. Peters, C. C., and Van Voorhis, W. R. *Statistical procedures and their mathematical bases.* N. Y.: McGraw-Hill, 1940.
5. Thibaut, J. W., and Coules, J. The role of communications in the reduction of inter-personal hostility. *J. Abnorm. Soc. Psychol.,* 1952, 47, 770–778.

THE VALIDITY OF RATINGS OF SEVERAL LEVELS OF SUPERVISORS*

Dean K. Whitla and John E. Tirrell

• SUMMARY

The following experimental procedure was developed to determine the validity of ratings of several levels of supervisors. Frequently the utilization of ratings necessitates the assumption that ratings are comparable when given by numerous raters or that the knowledge of the ratees is comparable when given by one rater. The procedure used involved the rating of 100 flight mechanics by three levels of supervisors and correlation of their ratings with the ratee's scores on a Job Knowledge Test. The results indicate that those raters on the supervisory level functionally closest to the ratees were best able to rate them.

• PROBLEM

Two assumptions that can be made when a large group of individuals is to be rated are:

1. Ratings are comparable when given by numerous raters. *or*
2. Knowledge of the ratees is comparable when given by one rater.

These hypotheses are not necessarily mutually exclusive. When a large group of people is to be rated, however, either can be made to have a predominating effect.

This experiment attempts to answer the question: When 100 people are to be rated, would more valid ratings be secured by having a number of immediate supervisors with intimate acquaintance with the ratees do the rating or by having some higher level supervisor who knows a larger number of the ratees perform the rating? In other words, does either intimate knowledge and acquaintance with the ratees or variability caused by having many raters have more effect on rating validity?

• PROCEDURE

The procedure consisted of securing ratings on 100 flight mechanics at Bolling Air Force Base. Ratings for the airmen were given by three commissioned officers, three non-commissioned officer flight chiefs, and 14 immediate non-commissioned officer supervisors.

The highest level of supervision consisted of the commissioned officers, who made frequent, almost daily, contact with their mechanics. The second level of supervision consisted of the non-commissioned officer flight chiefs (NCO flight chiefs), who did make daily contact with the mechanics in their flights

Note. This research was conducted under the auspices of the Air Force and was subsequently released for publication. The statements of findings, however, are solely the responsibility of the authors.

* From *Personnel Psychology,* Vol. 6, no. 4, Winter 1954, pp. 461–466.

but spent little time as direct supervisors of their work. The third level of supervision was the immediate NCO supervisor, who spent his time directly assigning, supervising, and overseeing the work of his group of approximately seven mechanics. When the study was completed, the minimum time of assignment in these flights was four months for mechanics, six months for the third level supervision, and nine months for the upper two levels of supervisors.

The result was three ratings for each mechanic; that is, one by an officer, one by the NCO flight chief, and one by the immediate NCO supervisor.

The rating instrument administered was divided into three sections, each of which was headed by a question and developed by explanatory statements. The first section was: "How Well Does He Get Along With Others?" the second: "How Much Does He Know About His Job?" and the third: "How Well Does He Do His Job?" Each of the three sections was graphically illustrated to present an idea as to how many men should be placed on each point of the six-interval scale to secure a normal distribution. Describing the six-interval scale was a series of words; poor . . . superior. The raters were instructed to rate all their men on one section of the scale before proceeding to the next section. A separate rating blank was used for each mechanic.

The Flight Mechanics Job Knowledge Test was used as a criterion measure for the rating scale. This test is the product of one of the Air Force test construction units, who devised this instrument to serve as a method of evaluation for bypassed specialists; that is, for evaluating people possessing civilian skills convertible into Air Force specialties. The items were written by selected master sergeants, who normally perform in this occupational specialty, under the supervision of test construction personnel. Item analyses have indicated high internal consistency, while administrations for standardization of the test have proven that it does discriminate between skill levels of flight mechanics. On the basis of such findings the Job Knowledge Test was accepted as the best available criterion. It was administered to the 100 ratees at the time they were rated and obviously the raters had no knowledge of the results.

• ANALYSIS

The method used to test whether the levels of supervisors differed in their ability to predict scores on the Job Knowledge Test was to correlate the ratings with the test scores. This was done separately for each of the three levels of raters. Since there were 100 mechanics in the study, each of the correlations has $N = 100$. The number of raters, however, varies from three in each of the two upper levels to 14 in the third level.

The correlation coefficients calculated are found in Table 1. Inspection indicates that low correlations were secured by all classes of raters in section 1 of the instrument "How Well Does He Get Along With Others?" There is no significant difference between these coefficients. Since this question has no face validity with the Job Knowledge Test, the results seem justified.

On the second portion of the rating instrument "How Much Does He Know About His Job?" the correlations are .24, .19 and .42 for the first, second, and third levels of supervision. Employing

Table 1

CORRELATION COEFFICIENTS AMONG THREE SECTIONS OF A RATING SCALE BY THREE LEVELS OF SUPERVISORS AND THE AIRMAN JOB KNOWLEDGE TEST ($N = 100$)

	SUPERVISORY LEVEL		
RATING SCALE SECTION	OFFICERS (1ST LEVEL)	NON-COMMISSIONED FLIGHT CHIEFS (2ND LEVEL)	IMMEDIATE NON-COMMISSIONED OFFICER SUPERVISOR (3RD LEVEL)
How well does he get along with others?	0.20	0.21	0.25
How much does he know about his job?	0.24	0.19	0.42
How well does he do his job?	0.25	0.18	0.40

Fisher's transformation it was found that the correlation of .42 is significantly higher than the other two coefficients at the 5% and 2% levels of significance, respectively. These results indicate that the third-level supervisors were more capable of evaluating the mechanics than either of the other two levels of supervisors. It further demonstrates that they were able to differentiate between the various sections of the rating instrument, an ability not demonstrated by the other levels of raters.

The third portion of the rating instrument, "How Well Does He Do His Job?" seems to be highly related with the second or knowledge section of the instrument. This is amplified, since the requirements of the mechanics job are man-to-machine rather than man-to-man duties. Such hypotheses are substantiated by the correlation coefficients found with the third level of supervision. In fact, the two coefficients .42 and .40 for third-level supervision are in the direction to support a higher relationship between the mechanics knowledge of the job, as shown by the Job Knowledge Test, and the rating of knowledge, than between the knowledge of the job and the rating of performance. However, the difference is not significant.

The three coefficients of .21, .19, and .18 for the second-level supervision of raters indicate that they were unable to differentiate between the sections of the instrument.

• DISCUSSION

The first-level supervisors were able to rate the mechanics in such a manner as to indicate the proper direction (i.e., an increase in coefficient size for the knowledge and performance sections of the instrument). This trend, however, is not statistically significant. One of the hypotheses for this study was the relating of more accurate ratings to the proximity of the supervisor to the ratee. This relationship is not found in the results between first- and second-level supervisors. In fulfilling this hypothesis the second-level supervisors would have to have obtained higher correlation coefficients. The reverse is true, however, although not at a significant level. Ferguson (2, p. 95) has demonstrated that the degree of accuracy of a rating is related in a direct and positive manner to the degree of acquaintance. The study reported here tends to support this position although the emphasis is more on the proximity of the level of supervision than on the amount of acquaintance.

To obtain ratings for the 100 mechanics, it was necessary on the third level of supervision to use the ratings of 14 supervisors. Obviously, their ability to make ratings and to give high or low ratings affects the correlation coefficients. These differences have been found to be minor by Ferguson (*1*) as compared with other variables in the rating situation. In the two higher classes of raters this equalization of ratings took place for only three raters. In this study ratings have been used for experimental purposes. It has been pointed out by Taylor and Wherry (3, p. 46) that this type of rating changes distributions and means when used for administrative decision. Under such conditions the ability of third-level supervisors should be determined by additional investigation to insure their ability to provide the most accurate ratings.

• CONCLUSIONS

The findings can be summarized as follows:

1. The level of raters closest to the ratees were best able to rate them.
2. The level of raters closest to the ratees, and only this level, was able to discriminate between sections of the rating instrument.
3. These results occur even when the group of raters closest to the ratees is composed of 14 raters while the two higher levels of raters were composed of three raters each.
4. Therefore in this rating situation of 100 flight mechanics it was better to combine the ratings from 14 immediate supervisors than to accept those from fewer higher level supervisors. Or as in the terms of the original hypothesis; the equality of ratings by various raters is more nearly satisfied than is the equality of knowledge about the ratees.

REFERENCES

1. Ferguson, Leonard W. The Effect upon Appraisal Scores of Individual Differences in the Ability of Supervision to Appraise Subordinates. *Personnel Psychology,* 1949, 2, 377–382.
2. Ferguson, Leonard W. The Value of Acquaintance Ratings in Criterion Research. *Personnel Psychology,* 1949, 2, 93–102.
3. Taylor, Erwin K., and Wherry, Robert J. A Study of Leniency in Two Rating Systems. *Personnel Psychology,* 1951, 4, 39–47.

THE IMPACT OF INTERPERSONAL RELATIONS ON RATINGS OF PERFORMANCE*

Verne Kallejian, Paula Brown, and Irving R. Weschler

Many administrative decisions, of necessity, are based upon evaluations of performance. These evaluations, involving judgments concerning individuals or groups, are usually formalized as performance ratings. Some factors which influence performance ratings, such as the "halo effect," "errors in central tendency," and "judgments of leniency" have been identified,[1] and various methods have been proposed to reduce the effect of these factors. Few studies, however, have directly investigated the effect of the interpersonal relationship between the superior and his subordinates upon the former's ratings of the latters' performance.

This investigation arose in connection with one of the long-range interests of the Human Relations Research Group, that of identifying effective work groups and isolating the leadership variables responsible for the effectiveness of groups. Up to the present time a large portion of the field work of the Group has been conducted at a local naval research and development laboratory. The formulation of valid, reliable criteria of effectiveness in a research and development setting is complex and raises a number of problems.

An approach to the evaluation problem was made in May, 1952, when our Group held a day-long invitational conference of leading local research administrators on the UCLA campus. This conference was largely devoted to eliciting those criteria which research administrators actually use in evaluating the work of their subordinates or subunits. Unfortunately, few criteria emerged which can be described as objective.[2] Analysis of the conference proceedings supported the following conclusions:

1. At present, evaluation of performance is based primarily upon the subjective judgments of "competent individuals."
2. A wide variety of characteristics of performance are used in the evaluation of research and development.
3. There is no substantial agreement as to which of these characteristics is most valid in evaluating performance, nor are the circumstances which favor

[1] For a discussion of some of these factors see Donald G. Paterson, "Rating" *in* D. H. Fryer and E. R. Henry (eds. *Handbook of Applied Psychology*, Vol. 1 (New York: Holt, Rinehart and Winston, 1950), p. 153. For a different critical investigation of the rating process, see Irving R. Weschler, Fred Massarik, and Robert Tannenbaum, "Experimenting With Federal Efficiency Ratings: A Case Study." *Journal of Social Psychology*, 36 (1952), pp. 205–222.

* From *Public Personnel Review*, October 1953, pp. 166–170. Reprinted from the October 1953 issue of *Public Personnel Review*, The Journal of the Public Personnel Association, with permission of the publishers.

[2] See Irving R. Weschler and Paula Brown (eds.), *Evaluating Research and Development*, Annotated Proceedings of a Conference of Research Administrators (Los Angeles: Institute of Industrial Relations, University of California, 1953).

the use of one criterion as against another specified.

A PRELIMINARY FIELD STUDY

In order to examine these conclusions in a field setting, a preliminary study was undertaken to determine what characteristics of performance superiors actually use in evaluating their units, and to determine what conditions, if any, favor the use of one characteristic as against another.[3] One department of the research and development laboratory was studied. At the time of the investigation, this department consisted of approximately 425 people, organized in five divisions, each of which was subdivided into four or five independently functioning branches. Some of these branches were in turn subdivided into sections.

The superiors in this department rated the groups they supervise in terms of their *over-all effectiveness of performance.* Next, they were asked to state what criteria of performance they used in arriving at these over-all ratings. Then, the raters were presented with a list of *17 specific characteristics of performance* (such as general technical competence of personnel in the group, communications within the group, administrative competence of the group leader, quantity of work accomplished, etc.), and were asked to rate their units again, independently, on each of these. Each item was defined and explained to the subjects. A scale ranging from 0 (very poor performance) to 10 (outstanding performance) was used. These ratings are referred to in this paper as the "actual ratings." Finally, the supervisors were asked to indicate the relative importance they attached to each of the items. The following findings emerged:

1. The criteria of performance which superiors stated they had actually used in the over-all evaluation of the groups they supervise can be readily grouped into four major categories: output, skills, supervision, and group variables (morale, cooperation, accepting group objectives). Within each of these categories, however, there is no significant agreement as to which specific characteristics are to be emphasized.

2. The ratings on the 17 characteristics of performance show some agreement as to the importance or lack of importance of certain specific items. Superiors at all levels within the department placed emphasis on four items: general technical competence of the personnel in the group, proper utilization of the personnel, technical competence of the head, and effectiveness of the head as a leader. There was a tendency to minimize the importance of such factors as planning, scheduling, and control procedures, systematic work methods, potential for group "growth," and conformity of the product to specifications.

3. The reliability of ratings, in those cases where two or more individuals rated the same groups on the 17 items, ranged from −.60 to +.94. This range was to be expected in view of the lack of agreement concerning the relative importance of specific characteristics in evaluating performance. The effect of this divergence of attitudes is also re-

[3] A more detailed description of this phase of our research can be found in Weschler and Brown (eds.), *op. cit.*, pp. 87–94.

flected in a lack of agreement with regard to the over-all ratings of performance, in those cases where two or more superiors rated the same groups.

• A CLINICAL INVESTIGATION OF THE RATING PROCESS

The results from the preliminary study clearly indicate that the evaluation of performance is subject to wide individual variation. This finding suggests that the problems associated with ratings of performance might profitably be studied in much the same way as other instances of interpersonal judgments. Since few guidelines exist for the evaluation of performance in research and development settings, it is likely that situational and interpersonal factors operate to influence ratings of performance. Considerable evidence is available which indicates that, particularly in ambiguous situations, the personality characteristics of the judge are also important determinants of his evaluations.[4]

One division of the department in which the preliminary study had been conducted was selected for further investigation. This division contained five branches, four of which had two or more sections.

A clinically skilled interviewer, who had no previous contact with the laboratory or the data obtained in the preliminary study, interviewed members of subordinate groups regarding their relationships with co-workers and superiors. After the interviews with subordinates, the interviewer formulated a diagnostic personality evaluation of the superiors who rated each group. From this personality evaluation of the superior and the interviewer's obtained knowledge of the group and the leader of the group being evaluated, he then attempted to predict the superior's actual ratings for the group. These are called "predictive ratings." They were made for the over-all ratings of performance as well as for all of the 17 specific characteristics of performance. The actual ratings of eleven superiors were predicted in this way. In addition, the interviewer gave his own impressions of each group by completing a set of "evaluative ratings."

Thirty-two people were interviewed. These included every member of two sections in each of two branches, all the branch heads and their assistants, and the division head and his assistant. The fifty-minute interviews were conducted in a private office at the laboratory and were recorded. The subjects were assured that the interviewer had no official connection with the laboratory and that no one at the laboratory would have access to any information obtained during the interview. After interviewing the subordinates of a given group, the predictive and evaluative ratings were completed, and an interview was held with the group's superior.

The evaluative ratings made by the interviewer were primarily based upon his evaluation of variables found within the group itself, i.e., the maturity and adjustment of the subordinate leader (e.g., the section head), the effectiveness of each leader-subordinate relationship, the general level of job satisfaction and morale, and the degree of cooperative effort among members of the group. The interviewer based his judgments pri-

[4] See J. S. Bruner, "Personality Dynamics and the Process of Perceiving," *in* Robert R. Blake and Glenn V. Ramsey (eds.), *Perception, An Approach to Personality* (New York: The Ronald Press, 1951).

marily on interpersonal factors and was not acquainted with the technical work.

The predictive ratings were based upon three classes of variables, i.e., the personality characteristics of the superior making the rating, his relationship with the persons being rated, and situational factors. The following assumptions served as a basis for the formulation of these predictive ratings:

1. Superiors will react to, and place greater importance on, those characteristics of performance which are related to their personal needs.
2. The quality of the relationship between the superior and the subordinate is a determinant of the superior's perception of that subordinate's performance. Those individuals who behave in such a way as to satisfy the personal needs of the superior will generally be rated higher. Those subordinates who interfere with the satisfaction of the personal needs of the superior will generally be rated lower. The specific ratings of superiors are likely to be determined by the more global, conscious or unconscious reactions to subordinates.
3. Superiors will be differentially influenced by the following situational factors: the actual performance itself, the nature of the rating task, the organizational setting (e.g., the structure of the work group, the attitudes and interests of higher echelons of management, the mission of the laboratory). Effects of these influences are reflected in the performance ratings.

The interviews were structured to obtain the information necessary to evaluate these variables. Some of the factors which were investigated included a consideration of the extent to which:

1. subordinates had favorable reactions to the superior;
2. subordinates felt that the superior is aware of the effect which he has on the group;
3. the superior followed a consistent behavior pattern in dealing with his group;
4. the superior was able to adapt his behavior to the different personality characteristics of individuals in the group;
5. the superior was perceived as being aware of the needs of his subordinates;
6. subordinates felt that they understood the objectives established by their superiors;
7. subordinates felt that they have contributed to decisions relevant to their particular jobs;
8. subordinates were aware of the relationship between their objectives, the objectives of the next higher unit, and the over-all mission of the laboratory;
9. subordinates felt at ease in discussing their problems, personal and technical, with their superior;
10. subordinates felt that differences in opinion between their superiors and themselves are expressed, understood, and accepted;
11. subordinates felt that the attainment of objectives, as they saw them, was worthwhile;
12. subordinates were willing to supplement each other's skills and knowledge;
13. subordinates felt satisfied with their own performance in relation to the over-all objectives;
14. subordinates were aware of the superior's attitudes toward the performance of the group; and
15. job satisfaction and morale were related to actual job activities, rather

than to other aspects of the work situation such as location, civil service employment, etc.

When the interview protocols concerning various superiors were analyzed, sharp contrasts appeared in the way in which subordinates reacted to their superiors. For example, the following remarks made by various subordinates all describe Superior A:

He gives orders indiscriminately and changes them without notice.

I talk to him as little as possible.

He may know his job, but we pay a high price to get it done.

I'm not sure he really knows what we are doing.

I don't think he knows my name.

I never ask questions and he rarely asks for my opinion.

Even if something is really wrong with work based on his orders, I have a tough time convincing him.

For a long time he would give orders to my group without telling me.

I don't think he respects anyone around here.

A similar set of subordinate responses for Superior B follows:

It's a real pleasure working for him.

He doesn't always do the things I like, but I respect his judgment.

He is the best man around.

I think other people may know more than he does, but he knows how to help you think through a problem.

If anything goes wrong, I know I can tell him about it and he'll look into it.

He is easy to talk to.

I think he knows everything that goes on.

He keeps on top of the operation.

From an analysis of all the interview material relating to Superior A, it was concluded that he was relatively unaware of his effect upon subordinates. His primary concern was with production and the promotion of his own ideas. He discouraged initiative among his subordinates and considered almost any deviation from his orders as a personal insult. He was very little concerned with the welfare of his subordinates and bolstered his own insecurities by maintaining rigid control, primarily by withholding information and depreciating the efforts of his subordinates. When predicting the ratings for Superior A, it was relatively easy to determine what characteristics of performance he would consider important and what factors would influence the level of his ratings.

The ratings for Superior B were more difficult to predict. From interviews with his subordinates it was possible to conclude that he was conscious of his effect upon people and also seemed to be aware of the needs of his subordinates. He actually delegated responsibility and encouraged his subordinates to communicate freely with him. He seemed concerned about maximizing the performance of each subordinate and promoting cooperative efforts toward common goals. Subordinates in his group were aware of what was going on and where they fitted into the total activity. It was concluded that Superior B would evaluate his subordinates in much the same way as an impartial observer. Thus, in this instance, the interviewer's predictive ratings were not greatly different from his evaluative ratings. For Superior B, the interviewer's predictions were not as accurate with regard to the technical items, since B's ratings on these items were less influenced by interpersonal factors.

The following illustrations show how many of these conclusions were substantiated by interviews with the superiors themselves after the evaluative and predictive ratings had been made. Consider these edited samples of two interviews with Superiors A and B. First, Superior A:

Interviewer: Tell me about Joe White.
Superior A: He is a good worker, fast, a good engineer.

I: Is there anything else about him you consider important to keep in mind as his supervisor?

A: No, he has had good training.

I: How do you get along with him?

A: All right. He doesn't give me any trouble.

I: You mentioned Jim Blue. How about him?

A: He is a slow worker. He is working on a new job, and always griping about something. As an engineer, he is fair.

I: What sort of person is he?

A: What do you mean?

I: Well, what is he like as a person?

A: Oh, I guess he is all right.

I: How about John Black?

A: He is a good man.

Next, a comparable interchange with Superior B:

I: Tell me about Bill Green.

B: He is coming along rather well. Some of the others don't quite understand his temperament. He is methodical. I try to give him jobs that require care and precision, and try to keep him away from work that requires a lot of decisions or new methods. He is very stable and consistent in his work. It took me a long time to learn that he needs time to think out an answer. Some people think he doesn't know very much because he is quiet. I ask him to give his reports in written form, and I pass them around. This has helped a lot.

I: Anything else?

B: Well, I could tell you a lot about him personally, his background and family.

I: How about Frank Brown?

B: He is a key man in the group. He is well liked by the other people. If I can get him interested in a project, the others seem to go along. Things were a little strained for a while as he wanted a promotion and I couldn't get it for him, but he knows I'm trying, so that's disappeared. He needs to ask questions and talk over every aspect of the problem before he feels comfortable about going ahead. I usually bring the group together when we start something new and his questions stimulate the others to do a lot of thinking.

I: Anything else?

B: He's been having some trouble. I suspect it's financial. Sometimes he slows down for a week or two. I leave him alone and he pulls out of it.

In comparing these two sample interviews, the differences in personality, which were already brought out in the interviews with the subordinates, were dramatically substantiated in a number of ways. Superior A seems to have little, if any, awareness of the personality differences between subordinates, while Superior B thinks in terms of relationships and personalities. Superior A sees people primarily as engineers with certain work habits, while Superior B is able to differentiate "engineers" by personal characteristics. Also, Superior A talks as though his reactions are determined exclusively by the nature of the subordinate. Superior B, on the other hand, is aware that some of his reactions are determined by his own personality make-up rather than by the characteristics of his subordinates, and he is aware of his effect upon subordinates.

• RESULTS AND CONCLUSIONS

The interviewer's predictive ratings, when compared with the superiors' actual ratings with regard to *over-all effec-*

tiveness of performance, were accurate at the 3 per cent level of confidence.[5] With the exception of one case, the predictions were thus accurate in terms of relative rankings of groups, the amount of difference between groups, and their absolute standing on the rating scale.

The interviewer's predictive ratings, when compared with the superiors' actual ratings with regard to the *17 specific characteristics of performance,* were accurate at the 5 per cent level of confidence.[6]

It was also found that there was a much closer relationship between the interviewer's predictive ratings and the superiors' actual ratings than between the interviewer's evaluative ratings and the superiors' actual ratings. Thus, the predictive ratings were accurate not only when they coincided with the evaluative ratings, but also when they failed to coincide.

On the basis of these results, we conclude that the interviewer was able to account for a significant portion of the variance of performance ratings on the basis of his clinical evaluation of personal, interpersonal, and situational factors.

The personality characteristics of the superior which influence his ratings consist of those attitudes and personal needs that determine the way he sees himself and responds to the world around him. The components of the relationship between superior and subordinate which affect the superior's ratings are, for example, tensions, likes, and dislikes. Among the situational variables which influence performance ratings are the actual performance itself, the nature of the rating task, and the organizational setting.

Most superiors are unaware of the factors which reduce the validity of their performance ratings. Their recognition of these factors should result in more objective judgments of individuals and groups. In addition, individuals whose administrative decisions are based upon performance ratings would do well also to recognize the limitations of this kind of information as a basis for action.

---

[5] Determined by point binomial for the number of correct predictions.

[6] Determined by product moment correlation.

PART TWO • TECHNIQUES OF APPRAISAL

Although we may be only beginning to find effective research on fundamental problems of interpersonal relations and of human judgment, a remarkable amount of effort has been put into research on the technique of rating and appraisal. This effort reflects a strong distrust of individual judgment. While men may be blind to the existence of their own biases, they are aware of bias in others. Consequently, the goal of social scientists and personnel experts alike has been to invent a scheme which either neutralizes or measures the biases of those who judge others.

The readings in this section constitute a description of the major rating techniques, together with some informed criticism (ordinarily growing out of research) of these techniques. Of particular interest are the articles that summarize research on particular techniques, such as the one by Hollander.

In terms of who in the organization rates the performance of others, the most pervasive answer is the individual's superior. Probably the oldest of the formal techniques used in ratings by superiors is the *graphic scale.* The alleged deficiencies of this scale have led to the invention of other techniques in the past thirty years. Among the newest techniques using the supervisor as rater are the *critical-incident rating* and the *forced-choice performance report.*

The most interesting current trend in performance appraisal is the criticism of the use of the supervisor as rater. An early modification of supervisory rating was the *field-review* technique, involving a third party who, in one or another of a variety of arrangements, acted as interpreter, questioner, and go-between, with reference to the rater and the person being rated. More recently, the findings in military research about the value of peer ratings and subordinate ratings have created interest in administrative circles elsewhere.

A. Rating by Supervisors

1. THE GRAPHIC SCALE—TECHNIQUES AND CRITICISMS

THE SCOTT COMPANY GRAPHIC RATING SCALE

DONALD G. PATERSON

MERIT RATING CRITICIZED

THOMAS ARTHUR RYAN

RELATION OF FORMAT AND ADMINISTRATION TO THE CHARACTERISTICS OF GRAPHIC RATING SCALES

ERWIN K. TAYLOR AND ROY HASTMAN

Donald Paterson launched the graphic rating scale in business nearly forty years ago. He and his colleagues felt that they had found a device which provided the busy supervisor the opportunity to make a clear and accurate rating of his subordinates. Although the graphic scale is still widely used, it has also been widely criticized, as it is in Ryan's article. An interesting example of such criticism put to an empirical test is given in the article by Taylor and Hastman. Their research serves as a warning to over-enthusiastic critics and provides a nice picture of some of the forces affecting the outcome of performance appraisal in the organization.

FURTHER READING

Taylor, Erwin K., "Supervised Ratings—Making Graphic Scales Work," *Personnel,* Vol. 27, no. 6, May 1951, pp. 504–514.

Uhrbrock, Richard Stephen, "Standardization of 724 Rating Scale Statements," *Personnel Psychology,* Vol. 3, no. 3, Autumn 1950, pp. 285–316.

THE SCOTT COMPANY GRAPHIC RATING SCALE*

Donald G. Paterson

Walter Dill Scott was the pioneer who introduced the method of rating the abilities of workers in industry prior to World War [I]. He invented what has come to be known as the Man-to-Man Comparison Scale, and as Director of the Committee on Classification of Personnel in the United States Army modified that scale for use in rating the efficiency of army officers. This scale supplanted the seniority system of promotion in the army and initiated an era of promotion on the basis of merit. It is natural, therefore, that the Scott Company, in its work in industry, should utilize the rating method as part of its technique in solving certain types of personnel problems. Man-to-man rating scales were developed for foremen and for executives and given a thorough trial in several large organizations. Considerable difficulty was experienced in this work primarily because of the time and effort necessary in getting executives to prepare their "master scales" carefully and to use their "master scales" in subsequently rating their subordinates. Without such care, it is well-nigh impossible to secure satisfactory results. The difficulty was ingeniously overcome by Ruml's suggestion that a simplified plan based on new principles should be adopted. The Graphic Rating Scale is the result and what follows is an attempt to describe this new method, its development, its uses, the results that have been achieved, and the steps that must be taken to safeguard its use.

DESCRIPTION OF THE GRAPHIC RATING SCALE

The Graphic Rating Method is a new method for securing the judgment of superiors on subordinates. Other methods, apparently similar, have appeared in the past, yet this new method includes two features which have not been brought together heretofore,[1] and which are basic in the Graphic Rating Method. These features are:

1. The person who is making the judgment is freed from direct *quantitative* terms in making his decision of merit in any quality.

NOTE. The development of the Graphic Rating Scale is the result of coöperative effort on the part of the members of the Scott Company, Philadelphia. Credit for originating the graphic rating method as well as supervising its experimental development belongs to Beardsley Ruml. The writer participated in its development and is indebted to all members of the Company for the opportunity of assisting over a considerable period in this interesting experiment. Full acknowledgment would necessitate mention of all the members of the Company. Special mention should be given, however, to Mr. L. B. Hopkins and Mr. R. C. Clothier, who contributed much to the development of the logic and uses of the scale in various industrial situations. Much of the present article is taken directly from the Scott Company Bulletins on the Graphic Rating Scale and is published with the permission of the Company's officers.

* From *Journal of Personnel Research*, Vol. 1, December–January 1922–1923, pp. 361–376.

[1] One early method of graphic rating is described by J. B. Miner, *Journal of Applied Psychology*, Vol. I, pp. 123–133.

GRAPHIC RATING REPORT ON WORKERS

Name of Employee.............................. Branch..............................

Position of Employee.............................. Department..............................

Employee Rated By.............................. Date..............................

Instructions for Making Out This Report:—Rate this employee on the basis of the actual work he is now doing. Before attempting to report on this employee, it is necessary to have clearly in mind the exact qualities which are to be reported on. Read the definitions very carefully. In each quality compare this employee with others in the same occupation in this company or elsewhere. Place a check (√) somewhere on the line running from "very high" to "very low" to indicate this employee's standing in each quality. It is not necessary to put the check (√) directly above any of the descriptive adjectives.

QUALITIES	REPORT				
I. *Ability to Learn:* Consider the ease with which this employee is able to learn new methods and to follow directions given him.	Very Superior	Learns With Ease	Ordinary	Slow To Learn	Dull
II. *Quantity of Work:* Consider the amount of work accomplished and the promptness with which work is completed.	Unusually High Output	Satisfactory Output		Limited Output	Unsatisfactory Output
III. *Quality of Work:* Consider the neatness and accuracy of his work and his ability constantly to turn out work that is up to standard.	Highest Quality	Good Quality		Careless	Makes Many Errors
IV. *Industry:* Consider his energy and application to the duties of his job day in and day out.	Very Energetic	Industrious		Indifferent	Lazy
V. *Initiative:* Consider his success in going ahead with a job without being told every detail; his ability to make practical suggestions for doing things in a new and better way.	Very Original	Resourceful	Occasionally Suggests	Routine Worker	Needs Constant Supervision
VI. *Co-operativeness:* Consider his success in effectively co-operating with his co-workers and with those exercising greater authority.	Highly Co-operative	Co-operative		Difficult to Handle	Obstructionist
VII. *Knowledge of Work:* Consider present knowledge of job and of work related to it.	Complete	Well Informed	Moderate	Meagre	Lacking

REMARKS: (See reverse side for suggestions).............................. Total ....

.... Final Rating ....

....

Fig. 1. A graphic rating scale for workers (*front*).

GRAPHIC RATING REPORT ON WORKERS

The Purpose of Periodic Rating Reports

1. The graphic rating report is a practical method by means of which each employee's ability and fitness for promotion can be known quickly, with a reasonable degree of accuracy and with uniformity throughout the company.

2. The ratings are converted into a numerical expression indicating the ability of each person in those qualities deemed most essential, such as ability to learn new methods, quantity of work, quality of work, industry, initiative, co-operativeness, and knowledge of work.

3. Because the Rating Report calls attention separately to each of these essential qualifications, it lessens the danger that opinions will be based on minor points, with a corresponding disregard of important qualities. It is to the interest of all concerned to replace snap judgments by carefully thought-out reports.

4. This rating report has been devised after careful consideration of the best practices throughout the country. Its chief claim for the support of the supervisor and the employee is the fact that it is simple, concrete, and definite. It reduces the time required to rate an employee to a minimum, yet it is so arranged that the interests of each employee are safeguarded as regards accuracy and fairness.

5. All rating reports are confidential. Any employee who is rated, however, may be told where he stands in order that he may improve himself if he so desires.

To Supervisors: Supplement Your Rating With Appropriate Remarks.

When you have completed your rating of the employee on the front of this report, enter under REMARKS any comments which are appropriate.

In doing so, consider the possible comments suggested here and write the numbers of any comments that are particularly pertinent.

1. Recommend that Personnel Department interview this employee to advise him
   (a) How he can improve himself.
   (b) Concerning his present and future opportunities.
2. Deserves promotion.
3. Desires transfer to other work.
4. Well liked by fellow-employees.
5. Would do well in a supervisory position.
6. Is handicapped physically as follows..................................
7. Is taking a course in..................................

Fig. 2. A graphic rating scale for workers (reverse).

2. The person who is making the judgment can make as fine a discrimination of merit as he chooses. These two facts eliminate the restrictions on natural judgments which other rating methods impose.

Figures 1 and 2 reproduce one of the scales that have been developed for rating the efficiency of factory workers. Figure 3 shows one form of scale constructed for use in rating executives by their superiors. Inspection of these two sample rating scales brings out clearly the two points mentioned above. The one doing the rating is freed from *quantitative* terms in indicating his opinion of the subordinate in any quality, for he simply records his opinion by making a check mark on the line following a defined

GRAPHIC RATING SCALE

FOR EXECUTIVES, DEPARTMENT HEADS, FOREMEN AND SUPERVISORS

Name of Executive Doing Rating .... Date ....

Branch or Division .... Name of Supervisor Being Rated ....

Department .... Supervisor's Department ....

Instructions for Making Out This Report:—Before attempting to rate this supervisor, re-read carefully the definition of each quality immediately before rating the supervisor in that quality. Base your rating on the work this supervisor is actually doing at this time. Indicate your rating in each quality by placing a check (√) on the line just where you think it ought to be. For instance, if in quality I, you think the person you are rating ranks somewhere between Indifferent and Favorable, put your check on the line somewhere between these two points.

QUALITIES	REPORT				
I. Consider his success in winning confidence and respect through his personality.	Inspiring	Favorable	Indifferent	Unfavorable	Repellent
II. Consider his success in doing things in new and better ways and in adapting improved methods to his own work.	Highly Constructive	Resourceful	Fairly Progressive		Routine Worker
III. Consider his success in winning the co-operation of his men, in welding them into a loyal and effective working unit.	Capable and Forceful Leader	Handles Men Well	Fails to Command Confidence	Frequent Friction In His Department	
IV. Consider his success in organizing the work of his department, both by delegating authority wisely and by making certain that results are achieved.	Effective Even Under Difficult Circumstances	Effective Under Normal Circumstances	Lacks Planning Ability		Inefficient
V. Consider his success in making his department a smooth running part of the whole organization; his knowledge and appreciation of the problems of other departments.	Exceptionally Co-operative	Co-operative	Not Helpful	Difficult to Handle	Obstructionist
VI. Consider his success in improving his men by imparting information, creating interest, developing talent and arousing ambition.	Develops Men of High Calibre	Develops Men Satisfactorily	Neglects to Develop Men	Discourages and Misinforms Men	
VII. Consider his success in applying specialized knowledge in his particular field, whether by his own knowledge of ways and means or through his use of sources of information.	Expert	Competent	Uninformed		Neglects and Misinterprets the Facts

REMARKS: .... | Total ....

Fig. 3. Rating scale for executives.

quality or ability. He is guided in this by short descriptive adjectives that define the various degrees of excellence in that quality. Furthermore, the rating executive is not forced to place a subordinate in one of several classes but may put his check mark anywhere on the line. This means that he may make as fine a discrimination of merit as he chooses. It is also important to note that the rating executive himself is not burdened with the task of summing up his ratings. This work is clerical in nature and is economically performed by clerks in the personnel department.

The steps involved in summing the ratings and in evaluating the ratings for use on permanent record cards is as follows: A stencil or scale divided into ten divisions, each numbered from 1 to 10, is provided for converting the various check marks into numerical scores. The directions printed on this scoring stencil are: Place the stencil so that the scale coincides with the line for Quality I. Note in which of the ten scale divisions the check mark falls. Enter this number in the column at the right of the line. Proceed similarly to score the report for Qualities II, III, IV, V, VI, and VII. Add the seven numbers you have entered in the column at the right of the report lines and enter this sum after the word "Total" in the lower right-hand corner of the report sheet. These "Total Ratings" are never used but are converted into Final Ratings by the following procedure: the reports made by a given supervisor or foreman are assembled and the "total scores" are arranged in a frequency distribution from high to low. This distribution is then divided into five parts so that the highest 10 per cent of the Total Scores are given a Final Letter Rating of A, the next 20 per cent are given a Final Letter Rating of B, the next 40 per cent are given a C rating, the next 20 per cent are given D, and the lowest 10 per cent are given E. The limiting points in Total Scores are noted and a "Key to Final Ratings" is prepared whereby future ratings made by this supervisor may readily be converted into Final Ratings. This procedure converts the actual ratings into relative ratings and is designed to do away with the error which otherwise arises because some supervisors rate too high and other supervisors rate too low. The necessity for some such statistical method of correction will be explained in greater detail in a later part of this paper.

PURPOSES OF RATING • METHODS IN BUSINESS AND INDUSTRY

A word or two about the purposes of such rating scales will clarify the actual presentation of results. These purposes may best be outlined in terms of three factors that have brought about the development of rating methods as one of the tools of personnel administration.

I. Rating methods have been developed because of a recognition of *the educational value of ratings* from the following points of view:

a. The educational effect on those who make the ratings. Making out the rating reports insures the analysis of subordinates in terms of the traits essential for success in the work.

b. The educational effect on the employee. The knowledge that he is being judged periodically in essential traits affords him knowledge of those things that are considered vital and important, encourages self-analysis and provides an incentive for self-improvement in those traits in which he is weakest.

II. The development of rating methods has also been due to a realization of the need of bringing about a more uniform method of expressing the opinions of superiors concerning subordinates in order to:

a. Avoid, as far as possible, snap judgments made at times when sudden decisions affecting individual employees are to be made.

b. Standardize the elements considered as essential by the Company, eliminating as far as possible disagreements among superiors concerning employees.

III. A more important reason for the development of rating methods is found in the need for bringing to the notice of the management the progress of individual employees so that:

a. Employees whose development seems to be rapid or whose ability seems to be unusual may be considered by the management for a wage increase or for promotion as a reward for exceptional merit.

b. Employees who are doing unsatisfactory work in a given department may be considered for transfer to other work where they will be more valuable to themselves and the company.

c. Employees who are unusually weak in certain traits may be given vocational counsel or given special training by the Educational Department.

Decisions under *a, b,* or *c* above should not, of course, be based on the rating reports alone. Such reports should be looked upon as of value in indicating those employees to whom the attention of the management should be directed. Decisions should be based upon a consideration of the qualifications of the individual as indicated by Mental Alertness rating, Trade Test rating, past and present ratings of supervisors, previous experience, education, physical condition, etc.

• THE EXPERIMENTAL DEVELOPMENT OF THE GRAPHIC RATING METHOD

The necessity for carefully determining the possibilities and limitations of this new method of rating was evident and steps were taken to conduct an extensive experiment in three large companies. The purpose of this experiment was to discover:

1. The reliability of judgments secured by the Graphic Rating Method.

2. Whether the need for "interpretation" (statistical method for correcting original ratings), due to differences in standards of judgment on the part of different executives exists when the Graphic Rating Method is used.

3. The general usefulness and practicability of the method.

• GENERAL SUMMARY OF RESULTS

1. Ratings made by the Graphic Rating Method are highly reliable. This is evidenced by the close relationship between ratings on the same men by the same judge for different months; and by the close relationship between the ratings on the same men by different judges.

2. Large differences were found in the rating tendencies or standards of different foremen. These differences are important enough to necessitate the use

of the statistical method of correction described in the Rating Scale Guide.[2] This correction method appears adequate for the adjustment of differences in rating standard on the part of different judges.

3. The method has been found simple and practicable in actual use.

• EXPERIMENTAL PROCEDURE

In subjecting the Graphic Rating Method to a thorough experimental trial, ratings were secured on the following kinds of workers:

a. Office clerks.

b. Maintenance workers – carpenters, millwrights, plumbers, electricians, motor repairmen, boilermen, painters, and laborers.

c. Tool designers–draftsmen, detailers and tracers, and machine designers.

d. Machine shop operators–drill press operators, lathe operators, hand screw machine operators, etc.

e. Assemblers–small and large machine parts.

Practically all the workers in the above groups were rated by at least two foremen or supervisors. For certain groups it was possible to have the same workers rated for each of three months by the same foremen. Care was taken to explain to the foremen and supervisors the purpose of the Graphic Rating Method as well as to instruct them how to make out their reports in accordance with the standard directions. In all, 1446 ratings were secured in the course of the experiment.

[2] The Rating Scale Guide is a bulletin issued by the Scott Company giving in detail all necessary directions for properly handling the rating sheets.

• RESULTS OF THE EXPERIMENT

The Consistency of Foremen's Ratings

Assuming that the same workers are of about the same general value to the company in one month as they are in the next month, we should expect a foreman's ratings of the same men to be consistent from month to month.

A foreman's ratings would be considered to be consistent:

1. If he gives approximately the same average ratings to his men as a group in one month as in another.

2. If he rates his men in approximately the same order from month to month.

1. Consistency in ratings month to month. Results bearing on consistency in ratings from month to month are available for nine foremen who submitted ratings on their workers for three successive months.

The *rating tendency* of each of these foremen is shown by the following comparison of the three monthly average ratings given to the same workers:

Table 1

RATED BY	AVERAGE RATING FIRST MONTH	AVERAGE RATING SECOND MONTH	AVERAGE RATING THIRD MONTH
Foreman A	58.9	60.9	61.0
Foreman B	52.2	51.1	53.4
Foreman C	51.6	50.7	52.2
Foreman D	46.2	46.8	49.2
Foreman E	54.3	58.6	60.0
Foreman F	50.1	58.1	52.0
Foreman G	38.6	45.9	44.5
Foreman H	46.3	46.3	55.3
Foreman I	55.3	43.7	45.5

The average ratings given by Foremen A, B, C, and D are remarkably stable from one month to another. Foreman E tends to give a slightly higher rating each succeeding month. Foreman F rates his men approximately the same during the first and third month while he rates them higher during the second month. Foremen G and I submit similar average ratings for the second and third month which differ from the average ratings for the first month. Foreman H rates his men on the same level for the first two months but rates them higher for the third month.

The practical conclusion resulting from this study is that great care must be taken in interpreting the rating results for each foreman at each periodic rating, until his rating tendency has become stabilized. Ratings from two or three months for a given foreman can be combined for the purpose of establishing more definitely a foreman's rating tendency and in computing a Key for Final Ratings only in case the rating tendency remains sufficiently constant. Hence it is necessary that a careful analysis be made of the ratings of each foreman at each periodic rating.

2. *Consistency in rating same workers month to month.* The *consistency* of these foremen's ratings from month to month is shown by the *agreements* between the individual ratings given to the *same workers* in the first month and those given in the second and third months by each of the foremen. These agreements are evaluated in terms of the coefficient of correlation. The correlations are shown in Table 2. A correlation over +0.75 is considered high.

The average correlation between the ratings given in the first month and those given in the second month by

Table 2

RATED BY	CORRELATIONS BETWEEN FIRST AND SECOND RATINGS	CORRELATIONS BETWEEN SECOND AND THIRD RATINGS
Foreman B	+0.91	+0.96
Foreman H	0.88	0.92
Foreman C	0.85	0.86
Foreman G	0.84	0.92
Foreman I	0.84	0.90
Foreman D	0.82	0.90
Foreman F	0.62	0.66
Foreman E	0.60	0.82
Foreman A	0.52	0.88
Average correlation	+0.76	+0.87

these nine foremen is +0.76. A correlation of +0.76 is high and indicates that the rating of these foremen meet the requirements of consistency.

The average correlation between the ratings given in the second month and the third month, is, however, much higher, +0.87. The ratings of these foremen are found to become even more consistent from month to month.

This tendency toward greater consistency in the later ratings is also demonstrated by the fact that the correlation for each and every foreman is higher for the second pair of ratings than it is for the first pair.

Only one of these foremen (Foreman F) exhibits an unsatisfactory degree of consistency in his ratings. The correlation for the first and second months for this foreman is +0.62 and for the second and third months is +0.66. It is probable that with further practice and instruction this foreman's ratings will also show a satisfactory degree of consistency.

Correlations of at least +0.75 should be attained before a foreman's ratings are pronounced "Satisfactory in Consistency." Ratings submitted by foremen who prove to be inconsistent in their judgments should be discarded because such ratings are unreliable.

This measurement of consistency from month to month is a definite and practical method whereby a foreman's ability to judge his workers can be determined. By this method foremen can be checked up on the consistency of their judgments of men.

The Agreement Between Foremen Concerning the Same Workers

A foreman should not only be consistent in agreeing *with himself* in the ratings he gives to the same workers from month to month but he should also agree with other foremen whose ratings of the same workers are equally consistent and reliable.

1. *Agreements between foremen as shown by correlations.* Ratings of the same workers by three pairs of foremen for three successive months as well as the first monthly ratings of the same workers by five additional pairs of foremen are available. The correlations are as follows:

Table 3

AGREEMENT BETWEEN	FIRST MONTH	SECOND MONTH	THIRD MONTH
Foremen A and F	+ 0.33	+ 0.40	+ 0.50
Foremen H and D	0.78	0.82	0.78
Foremen B and E			0.90
Foremen J and K	0.82		
Foremen L and M	0.63		
Foremen N and O	0.80		
Foremen N and P	0.75		
Foremen O and P	0.84		

The lower correlations between Foremen A and F are due to the lack of "consistency" found in the ratings of Foreman F. It is important to note that with the improvement in the consistency of Foreman F's ratings (noted in the preceding section) we find an increase from month to month in the correlations between his ratings and those of Foreman A.

The correlations between Foremen H and D are consistently high for each of the three months.

The correlations between Foremen B and E for their third monthly rating is very high (+0.90). Data are not available for previous months.

The correlation between Foremen J and K for their first monthly rating is high (+0.82). These two foremen have not yet submitted their second and third monthly ratings.

The correlation between Foremen L and M was +0.63. Their ratings were in close agreement with the exception of a radical disagreement concerning three of their workers.

Foremen N, O, and P rated the same workers. The correlations are uniformly high. The correlation between Foremen N and O is +0.80; between Foremen N and P is +0.75; between Foremen O and P is +0.84. The ratings given by three foremen were averaged and it was found that Foreman N's ratings correlated +0.93 with the average. Foreman O's ratings correlated +0.95 and Foreman P's ratings correlated +0.93.

In general, we find a close agreement between foremen who rate the same workers provided that each foreman's ratings are consistent.

2. *Agreements between foremen as shown by adjusted ratings.* Agreements in the ratings given to the same workers by two foremen can also be determined by comparing the Final Letter Ratings

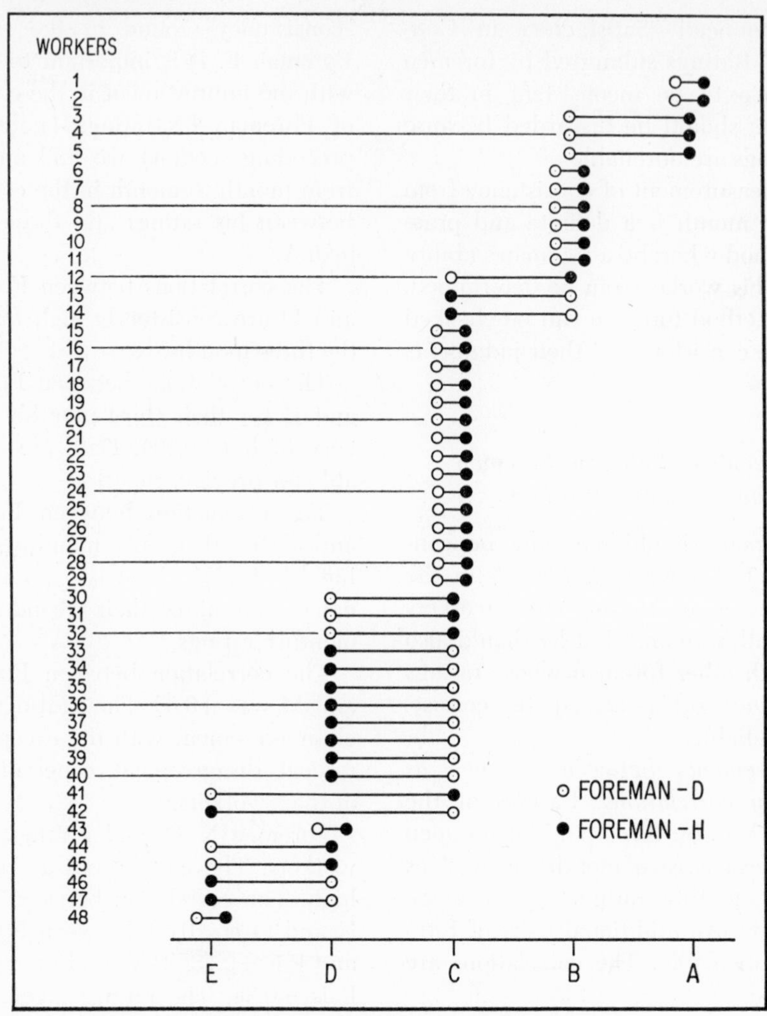

Fig. 4. Agreement between Foreman D and Foreman H on ratings of carpenters and painters.

given to those workers by the two foremen.

The Final Letter Ratings are derived in terms of a five division scale, i.e., A, B, C, D, and E. (A represents a very high rating and E a very low rating.)

Figure 4 presents the results of the first monthly ratings given to a group of carpenters and painters by Foremen D and H. Inspection of the agreements and disagreements shown on the chart may be summarized as follows:

	NO. OF CASES	% OF CASES
Perfect agreement	25	52
Disagreement of one letter step	21	44
Disagreement of two letter steps	2	4
Disagreement of three letter steps	0	0
Disagreement of four letter steps	0	0
Total number	48	100

These two foremen disagree radically on only two carpenters. They agree within one letter step on 46 of the 48 carpenters. In general it is apparent that Foremen D and H are in close agreement concerning the respective merits of these carpenters and painters.

Figure 5 shows the results of the first periodic ratings given to 47 tool designers by Foremen J and K. A summary of the agreements and disagreements shows:

	NO. OF CASES	% OF CASES
Perfect agreement	29	62
Disagreement of one letter step	16	34
Disagreement of two letter steps	2	4
Disagreement of three letter steps	0	0
Disagreement of four letter steps	0	0
Total number	47	100

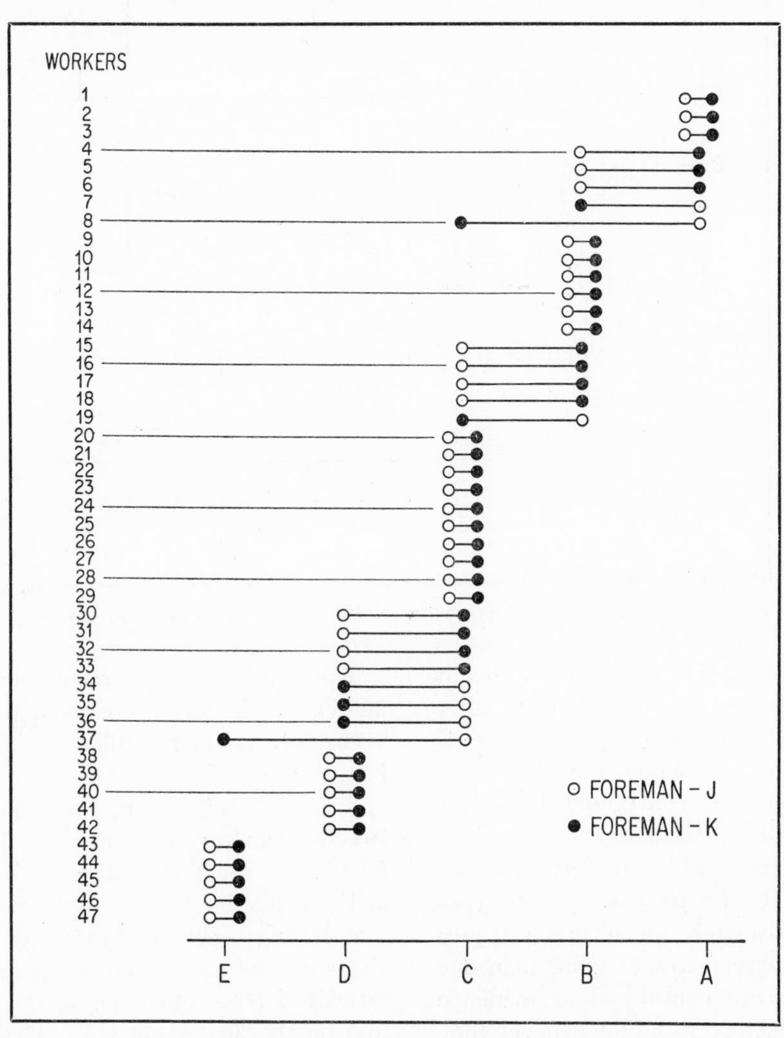

Fig. 5. Agreement between Foreman J and Foreman K on ratings of tool designers.

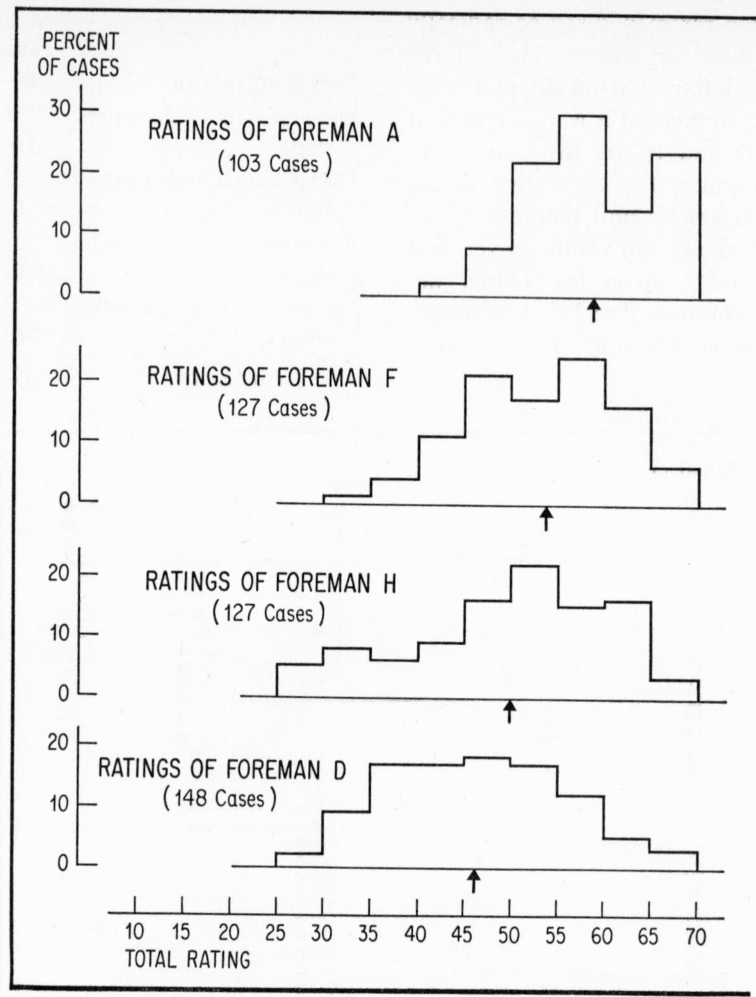

Fig. 6. Percentage frequency distribution of total ratings given by seven foremen

These two foremen disagree radically on only two tool designers. They agree within one letter step on 45 of the 47 tool designers. Foremen J and H are in close agreement concerning the value of these tool designers.

Agreements within one letter step on the A, B, C, D, E scale may be considered satisfactory for all practical purposes. Disagreements of more than one letter step are considered as evidence of unsatisfactory ratings whenever they occur.

The study of agreements and disagreements between foremen and supervisors has led to the following generalizations:

1. In general, the close agreement between foremen concerning their workers justifies the use of the ratings as an index of the general value of employees.

2. Ratings secured from two supervisors can be used safely for permanent records if they agree within one letter step on the final letter scale. Whenever a disagreement of two or more letter

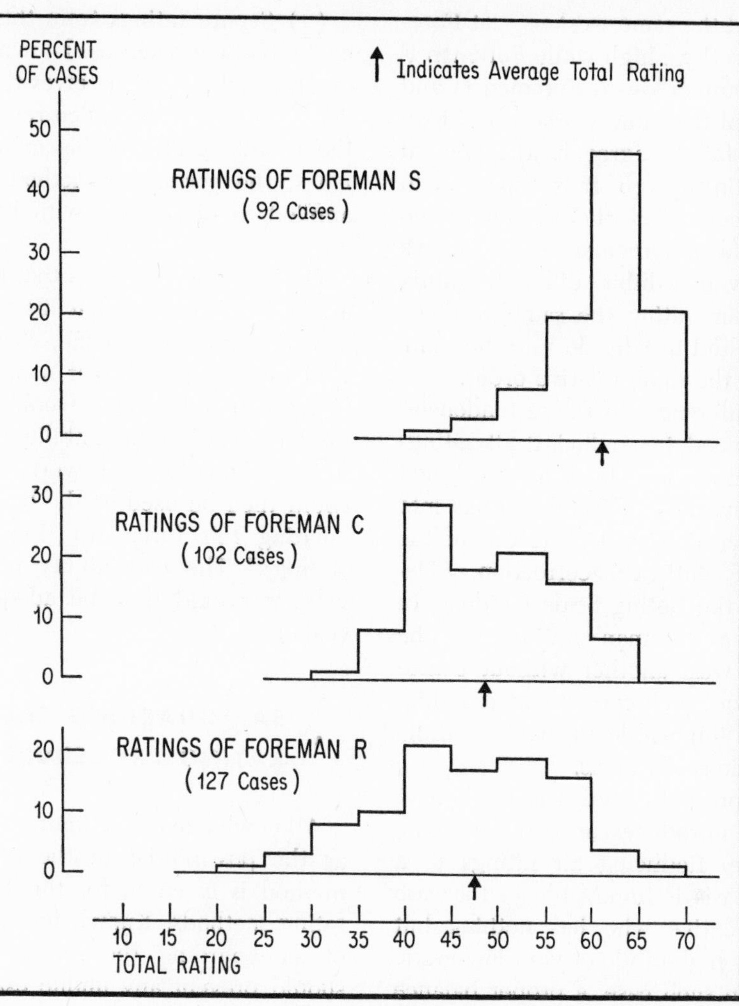

Fig. 6 (Continued).

steps occurs, a conference should be held with the disagreeing judges and re-ratings secured.

Differences between Foremen in Rating Tendency

Tendencies on the part of one foreman to rate all of his employees too high and of another to rate all of his employees too low were discovered by studying the rating tendencies of various foremen.

Figure 6 shows the percentage frequency distribution of the Total Ratings given by seven supervisors and foremen. It is apparent that Foremen A and S tend to rate their workers in the extreme upper range of the scale, i.e., for the most part over 55 points. The ratings submitted by Foremen D and R illustrate a tendency to rate in a much lower range of the scale.

These differences are not due to actual differences in the abilities of various groups. For example, Foremen A and F rated the same workers, yet Foreman A rates them high while Foreman F rates them much lower. Foremen H and D also rated the same workers and likewise they fail to agree in the general level of ratings given. It is important to note, however, that there need be no fundamental disagreement between two foremen who exhibit different rating tendencies in rating the same workers. They may and usually do rate the same workers in the same relative order.

These differences in rating tendencies show the need for reducing all ratings to a common basis. This is accomplished by the conversion of Total Ratings into Final Letter Ratings by the use of the method of statistical correction. (Described in the Rating Scale Guide.)[3] In this way one foreman's ratings may be compared wtih another without confusion. Without such corrections, it is difficult if not impossible to make accurate interpretations of ratings.

Unless properly used, the method of correction introduces an error of some importance. Reducing all ratings to a common basis is impossible in the case of an executive who has nothing but either very high-grade or very low-grade workers. In such case, a proper balance is secured by asking him to rate selected persons other than those in his department.

Experience has shown that the chance of a superior having as many as 40 men of exceptional ability is rather remote. However, if the condition is suspected, it should be investigated. If it is believed that any foreman is rating all of his workers high because of a real superiority of his workers, the procedure is as follows:

[3] Rating Scale Guide, op. cit.

(a) Secure ratings from this foreman on individuals who are known to be of mediocre ability. If he gives these mediocre individuals ratings corresponding to the middle group of his own subordinates, the correction method could be applied to his ratings with little or no error.

(b) In case it appears that his ratings are due to the fact that his workers as a whole are exceptional, it would be well to prepare a list of names for this foreman to rate which would include a random distribution in ability of workers in the same kind of work. This data could then be used as the basis for calculating this foreman's "Key to Final Ratings." The true ability of his own workers would then be adequately revealed.

• SAFEGUARDING THE RATING PROCEDURE

A knowledge of the limitations as well as the possibilities of the rating scale method is essential for the safe use of rating methods. Knowledge of methods of safeguarding the rating procedure should prevent any undue exaggeration of the value of ratings and should lead to greater care in handling the procedure so that errors in rating may be detected and so that different standards of judgment among the several supervisors may be minimized by adequate statistical treatment.[4]

[4] The writer can cite the costly experience of a very large organization as an example of the necessity for such statistical treatment. This company had built up a large file of ratings on their salesmen who were scattered throughout the United States. The sales manager was preparing to "scrap" all of the results and prepare a new rating scale on the assumption

The ways in which the rating procedure may be reasonably safeguarded are:

1. Rating supervisors should be instructed to follow closely the instructions on the Graphic Rating Sheets in making out their periodic reports.

2. Rating supervisors should clearly understand that reports are to be based on the work employees are actually doing at the time the ratings are made. This is necessary in order that all the ratings may be statements of facts as they are rather than guesses as to the future.

3. The need for reporting the ability of any given employee in comparison with other employees doing the same work should be pointed out to the rating supervisor. It is clear that a typist should not be compared with a messenger.

4. Each rating supervisor should be carefully instructed to report each employee on the basis of the defined qualities or traits. Otherwise some supervisors may report the worker on the basis of his own idea of what the names of the qualities mean to him. If this occurs it is evident that the ratings submitted by different supervisors will not be comparable.

5. It is found that better results are secured when the periodic ratings are scheduled at three-month intervals rather than at monthly intervals. Monthly ratings appear to many supervisors to be unnecessary and are apt to be made with insufficient care.

6. It is necessary to secure two or three independent ratings on each employee in order that any inaccurate ratings may be detected. Such inaccurate ratings will be made if any of the supervisors are lacking in a knowledge of an employee's real ability. When such inaccurate ratings are detected, it is well to have a conference of the three supervisors in order that the supervisor whose knowledge of the employee is limited may arrive at a better understanding and knowledge of that employee.

7. In securing three independent ratings on each employee the Personnel Department is in a position to detect any radical disagreements that may be due to bias or prejudice on the part of a supervisor. As in 6, it is well to have a conference of the three supervisors when such radical disagreements are found. Sometimes a supervisor unconsciously permits some trifling incident with an employee to influence his report. A conference will lead to a more definite understanding and greater agreement as to the real merits of the employee.

8. Consultations should be held with supervisors who tend to rate all their employees the same. It is only necessary to point out to such supervisors the differences between the distribution of the ratings they have given and the distributions of the ratings given by other supervisors. Such consultations should lead to a wider recognition of the real individual differences that exist among employees.

---

that the particular rating scale in use was responsible for the worthlessness of the ratings that had been accumulated at great expense. When asked what was wrong, he said that they could not safely use the ratings for they knew that all of their salesmen in Atlanta, Georgia, could not be poorer than all of their salesmen in St. Louis yet that was what the ratings revealed. He had failed to see that the error was due to a serious difference in the rating standards of his sales manager in Atlanta and his sales manager in St. Louis. It was obvious that a statistical method that would reduce the rating standards of the Atlanta and St. Louis managers to a common basis would have done much to increase the accuracy and usableness of these ratings filed in the central office at headquarters.

9. Careful statistical treatment of the ratings of each supervisor is necessary in order to correct any tendency to rate too high or rate too low. Frequently one supervisor will judge his employees too leniently, thus giving all of them very high ratings while another supervisor will judge his employees too severely, thus giving all of them very low ratings.

10. In addition to the statistical treatment that corrects these tendencies, consultations should be held with supervisors who tend to rate too high or rate too low. This tendency can be pointed out to them by reference to the distribution of their ratings in comparison with the distribution of the ratings of other supervisors.

THE USEFULNESS AND • PRACTICABILITY OF THE GRAPHIC RATING SCALE

The attitude of foremen and of workers toward the Graphic Rating Method is of considerable significance. Shop executives who have used the Graphic Rating Method have manifested a marked interest in the method and have given their hearty coöperation in preparing their rating reports. The statement of the purposes of the ratings is generally sufficient to arouse a foreman's interest in the possibilities of the rating method. Actual use of the scale, together with a knowledge of his rating tendency, his agreement with another foreman, etc., then brings the foreman to realize the importance of the information the Rating Method has made possible. No cases of objection to the method on the part of superiors or subordinates have come to our attention.

The following experiences are illustrative:

1. A section head states that the rating scale made him give greater consideration to his workers as individuals in the assignment of work. This section head also attributes part of his own progress during the past year to improvement of his weak points as revealed by a use of the rating scale on himself.

2. One foreman who was not friendly to the rating scale when it was first introduced, voluntarily remarked at the end of three months that the scale had been useful in bringing the merits of his workers to the attention of the higher executives.

3. One executive states that the Graphic Rating Method has greatly assisted him in adjusting the wages of certain dissatisfied workers. This executive emphasizes the confidence he felt in making these wage adjustments in contrast with his feeling under similar circumstances when Graphic Ratings, Trade Test Ratings, etc., were not available.

Less tangible evidence is available concerning the attitude of workers toward the Graphic Rating Method. A number of the workers voluntarily expressed their approval of the idea following the first periodic rating. One of these workers said that he wished he had known a year in advance just what qualities his supervisors considered to be important. He felt that he could have improved himself in those qualities he felt himself weakest in.

MERIT RATING CRITICIZED*

Thomas Arthur Ryan

Current books and periodicals devoted to personnel management techniques commonly present a strong case for the use of some form of graphic rating scale for progress or proficiency ratings, usually a standardized form which permits a total numerical evaluation of each worker. While the aims and advantages claimed for these rating techniques are highly laudable, the present writer sees little evidence that these aims are approached or that the supposed advantages really appear. In fact there are certain basic difficulties with these methods which indicate a need for intensive effort to discover new and quite different approaches, or, at least, drastic modifications in the way in which these ratings are employed in current practice.

• TAKEN ON FAITH

Few would question the importance of keeping track of the development and potentialities of workers for purposes of promotion, establishing differential pay rates based upon merit rather than upon seniority alone, or evaluating employment practices by checking upon the performance of men hired by these methods. The question to be raised is whether the methods now in use have any reasonable degree of demonstrated accuracy for these purposes.

We are asked to accept the rating scale technique largely on faith, since there is no way of testing its validity directly. The rating scale is ordinarily used in situations where there is no other way of obtaining an estimate of the worker's characteristics except, possibly, for records of his production. It is apparently believed necessary to know more than the productivity of the worker, else the rating scale would not be proposed. As a result of the impossibility of direct validation, we are told what the rating scale is *expected* to do or what it *ought* to do, with little or no support for these claims.

• SUPPOSED ADVANTAGES

In the following discussion we shall consider these supposed advantages of the graphic rating scale in some detail. We shall try to show that these claims are by no means easily acceptable; in fact, that some of them are logically contradictory. Throughout this discussion we shall assume that the merit rating system is satisfactorily administered, with proper instruction and training for the raters. The difficulties we shall discuss are inherent in the technique itself, even when it is administered under the best possible conditions. How often these conditions are met is another question, although some may admit that these rating scales are only too seldom used according to the plans of those who designed them.

Although it is not always explicitly stated, the graphic rating form in so frequent use apparently aims to secure

* From *Personnel Journal,* Vol. 24, no. 1, May 1945, pp. 6–15. Copyright 1945 by Personnel Journal. Reprinted by permission.

several advantages over unsystematized procedures which have been prevalent in the past and continue to be common. These expected advantages might be listed as follows:

These Advantages Listed

One. Requiring the rater to consider a number of different traits or aspects of the man rather than a single total evaluation without any explicit analysis.

Two. Defining these traits for the rater so that there is less likely to be disagreement upon the meaning of terms.

Three. Emphasizing that individual differences involve a number of levels along a continuous scale of each quality. Thus it prevents such vague terms as "dependable," "skillful," "honest," being applied to a worker, and requires instead an estimate of the *degree* of dependability, skill, or honesty possessed by the individual.

Four. By giving examples or definitions it is hoped that the raters will agree not only upon the general meaning of the trait under consideration, but that they will also be able to use a common standard for determining the various levels of the trait. If this purpose is attained, "average skill" would mean about the same thing to various supervisors. (Not all graphic rating forms make the attempt to define levels of a trait, and some even fail to define the traits themselves. We are considering here the more carefully worked-out rating techniques, and all of the possible advantages which might accrue through the use of all known precautions in composing the form. There are methods for "correcting" for errors due to failure to secure common standards of raters. These will be discussed later.)

Five. By deciding upon the relative importance of the various traits considered in the rating, and by assigning point values to each level of each trait, it is possible to produce a total score which would represent the over-all value of a particular employee and would provide ready comparison with other employees.

• INCOMPATIBILITIES

It is not usually recognized that the first and last of these expectations are incompatible with one another. If we are successful in getting the rater to consider a number of distinct traits and phases of the worker, there are several difficulties and a definite fallacy involved in applying a total numerical score to the result. The fallacy consists in the assumption that it is possible to substitute one trait for another. The use of a total numerical score means that the worker who is weak in skill can make up for that failing by getting an especially high rating in such a trait as dependability. Perhaps such compensation is possible within limits, but in cases where there is considerable divergence between the traits of a given individual his total numerical score may not represent at all his relative value to the company. In the above example we shall for simplicity suppose that three men are each rated on three traits. They all receive equivalent total scores but one would scarcely say that they are equivalent for purposes of transfer, promotion, or even for establishing relative pay.

H. M. Johnson has pointed out this fallacy in connection with aptitude test-batteries which take into account several

Table 1

Hypothetical Ratings of Three Workers with Equivalent Total Scores

TRAIT	POINT VALUES[a] OF RATINGS FOR		
	WORKER A	WORKER B	WORKER C
Skill	10	5	5
Cooperativeness	5	10	5
Capacity for future development	0	0	5
Total	15	15	15

[a] It is assumed that all three-traits are of equal importance (*i.e.,* each is allotted the same number of points).

distinct aptitudes (1). As an example, he describes the score which he might receive as an operatic tenor, based upon several component abilities. It is possible, he says, that his score for aptitude in this profession might be fairly good in spite of the fact that he is totally unable to produce a high note, and would therefore never have any chance of succeeding as a tenor.

Johnson's discussion was written primarily for psychologists. The point has received little consideration in discussions of merit rating which are aimed at the practical administrator, in spite of the probability that the fallacy is even more important in ratings than it is in the field of aptitude testing. In rating we are not even limiting ourselves to aptitudes but are considering all phases of the man, including a variety of traits which come under the broad heading of personality and character.

• WEIGHING OF TRAITS

Of course, there are some arguments which could be advanced to justify the procedure of totalling points or scores based upon several distinct aptitudes or even several disparate traits like those included in a merit rating form. First, it might be asserted that if a particular trait is so important that the worker is no good without a high rating in that trait, the trait will be weighted in proportion to its importance. Thus Johnson would not be able to get an extremely high score as an opera singer because ability to produce a high tone would be weighted very heavily in the total score.

Unfortunately, there may be a number of traits, all equally important, and such that a low rating would indicate almost certain failure on the job. No system of additive point scores could take this situation into account. When we are dealing with aptitude tests, the process of validation would be such that these possibilities would be examined. If there were minimum requirements on each trait, these could be established through an examination of the validation data which would be secured in developing the test. It would be possible to discover *critical scores* which would be taken into account before any composite score is determined. These critical scores would appear in the correlation tables which are used in analyzing the validation data. If an addition procedure is finally adopted for combining the test scores, it can be based upon observed correlations with job performance, and the weighting based upon the closeness of relation between test performance and job performance. If the additive procedure is successful, it must mean that some degree of substitution of traits is possible—that the worker can make up for his deficiencies in one aptitude by having an extra amount of another.

• OPINIONS CANNOT BE VALIDATED

These devices for overcoming the difficulty do not exist when we are dealing with merit rating. There is no way of weighting the various traits according to their importance, except by taking the consensus of opinion of those engaged in developing the rating scale. There is no way of validating these weights by a comparison with some independent measure as there is when aptitude tests are properly validated. Since there is no independent measure of the value of the worker, there is no way of determining whether a low rating on a given trait is indicative of certain failure in the job or in jobs to which the man might be promoted.

Thus, when we are discussing merit rating, it may be claimed that the system of weights attached to the various traits takes their relative importance into account. It may also be claimed that a worker can compensate to a certain extent for deficiencies in one trait by his higher degrees of other traits. These are only claims, however, unsubstantiated by any concrete evidence. In fact, it is not possible to test these claims by any means known to the writer.

• HALO EFFECT

The logical difficulty which has been discussed here at some length seems to be the most fundamental difficulty with merit systems based upon a point system. If the first four of the advantages we have listed as possible attainments of a carefully designed rating procedure are secured in any degree, we should abandon the attempt to summarize the results in a numerical form. The only case in which the numerical summary could be justified would be that in which the raters do not actually rate distinct traits. Discussions of the "halo effect" have pointed out the tendency of raters to rate men similarly on all traits. If the halo effect is extremely strong, we might find that the rater does not really rate distinct traits at all. His separate ratings may be no more than repeated ratings of the worker on a single scale—a scale of the supervisor's belief concerning the worker's value to the organization.

If this were the situation, a numerical total score might be justified as being somewhat more reliable than the individual ratings. The advantage would be so doubtful, however, that we should seriously question the value of the rating technique. We lose most of the advantages which might be expected of the graphic rating method if the halo effect is strong, and it no longer has much usefulness. Would it not be better to ask the supervisor to make a single careful rating of the over-all value of the man and let it go at that?

Ewart, Seashore, and Tiffin, in an analysis of a large number of ratings made in one industrial concern, found that there was a very strong halo effect

(2). It was so strong that ratings on one trait correlated with ratings on others to the extent of about .70, on the average. He suggests, however, that the result does not necessarily hold if the raters are given better training on the use of rating forms (3).

• TOTAL POINT SCORE UNJUSTIFIED

Thus we are faced with two possibilities. If the halo effect is as strong as Tiffin found it to be in his statistical study, few of the advantages which are claimed for graphic ratings are left. In such a case no elaborate rating system is justified. If, on the other hand, the halo effect is only moderate in size, as it may be under careful training of raters, we may secure the advantages of a more complete analysis of the individual and possibly some of the other benefits listed above under headings One–Four. We cannot in this case, however, justify the use of the total point score to summarize the results.

If the reader is still inclined to believe that substitution of traits is justified as a working hypothesis, in spite of the preceding discussion, we should like to point out other difficulties that still appear after this assumption is made. Another aim of the graphic rating method is to help the raters to adopt common standards of judgment. If this were fully successful, a man in one department who is rated at the "average" level in a certain trait would be equivalent to a man in another department rated at the same level. Students of the rating data do not believe, however, that this condition is met in practice, since they usually provide methods of "correcting" for the raters' differences in standards.

• NO ONE KNOWS THE FACTS

We shall not discuss the details of these techniques of correcting for constant errors of the rater in this paper. They may be found in numerous presentations of rating methods (4). These methods, regardless of their details, all have a common basis. If one rater differs from another in the average ratings for all men in the department, it is assumed that this difference *must be* an error due to differences in standard between the supervisors. Before men from the two departments are compared, their ratings must be corrected for this constant difference between the raters. To put it another way, these methods assume that if the raters differ it must be due to a difference in leniency or kindheartedness. The possibility that the men in one department are actually better than those in the second department is not taken into account.

It is equally unjustified to make the opposite assumption that the difference of raters is due to a real difference in the quality of their men. No one knows which is the case, and the facts, if they could be found, would probably indicate that part of the difference is due to difference in leniency of the raters, and part is due to real differences between men in the two departments. Either the "corrected" or the "uncorrected" ratings, or both, may be in error by unknown amounts. What we have said here concerning differences in average scores is equally true of differences between raters in the *spread* of their ratings—another difference which is usually taken into account in "correcting" the ratings.

Thus, even if we are willing to make the assumptions necessary for using point scores for rating, there is little chance that we could compare ratings which are given by different supervisors with any degree of confidence. It is even questionable whether men rated by the same supervisor could be accurately compared if they happened to be working upon different jobs. The same rater's leniency may vary with the type of work and we should be faced with the same dilemma we met in comparing results of different raters.

• RELIABILITY LOW

So far we have said nothing of the problem of reliability of the ratings. The direct study of the repeated ratings of a supervisor shows that they often have poor consistency, and the correlations between successive ratings by the same rater are moderate at best. As Tiffin points out, the reliabilities are such that a point system of rating based upon a range of four or five hundred points is absurd because differences in the last place and even in the tens place are likely to be the result of chance variations rather than real variations between the persons rated. This difficulty with reliability could be overcome by using only five to seven rough groupings for the total score rather than attempting to use a finer scale, and it might also be improved by better training of the raters. Improving the reliability of the ratings would not, however, overcome the objections to a point system which we have discussed in preceding paragraphs.

What is the solution of this problem? As we indicated at the beginning, there is a real need for intensive search for other modes of approach to the problem of evaluating employees. So far these other methods are not available. Until they are, however, the writer believes that little is accomplished by elaborating and complicating the rating methods. Instead, he would recommend proceeding on a much simpler common-sense basis. The following suggestion is presented as one possible way out, not as a final solution of the problem.

• THREE LEVELS SUGGESTED

For the lack of any better and more reasonable suggestion, we could assume that experienced supervisors ought to be able to distinguish on an *absolute* basis three levels of over-all value of men in their departments. If the men are engaged in quite distinct types of work, they would have to be divided according to occupation and rated separately and with reference to that occupation. In addition it seems reasonable that they should detect extreme degrees of certain specialized traits even though they do exhibit the halo effect and unreliability when they are asked to rate all men in the department on each trait.

The result of these suggestions would be a form like Figure 1 with certain changes dictated by the industry or the occupations involved in a particular application. The form which is reproduced in Figure 1 is not meant as a final version, and revisions of the instructions are probably necessary for use in any specific organization. The general approach is the thing which we are mainly

Inventory of Personnel

Department........................ (This should be a single job or group of similar, related
Jobs................................ jobs. Jobs requiring unrelated skills or training should be considered independently.)

1. *Outstanding men:* List names of the men who are doing an exceptionally good job, and whose all-round value to the department is very high. Consider their present ability and skill, not what you think they might develop later. Men placed in this group should be in about the top ten per cent of men in this line of work *anywhere,* not only in this shop. If you are doubtful about any man's belonging in this group, *do not include him.* List these men in order from top down, if that is possible.
2. *Poor workers:* List the names of all men who are doing an exceptionally poor job, and whose all-round value to the department is very low. Consider present ability and skill, but do not include those who are poor because they do not have sufficient training or experience. These will be listed separately. As in the top group, if you are doubtful about a man belonging in this group, do not include him. The men in this group should be those who would be considered as about the bottom ten per cent of men in this occupation *anywhere,* but they may include more or less than ten per cent of your own men.
3. *Average workers:* List all men who have not been included in the first two groups except those who are not fully trained or who lack experience. As you list them consider each one to make sure that he does not belong either in Group 1 (exceptional men) or Group 2 (poor workers).
4. *Trainees and inexperienced workers:* Include here all those who have not finished the normal training period or who have not worked long enough to show what they can do. Mark those who show promise with a *G* and those who do not appear to make normal progress with *P.*

Special Qualifications and Abilities

Listed at the left are a number of special characteristics which may be important considerations in promotions or transfers. List, for each of these qualifications, the names of those men in the job you are considering who are outstanding in this quality, and those who are especially poor in this respect. The names listed are not necessarily the same names you have given in your over-all estimates of the value of the employee on page 1.

QUALITY[a]	OUTSTANDING MEN	POOR WORKERS
1. Dependability (Does he follow instructions without close follow-up?)........		
2. Ability to get along with others (Is he respected and trusted by fellow workers?)........		
3. Specialized technical knowledge of the job....		
4. Ability to instruct others in his job........		
5. Interest in his work and in the department...		

[a] Other traits to be added to meet the needs of a particular organization. Instructions to be revised after conferences with supervisors and experience in application of the forms.

Fig. 1. Suggested form of employee appraisal.

interested in presenting at this time. It should be emphasized that this proposed form does not include anything radically new. In fact, it is basically a return to procedures of evaluation which are older and simpler than current rating techniques. It is an attempt to secure some of the advantages of a standardized rating technique without depending so heavily upon the assumptions required for the graphic scale-point method of evaluation.

• INVENTORY OF PERSONNEL

The writer believes that this "Inventory of Personnel," while it still has flaws which cannot be entirely eliminated, is more defensible than the graphic rating scale. It obtains an over-all estimate of the value of men in a job from the supervisor, which, in view of the halo effect, is all we can confidently expect of the graphic rating technique. It requires the supervisor to make only broad groupings, which, in the light of the known reliabilities of the graphic scale, are the only groupings justified. (If three groups are felt to be too broad, the same technique could be used with four or five categories instead of the three major groups illustrated in Figure 1). The method obtains these broad groupings without resort to dubious point-rating scales.

The method also allows us to obtain useful information upon special traits without forcing the supervisor to rate all workers on each trait. He can thus designate those who show noticeable excellence or deficiency without being asked to make ratings on these traits where no information is available.

• PAPER WORK REDUCED

Last, but by no means least, this procedure should reduce the amount of "paper work." While the supervisor has to write names instead of check marks, he is not overwhelmed with a rating form for each man. One form can serve for all the men on a job or a related group of jobs, so long as sufficient space is provided for listing the names. At the same time, the supervisor is required to consider each man because the form requires that each man must be listed somewhere.

Obviously, the inventory method here described cannot fit all requirements any more than any other single procedure can. It is felt, however, that it has advantages, both logical and practical, over the graphic rating method for a great many of the purposes for which the graphic method has been employed.

• USE OF EVALUATORS

If it is still felt that the graphic form of recording supervisor's judgments is desirable, some of its difficulties could be avoided by other methods of handling the information they contain. The rating forms might be sorted by inspection into three or four categories. With some training for those who do the sorting, it is possible that the method could be made quite reliable, and it would not be necessary to make the assumptions required by a point system of evaluation. The evaluators could take into account both the average level of the ratings for a given individual and any marked deficiencies on single traits. In this way a rough qualitative analysis of the forms might produce a more adequate evaluation than would be possible by the point system.

Even this procedure would not, however, settle the question of whether to "correct" for the rater's tendencies to rate higher or lower than normal. That problem can never be settled until there is some more objective criterion against which the ratings may be checked. If we had such a criterion, the ratings would no longer be necessary.

• SUMMARY

This article has supported the thesis that the graphic rating scale with numerical scoring has serious logical difficulties and practical inadequacies. These flaws are so serious that they more than offset any advantages which are claimed for these rating techniques, especially since there is little more than common-sense argument to support these claims.

There is a serious need for research to develop new and fundamentally different methods of evaluating workers for promotion, transfer, or validation of employment techniques. Until this development is carried out, the writer has proposed to return to simpler procedures which require fewer doubtful assumptions. This simpler approach was illustrated by a suggested form for recording information in an "Inventory of Personnel." Such an inventory is aimed at securing some of the advantages of currently popular rating techniques while making the task of the rater as simple as possible, and making fewer baseless assumptions.

REFERENCES

1. H. M. Johnson, Some neglected principles of aptitude testing, *Amer. J. Psychol.*, 1935, 47, 159–165.
2. E. Ewart, S. E. Seashore, and J. Tiffin, A factor analysis of an industrial merit rating scale. *J. Applied Psychol.* 25, 1941, 481–486.
3. J. Tiffin, *Industrial Psychology*, New York, 1942, p. 245.
4. J. P. Guilford, *Psychometric Methods*, New York, 1936, p. 274.

RELATION OF FORMAT AND ADMINISTRATION TO THE CHARACTERISTICS OF GRAPHIC RATING SCALES*

Erwin K. Taylor and Roy Hastman

• INTRODUCTION

The evaluation of the performance of individuals in their occupational activities has been a perennial problem for both military and civilian management. Formal rating programs for a variety of purposes have been instituted with enthusiasm and discarded with disgust in a wide variety of situations. Managerial as well as technical publications abound with articles, some praising and some criticizing merit rating in general or some scheme in particular. Self-styled experts, particularly among management personnel, abound. The authors of "cookbook" publications frequently promulgate rules for the establishment of merit rating systems on the basis of the results of a number of separate studies conducted under widely varying situations. Guilford (*2*), for example, lists 16 "rules for the construction of graphic scales." His first rule is: "1. Each trait should occupy a page by itself. This rule is rarely observed. When a number of individuals are to be rated, it is far better that all of them be rated in one trait before going on to the next." No evidence in justification of this "rule" is given. It may be assumed, although Guilford makes no reference to it, that he was familiar with the work of Stevens and Wonderlic (*3*), which incorporated this practice. While this has become a fairly accepted "principle," no controlled study of its influence on the results of ratings has to our knowledge been conducted. One of the purposes of this study is that of determining empirically in a controlled situation the extent to which the assumption made in this rule is a valid one.

Tiffin (*5*) suggests that those devising rating systems "have ratings made in conference or under supervision." Again, no basis is given for this "rule." A later publication by Taylor and Manson (*4*) provides some evidence to support this position. These studies, like those quoted above, were not conducted under controlled and comparative circumstances; rather, supervised ratings were gathered using the Stevens-Wonderlic techniques on a rather extensive clerical population. The distributions of the ratings were fairly symmetrical, the means not too high, the intercorrelations moderate, and alternate rater reliability satisfactory. Whether or not a traditional graphic form, unsupervised, would have yielded similar results is, of course, not known.

NOTE. This research was carried out under Contract No. NONR 1439 (03) between Western Reserve University and the Office of Naval Research.

* From *Personnel Psychology*, Vol. 9, no. 2, Summer 1956, pp. 181–206.

It is the second purpose of this study to determine whether or not the claims made for supervised ratings are justified.

• BASIC DESIGN

It was hypothesized 1) that the results of ratings obtained under the Stevens-Wonderlic format with respect to certain criteria of rating excellence (see p. 172) would be sufficiently greater than those obtained using the traditional graphic format to justify the increased cost and more elaborate procedure demanded by the former and 2) that on the basis of these same criteria sufficient improvement would ensue from the use of a qualified technician individually to administer the ratings to justify the increased cost of this procedure over that of having the technician supervise the ratings of a number of raters in a single session; and that this, in turn, would be superior to the use of the Stevens-Wonderlic format without supervision of the ratings by a psychologically trained technician.

A series of graphic rating scales appropriate to the positions under consideration was to be constructed. These scales were to be used without change in both formats and all administrations.

1. In Group 1 the traditional graphic method was to be employed. All of the scales to be used would be printed on a single sheet of paper. There would be a separate rating sheet for each ratee. The supervisor would complete his evaluation of the first individual before proceeding with the evaluation of the next, and so on. A rating manual would be prepared and after group orientation of the raters, manuals and forms would be distributed. Without further instruction or contact by the project personnel, Group 1 supervisors would return to their customary work space and perform their evaluations without assistance. When they had completed the task, they were to return their ratings to a central point.

2. Group 2 raters would follow the same administrative conditions as was followed by Group 1. Instead of using the traditional graphic rating format, however, the identical series of scales would be assembled in such a manner that the supervisors would rate all of the individuals in their respective groups on the first trait before rating any of them on the next trait. The administrative manual for these people would be the same in all respects as that for Group 1, with the exception of such differences as were required by the rating format.

3. Group 3 (group administered Stevens-Wonderlic) used the same rating scale format as Group 2 but instead of returning to their customary work places to fill out the forms without assistance after orientation, they would be scheduled to meet in groups of not less than four nor more than ten, with a trained personnel technician who would discuss with the group the problems and pitfalls of graphic rating, stimulate participation in a discussion, answer questions, etc. He would then begin the rating session by reading the definition and the steps of Scale 1 aloud while the raters read silently. He would answer any questions with respect to the trait definition or with respect to any of the steps it incorporated. He would then instruct the raters to select in each instance the best person with respect to that scale and to place him appropriately thereon. When all had accom-

plished this, he would instruct them to select the poorest person and rate him appropriately. He would alternate high and low until all of the raters had rated all of their people on the first scale. The process would be repeated for Scale 2 and for subsequent scales until the evaluations were completed.

4. This group (supervised Stevens-Wonderlic) differed from Group 3 only to the extent that project technicians would visit individually with each of the raters after the orientation sessions, and remain with him while the evaluations were performed. The approach to be employed would be the same as with Group 3, except that the ratings would be performed during private rating sessions with each supervisor, and more opportunity would be afforded for individual guidance and discussion than would be the case with Group 3.

Hypothesis 1, with respect to the influence of format upon the characteristics of the rating, would be tested by comparisons between Groups 1 and 2 for the various criteria to be set forth below. Hypothesis 2 would be tested by comparisons among Groups 2, 3, and 4 for the several criteria.

• CRITERIA OF RATING EXCELLENCE

Merit ratings, regardless of the use to which the end products are to be put, are performed for the purpose of evaluating behavior along certain stipulated continua. Like all other measuring devices, ratings are of necessity imperfect. That is, even when corrected for attenuation, they would not correlate unity with perfect criteria of whatever it was that the scales were to measure. The most important criterion of the format or administration of a rating scale would thus be its validity. But ratings are themselves frequently the criterion against which predictors are validated. To validate the ratings would require the construction of a more ultimate criterion. If such an ultimate criterion could be quickly and economically constructed, there would, of course, be no justification for the use of more remote measures of performance such as ratings. It would be desirable for research purposes to develop a costly and elaborate performance evaluation measure and to use it as a basis for determining which of the several more feasible performance evaluation procedures correlated most highly with the ultimate criterion, and thus should be employed for operating purposes. While it was hoped that some such procedure might be incorporated in this study, it was necessary to abandon plans to validate format and administrative procedure for several reasons. These were:

1. The resources of the study were not adequate enough to undertake the elaborate criterion research that would have been necessary for the development of an ultimate criterion.
2. The heterogeneity of assignments in the population precluded the construction of a relatively simple objective criterion.
3. Production records were not available nor was the time to construct, standardize, and collect them.

The concept, therefore, of the direct comparison of the validity of the four systems was abandoned in favor of inferring the relative merits of each by comparisons within a series of what we might call "secondary criteria of rating system qualities." These are:

1. Reliability

Graphic ratings have not infrequently been criticized because of the failure of two raters evaluating the same group of subordinates to agree with respect to their evaluations. In an ideal rating situation, the rating received by an individual should be independent of its source. That is, a given individual should receive the same rating regardless of who renders it. Ideally, of course, to test this, all of the raters for a given individual should bear identical relationships to him. Where superior ratings are employed, it is rarely possible to find two individuals who 1) have ample opportunity to observe the work performance of the ratee and 2) bear the same relationship to him.

As the closest feasible approximation to this situation, the usual practice of taking the first and second levels of supervision was followed in this study. Two unavoidable deficiencies may be noted in this practice: 1) First-line supervisors in most cases have a much closer relationship with and more opportunity to observe the ratees than do second-line supervisors, and 2) where this is the case, much of the variation introduced into the ratings by the second-line supervisor may be a function of reputation bias. That is, the second-line supervisor bases his ratings not upon direct observation of the performance of the individual being rated, but rather upon information transmitted to him previously by the first-line supervisor.

The first of these two factors would operate to reduce the between-rater correlations from what might be expected if both had an equal and adequate opportunity for firsthand observation in identical situations. The second factor would work in the opposite direction, resulting in spuriously high inter-rater reliabilities. Since the four rater groups were to be selected at random, it could be assumed that both inadequacy of opportunity to observe and reputation bias would vary from group to group only by chance. Thus, differences in inter-rater reliability, if found, could be assumed to be attributable to differences in format or administrative procedure.

2. Halo

Probably the most common criticism of graphic rating has been the oft-noted tendency of presumably independent scales to correlate extremely high with each other. In factor analyses of graphic ratings [*e.g.*, Ewart, Seashore, and Tiffin (6)] and the extensive studies conducted by the Adjutant General's Office, multiple scale ratings have always boiled down to two or three orthogonal factors. This has seriously raised questions with respect to the ability of raters to discriminate between performance in various behavior areas. To the extent that the several independent aspects of behavior being measured in a rating scale are not influenced by each other or by an over-all impression or bias that the rater may have for the ratee, the greater validity of the scale may be inferred.

In the present study the matrix of trait intercorrelations will be obtained for each group and the relationship between equivalent pairs of correlation coefficients will be studied.

3. Variability

There is a tendency in graphic ratings for raters to employ only a portion (usually the upper) of the rating scale. While objective measures of work performance indicate the existence of a wide range of productivity, graphic ratings are usually much more restricted in their range. Raters seem reluctant to use extreme categories, particularly the low extreme. Consequently, a large portion of those being rated fall into a small number of rating categories, thus precluding optimum use of the rating scale as either a criterion for validating predictors or as a basis for personnel action.

Two statistics will be employed to explore in this realm. First, comparisons will be made of the standard deviations of equivalent sets of scales across the four conditions to provide a comparison of dispersion on an absolute basis. In addition, g_2, a measure of kurtosis [Fisher (*1*)], will be employed to compare the tendency under the several conditions to concentrate cases about the measure of central tendency.

4. Leniency

The tendency of raters to be generous in the evaluation of their subordinates is one that has been frequently noted in the literature by critics of graphic ratings. The extent to which leniency characterizes each of the four experimental conditions of this study will be measured in two ways. The first of these will be on the basis of a comparison of the arithmetic means of the several scales. Second will be through the use of the statistic g_1 [Taylor].

Theoretically, if scales are properly designed, the mean should fall somewhere fairly close to the midpoint of the scale, and the cases should be distributed in a symmetrical manner about the mean. Thus, leniency may express itself in either or both of two ways. First, the mean of the scale may fall at a point considerably higher than mid-range. Here, if only a portion of the scales were being used and the lower interval omitted, the distribution could still be symmetrical. On the other hand, the mean could fall at a point only moderately above mid-range but with a substantially greater proportion of the cases above than below the mean. This would yield a negatively skewed distribution.

• THE POPULATION

Arrangements were made to conduct the study at the U. S. Navy Finance Center located in Cleveland, Ohio. It is the function of this organization to make monetary disbursements on a broad scale to Navy personnel. It is a sizable installation with more than 1300 civilian employees housed, for the most part, in an office building in downtown Cleveland.

Even among so large a clerical and administrative population it was not possible to find an adequate number of people doing the same or closely enough related work to constitute the homogeneous population desired for this study. An analysis of the personnel records of the Center indicated the availability of 712 production personnel who met the requirements for participation as ratees in the research. Analysis of the work performed by these personnel revealed

Table 1

DISTRIBUTION OF JOB FAMILY BY RATING CONDITION

JOB FAMILY	TRAD.	IND.	GRP.	SUPER.	TOTAL
Clerical	80	75	74	92	321
Auditing-accounting	63	68	69	75	275
Machine operator	28	25	33	30	116
Total	171	168	176	197	712

that they could be classified into three work groups:

1) Clerical job family
2) Auditing-accounting job family
3) Machine-operating job family

It was felt that while certain grade differences in work assignments existed within the several job families, these groups were about as homogeneous as we could expect to find in an operating situation. Instead, then, of randomizing the entire population for distribution among the four experimental conditions, randomization was accomplished within each of the job families. Randomization was not conducted on the basis of ratees, but rather on the basis of second-line supervisors. This course was taken to insure that no rater at either level would be required to use more than one of the four systems and that for each second-line supervisor, all of the first-line supervisors, rating the same people as he, would use the same format and administrative condition. Had this not been done, a comparison of reliabilities would have been impossible.

It had originally been planned to use 889 cases, and stratification was predicated on this basis, with an almost equal number from each job category in each of the four rating conditions. Illness, absence, transfer, and resignations reduced this to the 712 cases actually used. Their distribution across the four conditions by the three job categories are presented in Table 1.

There were 54 cases in which it was not possible to secure ratings from the second level of supervision, and 33 cases in which it was possible to secure ratings only from the second level of supervision. In one group, it was necessary to use a first-level supervisor who had only three ratees instead of the desired four ratees, while in another group, 28 individuals were supervised by one supervisor rather than the maximum of 20 set up in planning the study.

To simplify usage, the second-line supervisor throughout the study has been called "endorser." Actually, however, his ratings were completely independent of those of the first-line supervisor and he did *not* in any case see the ratings of his subordinates before making his own.

• THE SCALES

The situation with respect to rating scales is generally the same as with respect to format and administration, except for the subject of the number of intervals, which has been fairly well explored. Little systematic research concerning rating scale construction has been published. It was decided to construct what we wanted on an *a priori* basis considered to be in keeping with the best scale-construction practice. The following principles were arbitrarily established and followed:

1) All traits would be in job related terms. General characteristics would be avoided.

2) No trait name would be used, but rather we would employ a verbal description of the area of behavior with which the scale was concerned and the intended relationship of such behavior to job success.

It was arbitrarily decided that five points along each continuum would be described and that the area subtended by each description would be divided equally into two, thus yielding a ten-point scale.

The authors met with members of the U. S. Navy Finance Center Personnel Department in a series of conferences during which they studied and discussed the various jobs of the people to be evaluated. As a result of these discussions, eight scales were prepared and approved. The scales used in the Stevens-Wonderlic format were verbally identical with those used in the traditional format. Each of these scales was printed on a single 11″ by 4¼″ sheet, the cover sheet being the same as in the traditional graphic. On the bottom half of the inside back cover, numbered spaces for the insertions of the names of 24 people to be rated were provided. Where a rater had more than 24 subordinates, the ratees were randomly divided into two or three groups, as the situation required, and the requisite number of forms employed.

The eight scales covered the following areas. (The titles applied to the scale here are purely for expository purposes. They were devised *after* the study had been completed, appeared nowhere on the ratings, and were in no way employed in the study.)

1. *Interpersonal Relations:* The way in which the individual's interactions with other people in his work group influence the productivity of the group.
2. *Amount of Production:* The mere quantity without reference to quality of work produced.
3. *Acceptability of Production:* The evaluation without reference to quantity of the work produced.
4. *Leadership Characteristics:* Ability to direct the work of others and lead a work team without reference to technical skills, knowledge, or experience.
5. *Job Complexity:* The level of complexity which the individual under consideration is capable of managing.
6. *Supervision Required.*
7. *Effort Required:* This scale attempts to measure the difference between the worker's present level of effectiveness and the highest level of which he is capable.
8. *Over-all:* Effectiveness of the individual as a whole, considering factors already rated as well as any other which is relevant.

No attempt is made to justify the selection of these eight particular variables. They are predicated on the assumption that in order to test our hypotheses we would want to include closely job-related variables such as 2 and 3, personal qualities such as 1 and 4, and advancement possibilities such as 5 and 7, as well as generalized variables such as 6 and 8.

While it would have been desirable to have been able to prepare a scale oriented to more specific job duties, the heterogeneity of the ratee population made this unfeasible. The decision to use eight scales was an arbitrary one. These will yield 28 intercorrelations per matrix, an adequate number for the study of halo without placing too much of a burden upon the participating supervisors. On the basis of factor analyses of rating scales referred to above, the ability of raters to make even as many as eight meaningful discriminations is highly questionable. Thus, it is not believed that additional scales would have made any real contribution to the study.

Five rating categories were prepared to represent the steps on the continuum. These, too, were narrative in nature and attempted to describe in behavioral terms the activities of the individual to be properly assigned to that category. The rating categories were created on an *a priori* basis and no effort was made to scale them quantitatively.

• ADMINISTRATION

Conditions of administration were fairly rigidly defined by the experimental conditions. At the very outset of the research, the project director met with all of the supervisors who were to participate in the study. Without giving specific details which might invalidate results, he outlined the general nature and purpose of the research and solicited their cooperation in making it successful. Some of the pitfalls common to graphic ratings were described and the purpose of the study was said to be that of determining which of a variety of rating methods was the most effective. Members of the supervisory staff were invited to ask any questions that they cared to, and these were answered in the session.

Following these initial conferences, no additional contact with the supervisors occurred for a period of several weeks. During this time the project personnel busied themselves with the task of studying the organization's manning tables for the purpose of assigning raters to the various experimental conditions. This entailed careful study of the personnel rosters and job descriptions to assemble groups of four or more working under the same supervisor in homogeneous assignments. During this period the junior author was assigned desk space at the U. S. Navy Finance Center and worked full time in that organization. After assembling the ratee groups tentatively, he again established contact with the supervisors, this time individually by phone to verify the correctness of the personnel rosters and to determine the job tenure of both the ratees and raters. Opportunity to observe and familiarity with individual ratees was particularly stressed with respect to the second level of supervision. A small number of these supervisors were eliminated from the study because of the short or remote relationship of the available rater to the employee. Rating conditions, as has been noted, were assigned on the basis of the second-level supervisor in order to permit the determination of alternate rater reliability within each study. When the assignment of each rater to a particular condition had been completed, raters were again contacted according to the following procedure:

Traditional Graphic Ratings

All of the raters who were to follow this procedure met with a member of the project staff in a group. Since a number of them had not been in attendance at the original orientation session and because of the time that had elapsed since that session, an over-all review and summary was presented. Rating forms and manuals appropriate to the situation were distributed and a final check made on the accuracy and completeness of the rating forms.

Stevens-Wonderlic

The procedure followed for raters in this category was identical with that in the preceding. Only the rating forms themselves and the manual were different. The differences in the manual were confined to the actual rating operation. All other material was the same.

Group Stevens-Wonderlic

Five rating sessions were originally scheduled for supervisors participating in this condition. Since, for one reason or another, not all supervisors were able to attend their scheduled sessions, an extra meeting was held to pick up the stragglers. The scheduling was arranged so that supervisors rating more than one group attended more than one session. Arrangements were made so that different administrators made the presentation to the two levels of supervision. In addition to the general orientation, comments were made regarding the usual rating errors. These instructions paralleled the material covered in the rating manual used by the first two groups. Questions were answered and guidance was given during the session.

Supervised Stevens-Wonderlic

The first- and second-line supervisors who constituted Group 4 were individually contacted by telephone and a definite appointment made to participate in the study. These appointments were scheduled at the raters' convenience. The project technician went to the usual work place of the rater. If this were not too public, ratings were made there. If, however, it proved unsuitable because of the physical environment, the technician suggested that they seek out some more convenient location. The technician, after preliminary rapport-establishing remarks, conversed generally with the rater about the study, ratings in general, and the pitfalls that are common to them. The technician tried to answer any questions that the rater had with respect to ratings and then, when the rater indicated his readiness to proceed, started the actual rating session. Different administrators alternated in supervising the ratings obtained from the raters and endorsers in order to insure that the reliability of this method was not a function of unintentional intervention of the administrator.

• ANALYSIS AND RESULTS

Alternate Rater Reliability

Format. Table 2 compares the alternate rater reliability of the graphic and Stevens-Wonderlic formats. With the exception of Scale 7, as noted before, all are adequate for the purposes for which graphic scales are customarily employed. Three of the seven differences favored the Stevens-Wonderlic, and four favored the traditional graphic. None of the differences is, however, large enough to be of practical value.

Method of Administration. Approximately the same statement can be made with respect to the influence of administration upon reliability. These data are

Table 2

Comparison of Alternate Rater Reliability of Traditional Graphic and Individual Stevens-Wonderlic Rating Format

SCALES	TRAD. GRAPH	IND. STEV-W	STEV-W-TRAD.
1. Interpersonal relations	.55	.55	.00
2. Amount of productivity	.66	.69	.03
3. Accuracy of productivity	.69	.54	−.15
4. Leadership	.57	.48	−.09
5. Job complexity	.63	.59	−.04
6. Supervision required	.58	.65	.07
7. Effort required	.01	.37	
8. Over-all	.64	.65	.01
N	163	128	

presented in Table 3. No clear-cut trends can be recognized. It does seem, however, that the supervised ratings are inclined to be unimportantly lower with respect to reliability than the unsupervised, with the group-administered usually in an intermediate position. This gives rise to the possible inference that the magnitude of the alternate rater reliabilities might possibly be a function, in part at least, of reputation bias which is to some degree overcome in the group-administered and supervised situation. In any event, whether the differences are truly representative of reliability or are to some extent influenced by reputation bias, the results suggest that not enough practical difference exists among the four rating conditions explored in this study to justify the costs of the more expensive ones.

Dispersion

Format. In Table 4 are recorded the standard deviations and measure of kurtosis for the distribution of the eight traits yielded from the traditional graphic and Stevens-Wonderlic formats. For the traditional graphic, the standard deviations ranged from 1.61 to 2.13. For the Stevens-Wonderlic, they ranged from 1.75 to 2.26. With a ten-point range, a standard deviation slightly under 2 is

Table 3

Comparison of the Alternate Rater Reliability of Three Different Administrations of Stevens-Wonderlic Ratings

SCALES	IND.	GROUP	SUPERVISED
1. Interpersonal relations	.55	.41	.48
2. Amount of productivity	.69	.65	.54
3. Accuracy of productivity	.54	.59	.55
4. Leadership	.48	.40	.47
5. Job complexity	.59	.45	.50
6. Supervision required	.65	.59	.47
7. Effort required	.37	.02	.03
8. Over-all	.65	.62	.60
N	128	156	175

Table 4

COMPARISON OF THE STANDARD DEVIATION AND KURTOSIS OF DISTRIBUTIONS YIELDED BY TRADITIONAL GRAPHIC AND STEVENS-WONDERLIC RATING FORMATS

	S.D. (σ)		KURTOSIS (g_2)	
SCALES	TRAD.	S-W	TRAD.	S-W
1. Interpersonal relations	1.80	1.75	−.078	−.484
2. Amount of productivity	1.81	2.10	−.101	−.354
3. Accuracy of productivity	1.64	1.74	.422	.518
4. Leadership	2.11	1.95	−1.000	−.688
5. Job complexity	1.61	1.85	−.563	−.484
6. Supervision required	2.07	2.26	−.989	−.671
7. Effort required	2.13	2.15	−.794	−.877
8. Over-all	1.81	1.83	−.201	.191
N	171	145	171	145
σg_2			.37	.40

about what would be expected from a normally distributed population of the size of these. In no scale is the difference between the two standard deviations of sufficient magnitude to be noteworthy. The Stevens-Wonderlic standard deviations are larger than the traditional graphic standard deviations for five of the seven scales (omitting Scale 7). Again, there is no clear trend and no differences whose magnitude would justify a definitive statement with respect to the superiority of one procedure over the other.

The other statistic in Table 4 shown for each of the scales by administration groups 1 and 2 is g_2, a measure of kurtosis proposed by Fisher (*1*). The noteworthy aspect of this table lies in the fact that all scales except "Quality of Production," (Scale 3), are platykurtic. This phenomenon is rather unusual in graphic rating scales, where it is more usual to find the distributions more

Table 5

COMPARISON OF STANDARD DEVIATION AND KURTOSIS OF DISTRIBUTIONS YIELDED BY THREE DIFFERENT ADMINISTRATIONS OF STEVENS-WONDERLIC FORMAT RATINGS

	S.D.			KURTOSIS		
SCALES	IND.	GRP.	SUPER	IND.	GRP.	SUPER
1. Interpersonal relations	1.75	2.09	1.89	−.484	−.630	−.280
2. Amount of productivity	2.10	2.14	2.26	−.354	−.286	−.814
3. Accuracy of productivity	1.74	1.96	1.75	.518	.047	−.449
4. Leadership	1.95	2.04	1.98	−.688	−.819	−.905
5. Job complexity	1.85	1.89	1.67	−.484	−.146	−.410
6. Supervision required	2.26	2.28	2.23	−.671	−.645	−.787
7. Effort required	2.15	2.48	1.87	−.877	−1.164	−.277
8. Over-all	1.83	2.07	2.08	−.191	−1.62	−.526
N	145	170	193	145	170	193
σg_2	—	—	—	.40	.37	.35

peaked than normal, rather than less peaked. But again, this phenomenon does not appear to be a function of the rating format since it characterized both the traditional graphic and the Stevens-Wonderlic groups.

While the trend toward platykurtosis is definite for both sets of distributions, the magnitude is moderate. Except for Scales 4 and 6 for the graphic format, the null hypothesis with respect to kurtosis cannot be rejected at the one per cent level. The writers infer from these data (tests of significance to the contrary notwithstanding) that the parametric value of these statistics is somewhat less than zero—that, in other words, the distributions are truly but not importantly platykurtic.

METHOD OF ADMINISTRATION. Table 5 presents the standard deviation and kurtosis (g_2) for Groups 2, 3, and 4. Precisely the same comments that were made with respect to format obtain in relation to type of administration. The standard deviations range around 2.00. None of the distributions demonstrates a substantially greater variance than does the other. The distributions with minor exceptions are platykurtic but not extremely so. For all practical purposes, at least insofar as these scales are concerned, dispersion and kurtosis are unrelated to either format or administration.

Halo

FORMAT. The matrices of rating scale intercorrelations for the traditional graphic and individual Stevens-Wonderlic are presented in Table 6. Ignoring as we have been the correlation of unreliable Scale 7 with the others, the average correlation on z transformations is .60 for the traditional and .57 for the Stevens-Wonderlic. The average Fisher z's are .69 and .64, respectively. The standard error of the difference between these mean z's is .04. The probability that the parametric value of this difference is zero or negative is .12. There is an equal probability, of course, that the

Table 6

COMPARISON OF RATING SCALE INTERCORRELATIONS BETWEEN TRADITIONAL GRAPHIC AND STEVENS-WONDERLIC FORMAT RATINGS

CORREL. BETWEEN SCALES NUMBER	TRAD. GRAPH	STEV-WOND.	TRAD.-STEV-W.
1 and 2	.31	.36	–.05
1 and 3	.53	.48	.05
1 and 4	.45	.52	–.07
1 and 5	.36	.32	.04
1 and 6	.43	.45	–.02
1 and 7	.06	.12	
1 and 8	.53	.51	.02
2 and 3	.62	.57	.05
2 and 4	.44	.33	.11
2 and 5	.48	.46	.02
2 and 6	.53	.52	.01
2 and 7	.05	.13	
2 and 8	.76	.64	.12
3 and 4	.58	.42	.16
3 and 5	.66	.59	.07
3 and 6	.70	.72	–.02
3 and 7	.20	.10	
3 and 8	.78	.85	–.07
4 and 5	.65	.60	.05
4 and 6	.58	.46	.12
4 and 7	.27	.29	
4 and 8	.65	.49	.16
5 and 6	.75	.69	.06
5 and 7	.42	.37	
5 and 8	.69	.68	.01
6 and 7	.24	.26	
6 and 8	.75	.78	–.03
7 and 8	.15	.24	
$\bar{r}_z$	.60	.57	
$\bar{Z}$	.69	.64	

difference between the mean *z*'s is .10 or higher.

In 15 of the 61 possible comparisons between matched pairs of correlations, the value for the traditional graphic is higher than that for the Stevens-Wonderlic. These positive differences range from .01 to .16. Again, the Stevens-Wonderlic format does not demonstrate any marked superiority over the traditional graphic format.

Method of Administration. Statistics relevant to this point are presented in Table 7. The group-administered Stevens-Wonderlic shows the highest mean intercorrelation. The biggest difference is between the supervised Stevens-Wonderlic and the group-administered

Table 7

Comparison of Rating Scale Intercorrelations among Three Different Administrations of Stevens-Wonderlic Rating Format

CORREL. BETWEEN SCALE NUMBERS	IND.	GRP.	SUPER.	IND.-GRP.	IND.-SUP.	GRP.-SUP.
1 and 2	.36	.36	.36	.00	.00	.00
1 and 3	.48	.52	.32	–.04	.16	.20
1 and 4	.56	.48	.45	.04	.07	.03
1 and 5	.32	.37	.35	–.05	–.03	.02
1 and 6	.45	.38	.38	–.07	.07	.00
1 and 7	.12	.22	.02			
1 and 8	.51	.51	.44	.00	.07	.07
2 and 3	.57	.65	.46	–.08	.11	.19
2 and 4	.33	.51	.35	–.18	–.02	.16
2 and 5	.46	.57	.43	–.11	.03	.14
2 and 6	.52	.61	.46	–.09	.06	.15
2 and 7	.13	.34	.07			
2 and 8	.64	.80	.61	–.16	.03	.19
3 and 4	.42	.54	.43	–.14	–.01	.11
3 and 5	.59	.69	.66	–.10	–.07	.03
3 and 6	.72	.69	.63	.03	.09	.06
3 and 7	.10	.43	.17			
3 and 8	.85	.77	.77	.08	.08	.00
4 and 5	.60	.64	.55	–.04	.05	.09
4 and 6	.46	.55	.44	–.09	.02	.11
4 and 7	.29	.39	.09			
4 and 8	.49	.62	.45	–.13	.04	.17
5 and 6	.69	.73	.62	–.04	.07	.11
5 and 7	.37	.52	.35			
5 and 8	.68	.70	.61	–.02	.07	.09
6 and 7	.26	.41	.14			
6 and 8	.78	.76	.71	.02	.07	.05
7 and 8	.24	.43	.14			
$\bar{r}_z$	.57	.61	.52			
$\bar{Z}$	.64	.71	.57			

Stevens-Wonderlic. There is a probability of four per cent that this difference is zero or in favor of the individual Stevens-Wonderlic. Conversely, there is an equal probability that the supervised Stevens-Wonderlic average z is 14 or more points less than that of the group-administered. We may conclude from these data that a real reduction in halo is secured through the supervision of ratings. Whether it is or is not of sufficient magnitude to justify the added cost of the supervised administration is a moot question.

Leniency

Leniency in rating expresses itself primarily in two ways. First, the arithmetic mean of ratings given is frequently far in excess of the rating category characterized as "average." Secondly, the distribution of lenient ratings is generally negatively skewed. That is, there is a tendency for raters to put a greater proportion of their ratings in the categories above their mean than in those below. The arithmetic mean was taken in this study as the most desirable measure of central tendency to be used as a basis of comparison. Fisher's unbiased estimate of skewness, g_1, was used as a measure of asymmetry. The ten-point scale employed in the ratings were scored on a zero to nine basis. This would make a score of 4.5 represent the midpoint on the scale. Means in excess of this value would indicate leniency while those below it would be indicative of the opposite.

FORMAT. Table 8 presents the means and skewness measures yielded by the traditional and Stevens-Wonderlic rating formats. In six of the seven scales considered, the traditional graphic had a higher mean than did the Stevens-Wonderlic. The exception was for rating Scale 2, "Quantity of Production." However, the superiority of the Stevens-Wonderlic, while consistent (with this one exception), was most moderate. Only one difference, that for Scale 1, "Interpersonal Relationships," approached statistical significance. One other, Scale

Table 8

COMPARISON OF MEANS AND SKEWS OF DISTRIBUTIONS YIELDED BY TRADITIONAL AND STEVENS-WONDERLIC RATING FORMATS

SCALES	MEAN			SKEW	
	TRAD.	S-W	TRAD.-S-W	TRAD.	S-W
1. Interpersonal relations	5.37	4.84	.53	−.442	.017
2. Amount of productivity	5.39	5.50	−.11	−.017	−.184
3. Accuracy of productivity	5.49	5.35	.14	−.217	−.259
4. Leadership	3.73	3.56	.17	−.119	−.118
5. Job complexity	4.80	4.52	.28	−.088	−.059
6. Supervision required	5.25	5.24	.01	.030	−.245
7. Effort required	3.94	4.55	—	.301	−.099
8. Over-all	5.68	5.59	.09	−.456	−.321
N	171	145			
σg_1	—	—	—	.18	.20
5% lower limit g_1				.36	.39
$\sigma d = .23$					

5, "Job Complexity," was as large as its own standard deviation.

As is generally found in graphic ratings, all of the scales, with one exception in the traditional and one in the Stevens-Wonderlic, produced negative skewness. In Scale 1, "Interpersonal Relations," and Scale 8, "Over-all," for the traditional graphic these measures were significant at the five per cent level. In the case of the Stevens-Wonderlic format, the value of g_1 was in no case significantly different from zero at even the five per cent level. Examination of Table 8 indicates the amount of skewness apparently to be more a function of the scale than of the rating format. The evidence presented would not justify a statement to the effect that the difference in format substantially reduced skewness.

The effect of the nature of administration upon the two measures of leniency is presented in Table 9. The group administration produces the lowest means, but except for Scale 4, "Leadership Characteristics," the differences between the group and individually administered are extremely small. Throughout, however, the mean ratings on all scales center fairly closely about the middle of the distribution, except with respect to Scale 4, where they are considerably below what would ordinarily be ex-

Table 9

COMPARISON OF MEANS AND SKEWS OF DISTRIBUTIONS YIELDED BY THREE DIFFERENT ADMINISTRATIONS OF STEVENS-WONDERLIC FORMAT RATINGS

	MEAN					
SCALES	IND.	GRP.	SUPER	IND.-GRP.	IND.-SUP.	GRP.-SUP.
1. Interpersonal relations	5.37	4.89	4.97	.48	–.40	.08
2. Amount of productivity	5.39	5.46	5.41	–.07	–.02	.05
3. Accuracy of productivity	5.49	5.20	5.17	.29	.32	.03
4. Leadership	3.73	3.02	3.50	.71	.23	–.48
5. Job complexity	4.80	4.79	4.78	.01	.02	.01
6. Supervision required	5.25	5.02	5.13	.23	.12	–.11
7. Effort required	3.94	4.55	3.97	—	—	—
8. Over-all	5.68	5.31	5.06	.37	.62	.25
N	145	170	193			

	SKEW		
SCALES	IND.	GRP.	SUPER
1. Interpersonal relations	.017	–.056	–.013
2. Amount of productivity	–.184	–.301	–.105
3. Accuracy of productivity	–.259	–.267	–.147
4. Leadership	–.118	.404	–.069
5. Job complexity	–.059	–.077	.117
6. Supervision required	–.245	–.194	.023
7. Effort required	–.099	.077	.412
8. Over-all	–.321	–.325	–.107
σg_1	.20	.18	.17
5% lower limit	.39	.36	.34

pected. None of the differences among the three methods of administration is of a substantial enough nature to justify the added costs of the more complex ones.

With one exception in the group-administered Stevens-Wonderlic, the skewness of the distributions tends to be slightly but not importantly negative. The sizable positive skewness occurs in Scale 4, "Leadership Characteristics," which, as was previously noted, had an exceptionally low mean. For the most part, all of the scales were very close to being symmetrical and no important differences among them is evident. Thus, methods of administration in this study cannot be said to have had any substantial effect upon either the mean ratings given nor upon the skewness of the distributions.

CONCLUSIONS AND DISCUSSION

Broad generalizations are seldom justified on the basis of a single study. That is certainly true in this instance. In interpreting the results of this research, we must remain aware of the fact that it was conducted in a single installation and that the situational factors that existed there may be quite different from what would be found in another rating environment. One effect, however, does stand out. That is that the claims made by the champions of various rating techniques (including the senior author of this report) do not universally obtain and that there are circumstances in which the traditional graphic format administered in the usual manner yields substantially the same results that are obtained through the use of the more involved Stevens-Wonderlic format and more expensive procedures.

Perhaps the most outstanding finding of this study rests not nearly so much in the comparisons which the research was designed to make as in the attributes that were common to the ratings yielded by all four groups. In this study, under all four conditions we obtained ratings which were relatively free of those characteristics for which graphic ratings are most frequently criticized.

1. In almost all cases the entire range of ratings was used by the raters.

2. The standard deviations on a ten-point scale were in all cases approximately 2.00, which again indicates a desirable dispersion.

3. Rather than displaying peakedness, as is generally the case with graphic rating, these distributions were on the whole somewhat platykurtic but not extensively so.

4. The means of the several scales in all the groups were, for the most part, only slightly above the mid-point of the range and in the case of Scale 4, "Leadership Characteristics," were actually below this point for all four groups.

5. Skewness, while negative, was only moderately so and the scales by and large were not markedly asymmetrical.

6. Correlations among the traits were generally considerably lower than are usually found in graphic rating scales. The average based upon the z transformation for the four conditions ranged from .52 to .61. If the correlations of the individual scales with the Over-all are omitted from consideration, 29 of the 60 intercorrelations in the four groups are below .50. Only four of the 60 correlations are above .69, and there are none above .79.

These are rather unusual findings. They cannot be attributed to either the scale format or to the methods of administration, since with the possible exception of halo there was little difference among the four groups. Three possibilities suggest themselves:

1. The experimental nature of the ratings rendered them atypical of what would obtain in a "for keeps" situation. This may be something akin to the famous "Hawthorne Phenomenon" of the Western Electric studies. In order to minimize the influence the fact that this was an experimental study may have had on the raters, they were informed (in the rating manual for Groups 1 and 2 and orally in the other two groups) that the ratings would be added to the personnel files, providing the study showed that they are accurate and consistent. It is possible, also, that too good a job was done in "selling" the research to the raters and that they cooperated by being much more conscientious and careful than they would have been with the same forms used periodically and operationally.

2. Situational factors. The Navy Finance Center has an active and competent personnel department. It has been quite active in the area of improved supervisory procedures and in the training of supervisors. The jobs that were being rated were well defined and clearly structured. All of these factors may have operated in combination with each other to produce more desirable ratings and at the same time to reduce the differences which might have been found, under other circumstances, between the two formats and among the three administrations.

3. The rating scales. The term "graphic rating scale" covers a multitude of possible variations. These may range from the use of a single ambiguous trait name (e.g., "ambition" or "cooperativeness") with an equally ambiguous scale either in terms of mere numbers or equally uninterpretable adjectives such as "poor," "good," "average," "excellent," and "superior." In our scales, trait names were avoided entirely. We attempted to describe in behavioral terms the continuum on which we hoped to secure ratings. Even here we failed in the case of Scale 7 to create a usable continuum. A similar effort was made with respect to the steps in each continuum, using brief behavioral descriptions rather than merely adjectives which were prone to broad perceptual interpretations. These three probably do not exhaust the list of hypotheses which might be related to our findings. The fact does remain, however, that in this study ratings were produced which were markedly free of the defects that customarily characterize graphic ratings. Further research with respect to such factors as experimental conditions, supervisory climate, and particularly scale construction is indicated as a promising means of improving performance evaluation through graphic ratings.

The over-all findings of this research can, in a sense, be said to be unequivocally negative. While minor differences between the formats and among the administrations were found to exist, none of these was of an order of magnitude adequate to justify the increased complexity and cost of the more elaborate procedures. These negative results, it should be noted, were not a function of the fact that the more elaborate techniques were burdened with the defects that usually characterize graphic ratings, but rather that in this instance the traditional graphics were essentially free of such defects.

Broad generalizations cannot usually be legitimately drawn from a single experiment. We do not believe that it can be said on the basis of these results that there are no circumstances in which the Stevens-Wonderlic format and the use of group or individual administration by a qualified technician should not be employed rather than the traditional graphic. Rather, it should be said that the traditional graphic rating under usual administration has been demonstrated to be capable of yielding a rating practically as free from defect as the individually administered Stevens-Wonderlic. To determine the conditions responsible for these results is a task for future research.

REFERENCES

1. Fisher, R. A., *Statistical Methods for Research Workers.* Edinburgh, Oliver & Boyd, 1950.
2. Guilford, J. P., *Psychometric Methods.* New York, McGraw-Hill Book Co., 1936.
3. Stevens, S. N., and Wonderlic, E. F., "An Effective Revision of the Rating Technique." *Personnel Journal,* 1934, **13,** 125–134.
4. Taylor, Erwin K., and Manson, Grace E., "Supervised Ratings–Making Graphic Scales Work," *Personnel,* 1951, **27,** 504–514.
5. Tiffin, Joseph, "Merit Rating: Its Validity and Techniques," in M. J. Dooher and V. Marquis (Eds.), *Rating Employee and Supervisory Performance, A Manual of Merit Rating Techniques.* New York, American Management Association, 1950.
6. Ewart, E., Seashore, S. E., and Tiffin, J., "A factor analysis of an industrial merit rating scale," *J. appl. Psychol.,* 1941, **25,** 481–486.

A. Rating by Supervisors

2. FORCED DISTRIBUTION–TECHNIQUES AND CRITICISMS

THE FORCED DISTRIBUTION SYSTEM

JOSEPH TIFFIN

THE EVALUATION OF A METHOD FOR FINELY GRADUATED ESTIMATES OF ABILITIES

JAMES BURT MINER

PERFORMANCE EVALUATION–SUPERVISORY EMPLOYEES: An Example of a Forced Distribution Merit-Rating Form

Tiffin is one of the few researchers in performance appraisal who have strongly argued the case for forced distribution of direct judgments, at least in recent years. His brief statement is used as an introduction here. The article by Miner is one of the earliest to describe a rating technique which has since achieved some popularity. He found that the substitution of gross categories for fine differentiation among individuals did not substantially change the outcome of the rating process. The three-category distribution of the critical-incident technique described in a later section is the latest development in this kind of rating. An example of the sort of form used by a supervisor in forced distribution rating follows Miner's article.

THE FORCED DISTRIBUTION SYSTEM*

Joseph Tiffin

A final method which has much to recommend it may be called the "forced distribution" system. This method is very simple—perhaps the simplest of all merit rating systems. But its simplicity is based on the fact that very extensive statistical work with a variety of more complicated systems has shown that it not only gives all results yielded by more complicated systems but gives the results with even greater reliability than many more complicated systems.

With this system the employees are rated on only two characteristics; namely, job performance and promotability. Limitation of the traits to these two is not based on arbitrary judgment. It is based upon the results of statistical factor analyses of the "halo effect," which was discussed earlier. Since there is a marked tendency to rate men at about the same level on various traits—whatever those traits may be—a great deal of time and effort can be saved by having the ratings made on only one trait at the outset. Furthermore, most production men will agree that job performance is the basic factor in determining any employee's value to the company, and that the various other things such as cooperation, personality, etc., are worth considering only insofar as they contribute to job performance. Rating on this basic characteristic is, therefore, made the foundation of this system.

With this system a five-point job performance scale is used. One end of the scale represents best job performance; the other end poorest job performance. The supervisor is asked to allocate approximately 10 per cent of his men to the best end of the scale, 20 per cent in the next category, 40 per cent in the middle bracket, 20 per cent in the bracket next to the low end, and 10 per cent in the low bracket. By forcing the distribution in this manner, the problem of different supervisors' using different parts of the scale is avoided. All raters use the same percentage distribution, 10-20-40-20-10. This principle is discussed thoroughly when supervisors are trained to make the ratings.

In using this method no descriptive phrases should be printed under the five places on the scale; for if this is done, the descriptive phrases under the poor end of the scale will necessarily not be very flattering, and many supervisors will hesitate to check a man with such an uncomplimentary phrase. But they are usually willing to identify the poorest 10 per cent of their men.

Another advantage of this system is that employees may be rated where they belong even when on quite different jobs. The reason for this is that each employee is considered in terms of job performance on his or her particular job.

A question may well be raised about this system when the matter arises of discussing ratings with employees. An employee almost certainly will want to know why he was placed at a particular

* From "Merit Rating: Its Validity and Techniques" in *Rating Employee and Supervisory Performance,* edited by M. Joseph Dooher and Vivienne Marquis (pp. 17–19). New York, American Management Association, 1951. Copyright 1951 by the American Management Association, Inc. Reprinted by permission.

point on the scale. If rated low, he is very likely to want to know his particular weak points. This part of the program can be handled in advance by printing on the back of the card a check list of characteristics. The supervisor may check several of these to indicate the reasons for his rating. The selection of traits to be included in this list may well be decided by supervisors in conference. By so doing they will have a greater interest in the whole merit rating program, because they will have had a part in its construction. A man in a boat doesn't bore a hole in it. Asking the supervisors to help make out the check list increases their support of the program.

It should be emphasized that the checkmarks are not added to obtain a composite rating. The over-all rating has already been obtained by the forced distribution. If the checks are added to obtain an over-all rating, all the difficulties characteristic of the chart system will again arise.

With this system, employees are rated on only one other characteristic in addition to job performance; namely, *promotability*. This is rated on a three-point scale, with verbal descriptions. These are: "very likely promotional material"; "may or may not be promotional material"; and "very unlikely to be promotional material." This secondary rating serves to identify employees who later may be groomed for more responsible jobs, usually at a supervisory level.

With this system, the job performance rating and promotional rating are not added to give a single composite score. This is because each gives some information by itself, and the adding of the pieces of information is more likely to obscure the picture than to clarify it.

The forced distribution technique need not be limited to rating scales based on only a single item, job performance, or on the two items mentioned in the previous discussion. Some companies may wish to use this principle to insure the use of the whole range, even where using a chart system with several traits listed.

THE EVALUATION OF A METHOD FOR FINELY GRADUATED ESTIMATES OF ABILITIES*

James Burt Miner

Estimating abilities may be merely skirmishing in research, but the attack of the main army is often wisely or foolishly directed as a result of the skirmish. The technique of estimating accordingly assumes an essential place in psychological procedure. Any improvement in the discrimination or reliability of estimates promises to meet urgent needs, not only in the employment office but whenever questions of admission or promotions are considered in the school room, the store, the factory, or the business office.

Our immediate problem was connected with the employment office at the Carnegie Institute of Technology, which recommends students and graduates for positions ranging from civil engineer to actress, from plumber to musician, from architect to teacher. Can the scholarship records be supplemented by sufficiently reliable and significant ratings of personal traits to be of use in recommending these young people for work?

Beginning with the problem of estimating the traits of those about to graduate from the institution, we were at once confronted by the fact that all the seniors were not intimately enough known by one person to make it possible to have an order of merit for the whole class in a college arranged by the same person. This is a frequent problem in estimation. Thorndike has attacked it by a method of combining the judgments of numerous judges.[1] His method, however, requires that each individual in the final order of merit be compared by several judges with those on either side of him, a condition we could not fulfill.

We hoped to obtain sufficient accuracy by assuming that the average senior class in the various courses within the same school had roughly the same distribution of ability. On this assumption a single order of merit might be obtained for the seniors of each school, provided that some systematic method of grading could be discovered which would be used in approximately the same way by the different judges.

The method which we tried out is indicated by the sample rating blank shown in Figure 1. At least four of these blanks were prepared for each student in the senior classes and they were sent to members of the faculty who were supposed by the administrative officers to be best acquainted with the particular students. Three out of the four had come in contact with the students in either the laboratory or shop, which afforded them a better opportunity for judgment than is possible in many institutions.

* From *Journal of Applied Psychology,* Vol. 1, no. 2, June 1917, pp. 123–133.

[1] E. L. Thorndike, "The Technique of Combining Incomplete Judgments of the Relative Position of N Facts by N Judges," *J. of Phil., Psychol.,* etc., 1916, Vol. 13, 197–203.

The fourth judge was a teacher in one of the academic subjects. In order that no member of the faculty should be burdened, we limited the number of students to be graded by any one instructor to about a dozen. About 70 judges graded sub-groups of the 140 seniors.

One feature of the method consisted in grading the person by means of a dot placed on a line. This plan of placing a dot on a line was found in a blank prepared by the B. F. Clark Teachers Agency of Chicago. A somewhat similar plan with five divisions from 0-100, without definition of the meaning of the divisions or of the standard group, was tried at one time by the Appointment Committee at Teachers College, Columbia University. The method was adapted to our purpose by substituting divisions into fifths of a group instead of the divisions "superlative," "excellent," "satisfactory," "fair," and "poor," which were used on the teachers' agency blank. Psychologically the use of a dot on a line seems to have a decided advantage over the percentage method, which it most closely resembles, in that it gets rid of the habit of thinking that different percentages have qualitative significance as indicating passing or excellent grades.

The blank embodies four fundamental principles for securing systematic estimates which are here combined for the first time, so far as I know. They summarize the result of much of the systematic work which has been done in this field in recent years. (1) The person is rated relative to the members of a defined group which is known by the judges and is used as a standard. In our

Will you please rate the student named below for the traits indicated. Place a dot along the line after each trait, grading the student as finely as you care to. Please give the rating independently without consulting others. The record sheet is to be returned to the secretary's office within three days.

JONES, JOHN — Instructor–D

Among the members of *the average senior class in this student's course and school* the student would rank in the

	Lowest 5th	Fourth 5th	Middle 5th, Average	Second 5th	Highest 5th
Common sense					
Energy					
Initiative					
Leadership					
Reliability					
General ability					

Fig. 1. Sample Rating Blank.

Table 1

Combined Order of Merit for Traits in Recommending Graduates for Employment

	BY ALL (23)	Q.	EXTREMES	SEMINAR (6)	OFFICE (3)	STUDENTS (14)
Common sense	1	6.5	(1-23)	3.0	2.0	1.0
Judgment	2	10.5	(1-45)	8.0	3.0	8.0
Initiative	3	6.0	(1-39)	2.0	11.0	9.0
Reliability	4	9.5	(1-48)	13.0	13.5	4.0
Efficiency	5	8.5	(2-38)	7.0	19.0	6.0
Intellect	6	9.0	(1-39)	4.0	6.0	11.0
Clearness of thought	7	5.5	(2-44)	9.0	23.0	3.0
Understanding of men	8	10.0	(1-47)	22.0	7.5	7.0
Accuracy	9	10.5	(2-43)	23.0	35.5	2.0
Integrity	10	15.5	(1-47)	16.0	4.0	13.5
Energy	11	10.5	(4-43)	5.0	5.0	18.0
Technical skill	12	15.0	(1-45)	21.0	21.0	10.0
Loyal	13	13.0	(1-46)	12.0	1.0	29.0
Industry	14	13.0	(4-47)	1.0	9.5	37.0
Moral	15	18.0	(1-49)	31.5	13.5	12.0
Resourcefulness	16	7.0	(8-42)	17.0	15.5	5.0
Foresight	17	10.0	(7-39)	14.0	26.5	21.0
Thorough	18	11.0	(4-48)	28.5	34.0	19.0
Conscientiousness	19	12.0	(2-48)	10.0	22.0	27.5
Leadership	20	14.0	(1-44)	11.0	15.5	30.0
Ambition	21	11.5	(2-47)	26.0	28.0	17.0
Perseverance	22	13.0	(3-49)	6.0	42.0	25.0
Originality	23	11.0	(4-46)	19.0	25.0	24.0
Tact	24	12.5	(7-50)	27.0	20.0	23.0
Systematic	25	13.5	(5-47)	33.5	44.5	13.5
Self-reliant	26	13.5	(4-47)	15.0	12.0	39.0
Concentration	27	10.0	(2-44)	28.5	34.0	19.0
Broad-minded	28	16.0	(3-50)	24.5	26.5	26.0
Co-operativeness	29	11.0	(9-46)	24.5	17.0	36.0
Courage	30	15.5	(3-48)	35.5	7.5	33.0
Imagination	31	12.5	(5-50)	20.0	18.0	38.0
Well-informed	32	8.0	(1-49)	38.5	44.5	19.0
Stability	33	16.0	(5-48)	37.0	35.5	27.5
Careful	34	12.5	(6-48)	43.5	47.0	16.0
Practical	35	8.0	(3-48)	40.0	31.5	34.0
Enthusiasm	36	6.5	(6-45)	28.5	9.5	41.0
Adaptable	37	5.5	(14-48)	33.5	46.0	35.0
Memory	38	11.5	(7-49)	49.0	40.0	21.0
Patience	39	8.5	(3-49)	31.5	24.0	40.0
Observation	40	9.5	(10-50)	47.0	38.0	30.0
Quickness	41	7.5	(4-49)	47.0	37.0	32.0
Inquiring	42	8.5	(8-48)	41.0	33.0	44.0
Aggressive	43	10.5	(11-50)	45.0	29.5	47.0
Firmness	44	8.0	(17-48)	43.5	29.5	46.0
Oral expression	45	10.0	(5-50)	48.0	39.0	43.0
Presence	46	8.5	(1-50)	38.5	31.5	48.0
Apprehension	47	10.0	(4-50)	42.0	48.0	45.0
Profound	48	5.5	(6-50)	30.0	50.0	50.0
Dignified	49	3.5	(23-50)	50.0	49.0	49.0
Ease of learning	50	10.0	(5-50)	35.5	43.0	42.0

CORRELATIONS

	(r FROM R)
Seminar and employment office	.57
Seminar and students	.54
Employment office and students	.28

case the average senior class in the students' course and school was used as this standard. (2) All qualitative terms are avoided since it is impossible to define them so that they call up the same idea in the minds of different judges. Instead, we have used fifths of the group, a concept about which there should be no difference in opinion as to what is meant. (3) The method allows the discrimination to be made as finely as the judge desires and yet permits the investigator to determine approximately how small divisions in that grading have sufficient reliability to make them worth while. The results on this phase of the problem will be discussed later in the paper. (4) The units of measurement may be readily transmuted into equivalent units of the standard deviation on the basis of the distribution of the judgments. In our blank the measurements may be made in millimeters or any larger portion of the line and changed into units of the standard deviation by Thorndike's table.

Just a word as to the choice of the particular traits for use on the blank. A list of something over 300 traits was first compiled from the studies by Cattell, Wells, Yerkes, and LaRue, Davenport's Trait Book, Mann's study of engineers, etc. From this list, 50 were selected and submitted to three different groups to be arranged in order of their importance in recommending graduates for employment. These arrangements were made by the members of the seminar in psychology, the three men in the employment office, and a group of seniors and juniors in the teachers' training courses. The result is shown in Table 1.

Among the traits which were near the top of these lists we then selected five which seemed to represent different important factors in personality from the point of view of employment, and which were not sufficiently indicated by the scholarship records or "General Ability." The latter term allowed the judge to weigh the traits subjectively and to summarize his opinion of the student.

In evaluating the method, the first question is, how far may the judgments be relied upon? How sure are we that other capable judges equally acquainted with the individuals would give like estimates? The correlation of series of estimates on the same people seems to offer the best means of answering this question. The data are summarized in Table 2.

All the correlations are between a series of judgments selected at random from those made on each student and similar series selected in the same way from those judgments remaining. The same series of single judgments or of combined judgments on the same students is always used in the correlations compared, but the judgments are scored in different ways.

The first two rows of figures compared with all the others in the table indicate that a single judgment is not sufficiently reliable, but that two judgments combined give approximately a reliability of .70 and may be relied upon when no more judgments are practicable. Four judgments combined, which we use, should then give us a reliability of .83, if we apply William Brown's formula for estimating the number of combined judgments necessary to attain a desired degree of reliability.[2] It is interesting to note that, if the correlation between two single series is .55, as here, the correlation between the two series combined

[2] *The Essentials of Mental Measurements*, p. 101 n.

Table 2

RELIABILITY OF ESTIMATES
COLLEGE SENIORS JUDGED BY MEMBERS OF THE FACULTY
AT THE CARNEGIE INSTITUTE OF TECHNOLOGY

COLLEGE	GEN. A.	COM. S.	INIT'E	LEAD'P	RELIAB.	ENERGY	AV.
College of Applied Science							
Correlation of ranks							
Measured in millimeters							
1 Judgment and 1 other (64 cases)	.53	.54	.53	.64	.30	.67	.54
1 Judgment and 1 other (30-36 cases)	.63	.52	.42	.68	.50	.69	.57
2 Judgments and 2 others (30-36 cases)	.76	.62	.67	.77	.71	.78	.72
Measured in fifths							
2 Judgments and 2 others	.69	.60	.67	.77	.64	.73	.68
Product-Moment cor. of transmuted tenths							
2 Judgments and 2 others (30-36 cases)	.76	.52	.64	.79	.71	.70	.69
M.M. College for Women (24-26 cases)							
2 Judgments and 2 others	.44	.59	.69	.79	.61	.70	.64
Correlation of ranks measured in m.m.							
Product-Moment cor. of transmuted tenths	.44	.62	.68	.80	.69	.62	.64
College of Applied Science (30 cases)							
Correlation of ranks							
2 Judgments in fifths and the same 2 in m.m.	.98	.98	.88	.97	.90	.97	.94
2 Judgments in fifths and the same 2 in transmuted tenths	.86	.89	.91	.87	.96	.97	.91

and two other series should theoretically be .71. This agrees with our empirical findings.

In the Margaret Morrison Carnegie School it is possible to check the order of merit for the seniors which has been obtained by combining the estimates of various instructors, none of whom judged the whole class, by two orders of merit for the whole class furnished by the dean and by the secretary of the school who has charge of employment. The orders of merit arranged by each of these administrative officers correlates over .70 with the combined order of merit of the faculty judgments on the "general ability" of various parts of the class, taken from the estimate blanks. The combined order of merit of the administrative officers agrees with the result of the same combined faculty estimate with a correlation of .75. All correlation coefficients for rank orders in Table 2 are obtained by Pearson's method for calculating *P* and translating to *r*.

Important data as to the form of scoring these estimates are also provided in Table 2. Notice the three rows of coefficients in the second division of the table. The averages are .72, .68, and .69. They suggest that refinements of measurement make very little difference in the reliability of an order of merit obtained from two judgments chosen at random. This is true at least so far as the orders of merit of these thirty seniors in the engineering college were concerned. The results are corroborated by the next two rows of data on the seniors in the college for women, which show the same average, .64. Since four judgments are averaged, the students were fairly well discriminated in rank.

The last division of the table, moreover, shows that an order of merit obtained from two judgments combined remains practically the same whether the judgments are scored one way or another. Measurements in fifths give about the same order of merit as those in millimeters or transmuted tenths. The correlations are over .90. If an order of merit is all that is desired, records in less than fifths or the use of transmuted measures are probably unnecessary refinements. When the methods differ as to particular students, however, the refined method may be safer. With our blank the position of the dot can be read directly in tenths as easily as in fifths.

There is some tendency for students in certain divisions to be ranked higher than in others. This may raise the correlations. If present, however, the spurious correlation does not affect our conclusions. In the women's college the order of merit agreed well with that of the two administration officers who ranked the entire class. At least two judgments are necessary for reasonable reliability, and the measurement of combined judgments need not be in smaller units than fifths if conclusions are limited to the group as a whole, rather than directed to particular students.

If the reader will now turn to Table 3, the intercorrelations may give us some other hints in evaluating this particular rating card. Which of these specific traits gives the most unique information not afforded by the grades in scholarship? To answer this question we may note which trait shows the lowest correlation with scholarship. With this group of seniors in the engineering college the estimate of "leadership" is least indicated by scholarship. We also note that "general ability" shows the highest intercorrelations with these specific traits, even when we disregard the intercorrelations with scholarship. For a single term "general ability" would, therefore, probably give us the most additional information about the whole group of specific traits. If the problem justified the labor of the calculations, this conclusion could be checked by the partial intercorrelation of each of the traits with the others independent of their relations to scholarship.

When considering a particular person, what sort of numerical rating will be most usable? This is largely a question of practical convenience. The method we use is to record the average rating of the faculty judges in a particular trait; then to arrange these in ten equal groups. By this method the rating of the

Table 3

INTERCORRELATIONS OF ABILITIES

Thirty seniors in the College of Applied Science estimated by four judges in tenths of an average graduating class and the scores then transmuted into units of the standard deviation. Scholarship rated by the total scholarship in credit hours transmuted into units of the standard deviation. The correlations were calculated by the product-moment formula.

	SCHOL'P	GEN. A.	COM. S.	ENERGY	INIT'VE	LEAD'P	RELIAB.
Scholarship	----	.73	.58	.73	.62	.39	.72
General ability	.73	----	.85	.74	.78	.71	.84
Common sense	.58	.85	----	.68	.76	.68	.78
Energy	.73	.74	.68	----	.78	.46	.76
Initiative	.62	.78	.76	.78	----	.75	.80
Leadership	.39	.71	.68	.46	.75	----	.55
Reliability	.72	.84	.78	.76	.80	.55	----
Average	.62	.78	.72	.69	.75	.59	.74

student is in the *actual* tenth of his class in which he fell on the average for that trait. This is, of course, different from the average estimated tenth. For example, the separate judgments of the seniors in the engineering college distributed in the various estimated tenths in general ability as follows, beginning with the estimated lowest tenth and stated in percentages: 2, 3, 8, 3, 9, 29, 17, 8, 15, 6. We may note in passing that the transmuted value in terms of the standard deviations for an estimate in each of these tenths for this college was as follows, omitting decimal points: −24, −18, −14, −11, −8, −3, +3, +7, +11, +20.

In spite of the fact that there is a tendency to place more than a tenth in the middle and upper estimated tenths, the discrimination is probably better than with other methods of estimation. For example, the distribution of the grades in scholarship of the same class under the six marks used showed the following percentages of credit hours for each mark: 1, 7, 15, 54, 19, 4.

A more precise quantitative score also seems advisable, at least for general ability. For this purpose we have used estimated tenths transmuted into terms of the standard deviation. With this quantitative score a unit means approximately the same at one position on the scale as at another. This is not true of decile units or ranks in an order of merit, in which adjacent extreme tenths theoretically differ from each other about three times as much as those tenths near the middle.

The office should also be informed as to the variability of these ratings. For example, with the estimates of general ability of the 64 engineering seniors, we can say that the chances are roughly 9 out of 10 that a student would not be estimated more than 2 tenths of an average class differently, even in the most variable tenths, by a similar average judgment of four members of the faculty.

W. D. Scott has suggested a method by which the rating blank can be made more concrete if comparison can be made to a known group which is stable enough so that typical individuals may be selected for a standard scale. For example, when the divisions are in fifths, at the boundaries of the divisions may be inserted the names of those persons in the standard group who are highest, lowest, middle, etc. The estimator would then judge an individual to be between Mr. A and Mr. B, or between Mr. B and Mr. C, etc. In this form the method is being tried out by the Bureau of Salesmanship Research.

The complete answer as to whether it is worth while to supplement the scholarship ratings of college students by such estimates of ability as have been attempted here will be possible only after we can determine whether they assist in making a more accurate prediction of success in life. This must wait until we have data upon these graduates some years after they have left the schools.

That these estimates give illuminating information about certain students cannot be doubted, however, when one finds such records as those of Mr. A and Mr. B given in Table 4. Without such estimates of traits, an institution has no systematic record in available form of anything except scholarship. That would certainly be an inadequate basis for judging these individuals. On the other hand it must be recognized that for the great majority of the seniors the estimates and the scholarship records are quite similar. The record of Mr. C may be said to be fairly typical and that of Mr. D is the other extreme.

We may recapitulate the experience of the Carnegie Institute of Technology in regard to the method described above when applied to its seniors in 1916. The empirical test of the method under the conditions found in its four colleges shows: 1) The plan of estimating traits within fifths of an average class in the student's course in college by placing a dot on a line, is so easy to use that replies can be secured, without serious annoyance, from teachers who do not have to estimate more than about a dozen students for six traits. 2) The average of four estimates on each student was found to give fairly constant orders of merit when such estimates on personal traits were made by those as well acquainted with the individuals as instructors in laboratory courses with small groups. An estimate by one member of the faculty is unreliable. 3) The method allows for a quantitative estimate on a common standard without

Table 4

RECORDS OF INDIVIDUALS

Seniors	MR. A	MR. B	MR. C	MR. D
Standard deviation:				
Scholarship	−.24	+.18	+.26	+.82
General ability	+.36	−.30	+.30	+1.40
Actual tenths of the class:				
Scholarship	3	7	7	10
General ability	6	4	6	10
Common sense	8	1	4	10
Energy	8	6	6	10
Initiative	8	4	4	9
Leadership	10	3	7	8
Reliability	7	7	6	10

requiring all the members of the class to be known by the same person. 4) The records supplement the scholarship ratings of some students in a most suggestive way. 5) Five traits selected because of their estimated high importance in recommending graduates for employment, were common sense, energy, initiative, leadership, and reliability. Among these, leadership was least correlated with scholarship ratings. Estimates of general ability showed the highest intercorrelations with the special traits. 6) Scoring the estimates in divisions less than estimated fifths of the class or in transmuted measures did not give notably different orders of merit.

PERFORMANCE EVALUATION—SUPERVISORY EMPLOYEES*

STANINE ______

PERFORMANCE EVALUATION—SUPERVISORY EMPLOYEES

______ TOTAL SCORE

(Typical Jobs — Unit Head, Section Head, Supervising Clerk, Supervising Accounting Reviewer, Assistant Manager. If any questions arise concerning classification, contact the Personnel Division.)

DIV., DEPT., OR OFFICE	NAME	SEX	JOB DESIGNATION OR TITLE	APPOINTMENT			JOB CODE NUMBER		
				Mo	Day	Year	Div.	Sect.	No.

DATE ASSIGNED TO PRESENT JOB______ ADJECTIVE RATING______

Be sure to read the instructions on the reverse side before filling out this form.

FOR SCORING PURPOSES

1. Consider his attitude toward his work, his associates, toward management policies, and the Company as a place to work. This may be shown, in part, by his willingness to accept suggestion and to carry out instructions and by the enthusiasm he has for the job. Do not consider his leadership ability.

2 % ☐ ☐ 18 % ☐ ☐ 60 % ☐ ☐ ☐ 18 % ☐ ☐ 2 % ☐ ☐ Not Observed ☐

VERY POOR — ABOUT THE SAME AS MOST — VERY OUTSTANDING

2. Consider his ability to inspire confidence, to obtain cooperation, to maintain the morale of his group, and to organize his group into a smooth-running part of the whole organization.

2 % ☐ ☐ 18 % ☐ ☐ 60 % ☐ ☐ ☐ 18 % ☐ ☐ 2 % ☐ ☐ Not Observed ☐

VERY POOR — ABOUT THE SAME AS MOST — VERY OUTSTANDING

3. Consider what he knows about the methods and procedures of performing his job. Consider his knowledge of routine. Consider also his ability to grasp new ideas and to learn new methods and techniques. Do not consider his ability to maintain high morale in his group.

2 % ☐ ☐ 18 % ☐ ☐ 60 % ☐ ☐ ☐ 18 % ☐ ☐ 2 % ☐ ☐ Not Observed ☐

VERY POOR — ABOUT THE SAME AS MOST — VERY OUTSTANDING

4. Consider how well he decides what is important in the work and what is not. Consider his ability to choose the proper course of action. Do not consider his tact in handling subordinates.

2 % ☐ ☐ 18 % ☐ ☐ 60 % ☐ ☐ ☐ 18 % ☐ ☐ 2 % ☐ ☐ Not Observed ☐

VERY POOR — ABOUT THE SAME AS MOST — VERY OUTSTANDING

5. Consider his ability to explain the work to others in order that it is done quickly and accurately. Do not consider his ability to maintain high morale in his group.

2 % ☐ ☐ 18 % ☐ ☐ 60 % ☐ ☐ ☐ 18 % ☐ ☐ 2 % ☐ ☐ Not Observed ☐

VERY POOR — ABOUT THE SAME AS MOST — VERY OUTSTANDING

RATER:______ REVIEWER:______

Comb. 35352 Ed. 5-52 (W)

(OVER)

Fig. 1. Forced distribution merit-rating form (*front*).

* From *Supervisory Merit-Rating*, Bureau of National Affairs, Survey no. 14, September 1952, pp. 26–27. Copyright 1952 by the Bureau of National Affairs, Inc. Reprinted by permission.

COMMENTS: (The employee's training status, his promotability, or any other pertinent information or comments may be noted here.)

MANAGER'S SECTIONS

1. Consider this individual's over-all job performance as a supervisor. Disregard the importance of the job in your department or division. Then:

a — If you have ten or more supervisors in your division or department, is he in the

☐	☐	☐	☐	☐
HIGHEST 10 %	HIGH 20 %	MIDDLE 40 %	LOW 20 %	LOWEST 10 %

of the supervisors in your division or department?

b — If you have less than ten supervisors in your division or department, regardless of their job classification, rank them on over-all job performance. On the basis of this ranking, his rank is number______ of______ supervisors, where number 1 is best.

2. If you recommend this person for the Outstanding category, initial here__________.

If your immediate superior approves your recommendation, have him initial here__________.

3.

DATE:____________________ MANAGER:____________________

INSTRUCTIONS FOR RATERS

1. Check the information listed in the heading of this form and correct (preferably in red) anything listed incorrectly.
2. Fill in the "date assigned to present job."
3. Leave the spaces marked "stanine", "total score", "adjective rating", and "for scoring purposes" blank. They are used by your manager and the Personnel Division.
4. If you rate several supervisors you should follow the percentages above the boxes. On any one trait, about 60% of the supervisors rated by you should be rated in one of the three boxes in the middle. About 18% of them should be rated in the two boxes immediately above and another 18% should be rated in the two boxes immediately below the middle three. The middle seven boxes should be used in most cases. Very rarely should someone receive a rating in the boxes at the extreme ends of the traits.
5. If you rate only a few supervisors, use the percentages above the boxes as a guide. These percentages should be interpreted as follows: Use:
The lowest 2% — if the supervisor is inadequate on the trait under consideration. Very rarely would a person be marked here.
The low 18% — if the supervisor is adequate on the trait under consideration, but does not quite meet your standards or come up to most people.
The middle 60% — if the supervisor meets your standards for the trait or does as well as most people.
The high 18% — if the supervisor greatly exceeds your standards for this trait or does much better than most people.
The highest 2% — if the supervisor does so well on this trait that the usual standards don't apply or does much better than almost anyone else could. Very rarely would a person be marked here.
6. If you do not know where to rate an employee on a trait, don't guess. Check the box titled, "Not Observed."

RATING TIPS

1. Disregard your general impression of an employee and concentrate on one trait at a time. It will help you to do this if you rate everyone on the first trait before going on to the next, etc. Work sheets (Form Comb. 35352-A) have been provided for this purpose. Using them will also help you make comparisons and establish standards.
2. Rate an employee on his typical performance during the past six months. Do not be influenced by unusual instances which are not typical of his work.
3. Ratings should be based on facts so that you can explain the rating if asked to do so.
4. Don't be influenced by previous ratings. Above all, don't refer back to previous evaluation forms.
5. It is true that several of the traits on this form are related. However, when you rate an employee on a trait, try to disregard the ratings you have given him on other traits.
6. Remember that your best employee may have a few weaknesses while your poorest employee may have a strong point. Your evaluation should reflect these.
7. Disregard the importance of the job when rating. Consider only how well the person is doing his assigned job.

Fig. 2. Forced distribution merit-rating form (*reverse*).

Figures 1 and 2 are an example of a forced distribution merit-rating form. This form is used in a large insurance company. In Figure 1, note the percentages used along each scale; these encourage raters to place the employee in proper grouping in a "normal distribution curve." The raters are also requested to rank the individual on the basis of over-all job performance as a supervisor. (The reverse side of the form is shown in Figure 2.)

A. Rating by Supervisors

3. RANKING–TECHNIQUES AND CRITICISMS

RANKING METHODS

EDWIN E. GHISELLI AND CLARENCE W. BROWN

PAIRED COMPARISON TECHNIQUE FOR RATING PERFORMANCE OF INDUSTRIAL EMPLOYEES

C. H. LAWSHE, N. C. KEPHART, AND E. J. MCCORMICK

WAR DEPARTMENT INSTRUCTIONS FOR RATING COMMISSIONED OFFICERS

Ranking of individuals is an intuitively appealing way of expressing appraisals of their performance. Appraisal usually precedes discriminatory action of some kind, and discrimination presupposes some ordering or ranking. The ease with which simple ranking can be accomplished has led some psychologists to be suspicious of the process the rater goes through to reach his conclusions. Consequently some rather elaborate techniques have been developed to determine the rank order of merit of individuals. One of the earliest popular rating devices used an elaborate ranking system that forced the rater to compare each man with carefully chosen key men. This system, developed by the Army in World War I, is described by Scott and others. The paired-comparison ranking method has long been supposed to yield greater precision and reliability of rating. The technical gains have been offset, however, by its high cost. The study by Lawshe, Kephart, and McCormick reveals the degree of reliability and the magnitude of cost of this technique.

FURTHER READING

Jurgensen, C. E., "Overall Job Success as a Basis for Employee Ratings," *Journal of Applied Psychology*, Vol. 34, no. 5, October 1950, pp. 333–337.

RANKING METHODS*

Edwin E. Ghiselli

and Clarence W. Brown

• ADVANTAGES OF RANKING

Rating individuals by arranging them in order of merit has two major advantages: simplicity and naturalness. It is a very simple process to evaluate persons by merely arranging them in order from best to poorest or from most to least in terms of some characteristic. Furthermore, ranking is a very natural type of evaluation, involving a kind of judgment which is frequently made in everyday living. Hence this method is advised for use in situations where the raters are unfamiliar with problems involved in the appraisal of people or are unable to execute the more complicated rating procedures.

• DISADVANTAGES OF RANKING

There are two major disadvantages of these methods. First of all, the task of ranking a group of individuals becomes difficult when there are over twenty or thirty cases. Secondly, the magnitude of the differences in ability between ranks is not equal at different positions. For instance, the difference in ability between the fifth and sixth individuals may be much greater, in absolute terms, than the difference between the sixth and seventh. In terms of rank, however, the differences between these individuals are the same. Since absolute differences in ability between individuals are not taken into account, it is apparent that individuals ranked in one group cannot be compared with those ranked in another group.

If only a relatively few individuals are to be rated, and if the only requirement is to learn which ones are better or which ones are poorer regardless of absolute ability, then a simple ranking method may well suffice. With larger groups about whom some notion of absolute ability is important, some other method, such as the rating scale, should be used.

• AIDS TO RANKING

When the number of individuals to be evaluated is large, one of several methods may be used to reduce the labor of ranking. Each rater may simply assign each individual to one of a small number of groups, roughly classifying them as good, average, or poor. Then the individuals within each group are ranked. After possibly a few shifts of borderline cases, the ranked groups are then combined. Similar to this method is the "peeling" process wherein the rater selects the best and the poorest individuals, then he selects the best and the poorest of the remaining cases, and so on, through the entire group. The advantage of this method is that after several extreme pairs have been "peeled" off, there are fewer cases to differentiate in the middle range of ability where

---

* By permission from *Personnel and Industrial Psychology*, by Edwin E. Ghiselli and Clarence W. Brown. (Second Edition, Chapter 4, pp. 96–103.)

differences between people are likely to be smaller and harder to distinguish.

Since it is easier to judge which of two workers is superior than to arrange members of a large group of workers in order of excellence, the *method of paired comparisons* sometimes is used. In this method the rater compares each man in the group with every other man. The final ranking of the workers is determined from the number of times each was judged better than the others. Although the ease of judging is probably greater, the amount of work that must be performed is greatly increased. The rater must make $\frac{n(n-1)}{2}$ judgments, where n is the number of men to be ranked. Thus, if there are 50 men in the group, the rater must make 1,225 separate comparisons.

TRANSMUTING RANKS • TO VALUES ON A CONTINUOUS SCALE

Ranks are ordinal numbers; *i.e.*, they are numbers that indicate the relative position of an individual with respect to others in a group. The rank of an individual tells *how many other persons* he is better or poorer than, but it does not tell *how much* better or poorer he is than the other members of the group. Because ranks are ordinal numbers, they

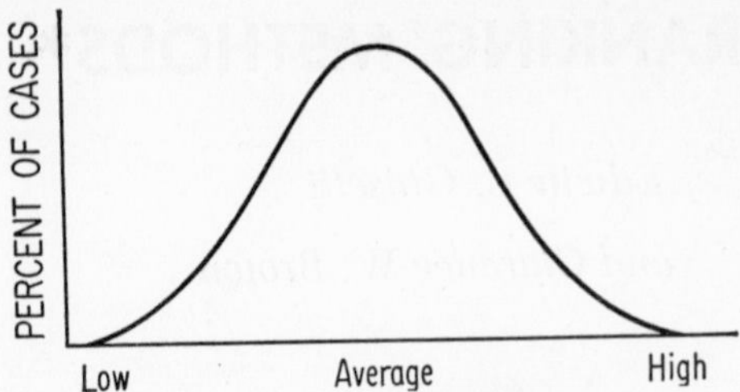

Fig. 1. Normal frequency distribution curve.

cannot be arithmetically manipulated as can numbers representing points on a continuous scale, such as amount of test intelligence, number of items produced per day, or accident rate per year. Consequently, when the workers in a group have been ranked by several supervisors, the final rank of each worker cannot be taken as the arithmetic average of all of the ranks assigned to him unless certain assumptions are made. If some average is required, the median, *i.e.*, the midmost, rank should be used.

Because of the ordinal nature of ranks and the difficulties involved in handling them arithmetically and statistically, several methods have been suggested for transmuting ranks into values on a continuous scale. In general, these methods are based upon the assumption that any characteristic of human beings that is measured on a quantitative scale will be distributed in accordance with the normal distribution curve. A distribution of this type is shown in Figure 1. If an ability under consideration is nor-

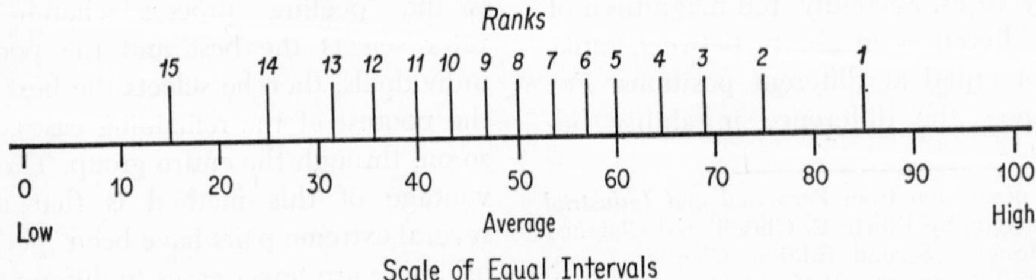

Fig. 2. Spacing of fifteen individuals along a scale, assuming a normal frequency distribution.

mally distributed, then the differences in absolute amount of ability between adjacent individuals at either end of the distribution will be greater than the differences in absolute amount of ability between adjacent individuals in the middle portions of the distribution. By way of illustration, the spacing of individuals along a continuous scale, assuming a normal distribution of ability, is shown in Figure 2. The marked differences between ranks at different points on the scale are very apparent.

On the basis of the mathematical relationship existing between ranks and scores on a continuous scale, assuming a normal distribution, tables have been prepared to facilitate the transmutation of ranks into scaled scores. These scaled scores are so devised that the average is 50, and the extreme values approach 0 and 100. A table of this kind is presented in Table 1. In effecting the transmutation, the following formula is employed:

$$\% = \frac{100(R - .5)}{N}$$

where the left-hand side is the percentage position, R the rank of the in-

Table 1

TABLE BASED ON THE NORMAL FREQUENCY DISTRIBUTION CURVE FOR TRANSMUTING PER CENT POSITION IN A RANKED SERIES INTO VALUES ON A CONTINUOUS SCALE

PER CENT POSITION	SCALE VALUE	PER CENT POSITION	SCALE VALUE	PER CENT POSITION	SCALE VALUE	PER CENT POSITION	SCALE VALUE
1	93	26	63	51	50	76	36
2	89	27	62	52	49	77	35
3	86	28	62	53	49	78	35
4	84	29	61	54	48	79	34
5	82	30	60	55	48	80	33
6	80	31	60	56	47	81	33
7	79	32	59	57	47	82	32
8	78	33	59	58	46	83	31
9	76	34	58	59	46	84	31
10	75	35	58	60	45	85	30
11	74	36	57	61	44	86	29
12	73	37	57	62	44	87	28
13	72	38	56	63	43	88	27
14	71	39	56	64	43	89	26
15	70	40	55	65	42	90	25
16	69	41	54	66	42	91	24
17	69	42	54	67	41	92	22
18	68	43	53	68	41	93	21
19	67	44	53	69	40	94	20
20	67	45	52	70	40	95	18
21	66	46	52	71	39	96	16
22	65	47	51	72	38	97	14
23	65	48	51	73	38	98	11
24	64	49	50	74	37	99	7
25	63	50	50	75	37		

dividual under consideration, and N the number of individuals being ranked. Thus the percentage position of the second-ranking person in a group of 10 would be

$$\% = \frac{100(2 - .5)}{10}$$
$$= 15$$

In Table 1 it will be seen that a scale value of 70 is obtained for a percentage position of 15. This value, 70, would be this individual's score on a continuous distribution, assuming that a normal distribution holds within the group of ten individuals for the characteristic on which they were ranked.

Although it is true that many physical and psychological characteristics are found to be distributed normally in the general population, it certainly does not follow that all characteristics in a specially selected group will be distributed in this manner. As a matter of fact, it is unlikely that a trait such as speed of work would be normally distributed in a highly proficient group of workers. It would be expected that, through a process of selection, elimination, and training, there would be a large number of "high" persons and a small number of "low" persons, a considerable variation from the normal distribution. Such a non-normal distribution is shown in Figure 3. For a distribution of this type the spacing of individuals along a scale would be like that shown in Figure 4. It is apparent that the differences in absolute amount of ability are greater between adjacent persons at the low end of the scale than between adjacent persons at the high end, and that the smallest differences occur in a region above the average.

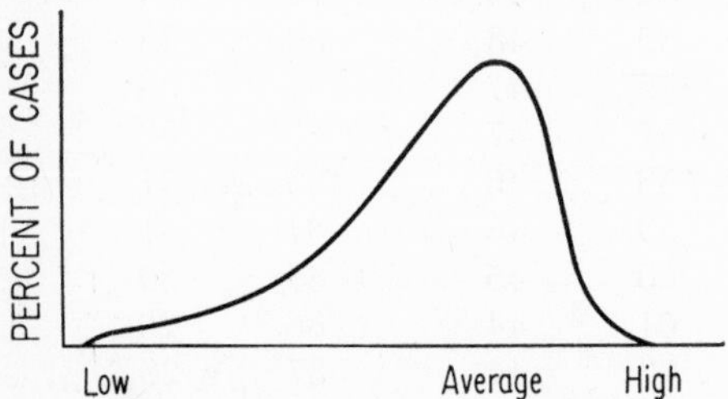

Fig. 3. Example of a skewed (non-normal) frequency distribution curve.

In view of the fact that for any group of workers, the shape of the distribution of the trait on which the workers are to be ranked will be unknown, the transformation of ranks into values on a continuous scale will introduce an error of unknown extent. As a consequence, such transformations must be applied with caution.

• GROUP-ORDER RANKINGS

In some instances a complete ranking of all individuals in order of merit is not necessary. Sometimes what is desired is to know in which half, fifth, seventh,

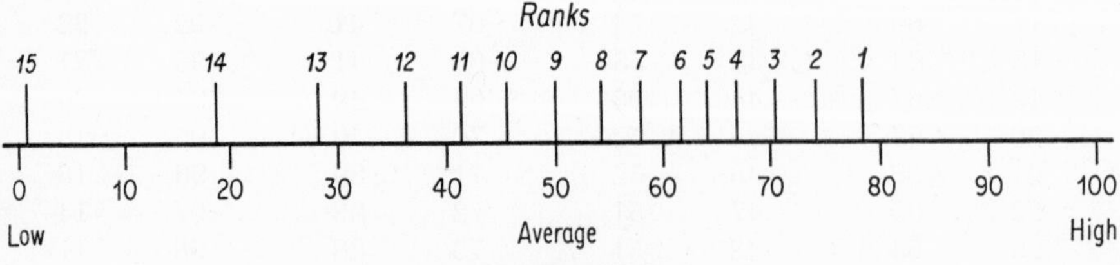

Fig. 4. Spacing of fifteen individuals along a scale of equal intervals, assuming a distribution skewed as in Fig. 3.

Table 2

EXAMPLE OF GROUP-ORDER RANKING PROCEDURE

HIGHEST FIFTH	NEXT HIGHEST FIFTH	MIDDLE FIFTH	NEXT LOWEST FIFTH	LOWEST FIFTH
Outstanding, among best agents in the company	Superior, above average but not outstanding	Average, neither superior nor inferior	Below average but not poor	Falls among the poorest agents in the company

NOTE: For the over-all rating, consider both the individual's success as a casualty insurance agent and his loyalty to the X company. When making this judgment, keep in mind all the X company's agents. The phrases above were chosen to aid in describing successive fifts of all casualty agents in general job sucess. Therefore, 20 per cent of the agents should be placed under each heading.

etc., of his group a person belongs. In this case, the group of workers is divided into whatever proportions appear to be desirable. Ratings of this kind are termed group-order rankings and are illustrated in Table 2.

When the group-order method is used, it is customary to assign a series of numbers to the categories. If the group is divided into fifths, those in the lowest fifth are assigned a rating of 1, and those in the highest fifth a rating of 5, with the intermediate categories being assigned the appropriate numbers between. These final ratings are then treated as if they were values on a continuous scale. Although this may be satisfactory for rough work, as pointed out earlier, such a procedure in the treatment of ordinal numbers is not logically sound.

To overcome this deficiency the proportion of individuals assigned to each group may be allotted in accordance

Table 3

PERCENTAGE OF CASES EXPECTED ON THE BASIS OF A NORMAL FREQUENCY DISTRIBUTION TO FALL INTO EACH STEP ON RATING SCALES OF VARYING NUMBERS OF STEPS

	NUMBER OF INTERVALS																				
	3			4			5			6			7			8			9		
NO. OF CASES TO BE RATED	20	40	60	20	40	60	20	40	60	20	40	60	20	40	60	20	40	60	20	40	60
STEPS IN SCALE										PER CENT											
1	25	21	20	14	12	10	9	7	5	8	5	5	6	4	4	5	3	2	4	3	2
2	50	58	60	36	38	40	24	25	26	16	16	15	11	11	10	9	8	8	7	6	6
3	25	21	20	36	38	40	34	36	38	27	29	30	20	21	22	15	16	16	12	12	12
4				14	12	10	24	25	26	27	29	30	26	28	28	21	23	24	17	18	19
5							9	7	5	16	16	15	20	21	22	21	23	24	20	22	22
6										8	5	5	11	11	10	15	16	16	17	18	19
7													6	4	4	9	8	8	12	12	12
8																5	3	2	7	6	6
9																			4	3	2

with the normal distribution curve. By having larger numbers of persons assigned to those groups in the central positions and fewer to the more extreme groups, an approach to normal distribution can be achieved. If this procedure is accurately carried out, the differences between successive groups in terms of the ability under consideration can be considered to be equal.

In effecting this type of grouping, the total range of individual differences is divided into whatever number of categories is desired, and frequencies are set up for each category in accordance with the normal frequency distribution. Table 3 gives appropriate proportions for dividing a normal population into varying numbers of steps. Since the effective range of individual differences is greater when the number of persons in the distribution is larger, separate frequencies have been presented for situations where 20, 40, and 60 individuals are to be rated. An example of a rating form employing this principle is shown in Table 4.

In the earlier discussion concerning the transformation of ranks into values on a continuous scale, some of the problems involved in the assumption of a normal frequency distribution were considered. The same limitations hold in the assumption of this type of distribution in the group-order ranking method.

Table 4

Rating Scale for Clerical Workers Employing the Group-order Method of Ranking, with Proportions Distributed among the Groups in Accordance with the Normal Frequency Distribution

Rate each of the clerks in your department on the following characteristics. Rate all of them on the first characteristic, Amount of Output, then rate all of them on the second characteristic, Quality of Output, etc. Assign the ratings as follows:

A = 7% B = 25% C = 36% D = 25% E = 7%

These percentages must be adhered to as closely as the number of clerks you are rating will permit. For each characteristic enter all names in the appropriate spaces provided.

	E	D	C	B	A
Amount of output					
Quality of output					
Accuracy					
Punctuality					
Initiative					
Interest					

THE PAIRED COMPARISON TECHNIQUE FOR RATING PERFORMANCE OF INDUSTRIAL EMPLOYEES*

C. H. Lawshe, N. C. Kephart, and E. J. McCormick

The method of paired comparisons has been used occasionally for making subjective ratings of job performance but has not been commonly adopted for this purpose, presumably because of certain disadvantages involved in its usual application. These disadvantages especially center around two factors: first, the time required, including the preparation of the pairs of names of the subjects, the actual rating process, and the summarizing of the results; and second, the rating process has been considered wearying to the raters, particularly if a considerable number of individuals are to be rated.

• THE PERSONNEL COMPARISON SYSTEM[1]

The *Personnel Comparison System* provides for the rating of job performance by the paired comparison technique, but the mechanics of its administration were specifically designed to simplify the various procedures.

The system lends itself to rating any aspect of employee performance, although in most of its applications it has been used for rating over-all job performance. The cue for the use of this basic factor as a measure of job performance is derived from such studies as that of Ewart, Seashore, and Tiffin (*1*) which brings out high degrees of communality among factors typically "measured" on rating scales. These authors identified the factor "Ability to do the present job" which accounted for most of the variability of the ratings.

The *Personnel Comparison System* provides the rater with a booklet that is composed of slips of paper approximately one inch wide and six inches long. Each slip contains one pair of names. To facilitate preparation, eight slips are initially arranged on one 8½ by 11 form. Pairs of names are typed on each slip and the slips are later separated by tearing along perforated lines.

The procedures involved in the administration of the system and the subsequent scoring of results follow:

1. The names of individual pairs are typed on the separate sections of the forms according to a pre-determined order which is presented in table form. The table provides for pairing each employee with each other employee.
2. The sections are separated on the perforations and the slips are assembled into a

[1] The *Personnel Comparison System for Rating Employee Performance* (Copyright 1948 by C. H. Lawshe and N. C. Kephart) is available from Mayer and Company, 15 East Eighth St., Cincinnati 2, Ohio.

* From *Journal of Applied Psychology,* Vol. 33, no. 1, February 1949, pp. 69–77. Copyright 1949 by the American Psychological Association, Inc. Reprinted by permission.

booklet by means of a paper fastener inserted through prepared holes.

3. The rater checks the preferred name on each slip.

4. The number of times each individual is preferred is tallied on a summary sheet.

5. A performance rating index is derived from a table,[2] the specific index being determined by the number of times each individual was preferred and the number of individuals being rated.

APPLICATION OF THE SYSTEM

For the purpose of experimentally applying the *Personnel Comparison System* in an operating situation, arrangements were made with a paper form manufacturing company to rate employee performance in two selected departments. This experimental tryout was directed toward the establishment of a criterion for the validation of personnel tests, rather than as a merit rating procedure. The raters were asked to rate the individuals with the following question in mind, "Which of these two employees is performing his present job better?" The two departments in which the system was tried, and the specific provisions for the application of the system in each, are given below.

1. *Offset press department.* Twenty-four of the offset pressmen who were oldest in point of service were rated by three supervisors and an instructor. All four raters had had an opportunity to become familiar with the work of each pressman through the systematic rotation of the pressman from one shift to another. One booklet including all pairs of employees was provided for each rater. Ratings were made independently.

2. *Stereo press department.* Eight stereo pressmen on each of three shifts were rated. These 24 men had had five or more years of experience on the job. While each man had previously been rotated between all three supervisors, they were classified in terms of their present shift position and the men on each shift were divided into random halves, called, 1–1, 1–2, 2–1, 2–2, 3–1, and 3–2.

Table 1

Subgroups Rated by Each of Three Supervisors on Two Days

	Supervisor Making Rating			
Group	First Day	Second Day		
1–1	A	A		C
1–2	A	A	B	
2–1	B	A	B	
2–2	B		B	C
3–1	C		B	C
3–2	C	A		C

On one day, each of the three supervisors (designated A, B, and C) rated those men then on his shift. On the next day, each supervisor rated the same men along with one-half of the men then on each of the other shifts. The groups rated by the three supervisors on the first and second days are indicated in Table 1. In addition, an instructor (Rater D) rated all of the 24 men.

RESULTS OF OFFSET PRESSMEN STUDY

The first study, involving the 24 offset pressmen, was conducted to determine the reliability of the ratings of different raters.

The agreement between the four raters

[2] The indexes in the table are based on the proportion of times each individual is preferred, converted to standard score units. These units are based on a mean of 50 with a standard deviation of 10. Indexes range from approximately three standard deviations below the mean to approximately three standard deviations above the mean (actually from 23 to 77).

is shown in Table 2. This table shows the number and per cent of pairs in which the same individual was preferred by all four raters; the number of pairs in which three raters chose the same man; and the number of pairs in which the raters split two-to-two. Of the 276 different pairs rated, all four raters preferred the same individual in 227, or 82.3 per cent, of the pairs. In 36 pairs, or 11.1 per cent, three raters preferred the same individual. In the 13 remaining pairs, or 4.7 per cent of the total, two of the raters preferred one of the individuals, and the other two raters preferred the other individual.

Table 2

DISTRIBUTION OF PREFERENCES OF FOUR RATERS ON PAIRS OF TWENTY-FOUR OFFSET PRESSMEN BY NUMBER AND PER CENT OF PAIRS

DISTRIBUTION OF PREFERENCES OF FOUR RATERS ON PAIRS OF EMPLOYEES	NO. OF PAIRS	PER CENT OF PAIRS
4–0	227	82.3
3–1	36	13.0
2–2	13	4.7
	276	100.0

Intercorrelation of Ratings

Further analysis of the agreement among the four raters was accomplished by means of an average intercorrelation coefficient of the rank orders of the 24 men as resulting from the ratings of each of the four raters; the resulting average intercorrelation coefficient of the four rank orders was .94.

Reliability of Ratings on Halves and Quarters

In order to examine possible differences in reliability that would result from the rating of smaller groups of the same employees by the four raters, average intercorrelations were also computed for chance halves and chance quarters of these 24 offset pressmen. The two chance halves included odd-numbered and even-numbered employees respectively, the numbers having been assigned by alphabetical order of names. The chance quarters, in turn, were made up of every fourth name in the list in the same fashion. Only the preferences on pairs of employees included in the particular chance half or chance quarter in question were considered. Within each such group the number of times each employee was preferred was tallied, and rank orders of the men in each group were subsequently determined. The average intercorrelations, computed by the rank-order method, are given in Table 3. These average intercorrelations closely approximate the coefficient of .94 obtained with the whole group. Even the correlation of .85 can reasonably be considered as satisfactory since only six men are involved.

Table 3

AVERAGE INTERCORRELATIONS OF RANK ORDER OF TIMES PREFERRED OF CHANCE HALVES AND CHANCE QUARTERS OF TWENTY-FOUR OFFSET PRESSMEN

GROUP	AVERAGE INTERCORRELATIONS
Chance halves	
1st half	.96
2nd half	.93
Average of 2 halves	.94
Chance quarters	
1st quarter	.97
2nd quarter	.85
3rd quarter	.93
4th quarter	.94
Average of 4 quarters	.92

Reliability of Ratings on Restricted Range Group

A further analysis of this same character was made with respect to a selected group of the 24 pressmen representing a restricted range of talent. The over-all group included three floormen (working supervisors), thirteen "A" pressmen, seven "B" pressmen, and one helper. The 13 "A" pressmen (who operate somewhat more complex offset presses) were selected from the group for separate analysis, and the number of times each of these was preferred over the others within this same group was tallied. The resulting average intercorrelation of the rank orders of this group was .79.

This reduction in average intercorrelation from that of the over-all group and from those for the chance halves and chance quarters would be expected, since the group of "A" pressmen was much more restricted in its range of talent, and, generally speaking, tended to fall within the central and above-average (though not extreme top) range of the distribution of the entire group. The floormen consistently were rated above the "A" pressmen, and to a considerable extent the "B" pressmen and the helper tended to be rated toward the lower end of the over-all group.

The ratings of these 13 "A" pressmen were then subjected to a different type of analysis. The relative rank orders of these 13 men were "extracted" from the rank orders of the entire group; they were then compared with the rank orders resulting from the preferences on *only* the pairs of men in this sub-group. The rho correlation between these two rank orders was .996, indicating that there was practically no displacement in rank-order position among these 13 men when their rank order was derived from the ratings made exclusively on this group, as compared with their relative rank orders when "extracted" from that of the whole group.

• RESULTS OF STEREO PRESSMEN STUDY

As indicated before, the eight stereo pressmen on each shift were split into chance halves. On one day each supervisor rated the eight men together, and on the subsequent day each supervisor rated the same eight men along with one of the halves of each of the other shifts. The instructor rated all 24 men on one occasion.

In order to determine the correlations between subsequent ratings on men rated twice by the same supervisor, or on ratings by two or more raters on men rated in common, only the pairs of names pertinent to any such specific analysis were used in tallying the number of times each man was preferred. The rank-difference correlation coefficients (rho) between the several combinations of ratings are given in Table 4.

Reliability of Two Ratings by Three Supervisors

The initial analysis of the ratings of the stereo pressmen was that of the reliability of the two ratings made by each of the three supervisors of the eight men who were then under their respective supervision. The rank-difference correlations (rho) between the two ratings made by each of the supervisors ranged from .94 to 1.00, with an average of .97, which reflects a highly satisfactory degree of consistency between the ratings.

Table 4

RANK-DIFFERENCE CORRELATIONS (RHO) OF VARIOUS RATINGS ON TWENTY-FOUR STEREO PRESSMEN

RATER	GROUPS RATED	NO. OF MEN IN GROUP	COEFFICIENT OF CORRELATION (RHO)
First and second ratings by each of three supervisors			
A	1–1, 1–2	8	.98
B	2–2, 2–2	8	1.00
C	3–1, 3–2	8	.94
Average			.97
Ratings by two different supervisors			
A & B	1–2, 2–1	8	.81
A & C	1–1, 3–2	8	.83
B & C	2–2, 3–1	8	.86
Average			.83
Ratings by each of three supervisors and one instructor			
A & D	1–1, 1–2 2–1, 3–2	16	.88
B & D	1–2, 2–1 2–2, 3–1	16	.90
C & D	1–1, 2–2 3–1, 3–2	16	.83
Average			.87

Reliability of Ratings Among Three Supervisors

As indicated above, eight men were rated in common by supervisors A and B, eight others were rated in common by supervisors A and C, and eight others were rated in common by supervisors B and C. The rank-difference correlations between the two ratings of each of these three groups ranged from .81 to .86, with an average of .83. While these coefficients between ratings made by different supervisors are somewhat below the coefficients of the two ratings made by the same supervisors on men whom they rated on successive days, they can nevertheless be considered as reflecting an adequate degree of consistency among the three raters.

Reliability of Ratings Between Three Individual Supervisors and One Instructor

Each supervisor rated 16 men, while all 24 were rated by the instructor. The rank-difference correlation coefficients between the ratings of each of the supervisors and the ratings of the instructor ranged from .83 to .90, with an average of .87.

Reliability of Ratings of Three Raters

Since each of three groups of eight stereo pressmen was rated by two different supervisors and by the instructor, it was possible to determine the average intercorrelations of the rank-orders resulting from the three ratings on each

Table 5

AVERAGE INTERCORRELATIONS OF RATINGS BY THREE RATERS OF THREE GROUPS OF EIGHT STEREO PRESSMEN

RATERS	GROUPS	AVERAGE INTER-CORRELATION
A, B, D	1–2, 2–1	.84
A, C, D	1–1, 3–2	.76
B, C, D	2–2, 3–1	.87
Average		.82

of these groups of eight men. These average intercorrelations were .76, .84, and .87, the average of the three being .82. (See Table 5.) This average is lower than the average of the other measures of reliability previously mentioned, but is within the same relative range as those of the other measures of reliability.

• ADMINISTRATION OF RATING SYSTEM

Time Required for Administration

The time required for applying the rating system to the 24 offset pressmen may give a rough indication of the practical feasibility of the system in somewhat comparable circumstances. It was estimated that it took a total of 12 hours to type the slips for the 276 pairs (including carbon copies for the four raters), to assemble the four booklets, to rate the workers, and to derive the rating indexes. This time did not include planning, conference, or administrative time, but did include the time required for the rating by all four raters. In view of the fact that time required for functions such as typing and separation of the slips does not increase proportionately with the number of different raters, the over-all time is not indicative of the time that would be required if the rating were done by one rater rather than by four. It is estimated that the time required to prepare material and to summarize results for a complete rating of the 24 men by one rater would be about five or six hours.

The actual time required for each rater to rate the 276 pairs, however, was only about 30 minutes. This time required for actual rating is sufficiently reasonable to raise a question about the comments made by Guilford (2) and made in the report of the National Industrial Conference Board (3) to the effect that the method of paired comparisons is, by its nature, excessively wearying to the raters. More specifically, there is reason to doubt the limit of 15 subjects implied by Guilford as the upper limit of the practical application of the technique. Perhaps the mechanics of the specific scheme provided for making the ratings have a significant bearing on the degree to which the system is acceptable to the raters, and consequently on the total number of subjects that can reasonably be rated by one individual.

In considering the over-all time required for all the processes, there was no suggestion that this time was considered excessive by the company applying the system to these two groups of workers.

• SUMMARY AND CONCLUSIONS

Two groups of 24 workers each were rated by the paired comparison technique using the *Personnel Comparison System.* One of the groups included 24 offset pressmen who were all rated by three supervisors and one instructor. The other group included 24 stereo pressmen, eight from each of three shifts; each supervisor rated the eight men on his own shift on one day, and on the next day he rated the same men along with one-half of the men on each of the other shifts, making a total of 16 men. An instructor rated all 24 stereo pressmen once.

Analyses of the resulting ratings brought about the following primary conclusions:

1. There was a high degree of reliability between the ratings of two or more raters who rated the same employees.

2. There was a high degree of reliability between successive ratings, made on different days by each of three raters, on the employees whom they individually supervised.

3. The analysis of the ratings of a selected subgroup of employees revealed very little relative displacement in their rank-order position derived from the ratings on only the selected employees, as compared with their relative rank-order positions "extracted" from the ratings of the larger group of which they were a part.

4. The evidence accumulated did not indicate that the time required of raters was excessive.

REFERENCES

1. Ewart, E., Seashore, S. E., and Tiffin, J., "A factor analysis of an industrial merit rating scale," *J. appl. Psychol.*, 1941, **25**, 481–486.
2. Guilford, J. P. *Psychometric methods.* New York, McGraw-Hill Book Company, Inc., 1936.
3. *Employee rating; methods of appraising ability, efficiency, and potentialities.* National Industrial Conference Board, Studies in Personnel Policy No. 39, 1942.

WAR DEPARTMENT INSTRUCTIONS FOR RATING COMMISSIONED OFFICERS*

• SIGNIFICANCE OF THE RATING SCALE

1. Under General Orders 46 and 85 (W. D., 1918) all officers in the Army below the rank of Brigadier General will be rated quarterly according to the Officers' Rating Scale. Circular No. 73 (W. D., 1918) provides that a final rating will be given each officer just prior to separation from the service. The rating of an officer is a numerical expression of the degree in which he possesses the five essential qualifications of an officer, namely; (1) Physical Qualities, (2) Intelligence, (3) Leadership, (4) Personal Qualities, and (5) General Value to the Service. The rating is made by comparing him in each of these respects with officers of the next higher rank.

2. Promotions, discharges, and subsequent appointments are determined as a rule by ratings. Making just and accurate ratings is therefore one of the most serious duties of an officer. Proper rating is largely dependent on the possession of an accurate Rating Scale. Each rating officer makes his own scale, using the reverse of this form.

• HOW TO MAKE THE SCALE

3. Write on small slips of paper the names of from 12 to 25 officers of your own rank and not above the average age of that rank. They should be men with whom you have served or with whom you are well acquainted. Include officers whose qualifications are extremely poor as well as those who are highly efficient. If these names do not include all the grades for each of the five qualifications, others may be added.

4. Look over your names from the viewpoint of Physical Qualities only. Disregard every other characteristic of each officer except the way in which he impresses his men by his physique, bearing, neatness, voice, energy, and endurance. Arrange the names on the slips of paper in order from highest to lowest on the basis of the physical qualities of the men. Select that officer who surpasses all the others in this qualification and enter his name on the line marked Highest under Physical Qualities. Then select the one who most conspicuously lacks these qualities and enter his name on the line marked Lowest. Select the officer who seems about halfway between the two previously selected and who represents about the general average in physical qualities; enter his name on the line marked Middle. Select the officer who is halfway between middle and highest; enter his name on the line marked High. Select the one who ranks halfway between middle and lowest; enter his name on the line marked Low.

5. In the same manner make out scales for each of the other four qualifications (Intelligence, Leadership, Personal Qualities, and General Value to the Service).

---

* By permission from *Personnel Management,* by Walter Dill Scott, et al. (Second Edition, pp. 217–218.) Copyright, 1941, McGraw-Hill Book Company, Inc.

6. Each officer whose name appears on the scale should be one who exhibits clearly and distinctly the qualification and the degree of the qualification for which he has been chosen.

7. The names for Highest and Lowest on each section of the Scale must represent extreme cases. The name for the Middle should be that of an average officer, halfway between extremes. High and Low should be halfway between the Middle and the extremes. An even gradation of merit is important.

8. In making or using any section of the Scale, consider only the qualification it covers, totally disregarding all the others.

9. In rating subordinates of more than one grade the best practice is to make separate scales for each grade, using always the names of officers one grade higher than that of the subordinate to be rated. However, in exceptional cases good results have been secured where a Scale constructed of captains is used for rating both lieutenants and captains, and a Scale constructed of colonels is used for rating all ranks of field officers.

• POINTS FOR SPECIAL ATTENTION

10. Rate your subordinate for Physical Qualities first. Consider how he impresses his men by his physique, bearing, neatness, voice, energy, and endurance. Compare him with each of the five officers in section I of your Rating Scale, and give him the number of points following the name of the officer he most nearly equals. If he falls between two officers in the Scale, give him a number accordingly (e. g., if between Low and Middle, give him 7, 7½, or 8).

11. Rate the subordinate in a corresponding manner for each of the other four essential qualifications.

12. In rating, make a man-to-man comparison of the subordinate with the officers whose names appear on your scale. Disregard the numerical equivalent until you have made these concrete comparisons.

13. When rating several subordinates, rate all of them on each qualification before adding the total for any one.

14. This is not a percentage system and you should not allow yourself to fix in mind any particular number of points you think the subordinate ought to get.

15. The total rating for a subordinate is the sum of the ratings you give him in the five separate qualities. If these directions are followed carefully, the average of any considerable group of officers rated will not be over 60 points.

16. Each officer below the rank of Brigadier General will be rated by his immediate superior. Ratings will be revised or approved by the immediate superior of the officer making the rating. Each revising officer will be held responsible for the ratings made by his subordinates.

I. Physical Qualities

Physique, bearing, neatness, voice, energy and endurance. (Consider how he impresses his men in the above respects.)

Highest	15
High	12
Middle	9
Low	6
Lowest	3

II. Intelligence

Accuracy, ease in learning, ability to grasp quickly the point of view of commanding officer, to issue clear and intelligent orders, to estimate a new situation, and to arrive at a sensible decision in a crisis.

Highest	15
High	12
Middle	9
Low	6
Lowest	3

III. Leadership

Initiative, force, self reliance, decisiveness, tact, ability to inspire men and to command their obedience, loyalty, and cooperation.

Highest	15
High	12
Middle	9
Low	6
Lowest	3

IV. Personal Qualities

Industry, dependability, loyalty, readiness to shoulder responsibility for his own acts, freedom from conceit and selfishness, readiness and ability to cooperate.

Highest	15
High	12
Middle	9
Low	6
Lowest	3

V. General Value to the Service

His professional knowledge, skill and experience; success as an administrator and instructor; ability to get results.

Highest	40
High	32
Middle	24
Low	16
Lowest	8

A. Rating by Supervisors

4. FREE-WRITTEN (ESSAY) RATINGS

THE FREE-WRITTEN RATING

MARION W. RICHARDSON

QUOTES FROM OFFICER EFFICIENCY REPORTS

AN AIR FORCE OFFICER

Though in practice seldom used alone, essay ratings are nonetheless significant. In the first place, as Richardson points out, this rating technique is important in the development of a forced-choice rating. In addition, space is almost always provided on any sort of rating form for a brief essay, or narrative statement, about the person being rated. As the second reading illustrates in humorous fashion, a single sentence can often tell more than a sophisticated scale.

In Part Four, the article by Kenneth Richards presents an example of an important application of the essay rating.

THE FREE-WRITTEN RATING*

Marion W. Richardson

One way to approach the problem [of appraisal] is to ask someone who is in a position to know thoroughly a man's work performance to describe that performance and tell how good it is. In practice, something of the sort is always done in any organization, with or without benefit of a formal merit-rating procedure. The general idea seems simple but is actually complicated for the following reasons:

1. Some supervisors can do a good job of reporting the work behavior of subordinates, and others cannot. Some are good observers but cannot write with skill or give a good oral report. One organization that tried to get its supervisors to make free-written ratings with only a general guide to help them came to the conclusion that ratings were more affected by the writing skill of the executive than by the actual merit of the subordinate. Moreover, it became clear that mere willingness to take pains in making the report was a factor in determining how high a man would be rated.
2. The method is time-consuming as compared with formal rating methods.
3. Equally competent executives tend to differ with respect to the aspects of job performance they consider most important. Obviously, value-systems of responsible executives have significance, but a consensus as to what is most important in job performance has more value in the long run than any individual opinion.
4. The method does not lend itself to any form of expression in numerical terms; thus it would be almost impossible to place a group of men in rank order for promotion purposes.

Although this method is impractical in operation, it does serve as a one-time research technique for the development of a modern forced-choice performance report.

* From "Forced Choice Performance Reports," in *Rating Employee and Supervisory Performance*, edited by M. Joseph Dooher and Vivienne Marquis (p. 37). New York, American Management Association, 1950.

QUOTES FROM OFFICER EFFICIENCY REPORTS*

Once a year, commanding officers throughout the military sharpen their pencils and compose volumes of what you'd imagine is extremely dull reading —"efficiency" reports on the officers in their command.

By the rules of the game, these 50- to 100-word comments should size up a man's ability accurately, objectively, and solemnly. Promotions and careers hinge on good efficiency ratings. Bad ones can be appealed, and all must be endorsed and reviewed. All become part of the officer's permanent file in the Pentagon.

But actually many ratings are not solemn at all. They make up one of the

* This edited excerpt is taken from a paper submitted by a U. S. Air Force officer enrolled in a university school of business.

nation's richest veins of off-guard humor. Asked for an evaluation, many a CO responds with a punch line. Others simply get their verbal feet mixed up. And often, the rating tells more about the CO than about the subordinate—as some of these examples mined from Air Force files will show:[1]

This officer has talents but has kept them well hidden.

Combs his hair to one side and appears rustic.

A quiet, reticent, neat appearing officer—industrious, tenacious, diffident, careful, and neat. I do not wish to have this officer as a member of my command at any time.

Does not drink but is a good mixer.

Can express a sentence in two paragraphs at any time.

His leadership is outstanding except for his lack of ability to get along with his subordinates.

He has failed to demonstrate any outstanding weaknesses.

He hasn't any mental traits.

His departure is in no way considered a loss. In fact, it is a gain. His transfer was concurred in by all commanders with relief.

He needs careful watching since he borders on the brilliant.

A particularly fine appearance when astride a horse.

Believes sincerely in the power of prayer and it is astonishing to note how many times his prayers are answered.

A tall stocky officer.

[1] Original source unknown.

Open to suggestions but never follows same.

Never makes the same mistake twice but it seems to me that he has made them all once.

Has begun to fraternize without realizing it.

In any change of policy or procedure, he can be depended upon to produce the improbable hypothetical situation in which the new policy will not work.

Gives the appearance of being fat due to the tight clothes he wears.

Is stable under pressure and is not influenced by superiors.

Is keenly analytical and his highly developed mentality could best be used in the research and development field. He lacks common sense.

Has developed into a good round staff officer.

Tends to over-estimate himself and under-estimate his problem, being surprised and confused by the resulting situations.

An independent thinker with a mediocre mentality.

Maintains good relations unilaterally.

Recently married and devotes more time to this activity than to his current assignment.

An exceptionally well qualified officer with a broad base.

Tends to create the impression of unpositive personality through needless and undiscerning gentility and softspokenness.

Of average intelligence except for lack of judgment on one occasion in attempting to capture a rattlesnake for which he was hospitalized.

A. Rating by Supervisors

5. FORCED-CHOICE PERFORMANCE REPORTS —TECHNIQUES AND CRITICISMS

FORCED CHOICE—THE NEW ARMY RATING

DONALD SISSON

FORCED CHOICE: BETTER THAN OTHER RATING METHODS?

LEE W. COZAN

A STUDY OF LENIENCY IN TWO RATING SYSTEMS

ERWIN K. TAYLOR AND ROBERT J. WHERRY

FORCED-CHOICE PERFORMANCE RATING—A METHODOLOGICAL STUDY

JAMES R. BERKSHIRE AND RICHARD W. HIGHLAND

A highly popular form of rating is that known as the forced-choice performance report. Its main appeal is the apparent objectivity it introduces into the rating process. The readings in this section describe the method and take some critical looks at its value.

FURTHER READING

Huttner, Ludwig, and Raymond A. Katzell, "Developing a Yardstick of Supervisory Performance," *Personnel,* Vol. 33, no. 4, January 1957, pp. 371–378.

Kay, Brian R., "The Use of Critical Incidents in a Forced-Choice Scale," *Journal of Applied Psychology,* Vol. 43, no. 4, August 1959, pp. 269–270.

Richardson, Marion W., "Forced-Choice Performance Reports: A Modern Merit-Rating Method," *Personnel,* Vol. 26, no. 3, November 1949, pp. 205–212.

Wherry, Robert J., "An Evaluative and Diagnostic Forced-Choice Rating Scale for Servicemen," *Personnel Psychology,* Vol. 12, no. 2, Summer 1959, pp. 227–263.

FORCED CHOICE—THE NEW ARMY RATING*

E. Donald Sisson

• SUMMARY

The origin of the use of efficiency reports for Officers of the U. S. Army is lost in history, as is the story of the evolution of the formal procedures of reporting. Sometime after the first World War, however, a standard form was adopted and a procedure regularized for acomplishing this report. Thereafter, twice each year—on June 30th and on December 31st—every officer in the Army has been rated by his immediate superior, and this rating submitted to the War Department. Though early recognized as not completely satisfactory, the original rating form remained in force (with sporadic minor amendments) until it was superseded in July of 1947.

The new form is the product of many months of concentrated research. It is radically different in many respects from the old form, and from other rating devices currently in use in industry. Its most novel feature is the use of what has been called the "forced-choice" rating method. Rather than indicating how much or how little of each characteristic an officer possesses, the rater is required to choose, from several sets of four adjectives or phrases, which best characterizes the officer and which is least descriptive. In other words, it calls for objective reporting and minimizes subjective judgment. And because of the way in which the tetrads—sets of four rating elements—are constructed, it reduces the rater's ability to produce any desired outcome by the choice of obviously good or obviously bad traits. It thus diminishes the effects of favoritism and personal bias.

The technique, and the form embodying it, has been tried out on fifty thousand officers—in both experimental and official trials—and the results obtained with it have been compared with independent criteria of efficiency arrived at through group ratings. The new method is superior to all other methods examined. It produces a better distribution of ratings relatively free from the usual pile-up at the top of the scale. It is less subject to influence by the rank of the officer being rated. It is quickly and objectively scored by machine. And above all, it produces ratings which are more valid indices of real worth.

The particular form developed for rating Army officers would probably be of little value for other groups—largely because of the specificity of the rating elements it contains. The technique, however, has already proved of value in other situations and there is every reason to believe that it is even more generally applicable.

NOTE. The research reported in this study represents the combined efforts of the entire professional staff of the Personnel Research Section, AGO in 1945. The opinions expressed, however, are those of the author and do not necessarily represent those of the Department of the Army.

* From *Personnel Psychology,* Vol. 1, no. 3, Autumn 1948, pp. 365–381. Copyright 1948 by Personnel Psychology, Inc. Reprinted by permission.

• THE OLD RATING SYSTEM

It can generally be assumed that the main value of efficiency ratings—usually their sole purpose—is in providing a sound basis for personnel actions. Yet when the clouds of war rolled up in 1940 and it became evident that the Army needed to promote a rather large number of top-ranking officers immediately to serve as generals of the rapidly mobilizing forces, it was suddenly discovered that the years of regular efficiency reporting had provided no basis for the important decisions that had to be made. To quote one of the men responsible for making the selections at that time: "Efficiency reports, instead of showing the 150 best, showed only that of 4000 ground officers of suitable general officer age, 2000 were superior and best. As such a showing was perfectly worthless for the purpose, the selecting authorities reluctantly fell back on personal knowledge, which is exactly what the Army thought it was getting away from when, twenty years ago, it inaugurated the existing system."[1]

The existing system was not as bad as this recital might make it appear. As such systems go, in fact, it was fairly typical and quite respectable; it would even compare rather favorably with the run-of-the-mill of systems currently in use in business and industry. It contained some ten numerical scales covering such general traits as "force," "leadership," "attention to duty," "ability to obtain results," and so forth; and each scale, as well as the net numerical score, was divided into areas which were assigned the five adjectival ratings of superior, excellent, very satisfactory, satisfactory, and unsatisfactory. It was generally filled out with great care, and undoubtedly with great seriousness—nothing is more important to the Army officer than his efficiency index. Moreover, its validity as determined through extensive tests was shown to be at least fair, particularly with respect to the identification of a very small number of outstandingly poor officers.

If a superior officer really and honestly wanted to point up the deficiencies in a truly poor subordinate, the form was adequate to the purpose. But therein lay its greatest weakness; the rater could control the outcome at will. And because of traditions, the pressures of circumstances and for a host of other reasons—personal or general—he usually made it come out high. He said only the best of his men or else "damned with faint praise" by saying the next best about those whose performance was low. Or if his conscience pricked, he said nothing, and left the trait unrated with a cryptic "unknown." "Nothing but good" was the general rule, with the consequence that the whole scale was distorted; what was supposed to be outstanding became typical; and to be labelled "satisfactory" was to be called "intolerably inefficient." To correct these deficiencies in the system, and to provide a more valid procedure for rating Army officers, work was begun in 1945 on the development of a new efficiency report.

• THE NEW OFFICER EFFICIENCY REPORT

At the outset the research leaned pretty heavily on the finding of a recently completed program for screening

[1] Details of the comparative validity of a number of rating systems will be published in the near future.

wartime officers to be offered commissions in the Regular Army. One of the instruments developed in that program—and shown to possess a high degree of validity—was a rating form which incorporated, among other elements, a forced-choice section. In addition, a by-product of the earlier research program—a method for constructing an acceptable criterion—was of equal importance to the present problem. This latter will be discussed first.

The Criterion

The crucial importance of the criterion in research of this kind cannot be overemphasized. To determine the validity of any rating system, it is obviously necessary to compare ratings produced by it with some independent measure of each man's "true" merit. In this case, the criterion problem was attacked by identifying groups of officers who were clearly outstanding in efficiency or competence and other groups clearly less competent. This identification, of course, could not be based on existing efficiency reports since to do so would beg the whole question. Nor could it be based solely on other such opinions of superiors. It was decided, therefore, to use the consensus of fellow-officers in identifying the Army's best and poorest. The procedure followed was somewhat as follows. Officers belonging to the same unit, and in a position to know each other's work and qualifications, were assembled in groups of about twelve to forty. Each was furnished a form on which all names appeared in alphabetical order, regardless of rank. Without signing the form or identifying himself in any way, each officer was asked to select the best—most competent—of the group, then the least competent, and to continue selecting most and least competent until all but about five names on the list had been selected as among the most or least competent. By tallying these nominations, it was possible to earmark the two or three in each group who were clearly best, the two or three clearly poorest, and finally, from among the names not rated either high or low, some truly average officers. By repeating the process in literally hundreds of such units, comprising almost 50,000 officers, rather sizable groups of high, middle, and low officers were identified.

Members of these three widely divergent criterion groups were rated in the normal manner on various types of rating forms. Needless to say, no rating officer was apprised of the criterion status of the ratee. Results obtained with these independent ratings were correlated with criterion-group membership. In all comparisons, one particular form stood out as most valid. This was the form containing the forced-choice elements mentioned above.

How Forced Choice Items Are Made

Forced-choice rating elements are sets of four phrases or adjectives pertaining to job proficiency or personal qualifications. The rater indicates which of the four is most characteristic of the ratee, and which is least characteristic; and repeats this selection for each of the sets included. A sample set is the following:

A. Commands respect by his actions
B. Coolheaded
C. Indifferent
D. Overbearing

It is at once obvious that two of these are relatively favorable terms, and the

F 1423 REV. 3

EFFICIENCY REPORT

WD AGO Form 67-1 Part 2 See AR 600–185 for details.

Unit Adjutant or Personnel Officer will complete Sections I and III.
Rating Officer will complete Sections II, IV, V, VI, VII, VIII, and IX.
Indorsing Officer will complete Sections II, V, VII, and IX.

Section III. OFFICER REPORTED UPON
Enter same information as for Section I.

LAST NAME FIRST NAME INITIAL	SERIAL NUMBER	GRADE	ARM OR SERVICE	COMPONENT	PERIOD OF REPORT FROM	TO	DO NOT WRITE IN THIS SPACE

THEATER OR CONTINENTAL COMMAND	UNIT, ORGANIZATION, AND STATION	PRIMARY MOS	DUTY ASSIGNMENT (MOS CODE)	DAYS OF DUTY	LEAVE	OTHER NON-DUTY	JP

DATE OF REPORT	FOR REPORTS RENDERED BECAUSE OF PERMANENT CHANGE OF STATION, SUPPLY ADDRESS OF UNIT AND INSTALLATION WHERE OFFICER WILL REPORT	PQ
		OA

READ INSTRUCTION SHEET CAREFULLY BEFORE MARKING THIS SECTION

Section IV. JOB PROFICIENCY

	1 MOST	LEAST		4 MOST	LEAST		7 MOST	LEAST		10 MOST	LEAST
A. Becomes dogmatic about his authority.			A. Always criticizes, never praises.			A. Fails to work for the best interest of all.			A. Fails to support fellow officers.		
B. Careless & slipshod in attention to duty.			B. Carries out orders by "passing the buck."			B. Has a high degree of initiative.			B. Oversteps his authority.		
C. No one ever doubts his ability.			C. Knows his job and performs it well.			C. Never makes excuses for his mistakes.			C. Gives clear and concise directions.		
D. Well-grounded in all phases of Army life.			D. Plays no favorites.			D. Slow in accomplishing his work.			D. Very exacting in all details.		

	2 MOST	LEAST		5 MOST	LEAST		8 MOST	LEAST		11 MOST	LEAST
A. Follows closely directions of higher echelons.			A. Constantly striving for new knowledge and ideas.			A. Criticizes policies of superiors.			A. Blames others for his mistakes.		
B. Inclined to "gold-brick."			B. Businesslike.			B. Others can't work with him.			B. Always demands strict discipline.		
C. Criticizes unnecessarily.			C. Apparently not physically fit.			C. If he is wrong, will admit it.			C. Excellent at constructive criticism.		
D. Willing to accept responsibility.			D. Fails to use good judgment.			D. The men know they can rely on his judgment.			D. Hesitant about rendering decisions.		

	3 MOST	LEAST		6 MOST	LEAST		9 MOST	LEAST		12 MOST	LEAST
A. A go-getter who always does a good job.			A. Cannot assume responsibility.			A. Doesn't try to "pull rank."			A. Can take over in an emergency.		
B. Cool under all circumstances.			B. Knows how and when to delegate authority.			B. Knows men, their capabilities & limitations.			B. Fair and just in his dealings.		
C. Doesn't listen to suggestions.			C. Offers suggestions.			C. Low efficiency.			C. Lacks interest in his job.		
D. Drives instead of leads.			D. Too easily changes his ideas.			D. Uses a steady monotone in his speech.			D. Questions orders from superiors.		

READ INSTRUCTION SHEET CAREFULLY BEFORE MARKING THIS SECTION

Section V. JOB PROFICIENCY

DO NOT WRITE IN THIS SPACE

1 Management and operation of military matters not included in tactics and strategy.
2 The directions of the over-all operation of a military unit.
3 Presenting learning materials in a classroom situation in a military or civilian component.
4 Exercise of specialized knowledge, requiring lengthy technological training.
5 Assisting commanders of battalions or larger units in devising methods of meeting the requirements of military situations.
6 Duties involving aeronautical skills performed by rated officers.
7 Training at service schools, Air University, Army Industrial College, etc.

	FOR RATING OFFICER		FOR INDORSING OFFICER
PRIMARY	1 2 3 4 5 6 7 8 9 10	PRIMARY	1 2 3 4 5 6 7 8 9 10
SECONDARY	1 2 3 4 5 6 7 8 9 10	SECONDARY	1 2 3 4 5 6 7 8 9 10

DO NOT WRITE IN THIS SPACE	1	2	3	4	5	6	7	8	9	10	11	12	13	14	15	16
	17	18	19	20	21	22	23	24	25	26	27	28	29	30	31	32

Fig. 1. Job proficiency section of new officer efficiency report.

other two relatively unfavorable. One of the two favorable terms, checked as most characteristic, gives plus credit; selecting the other, gives no credit. In the same way, picking one of the two unfavorable items as least characteristic adds credit whereas the other adds nothing.

The construction of these tetrads and the determination of the scoring key are the crucial problems in the development of a rating scale of this type. Rundquist (2) outlined six steps in the process.

1. Collection of brief essay descriptions of successful and unsuccessful officers.

2. Preparation of a complete list of de-

scriptive phrases or adjectives culled from these essays, and the administration of this list to a representative group of officers.

3. Determination of two indices for each descriptive phrases or adjective—a preference index and a discrimination index.

4. Selecting pairs of phrases or adjectives such that they appear of equal value to the rater (preference index) but differ in their significance for success as an officer (discrimination index).

5. Assembling of pairs so selected into tetrads.

6. Item selection against an external criterion and cross-validation of the selected items.

F 1429 REV. 4

Section VI. PERSONAL QUALIFICATIONS

Use ELECTROGRAPHIC PENCIL, following same directions as for Section IV. Make ONE mark in EACH column for each set of items.

	MOST	LEAST
1		
A. People work for & with him because of his personality.		
B. Never rank-conscious.		
C. Thinks only of himself.		
D. Worries a great deal.		
2		
A. Active in athletics.		
B. Firm but not overbearing.		
C. Egotistical.		
D. Rubs people the wrong way.		
3		
A. Compliments a man on his good work.		
B. Loses his head, gets excited.		
C. Has admiration of officers & men alike.		
D. Poor in dress & appearance.		
4		
A. Lacks ability to inspire confidence of men & officers.		
B. Easygoing.		
C. Type of man everyone likes for a friend.		
D. Has a quiet, dignified bearing.		
5		
A. Hot-tempered.		
B. Fails to demonstrate originality.		
C. Reserved.		
D. Impresses people favorably.		
6		
A. Boastful.		
B. Inspires pride in the organization.		
C. Lacks tact.		
D. Thoughtful of others.		
7		
A. Plenty of military snap, bearing, & neatness.		
B. Normally cheerful.		
C. Can't take criticism.		
D. Doesn't get along with people.		
8		
A. Modest & reserved.		
B. Doesn't have drive or force he should.		
C. Antisocial.		
D. Respected by all fellow officers.		
9		
A. A quiet, unassuming officer.		
B. Follows rather than leads.		
C. Has an attitude of superiority.		
D. Tactful.		
10		
A. Obtains respect & obedience without causing resentment.		
B. Lacks aggressiveness.		
C. Has an excellent command of language.		
D. Lacking in good conduct & moral habits.		
11		
A. Coolheaded.		
B. Commands respect by his actions.		
C. Overbearing.		
D. Indifferent.		
12		
A. Immature.		
B. Modest but not retiring.		
C. Nervous.		
D. Thoroughly cooperative in his work.		

Section VII. PERSONAL QUALIFICATIONS

Use ELECTROGRAPHIC PENCIL, following same directions as for Section V. MARK ALL SIX QUALIFICATIONS.

	FOR RATING OFFICER	FOR INDORSING OFFICER
The degree to which he is able to meet situations without bias and without emotional upset.	1 2 3 4 5 6 7 8 9 10	1 2 3 4 5 6 7 8 9 10
The degree to which he is able and willing to work with other officers and enlisted men.	1 2 3 4 5 6 7 8 9 10	1 2 3 4 5 6 7 8 9 10
The degree to which he is able to act on his own responsibility in absence of orders.	1 2 3 4 5 6 7 8 9 10	1 2 3 4 5 6 7 8 9 10
The degree to which he is able to discriminate & evaluate facts to arrive at logical conclusions.	1 2 3 4 5 6 7 8 9 10	1 2 3 4 5 6 7 8 9 10
The degree to which his appearance and behavior cause people to react favorably.	1 2 3 4 5 6 7 8 9 10	1 2 3 4 5 6 7 8 9 10
The degree to which he is able to carry out orders with consistency & firmness to achieve objectives.	1 2 3 4 5 6 7 8 9 10	1 2 3 4 5 6 7 8 9 10

Section VIII. OVER-ALL RELATIVE RANK

FOR RATER ONLY

The number of officers in this grade rated by me at this time is______	If these officers were arranged in order, considering over-all future usefulness to the Army, from highest (No.1) to poorest, this officer would be No.______ of the total group rated.

Section IX. AUTHENTICATION

Use typewriter (except for signatures) or ink.

I certify that I have read the current AR 600-18 and that all ratings are made in accordance with instructions contained therein, and that to the best of my knowledge and belief all entries contained hereon are true and impartial.

SIGNATURE OF RATING OFFICER	SIGNATURE OF INDORSING OFFICER
NAME, GRADE, AND ORGANIZATION OR UNIT	NAME, GRADE, AND ORGANIZATION OR UNIT
OFFICIAL STATUS OF RATED OFFICER WITH RESPECT TO RATING OFFICER	OFFICIAL STATUS OF RATED OFFICER WITH RESPECT TO INDORSING OFFICER

Fig. 2. Personal qualifications section of new officer efficiency report.

The New Officer Efficiency Report, as it was approved for official use, consists of twelve of these forced-choice tetrads relating to job proficiency, followed by two ten-point graphic scales concerning the ratee's primary and secondary duties (Figure 1). Then there are twelve more tetrads pertaining to personal qualifications, followed this time by six ten-point scales concerning such general characteristics as cooperation—spelled out as "The degree to which he is able and willing to work with other officers and enlisted men"—or initiative, the "degree to which he is able to act on his own responsibility in the absence of orders."

EFFICIENCY REPORT

See AR 600–185 for details.

Unit Adjutant or Personnel Officer will complete Sections I and III.
Rating Officer will complete Sections II, IV, V, VI, VII, VIII, and IX.
Indorsing Officer will complete Sections II, V, VII, and IX.

Section I. OFFICER REPORTED UPON

Use typewriter or print in ink. Use carbon paper to fill out Section III at same time. See AR 600–185.

LAST NAME	FIRST NAME	INITIAL	SERIAL NUMBER	GRADE	ARM OR SERVICE	COMPONENT	PERIOD OF REPORT FROM	TO	DO NOT WRITE IN THIS SPACE

THEATER OR CONTINENTAL COMMAND	UNIT, ORGANIZATION, AND STATION	PRIMARY MOS	DUTY ASSIGNMENT (MOS CODE)	DAYS OF DUTY	LEAVE	OTHER NON-DUTY	JP

DATE OF REPORT	FOR REPORTS RENDERED BECAUSE OF PERMANENT CHANGE OF STATION, SUPPLY ADDRESS OF UNIT AND INSTALLATION WHERE OFFICER WILL REPORT	PQ

NAME, GRADE, AND ORGANIZATION OR UNIT OF RATING OFFICER	NAME, GRADE, AND ORGANIZATION OR UNIT OF INDORSING OFFICER	OA

Section II. DATA AND SUGGESTIONS FOR USE IN ASSIGNMENT

NOTE: Information on this page will be forwarded to the Career Branch of the Personnel and Administration Division by TAG after ratings have been determined. Proper future assignment and utilization of the officer will depend upon the care with which information in this section is formulated and reported. Use typewriter or print in ink.

A. DUTIES ACTUALLY PERFORMED ON PRESENT JOB. To be supplied by Rater. Be specific. Give his duty assignment and all additional duties with enough specific detail to show scope of job in each area.

B. DESCRIPTION OF OFFICER RATED AND COMMENTS. These paragraphs should cover physical, mental, moral qualities of rated officer, specialties of value to the Army, and any special defects or weaknesses affecting his ability to do certain assignments.

COMMENTS OF RATING OFFICER	COMMENTS OF INDORSING OFFICER

C. ESTIMATED DESIRABILITY IN VARIOUS CAPACITIES. Assume you are a commander of a major unit in war. Indicate to what extent you would want the rated officer to serve under you in the next higher grade in each type of duty described below. Place an X in the proper box, using the shaded NA area if the duty is not applicable. If line h is used, specify the nature of the specialty.

	RATER NA	1 NOT WANT HIM	2 TAKE A CHANCE ON HIM	3 HAPPY TO HAVE HIM	4 PREFER HIM TO MOST	5 FIGHT TO GET HIM	INDORSER NA	1 NOT WANT HIM	2 TAKE A CHANCE ON HIM	3 HAPPY TO HAVE HIM	4 PREFER HIM TO MOST	5 FIGHT TO GET HIM
a. Represent your viewpoint and make decisions in your name at a higher headquarters.												
b. Command a unit immediately subordinate to you on a combat mission.												
c. Be responsible in an emergency calling for initiative, coolness, forceful leadership.												
d. Work on an assignment requiring great attention to detail and routine.												
e. Plan all aspects of a military situation, using judgment, initiative, and coolness.												
f. Carry out an assignment in a civilian component such as ROTC, NG, or ORC.												
g. Represent you where tact and ability to get along with people are needed.												
h. Work on an assignment as specialist or technician. (Specify.)												
i. Carry out the duties of the type of work to which he is now assigned.												

D. IMMEDIATE RECOMMENDATIONS FOR CAREER DEVELOPMENT. Be specific.

RATER'S RECOMMENDATION FOR ASSIGNMENT (MOS CODE)	INDORSER'S RECOMMENDATION FOR ASSIGNMENT (MOS CODE)
RATER'S RECOMMENDATION FOR FURTHER TRAINING	INDORSER'S RECOMMENDATION FOR FURTHER TRAINING

E. ENTRIES ARE BASED ON ➔ (RATER WILL CHECK)	INTIMATE DAILY CONTACT	FREQUENT OBSERVATION OF THE RESULTS OF HIS WORK	INFREQUENT OBSERVATION OF THE RESULTS OF HIS WORK	ACADEMIC RECORDS	OFFICIAL REPORTS

Fig. 3. Front sheet of new rating form incorporating personal information.

```
                STANDARD SCORE SCALE
-.6 -.5 -.4 -.3 -.2 -.1  0  1 .2 .3 .4 .5 .6 .7 .8 .9 1.0 1.1
            X_____X______X___________X_____X_____X  FORM 67
              0____0_____0____0_______00  0E CRITERION
                           00_0_______0__0____0    SECTION III, FORM 67-1 (RATER)
                        N---N---N---N----N-----N   SECTION II, FORM 67-1

   2nd Lt.——1st. Lt.——Capt.——Major——Lt. Col.——Col.
```

Fig. 4.

(Figure 2.) These sections, which constitute the scorable part of the form, are printed on an IBM answer sheet. Preceding this, and attached to it but perforated to permit easy detachment, is a sheet calling for identifying information, a verbal description, recommendations, and other information of an administrative nature (Figure 3).

The "For Keeps" Trial

As already indicated, various preliminary forms of this report were tried out experimentally, validated against the criterion described above, and compared with other types of reports. In all of these experiments involving the experimental rating of almost 50,000 officers, the new report proved more valid and more acceptable in several other respects. But since these were experimental trials, in which the pressures and circumstances surrounding official reports were not called into play, it was recommended that a real test be made in an official reporting period. Consequently, both the old form (known as Form 67) and a later version of the new report (to be labelled Form 67-1) were used on all officers throughout the country for the regular semiannual efficiency report in June 1946. At the same time, but with precautions to prevent cross-contamination, criterion information was collected on fifteen thousand of these same officers.

Analysis of the data obtained in these studies led to the conclusion that the new form (67-1) was clearly superior to the old form (67). This conclusion was based on several particulars:

1. The new form produced ratings which were definitely less influenced—less biased—by the rank of the rated officer. As a matter of fact, all ratings, and the criterion itself, were influenced by grade to some extent. This is indicated in Figure 4, where the various scales are made comparable by converting each to standard score terms. This figure shows the average score for the officers in each grade group from 2nd Lt. through Colonel on the criterion[2] and on the various ratings. Two ratings

[2] The criterion, in this case, was quantified by assigning values of 3, 2, or 1 for each "nomination" of most competent, second most competent, or any other high position, respectively, and values of −3, −2, or −1 for "nominations" of least competent, next least competent, or any other low rating; by dividing the number of "nominators," multiplying by 10 to clear decimals and adding a constant of 30 to avoid negative values.

are shown for the new form. One (labelled Section II, 67-1) is the score on the forced-choice elements—not separated in this version into the two areas of job proficiency and personal qualifications. The other (labelled Section III, 67-1) is the "over-all" rating—in this case a single 20-point scale on relative standing of the ratee in comparison with other officers *of his grade.* The fact of influence by grade can be attributed partly to real differences (colonels in general are doubtless somewhat more efficient than second lieutenants in general because of the Army's promotion policy) and partly to bias based on the prestige of rank. In any event, the older rating form (67) showed much more effect from rank than would be expected (more than the criterion index) while the two parts of the new form showed much less.

2. Scores on the new form are distributed in a way which permits better discrimination among officers rated at the two extremes of the scale. In testing terminology, the new form would be said to possess more "floor" and more "ceiling." As indicated in Figure 5, which shows the actual distributions of scores on the two forms with range of scores equated, this advantage is more marked at the lower end of the scale, which means that the new form is particularly more effective in discriminating among officers rated low in competence.

3. Scores derived from both forms showed an unmistakable tendency to be higher when the ratings were rendered officially rather than in an experimental trial, but this tendency was much less marked for the scores on the new form than for those made on the old form 67.

4. When scores on the two forms were compared with the independent criterion ratings of the same officers, the new form was generally shown to be more valid.

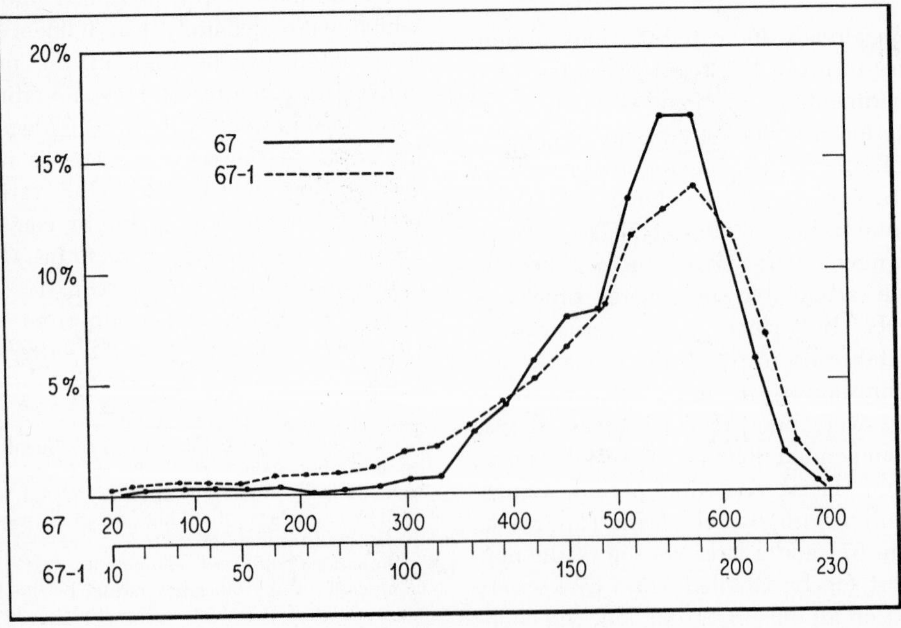

Fig. 5.

After further revision along the lines already described, the form was again submitted to experimentation. The results corroborated these earlier findings in every important respect. In fact, its tested validity was demonstrated to be even higher than before. After nearly two years of research, it was felt that the form was definitely superior to any other yet devised and tested in fulfilling the requirements of an adequate rating system for Army purposes—requirements outlined by General Witsell (3), the Adjutant General, in the following terms:

> It (an adequate rating system) should be capable of distinguishing between the best and the next best in the Officer Corps instead of lumping them altogether in the same category. It should likewise indicate which are least efficient and which next least instead of merely labelling a microscopic few at the bottom of the scale as "unsatisfactory." And finally, it should at long last and without fear or favor, admit that the average officer is truly average!

• TECHNICAL DISCUSSION

Construction of the Forced-Choice Tetrads

As already noted, the scaling and selection of the rating elements to compose the forced-choice tetrads is the nub of the problem. The basic assumptions underlying the method can be stated as follows:

1. Any real differences which exist between officers in competence or efficiency can be described in terms of objective, observable items of behavior.

2. These "behavior items" differ in the extent to which people in general tend to use them in describing other people, i.e., in general favorableness,[3] and this tendency can be determined statistically.

3. These items also differ in the extent to which they characterize officers at one extreme of the true scale of competence as opposed to officers at the other extreme. The index of this difference, the "discriminative" value, can also be determined statistically.

4. Pairs of items can be selected such that they are equal in preference value but different in discriminative value. A rater forced to say which item is most (or least) characteristic of a ratee is thus unable to select solely on the basis of prejudice for or against him (since the preference values are equal). The rater is compelled to consider both alternatives and—theoretically at least—to do a more objective job of reporting.

The first step in the process of constructing the tetrads of items, as stated above, is obtaining brief descriptive essays of good and poor officers. These essays serve as the source of the behavior items pertinent to the job—in this case, the job of being an Army officer. This step is essential, not only to focus agreement on the nature of the traits involved, but also to insure that the behavior items are worded in the language familiar to those who will later be using the scale.

In the second step, a large pool of behavior items culled from these essays is prepared in list form and submitted to another group of officers—a group numbering in the neighborhood of 300 is generally used. Each man in the group is asked to select from among his ac-

[3] Though not a necessity of the logic involved, those items which tend to be used most often, i.e., are generally "preferred" by raters in describing others, are invariably more favorable items—nice things to say.

quaintances some one officer whom he knows well enough to rate with confidence, and to indicate for that officer the extent to which each of the items in the list applies to him. The following key is used for this purpose:

1—to an *exceedingly high* or to the *highest possible* degree
2—to an *unusual* or *outstanding* degree
3—to a *typical* degree
4—to a *limited* degree
5—to a *slight* degree, or *not at all*

After completing the entire list in this fashion, each man is asked to evaluate the officer he is rating on a scale showing his position with respect to over-all competence in a representative group of 20 officers of the same grade.

All lists are collected, arranged in order of the rating of over-all competence, and separated into upper (U), middle (M), and lower (L) thirds. An analysis is then performed on each of the items, and a determination made for the three groups separately, of the frequency with which each of the five alternatives was chosen for that item. Two values are then computed for each item.

1. *Preference value.* Assume that there are exactly 300 officers in the group checking the lists, and consequently 300 officers rated, divided into the three groups of 100 U, 100 M and 100 L. For each item, the frequencies of each alternative are summed across the three groups (U, M, and L) multiplied by the alternative weight (one less than the number preceding that alternative in the key presented above), and these five weighted alternative frequencies in turn added to yield a weighted total sum for the item. This weighted total sum (which has limits of 0 to 1200 where *N* is 300) is divided by *N* and multiplied by 100 to give the *preference index.* As indicated, this value (with limits of 0 to 400) indicates the tendency of raters to mark people high or low on the particular behavior item. As here computed, low values of the index indicate a tendency to mark the item as applying to a high or outstanding degree; high values indicate little or no applicability for the item.

2. *Discriminative index.* For each of the alternatives of a given item, the difference between its frequencies in the upper and lower groups is computed. These five differences are then added, *without regard to sign,* to give the *discriminative index.* At one extreme, where the distribution of alternative frequencies is identical for the upper and lower groups, this index will be zero. At the other extreme, where the two frequency distributions have no overlap, the value will (in this case) be 200. Low values of the index, obviously, indicate that the item is equally applicable to good and poor officers and consequently does not discriminate. High values, on the other hand, indicate gross differences between the groups in applicability of the item, and suggest that it represents behavior which has significance for success (or failure).

Figure 6 illustrates the method of calculating these two indices for a typical item.

Item pairs are made up by selecting insofar as possible two items equal in preference value and widely different in discriminative value. This selection is facilitated by plotting each item (identified by its number on the list) on a double-entry table with preference values along the abscissa and discrimi-

Alternative	1	2	3	4	5	
Weight (w)	0	1	2	3	4	
Frequency (f)						
Upper (U)	1	0	6	6	87	($N = 100$)
Middle (M)	3	5	13	15	64	($N = 100$)
Lower (L)	4	11	27	23	35	($N = 100$)
Σf	8	16	46	44	186	($\Sigma n = 300$)
$\Sigma f{\cdot}w$	0	16	92	132	744	($\Sigma fw = 984$)
$d\|U - L\|$	3	11	21	17	52	($\Sigma d = 104$)

$$\text{Preference index: } \frac{\Sigma fw}{\Sigma n} \times 100 = \frac{984 \times 100}{100} = 328$$

$$\text{Discriminative index: } \Sigma d = 104$$

Fig. 6. Setup for determining preference and discrimination indices of forced choice items.

native values along the ordinate—both in suitable intervals. By entering any row in this table, two items close in preference can be picked that are widely separated on the ordinate scale. It is wise to avoid choosing items which are opposites in meaning since this eliminates the forced-choice element. Also, though the same item may be used in several pairs, it is wise to avoid too much repetition of this sort, since it tends to reduce the "scope" of the scale and necessarily raises the item intercorrelation; it may also inject an extraneous factor if the rater strives for "consistency."

Finally, pairs of items are combined to form tetrads. One pair with low preference indices (favorable) is combined with a second pair having high (unfavorable) preference indices. There is no logical basis for this step, but experience has demonstrated that if single pairs are used with instructions to indicate the most characteristic, there is considerable rater resistance to those pairs that have high (unfavorable) preference indices. By combining high and low preference pairs with instructions to choose the most and the least characteristic, rater resistance is materially reduced. The same end can be achieved by presenting high and low preference pairs (as pairs) separately with appropriate instructions for each.

• SCORING FORCED CHOICE RATING SCALES

Tetrads are formed from two pairs of items. The members of each pair are matched for preference value. One member of each pair differentiates good from poor officers. The other does not. It is possible, because of the way items are thus combined into tetrads, to key forced-choice scales by assigning a point (plus or minus as the direction of the discrimination indicates) to each of the two discriminating members of each tetrad.

Forced-choice items may, however, act differently in combination with other items than they do by themselves. Consequently, it is always desirable to establish the key on the final set of tetrads. In doing this it is necessary to include enough tetrads so that those which fail to stand up on the final cross-validation can be eliminated from the scoring key. Needless to say, the cross-validation should employ an external criterion.

In one experiment on a group of 24 tetrads (96 items, each of which could be marked as most or as least characteristic of the ratee), 75 percent of the items were scored in the same way after cross-validation as they would have been scored by a pre-determined key based on the original preference and discrimination values. It should be noted that while items which had discrimination value (either positive or negative) in the predetermined key may have lost their value, and while some items which did not discriminate in the original study came to do so in the cross-validation run, there was no instance in which an item which discriminated in one direction in the first experimental situation reversed its direction of discrimination in the cross-validation run.

The establishment of keys on the basis of a cross validation experiment rather than from the use of the discrimination indices increases the validity of the rating. The experience of the Personnel Research Section indicates that the extra work involved in this additional step is justified by the increased validity that results from it.

REFERENCES

1. Herron, C. D., Maj. Gen., Efficiency Reports. *Infantry Journal,* April 1944, pp. 30–32.
2. Staff, Personnel Research Section, The Forced Choice Technique and Rating Scales. *The American Psychologist,* 1946, 1, p. 267.
3. Witsell, E. F., Maj. Gen., The New Officer Efficiency Report. *The Reserve Officer,* 1947, Vol. 24, No. 6, pp. 8–10.

FORCED CHOICE: BETTER THAN OTHER RATING METHODS?*

Lee W. Cozan

Even at their best, the conventional rating scales, such as rank order, forced distribution, graphic, and check list, have been found to yield only a semi-objective evaluation of performance on the job. Dissatisfaction with the results of these techniques led, during World War II, to the development by a group of Army research psychologists, of the forced-choice performance scale. Based on the concentrated application of sound psychological theory, the forced-choice rating method was given experimental tryouts before its release in 1947, and was almost immediately hailed as a signal advance over older techniques.

Since that time, a number of attempts have been made to evaluate the validity of forced-choice performance scales as indicators of employee performance. But the findings of these studies have been scattered over a variety of technical reports and publications, making it difficult for the personnel practitioner to arrive at an over-all assessment of the merits of forced-choice performance rating. It is my purpose here to offer an overview of these findings, and in so doing to provide at least a provisional answer to the question: Is this new technique superior to the older types of ratings in achieving an objective evaluation of employee performance?

Since the development of the forced-choice method has been fully reported elsewhere,[1] no attempt will be made here to cover this aspect of the subject. But it may perhaps be worth recapitulating that a forced-choice performance scale consists of a series of tetrads, i.e., sets of four phrases or adjectives, relating to work performance and/or personal qualifications. A typical forced-choice scale usually contains from 15 to 50 tetrads, depending upon the level of the job being evaluated and the complexity of its duties.

The rater is asked to indicate which of the four statements is most, and which is least, characteristic of the ratee. If one of the two favorable phrases is checked as most characteristic of the ratee, he receives a plus credit; if, however, the unfavorable element is checked, no credit is given. Similarly, credit is given when one of the unfavorable elements is checked as least characteristic.

"Rater halo" and other shortcomings of conventional techniques, it is claimed, are eliminated by the fact that only one of the favorable elements is related to success on the job and only one unfavorable item is associated with poor performance or personal shortcomings—but the rater is not told which is which.

NOTE. The opinions expressed in this article are those of the author and should not be construed as reflecting the views or endorsement of the Department of Health, Education, and Welfare.

* From *Personnel,* Vol. 36, no. 3, May–June 1955, pp. 80–83.

[1] Staff, Personnel Research Branch Section, Adjutant General's Office, U.S. Army, "The Forced Choice Technique and Rating Scales," *American Psychologist,* Vol. 1 (1946), p. 267; D. E. Sisson, "Forced Choice, The New Army Rating," *Personnel Psychology,* Vol. 1 (1948), pp. 265–381; and M. W. Richardson, "Forced-Choice Performance Reports," *Personnel,* Vol. 26 (1949), pp. 205–212.

• U. S. ARMY STUDIES

Among the evaluation studies that have been carried out on the forced-choice performance scale, let us consider first four conducted by the U. S. Army:

1. In the first study, 286 brigadier and major generals who had been rated on a forced-choice performance scale were then rated by their peers, each officer being asked to evaluate those generals whom he knew well enough to rate. The validity coefficients, corrected for the restricted range of the sample, were .46 and .43, respectively.[2]

2. In another study, little difference in validity between ratings of 400 officers made on an over-all evaluation form and a forced-choice performance scale was found.[3]

3. Of three types of ratings on 400 officers in another investigation, an eight-step graphic scale had the highest validity (.53). A check list had .44, and a forced-choice rating scale, .41.[4]

4. In a comparative study involving two types of forced-choice items that were used on a group of Army officers in 1946 and 1949, the validity coefficients remained reasonably the same. The validity indices for the two years in question showed correlation coefficients of .60 for favorably worded phrases and .52 for unfavorably worded phrases.[5]

Now let us look at the findings of some studies that have been made by investigators outside of the Army.

• OTHER STUDIES

1. In an independent investigation, forced-choice and graphic ratings were obtained on Army personnel. The findings indicated that, for administrative purposes, the graphic ratings had a higher meaning and were skewed.[6]

2. In another study, the forced-choice method was used to develop a rating scale for evaluating personnel counselors and was experimentally applied in measuring the job proficiency of 37 of the counselors. Comparisons with graphic scale and peer ratings on the same group revealed some advantages of the forced-choice scale over the other two types of ratings.[7]

3. A 28-tetrad forced-choice evaluation scale was used in another instance to rate retail store managers. The scale was constructed according to the standard procedures established by the employee relations staff of a well-known industrial firm.[8] An *a priori* key was de-

[2] *The Validity of Officer Efficiency Report, WD-AGO Form 67–1, for General Officers,* Personnel Research Branch Report No. 792, Department of the Army, AGO, Washington, D. C., American Documentation Institute, 1952.

[3] *A Study of Officer Rating Methodology, IV: Effect of Forced-Choice Items on Validity of Rating Scales,* Personnel Research Branch Report No. 903, Department of the Army, AGO, Washington, D. C., American Documentation Institute, 1952.

[4] *A Study of Officer Rating Methodology, VIII: Validity of Two Types of Rating Techniques: Forced-Choice Items and Rating Scales,* Personnel Research Branch Report No. 907, Department of the Army, AGO, Washington, D. C., American Documentation Institute, 1952.

[5] *Studies of Officer Efficiency Report, WD-AGO Form 67–1, in Operation II: Consistency of Vadidity of Forced-Choice Phrases,* Personnel Research Branch Report No. 8173, Department of the Army, AGO, Washington, D. C., American Documentation Institute, 1952.

[6] E. K. Taylor and R. J. Wherry, "A Study of Leniency in Two Rating Systems," *Personnel Psychology,* Vol. 4 (1951), pp. 39–47.

[7] L. Stangas and L. L. McQuitty, "A New Application of Forced-Choice Ratings," *Personnel Psychology,* Vol. 3 (1950), pp. 413–424.

[8] E. K. Taylor *et al.,* "Short Forced-Choice Ratings Work," *Personnel Psychology,* Vol. 7 (1954), pp. 245–252.

veloped but, because of the limited size of the available sample, item analysis was precluded. Previous research had indicated that adequate validity could be secured with considerably fewer than 28 tetrads. Consequently, 10 sets of 10 tetrads each were selected on a random basis and adjusted for excessive overlap. These were then validated against a supervised adjusted objective criterion, with the validity coefficient of the 28-tetrad *a priori* key being .60. The resultant validities of the 10 random 10-tetrad keys ranged from .52 to .62.

4. In a research project conducted by a leading flour milling company, scores on a forced-choice performance report made by 61 first-line production foremen showed a correlation coefficient of .73 when validated with over-all evaluations given by 30 department heads and plant managers.[9]

5. Another study concluded that the forced-choice section of an experimental work performance report was highly effective for evaluating the proficiency of physicians, dentists, research personnel, and nurses. Of 24 validity coefficients, it was found that 41.7 per cent were .62 or higher with all but one being significant at the .01 level or below.[10]

6. In a more recent investigation[11] designed to construct a valid forced-choice performance rating scale for pharmaceutical salesmen, it was found that, on the basis of a rank difference correlation between scores on the proposed evaluation scale and ratings for 200 salesmen made by 15 divisional sales managers, the forced-choice performance ratings were valid in all but two sales divisions on at least the .05 level of confidence. The coefficients of correlation were found to range from .53 to .89.

• CONCLUSIONS

The findings of these studies indicate that although there is much to be said in favor of the forced-choice technique, some of the early claims about the consistently higher validity afforded by this type of rating procedure have not been borne out by experience thus far. On the other hand, while it must be conceded that this new rating method does not have a clear-cut superiority over older techniques in producing more valid performance evaluations, it does appear to insure greater objectivity in the rating process.

This, however, hardly seems a sufficient reason for an organization to scrap its present rating procedure in favor of one based on the forced-choice method, especially in view of the fact that the adoption of this technique entails the following prerequisites:[12]

Trained technicians to develop the performance scale.

A different collection of tetrads for each job or occupational group.

A fair agreement on the criteria of success and failure.

[9] L. Huttner and R. A. Katzell, "Developing A Yardstick of Supervisory Performance," *Personnel,* Vol. 33 (1957), pp. 371–378.

[10] S. H. Newman *et al.,* "Forced Choice and Other Methods for Evaluating Professional Health Personnel," *Psychological Monographs: General and Applied,* Vol. 71, No. 10 (1957), pp. 1–27.

[11] J. H. Nagel, "The Construction and Validation of the Forced-Choice Performance Rating for Pharmaceutical Salesmen and Analysis of the Characteristics Contributing to Overall Competence and Efficiency of These Men," *Doctoral Dissertations Abstracts,* Vol. 15 (1955), pp. 229–230.

[12] N. R. F. Maier, *Psychology in Industry,* Second Edition. Houghton, Mifflin Company, Boston, 1955.

Willingness on the part of supervisors to rate their employees when they cannot even tell whether they are giving one person a more favorable rating than another.

On the whole, therefore, there would seem to be little to choose between forced-choice and traditional ratings, and further research is clearly needed to establish any decisive advantage in the new method. In particular, we need more studies comparing the validity of forced-choice ratings with that of other types of ratings. Validating forced-choice ratings against other criteria, such as peer ratings, may give us some clue as to their reliability, but do not tell us whether the same degree of effectiveness, if not more, might not have been achieved by the use of traditional rating methods.

A STUDY OF LENIENCY IN TWO RATING SYSTEMS*

Erwin K. Taylor
and Robert J. Wherry

• IN BRIEF

Forced-choice and graphic ratings were obtained in both "experimental" (results used for research purposes only) and "for keeps" or real (results had administrative implications) situations. Results show that with graphic ratings the average is much higher in the "for keeps" than in the "experimental" situation. There is also a marked distortion of the shape of the distribution with considerably poorer discrimination at the top of the scale for the "for keeps" ratings.

In shifting from the "experimental" to the "for keeps" situation, there was an increase in the mean score on both forms. This increase was much more extensive for the graphic than for the forced-choice form. In addition, the slope of the distribution of forced-choice scores changed only slightly with the shift from "experimental" to "for keeps" conditions. The distribution of graphic scores, however, was much steeper at the high extreme, making discrimination in that area much cruder in the "for keeps" than in the experimental situation.

While the forced-choice technique cannot be said to have solved the problems of leniency and bias, a step in that direction appears to have been taken. More research in the development of the forced-choice technique is needed before a final evaluation of it may be made.

• TESTING A THEORY

Research workers, in developing criteria for test validation, have often asserted that special ratings had to be collected for the purpose because existing employee evaluations were too biased to be useful, because of attempts on the part of raters to insure desired administrative action. This statement has been taken pretty much for granted. To the knowledge of the authors, no definitive research establishing or refuting this contention has ever been published.

The extensive research conducted in connection with the development and validation (*1*) of the Army Officer Efficiency Report provided (as a by-product) the data on which a comparison of experimental and official ratings could be made.

In September 1945, more than 5,000 officers were each rated on three different forms. One of these (which was common to the entire population) was the ten-scale graphic form which was then in official use. A subpopulation of 2,000 was also rated on a forced-choice form (FCL 2b), which was later to be reused. These ratings were experimental and all raters were informed that the results would be used for research purposes only.

Note. The opinions expressed are those of the authors and do not necessarily reflect official Department of the Army policy.

* From *Personnel Psychology,* Vol. 4, no. 1, Spring 1951, pp. 39–47.

In the regular official rating period of June 30, 1946, all officers in the U. S. were rated on two forms: the usual ten-scale graphic (WD AGO Form 67) and the new[1] type (WD AGO Form 67-1), the forced-choice portion of which was identical with FCL 2b referred to above. These ratings were administered in the usual official manner and were submitted to the Department of the Army through normal channels. The only aspect of this rating period that distinguished it from any other was the fact that two forms rather than the usual one form were used.

After the ratings had been submitted to the department, technicians visited a number of Army installations and collected criterion data on almost 15,000 officers. For almost 9,000 of these, ratings were matched with the criterion forms. The criterion instruments used were identical with those which had been collected in the earlier study and thus provided a basis for comparing the shifts that took place under the change from the experimental to the for keeps situation.

• COMPARING GRAPHIC RATINGS

Several different comparisons are possible. For the associate rating criterion, and for the Form 67 (graphic) ratings, it is possible to compare the total population in both studies.

The mean value of the criterion in the experimental group was 29.85. In the "for keeps" population it was 29.29. The nature of these ratings were such that the mean for each total rating group was 30.00. This comparison of criterion means serves merely to indicate that in neither the "for keeps" nor the experimental population was there any systematic bias in the selection of those cases appropriate to the needs of this study.

The comparisons for the Form 67 (graphic) ratings are given in Table 1.

The difference between the means (.34 points) amounts to 40 per cent of a standard deviation of the "for keeps" distribution. The critical ratio of the difference is 23.9. The probability that the true difference is less than .307 is 1 in 100. In other words, the true difference between these means is probably

Table 1

RELATIVE FREQUENCY DISTRIBUTION WD AGO FORM 67 (GRAPHIC RATING) GIVEN UNDER EXPERIMENTAL AND FOR KEEPS CONDITIONS

SCORE	FOR KEEPS	EXPERIMENTAL
	%	%
6.60–7.00	1.22	1.40
6.10–6.59	10.62	6.11
5.60–6.09	25.96	14.42
5.10–5.59	24.74	20.40
4.60–5.09	16.62	22.53
4.10–4.59	11.34	17.79
3.60–4.09	5.61	10.90
3.10–3.59	2.51	4.66
2.60–3.09	.64	1.11
2.10–2.59	.30	.36
1.60–2.09	.20	.19
1.10–1.59	.06	.07
.60–1.09	.06	.00
.10– .59	.12	.03
.00– .09	.00	.03
N	8934	5778
M	5.24	4.90
σ	.82	.86
Diff. between means		.34
CR		23.9

[1] This is not the form currently in use but an earlier version which has since been revised.

at least .307 or 37 per cent of a standard deviation.

The two frequency distributions are presented in Figure 1. Although the possible score range on the Form 67 (graphic) is from −4 to 7, no negative scores appear. To all intents and purposes only a little more than four of the eleven possible scale points are used. This appears to be equally true of both conditions. Considering the range from 2.60 to 7.00 (this omits the lowest 1.38 per cent of the "for keeps" and the lowest .68 per cent of the experimental population), the distribution for the experimental population appears to be quite symmetrical while that for the "for keeps" ratings is still quite skewed. There is an obviously greater peakedness in the for keeps than in the experimental distribution.

From these comparisons of graphic rating scales on the two populations, we may draw the following conclusions:

1. The lower extreme of a graphic scale is not likely to be used in either situation.

2. There is an important and highly significant difference between the mean of ratings collected for experimental purposes and that of those which have administrative implications.

3. In the functional part of the scale there is less skew and less peakedness under experimental conditions.

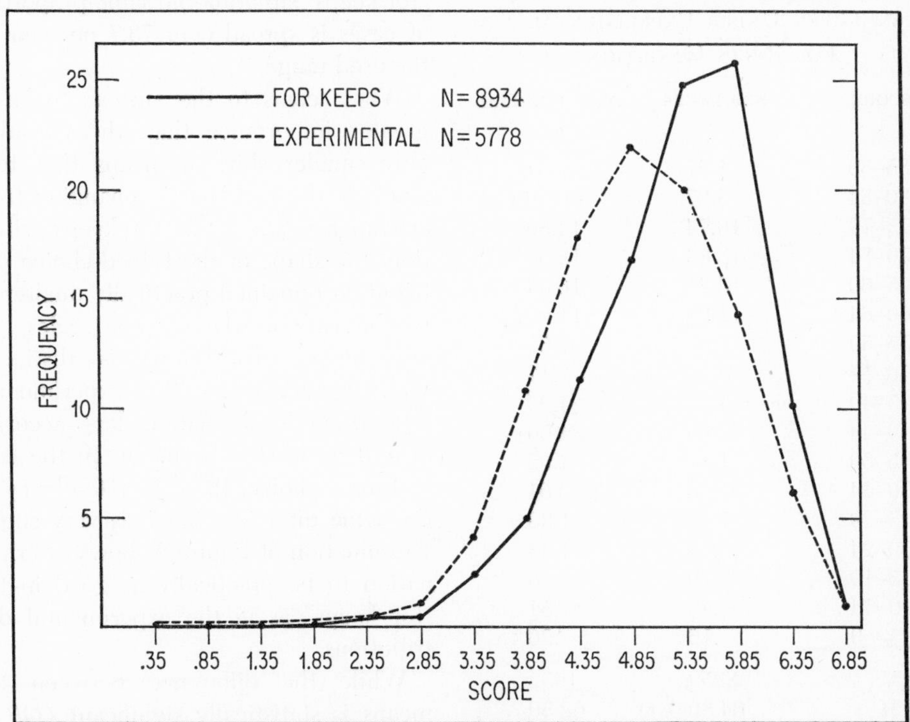

Fig. 1. Comparison of relative frequency distributions of graphic rating scores.

	Mean	σ
Experimental	4.90	.86
For keeps	5.24	.82

4. In "for keeps" ratings differentiation is poorest in the upper range where it is important for selection, assignment, and promotion.

• COMPARING FORCED-CHOICE RATINGS

The comparisons for the two administrations of the forced-choice ratings are given in Table 2.

The difference between the means amounts to 15.8 per cent of a standard deviation of the "for keeps" population. To the extent that this may be taken as an index of the bias introduced when evaluations are known to have administrative implications, it may be said that the shift in graphic ratings is more than two and one-half times that in forced-choice ratings.

Table 2

Relative Frequency Distribution of Scores on a Forced-Choice Rating Form Given Under Experimental and For Keeps Conditions

SCORE	FOR KEEPS	EXPERIMENTAL
	%	%
85–89	1.67	.51
80–84	8.87	6.56
75–79	16.74	14.86
70–74	18.83	18.55
65–69	15.21	16.34
60–64	11.60	11.99
55–59	7.64	7.63
50–54	5.23	5.17
45–49	4.23	4.05
40–44	2.98	4.00
35–39	1.87	2.92
30–34	1.58	2.61
25–29	1.24	1.33
20–24	.84	1.43
15–19	.79	1.28
10–14	.48	.51
5– 9	.16	.26
N	8959	1952
M	64.80	62.50
σ	14.56	15.65
Diff. between means		2.30
CR		5.99

The percentage frequency distributions for the forced-choice ratings are shown in Figure 2. These distributions, like those of the graphic scales, have a decided negative skew. One obvious difference between the two sets of distributions is that in the case of the graphic situation 98.6 per cent of the cases are distributed over the upper 56 per cent of the used range. In the forced-choice "for keeps" situation the same proportion of cases is spread over 78.7 per cent of the used range.

What seems to the authors to be of greater importance than the considerably smaller shift in means that took place, is the fact that in changing from an experimental to a "for keeps" situation, the shape of the forced-choice distribution remained practically unaltered. In the case of the graphic scales, the "for keeps" distribution is distinctly more peaked than the experimental, rendering discrimination less accurate on either side of the mean. In the case of forced-choice, there is a tendency in the same direction, but it is very slight. Examination of Figure 2 shows discrimination to be practically as good in the "for keeps" as in the experimental distributions.

While the difference between the means is statistically significant (CR = 5.99), its magnitude is not great. The probability is less than one in one hundred that the true difference *exceeds* 3.2

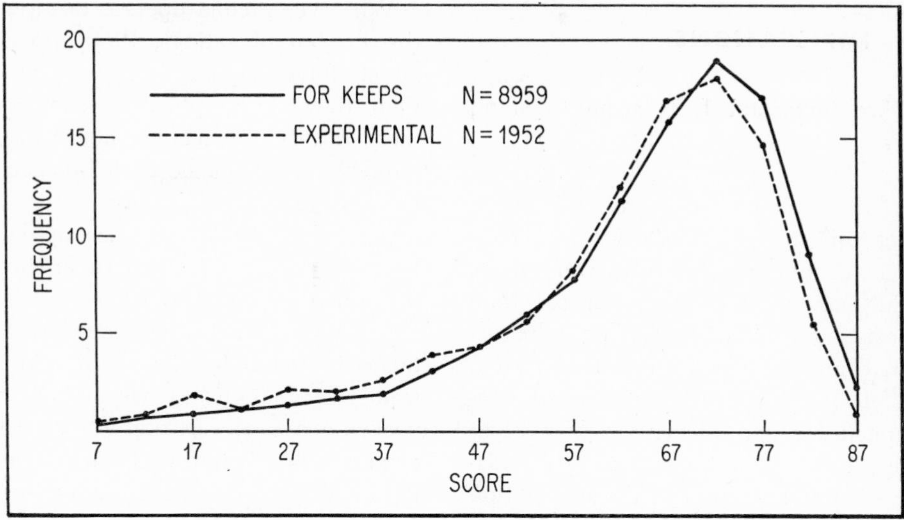

Fig. 2. Comparison of relative frequency distributions of forced-choice scores.

	Mean	σ
Experimental	62.50	15.65
For keeps	64.80	14.56

score points or about ⅕ standard deviation.

GRAPHIC RATINGS • FOLLOWING FORCED-CHOICE

In both the experimental and "for keeps" studies, the forced-choice forms consisted of fifty tetrads followed by a single twenty-point graphic rating of overall value to the Army. This rating was accomplished on the same answer sheet as the forced-choice items and immediately after their completion.

It will be recalled that in the graphic form the mean rating in the "for keeps" study was approximately .40 of a standard deviation higher than in the experimental study. In the case of the graphic ratings in the forced-choice forms, the reverse situation obtained—the mean graphic rating in the "for keeps" run was about .1 of a standard deviation lower than in the experimental study. The mean rating in the experimental study was 13.97; in the "for keeps" study it was 13.60. In addition to the lower mean, there was a considerably greater dispersion in the "for keeps" than in the experimental study. The standard deviation in the experimental study was 3.58; in the "for keeps" study it was 4.04.

This reversal of the direction of change in both mean and standard deviation in graphic ratings accomplished after forced-choice is worthy of special note. To the extent that the finding is supported by future research, it may be that forced-choice ratings, quite aside from their own merit, may provide a means of reducing bias in graphic ratings used in conjunction with them.

• IMPLICATIONS

Two important facts seem to stand out:

1. If graphic ratings are to be used as criteria in research studies, better results will probably be obtained if special ratings are used for that purpose than if existing evaluations having administrative implications are to be employed.

2. If graphic ratings are being constructed for periodic employee evaluations, it may be anticipated that the distribution of ratings after the installation of the system will have a considerably higher mean and be more skewed than would be expected from the results of ratings collected under experimental conditions.

Whatever factors operate to alter the distribution of ratings, they appear to affect forced-choice forms much less than they do graphic. In considering these results, the reader should bear in mind the fact that the forced-choice rating here employed was one of the earliest to be used with a large population. We still have much to learn in the improvement of this technique.

It appears that one step has been taken in the reduction of bias in personnel evaluation. As we develop improved ways of securing forced-choice elements, find better methods for the determination of preference and discrimination values, and learn more about the process of matching elements, we may anticipate further advances toward the goal of less biased and more valid evaluations.

REFERENCE

1. Sisson. E. D., Forced-choice—the new Army rating. *Personnel Psychology,* 1948, *1,* 365–381.

FORCED-CHOICE PERFORMANCE RATING

A Methodological Study*

James R. Berkshire
and Richard W. Highland

SUMMARY AND CONCLUSIONS

1. Six kinds of forced-choice forms for rating Air Force technical instructors were compared under experimental conditions and under instructions to give as high a score as possible (bias). The comparisons included relative resistance to leniency effect, split-half reliability, validity, and relative acceptability to raters.

2. Four of these forced-choice forms and a graphic rating scale were further compared under operational conditions. Comparisons included relative evidences of leniency effect, test-retest and interform reliability, and validity.

3. Based on the above comparisons the following conclusions concerning the forms seem justified:

Form A (two statements per block, both favorable *or* both unfavorable, choose the more descriptive *or* the less descriptive). While this form had relatively high reliabilities and validities and was one of the two best-liked forms, it was markedly unsatisfactory in its failure to resist leniency effects.

Form B (three statements per block, all favorable *or* unfavorable, choose the most and least descriptive statements in each block). The sole virtue of Form B was its apparent resistance to skewing under instructions to bias. Other than this it was relatively low in validity, lowest in reliability, and least liked by the raters. Additionally, both Form A and Form B were uneconomic, in that over half the blocks included in the original forms failed to discriminate when subjected to item analysis.

Form C (four statements per block, all favorable, choose the two most descriptive statements). This form was most bias-resistant, yielded consistently high validities under various conditions, was one of the two best-liked forms, and had adequate reliability. It seems reasonably clear that this method of constructing forced-choice forms is superior to the other methods tested in this experiment.

Form D (four statements per block, all favorable, choose the most and least descriptive statements). While Form D compared favorably with Form C in validity and reliability, it was more susceptible to leniency effects and less well liked.

NOTE. The data reported in this study were collected as part of the United States Air Forces Human Resources Research and Development Program and are described in HRRC Research Bulletin 51–9, "A Methodological Study of Forced-Choice Performance Rating" and in an as yet unnumbered HRRC Research Bulletin, "Studies of the Forced-Choice Methods: Comparisons Among Five Rating Forms" now awaiting publication. The opinions or conclusions contained in this report are those of the authors. They are not to be construed as reflecting the views or indorsements of the Department of the Air Force.

Form E (four statements per block, two favorable and two unfavorable in appearance, choose the most and least descriptive statement). This appears to be a generally inadequate method of constructing forced-choice forms. The form was easily biased, had relatively low validity under experimental conditions, and was not liked as well as Forms A, C, and F.

Form F (five statements per block, two of which were favorable, one neutral, and two unfavorable in appearance, choose the most and least descriptive). This form was also too easily biased to be given serious consideration for regular administrative use. Under experimental conditions it was exceeded in validity by Forms A, C, and D, although it was moderately well liked.

Graphic rating scale. Scores from the graphic scale, at least on this first operational administration, exhibited relatively little bias and had as high validity and reliabilty as the best of the forced-choice scales. Combining the scores from the graphic scale with those from the forced-choice scales yielded validity coefficients substantially higher than for either alone.

The over-all methodological implications of the data can only be stated as hypotheses, pending further investigation. For the psychologist faced with the necessity of constructing forced-choice forms without the benefit of this future research, the available data support the use of the following methods:

1. The favorableness index seems to fit into the forced-choice rationale better than does the preference index. It is quite possible that other indices may prove superior to either.

2. All statements within a forced-choice block should have approximately the same favorableness index.

3. There should be at least four statements in each block.

4. The instructions should require the rater to check the two most descriptive statements rather than the most and least descriptive.

5. Until demonstrated otherwise, it is probably better to combine with the forced-choice rating procedure some more conventional kind of rating form.

One of the more interesting psychological research products of World War II was the forced-choice performance rating method developed in the Personnel Research Section (now Branch) of the Adjutant General's Office. Officer ratings obtained on forced-choice rating forms were reported to be substantially less biased and more valid than comparable data obtained by other rating methods (*1, 3, 8, 12*). Subsequent to the war, the development of forced-choice rating forms for industrial supervisors has been favorably reported by Richardson (*5, 6*), and Seeley (*7*) reports success in the use of the method in constructing rating forms for Naval Air Ground School instructors.

These forced-choice rating forms differ considerably from earlier rating methods. Earlier methods almost universally required that the rater indicate, on one or more good-poor dimensions, the standing of the individual being rated. A forced-choice rating form requires instead that the rater indicate, from groups of descriptive statements, which statements are most (and/or least) descriptive of the person being rated. The extent to which each statement discriminates between effective and ineffective workers has been predetermined. So also has the extent to which each statement appears to raters to be a favorable (or unfavorable) thing to say about a worker. The statements are usually arranged in pairs that are equal in apparent favorableness, but which differ in discrimination. (Procedures for constructing such forms are described in more detail later in this article.)

These authors, however, used three different kinds of forced-choice forms. The form reported by Sisson (8) was made up of a series of blocks of four statements each, two favorable and two unfavorable in appearance. Richardson's (5) form had five statements per block, two favorable, two unfavorable, and one rather neutral in appearance. Both these forms required the rater to check the statement in each block that was most descriptive, and the one that was least descriptive, of the person being rated. The Seeley (7) form used only statements that were favorable in appearance. There were four statements to each block, from which the instructions required the rater to check the two most descriptive statements.

When the Human Resources Research Center was asked to develop an improved method of rating Air Force technical (nonflying) instructors, the forced-choice method appeared to the authors to offer the best promise of being satisfactory. No information was available, however, concerning the relative merits of the different forced-choice forms that had been previously reported. Therefore this study was made with the dual objectives of comparing the efficacy of various methods of constructing forced-choice forms and of developing a technically and operationally adequate procedure for the routine rating of Air Force technical instructors.

• CONSTRUCTION OF THE RATING FORMS

Collecting statements describing instructor performance. These statements were collected from several sources. Among these were the written remarks of instructor supervisors in "comment" sections of instructor rating forms (collected from files of previous rating forms), descriptive statments from other instructor rating forms, and descriptive statements from rating forms used for rating personnel other than instructors. The list of collected statements totaled 949.

Collecting performance rankings. In order to establish a criterion for use in evaluating the statements which had been collected, the immediate supervisors of the technical training instructors at one Air Force base were asked to rank their instructors as to over-all performance. Only those supervisors were included who had under their supervision at least five and not more than 20 instructors.

Obtaining ratings of applicability of the statements. On the basis of the rankings collected in Step 2, two extreme groups of instructors were picked. One group consisted of instructors who had been identified as being highly effective. The other group consisted of instructors who had been identified as being relatively ineffective. The 949 statements were divided among four forms. Fifty-four instructor-supervisors were asked to use one of these forms in describing each of two specific instructors. They were to indicate on a five-point scale the extent to which each of the descriptive statements applied to the designated instructors. The fact that the instructors selected were members of the "high" and "low" groups was not mentioned to the instructor supervisors.

Computing discrimination indices. Indices of discrimination (*DI*) were computed by use of the formula: $DI = (\overline{D}_H \; \overline{D}_L) \frac{pq}{y}$ in which $\overline{D}_H$ is the mean applicability of the statement for effective instructors, $\overline{D}_L$ is the mean applicability of the statement for ineffective instructors, p is the proportion of the total number of instructors in the "high" group, q is the proportion of the total number of instructors in the "low" group, and y is the ordinate of the normal curve corresponding to the values of p and q.

The preference index. The authors previously cited, computed measures of the apparent favorableness of statements which they called "preference indices." Sisson (8) refers to the preference index or value of a statement variously as (a) "the extent to which people in general tend to use (it) in describing other people," (b) "general favorableness," and (c) as "the tendency of raters to mark people high or low on the particular behavior item." The formula used for obtaining the index can be related only to definition (c): Preference Index $= \frac{\Sigma fw}{\Sigma n} \times 100$ where Σf is the sum of the response frequencies on each of the five points of the applicability scale, w is the numerical weight assigned to each of the different points of the scale, and Σn is the total number of persons rated.

Richardson (6) lists as separate characteristics of a statement (a) "generally judged favorableness or unfavorableness of the stated behavior" and (b) "popularity (preference-value, or more explicitly, use-frequency) of the element." He does not specify the operations for obtaining indices of either.

Seeley's (7) definition is "preference index, i.e., an average rating or measure of popularity for each phrase as used to describe instructors." He computed this index for individual items by taking half the sum of the mean scores of "best" and "poorest" instructors. These mean scores were obtained from ratings, on a 5-point scale, of the degree to which the items described the instructors. This is essentially the same procedure used by Sisson.

Semantically, it would appear that "extent to which people tend to use a statement" is a different thing from "apparent favorableness" and that neither of these would be measured by the operations described. Therefore, in the present experiment, an attempt was made to get ratings of the "favorableness" of each statement and to compare these with the "preference index."

Obtaining favorableness indices. Forty-six instructor-supervisors not used in Step 3 were asked to indicate on a five-point scale how favorable each statement was when used with reference to an instructor.

Computing preference and favorableness indices. The preference indices were the mean applicability ratings of the statements when ratings of applicability to "high" and "low" groups (obtained in Step 3) were combined. The index of favorableness was the mean of the favorableness ratings obtained for each statement in Step 6.

Comparison of preference and favorableness indices. The distributions for both preference and favorableness indices were bimodal. For this reason, the distribution of favorableness indices was divided at the midpoint of the scale and the upper and lower halves were correlated with the preference indices of the same statements. The resulting coefficients were −.03 and +.06, respectively. Apparently the indices for preference and favorableness are not indices of the same thing.

The reasons for this lack of agreement appear to lie in the nature of the two indices. The preference index is the mean degree of applicability of a statement to the entire population (or to the high and low extremes thereof). The same mean degree of applicability could result from statements that differed considerably in their degrees of applicability to the high and low groups. For instance, three statements with applicability (or descriptiveness) mean scores of 4, 3, and 2 for the high group would yield the same preference index when the mean scores for the low group were 0, 1, and 2, respectively. But the purpose of computing such an index is so that statements that appear equally favorable can be paired in the forced-choice blocks. And statements with descriptiveness means of 4 and 0 for the high and low groups, respectively, inevitably appear to be more favorable than statements for which the descriptiveness is the same for both groups. The preference index, being an average, obscures these differences.

The favorableness index, on the other hand, was a direct attempt to ascertain how favorable a statement looked to the supervisors who were ultimately to use the forced-choice form. Since the preference and favorableness indices were dissimilar, and since the latter seemed more likely to represent a statement's appearance of favorableness, the favorableness index was used for the balance of the study. This should not be interpreted as implying that the favorableness index is the only satisfactory index to use in constructing forced-choice forms. The Personnel Research Branch of the Army (*11*) found a "promotability index" to be very satisfactory. In their research this was defined as "expressed willingness to promote an officer about whom the phrase was felt to be true."

Constructing the rating forms. The forced-choice method calls for the pairing, within blocks, of statements that are of equivalent favorableness, but that differ in discrimination. In this study a discriminating statement was defined as one which had a discrimination index of .60 larger than the nondiscriminating statements of equivalent favorableness in the same block. This particular discrimination difference was chosen solely because it was the largest difference that would make available the number of statements necessary for what was considered, on an *a priori* basis, to be optimal form length.[1]

Six forced-choice forms were constructed as shown below. The favorableness indices (FI) and discrimination indices (DI) given for each statement are merely illustrative—they are not the correct indices for the statements shown.

Form A

Seventy-three blocks, two statements per block. There were roughly equal numbers of favorable and unfavorable blocks.

Summary of Directions:

> Pick the statement which is more descriptive (favorable blocks), or less descriptive (unfavorable blocks).

---

[1] Other investigators have used other discrimination differences. Actually, the precise difference necessary to maximize validity, reliability, and resistance to leniency effects has not yet been determined. One might expect that, as larger discrimination differences were used, reliability would increase, validity might increase, but that resistance to leniency would decrease.

Sample Blocks:

a. Aim of lesson is clearly presented. (FI 2.78, DI .63)
b. Refrains from spending too much time boasting of his experiences. (FI 2.61, DI .02)

a. May "bawl out" or ridicule a student in the presence of others. (FI .90, DI −.95)
b. Doesn't get to know each student's problems. (FI .87, DI −.34)

Form B

Thirty-four blocks, three statements per block. One of the three statements had a discrimination index .60 higher than the other two. There were roughly equal numbers of favorable and unfavorable blocks.

Summary of Directions:

Pick the statement which is most descriptive and the one which is least descriptive in each block.

Sample Blocks:

a. Does not answer all questions to the satisfaction of the students. (FI 1.43, DI −.20)
b. Does not use proper voice volume. (FI 1.47, DI −.80)
c. Supporting details are not relevant. (FI 1.40, DI −.15)

a. Conducts class in orderly manner. (FI 2.22, DI 1.20)
b. Repeats questions to the whole class before answering them. (FI 2.29, DI .57)
c. At ease before class. (FI 2.35, DI .53)

Form C

Thirty-one blocks, four statements per block. All statements had high favorableness indices.

Summary of Directions:

Pick the two statements which are most descriptive.

Sample Block:

a. Patient with slow learners. (FI 2.82, DI 1.15)
b. Lectures with confidence. (FI 2.75, DI .54)
c. Keeps interest and attention of class. (FI 2.89, DI 1.39)
d. Acquaints classes with objective for each lesson in advance. (FI 2.85, DI .79)

Form D

This form was identical with Form C except for the directions.

Summary of Directions:

Pick the statement which is most descriptive and the one which is least descriptive in each block.

Sample Block: Same as Form C.

Form E

Thirty-two blocks, four statements per block. Two had high and two had low favorableness indices.

Summary of Directions:

Pick the statement which is most descriptive and the one which is least descriptive in each block.

Sample Block:

a. Fine personal bearing. (FI 3.01, DI 1.21)
b. Adapts himself readily to new duties. (FI 2.98, DI .59)
c. Is not well qualified to instruct in all phases of his subject. (FI .65, DI −.75)
d. Does not put class at ease. (FI .78, DI −.13)

Form F

Thirty-six blocks, five statements per block. Two had high and two had low favorableness indices; the fifth statement had favorableness and discrimination indices midway between the high and low pairs.

Summary of Directions:

Pick the statement which is most descriptive and the one which is least descriptive in each block.

Sample Block:

a. Works hard. (FI 3.26, DI 1.39)
b. Somewhat antagonistic about what he is instructed to do. (FI 1.22, DI –.96)
c. Could improve cleanliness of classroom area. (FI 1.89, DI .05)
d. Not willing to adapt to changing situations. (FI 1.26, DI –.30)
e. Can take criticism. (FI 3.30, DI. 78)

Form C uses Seeley's (7) method of constructing blocks, Form E uses the AGO method reported by Sisson (8), and Form F follows Richardson (5). Forms A, B, and D are rather obvious alternative constructions developed for this experiment.

The graphic rating scale. In addition to these forced-choice forms, a graphic rating scale adapted from Seeley (7) was used in the research. Its primary purpose was to provide instructor-supervisors with an easily understood device for identifying the areas in which the instructor was strongest and weakest, in order that these might be discussed with him.

• PROCEDURES

Experimental Testing

All instructor-supervisors at six Air Force bases rated all their instructors, using the forced-choice forms. As far as possible, each supervisor used all six forms, rating different instructors on each form.

At two of the bases a separate group of supervisors was asked to fill out the forms as if "you are rating your best friend and want to make certain he obtains as high a score as possible." The data gathered in this manner will be referred to hereafter as resulting from the "bias experiment."

In addition, a random sample of the supervisors was asked to rank the six forms in order of their preference for the forms as a rating instrument.

A sample of 429 instructors was rated on the graphic rating scale in addition to being rated on a forced-choice scale.

Following collection of the ratings, supervisors were asked to rank their subordinates as to their over-all effectiveness as instructors. These ranks were to be used as the criterion measure.

In order to give ranks from groups of different sizes a comparable meaning, the rankings were converted to normalized standard scores. This procedure makes the assumption that the means and variances of performance in all groups were equal. To the extent that this assumption is unwarranted, these normalized scores will give an inaccurate report of the relative abilities of instructors from different groups. Since these are the criteria against which the rating form scores were validated, it can be assumed that the validity coefficients obtained are conservative estimates.

In connection with the foregoing ratings and rankings, supervisors were assured that the data were for research use only—that none of the scores of individual instructors would be reported to anyone.

Operational Testing

In the light of results from the experimental testing, four of the forced-choice forms (A, B, C, and D) appeared to merit further evaluation under operational conditions. In this evaluation the forms were printed and distributed by Air Training Command Headquarters. They were accompanied by a directive from that headquarters officially requesting execution of the ratings. An instruction booklet distributed to the supervisors discussed the administrative uses of the scores. Upon completion of scoring, the scores were reported back to the bases for their use. In other words, in contrast to the experimental testing, the operational testing tried to make it evident that this was a "for keeps" rating.

The graphic rating scale had been intended originally for diagnostic and counseling use; but following publication of an article by Baier (*1*), it was decided to include the graphic rating scale scores in the operational evaluation, since Baier had reported higher validities for combined forced-choice and graphic scores than for either alone.

All instructors were rated on the graphic rating form and one of the four forced-choice forms. Each supervisor used only one kind of forced-choice form. After completing the ratings, the supervisors ranked their instructors on overall ability.

Approximately 30 days later the supervisors were asked to rerate certain of their instructors on either the same form or on a different form. These reratings provided data for a study of the test-retest and interform reliabilities.

• SCORING

For the development of scoring keys, the data from the experimental administration were divided into two groups. Ratings and rankings collected from three Air Force bases constituted one group (Group I); ratings and rankings from three other Air Force bases constituted the other group (Group II).

Five experimental scoring keys were made for each of the six forced-choice rating forms:

Key 1—This was an *a priori* key based on the individual item discrimination indices (See Step 4 of "Construction of Rating Forms" for computation of discrimination indices).

Key 2—This key was based on an item analysis of Group I data.

Key 3—This key used item analysis results, but unit weights were assigned in accordance with the logical relations of the various response positions. That is, opposite responses ("most descriptive" vs. "least descriptive") to the same statement either got opposite weights or no weight at all.

Table 1

EFFECT OF ITEM ANALYSIS ON LENGTH OF FORMS[a]

FORM	ORIGINAL LENGTH BLOCKS	ORIGINAL LENGTH STATEMENTS	SCORABLE LENGTH BLOCKS	SCORABLE LENGTH STATEMENTS	PER CENT SHRINKAGE
A	72	144	32	64	55
B	34	102	16	48	53
C	31	124	26	104	16
D	31	124	20	80	35
E	32	128	30	120	6
F	36	180	34	170	6

[a] Based on Group I data and Key 2.

Table 2

DISTRIBUTION STATISTICS FOR SEVEN RATING FORMS UNDER THREE CONDITIONS OF ADMINISTRATION

	EXPERIMENTAL			BIAS			OPERATIONAL		
FORM	N	MEAN	SD	N	MEAN	SD	N	MEAN	SD
A	127	17.1	6.2	90	21.5	4.0	1086	18.7	6.0
B	133	1.2	11.1	94	7.9	7.0	1171	3.7	10.0
C	129	−1.5	13.2	88	4.3	8.5	1183	−2.2	12.6
D	129	−0.2	13.6	93	9.8	9.7	1140	3.5	12.2
E	132	8.5	26.7	93	28.3	18.0	[a]		
F	128	15.8	30.0	95	37.9	13.6	[a]		
GRS	429	20.4	5.8	[b]			3624	20.9	4.8

[a] Forms E and F were not included in the operational administration.
[b] The graphic rating scale was not included in the bias experiment.

Key 4—This key was developed in the same manner as Key 2, but used Group II data.

Key 5—This key was developed in the same manner as Key 3, using Group II data.

Many of the statements which had been found to be discriminating when they were considered alone were no longer discriminating when they were combined into forced-choice blocks. This is an indication that either the original discrimination indices were only a rough indication of the relative dscriminating power of the statements or the discriminating power of a statement may be different when considered alone than when considered in comparison with certain other statements.

Table 1 shows the extent of shrinkage of each form when nondiscriminating blocks are eliminated after analysis of Group I data. From these data it would appear that, if two- or three-choice blocks are used, considerable shrinkage should be anticipated. Under cross-validation the coefficients obtained when forms were scored by means of Key 2 were generally higher than for the other keys.[2] Therefore the forced-choice analyses reported herein are based on Key 2 scoring.

The graphic rating scale was scored by assigning to the five scale positions weights of from zero to four, zero being given for a checkmark in the "Generally weak" column and four being given for a checkmark under "One of the best." Since nine categories of behavior were rated, this gave a possible range of scores from 0 to 36.

• ANALYSES

Resistance to Leniency Effects

Since a major claim for the superiority of forced-choice rating forms over graphic rating forms lies in the presumed resistance of the former to leniency effects (or bias), data pertinent to this problem will be dealt with first. Table 2 shows the means and standard deviations obtained under each condition and the numbers of cases (N) involved in each.

[2] Validity coefficients for all keys are reported by Highland and Berkshire (*4*).

Table 3

MINIMUM AND MAXIMUM SCORES POSSIBLE ON EACH FORM, AND BIASED MEANS

FORM	MIN. POSSIBLE SCORE	MAX. POSSIBLE SCORE	BIAS MEAN
A	0	+32	21.5
B	–32	+32	7.9
C	–45	+36	4.3
D	–42	+40	9.8
E	–60	+57	28.3
F	–67	+66	37.9

It will be noted that all mean forced-choice scores were highest and SD's smallest under instructions to bias. All the forms, therefore, are susceptible to leniency effects. On the other hand, all the forced-choice forms possessed some resistance to leniency effects, as shown by the raters' failure to give the maximum scores possible on the forms. These results are shown in Table 3.

If one assumes that the mean scores obtained under experimental conditions were unbiased, then the differences between these means and the means obtained under instructions to bias can be considered as indicating the biasability of the forms. Similarly, the differences between experimental and operational means can be considered to indicate the amounts of leniency effect appearing under operational conditions. The critical ratios of these various differences between means can be compared in Table 4.

Inspection of these critical ratios yields two salient facts: first, that Form C had superior resistance to leniency effects under both conditions; and second, that the graphic rating scale scores showed relatively small leniency effects under operational conditions.

This latter result was somewhat surprising. Because of the reported experience of other investigators (*1, 5, 12*), it had been expected that a substantial increase in GRS raw scores would accompany operational use. A possible (but highly speculative) explanation of the

Table 4

CRITICAL RATIOS OF CHANGES IN MEAN RATING SCORES FROM EXPERIMENTAL TO BIAS AND TO OPERATIONAL CONDITIONS

	BIAS MEAN MINUS EXPERIMENTAL MEAN		OPERATIONAL MEAN MINUS EXPERIMENTAL MEAN	
FORM	DIFFERENCE	CR[a]	DIFFERENCE	CR[a]
A	4.4	6.32	1.6	2.76
B	6.7	5.54	2.5	2.47
C	5.8	3.92	–.7[c]	–.58[c]
D	10.0	6.37	3.7	2.96
E	19.8	6.62	[d]	
F	22.1	7.35	[d]	
GRS	[b]		.5	1.76

[a] Using a single tailed test (since direction of shift of means is considered important) all critical ratios larger than 1.65 are significant at better than the 5 per cent level, and those above 2.35 are significant at better than 1 per cent level.

[b] The graphic rating scale was not included in the bias experiment.

[c] The negative signs indicate that the mean score shifted downward.

[d] Forms E and F were not included in the operational administration.

nonappearance of such an increase may lie in the fact that the raters felt that the accuracy of their graphic rating could be checked against the result of their forced-choice rating. Because they could not tell at what *level* they rated a man on the latter, their best hope of consistency lay in an accurate, unbiased rating on the former.

Since we do not know that such a result will continue on future ratings, further analyses of semiannual ratings are planned, both for the purpose of comparing the extent to which leniency effects appear in the graphic and forced-choice parts of the form, and to make sure that they do not become of sufficient magnitude as to impair the form's validity and administrative usefulness.

The distributions of bias scores from Forms E and F appeared to be considerably more skewed than those from the other forms. In order to compare the skewnesses of the six distributions, an index of the amount of skewness of each was calculated.[3] These indices were (in descending order of amount of skewness) Form E = −1.12, Form F = −.75, Form A = −.68, Form D = −.46, Form C = −.28, and Form B = .00. Only Form B scores have no skew, Forms E, F and A scores have substantial skew, while scores from D and C are moderately skewed.

Considering both shift of mean and amount of skewness, it is clear that Forms E and F are inferior in resistance to leniency effects and it seems probable that Forms B and C are the most resistant. Form B is slightly superior to C in lack of skewness of the bias distribution, but appears markedly inferior to C in the degree to which the whole distribution shifted under instructions to bias.

In an attempt to discover the reason or reasons for the differences in bias-resistance among the forms, an analysis was made of the scoring keys for the six forced-choice forms. On Forms A, B, C, and D, considering all possible ways of marking the blocks, the percentages of these possibilities yielding various block scores were computed. On Forms E and F, in computing the possibilities, the assumption was made that a rater who wanted to be lenient would check a favorable-appearing statement as "most descriptive" and an unfavorable-appearing statement as "least descriptive." Table 5 shows these possibilities for the six forms.

Table 5

PERCENTAGES OF POSSIBLE CHOICES YIELDING VARIOUS BLOCK SCORES

	SCORES				
FORM	2	1	0	−1	−2
A		50	50		
B	23	19	15	19	24
C	6	15	45	21	13
D	13	19	26	22	20
E	31	30	25	12	2
F	35	43	20	2	

Form C has the lowest proportion of favorably scoring combinations. If, in the situation in which the rater is trying to be lenient, we consider favorably scoring combinations as "correct" responses, then it can be said that Form C had a higher ratio of misleads to correct answers. And it seems quite reasonable that, in a situation in which discrimination is somewhat difficult, the provision of a greater proportion of plausible misleads will decrease the probability of

[3] G. U. Yule and M. G. Kendall, *An Introduction to the Theory of Statistics,* p. 162. London: Chas. Griffin & Co., Ltd., 1947.

the raters being able to identify the favorably scoring combinations.

Despite the apparent reasonableness of the foregoing, it cannot be said with complete assurance that this was the only, or even the major, factor in the superiority of Form C. All of the experimental forms differed from Form C in a variety of ways (directions, number of statements per block, etc.). It is conceivable that any of these differences, either alone, in combination, or in interaction with the difference in the characteristics of the scoring keys, might have made the forms inferior to Form C.

Further, we do not know whether a scoring key having this characteristic (low ratio of favorably scoring responses) would always result from item analysis of a form constructed as was Form C, or whether this was an atypical case. It is possible, in devising keys by item analysis methods, to intentionally hold down the ratio of favorably scoring responses by demanding higher levels of discrimination for items that are to be scored favorably. By this method several keys, with varying proportions of favorably scoring responses, could be developed for the *same* form. Further research is needed to establish the certainty of the relationship of this factor to resistance to leniency effects, and to ascertain what proportion of favorably scoring responses yields an optimal combination of reliability, validity, and resistance to leniency effect.

It should be emphasized that the discrimination levels referred to are those that result from item analysis of already assembled forms. They are *not* the discrimination indices or the discrimination differences used in the construction of forced-choice blocks. It is the authors' opinion that the use of large discrimination differences in constructing forced-choice blocks *decreases* resistance to leniency effects by making the discriminating statement more identifiable.

Another point of some methodological interest lies in the fact that Forms C and D, which were identical in block content, differed in their resistance to leniency effect. It will be remembered that Form C required the respondent to check the two most descriptive statements in each block, while on Form D, from each block, he was to choose the most and least descriptive statements.

If we examine the scoring key for Form C, we find nine blocks scored + + − −, 10 scored + − − 0, six scored + − 00, and one scored + + − 0. (The remaining five blocks were not scored on this key.) On Form D, except for sampling errors in the item analyses, one would expect the scoring patterns within the blocks to be the same as on Form C when a statement was checked as "most descriptive," and reversed when checked as "least descriptive."

Table 6 shows the effects of the differences in instructions for forced-choice blocks containing four favorable-appearing statements on the probabilities of obtaining various possible scores. It will be seen that, in the three most frequently occurring patterns, the probabilities of getting a favorable score by chance are greater for the "Most-Least" instructions. Thus, if tendencies toward leniency are operating, the odds against the raters being able to identify favorably scoring combinations are higher when the rater is instructed to choose the two most descriptive statements.

Here again we cannot be sure that these differing probabilities of getting favorable scores are the sole reason for the superiority of Form C over Form D.

Table 6

PROBABILITIES OF OBTAINING VARIOUS CHANCE SCORES UNDER DIFFERING INSTRUCTIONS—FOUR-CHOICE BLOCKS

SCORING PATTERN	SCORE PER BLOCK	PROBABILITIES[a] TWO MOST	MOST-LEAST
++−−	2	.166	.333
	0	.667	.333
	−2	.166	.333
+−−0	2	000	.166
	1	.166	.166
	0	.333	.333
	−1	.333	.166
	−2	.166	.166
+−00	2	000	.083
	1	.333	.333
	0	.333	.166
	−1	.333	.333
	−2	000	.083
++−0	2	.166	.166
	1	.333	.250
	0	.333	.166
	−1	.166	.250
	−2	000	.166

[a] The probabilities shown in the column headed "Two Most" are actual probabilities computed from the scoring key for Form C. The probabilities shown in the column headed "Most-Least" are hypothetical; i.e., they are the Form D probabilities that would have been obtained if the only differences between the scoring keys for Forms C and D had been reversals in scoring for items checked "Least" on Form D.

The possibility also exists that the lenient rater found it easier to identify the favorably scoring choices when these were the behavioristically best and worst statements in each block (as in Form D) than he did when they were the two behavioristically best statements in Form C.

The methodological implications of the foregoing analyses can be summed up in the following hypothesis: Within some as yet undefined limit, the lower the proportion of favorably scored choices in a forced-choice rating form the greater will be the form's resistance to leniency effects.

Reliabilities

Split-half reliability coefficients were computed for the six forced-choice forms using data from the experimental administration. Data for computation of test-retest and interform reliabilities on four forced-choice forms and the graphic rating scale were obtained by asking the raters, approximately 30 days later, to rerate a random sample of those previously rated on the operational administration. Table 7 presents these reliability coefficients.

It will be noted that when the split-half method is used, the magnitude of the reliability coefficients appears closely

Table 7

RELIABILITY COEFFICIENTS FOR INSTRUCTOR RATING FORMS

1 FORM	2 NO. SCORED STATE-MENTS	3 SPLIT-HALF r^a	4 TEST-RETEST r^b	5 INTER-FORM r^c
A	64	.82	.74	.63[c]
B	48	.74	.59	.52[c]
C	104	.90	.72	.60[c]
D	80	.85	.72	.61[c]
E	120	.95	[e]	
F	170	.96	[e]	
GRS			.78	.56[d]

[a] Stepped up by Spearman-Brown formula.

[b] Same form, readministered 30 days later.

[c] Each r is an average of that form's r's with all other forced-choice forms, administered 30 days apart.

[d] Average r of GRS with four forced-choice forms—operational administration.

All r's averaged by means of Fischer's z transformation.

[e] Forms E and F were eliminated from the study after the experimental testing.

related to the length (number of scored statements) of the form. Magnitudes of test-retest and interform coefficients, with the exception of those for Form B, do not appear to be so directly related to form length.

The differences in magnitude between the split-half and the test-retest coefficients can be accounted for, at least in part, by the fact that the test-retest situation includes two possible sources of unreliability in addition to that contributed by the forms themselves: the occasion-to-occasion unreliability of the raters and actual changes in the work behavior of the ratees. The extent to which these factors influence the validity coefficients is discussed in the following section.

Validities

The "validity" of the various forms, as defined here, means the correlation of the scores obtained from the forms with a "criterion" consisting of supervisors' rankings of the men on their over-all ability as instructors. It is recognized that such a criterion is not necessarily an accurate measure of the "true" relative ability of these instructors. The "true" criterion would probably be a composite of scores resulting from measures of average student gain under different instructors, of the extent to which the instructors contribute to the accomplishment of the over-all mission of the school, of their influence on the morale of students and fellow-instructors, of their faithfulness in the execution of routine administrative duties, etc. Since such measures were not available, and since the primary purpose of the rating forms is to place supervisors' opinions on a comparable basis and make them available for administrative use, a ranking criterion seems a justifiable expedient.

Table 8 shows the coefficients of correlation between the forced-choice portions of the forms as scored with Key 2 and the rank-order data. These are presented for Forms A, B, C, and D under both experimental and operational conditions, for Forms E and F under experimental conditions only and for the graphic rating scale scores under operational conditions only. In addition, because the retest reliabilities of the forms

Table 8

VALIDITIES[a] OF RATING FORMS UNDER EXPERIMENTAL AND OPERATIONAL CONDITIONS

	EXPERIMENTAL		OPERATIONAL		RETEST	
FORM	N	r^{b}	N	r	N	r^{c}
A	127	.61	847	.56	146	.55
B	133	.53	828	.50	123	.52
C	129	.69	898	.58	130	.59
D	129	.66	871	.50	117	.60
E	132	.56	d			
F	128	.58	d			
GRS			2338	.59		

a Correlations of rating scores with supervisor rankings of over-all performance.
b Cross-validation correlations. The scoring key was developed on a different sample.
c Correlation of reratings with rankings obtained 30 days earlier.
d Forms E and F were eliminated from the study after the experimental testing.

Table 9

COMBINED VALIDITIES—
TOTAL RATING SCORE VS. RANKS

FORM	N	KEY 2
A + Graphic rating scale	691	.64
B + Graphic rating scale	674	.60
C + Graphic rating scale	733	.66
D + Graphic rating scale	677	.60

were not particularly high (see previous section) the correlations of these reratings with rankings of the same individuals obtained 30 days earlier were computed. These are shown in the column headed "Retest."

All validities decreased under operational as contrasted with experimental administration. However, despite the relatively modest retest reliabilities, (Table 7), the retest validities were of the same order of magnitude as the operational validities. The graphic rating scale yields a relatively high validity coefficient, conforming in this respect to findings reported by Baier (*1*) when the two types of scales were used together.

Table 9 reports the correlation coefficients between the forms and the rankings when the scores from the forced-choice portions were summed with scores from the graphic rating scale. Substantial increases in the correlations with the rankings likewise confirm Baier's findings.

Desirability

A number of supervisors who participated in the experimental testing were asked to state which of the six forms (or however many forms they used in rating their group of instructors) they liked best, next best, etc. If a supervisor rated six or more instructors, he made use of all six of the rating forms. If he had less than six instructors, he used as many of the forms as he had instructors. In other words, each instructor was rated on only one form, but as many of the forms as possible were used by each supervisor in rating his instructors. This resulted in from 80 to 83 rankings of each form.

The mean ranks in the order of most desirable to least desirable were:

1. Form C–2.89
2. Form A–2.90
3. Form F–3.12
4. Form E–3.40
5. Form D–3.69
6. Form B–4.66

It should be recognized that these data reflect only the ranked desirability of the forced-choice forms presented. Such a ranking cannot show intensity of feeling; i.e., it is conceivable that two forms having adjacent ranks might be widely separated on a like-dislike continuum. It is also possible that the raters may have very much liked or very much disliked all forms.

The most useful conclusion from the data would seem to be that if forced-choice forms are to be used, then forms arranged as are Forms C and A are somewhat less likely to be disliked than are the others.

REFERENCES

1. Baier, D. E. Reply to Travers' "A critical review of the validity and rationale of the forced-choice technique." *Psychol. Bull.*, 1951, *48*, 421–434.
2. Berkshire, J. R., and Highland, R. W. "The development and evaluation of procedures for rating Air Force technical training instructors," *Research Note* TECH: 52-2, May, 1952.

3. Fry, J. C. All superior officers. *Infantry Journal,* 1948, *63,* 21–26.
4. Highland, R. W., and Berkshire, J. R. A methodological study of forced-choice performance rating, USAF Air Training Command Human Resources Research Center. *Research Bulletin,* 51-9, May 1951.
5. Richardson, M. W. Forced-choice performance reports: a modern merit-rating method. *Personnel,* 1949, *26,* 205–212.
6. Richardson, M. W. An empirical study of the forced-choice performance report. Paper read at the 57th Annual Meeting of the American Psychological Association, Denver, September, 1949.
7. Seeley, L. C., "Construction of three measures of instructor evaluation," *Technical Report*–SD 383-1-5, Office of Naval Research, July 20, 1948.
8. Sisson, E. D., "Forced-choice–the new Army rating," *Personnel Psychol.,* 1948, *1,* 365–381.
9. Staff, Personnel Research Section, Adjutant General's Office. "Analysis of an officer efficiency report (WD AGO Form 67-1), using multiple raters. PRS Report 817, 13 April 1952.
10. Staff, Personnel Research Section, Adjutant General's Office. "A study of officer rating methodology IV. Effect of forced-choice items on validity of rating scales." PRS Report 903, 17 April 1952.
11. Staff, Personnel Research Section, Adjutant General's Office. "Determination of preference and discrimination values of phrases for forced-choice check lists of officer efficiency report forms." PRS Report 846, 10 April 1952.
12. Staff, Personnel Research Section, Adjutant General's Office. Major study of comparative validity of five periodic officer efficiency reporting methods." PRS Report 670, 5 December 1945.
13. Staff, Personnel Research Section, Adjutant General's Office. "Studies of officer efficiency report WD AGO Form 67-1 in operation. II. Consistency of validity of forced-choice phrases." PRS Report 873, 17 April 1952.
14. Thorndike, R. L. *Personnel Selection.* New York: John Wiley & Sons, Inc., 1949.

A. Rating by Supervisors

6. CRITICAL INCIDENT RATINGS—TECHNIQUES AND CRITICISMS

THE EMPLOYEE PERFORMANCE RECORD: A NEW APPRAISAL AND DEVELOPMENT TOOL

JOHN C. FLANAGAN AND ROBERT K. BURNS

THE G COMPANY

THOMAS L. WHISLER

The most recently developed rating technique grows out of the empirical observations of the unreliability of human memory and of human ability to make fine discriminations. The sort of common-sense analysis presented in "The Nature and Interpretation of Employee Ratings" (in Part One–B–1) finally flowered into a formal way of dealing with the "zone of uncertainty" and capitalizing on human ability to discriminate between extremes.

While the technical effectiveness of this method is impressive, its high cost in time and effort is illustrated in the case of the G Company, part of which is reproduced here as an excerpt from Part Four–A.

FURTHER READING

Flanagan, John C., "The Quantitative Measurement of Employee Performance." In: *Workshop Report on Performance Review*. Industrial Relations Center, The University of Chicago (1949), Reissued 1953. (Occasional papers, no. 1) pp. 9–17.

———, "The Critical Incident Technique," *Psychological Bulletin*, Vol. 51, no. 4, July 1954, pp. 327–358.

———, "The Critical Incident Approach to the Study of Psychopathology," *Journal of Clinical Psychology*, Vol. 15, no. 2, April 1959, pp. 136–139.

Kay, Brian R., "The Use of Critical Incidents in a Forced-Choice Scale," *Journal of Applied Psychology*, Vol. 43, no. 4, August 1959, pp. 269–270.

U. S. Office of Naval Research, Manpower Branch. *Procedures for Evaluating Research Personnel with a Performance Record of Critical Incidents.* Pittsburgh, American Institute for Research, June 1950. (Third in a series of reports prepared under the sponsorship of the Manpower Branch, Human Resources Division, Office of Naval Research.)

Hendrix, Algie A., and Byron Stewart, *Appraisal of Employee Performance*. Ann Arbor, University of Michigan, Bureau of Industrial Relations, May, 1957. (Addresses on Industrial Relations.)

THE EMPLOYEE PERFORMANCE RECORD

A New Appraisal and Development Tool*

John C. Flanagan
and Robert K. Burns

"Had to get ladder to reach raw stock near machine. Time wasted getting and returning ladder each time."

A brief, factual observation like this is typical of the notes that foremen in a number of General Motors divisions have started making on employees' performance. And they are both pleased and astonished by the good use to which they are able to put this simple recording of incidents—a recording made daily, almost on the spot, and without opinion or judgment.

Such notations, made on a specially diagrammed, blue and red,[1] two-page record (see Figure 1), are the basis of the new Performance Record program developed in the Delco-Remy Division of General Motors. Entries in blue boxes on the right-hand side of each page are positive instances of on-the-job performance; those in the red boxes on the left-hand side indicate ineffective performance. A glance at the two-color spread for each employee tells his foreman immediately whether or not the particular employee has contributed significantly to production and morale in recent months through his actions and remarks.

The foreman will tell you readily that both they and the employees much prefer their new procedure for appraisal and development to previous systems of assigning numerical ratings or writing descriptive paragraphs on the basis of general impression and opinion. In back of these results lies a four-year trial of the program at GM; in back of this experiment, in turn, lies a need shared by most managements.

• THE NEED FOR FACTS

Management generally does not have sound, objective, factual data regarding the qualifications and performance of its employees. The need is for objective observation of an employee's performance, followed by discussion with him of his strengths and weaknesses which can contribute materially to his development.

This need came to the fore as an explicit problem at the final session of the General Motors Corporation Conference for College and University Educators in June 1948. During a searching discussion of employee appraisal and development, the educators present, who were specialists in personnel administration and industrial relations, raised questions about the procedures used in various GM divisions.

Harry W. Anderson, Vice President for Personnel, called on Byron Stewart, Director of Personnel of the Delco-Remy Division, to comment on what was being

[1] In the original article, the right-hand panels of the record were shown in blue, and the left-hand panels in red.

* From *Harvard Business Review,* September–October 1957, pp. 95–102. Copyright 1957 by the President and Fellows of Harvard College. Reprinted by permission.

done in his division. After briefly describing the program, Mr. Stewart expressed the need for further research, stating that in light of the discussion "the first and most important task to be undertaken is the development of a yardstick that would provide a set of standards which would make the result for a particular employee the same no matter who did the rating."

Establishing a Program

Following this meeting, Mr. Stewart conferred with two of Mr. Anderson's staff members, George Jacoby, Director of Personnel Services, and Algie Hendrix, Director of Employment Practices. It was agreed that a development study would be initiated at Delco-Remy for the purpose of obtaining more effective procedures for use in the corporation's employee development program. With the support of the general manager of the division, H. D. Dawson, a committee was set up which included two foremen from each of Delco-Remy's ten plants and several representatives of the personnel department.

The committee held a number of meetings over a period of several months and critically reviewed the aims of the merit-rating program and evaluated the system then in use. The group outlined a number of the requirements for an effective procedure and then decided to get some outside assistance to check on their plans and to help in the later developmental stages of the studies.

At this point, the authors of this article were brought into the picture.[2] The committee quickly agreed to the desirability of obtaining a relatively objective check on the aspects of performance which should be covered. Interviewing forms were developed, and the foremen on the committee collected from the other foremen in the plants the records of more than 2,500 critical incidents describing specific deeds they had seen employees do recently which represented either an outstanding contribution to the productivity or morale of the department or an act of behavior definitely detrimental. Here are two examples:

"I observed an employee looking through the scrap tub. Shortly after, he came to me stating that someone had thrown a large piece of cast-iron piston into the scrap tub. We salvaged this piston and a short time later used the piece to make a pulley for a very urgently needed job."

"This man was operating a trim press and was having considerable trouble with the magazine. He failed to see that all that was needed was to increase the clearance. This was a very simple adjustment—one he had often done."

Analysis and Classification

These 2,500 incidents were turned over to the staff of the American Institute for Research for analysis and classification. It was found that the incidents included about 500 different kinds of behavior. These were first grouped into 33 categories—later reduced to 16 critical job requirements for hourly wage employees under two general headings, as follows:

Physical and Mental Qualifications

1. Physical condition
2. Coordination
3. Checking and inspecting
4. Arithmetic computation

[2] Dr. Harley O. Preston and Dr. Robert B. Miller of the American Institute for Research staff also played leading parts in the early phases of the program.

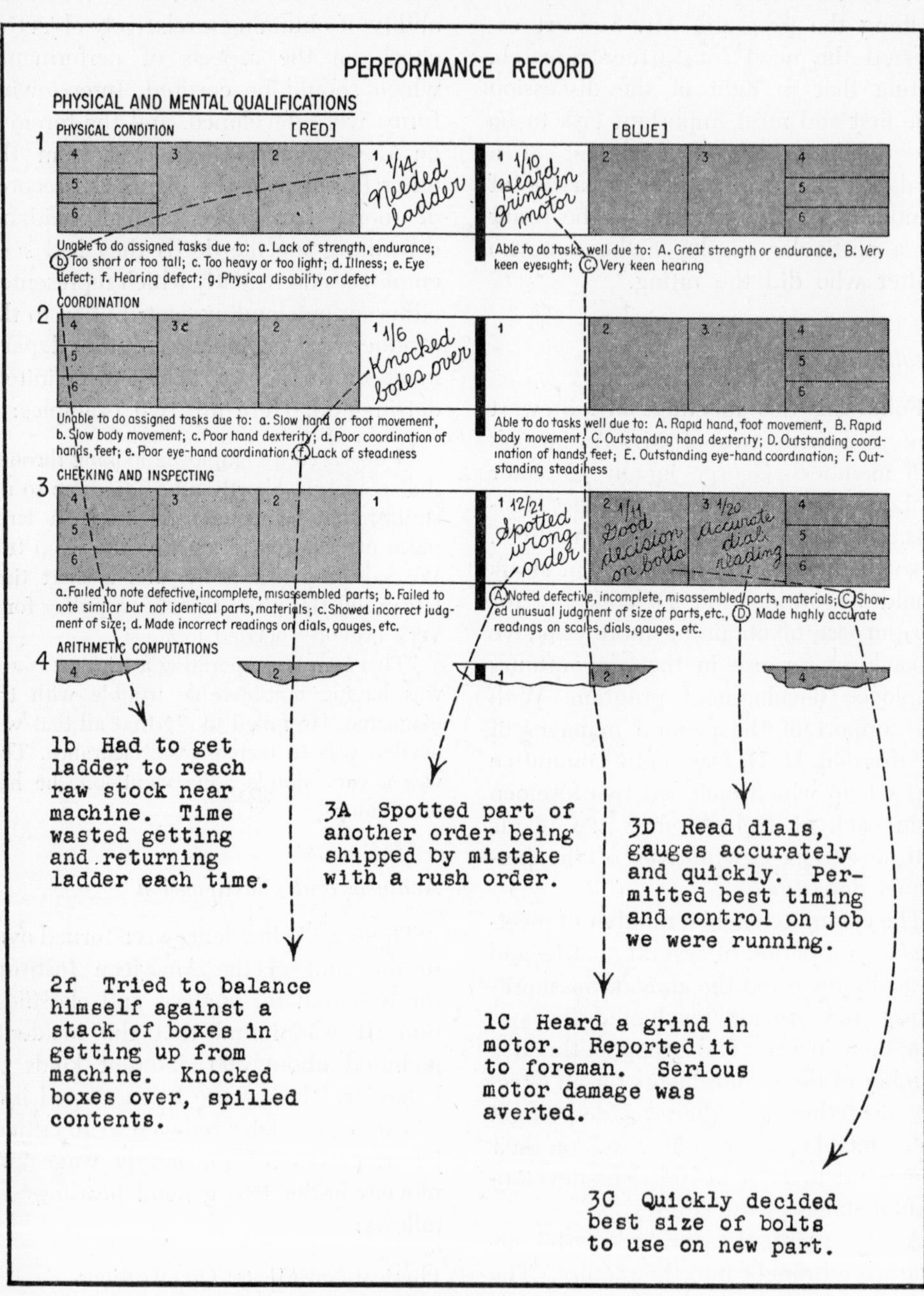

Fig. 1. Section of the performance record kept on an hourly-wage employee in a division of General Motors Corporation.

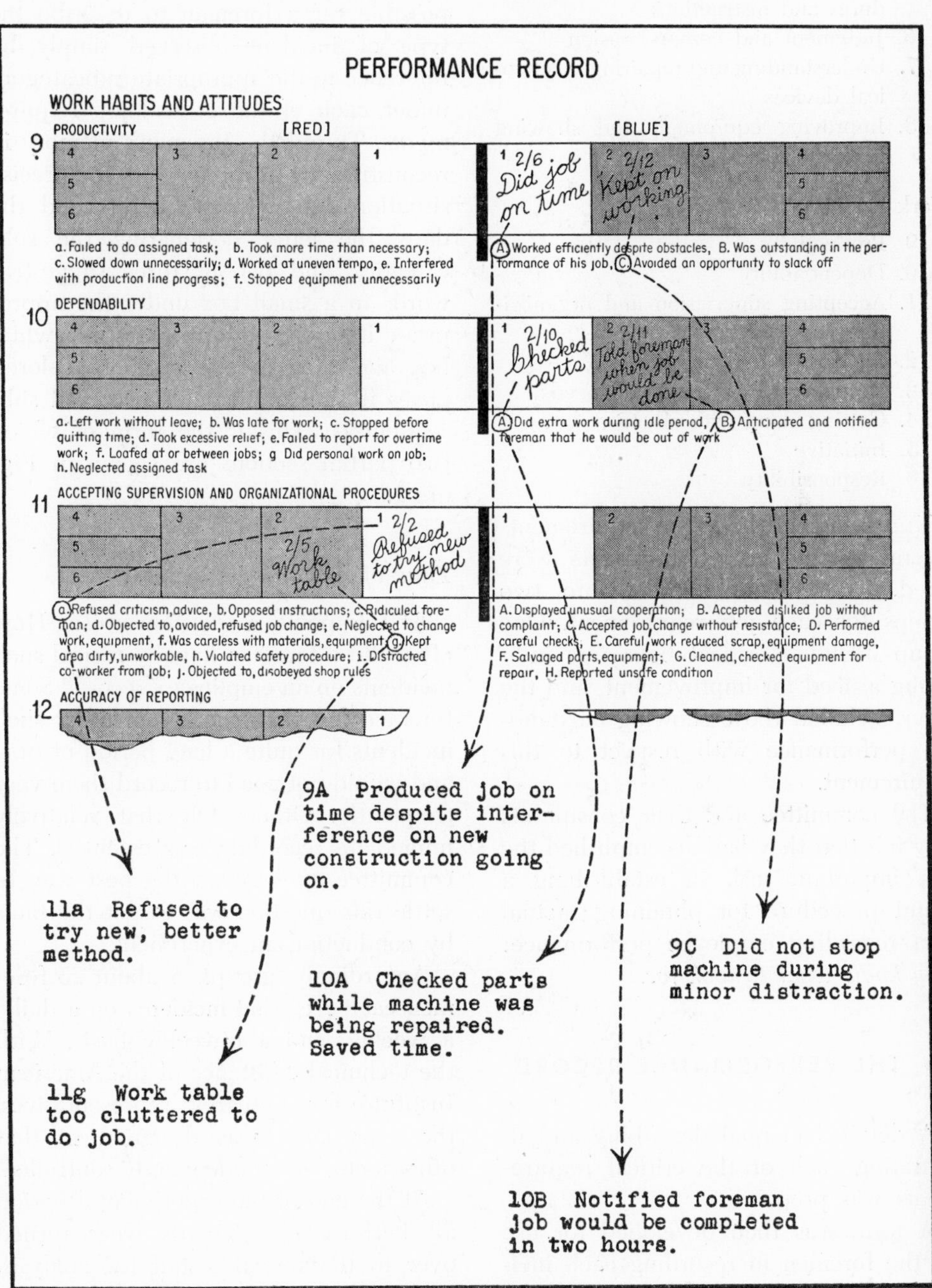

Fig. 1 (Continued).

5. Learning and remembering procedures and instructions
6. Judgment and comprehension
7. Understanding and repairing mechanical devices
8. Improving equipment and showing inventiveness

Work Habits and Attitudes

9. Productivity
10. Dependability
11. Accepting supervision and organizational procedures
12. Accuracy of reporting
13. Response to departmental needs
14. Getting along with others
15. Initiative
16. Responsibility

Under each of the 16 job requirements several specific critical behaviors were listed. These were divided into two groups for each job requirement. One group included critical behaviors indicating a need for improvement, and the other included those showing outstanding performance with respect to this requirement.

The committee and their consultants now felt that they had accomplished the first important task in establishing a sound procedure for obtaining factual data regarding employee performance: *they knew what to look for.*

• THE PERFORMANCE RECORD

A detailed manual describing and illustrating each of the critical requirements was prepared.

A form was then developed for use by the foremen in recording each incident of the types described on either the effective (blue) or the ineffective (red) half of the page for the employee involved. The purpose was to make it possible for a foreman to describe the type of incident observed simply by reference to the appropriate subcategory under each of the critical job requirements. To aid the foreman's memory in reconstructing at a later date the precise situation and actions, he recorded the date, the letter designating the subcategory, and two or three suggestive words in a small box under the appropriate item on the form (first in a white box and then in one or more colored boxes if similar incidents occurred subsequently). This is the form of which two partial sections are shown in Figure 1.

Time of Recording

At this point, a question arose: How often did a foreman have to record such incidents on an employee's record? Some foremen felt they could remember such incidents for quite a long period of time and would not need to record them very frequently. Others felt that relatively immediate recording was essential. The committee agreed that the best way to settle this question was to get the facts by conducting an experiment.

Accordingly, groups of about 25 foremen each recorded incidents on a daily, a weekly, and a biweekly basis. With the technical assistance of the American Institute for Research representatives, the experiment was designed so that other factors were adequately controlled.

At the end of the experimental period all Performance Records were turned over to the research staff for analysis. It was decided that the foremen who had participated in the experimental study would be brought together to be given a report of the findings and to obtain their personal suggestions and preferences regarding the use of the procedure.

Foremen's Reactions

The participating foremen were enthusiastic about their experience with the forms, although they had a number of specific questions and individual problems.

Before the findings were reported to them, the foremen had been asked to express a preference for one of the three types of incident recording which had been tried out. All but one of the 100 foremen indicated that they would prefer to make daily records of their observations of employee performance, and the remaining foreman changed his mind after hearing the report of the experimental results:

> Foremen recording weekly had on the average less than half as many incidents on the record as those recording their observations daily.
>
> Foremen who recorded their incidents only once at the end of the two-week period had less than one-fifth as many incidents on the record as the daily recording group.

These findings clearly corroborated the foremen's impressions. To accumulate adequate factual data regarding employee performance, observations must be recorded soon after they have been made. The foremen also reported that daily recording for all of their employees usually took less than five minutes of their time each day. When the recording was less frequent, much more time was spent in trying to recall specific incidents.

• USING THE RECORD

It is certainly essential to know what facts to collect, and to have a practical, efficient procedure for collecting them. However, such methods are of little value unless they are accompanied by an effective program which uses these facts regarding employee performance.

Early in the study it was agreed that the facts were being collected not for the personnel department, not for the plant manager, nor for the files, but rather for active use by the foreman himself. It was also agreed that this factual record was being accumulated not primarily to prove that a specific employee was effective or ineffective and certainly not as a basis for disciplinary action. The record of performance was designed as a tool for the foreman to use for the employee's benefit.

By providing a basis for commending and reinforcing effective performance and for objectively and clearly defining ineffective performance, the Performance Record gives the foreman a means of communicating with the employee with a minimum of personal feeling and a maximum of acceptance and insight. The program for using the data collected was set on the basic premise that the record of performance is made by the employees themselves. The foreman's function is one of observing, recording, and summarizing. Since only specific incidents are recorded, the foreman's opinion and judgments play an altogether minor role in making the record. *What is recorded are the facts regarding performance on which all observers would tend to agree.*

Observed and recorded performance,

based on the critical requirements of the job, provide an ideal basis for discussion between the foreman and the employee. In striking contrast to the effectiveness of employee-performance reviews based on this type of factual record were the merit-rating reviews previously conducted by foremen in a number of plants.

Development Interview

Interviews centering around general impressions are likely to accomplish very little. Thus:

> If a foreman starts the interview by saying that during the past six months he had to rate the employee low on both quality and quantity of production, and that he had indicated the employee was sometimes careless and inclined to be lazy, the natural reaction is to regard this as merely an expression of personal opinion by the foreman. The employee's attitude is almost always a defensive one, and his conclusion is merely that this foreman doesn't like him and "has it in for him."

When using the Performance Record, however, the foreman makes no over-all judgments. He merely cites the incidents he has observed and recorded, and discusses both the causes and consequences of these types of performance. If the foreman is experienced and has acquired skill in presenting such facts, the employee is quick to agree that these are the facts and to proceed to a discussion of their importance, their basis, and their implications for his future plans and conduct. For example:

> It is comparatively easy for the foreman to discuss objectively the fact that when a pan of parts was accidentally spilled and an assembly line had to be shut down until more parts could be obtained, this employee was the only one who sat down and waited until the parts were available and made no effort to help pick up and sort the spilled parts. A frank discussion of this situation is likely to promote better insight on the part of the employee and improve the understanding between the employee and the foreman.
>
> Similarly, if the foreman can open the interview by referring to an effective incident, such as his record that this employee called his attention to the loosening of a guard on an overhead conveyer and suggested a different style guard which would be more effective and durable, he is likely to make the employee feel that his efforts are appreciated and also to stimulate him to make further suggestions in the future.

While the interviews at the end of each six-month period should certainly not be allowed to replace the immediate and daily commendation and correction of the employee by the foreman, there are many times when the work situation does not permit an adequate discussion of an observed incident. There is also much to be gained from a deferred and a more detached discussion of all the facts regarding the employee's recent performance than is likely to be expedient in the normal supervision of the employee's daily record.

Basis for Action

In addition to its use as a basis for talking with the employee about his job and his plans, the Performance Record is a valuable aid to the foreman in making decisions on such problems as employee selection, training, placement, transfer, promotion, and demotion. These are day-to-day problems which should be solved by having facts available for ready use, rather than by groping for hunches or unreliable impressions.

Furthermore, the foreman is better able to make use of the motivating effect of praise or reward, which psychologists have found more useful in improving behavior than criticism or punishment. Though it is possible that foremen would tend to use the procedure negatively, exploiting the "red" incidents as a disciplinary device—and in fact there were some fears on this score before the program was tried out—experience has shown that the positive aspects get the most emphasis. Thus at Delco-Remy during the first year of the program (1951):

> More than 100,000 specific incidents were recorded by foremen. Of these, 98,566 were of effective performances, and 7,670 were of ineffective performances.
>
> During this same year about seven out of ten employees were observed doing something especially effective which got recorded on the blue side of their Performance Record, including some who had also been noted occasionally as ineffective.
>
> A very small percentage had only ineffective incidents of performance on their record.
>
> About one-fourth of the employees had neither effective nor ineffective incidents recorded. That is, nothing they did was worthy of special note either positively or negatively. Their work was satisfactory—that and nothing more.

• EVALUATING RESULTS

After the procedures described above had been in use for a substantial period of time, the foremen were asked to report specific examples of ways in which the Performance Record had been useful to them. Of several hundred foremen, only two reported that they had not found the procedures valuable. The balance submitted result stories from their experience like these:

1. *Anticipated job needs*—"I had one utility man who just did not anticipate job needs. When he had several entries in the red under this item, I again showed him his record and talked to him about it. Although I had mentioned this sort of thing before to him, he just didn't understand what was required. He is still somewhat weak on this characteristic, but much better than he was."

2. *Improved performance* — "An employee whom I had always considered above average in many respects had begun to drift. When we reviewed his Performance Record at the end of the first rating period, he showed some surprise at some of the blue marks he had earned, which gave me an opening I had been looking for without hurting him. He had begun to get the 'what's the use' attitude, thinking that he was not getting any more for his efforts than our worst employees. Realizing that he is getting credit where credit is due, he is now more like his old self again."

3. *Changed attitude toward job duties* —"A new man had been hired into the department, and after a few days he was observed spending time on the job without producing. He was taken aside and reminded again what was expected of him. Some time later he was taken to the department desk and shown his record and the times he was seen by the foreman spending time on the job without producing. Immediately following, his attitude toward his work changed and to date he is doing a good job of producing while at work."

4. *Improvement in production methods*—"I had an employee who came up with a good idea on changing a die to

increase the life of a punch and improve production. He also is keeping a record of pieces run after changing to a new punch. When going over the Performance Record with him we came to Item 11 on the blue side and I asked him if he recalled the incident. He said 'no.' By explaining the incident to him it brought out other ideas to improve jobs."

5. *Increased interest in making suggestions*—"I gave a man a blue mark for suggesting a better way to paint some parts. He then turned in another suggestion and was given a good cash award. We gained on production in a place where we were in trouble."

6. *Better communication and work performance*—"I have noted that in every case where I have sat down and talked to the employee about his record, he has returned to his job and done a better job—maybe just a little bit, but better—than he had previously been doing."

• NEED FOR TRAINING

In using the Performance Record procedures in several GM divisions, the great importance of proper foreman training has shown up.

It has been the general finding that if supervisors are properly instructed, they regard the Performance Record as a valuable timesaver. By devoting a few minutes a day to keeping records of their important observations with respect to employee performance, many benefits are obtained. For example, the new employee is apt to be started out right on the job because specific facts regarding his performance are brought to his attention before he makes repeated errors or gets into bad habits. Similarly, good work is immediately recognized and encouraged.

The supervisors learn to mention to the employees both outstanding performances and behaviors needing improvement at the time they occur and are recorded. This prevents the development of any attitude on the part of employees that the foreman is spying on them or recording things behind their backs.

The supervisors report that keeping systematic records of this type saves them both time and trouble by augmenting knowledge of what each employee can and will do, by eliminating disciplinary problems before they become serious, and by improving morale generally.

• TEST OF EXPERIENCE

In summarizing the first four years' experience with the system, Delco-Remy reported that the proportion of employees turning in suggestions had increased from 10.8% to 21.9%, while disciplinary warnings were cut in half. There has also been an encouraging rise in the ratio of effective to ineffective incidents observed and recorded by the foremen—which now stands as 4 to 1 in the unskilled group, 8 to 1 in the semiskilled, and 15 to 1 in the highly skilled group.

Mr. Stewart evaluated GM's four years' experience with this program as follows:

"I wouldn't be so naive as to try to tell you that every one of our 700 foremen is handling this thing perfectly. We keep everlastingly at the foremen to do a better job in dealing with their employees.

"Establishing a good basis for the foreman to talk to his people in a constructive way appears to us to be the main contribution of this program. People want to be talked to by their foremen.[3] When they know that their efforts are being evaluated and the foreman is taking the time to pat them on the back for a job well done, they respond accordingly.

"Furthermore, the vast majority of people would rather not do things that are wrong, and if a foreman takes the trouble to discuss these shortcomings with them, they will strive to correct them.

"This appraisal system is more realistic and practical than any we have tried to date, but it can be no better than the understanding and support given it by top management. The program's effectiveness depends on thorough familiarity with its basic concepts by supervision at all levels, and especially at first-line supervision or foreman level. The Performance Record program will never be any better than your foremen choose to make it."

• CONCLUSION

The Performance Record is not a yardstick. It is not a rating method. It is a procedure for collecting the significant *facts* about employee performance. These facts are gathered in such a way that they will be of maximum usefulness to supervisors and management both in improving the employee's understanding of the requirements of his present job and in developing his potential for more responsible positions. It is not simply a new form but *a new approach.* (To install this system of course requires comprehensive manuals and a training program. Such materials are now available.[4])

Various features in the Performance Record employee development program have been used by other organizations. The differences between the GM program and earlier ones refer primarily to aims and attitudes. Although it is not believed that supervisors' aims and attitudes can be changed by merely reading a manual and using a new form, it has been shown that these *can* help.

In extending the program from the Delco-Remy Division to a number of other divisions, GM has followed the principle that the procedure can only be effective if all groups concerned are fully aware of its advantages and limitations before it is installed. Experience indicates that the Performance Record program is based on sound principles and is an efficient tool to add to personnel programs of employee development.

---

[3] See Theodore V. Purcell, "Observing People," *HBR* March–April 1955, p. 90.

[4] John C. Flanagan, Robert B. Miller, and Robert K. Burns, *The Performance Record Manuals.* Chicago, Science Research Associates, 1955.

THE G COMPANY*

Thomas L. Whisler

AN EVALUATION OF PERFORMANCE APPRAISAL IN THE G COMPANY

Evaluation of performance appraisal in this company is nearly equivalent to evaluation of the critical-incident technique, as such. All other procedures—termination ratings, probationary employee ratings, etc.—have been replaced by this single plan.

It is clear that this technique, to be properly done, requires a great deal of the supervisor's time. Since the problem of finding the time is left to the supervisor, the question arises as to how much time the supervisor actually gives to it. The personnel department sampled 1,100 records to find the number of incidents recorded on employees over a six-month period. Some departments averaged as low as one-half item (good or bad) per employee, while one averaged around seventeen. This difference can reflect a number of things. It is possible that it reflects accurately a difference in employee behavior as among these departments. It may reflect a difference in supervisor interest and effort. Personnel officials know that some supervisors are not too strongly convinced of the worth of the plan, while others are quite enthusiastic. According to one foreman, most supervisors, their day already full of making reports and handling problems of supervision, cannot do as good a job as they would like in keeping the record.

Some pressure is brought to bear on the individual supervisor to make him give sufficient time to maintenance of the record. Statistical summations of departmental differences, such as that previously cited, are sent to plant superintendents. Many of these superintendents, in turn, call their foremen together to discuss the results. It is alleged that these superintendents, while visiting the different departments in their respective plants, frequently ask for the record book and look it over. The employee is given a small handbook explaining the rating procedure. He is told that his foreman *will* record incidents of performance, and he is encouraged to ask to see the record when he wishes. When foremen make recommendations for promotion, discharge, or disciplinary action, they can expect the plant superintendent or, in some cases, the personnel department to examine the record as a check on this recommendation. In addition to these pressures, some degree of positive motivation to make adequate use of the plan probably derives from the fact that the company foremen were utilized in building the plan.

Although most of the foremen appear to be reasonably faithful in maintenance of the report, admittedly a number of them fail to review regularly the record with the employee every six months, as they are supposed to. This again is largely a matter of finding time. One department foreman who, with two assistants, supervises 170 men finds it necessary to take over the direct supervision duties of his assistants for a day or two at a time to permit them to carry

* From *Merit Rating: A Management Tool.* Chicago, Ph.D. Dissertation, 1953. Appendix pp. 234–243.

out this interviewing. He has found that, if the incident is discussed with the employee at the time it occurs and is recorded, considerable time is saved at the regular review session. Some foremen apparently make this on-the-spot discussion but do not consistently perform the six-month review. If neither is done, the stated prime purpose of this plan—to keep the employee informed as to the specific things he is doing poorly and doing well—is not achieved.

This plan has never been used for wage-administration purposes. All except about one thousand of the production employees are on jobs carrying fixed rates. The remainder are on rate-range jobs. No serious attempt has been made to set up merit increases based upon the record, for the simple reason that in a large number of cases those employees currently at the top of the rate range do not have the best records.

The records are maintained on file in the offices of the plant superintendents. Discretion as to the use of these records in matters of discipline (usually layoff for poor performance or violation of rules), promotions, and discharges is thus largely left to these superintendents. The employment director indicates that these men are inclined to check all personnel decisions against the records. A recent instance occurred when it was necessary to promote someone to a foreman's position. An employee was recommended by a general foreman (who supervises several departments). The recommendation was rejected by the plant superintendent when he found that this employee's record contained no "good" incidents. This sort of control action conceivably could result in future manipulation of ratings by means of padding the record with "good" items. However, it may also motivate a foreman to spend more time getting relevant information on the record.

The union officially refuses to recognize this appraisal plan. This, of course, is the standard union position with respect to any management-rating device. Personnel officials indicate that "unofficially" the union shows considerable respect for the record. This means that, where the record shows, on balance, a substantial difference in the performance of two individuals, union officials are not inclined to "push" a grievance very far. Grievances inevitably involve decisions that violate length of service. In several cases the union has made the record part of its brief. In these cases it has been able to show that the senior man, who was not promoted, had a better record than the man promoted. These, of course, were cases of foreman error, and the company conceded. The union, in introducing this record as evidence, is, in effect, giving partial recognition to the worth of the plan.

The common tendency to rate the job as well as the man seems to be minimized by the critical-incident technique. Whereas in most traditional rating plans relying on the use of words such as "average," etc., there is a strong tendency to rate those in high-skill jobs "average" or "better" and those in low-skill jobs "lower than average." This tendency is less evident in the G Company plan. From the sample of 1,100 records previously mentioned, a summation was made, by departments and plants, of the percentages of employees who had received only blue (good) entries, only red (bad) entries, and no entries. Two of the nonproduction departments show wide divergence in the general level of skill content in jobs. The maintenance department has a preponderance of high skills; the production-control department a preponderance of low skills. The sample showed that 55 percent of the maintenance employees received only blue entries; 9 percent, red entries; and 27 percent, no entries. In the production-control department 63 percent received only blue entries; 3 percent, red entries; and 21 percent, no entries. A summary of entries for the whole company, classified by general skill levels, shows that there is a tendency to make more entries, both red and blue, on employees in high-skill jobs than on those in low-skill jobs. This may reflect a greater opportunity for variation in performance in high-skill jobs; or it may reflect only a more conscientious reporting job by supervisors of these jobs, or simply that, with fewer people to appraise, the supervisor gives each more attention.

Performance appraisal seems to be carried out with more enthusiasm and earnest effort in the G Company than in most other companies included in these cases, perhaps partly because of the novelty of participation in the development and installation of a new appraisal technique. To some extent objectives have been altered to conform with the nature of the rating device. The value of the incident record for substantiating management decisions accounts for much of its appeal to line supervision. This type of rating device provides many opportunities to make cross-checks on rating effectiveness. Few of these opportunities are currently being exploited, although management personnel indicate that they are aware of their existence and that they plan to make use of such opportunities.

B. The Field Review Technique

THE FIELD REVIEW METHOD OF EMPLOYEE EVALUATION AND INTERNAL PLACEMENT

GUY W. WADSWORTH, JR.

MERIT RATING—PLUS

STEPHEN HABBE

The problems of interpersonal relations arising out of the use of the supervisor as rater have led staff men to seek ways of modifying the appraisal procedure. A number of years ago the field review technique was introduced as one solution. It seeks to incorporate reliability and comparability into the ratings made by different supervisors through the device of having a staff man present when appraisals are being made. The two readings in this section discuss this technique.

FURTHER READING

Adriance, E. H., and H. M. Wisely, "The Operation of the Field Review Method of Performance Review," *Workshop Report on Performance Review,* Industrial Relations Center, The University of Chicago (1949). Reprinted 1953 as Occasional Paper no. 1, pp. 18–33.

THE FIELD REVIEW METHOD OF EMPLOYEE EVALUATION AND INTERNAL PLACEMENT*

Guy W. Wadsworth, Jr.

FUNDAMENTALS OF A SOUND EMPLOYEE EVALUATION AND INTERNAL PLACEMENT PROGRAM

If a personnel man fully accepts the responsibility which is his for developing and maintaining an effective working force in his company, his need for an adequate employee evaluation and internal placement program will be apparent to him. It is his business to know how well or how poorly the employees placed on jobs under the guidance of the Personnel Department are actually making out in their work. If he does not know the cases in which the company is getting its money's worth from given hirings, and the instances in which employee selections have missed fire, he does not know how good his hiring procedures really are or if they are actually any good at all.

Likewise, unless the personnel man can prompt the exercise of good judgment in the routine of promotions, transfers, and reassignments that follow initial employment, the care he uses in clearing new workers for jobs can come to nothing. It should be apparent that the act of hiring an employee merely starts him off in the direction of a job which he presumably can perform. If he is ultimately to land in the job in which he can serve the company to best advantage, adequate steps must be taken to follow his progress in his work and to plan the moves necessary to get him there. Such a result can be accomplished only by continuous, joint planning by the operating supervisors and the Personnel Department, supported by competently developed employee evaluations.

Author's Note: The employee evaluation and internal placement procedures described in this series of articles were first published in manual form by Army Service Forces (ASF M213, May 1945) from the pen of the same author. The Field Review Method itself was an outgrowth of extended employee rating and internal placement research carried on initially in Southern California Gas Company and Southern Counties Gas Company of California in the 1930s. Its principal features were placed at the disposal of the Employee Evaluation and Placement Section, Industrial Personnel Division, Headquarters, Army Service Forces, during World War II. There the method as a whole was developed in instructional form for use in Army Service Forces Civilian Personnel Officers' School. Special indebtedness is acknowledged to Judson Ford, Millicent Pond, E. Hardy Adriance, Robert E. Barmeier, J. Jerome Kravitz, Vincent P. Brennan, Peter Duignan, and Theodore Sharp, who were the author's co-workers in this undertaking. None in this group is more deserving of special mention than Captain Robert E. Barmeier, whose ability to develop creative ideas and to get results with them is reflected in much of the text that follows. As might be surmised from these acknowledgements, this series of articles is essentially a joint work in which the author served primarily in the capacity of editor. The text that follows has been revised to restore adaptations of the Field Review Method to the industrial (as opposed to governmental) setting in which its basic features were originally worked out.

Personnel Department Must Follow Up Hirings

This, in brief, is the case for an adequate employee evaluation and internal placement program, and establishes the basis for the discussion that follows. It is a departure from the tradition that, once an applicant has been cleared by the Personnel Department for employment, what happens to him from then on is strictly the business of the operating supervisors. Similarly, it presupposes a need within the Personnel Department for considerably more working knowledge of how employees are actually getting along on their jobs than is likely to be gained from perusing efficiency reports or ratings turned in by the supervisors at required intervals. In a word, the general proposition is that the personnel man must really follow up his own hiring activity. He must make sure that the methods used in his office result in successful initial placements, and the only way he can do this is to actually count the "hits" and "misses" reflected in fair and factual evaluation of each employee's work. He must also make sure that changes that affect employees throughout the course of their service with the company are based upon well-considered decisions, in which careful evaluation of their performance plays an adequate part. It is only as the steps necessary to accomplish these objectives are actively planned and carried out that the personnel man can fully accomplish the most ancient and honored of all personnel objectives—that of placing (and incidentally keeping) "square pegs in square holes, and round pegs in round holes."

The Field Review Method is a combination of employee evaluation and placement activity, in which expressions of employee value or of success on the job are developed not only for their usefulness in determining the predictive efficiency of hiring procedures used in the Personnel Department, but for immediate or eventual application in internal placement work. This provides a basis not only for checking employee selection methods, but a working basis for directly planning with the supervisors the personnel moves necessary to ensure proper assignment of workers at all stages of their service with the company.

Essentials for Employee Evaluation

The steps directed toward *employee evaluation,* as such, are based upon the following premises:

1. That most, if not all, employee evaluation rests primarily upon supervisory opinion, and that this holds even when tangible measures of production are available.

2. That the supervisor's opinion of his subordinates is no better than the factual observation behind it.

3. That supervisors develop the habit of systematically checking individual performance only as they are prompted to do so. As a corollary, it takes considerable factual evidence to induce a supervisor to revise an opinion, once formed.

4. That the distinctions which the supervisor makes between one employee and another are neither fine cut nor charged with profound meaning. Such distinctions do not lend themselves to numerical expression nor necessarily to statistical distribution. They may be characterized in a general way by saying that most supervisors, even when

capable of supporting their opinions with adequate facts, can point out little more than that, in their best judgment, (a) certain employees are doing good work and should be slated to move up, (b) others are satisfactory where they are, and (c) still others are unsatisfactory and give no promise of really making good on the job. These distinctions, if they actually hold water, are both practical and sufficient for all really necessary employee evaluation and internal placement purposes.

5. That employee evaluations are essentially negatively diagnostic. Appraisals of ability *not* shown in a task often have more tangible support in fact and are more clearly significant than are distinctions between "average" and "superior" performance.

Requirements for Good Placement

The internal placement aspects of the Field Review Method are based upon the following assumptions:

1. That the supervisor, who is immediately responsible for output, can achieve good results only through effective use of the people who work for him, and that he is better situated than anyone else to gauge the capacities and possibilities of his employees through direct observation of their performance.

2. That if the best use of personnel is to be achieved, it will result primarily from adequate performance of the internal placement function at the working level by the supervisor in charge.

The fact that initial responsibility for good internal placement lies with the supervisor does not imply that we need only let him alone and a good internal placement job will result. This is contrary to experience, and as absurd as to assume that a production line will function if operating jobs are merely parcelled out to the supervisors, who are, in turn, permitted to go about their work in any manner that appeals to them. The supervisor is responsible for results principally in the sense of making a success of his immediate job, within the production requirements placed upon him, and with the employees and equipment placed at his disposal. It remains the responsibility of the personnel department to see to it that the supervisor receives all necessary guidance in placing and using his workers to best advantage.

The essentials of a good employee evaluation and internal placement job, as performed by the supervisor, are:

Requirement 1. A well-considered current job assignment for each of his employees, established with due regard to the abilities of each worker, with appropriate attention to the training needed by the employee to make a success of the job.

Requirement 2. An accurate evaluation of the performance of each employee who reports to him, both as a measure of the worker's efficiency in his immediate job and as an indication of his ability to develop and make progress.

Requirement 3. A plan for anticipated changes in the jobs and in the personnel of the working unit. This means continuously scheduling in advance, so far as possible, all of the personnel moves which are in early prospect within the working unit, such as new assignments, promotions, reassignments, replacements, and terminations.

Making Current Job Assignments (Requirement 1)

This is primarily the attention given to matching the worker to his immediate job. Initially it means determining whether the worker has the capacity either as the result of previous working experience or the training given him to perform the job after it has been lined out for him. The first test of a satisfactory current job assignment is whether the employee can do the work, or can be trained to do the work, that the job calls for. This is a proper initial concern, but the worker who meets this test is not necessarily well matched to his job.

Of equal importance over the long term is the degree to which the job itself, assuming that it is well performed, is the right job for the employee. This involves the question of his ability to develop and advance, and whether the job itself is located organizationally so as to provide a logical line of advancement for him. The employee who has what it takes to get ahead and to perform increasingly more responsible or difficult work is as misassigned in a job which has no apparent future as in a job for which he is inadequate. The same principle operates in reverse in relation to the employee who can turn out an acceptable day's work in his current job, but whose ability to get ahead is doubtful. If his job is so placed as to arouse expectations of a promotion for which he would not be seriously considered, the work which he is actually capable of performing will ultimately suffer.

Matching the worker to the job involves, in addition, the choices which must be made between one worker and another in deciding job assignments. When two employees in the same payroll classification and of approximately equal qualifications are considered for a higher position, length of service should be an important factor in the choice. If the newer employee is clearly more qualified both in terms of immediate ability to produce on the higher job and in capacity for further advancement, he is the logical selection. In any case, consideration of current job assignments must include not only analysis of the qualifications of the employees as individuals, but comparison of one employee with another in the total working unit.

The worker is well matched to his immediate job (a) when he can adequately perform its duties, (b) when he is well placed in relation to his ability to get ahead, and (c) when he is assured of logical consideration in the group in which he works. None of these conditions is likely to exist unless considerable thought is given to the specific training needs of each employee in the working unit, reinforced by the training itself. The supervisor should not be required to labor indefinitely with workers who are not qualified or who cannot be qualified through adequate training. However, he should be expected to think through this part of his placement job. The workers will not perform at capacity unless it is obvious that their assignments are based upon logical consideration of all of these factors.

Evaluating Employees' Performance (Requirement 2)

The supervisor must make a considered evaluation of each employee in the working unit at sufficiently frequent intervals to determine the adequacy of his performance on his current job and to appraise his possibilities in general.

At first glance, this requirement would appear to be satisfied by preparation of a periodic rating or efficiency report at annual or semi-annual intervals. Actually, most ratings and formal reporting systems do not serve the purpose under discussion here. For one thing, periodic ratings often represent primarily a formal evaluation placed upon past services. Such evaluations, even when they are good, are not sufficient for detailed personnel planning.

In the planning job, the concern is not so much whether the performance of Henry Smith, junior mechanic, was excellent or very good in the abstract sense during a rating period which has elapsed. The point really at issue is whether or not Henry Smith is currently getting on well enough to be regarded as the next man in line for the job presently held by Frank Green, journeyman mechanic, if Frank should move up or leave the working unit. Or, if Henry's performance is weak in some respect, the important thing is to find out how and why, and what the chances are that he will really improve. Such information must be directly related to the particular duties or operations in which Henry is falling down. The end objective, of course, is a plan of action rather than that of developing a record, as such.

The most important element of employee evaluation for placement purposes is that of making sure that each employee in the working group actually receives individual study and attention. Frequently the supervisor who is questioned out of hand regarding his reasons for moving up one employee rather than another has no facts drawn from systematic observation of both employees on the job with which to back up his choice. This accounts in large degree for the insistence by employee groups, particularly unions, upon hard and fast seniority rules in assigning jobs, especially when promotions are involved. If the difference between two candidates for a given promotion is not substantial enough to be stated in terms of specific work behavior and actual output, there is considerable justice in the position that the employee who has worked the longest for the next job up and whose performance has been acceptable, should get it. This, of course, is the "straight seniority" argument.

Don't Be Deceived by First Impressions. Supervisors, in the interests of fair play as well as good placement, must guard against the common tendency of people in authority to form fixed opinions regarding subordinates which may or may not be consistent with their actual development. In some cases, casual impressions of a new employee formed in the early course of his employment, based upon the way that he appears to take hold of his job rather than upon an actual check of results, influence the supervisor without his being aware of it. As a result, certain workers are groomed for promotion or earmarked as mediocre, when an actual count of operations successfully completed (or of spoiled work) might easily change the supervisor's estimate. Developing a really considered evaluation of employees is necessarily a painstaking activity, in which the supervisor who forms the habit of taking another look, particularly when he feels most sure of himself, will do the best job.

Essentially, any sound evaluation entails determination of what each employee does, or fails to do, in relation to some reasonably tangible standard of good performance. The measure in one case may be total output. In another, such as a service operation where the amount of work varies from day to day, good performance may require ability to change pace and may be related to finishing the day's work as much as to anything else. In a third job, the difference between success and failure may be quality as measured by freedom from errors or spoiled work. Adherence to instructions or regulations may be another factor, etc. So far as possible, standards should be determined in a manner which permits comparison of the performance of one employee with that of another. Attitudes, personality, maturity, and other qualities which are individual to the worker should be considered only as they bear upon satisfactory performance of the work which the job calls for, or as they condition the employee's ability to move ahead.

The ultimate success of internal placement activity, so far as it depends upon employee evaluation, rests only in part upon the ability of the supervisor to name a candidate when a promotion is in the offing or to bring about occasional replacement of grossly incompetent employees. It rests to a much greater degree upon the supervisor's disposition to discover and to develop the abilities of the employees who work for him, for the good of the company as a whole. When he takes a second look at the case of each employee who at first appeals as the proper choice for promotion (from the viewpoint of other employees who would be ruled out by the decision), he may turn up additional deserving talent. When he makes an actual comparison of the mistakes of an employee who appears substandard with the mistakes of employees whom he considers satisfactory, he may avoid an unintentional unfairness. No test of leadership placed upon the supervisor requires more analytical ability than sound employee evaluation.

Anticipating Personnel Changes (Requirement 3)

Many supervisors face a changing situation with respect to jobs and to personnel. Some of these changes are unlooked for and unavoidable; some can be foreseen and forestalled by positive planning. Increases in the work load, changes in the character of the work, the development on the job of abilities for which the employee may be expected to seek an outlet, all present opportunities to plan personnel moves in such a way as to maintain so far as possible a stable, well-adjusted working force. The supervisor's placement job will succeed only as he weighs possible contingencies and develops a working plan in which all personnel moves reasonably in prospect are scheduled against the staffing requirements of the working unit, and as he keeps this plan continuously up to date.

Essentially, this amounts to lining up the job assignments in logical order, ranging from the simpler tasks ordinarily assigned to newcomers to those requiring more extended experience, with a clear indication of the normal lines of promotion and of the relationships which permit transfers from one job to another. A simple sketch will often serve this purpose as well as an elaborate one, and will not only enable the supervisor to schedule necessary personnel moves well in advance, but will assist him in preparing the employees for such moves.

The requirements of good internal placement properly placed upon the supervisor may be summarized as follows:

First, he must carefully line out the job assignments within his working unit which are currently necessary to get the work done. Second, he must compare the possibilities and weaknesses of each employee in the working unit in relation to possible personnel changes, with special emphasis upon detailed checking of current performance against reasonable standards. Third, he should have a plan of action which anticipates, so far as possible, all personnel changes in prospect, whether additions, promotions, reassignments, replacements, or terminations.

Most Supervisors Need Help in Placing Workers

Although the basic placement responsibilities of the supervisor which have just been described meet ready acceptance in principle, the evidence is that the average supervisor needs to have them pointed out and clarified for him. Most of all he must be shown how to go to work on his placement job. Anyone who has had the experience of undertaking an initial cross-table discussion with a supervisor concerning what he has in mind with regard to each of his workers will tell you that such discussion, employee by employee, through the whole of a working group, usually bears the indication of being the first thought through his personnel set-up in its entirety. Foresighted personnel plan- time that the supervisor has really ning has to be encouraged, developed, and guided, as does any other type of planning.

Theoretically the necessary guidance of placement activity at the working level is the responsibility of the top operating official in each department or section of the company. In practice, experience shows that he seldom takes hold of this job and pushes it to completion. It is much more typical to discover the top man charging off wastages of personnel to the inadequacies of subordinate supervisors, than to find him actively prompting the supervisors to perform a competent employee-evaluation and internal placement job. On this basis, placement activity is made effective at the working level largely through the attention it receives from representatives of the personnel office. This does not mean assumption by the personnel department of any decisional responsibility which logically rests with the line supervisors, but it does mean seeing to it that the employee evaluation and placement job, which must be carried on at the site of work, actually gets done.

PERSONNEL DEPARTMENT • RESPONSIBILITIES AND METHODS

Thus far we have considered the broad requirements of employee evaluation and internal placement activity from the viewpoint of desired end results. The remainder of the discussion will be related to the immediate responsibilities that the personnel department must assume and methods it can employ to achieve the results in question. First, and most obviously, as a staff and service agency, there are certain activities that the personnel department itself must carry out. These are (a) rendering service to operating supervisors, such as locating candidates for job vacancies, whether inside or outside of the company, (b) guidance of the supervisors in the handling of their responsibilities for assignment of jobs, evaluation of employee performance, and personnel planning, and (c) coordination of the employee evaluation and internal placement activities of the various departments and sections of the company so that the organization as a whole will have a unified and balanced program for the effective use of personnel.

Locating Candidates for Jobs

Recruitment and hiring procedures, as such, will not be directly considered in this discussion. They are mentioned, first, because these procedures may figure directly or indirectly in any situation that involves furnishing candidates for job vacancies, and, second, because they represent one of the services that the personnel department performs for the company as a whole that is closely interlocked with employee evaluation and internal placement activity. It goes almost without saying that in recruiting applicants and "selecting the right man for the job," the personnel department properly acts primarily in the capacity of clearing eligibles for employment. Eligible candidates should then be sent to the operating supervisors, who should exercise final choice and perform the act of conferring employment. There is no sound hiring system that thrusts any candidate for work down a supervisor's throat, so far as hiring from the outside is concerned. Sometimes the supervisor's choices may have to be restricted in internal placement, but that is another story.

In some instances the personnel department, by arrangement with individual supervisors, in effect, makes the final choice of new employees for lower level jobs and "hires" them without a supervisory interview. This arrangement may be acceptable (a) when the supervisor has "asked for it," based upon his satisfactory experience with the services of the personnel department, and (b) when it is not based upon an indifference on the part of the supervisor toward his responsibility for looking over new workers. Such an arrangement should not be forced upon supervisors who prefer to review their own candidates. However, the personnel department itself should not in any case pass up an initial review of applicants and turn them over to the supervisors sight unseen. There is no basis, even within the limited choices that prevail in a tight labor market, for failure on the part of the personnel department to screen carefully all candidates for employment, and to clear applicants only when there is some positive reason to believe that they can perform the work in the jobs that are being filled.

Promote from Within. Before outside recruitment activity is started in connection with any vacancy, however, the personnel department should locate all suitable candidates who may be available within the company, and see to it that they receive consideration. Recruitment from the outside is in order only when qualified employees cannot be located within the existing force. Particular care should be taken to see that the higher level jobs are filled whenever possible by promotion from within the company. Even in the lower level jobs a vacancy may provide the opportunity to improve the assignment or prospects of some employee already on the payroll. Granted that this principle cannot invariably be followed, and that it is sometimes defeated by hard and fast seniority rules, it is nonetheless the keystone of good internal placement work. It should, of course, be added that in considering employee candidates for a vacant position, not only must care be taken in appraising their qualifications, but the strengths and weaknesses of staff in working units from which employees may be transferred to fill the vacancy must be taken into account.

Employee evaluations that indicate the particular duties which each employee performs well (or poorly) are essential to effectiveness in this phase of internal placement work. A process by which such evaluations can be developed will be described in detail later on.

An important feature of the general activity of locating candidates for jobs is that of replacing employees who cannot be so assigned that their services are of real value to the company. The employee who does not or cannot pull his own weight is a liability both as regards his own work and the extra burden he imposes upon other employees.

The personnel department thus has a very direct concern in all terminations of service contemplated by the supervisor. Cases of poor performance should be analyzed for possible mis-assignments that can be corrected. When terminations are planned because of an existing surplus of satisfactory employees, such employees should be transferred whenever practicable to other units of the company where the staff is known to be weak.

Guidance of the Supervisors

The employee evaluation and internal placement staff of the personnel department in its dealings with the supervisors acts in the capacity of working consultants. Such staff must not only be grounded in sound employee evaluation and internal placement principles, but must likewise be qualified to assist the supervisors in applying those principles in actual situations. Situations which need attention at the site of work are best brought to light in individual cross-table contacts with the supervisors, undertaken for the purpose of dealing with the placement problems of a specific working unit. There is little reason to believe that necessary applications of sound employee evaluation and internal placement principles will result from generalized discussion of the subject in conferences with the supervisors. Even when these applications are understood and accepted in principle, the supervisors are not necessarily inclined to transpose them into action. The best guarantee of results is to work directly with individual supervisors on actual employee evaluation and internal placement problems of the working units of which they are in charge.

Company-Wide Coordination of Employee Evaluation and Internal Placement Activities

While employee evaluation and internal placement activity in the practical sense begins and ends at the work place, and necessarily entails dealing with the problems of individual working units, the personnel department has a responsibility for the employee evaluation and internal placement program of the company as a whole. Among other things this means achievement of a general state of balance in the assignments of the total working force which ensures a fair distribution of qualified staff throughout the company.

Individual supervisors naturally place primary emphasis upon their own personnel needs. They may be reluctant to give up competent workers even for the good of the company as a whole. One of the key purposes of a sound employee evaluation and internal placement job is to correct this attitude. This can be accomplished only by an order of procedure which progressively gains the confidence of the supervisor in the intentions of the personnel office as regards "proselyting." It must be made clear to the supervisor that first concern lies in seeing to it that his own requirements are satisfied. This means that his key jobs are adequately filled and understudied, and that all of the jobs under his supervision are competently staffed. It is reasonable to discuss with him the requirements of other working units when it develops that the supervisor has a surplus of capable individuals for whom no really desirable assignment or promotion is in prospect. The same point may be brought home to him when the principle operates in reverse, in the supervisor's favor. This applies, of course, to instances in which the personnel department fills vacancies for him with qualified staff drawn from other working units of the company, illustrating the reciprocal nature of these transactions. It goes without saying that unless such exchanges of personnel are brought about by a uniform practice of give and take between working units, no actual balance in the distribution of qualified personnel throughout the company as a whole can be achieved.

When the personnel department can encourage the necessary exchanges of staff between working units of the company by dealing individually with the supervisors, necessary results can be achieved informally. Supervisors may not be disturbed by an individual transfer which has been thoroughly discussed, even when they may take exception, on principle, to a company-wide activity that implies wholesale exchanges of staff. Therein lies the disadvantage of a mandatory placement policy that calls for company-wide transfers as directed by the personnel department. It is best, at least initially, to undertake coordination of placement activity on an individual, voluntary basis. Where placement staff finds through experience that certain supervisors, who have been given every opportunity to cooperate, fail to do so, it is time enough to require rather than request necessary action.

Personnel Department Must Know Supervisor Problems

This brings us directly to consideration of the principal feature of the Field Review Method. The basic premise underlying this procedure is that the personnel department can adequately discharge its responsibility for guiding the supervisors in the handling of their placement problems and for coordinating employee evaluation and internal placement activities in the company as a whole *only as representatives of the personnel department become thoroughly familiar with the supervisors and their problems through personal contact at the site of work.* A corollary is that supervisors, like other people, will discuss a variety of problems much more freely in oral conversation than they will express themselves on the same problems in writing. This is an obvious departure from the tradition that the personnel department must deal at arm's length with the supervisors through the medium of written instructions, periodically required reports, or perhaps through occasional group meetings. It is submitted, however, that assisting someone else with a problem when you do not really know what the problem is, or trying to guide someone in a situation about which he knows considerably more than you do is a tall order. Accordingly the Field Review Method is essentially a program of planned supervisory contacts undertaken to make the employee evaluation and internal placement job effective, and includes everything that ordinarily transpires in those contacts.

The personnel manager is, of course, responsible for use of the Field Review Method throughout the company, whether he applies it himself or delegates it to a special placement staff. Included in this responsibility is decision regarding the level of supervision at which the necessary contacts should be established and maintained. In general, the supervisor who should be dealt with in applying the Field Review Method should be the one nearest to the jobs under consideration who has sufficient authority to make the necessary placement decisions. An individual who does not have this authority, even though he is called a supervisor, is not the person to see. On the other hand, an operating official who is located at a place remote from the site of work and who does not know the personnel situation on the job cannot supply the necessary information. This is true even in cases where an upper level supervisor insists on personally making decisions regarding employees concerning whom he really knows very little. The point in any case is to develop access to the job at a supervisory level in which the work and the workers are intimately known.

Where first-hand relationships with supervisors have not been established as a matter of course, any personnel situation demanding immediate attention can be used as an opportunity to establish necessary contacts with the supervisors. Requests to fill vacancies justify visits from the personnel manager or his placement representatives, which can be used to develop fairly complete job information. Systematic follow-up on new hirings, undertaken to see how new employees are working out, may easily be turned toward discussion of the supervisor's entire working force.

The personnel manager, or his placement staff, bearing in mind that the objective is to have at all times a current picture of personnel requirements of the company as a whole, should coordinate field review activities so as to cover all operating units within the company at given periods, preferably at least three or four times a year.

Keeping Placement Information Up to Date

Once the basic placement information on each working unit has been developed with the supervisors in charge, and once the supervisors have scheduled a tentative plan with respect to each employee on the force, the task of keeping the employee evaluation and internal placement job up to date can be accomplished by periodic contacts in which basic plans are merely checked and brought forward. The process of securing employee evaluation and internal placement information is thus accumulative. Contacts following the initial visit will be less detailed and time-consuming.

Field Review contacts succeed only as they are carefully planned in advance with respect to a suitable approach, a logical order of inquiry, and development of a specific plan of action for all personnel moves that appear in the offing in each working unit. This includes consideration of how to prepare for the contact, how to open the discussion, and how to lead the interview to a conclusion that puts the supervisor to work on the problems developed in the course of the discussion. A "canned" list of questions has its place at least in preparing for the Field Review contact, and sometimes in the interview itself. However, as the personnel man or his representatives gain some experience, they will ordinarily vary the wording of the questions. It is, of course, undesirable to leave behind an impression of stilted conversation or that the Field Review contact was a planned inquisition. The preliminaries to the contact and the opening steps of the interview itself are as follows.

Preparation for the Interview. Before going to see the supervisor to secure employee evaluation and internal placement information regarding any given working unit, the personnel manager or his representative should gather together such data on the jobs and the personnel of the working unit as are available in the files of the personnel department. These usually include names of the employees in the working unit, their job titles, pre-employment test results (if any are in hand), and such information on their individual performance as can be determined from past conversations or past ratings. This merely amounts to getting a line on the jobs and on the employees of the working unit to the extent that the information on record provides it. The contact at the working level can then be undertaken with all of the information in hand which the personnel department would reasonably be expected to have. Such information also assists in planning the contact and deciding how much time will be required to cover the ground.

Getting Information during the Interview. The interview at the work place will be directed toward certain specific objectives. First, it is necessary to give some reason for undertaking the interview itself. The approach may be keyed to some immediate request for new staff, or it may be based upon the desire of the personnel office to check the service it has been rendering to the supervisor, or it may be based on the desire of that office to get a line on the personnel situation in the working unit in general. Often the most direct approach will serve the best purpose. In any case there should be some introductory statement that will get the interview under way.

Initial Questions. Initial questions should deal with the current accuracy of the list of employees, and any other records which have been assembled for the interview. This is a necessary precaution in lining out the discussion and permits making any necessary corrections.

Job Set-up. The next step is to find out how the jobs in the working unit are set up in relation to each other. This means checking the organization chart of the working unit if one is available or sketching out such a chart if there is none at hand. The line-up of positions should be discussed to any extent necessary to get a clear picture of lines of promotion and how personnel moves are actually made in the working unit.

Special Requirements. In addition to determining how the jobs are set up, it is important to note any special requirements attaching to given job assignments that may not be apparent in the job title. These would be represented in any unusual working conditions, special emphasis on given operations, irregular hours, special overtime exactions, unusual workload pressure, etc.

Job Design and Job Relationships. To this point discussion will have developed a picture of the jobs in the working unit, of general relationships between one job and another, and of any special requirements attaching to given jobs. It is, of course, important to find out if any changes, either in the total number or in the nature of these jobs, are contemplated, as such changes must necessarily be considered in studying the placement needs of the working unit. Another important point is to check the influence of the line-up of jobs itself upon qualifications which develop (or fail to develop) in performing the various jobs. For example, does experience in a given job actually prepare the employee for the next job up the line, or must such experience be supplemented by training? If there is a gap between the skills acquired in performing a job and those required in the next higher job, it should be noted and the training requirement should be earmarked and transmitted to the training staff of the personnel department later on. Likewise, instances in which experience in given jobs permits interchanges of staff from one line of jobs to another should be noted. "Dead end" jobs also should be noted. The point is to identify, within the line-up of jobs in the working unit, the cases in which the organizational location of the job conditions the development or chances for promotion of the employee placed on it. These steps will round out the information necessary to an understanding of the jobs themselves.

Qualifications Required. The next step is to discuss the abilities and qualifications that employees holding the respective jobs within the working unit should possess. The supervisor should be pinned down as definitely as possible with respect to the particular abilities needed in the performance of each job. The ability to perform any job will be determined to some extent by previous experience and training. The necessary kind and amount of experience or training should be reduced, if possible, to a standard that can actually be used in locating suitable candidates within the existing force, or in hiring new workers for the job. The same applies to age, sex, physical and other characteristics when discussing job qualifications.

It is not sufficient, however, merely to accept the off-hand opinion of the supervisor as to what kind of qualifications are needed. Experience has shown that the supervisor in many cases will dream up arbitrary requirements which have little real validity and which are, in fact, at marked variance with the qualifications of successful workers with whom the supervisor deals every day. It is best therefore to direct the discussion of qualifications to considerations of the experience, education, and other characteristics of employees within the working unit whom the supervisor regards as successful. This is accomplished by asking the supervisor to name an employee or two on each job who is making good. It can then be determined, as between one example and another, whether the supervisor's views on necessary qualifications are really consistent with the qualifications of workers whom he regards as adequate or perhaps highly successful. This will be important later on, because the selection of candidates for the supervisor can then take on the aspect of seeking out persons who are like the workers who have already made good, rather than searching for people with qualifications which have been, in effect, "picked off the ceiling."

Recording Information. The information developed in the foregoing steps should be noted down in some convenient form. The amount of necessary record keeping will vary with the size of the working unit, the number of different types of jobs involved, and the complexity of the jobs themselves. In a small company where the working units are small and few jobs are involved in each, a single sheet of paper may serve to record (in field note style) the line-up of jobs in each working unit. This may be an informally sketched organization chart with the job titles jotted in, with abbreviated notes necessary to supplement information not available with respect to any particular job.

In a large organization where there are many working units and many types of jobs, the record keeping can start with noting the job information developed in the placement interview, in longhand, somewhere on individual field sheets. These notes, plus a sketch of the line-up of jobs in the working unit (whether the existing organization chart or one sketched out during the interview), will provide a satisfactory working record. This arrangement is basically simple even in a large organization.

These steps complete the preliminaries to developing employee evaluations and developing a plan for any personnel moves in prospect in the working unit.

FIELD REVIEW CONTACTS • FOR EMPLOYEE EVALUATION

With the Field Review contact under way, and the preliminary of developing information about the jobs in the working unit accounted for, the remainder of the interview is devoted to getting information about the employees as individuals (employee evaluations) and to planning personnel moves. Information concerning employee performance and estimates of their individual possibilities are quite easily obtained by using the same informal sort of inquiry as is used in developing information about jobs. Experience shows that the average supervisor has an opinion regarding the competence of each employee who reports to him, and that this opinion is likely to govern what happens to the employee in the long run, whether it is well founded or ill founded. It is important that this opinion should, as a matter of habit, be shaped by systematic observation of what the employee specifically does, or fails to do, in relation to the duties imposed upon him by his job.

The supervisor's impression of an employee is seldom developed as precisely as should be desired without some prompting. His opinion may, in actuality, be based only upon casual impressions, colored in some degree by his personal reactions to the employee as an individual. Most of us tend to believe that we can "take in" a situation on which we have, in fact, focused no really detailed attention, particularly in judging other people. That our ideas can be wrong is frequently demonstrated when we are called upon to say explicitly where, when, and under what circumstances a given impression has developed. Even the most fair-minded supervisor is not very likely to check himself or to look for evidence which might revise his opinion of an employee, unless something happens to prompt him to do so.

A Planned Interview

It is the purpose of a Field Review contact, particularly the part of it devoted to getting employee evaluations, to provide the occasion for the supervisor to think through this part of his employee evaluation and internal placement job. This is accomplished by a planned pattern of inquiry. The supervisor is questioned about each employee in the working unit in relation to the employee's current performance, his possibilities for advancement, or possible usefulness in other work. The interview at each step is calculated to bring out facts that the supervisor could obtain only by direct and systematic observation of the employee on the job. The result is usually a well-considered, or at least a markedly improved, evaluation of each employee in the working unit. In line with these findings, the supervisor is questioned on his plans with respect to each employee and encouraged to schedule appropriate action in each case.

As previously stated, the evaluation and planning discussion in the interview ordinarily represents a second main step in the Field Review contact and normally can be started when the discussion of job requirements has been completed. There is no reason why this discussion cannot be undertaken separately if it serves any point of convenience. However, there is some logic in proceeding directly from the discussion of job requirements to the evaluation of the people holding the jobs and the development of a plan of action while all of the facts about the job requirements are fresh in mind.

The equipment needed for the evaluation inquiry is merely a roster that includes the names of employees in the working unit and the titles of their jobs. They may be listed in any convenient order, whether alphabetically or by grades or categories of jobs. Sometimes the names are listed in an order which corresponds to the line-up of jobs on the organization chart of the working unit, and this is of special advantage later on in the interview. There should be sufficient space opposite each name to permit making notes.

The order of inquiry and pattern of questioning at this point has two principal steps, (a) initial evaluation and informal analysis, and (b) supplementary analysis and planning. In the first step, the representative of the personnel department gets the supervisor's offhand opinion of each employee's performance, along with the specific reasons which substantiate that opinion. In the second step, he either determines what plans the supervisor has, or what plans he might be prompted to make, for each employee who is better than satisfactory or who is not making good.

Initial Evaluation and Informal Analysis

The first order of business is to get from the supervisor an offhand, over-all opinion of each employee on the roster. The primary objective at this stage in the interview is to draw from the supervisor an estimate of each employee in the working unit, which tentatively identifies him as satisfactory, better than satisfactory, or less than satisfactory. This will serve to show where each employee stands with the supervisor in relation to the following categories of evaluation, and, so far as possible, why:

EVALUATION	SYMBOL*
1. Definitely outstanding	+ (plus)
2. Satisfactory	OK
3. Definitely a problem	– (minus)

The questioning process is as follows:

Step 1. Starting with the first employee on the list, the representative of the personnel office first asks a general question, such as "*How is this employee getting along?*", or any equivalent general question. The supervisor's response will indicate which way his evaluation leans, whether toward the high side (+), the low side (–), or toward the middle (OK) evaluation.

Following Up a "High Side" or a Satisfactory Evaluation. Step 2. If the supervisor apparently leans toward a high side (+) evaluation, or toward satisfactory (OK), the next question is:

"In what way is he good (or particularly good)?" The response to this question may be (a) general ("he is my best worker," "he is a good worker"), or (b) specific ("he is 'tops' in finding what is wrong with an engine," "he can spot engine trouble," "she is a very fast typist," "she types accurately"). The distinction between general and specific responses, of course, lies in whether the response is merely a complimentary remark, as opposed to a statement that the employee *does* something well or in superior fashion. Any specific comment is preferred to a general comment, as the purpose is to draw out what the employee does, or fails to do, in relation to the requirements of his job. Another point which should be noted is the "shading" of the supervisor's comment, whether specific or general. Such expressions as "best worker," "tops," and "very fast" may suggest a higher degree of excellence, and are more indicative of a probable +, or outstanding, evaluation, than "good worker," "he can do (such and such)," "he is good (in a given operation)", etc. The latter responses generally point to satisfactory (OK) evaluations. Abbreviated notations of the supervisor's responses, whatever they are, at each step in the questioning process should be entered opposite the employee's name on the roster.

Step 3. If the question asked in Step 2 has elicited a general response or has drawn out only one specific answer, the next question is:

"What (or what else) is he doing well?" Here again the purpose is to "pull for" specific responses, developing if possible a series of duties or operations that are performed outstandingly well or satisfactorily. The point at this step is to *bleed out* specific information on workmanship that not only establishes the supervisor's leaning toward a + or OK rating, but supports that leaning. The response at this point again can be general ("He does everything the way I want him to do it"), or it may be

* The symbols indicated are used in noting the respective evaluations given by the supervisor as the discussion proceeds.

specific ("The motors he turns out are tuned perfectly," "he does a good tuning job," "she proofreads her own work and almost never makes a mistake," "she doesn't make many errors"). In most instances a sufficient number of specific responses are forthcoming at this point, as the questioning is continuously directed toward what the employee does on the job, rather than toward his general attributes.

Step 4. If responses of the supervisor thus far have been continuously general rather than specific, one further question can be:

"Why do you believe that he is good (in given operations)?" This may either elicit a specific response, or it must be concluded that the supervisor's good opinion of the employee, whether he leans toward a + or an OK evaluation, is based upon very general considerations. This may not be highly convincing, but it at least shows where the supervisor stands.

Step 5. If responses have been generally favorable to the employee, it is well advised to use a single check question at this point:

"Does he have any weaknesses?" The response may be general or specific, but may serve a purpose if a borderline rating (which will be discussed later on) has to be made.

Step 6. This is the "pin-down" step. The supervisor is given a choice or leading question to elicit either an outstanding (+) or a satisfactory (OK) evaluation:

"Is this a definitely outstanding employee, or would you describe him as fully satisfactory?" The supervisor's evaluation is then recorded opposite the employee's name on the roster, alongside the supporting comment that has been noted during the preceding steps (by appropriate symbol) as + or OK.

Following Up a "Low Side" Evaluation. Where the supervisor's response to the question in Step 1 (*"How is this employee getting along?"*) indicates that the supervisor leans toward a low side evaluation, the steps are undertaken in the same order as those used in following up an apparently high side or satisfactory evaluation. The questions, which are similarly intended to draw out as many specific answers as possible, are as follows:

Step 2. "In what way is he particularly weak?"

Step 3. "What is he doing poorly?"

Step 4. "Why do you think he does poor work?"

The line of questioning is reversed, but is in all other respects the counterpart of the follow-up on a high side or satisfactory evaluation. Where the process draws out a series of general or specific weaknesses, the "check" question is:

Step 5. "Has he any good qualities?"

Finally, the "pin-down," leading question is:

Step 6. "Is he definitely a problem, or do you regard him as a satisfactory employee with some weaknesses?" The supervisor's evaluation is then noted on the employee roster opposite the employee's name, and the supporting comment. This concludes the follow-up on a low side evaluation.

Field Review Questions

(Initial Evaluation and Informal Analysis)

Step 1. How is this employee getting along?

(*Follow-up on "high side"*)

Step 2. In what way is he good (or particularly good)?

Step 3. What (or what else) is he doing well? ("Bleeding" Step)
Step 4. *Why* do you believe that he is good (in given operations)?
Step 5. Does he have any weaknesses? ("Check" Question)
Step 6. Is this a definitely outstanding employee, or would you describe him as fully satisfactory? ("Pin-down" Step)

(*Follow-up on "low side"*)

Step 2. In what way is he particularly weak?
Step 3. What is he doing poorly?
Step 4. *Why* do you think he does poor work?
Step 5. Has he any good qualities? ("Check" Question)
Step 6. Is he definitely a problem, or do you regard him as a satisfactory employee with some weaknesses? ("Pin-down" Question)

These steps, started with the first employee named on the roster, and carried on down the list to the end, complete the initial evaluation and informal analysis. Up to this point, the effort has been to bring out the supervisor's offhand opinion of each of his employees by questioning him. The representative of the personnel department has made no suggestions and has challenged nothing that the supervisor has had to say. He has merely noted the apparent leaning of the supervisor toward high, satisfactory, or low evaluations in each case and has jotted down such supporting reasons, whether general or specific, as the supervisor has offered. He has, of course, varied his questioning to adapt certain of his questions to the job information already in hand or to fit the pattern of the supervisor's responses. Where the supervisor has "picked up the ball" and given detailed and specific information with a minimum of prompting, the representative of the personnel department will have passed up a one, two, three order of questioning so long as he has been getting the answers he needs. In the end the supervisor has furnished his own evaluation of each employee in the working unit, and it is altogether possible that some of them will have been moderated or improved during this initial review. In any case, discussion carried on up to this point will have provided a general picture of each employee in the working unit and will have laid the groundwork for the final steps in the placement interview.

Borderline or Intermediate Evaluations. It will have been noted that evaluations have been discussed thus far on a three-point scale (outstanding, satisfactory, problem). There is probably no such thing as a standard scale of employee evaluations that will mean the same thing to every person who uses it. Wagonloads of definitions have been written ostensibly to "clarify" shades of difference between such terms as Very Good and Excellent (in "five-point" rating scales) and such terms as Outstanding or Superior suggest a similar labor of definition. Effort along this line frequently serves only to transpose the confusion over the meaning of descriptive adjectives into an equal, if not greater, confusion revolving about the interpretation of the "definitions."

A great many supervisors are sparing in praise and regard a top evaluation as representing an almost unattainable ideal. Others are reluctant to go on record with poor ratings and do not want to place a black mark on anyone's record. The personnel man, on his part, fundamentally wants to identify three classes of employees: (a) those of whom the supervisor thinks well and whom he regards as candidates for better jobs, (b) those whom the supervisor regards as adequate, but who are likely to stay where they are, and (c) those of whom the supervisor thinks poorly, whether they are merely misassigned or definitely lacking in ability. The better than satisfactory employee and the less than satisfactory employee represent the two classes of individuals that require most of the attention in planning for better placement.

Some Supervisors Will Not Take a Stand. In some instances, the representative of the personnel department will find that the supervisor will not positively commit himself on evaluations above and below satisfactory. The supervisor, in such cases, will want to use intermediate evaluations such as OK + (plus), representing a satisfactory employee with some outstanding qualities. In others, the supervisor may suggest an OK − (minus), or a satisfactory employee with some weaknesses. Individuals who labor in this fashion with terms take the issues involved very seriously, and the personnel man may find that the only way he can get the supervisor to "come down to cases" is to accept or even suggest such intermediate evaluations. He will know when he does this that the supervisor's OK + (plus) is probably his individual way of describing an outstanding employee, and that the OK − (minus) is as far as the supervisor is willing to go in describing a problem employee. In some few instances these intermediate distinctions may appear entirely justified, based on the facts drawn out in the questioning process. The personnel manager or his representative should observe two principles in dealing with the issue of intermediate ratings:

(a) He should not unnecessarily suggest the use of intermediate or borderline ratings, as he will find the distinctions more typical of the evaluation habits of the individual supervisor than characteristic of any real differences between employees from one working unit to the next. In addition he will find more disparities of meaning in using what might be termed a "five-point scale" (+, OK +, OK, OK −, and −) than in the use of a three-point scale, merely as a mathematical proposition (that is, the greater the number of distinctions, the greater the difficulty in interpreting individual evaluations from one supervisory interview to the next).

(b) He does not want to bog down the placement interview with abstract discussion. Considered in terms of field review objectives, the personnel man primarily wants to spot talent in the working force which can be put to better use, to identify the employees who are "all right where they are," and to single out individuals who are misassigned, need special attention, or who should not be on the payroll at all. Where he can secure the simplest practical distinctions on the three-point scale that has been suggested, he is situated to move ahead to the supplementary analysis and planning activity which is the pay-off in the Field Review contact.

SUPPLEMENTARY • ANALYSIS AND PLANNING

With completion of the initial evaluation and informal analysis step of the Field Review contact, the personnel manager or his representative will have before him substantially complete information about the jobs in the working unit, and about the relationships between one job and another. He will also have the supervisor's offhand opinion on how each employee is getting along on his current job, a number of specific facts which presumably underlie that opinion in each case, and the supervisor's evaluation of each employee, whether outstanding, satisfactory, or a problem. All of this adds up to a balance sheet of the personnel situation in the working unit as it stands on the date of the Field Review interview.

It is to be remembered, however, that the discussion of the employees thus far has considered them primarily as individuals in given jobs where their performance presumably is a known quantity. It has not necessarily included consideration of the employee in relation to his current job, plus his "potential"; that is, his suitability for the next job up or in relation to jobs other than the one he holds. The personnel manager or his representative is necessarily concerned both in the personnel situation as it exists and in what is likely to happen to it when job changes occur. In undertaking the supplementary analysis, which is immediately in order, he must "mesh in" the job information with what he has learned of the employees with particular reference to lines of promotion and prospective changes in jobs within the working unit. This means that he must consider the organizational setting of each job and its "prospects," in reviewing the case of each employee.

By way of illustration, an employee may be outstanding in his current assignment, but even so, if he is admittedly as far as he can go, he is a poor placement in a job in which the incumbent is the logical understudy for the next job up. Similarly, an employee who can manifestly perform more important work is a poor placement in a job that leads nowhere, even when his current performance is definitely outstanding. The representative of the personnel department must undertake the final step of the Field Review contact with such relationships in mind, viewing each employee as (a) a producer or a nonproducer where he is and (b) as a possible candidate for some other job, whether the one next up in line of promotion or one which represents a change in occupation. To do this, he must actively relate all of his findings to the organizational line-up of jobs in the working unit and work toward a balanced distribution of the best qualified employees in it.

Supplementary Analysis of "Problem" Employees

The supplementary analysis begins with checking back through the employee list, taking up the cases of the problem employees in the first instance. At this stage in the interview the employees with less than satisfactory OK-evaluations should be considered along with the problem cases. Sometimes "OK" is the lowest evaluation given by the supervisor, and probably represents a problem. A suggested order of questioning in reviewing problem cases is:

Step 1. "What help have you given him?" The point here is to proceed on the assumption that the supervisor has made some effort to help the employee and has concluded that he is a problem only after the failure of such effort. This serves to bring out the problem itself more clearly and may indicate whether or not there is a real cure for it. On the latter point, a second question may be needed to bring out the facts, as well as to determine whether the supervisor's conclusions are tentative or final.

Step 2. "What results have you had?" This, of course, refers to the supervisor's effort to help the employee. His answer may determine whether he should be expected to do anything further to help the employee, or whether a change should be made.

"Problems" usually fall into two general categories: (a) a *problem of the job assignment* itself—that is, inability of the employee to perform the work or (b) *something else.* The latter may be something inherent within the employee such as a quirk of personality, inability to work with others, indisposition to turn in a day's work, nervousness or some other incapacity. It may have to do with the job environment as opposed to inability to perform, which points to examination of the prevalence of such cases in the working unit as discussion of the problem employee proceeds. Where an unusual proportion of the employees cannot get along with one another or with the supervisor, the conditions surrounding the job will bear looking into. Something may be wrong with some phase of the total personnel job that brought the employees in the working unit and their jobs together, such as an inadequate hiring procedure; or there may be poor employee relations or substandard working conditions. Such findings should be referred back to the personnel office for appropriate follow-up.

Where the employee falls down in the job operations and simply cannot do the work, two questions should be added:

Step 3. "What training has he had?"
Step 4. "What training does he need?"

These questions are in reality a follow-up, first, to determine whether or not the employee immediately under discussion has been given the training for the job that normally proves adequate and, second, to determine the status of the training job itself, whether conducted by the supervisor on the job or provided off the job. In addition, the supervisor's response may indicate whether he has gone as far as he can or as far as he is likely to go with the employee.

The final step in discussing a problem case is to prompt the supervisor to plan some disposition of it. He should decide to:

Solution 1. Place the employee on notice that his work is not up to standard, and offer to help him to improve; or, failing that,

Solution 2. Plan demotion of the employee to a lower grade job within the working unit, or arrange with the personnel department to relocate the employee in less difficult work in some other working unit; or, failing that,

Solution 3. Take steps to release the employee and secure a replacement if one is needed.

The supervisor's decision should be sensibly related to the background of the case, as it has been discussed. If the employee has repeatedly been told and assisted (Solution 1) with no resulting improvement, consideration of a demotion (Solution 2) is in order. Demotion is very often precarious. If considered at all, it should be based upon the supervisor's honest conviction that the employee has merely been misassigned, coupled with a good opinion of him otherwise. However, the employee himself must be reckoned with in considering a demotion. It entails considerable loss of face to the employee to step down either within the immediate working unit or elsewhere in the company. He must be a pretty good man to take it and still try to make good. In addition, the game of "pass the lemon" is so old in most companies that transfers are suspect, even when the employee apparently has a clean bill of health. Certainly where either the supervisor or the personnel department representative regard demotion as a doubtful solution, the logical action is to plan to release the problem employee (Solution 3). In any case, all of the discussion of the problem employee to this point has been developed for one single purpose: *to prompt an appropriate action.* When the problem employee has been fully discussed the pin-down question is:

Step 5. "What action should be taken in this case?" This question may be varied to suit the immediate interview situation. It might be: "What do you propose (or intend) to do?" However the question is shaped, the answer should be the supervisor's own solution, and carefully emphasized as such. If no proposal is forthcoming, the personnel man then assumes the responsibility for prompting the supervisor to come up with some plan *without taking the position of an expert.* This can be done effectively by offering suggestions in the form of questions so worded as to indicate clearly what the plan or alternate plans are, the beneficial results to be obtained therefrom, and at the same time offering the supervisor an opportunity to embrace the idea as his own, as follows:

> "*Had you considered investing* a few minutes (hours) of your time, sitting down with him, and working with him (talking to him), with the possibility of correcting the problem?"

On the other hand, the supervisor may counter the question used in Step 5 with another question ("What do *you* think I should do?") based upon reluctance to make a firm decision or upon an honest desire to secure advice from the personnel department representative who may enjoy some repute as a specialist. Whatever turn the interview takes at this point, it is imperative that the supervisor should decide the issues himself and that the action should be his own. The supervisor's question should be countered as follows:

> "In view of your immediate knowledge of the situation, *do you believe* that this employee should be dropped or demoted?"

Unless something positive is done to keep it definitely understood that the supervisor is to make the decision and to initiate action, the personnel department will subsequently face a backfire. Someone will show up in the personnel office and say: "My supervisor says that the personnel department ordered him to fire me, and I want to know why." The only cure for this sort of thing, which is bad for everyone involved, particularly the supervisor, is precaution.

Ironically enough, in face of the traditional complaint that personnel department activities tend to interfere with the authority and responsibility that properly rests with the supervisor in dealing with his workers, the personnel department representative finds himself a welcome interloper when it comes to firing undesirable employees. The supervisor will tend to pass an unpleasant responsibility of this sort up the line, if he is allowed to get away with it. The result is that the supervisor fails to take hold of his own placement job and perform it. Therefore, the representative of the personnel office, in pinning down the solution of a problem case, should uniformly add to any variation of the question on what the supervisor intends to do (Step 5), the question:

Step 6. "Would it be agreeable with you if I make a note here (on the roster) that you intend to (demote or dismiss) this employee by (such and such date)?"

As the supplemental analysis of problem employees proceeds from one case to the next, the planned action should be noted on the employee roster in each instance and the date upon which the supervisor is to initiate it or complete it. The term "initiate" is used advisedly to cover cases where the supervisor can only start the action due to restrictions of a union contract or for some other reason. Where the solution is to place the employee on notice and to offer further assistance to him, the supervisor can, of course, start the action and carry it through. The same applies to dismissals and to demotions within the working unit. However, where the problem employee is to be relocated outside the working unit, the supervisor can take only the initial step of advising the employee that he is to be transferred. The personnel department representative should "flag" such cases in his notes for follow-up, including the necessary reference to another supervisor, after the employee has been advised.

FIELD REVIEW QUESTIONS
(*Supplementary Analysis of "Problem" Cases*)

Step 1. What help have you given him?
Step 2. What results have you had?
Step 3. What training has he had?
Step 4. What training does he need?
Step 5. What actions should be taken in this case?
    5-a "Had you considered . . . ?"
    5-b "Do you believe . . . ?"
Step 6. Would it be agreeable with you if I make a note here (on the roster) that you intend to (demote or dismiss) this employee by (such and such) date?

The Yardstick of Fair Play

At the expense of appearing to backtrack in discussion of the supplementary analysis and planning step of the Field Review contact, it must be noted that consideration of problem employees as described to this point has been largely a question and answer process without a standard other than the preference for specific rather than general supporting comment from the supervisor. The effort has been to draw facts from the supervisor and to prompt him to act on solutions of his own making. This is based on the common experience that without some such prompting the supervisor fails to put the facts together and to act on them, even when he is fully aware that the employee is not making good. The immediate point is that the personnel man cannot assign the same value to all of his findings, nor can he afford passively to condone every solution reached by the supervisor. He has an equal responsibility to the employees themselves. The latter are entitled to some safeguard which assures that decisions affecting them meet some reasonable test of fairness and factuality.

Most mistakes in employee evaluation and placement activity as well as in other phases of personnel work are based upon neglect of the obvious. A job consists of things to be done, most of which are sufficiently tangible that the man in charge should be able to tell what they are. He should also be able to tell whether they are done or left undone. Yet experience shows that supervisors, by and large, are careless in their treatment of facts that bear upon employee performance or job behavior. Placement moves can be no better than the facts upon which they are based, and these, in turn, depend upon (a) the supervisor's powers of observation and (b) his disposition, as a matter of habit, to put them to use. Obviously there is wide variation, as between supervisors, in both respects.

Thus far the personnel department representative has been pictured in the Field Review contact largely as an interrogator and a prompter. At what point does he figuratively flash "green lights" or "red lights"? On what basis does he push for an obviously logical action, or hold back in his questioning when the supervisor obviously wants to go too far? What is a reasonable measure of the supervisor's facts and of the fairness of his solutions?

A four-point yardstick of fair play has been developed to test each placement move that is planned in the Field Review contact. It is applied both to the solutions of problem cases and to proposed action affecting satisfactory and outstanding employees. It will be discussed at this point, however, only with respect to its use in problem cases, where the employee faces some form of discipline or the loss of his job.

The yardstick may be applied as a final check in each problem case in "one, two, three" order, or the questions in the yardstick may be used individually at various stages of the interview, so long as clear and acceptable answers are developed to all of them before the discussion of any problem case is brought to a close.

The first application of the yardstick to a problem case lies in securing an answer to the following question, whether it is asked formally or whether the answer is apparent from the facts drawn from the supervisor:

Point One: Has the employee's performance really been substandard?

This is answered by the evidence of immediate and direct observation of the employee at work that is apparent (or lacking) in the statements which the supervisor makes about the weaknesses of the employee. Has he personally seen the employee do poor work? Has he cited actual instances of poor performance, so identified as to time, place, and attending circumstances that there can be no doubt as to what the employee has done, or failed to do, in relation to the requirements of his job? Anyone who has seen the supervisor under fire during grievance procedure knows that he is very often short on specific facts. Where the personnel department representative feels any doubt regarding whether or not the weaknesses attributed to the problem employee are based on something that has really happened, he should call for examples with questions which bring out "where?", "when?", and "under what conditions?"

Point Two: Has substandard performance actually been typical of the employee?

This adds to the basic question "Did it happen?" (*Point One*) an equally important question: "Was it representative?" (In other words, did a single fault that happened to be observed give the supervisor the impression that the employee's work is always deficient, or did the supervisor follow-up to make sure that the weakness was consistently present in the employee's performance? Viewed in another way, the question means: "Does the supervisor regard the employee as lazy or incompetent, because he happened to observe him on an occasion or two when he did not look 'too busy,' or has he reviewed the employee's work on a sufficient number of occasions to really know his weaknesses?" Again: "Do all of the facts make up a convincing picture of consistently poor work?" Certainly a proposed dismissal should meet this test.

Point Three: Is the employee's performance or job behavior really worse than that of other employees who are *not* regarded as problems?

Fundamentally the personnel man wants to make sure that the employee is not being picked on for weaknesses that other employees are allowed to get away with. From early childhood on up human beings defend themselves, sometimes very successfully, by making the point that they are no worse than someone else, even when clearly guilty of a fault. For this reason, the personnel department representative should ask the supervisor, in effect: "Are you sure that other employees in the working unit do not have the same weaknesses as this particular problem employee?", or some comparable question. If he can clear the problem evaluation in this regard, an uncomfortable situation can be avoided later on, when action is taken.

Point Four: Has the employee received fair warning as to what is wrong, and has he been given a real chance to improve?

This means essentially: "Did you tell him about his weaknesses, and help him to correct them?" This point may be cleared up in Steps 1 and 2 of the supplementary analysis ("What help have you given him?"; "What results have you had?") In any case, a full measure of fairness in evaluating employees requires some attention to the employee's response to correction, when it is actually undertaken. *The supervisor does not discharge his responsibility by merely observing and recording faults. He is expected to develop as well as to direct those under him.* A disposition to allow the problem employee to "hang himself" is inconsistent with a decent attitude toward people who work, even when their best is not very good.

Applications of the yardstick of fair play are necessarily more specific in some problem cases than in others. Where the supervisor has a typically "sour" outlook with respect to a substantial percentage of his employees, the yardstick should be applied in all of the problem cases, even if the time requirement is considerable. It should serve to clear up his thinking to some extent, and in any case provides a basis for holding back when the supervisor too readily considers dismissals. Certainly when an employee is to be fired, unless it is obvious that he has been guilty of overt misbehavior, flagrant dishonesty or willful violation of rules, the facts underlying the decision to release him should at least stand the tests of a problem evaluation which are included in the yardstick.

YARDSTICK OF FAIR PLAY

Test of a Problem Evaluation

Point One: Has the employee's performance really been substandard?

Point Two: Has substandard performance actually been typical of the employee?

Point Three: Is the employee's performance or job behavior really worse than that of other employees who are not regarded as problems?

Point Four: Has the employee received fair warning as to what is wrong, and has he been given a real chance to improve?

Taking Action in Problem Cases

In Steps 5 and 6 of the supplementary analysis of problem employees, the supervisor is asked: "What action should be taken in this case?" His idea of what *should* be done is likely to be conditioned by what he thinks *can* be done. The representative of the personnel department should therefore make sure that the supervisor has a clear understanding of the actual requirements related to demotions, dismissals, and other types of discipline, whatever these requirements are. Any proposed action must, of course, be checked carefully against top management policies and the collective bargaining commitments of the company. Where the supervisor exercises the "right to fire" indirectly (*i.e.* he must secure clearances before he acts, or he "effectively recommends" discharge action which sets dismissal procedures in motion) he must clearly understand what steps he is to take, when he is to take them, and what happens from then on.

Probably more supervisors fail to act in matters involving discipline because they do not know what they are expected to do, than for any other reason. In all too many instances, clearances required up the line to ensure uniformity in the administration of discipline throughout the company are interpreted by the supervisors as a signal that the best way to keep out of trouble is not to enforce any discipline at all. The Field Review discussion of "problem" employees affords an excellent opportunity to directly clear up any misgivings of the supervisors on this score.

• SUPPLEMENTARY ANALYSIS OF "SATISFACTORY" AND "OUTSTANDING" EMPLOYEES

The Field Review contact discussion of employees who are satisfactory, or better than satisfactory (which in some cases will include "OK +" employees) is largely a matter of questioning the supervisor regarding what he has in mind in the way of future placement moves, or prompting him to plan such moves by using the same pattern of questioning used in connection with problem employees. Depending upon the line-up of jobs in the organization plan of the working unit, and upon such personnel changes as can be foreseen on the date of the Field Review contact, three possibilities should be examined in the case of each "OK," "OK +," or "+" employee on the roster:

1. The employee is satisfactory (or better than satisfactory) where he is, and regarded as a likely candidate for a specific promotion within the working unit. In this case some notation earmarking the employee for the promotion should be made with the probable date indicated whenever practicable.

2. He is satisfactory (or better than satisfactory) where he is, and a likely candidate for more important work, but there is no suitable promotion in prospect within the working unit. In this case some notation to the effect that the employee is "underloaded; no promotion in sight" should be made.

3. He is satisfactory (or better than satisfactory) where he is, but "as far as he can go." In such case, some notation such as "limited to present job" should be made on the roster. If, in addition, the limited employee holds a job that puts him in line for a next job up or a definite understudy position reinforcing a key job, it is particularly important to note the fact for further discussion.

These possibilities can be established ordinarily by questioning the supervisor as follows:

"*Had you considered* assigning this employee to more responsible work or letting him understudy (the employee in the next job up) Mr. Jones in order to cash in on the fact that he can really turn out good work, or is he likely to stay where he is?

Any variation of this question which establishes the distinctions between promotional possibilities that can be used (within the working unit) or promotional possibilities that cannot be so used will serve. The same goes for any question which brings out the point that the employee is satisfactory in his present job, but not likely to move ahead. The objective is to draw out the supervisor and get some decision from him in each case. This process, carried on through the cases of all "OK," "OK +," and "+" employees in the working unit will show where each employee stands with the supervisor and what is likely to happen to him when promotions are made.

Applying the Yardstick of Fair Play to Satisfactory and Outstanding Employees

The fairness of decisions regarding promotion (or not to promote) has an important bearing upon the success of the employee evaluation and internal placement job that transcends the fairly obvious possibility that the supervisor may (or may not) play favorites in earmarking employees for promotion. It should be borne in mind that a fundamental purpose of the Field Review contact is to produce such stability in the working force as may result from positive planning of placement moves. The thesis is that employees of good caliber will ordinarily stay with jobs only when they are employed in a capacity in which they can succeed and in which their success will receive reasonable recognition. Unless there is some evidence of a planned effort to direct the rewards of good work to people who deserve them, a company policy subscribing to the principle of "promotion from within" merely takes on color of something from the "joke book."

Promotions cannot be made solely upon the reward theory. It is no favor to an employee to move him up into a job that he cannot handle. Nonetheless no one should labor under the delusion that the average employee is pleased, or that he automatically tends to congratulate the other fellow, when a promotion which he wants goes to someone else. Even when his best interests are served by keeping him where he is, the choice of someone else for a promotion is an intimate, personal affront, unless the superiority of the individual who is given the call is fairly obvious, and unless the choice was based upon manifestly impartial considerations directly related to the work. On this basis, it is desirable to test the cases in which an outstanding (or an "OK +") evaluation may underlie a proposed promotion, against the yardstick of fair play.

Here again, answers should be secured to four basic questions, whether they are asked formally or whether the answers are apparent from the information drawn from the supervisor at some previous point in the interview:

Point One: Has the employee's performance actually been superior?

The evidence of superior performance is ordinarily that the employee does certain things beyond merely going through the motions required to hold his job. Superiority may be manifested in going ahead with a job without being told what to do, and it may be evident in varying respects and degrees. Has the supervisor personally observed and cited instances of superior work? Has he indicated where, when, and under what circumstances? The point is to relate the outstanding evaluation to things that have happened on the job and that have been observed, pointing to a caliber of performance which obviously goes the normal standards of the job one better.

Point Two: Has superior performance been really typical?

Here again the point is to establish the consistency of the employee's performance. Has the employee typically turned in a high grade performance from day to day, or did the supervisor merely happen to be looking at some time when the employee was particularly "on the ball"? The point is to multiply the examples as far as necessary to be sure that the supervisor's estimate of the employee has been based upon continuing, as opposed to chance, observations.

Point Three: Is the employee really better than others who might be considered?

This is the pay-off question in applying the yardstick to outstanding employees. For practical purposes, superior performance must often be identified by comparison. This means comparing the outstanding employee's performance with that of other employees who are figuratively or actually "in competition" with him. What has *he* done, in relation to what *they* have done, that marks him as superior? Has the supervisor cited examples in which the performance of the outstanding employee was actually compared with that of other employees whom he regards as satisfactory, thus establishing that such other employees have actually been considered? If he has not, the personnel department representative should call for such comparisons and see to it that the other employees are looked over. This provides no guarantee that promotion of the outstanding employee will meet a favorable reaction on the part of employees who are passed up, but it will go a considerable distance in establishing a factual basis for the action. As general practice, therefore, the representative of the personnel department should single out satisfactory employees, if any, who perform the same work or operations as the outstanding employee and pin down the evidence of superior performance in the given case. In the process the supervisor may discover other superior talent, or he may conclude that he had better look things over some more.

Point Four: Has the employee been tried out in the more important duties for which he appears qualified to the extent it has been practical to do so; or has any proposed salary increase been considered from the viewpoint of its effect on other employees?

These are really two questions, but one or the other may be applicable in applying the yardstick to an outstanding employee who is to move up or who is being considered for a salary promotion. As regards the try-out in a higher job, the average employee is ordinarily a known quantity only in the job he holds. Most promotions tend to stick even when they prove to be mistaken, as supervisors (and, for that matter, many top management people) do not like to back up on their decisions. For this reason, where vacations or absences due to sickness (or other causes) permit actual trial of the outstanding employee on the higher job, his real ability to hold the job can at least be looked over in advance of a final commitment. This is particularly important when the higher job is a supervisory position. A great many people who can do excellent work themselves cannot direct other people successfully. On this basis it is a good idea to check on whether or not the trial step has been taken, or to suggest that it should be, if it has not.

Yardstick of Fair Play

Test of an Outstanding Evaluation

Point One: Has the employee's performance actually been superior?

Point Two: Has superior performance been really typical of the employee?

Point Three: Is the employee really better than others who might be considered?

Point Four: Has the employee been tried in the more important duties for which he appears qualified to the extent that it has been practical to do so; or, has any proposed salary increase been considered from the viewpoint of its effect on other employees?

As regards salary increases from the viewpoint of their effect on employees who may be left out, there is probably no practice which causes more ill feeling than carelessness in handling the steps leading to a salary promotion or assignment of "merit" pay. In the nature of things, only a small proportion of the employees in the working unit are likely to receive merit increases. The employees who continue on the regular base rates are likely to see no element of rewarding good work in a particular salary or wage increase, but merely a case in which someone who does no better work than they do just gets more money. There should be some tangible and preferably obvious evidence of superior performance in any case where a merit pay increase is seriously considered. Otherwise the reward appears to go merely to favorites, or, worse, to have no connection whatever with the caliber of performance.

Summary Discussion of Findings

With all available facts about the line-up of jobs and about the employees in the working unit in hand, plus evaluations that have been tested and a plan of action developed in each case, the final steps in the Field Review contact are as follows:

Step 1. Over-all findings should be looked over by the representative of the personnel department to determine the degree to which key jobs in the working unit are properly staffed and competently understudied if need be. The need for understudies will depend somewhat upon what is known of the status and perhaps intentions of employees occupying key jobs. In some instances the employee currently holding key job will be known as a steady customer, not likely voluntarily to change his job. The general state of balance (or lack of it) of placements in the working unit should likewise be reviewed, to determine whether there is a shortage or surplus of qualified staff, aside from the problem employees who are to be replaced.

The supervisor is entitled to the qualified personnel which he actually needs, but not to overstaff even on a small scale. *A balanced working unit is typified in a situation where the employee on each job is competent to perform it, and where the probable development of employees in understudy jobs is such as to ensure getting the key jobs properly filled as need arises.* The need for a few replacements particularly in the lower grade jobs does not necessarily signify understaffing in the unit. *It is overstaffed when it has more capable people than can be used at capacity,* irrespective of a numerical shortage or prospective changes involving the personnel in the less important jobs.

As the personnel department representative moves from one working unit to the next, he will develop requisite skill in spotting shortages and surpluses of qualified staff. Conclusions on this score are of special importance in a later step. This summary review can be undertaken with the supervisor, and it is desirable to do so if it is done in the spirit of "adding up our findings to see where we stand." It is extremely ill advised to say: "Let's see whether or not you have too many people."

Step 2. Satisfactory (or better) employees who have been marked as "limited to present job," but who hold positions that place them in line for promotions for which they will not receive favorable consideration, should be specially discussed to develop a possible reassignment, for two reasons: (a) the employee involved is almost certain to become disgruntled when the time comes to move up and he is passed over and (b) if a competent understudy is really needed, the supervisor is borrowing trouble by failing to train one. It is much better to relocate the limited employee in a comparable job (which does not involve understudying a key job), with a frank statement of reasons, than to await the evil day. His fellow employees are less likely to take sides over a change in the employee's job than over the rebuff implicit in moving someone over his head in making a promotion for which he has been in line.

Step 3. Satisfactory (or better) employees who are underloaded in the sense of being capable of doing more important work but for whom no better job is in sight should either (a) be relocated in the working unit in a job which has a future or (b) be discussed with a view to a possible transfer to some other working unit. It should be explained to the supervisor that such exchanges work both ways and that in all probability some of the replacements he needs will be drawn from other working units in the installation. Where each case of this type is discussed individually, *after* it has been determined that the supervisor has all of the qualified staff he needs (or arrangements have been set up to make good any shortage), he is more likely to assume a cooperative attitude than if discussion of such cases has entered the interview prior to this point. A great many supervisors like to see people whom they have developed get ahead, and some of them may even volunteer to make transfers in such cases. In any event, it is only as people who are well thought of figure in interworking-unit transfers that the transfer process gains respectability and acceptance. *A balanced distribution of qualified staff throughout the company cannot be achieved unless logical exchanges of underloaded employees who have no future in their current jobs are brought about.* The supervisor has no right to hold on to an employee whom he cannot use at capacity merely because he has spent the time it takes to train him. In cases where the supervisors refuse to cooperate on such a basis, it may be necessary to establish and enforce some form of priority in connection with necessary transfers.

Step 4. A summary review of needed replacements, if any, should be undertaken at this point, so that it will be clear that the personnel department is going to go to work on the staffing requirements of the supervisor. It also reminds the supervisor that he must prepare the employees who are to be replaced, for the change.

Step 5. Finally, all of the findings and conclusions developed in the interview should be read back to the supervisor and checked with him. This includes the comment, the planned solution in each case (or the conclusion that no change is to be made), plus the tentative or agreed date of each change.

This concludes the Field Review contact as it is carried on in a given working unit. There must, of course, be provision within the personnel department for follow-up upon individual personnel moves that have been planned. This should ordinarily be accounted for in the routine of checking personnel changes and in occasional follow-up contacts in between the regularly scheduled Field Review interviews. In placement work, as in other forms of human endeavor, not everything that is agreed upon actually happens.

Our final discussion will concern some of the fairly general problems entailed in using the Field Review Method.

SPECIAL PROBLEMS • IN PLANNING FIELD REVIEW CONTACTS

A few fairly common problems have arisen in applying the Field Review Method in working organizations. They are definitely of a "fringe" order. Businesslike application of the method does not often encounter obstacles based alone upon resentment of personnel department "intrusion" into the affairs of the operating supervisors. As general experience, the more the personnel manager or his representative tackles the job as a legitimate undertaking of the personnel department and the less he tries to "sell" the method, as such, the better things are likely to go. In many instances the method "sells itself" because of the direct and pointed interest taken in problems that in many instances have been really troubling the supervisor. The fact is that worrying about "how the supervisors will take the questioning" is another case of worrying about the wrong thing. However, depending upon the nature of the company's operations, it is well to give some forethought to the following.

Exemption of Certain Employees from Field Review

In general the Field Review contacts should cover all employees on the regular working force of the company. By this is meant all classes of employees below top management level who for practical purposes compose its permanent staff. It may be desirable to exclude from the Field Review process strictly temporary (short term) employees such as casual labor hired from day to day, where the individuals involved are not in any sense candidates for continuing employment. However, these exemptions should be made with due regard to the fact that numbers of people who are theoretically temporary may actually remain on the force for extended periods and thus automatically become regular employees. Provision must be made to review their performance and their possibilities when it develops that they are, practically speaking, in line for jobs ordinarily covered in the Field Review.

It may be advisable to exempt certain specialists and highly trained technical and professional staff in the upper grades, where the nature of their abilities and duties excludes them from consideration for transfers and where their jobs are relatively static. The representative of the personnel department should decide the necessary exemptions as common sense dictates. Where the Field Review will obviously serve no real purpose as a continuous planning operation in dealing with the placement of given individuals, small technical groups, or even large groups of casual employees, exemptions are in order.

Confusions between Levels of Supervision

Sometimes the relationship between the head of a working unit and his next higher supervisor has never included any real assignment of responsibility and authority to the unit head. In such instances, the higher supervisor sits in on the Field Review discussion and, although not really equipped through direct observation of the employees at work to evaluate them or discuss their possibilities, nonetheless contradicts the statements of the subordinate supervisor and generally turns the discussion into an argument. The only course in such cases is for the representative of the personnel department consistently to keep his questions directed toward things which the employees have done or not done on the job, and to keep pushing for specific answers. The subordinate supervisor is less likely to be challenged on statements of fact drawn from direct observation than on his conclusions. In some instances, the facts will win the day and result in the development of sound answers. In others, it will be evident that the subordinate supervisor properly should be challenged and that the higher supervisor has good reasons for sitting in. In still others, it will be evident that the higher supervisor neither wants to do the job himself nor to allow anyone else to do it. The last is a management problem which should be "referred." When the usefulness of the Field Review has become generally recognized, instances in which it is obstructed in this manner can be brought to the attention of the top operating officials for appropriate action.

Privacy in Field Review Contact

Obviously, considerable that is discussed in the Field Review contact is of a confidential nature. To talk things over with a supervisor who presides over an open working space while all of his employees are within hearing distance can defeat the objectives of the undertaking. There is no real objection to the attendance of the supervisor's secretary, if he has one, to take notes for him, provided the secretary knows how to maintain confidences. It must be borne in mind that any visitation from the personnel department tends to arouse speculation in an employee group. While the individual employee should be informed of any action affecting him at the proper time, there is no reason why the details of a planning discussion should become common property. The Field Review should uniformly be conducted in some privacy, and the personnel department representative should make this clear to the supervisor before the discussion starts.

Extending Field Review Throughout the Company

Extending the Field Review to obtain complete coverage of the working force requires lining up the working units throughout the company, scheduling the necessary clearances and contacts, and repeating in each working unit the steps that have been described. The most obvious question, of course, is the time requirement. How long does it take to complete the initial contacts and how much time is required to keep the information up to date?

Any consideration of the time required to apply the Field Review Method must logically take into account what the personnel department needs to know about jobs and about the true state of the working relationships at the job level into which it is the business of the department to fit people. The personnel manager cannot make more than a gesture toward effective placement of personnel without some comprehensive program for determining what the personnel situation really is throughout the company. Therefore the real question lies not in whether live contacts with the supervisors are necessary but in what form they will take.

The Field Review process, like any other activity reduced to written description, appears more detailed and time-consuming than the job itself proves to be. The questions and the order of questioning are readily committed to memory. In practice, actual use of the Field Review Method to date shows clearly that the precise order of inquiry affords a short cut in securing the minimum of information needed by the personnel manager to get a sound placement job done. It should be added that if he knows a better way, there is no reason why he should not use it, provided only that he does not try to perform his job by staying in his office, and provided further that he otherwise adheres to the principles that underlie the Field Review Method.

Time Required for Initial Contacts

The first interview and the initial contacts will require the least time per job discussed and per employee, if they are undertaken in relatively small working units. The representative of the personnel department must gain some experience in using the questions and in prompting decisions before he can really hit his stride. When he is moderately experienced, he should be able to complete the initial field review in a working unit which includes 50 employees in the space of a morning (4 hours working time), provided he stays with the uniform line of questioning. A complete set of initial Field Review contacts has been completed in one company with 1,000 employees in less than 10 days working time. As stated in this instance:

> "The job itself not only goes rapidly, but results in surprises which show clearly how really useless it is to try to dope out the personnel set-up in a working unit without discussing it directly with the supervisor. Employees who looked good on paper proved not to be such at all. The supervisor in one instance had not really looked over more than half of his people. Most of them had no plans at all. On the average, I learned more that was worth knowing about one working unit in 3 hours than I could have figured out in twice that time pouring over charts and forms and rating reports in my office.

Stated in another way, the initial Field Review, including development of job information and information regarding the employees up through the planning steps, requires an average of about 5 minutes per employee where the group numbers as many as 50 or more. Where the unit is smaller, the total time required is less, but the average time per employee may be greater. If discussion of any individual employee turns up a single case of unsuspected talent that is badly needed, or rids the company of one nonproducer, the time required to cover all of the cases in the working unit, whatever it is, is more than well repaid.

Time Required for Follow-Up

As has been indicated, the Field Review process is necessarily continuous and should be repeated at stated intervals, at least three or four times a year. The time required for follow-up depends upon the degree of change, either in the job information or in the personnel of each working unit that has occurred since the preceding interview. It can be devoted virtually in its entirety to such changes, barring only a general checking of the total situation for balance (or imbalance) in relation to initial findings. Probably one-third to one-half of the time devoted to initial contacts is a fair estimate of the requirement for follow-up interviews. This presumes that ample notes have been taken and maintained.

Field Review Records

The field notes developed in getting job information, employee evaluations, and in planning placement moves are essentially work sheets and should be preserved intact so long as they include any current information. One plan which has worked out well in handling such records is to keep the organization charts and employee roster sheets in 8½ x 11 inch, three-ring binders that are large enough to include data drawn from several working units, preferably those in which work is somewhat comparable.

As the representative of the personnel department proceeds from one working unit to the next, he may in one case find an employee who can fill the bill as a replacement needed in a working unit which has just previously been analyzed. In another he may find a spot for an employee who has been earmarked for a transfer. The field notes thus have cumulative value as the contacts are continued. In many instances transfers can be arranged directly from these notes, and the records of the working units at interest can be cleared so far as given changes are concerned. To the extent that contacts can be planned to permit this, the necessity for posting some of the findings on permanent records can be obviated.

Some of the data in the field notes should be posted on permanent records or at least on centrally maintained master lists or in finder files. For example, evaluation comment should be entered on the employee's individual record, in whatever form it is maintained. Cases in which some action is pending should be posted on promotion lists or other records maintained to keep "on top" of possible transfers.

• SUMMARY

The point has already been made that the Field Review Method provides a necessary foundation for a number of phases of personnel work. Obviously, a continuing working knowledge of the personnel situation at the job level is indispensable to sound performance of any personnel activity. Detailed planning of personnel moves in particular insures a better fit of the average worker to his job and proper recognition of his success.

Specifically, the primary service of the Field Review Method is to prevent that part of the total turnover of the company which can be avoided by a considered evaluation of each worker and by definitely planning his future in keeping with the ability he shows on the job. It provides a cushion against particularly damaging turnover in key jobs by focusing attention upon the need for competent understudies. It turns up the cases in which a particular employee needs training in order to move ahead, as well as identifying the cases in which training for the current job has either been lacking or has failed to serve its purpose. In addition, the Field Review contact not only identifies the workers who are regarded as successful (or unsuccessful) by the supervisors, but verifies the supervisors' opinions in this regard. These tested findings are essential in hiring procedures where success rests in large part upon searching out prospective workers whose experience, education, and other characteristics match, so far as possible, those of employees who have made good. They likewise enable the personnel manager to keep a valid score on the "hits" and "misses" that result from the hiring procedures he uses. Beyond this, the personnel manager or his representative can hardly conclude the Field Review contacts without becoming intimately informed on the tone of the personnel situation in each working unit. While he deals primarily with the supervisor, indications of rough edges in the job environment, dissatisfaction with salaries and wages, etc., inevitably figure in any detailed discussion of how workers are getting along on the job. All of these findings must be made the common property of the key staff of the personnel department.

Proper application of the Field Review Method provides a sense of direction for the total personnel program of the company. The situation that prevails at the working level is the pay-off in all personnel administration. No functionary within the personnel department can direct his effort to the solution of personnel problems unless he knows what they are and where they are. He will find most of them "down where the work goes on." Information drawn from the Field Review contacts thus provides the basis for performing a total personnel job of management stature that "knows where it is going."

MERIT RATING—PLUS*

Stephen Habbe

It is not enough merely to say that a company has a rating program or that it does not have one. A rating program may take one of many forms. It may be of limited scope and coverage, or it may be a fully developed program reaching into all parts of the organization. Also, it may serve important company functions, or it may be regarded as so much falderal by those involved.

A rating program may begin and end with the ratings themselves. Once or twice a year the supervisor appraises each of his workers on a prepared sheet and sends the completed form to the personnel office, where it is filed with the individual's personal record folder.

But a rating program may be more than this. It may include a review period, too. The review period, following the rating, gives the supervisor and the worker an opportunity to talk things over. The managements of many companies today take the position that the worker has a right to know how he is doing—and that it is a good thing all around to tell him.[1]

It is news in rating circles when an organization goes beyond both the evaluation and the review steps. For more than three years now, Gimbel Brothers in New York City (a department store) has rated its employees, has conducted review periods, and has obtained periodic checks on the management and efficiency of each of its departments.[2] This three-way approach is operated by the store's personnel department. Gimbels refers to the Field Review Method (FRM) in identifying its over-all rating program. In some respects its program is a modification of FRM and in others an extension.

• WHAT FRM IS

The Field Review Method of employee appraisal, although twenty years old, is not well-known in industry today.[3]

It may be explained here that FRM derives its name from the fact that a representative of the personnel department goes into the "field"—that is, he leaves his desk and goes to the work place of the supervisor to obtain information about the work of individual employees. He is equipped with a register of the persons who work in a given unit and with the name of their supervisor. He is also equipped with a definite list of questions, usually memorized in advance, which he will ask the supervisor about each employee.

[1] Four companies in ten surveyed rate their employees. Half the companies with rating programs follow through with the review period. See tables 9, 10, 128 and 129 in "Personnel Practices in Factory and Office," *Studies in Personnel Policy,* No. 88, National Industrial Conference Board, 1948.

* From *Management Record,* Vol. 15, no. 9, September 1953, pp. 323–324.

[2] The ratings, made semiannually in February and August, are of the usual sort. Separate forms are used for sales, stock, and clerical personnel. Instruction and training in making the ratings and in conducting the individual reviews are given every year.

[3] It has been described in a series of six comprehensive articles by Guy W. Wadsworth, Jr. in the *Personnel Journal,* issues of June to December, 1948.

An application of FRM in the rating of executives is contained in a recent Conference Board report, "The Appraisal of Job Performance," *Studies in Personnel Policy,* no. 121, 1951, p. 48.

The questions are asked and answered orally. The interview may be likened to an informal conversation. The personnel representative makes notes, or a secretary may be present for this purpose. No paper work is done by the supervisor. This is a feature of FRM which appeals to those supervisors who feel they already have too much paper work to do.

After the interviews have been completed, the personnel representative returns to his office and dictates his notes. The reports are sent to the supervisor, who revises them if necessary, and then signs them to indicate his approval.

OBTAINING THE EVALUATIONS

Three full-time workers and one half-time worker are able to carry the load of work involved in Gimbel's rating program. At the beginning, when the plan was new and the employees relatively unknown, a full year was needed to complete the field visits and the supplementary work. Now the rounds can be made in about nine months. The average worker, therefore, is "field-checked" four times every three years. All clerks, sales and stock personnel are included in these appraisals, making a present total of 3,500 individuals.

An over-all rating is obtained for each employee, with a three-way classification scheme followed. The supervisor rates the employee as *outstanding, satisfactory* or *unsatisfactory*. If the supervisor describes a particular worker as outstanding, the analyst (personnel representative) asks such questions as:

Do you believe this worker would be outstanding on other jobs?

Is he promotable?

If so, to what type and level of jobs is he promotable?

Other questions are asked about workers who are rated satisfactory, such as:

How could this person be helped to improve his performance?

Is additional training indicated?

If so, what kind of training is needed and when could this training be provided?

Should the worker be adjudged unsatisfactory, the analyst attempts to find out why and in what respects the quality of the work is low. Possible remedial programs are considered. But if the supervisor feels that the individual has been given a fair chance to improve and has failed to respond, a termination date usually is set without further ado. In certain instances, the employee is transferred to another work assignment (but not, of course, to one at a higher rate) in the store.

The analyst probes for supporting evidence, whatever the individual's rating may be. "What facts can you cite to support this rating?" is a question almost always asked. The supervisors, aware of this, have learned the advantages of keeping a running record of notes and comments on each of their workers. The analysts report that this procedure has trained the supervisors to make fairer, more accurate appraisals and to avoid the "halo" or "halitosis" extremes which have been noted so frequently in traditional ratings.

THE DEPARTMENTAL ANALYSIS

An important "plus" phase of the Gimbel plan, not usually thought of as a part of FRM, is the report which the

REVIEW NUMBER *(Deleted)*

FIELD REVIEW REPORT

DEPARTMENT NUMBER *(Deleted)* NAME *Men's Furnishings*

DEPARTMENT HEAD *(Deleted)*

REVIEW MADE BY *F. H. S.* DATE *March, 1953*

PERSON INTERVIEWED *(Deleted)*

* * * * *

1. DEPARMENT EFFICIENCY

(Deleted)

2. PERSONNEL

Full Time Sales *21* Assistant Buyer *1*

Part Time Sales *1*

"700's" ______

"800's" *1*

Full Time Stock ______

Part Time Stock ______

Clericals ______

Number Over 60 Years ______

	Floor	Stock
Is coverage adequate? Buyer's opinion	*No*	*No*
Reviewer's opinion	*Yes*	*No*

Recommendation For Change:

Stock help is needed for special days

3. SUPERVISORY ACTIVITIES

Job descriptions used *None*

Employee training scheduled to training department *None*

Employee meeting:

When *Saturdays*

By whom *Asst. Buyer*

Subject matter:

Merchandise information *x*

System ______

Suggestions ______

Others *New stock; promotions*

Are Personnel Relations Reports written? *Yes*

Commendations? *x*

Disciplinary? *x*

4. EMPLOYEE PERFORMANCE

Department:	No. Outstanding	No. Satisfactory	No. Unsatisfactory
	7	*10*	*4*

Per cent unsatisfactory in department *19%*

Sample Field Review Report Used by Gimbel Brothers

(Confidential entries or entries that might reveal identifications are marked "deleted" in parentheses.)

5. Human Relations in Department
   a) Asst. Buyer—sales force relationship, v. good
   b) Morale—good
   c) Asst. Buyer is excellent trainer

6. Training Needs in Department

   (Deleted)

7. Housekeeping *good*

8. Equipment *Very good in general, but more stock room space is needed for special days*

9. Situations Requiring Action

   (Deleted—three items mentioned)

10. Department Efficiency (current month)

Department selling cost		Percentage of return for month	
This year	*5.8*	This year	*8.49*
Last year	*7.9*	Last year	*7.12*

Percentage of gross margin		
This year	*35.96*	*(Three other ratios not shown)*
Last year	*32.69*	

11. General Comments

This is one of the departments where the management is left almost entirely to the Assistant Buyer, and in this case it is well handled. The personnel problems in the department are at a minimum. There is nothing in the department that cannot be handled through corrective interviewing by the Assistant Buyer.

(2nd and 3rd paragraphs not shown)

The Assistant Buyer complained that the delivery of mail and phone orders at or after 5 P.M. hampers customer service. Because of the late hour these orders reach the floor, it is impossible to fill them and get them out that day. He suggested that there be more frequent deliveries or at least an earlier delivery in the afternoon.

There is a problem of protection brought by the Assistant Buyer. He feels more concentration should be made on the doors near the department. There is too great an opportunity to steal the merchandise so close to the exits. The writer feels that this condition will be alleviated with the new physical setup.

Other phases of the department are well run and present a good organizational picture.

Sample Field Review Report Used by Gimbel Brothers (Continued) analyst makes, department by department. It is called the "Field Review Report." Excerpts from a sample report are shown on pages 314-315.

Two sections of this report require some explanation. Section 4 shows a summary of the ratings of the twenty-one employees in a certain department. These are the bare statistics which are derived from the discussions between the supervisor and the personnel representative about each of the workers. Management pays special attention to the figures in the outstanding and in the unsatisfactory columns.

The ratios in Section 10 will not mean much to the average reader. But three of the six that appear on the form are shown to suggest the kinds of information included in this report. Some will ask how a personnel man can rate the efficiency of an operating department of a store. Gimbel's answers: "Actually no person is doing this rating—the rating comes directly from the figures and from the resulting ratios. Our analysts simply collect, apply and report the figures and the ratios. The ratios are well understood and well accepted by our supervisors."

The analysts, it may be added, are selected for their work with extreme care. Two have been personnel directors of other companies. All have had supervisory experience, thus having gained the point of view of the line worker. At Gimbels the analysts are looked upon as persons who are trying to help the supervisors with their problems. They are constantly moving about the store, picking up good ideas and passing them on to others who can make use of them. Although it may seem at times that they are exposing department people to possible censure, the effect is usually just the opposite of this.[4]

When a situation which needs correcting is called to management's attention, there is a chance to get action. The "Field Review Report" serves to bring to light situations of all kinds, periodically and as a matter of routine. Without such a device, problem areas tend to be ignored and remedial measures delayed.

• EVALUATING THE PLAN

As Gimbels looks back on three years of experience with its rating plan, it is well pleased. To other companies that have become interested in a similar program, Gimbels has stressed two essentials of a successful operation: highly competent personnel representatives (analysts) and strong line support, including the full backing of top management.

In conclusion, there are three values that Gimbels believes are inherent in its Field Review Method. They may be described briefly.

FRM results seem to support the theory that supervisors prefer an oral rating plan to a written one, and that more accurate and more complete appraisals can be developed by the conversation approach. Also, the reports get done on time and no one is passed by.

The several ratings that are made keep the personnel department and management well acquainted at all times with

[4] The highly confidential nature of the information passed on to management by the analyst can be guessed from various sections of the report. Section 11, only parts of which could be reproduced, is an example of this.

the work of the individual employee and with the work of each department in the store. FRM gets the analyst out on the floor where he can observe conditions at first hand, whereas the usual rating plan is carried out by the supervisor working alone.

The program is dynamic. In some rating plans little or nothing happens after the appraisals have been made. At Gimbels, next steps are indicated. Time schedules for changing the assignments of individuals or for correcting a departmental situation are established.

C. Ratings by Self and by Groups (Peers, Subordinates, Others)

During World War I an interesting experiment took place in a rapidly expanding federal agency. The duties of the agency were multiplying so rapidly, and the organizational structure shifting so often, that in order to get information on the performance of thousands of employees, the head of the agency resorted to having everyone rate everyone else he knew.

On a less chaotic basis, the possibility of using ratings by peers, subordinates, and others instead of the superior has been explored in a number of settings. The advantages and disadvantages of group rating versus individual rating have also received examination. Interest is growing in these experiments and new techniques. The readings presented here illustrate the gains and problems of these rather unorthodox rating methods.

FURTHER READING

Hall, William B., "Employee Self-Appraisal," *Personnel Journal,* Vol. 29, no. 4, September 1950, pp. 134–136.

Hollander, E. P., "The Friendship Factor in Peer Nominations" *Personnel Psychology,* Vol. 9, no. 4, Winter 1956, pp. 435–447 (incl. bibl.)

"Is Group Appraisal the Best Way to Evaluate Top Executives?" *Personnel Administration,* Vol. 22, no. 2, March–April 1959, pp. 30–32.

Shelton, Henry Wood, "Mutual Rating: A Contribution to the Technique of Participation," *Bulletin of the Taylor Society,* Vol. 5, no. 2, April 1920, pp. 59–67.

Tupes, Ernest C., *Relationships Between Behavior Trait Ratings by Peers and Later Officer Performance of USAF Officer Candidate School Graduates.* Lackland Air Force Base, Texas, Air Force Personnel and Training Research Center, October 1957. (Research Report AFPTRC-TN-57-125, ASTIA Document no. 134 257.)

Turner, William D., "A Multiple Committee Method of Merit Rating," *Personnel,* Vol. 25, no. 3, November 1948, pp. 176–194.

Webb, Wilse B., "A Procedure for Obtaining Self-Ratings and Group Ratings," *Journal of Consulting Psychology,* Vol. 20, no. 3, June 1956, pp. 233–236.

Wherry, Robert J., and Douglas H. Fryer, "Buddy Ratings: Popularity Contest or Leadership Criteria?" *Personnel Psychology,* Vol. 2, no. 2, Summer 1949, pp. 147–160.

BUDDY RATINGS: MILITARY RESEARCH AND INDUSTRIAL IMPLICATIONS*

E. P. Hollander

• SUMMARY

From a base provided by sociometry, a relatively new procedure for personnel assessment through coworker evaluations has been developed. Particularly within the armed forces, recent years have seen the employment of such evaluations as an integral part of personnel research programs. One notable technique, "buddy ratings"—sometimes called "peer ratings" or "peer nominations"—has achieved prominence for the unique supplementary data on personnel which it can yield. Furthermore, the research on the buddy ratings technique affords extensive evidence in support of its validity and reliability. Approached from an industrial standpoint, this material suggests a variety of promising applications. While not conceived to be encyclopedic in its coverage, this paper presents an overview of the accumulated evidence with the intent of highlighting the possible utility of the buddy ratings technique within industrial settings.

• THE TECHNIQUE

Taken in its basic form, the buddy ratings technique involves each group member's rating of every other group member on a recognizable quality; for example, leadership. From these ratings, a composite score is obtained which may then be related to a criterion, or may itself be used as a criterion against which other factors are validated. There are two essential variations of this fundamental process, both of which are covered by the generic term "buddy ratings." In the first variation, each group member literally *ranks* the others through the assignment of a score or by an actual process of ranking. In the second, each individual *nominates* a specified number of his fellows whom he considers "high" or "low" on the quality being measured; this is sometimes called a "buddy nomination." Both procedures yield a score which serves as an index of the individual's status within his group on the pertinent factor. They both rest on the presupposition, however, that members of the group are familiar with one another. Quite obviously, close contact among group members over a period of time is central to the validity of their appraisals.

• THE EVIDENCE: VALIDITY AND RELIABILITY

When considering the value of any new measurement device, two questions immediately arise: Is the device valid? Is it reliable? In appraising the buddy ratings technique, therefore, we shall

* From *Personnel Psychology*, Vol. 7, no. 3, Autumn 1954, pp. 385–393.

present as basic evidence the data currently available concerning these dual issues.

Perhaps the first substantial work with the buddy ratings technique, so far as personnel research is concerned, was done during World War II within the armed services. The Navy, in a study of aviation squadrons, made wide use of a nominating technique described elsewhere (*6, 10*). From this substantial project came evidence of the utility of this mode of evaluation in pin-pointing the qualities making for the "wanted" pilot, as opposed to the "unwanted" pilot. This has been well documented in a comprehensive article by Jenkins (*6*).

Within this same era, Williams and Leavitt (*12*), two Navy psychologists at the Marine Corps Officer Candidate School (OCS), were utilizing buddy ratings with officer candidates to predict their field performance in combat. Their results were particularly striking. They found that ". . . sociometric group opinion was a more valid predictor both of success in Officer Candidate School and of combat performance than several objective tests . . ." (*12*, p. 291). Furthermore, buddy ratings were significantly better than superiors' ratings in predicting the criteria.[1] Considering this, they conclude that the buddy ratings technique has greater validity than these other measures because group members have more time to observe each other than do the superior officers, they know each other in a realistic context, and react more directly to each other's social behavior. These are all conditions, they observe, which are favorable to "informed judgments" (*12*, p. 291).

In a definitive study done at the Signal Corps OCS, and reported some years ago in this journal, Wherry and Fryer (*11*) found support for the higher validity of buddy ratings, as against superior ratings, in predicting leadership performance. "Buddy ratings," they contend, "appear to be the purest measure of 'leadership' . . . Nominations by class appear to be better measures of the leadership factor than any other variable" (*11*, p. 157). With this evidence at hand, they reject the argument that these ratings are mainly a contest for popularity rather than a valid criterion. Specific additional support for their position has been provided by a newly completed study cited below (*5*).

More recently, McClure, Tupes, and Dailey (*7*) conducted an evaluation of buddy ratings among trainees at the Air Force OCS. In their procedure, each candidate was required to rank all of the other candidates in his flight, with the number-one ranking going to the man he considered the most outstanding of the 40 or 50 men in his flight. Scores for each candidate were derived from an average of all of the ranks assigned him. They report that of the variables considered in their study, this technique yielded ". . . the most promising OCS criterion found . . ." (*7*, p. 6).

Shortly before the onset of hostilities in Korea, a buddy nomination form for leadership was introduced at the Naval

---

[1] Similar results were obtained in follow-up studies of West Point cadets conducted by the Personnel Research Branch, A.G.O. Cf. PRS Report #767, *Follow-up Study of Officer Performance of West Point Graduates.* Personnel Research Section, AGO, 1948. This report has been summarized in an article by Gaylord, R. H., and Russell, Eva. West Point Evaluative Measures in The Prediction of Officer Efficiency. *Ed. and Psych. Measmt.*, 1951, *11*(4), 605–611. Cf. PRS Report #811, *Follow-up Validation of Predictor Instruments for West Point Classes of 1944, 1945, and 1946 against 1948 ratings on DA AGO form 67–1.* Personnel Research Section, A.G.O. 1949.–Ed.

School of Pre-Flight in Pensacola.[2] One notable feature of the procedure used there was the solicitation from the cadets of reasons *why* they had nominated men "high" or "low" on this quality. This had been tried previously with some success by Jenkins (*6*) and his colleagues. Drawing on these data, Richardson, Bellows, and Henry (*13*) extended this investigation to the development of a forced-choice rating form which embodied descriptive phrases actually used by the cadets. Two interchangeable forms were ultimately designed; they report that when these forms are completed on a cadet by two classmates chosen at random, the forms correlate with the buddy nomination criterion at the .76 and .77 levels respectively (*13*, p. 19).

In a still later study at Pensacola, the writer (*3*) found that buddy nominations on leadership, among Naval Aviation Cadets at the pre-flight level, significantly predicted the pass-fail criterion for the total flight training program. The validity of these nominations was matched only by that of final pre-flight average. Superiors' ratings on "officer-like qualities" and other measures from the same level of training were not found to significantly predict this same criterion. The fact that buddy nominations on *leadership alone* can predict such a complex criterion as successful completion of a flight training program extending some 14 months beyond pre-flight raises enthusiasm for the potential inherent in this technique (*3, 4*).

At this point, one may properly begin to raise a query concerning the composition of buddy ratings data. What are the kinds of considerations which go to make up these ratings in the first place? An answer to this has to some degree been provided by valuable research done by Tupes, Borg, and Friedman (*9*) in the Air Force. In their study, they factor analyzed data drawn from OCS buddy ratings of the "paired comparison" variety. Effectively, this modification requires each candidate to evaluate each of his fellow flight members on some 30 specific areas of behavior plus evaluation on a general proficiency variable. From the analyses, six factors were obtained which, after rotation to orthogonal simple structure, appeared as one general factor, four group factors, and one residual factor. The group factors are described as: administrative ability, working effectively with others, striving to do a good job, and acceptance of organizational responsibility (*9*, p. 6). Notice how these can account for effective interpersonal qualities, personal involvement with a task, and assimilation to organizational structure and goals. The authors conclude that ". . . OCS candidates, although not able to discriminate satisfactorily among the 30 specific behaviors . . . do consider several different variables when evaluating each other" (*9*, p. 7).

A concern with the meaning of "low" leadership scores on buddy nominations led to a study recently completed by the writer with Webb (*5*). Working with a Naval Aviation Cadet sample, the question of whether such "low" leadership scores implied "high" followership was considered. The technique utilized involved the administration of three separate buddy nomination forms:

---

[2] Credit for the initiation of this research deservedly belongs to Dr. Howard E. Page, then of the Staff, Naval Air Training Command (*13*, p. 4).

one each on leadership, followership, and friendship. An analysis of interrelationships revealed a high positive correlation ($r = .92$) between leadership and followership nominations. It would appear, then, that "high" leadership, within this social context, is indicative of "high" followership, as well. As for the friendship nominations, the results indicated that an average of *more than two out of the three friends* each cadet listed were *not* nominated by them for any of the three "high" leadership positions. Followership nominations were, however, considerably more related to friendship. As has been noted above, this tends to substantiate the positions taken by Wherry and Fryer (*11*).

In addition to presenting adequate validity, buddy ratings have been found to meet acceptable standards of reliability. Thus, McClure, Tupes, and Dailey (*7*) report that the "correlation between the average rankings at the end of the third and fourth months was .91 and between those of the first and fourth months, .61" (*7*, p. 6). Wherry and Fryer (*11*) found that ". . . the reliability of nominations after four months is outstandingly higher than that of any of the other variables upon which the test was made. This is probably further evidence of the fact that the nominating technique has the property of early identification of the members of the group who constitute the two extremes of the leadership distribution" (*11*, p. 159).

From a recent study with trainees in the Marine Corps Officer Screening Course, Anderhalter *et al.* (*1*) report an average reliability of .71 from ratings made during the first and third weeks. With the leadership nomination form utilized among Naval Aviation Cadets, an uncorrected split-half reliability of .89 has been obtained (*4*). All considered, whatever the technique of reliability determination applied, the relatively high reliability of buddy ratings appears to persist.

• IMPLICATIONS AND APPLICATIONS

The evidence supporting the validity and reliability of the buddy ratings technique is consistent and substantial. Buddy ratings *do* predict such diverse phenomena as OCS performance, success or failure in flight training, and leadership adequacy. But this stands as a mere beginning. It will be apparent even to the casual reader that the potential inherent in the technique has yet to be seen in its fuller aspects.

Viewed broadly, the implication of the work already completed is that group opinion, taken as a composite, may yield information about an individual which is not being tapped at present by other measures. The very core of the matter, as has been suggested by Williams and Leavitt (*12*), is that such group evaluations are based upon "informed judgments" drawn from personal interactions. This suggests that still other qualities may be measured through buddy ratings and that advances into the general field of personal assessment may be made, if indeed they are not already underway.

As an illustration, consider for a moment potentialities for the use of buddy ratings in industrial training courses. One might argue, of course, that such an application might not be legitimate since the evidence presented stems entirely from military training programs.

This is partly so; yet, the buddy ratings technique rests not so much on situational considerations as it does on the stability of the group and its potential for inter-member contact. Thus, a group of industrial trainees could readily be assessed by this method, so long as they had been together for some minimal period of time. A variety of relevant criteria might be predicted with such groups. Incidentally, reports on applications of this kind are sorely needed for the enrichment of the personnel research literature.

Still further, the buddy ratings technique has utility for assisting in administrative decisions affecting personnel promotion. Admittedly, this requires some degree of subtlety on the part of administrators lest employees gain the erroneous impression that this constitutes the *sole* standard of evaluation. Nonetheless, the selection of personnel for key jobs may be considerably facilitated through the availability of information relative to their coworkers' view of them. Doubtless, some will raise the objection that this procedure puts a kind of administrative decision in the hands of employees. But that is precisely the point: information from buddy ratings is more than a simple tabulation of votes—it predicts criteria; it bears directly on organizational goals of optimum performance and effectiveness.

Possible applications to problems of morale are equally promising. It is entirely feasible that an index of morale for employee units could be gleaned through the implementation of a buddy ratings form specifying "interest in the job," "acceptance of company policies," or some such related characteristic. While this is still an exploratory modification, it presents a method for obtaining morale data which is thoroughly practicable and of ultimate usefulness. The only complication is the possible unwillingness of employees to make such ratings if it were felt that *individual scores* would be reported to management; such a situation could be obviated, however, by having the data gathered by an agency external to the organization which would report only group scores to the administrative level.

Along the same line, measures of group cohesiveness—another approach to morale—can be elicited from buddy ratings data. The extent to which individuals in a group are "underchosen" or "underranked" affords a useful index of this group characteristic (Cf. *8*). It has long since been observed that morale is closely bound up with the cohesiveness, or solidarity, of a group. And this is the kind of information which is most readily obtainable from applications of this technique.

Still another addition to the basic buddy ratings method is offered by Anderhalter *et al. (1)*. In their work they have evolved an index which reflects the degree to which group members, either individually or collectively, are accurate in ranking each other. Put simply, this procedure compares the rankings made by each individual with the rankings secured from the pooled judgment of the group. Where the average index for the group is small, group members have a superior awareness of how the others "stack up" on the quality being measured. Where the index is large, group members are inaccurate in their appraisal of the status of others on this quality. In a sense, then, this procedure also serves as a method for indexing group cohesiveness or solidarity.

A related method of extracting supplementary data from buddy ratings is now being studied at Pensacola. The procedure in use there is to request each individual to give his own self-rank on leadership, and then an estimate of the actual leadership rank he will secure from the pooled judgments of the group. This is directly incorporated into the leadership nomination form. Discrepancy scores from the actual group rank are then derived for each of these two "personal ranks." These scores, in turn, can be related to the basic nomination score or some other criterion. Another exploration of this method has recently been reported from a study in the Air Force (2).

The applications cited represent a sampling among those which now seem feasible with the buddy ratings technique. There are undoubtedly others of material usefulness which should come into currency as time proceeds and inventive research progresses along these lines. In any event, this much seems true: the combined judgments of a group bear latent information of appreciable worth to the personnel technician and administrator.

REFERENCES

1. Anderhalter, O. F., Wilkins, W. L., and Rigby, M. K. Peer Ratings. *Technical Report No. 2*. St. Louis: St. Louis University, 30 November 1952.
2. Flyer, E. S., Barron, E., and Bigbee, L. Discrepancies Between Self-Descriptions and Group Ratings as Measures of Lack of Insight. *Research Bulletin 53-33*. San Antonio: Human Resources Research Center, Lackland Air Force Base, September 1953.
3. Hollander, E. P. Peer Nominations on Leadership as a Predictor of the Pass-Fail Criterion in Naval Air Training. *Journal of Applied Psychology,* 1954, 38, 150–153.
4. Hollander, E. P. Studies of Leadership Among Naval Aviation Cadets. *Journal of Aviation Medicine,* 1954, 25, 164–170, 200.
5. Hollander, E. P., and Webb, W. B. Leadership, Followership and Friendship: An Analysis of Peer Nominations. *Journal of Abnormal and Social Psychology,* 1955, 50, 163–167.
6. Jenkins, J. G. The Nominating Technique as a Method of Evaluating Air Group Morale. *Journal of Aviation Medicine,* 1948, 19, 12–19.
7. McClure, G. E., Tupes, E. C., and Dailey, J. T. Research on Criteria of Officer Effectiveness. *Research Bulletin 51-8*. San Antonio: Human Resources Research Center, Lackland Air Force Base, May 1951.
8. Proctor, C. H., and Loomis, C. P. "Analysis of Sociometric Data." In *Research Methods in Social Relations.* (Part 2) Jahoda, M. *et al.* (Eds.) New York: Dryden Press, 1951, 561–585.
9. Tupes, E. C., Borg, W. R., and Friedman, G. A Factor Analysis of the OCS Paired-Comparison Evaluation System. *Technical Report 53-10*. San Antonio: Human Resources Research Center, Lackland Air Force Base, June 1953.

10. Vaughn, C. L. The Nominating Technique. In *New Methods in Applied Psychology.* College Park: University of Maryland, 1947, 22–25.
11. Wherry, R. J., and Fryer, D. H. Buddy Ratings: Popularity Contest or Leadership Criterion? *Personnel Psychology,* 1949, 2, 147–159.
12. Williams, S. B. and Leavitt, H. J. Group Opinion as a Predictor of Military Leadership. *Journal of Consulting Psychology,* 1947, XI, 283–291.
13. *A Report Evaluating Leadership Potential of Pre-Flight NavCads.* ONR Contract Nonr 0-3400 (RBH Project 203). New York: Richardson, Bellows, Henry and Company, 1951.

THE MECHANICS OF GROUP APPRAISAL*

Virgil K. Rowland

The group summary appraisal is the simplest of the many types of appraisal in use today. No set form or graduated scale is required. The only tools actually essential are a few sheets of blank paper and a pen or a pencil.

Under this plan the manager who wants to determine how well one of his subordinate managers is doing, and how he can be helped to improve his performance, invites a group of people to discuss the matter informally. The points on which all agree constitute the written appraisal.

The appraisal group generally consists of three or four people, including the immediate superior of the man who is being appraised. Four makes for the best discussion; five can handle the job satisfactorily; but a group of six is apt to be unwieldy.

The immediate superior may think that he alone is equipped to appraise his subordinates, and he is, of course, more familiar with their work than anyone else. But if he undertakes to appraise them without assistance, he is likely to overlook important points—because he cannot remember everything, because he has some unconscious bias, or simply because he is ignorant of all the consequences of their acts.

"He saved $15,000 by that change in procedure he made last January," is a point that is likely to stick in the superior's mind. But it may be that the $15,000 was saved only by increasing the costs of other departments by $16,000. If this is so, the immediate superior may not be aware of it.

Nor does the superior always know all the possible approaches that can be used to help his subordinate. Often he has seen only one side of him, and needs to have others fill out the picture.

One department head objected strongly to the group appraisal method. He would wager almost everything, he told his own superior, that no one could tell him anything about any of his subordinates that he did not already know. Yet after the first appraisal he admitted he had not known that one subordinate had for years acted as semi-professional adviser to a company-wide group of employees interested in one of the arts. Further, he realized that this fact could be used to help the subordinate correct one of his shortcomings—an inability to get along with those not under his supervision. "Why not," the superior decided to suggest, "use the same approach that you have used successfully with the extracurricular group?"

• DOES THE GROUP NEED TRAINING?

Participation in the group appraisal does not require special experience or training. Members will be asked to make only the kind of judgment they are making every day in their own minds, and sometimes vocally to their intimates. They should, of course, be people who have some contact with the man who

---

* From *Improving Managerial Performance*, by Virgil K. Rowland. New York, Harper and Brothers, Copyright 1958; as reprinted in *Personnel* (American Management Association), May–June 1958, pp. 36–43. Reprinted by permission.

is being appraised, preferably (and this is usually possible) those whose own work is affected by the quality of his performance. In addition—and this is very important—they must be managers on a higher level than the man they are to appraise.

Some authorities have suggested that men on the same level, or even subordinates, be parties to the appraisal; but in view of the facts of business life, this is unrealistic. Men on the same level are apt to be rivals or personal friends, and hence biased one way or the other. In any case, if George appraises Bill and Bill appraises George, logrolling is likely to ensue and vitiate the whole process.

Subordinates may not be subject to exactly the same temptations, but they have a set of inadequacies of their own. In the first place, they are not always free from fear of swift reprisal, even when they are assured their comments will be held in confidence. And sometimes their fears are justified. There have been instances where superiors attempted to ascertain "who said that." A more important objection is that subordinates do not see the whole picture; they tend to judge their superior mainly by the way he treats them; and though his attitude towards his subordinates is important, it is only one facet of the appraisal. Finally, and most important of all, people are not hired to judge the qualifications of their equals or their superiors; doing so is no part of their job.

Sometimes one or two high-level staff people may be included in the group, but it is generally more satisfactory to select higher line executives with whom the man "does business." For example, an accountant might be appraised not only by his boss, the controller, but by two or three of the department heads to whom he furnishes reports.

Where plants are widely scattered, it is conceivable that the plant manager may have no one of his own or higher status there to appraise his subordinates. Many companies have found that a satisfactory way to meet this situation is to utilize higher-level staff personnel from the home office. Often these people have the technical knowledge that enables them to contribute a good deal to the appraisal of a department head.

• SELECTING THE APPRAISERS

There are two ways of selecting the appraisers. In some cases the immediate superior selects them. In many companies, however, there seems to be a growing tendency to allow the person who is to be appraised to suggest some names. This has an advantage in that it is likely to give the man confidence in the fairness of the procedure and make him realize that the appraisal is designed to help him improve his performance, not to "get something on him." Nor is this likely to result in a more favorable estimate than he deserves. If a man can suggest three or four members of higher management all of whom believe he is outstanding, the chances are that he really is outstanding. If he succeeds in getting one biased appraiser into the group, little harm will be done because all opinions that go into the record must be unanimous.

If the subordinate tends to be suspicious of any of the appraisers his superiors selects, it may be particularly worth while to be guided by his views in the next appraisal. How this tends to promote acceptance of the appraisal process is illustrated by an incident that occurred in one company. A man who considered that he had been appraised unfavorably and attributed the disappointing result to one appraiser in particular was permitted to select the group the next time around. The second appraisal proved to be very little different from the first. For this third appraisal, the man voluntarily suggested the name of the executive on whom he had formerly centered his suspicions.

Two other points are important in the selection of appraisers. First, they must understand that the primary purpose of the appraisal is to help the man improve his performance on the job, and perhaps fit him for a future vacancy on a higher level; not to determine whether he gets a raise or gets fired. Second, they must believe that participation is worth while; that it is genuinely beneficial to the company. If they regard the whole procedure as a kind of boondoggle, they are not likely to contribute anything of value.

An appraisal group is always headed by a chairman, and that chairman is always the man's immediate superior. The immediate superior may select one of the appraisers to act as secretary of the group, though in most cases the chairman has acted as his own secretary. This, however, is not a hard and fast rule. Some department heads prefer to rotate the secretaryship, which is feasible if the same appraisers are used for all the managers in the department. The secretary participates in the appraisal himself, and, in addition, makes notes of his own and others' comments. As mentioned, he can use any blank sheet of paper for this, though it may be better to group the comments under three headings that can be printed on an appraisal form: results, methods, and personal qualifications. Such a division will help later on when the department head reviews the appraisal with his own superiors, since it will permit him to present the conclusions in logical order.

The secretary must be alert to everything that is said. He may jot down sentences or merely one-word hints, but he must be careful not to omit anything. Complete notes are extremely important. Often the most acute remarks are made at the beginning of the session, and the success of the discussion that follows will depend in large measure on the way in which these first off-the-cuff judgments are followed up. Probably he will find it better not to wait until there has been agreement on a point before jotting it down. He can later underline it, or place a checkmark in the margin, if the appraisers appear to be in accord on it. The points that are checked or underlined will constitute the notes he later reads to the group, but he will be in a position to read back other parts of the discussion if he is requested to do so.

Because his job is exacting, the secretary may not be able to do much talking during the greater part of the session, but his chance will come when the chairman determines that all the salient points have been brought out and asks that the notes be read. After the reading the secretary can express his own opinions fully; then the group can analyze what has been said and complete the appraisal while the secretary clarifies and adds to his notes.

It should be noted that this is the way the average appraisal is actually conducted. Every member is able to participate to his own satisfaction, and it is a rare person indeed who feels that secretarial duties keep him from getting his opinions into the discussion.

When the group has disbanded, the secretary writes up the completed appraisal and sends it to each member of the appraisal group for his approval and signature.

FUNCTIONS OF THE CHAIRMAN

The chairman, too, has definite duties. The final success of the session, in fact, depends largely on the way in which he conducts the meeting. It is up to him to start the ball rolling. He may begin, particularly in the case of a first appraisal, by stressing the confidential nature of the session and its purpose. He should also read the man's job description or make copies of it available to the appraisers. This is of the utmost importance. All appraisers must know what the man is supposed to do before they can judge the extent to which he is meeting his responsibilities, and frequently those from outside the department are not too clear about this.

One of the points the chairman must watch, however, is the extent to which he dominates the meeting. Though he must provide positive leadership, he must also take care not to impose his own opinions on the group or shut off discussion of any point too soon. This may be difficult for him if he has spent years dealing with subordinates and has become accustomed to issuing ex cathedra judgments. If he succeeds in smothering all dissent, he is merely wasting his time; he might as well conduct the appraisal by himself. Of course, no chairman can be expected to change the habits of a lifetime at the first session, but the executive who really believes in the value of a group opinion can gradually adjust himself.

Experience has shown that it is wise for the chairman—whether or not he believes himself too inclined to dominate—to spend the first part of the meeting asking leading questions. This, of course, forces him to keep his opinions in the "nod and grunt" stage while other members of the group talk.

Here, too, the staff "coach" who is present at the session as an observer can help him. For the chairman, if the other executives in the group are subordinate to him, does not have to speak to enforce his opinions. A lift of the eyebrows, a smile, a look of agreement or disagreement may be sufficient to prevent the others from pressing views contrary to his own. If the chairman really wants to make the appraisal procedure a successful group effort, he must be willing to accept later criticism from the coach.

Drawing out the opinions of all the members of the group is one of the most important parts of the chairman's job. Sometimes he may have to prod one or more of the others before they will enter freely into the discussion. He can do this by asking the man who hangs back whether or not he agrees with what has been said. Or he may ask a more specific question: "George thinks Stu always gets his reports in on time. Does he always meet the deadline on the reports he prepares for you?"

• WHEN SOMEONE HOLDS BACK

Sometimes, despite the best possible briefing by the chairman, some member of the group may feel he is not in sympathy with the appraisal process. He may go so far as to remark that he is not going to say anything derogatory about anyone.

In one actual case, an appraiser brought from a distant section of the company not only announced that he would make no derogatory remarks, but emphasized his detachment from the whole procedure by not removing his hat and coat. The chairman realized that urging or further explanations would be fruitless at that point; he merely asked the man to sit down and listen. Soon the detached observer became so interested in the discussion that he began offering his own opinions. Ten minutes later, he was participating freely. The chairman wisely made no comment on the change of attitude, then or later. When the meeting was over, he said only: "Well, thanks for helping us. You gave us several good points to consider." And the man left the meeting apparently unaware that he had executed a complete about-face.

Though it is best not to take issue with such a man directly, the chairman can keep stressing the fact that the purpose of the meeting is to help the person being appraised improve on the job, and the chairman can demonstrate this by the tenor of his questions. He should emphasize this point particularly whenever there is one of the best ways of helping the hesitant man feel free to talk frankly.

But drawing out the members of the group is not the chairman's only duty as a leader. He must be alert at all times to the worth of the discussion. He must determine whether any particular argument is leading to a worth-while conclusion or only to an impasse. Since he is trying to get unanimity, he will have, at times, to detach himself from the discussion and determine just where it is heading. If he feels that it is likely to be productive, he can let it go on, even though some members of the group are merely repeating themselves. If, however, he feels that no further benefit can be derived from an argument, two courses are open to him: (1) he can drop the point completely; or (2) he can put it aside temporarily and come back to it later. In either case, he will have to exercise diplomacy; for if he is not careful, one or two of the appraisers may adopt an attitude of passive resistance and contribute nothing of value for the rest of the session.

The chairman must also determine when there has been enough free discussion of any point on which there is substantial agreement. Some executives believe that there cannot be too much discussion, that all of it is good. This view is based on the assumption that more and more ideas come out as the talk continues, and that real opinions emerge only after a good deal of beating around the bush. Often they feel that if the first comments are accepted and incorporated, the conclusions will be inaccurate. There is some truth in this, and the chairman should be careful not to change the subject too abruptly. However, when nothing new has been contributed for some time, it may be well to leave a particular phase of the appraisal and start in on a new point, even though some members of the group may seem inclined to continue belaboring the old one.

• HOW MUCH GOSSIP?

A related consideration is the extent to which the chairman should permit gossip. Gossip is a natural part of any gathering, and appraisal sessions are not likely to be an exception. It is part of the chairman's responsibility to keep the conversation on an objective plane, but this does not mean that he must rule out gossip completely. A little of it may lead to some new thinking on the part of the appraisers. However, the chairman must keep gossip within reasonable bounds or too much time will be consumed. If the meeting shows signs of running on for more than two hours, the chairman would be well advised to steer the discussion back to more factual material.

After the first part of the discussion has come to a close and the secretary has read his notes, the chairman should ask the group whether they want to include all the comments on which there is general agreement. Sometimes the members may not care to do so because evidence to support some of the opinions is lacking. The chairman can then decide whether any of the points should be considered further in an effort to bring out the evidence.

The chairman's responsibility to bring out the consensus of the meeting is one that cannot be met in a routine manner. A good chairman will vary his approach with each point so that he will not appear to be following a definite pattern. No member should be able to close his eyes and say, "Next item."

Even when discussion has brought out a point that is obviously pertinent, further discussion will be required to phrase the final statement in such a way that all participants can agree to it. An alert chairman will not ignore the man who, though he remains silent, gives evidence of mental reservations. From a practical standpoint, of course, not all participants can be expected to concur positively in all statements; some of them may not know enough about the man who is being appraised to judge all phases of his performance. No statement should go into the record if there is any opposition to it. But if an appraiser who does not volunteer agreement is asked whether he has any evidence to the contrary and says "No," this can be considered agreement from a practical standpoint.

When agreement has been reached on all points covered in the appraisal and they have been phrased in a way that everyone can subscribe to, the chairman has one final duty before the meeting is brought to a close: he must stress again the confidential nature of the discussion. Some executives feel that this is unnecessary after the first few meetings; once the procedure has been established, they contend, no one is likely to forget this point. However, there is the possibility that a rule no longer stressed will eventually be ignored, and any breach of confidence could have serious consequences. If the results are broadcast widely, opposition to the whole procedure could develop. The man who has been appraised should learn of his standing from his immediate superior, the person from whom he naturally expects guidance; hints from anyone else are likely to make him uneasy.

• THE RULES ARE SIMPLE

It can be seen that the rules for conducting the sessions are few and simple. But a successful session is not merely a matter of rules. As he gains experience, the chairman will acquire new skills, and the meetings will gain in value. Appraisers, too, are trained through practice.

Some variations in the procedure outlined is permissible when the man who is being appraised is high in the management organization and the appraisers are, therefore, the operating heads of the company or the corporate officers. In such a case, a high-level staff man can act as secretary, and the top people can agree to allow him to phrase the conclusions later. In instances of this kind, the secretary is usually able to reflect the flavor of the discussion accurately, and few changes in his first draft will be necessary.

This may appear to be a violation of one of the principles pointed out earlier: that the appraisers themselves should agree on the phraseology and work it out together. Experience will show, however, that the higher up in the organization the appraisers are, the more likely they are to express their opinions with precision. At no time should an appraisal session take longer than is necessary, and at the top level this is particularly important.

RATINGS OF CANDIDATES FOR PROMOTION BY CO-WORKERS AND SUPERVISORS*

Doris Springer

The primary purpose of this study was to compare ratings made by supervisory personnel and by co-workers on candidates for promotion to leadman jobs. Specifically, answers to the following questions were sought:

1. To what extent do supervisory personnel and co-workers agree in their ratings of workers?
2. How does the extent of this agreement compare with (a) the extent to which members of supervision agree with each other, and (b) the extent to which co-workers agree with each other in the ratings given workers?

In analyzing the data to answer these questions, answers were suggested for other questions, such as:

3. How do judgments on different items in the rating form compare with each other?
4. Is there any evidence that supervisors tend to rate candidates lower or higher than do their co-workers?
5. How do the totals of the ratings on the individual characteristics compare with the ratings on the suitability of the candidate for promotion?

The problem is of practical importance in determining the reliability of ratings by supervisors and co-workers and in arriving at the appropriate weights to be given ratings made by them in an over-all evaluation of candidates for promotion. The provision in many union contracts which states that promotions to jobs covered by the contract are to be governed by seniority only when ability, skill, and job performance are equal draws attention to the need for devising techniques for determining workers' suitability for promotion. These techniques must be acceptable to the union and management and, at the same time, be statistically sound. It then becomes important to analyze the results of these techniques in their actual application. The present study provides data on two of these techniques, namely, co-worker ratings and supervisory ratings.

From a theoretical standpoint, the study contributes some data on the attitudes of two distinct groups in the economic structure and on the relative homogeneity of thought of these two groups with respect to one aspect of their work environment. An accumulation of such data will enable us at some future time to arrive at a psychological and sociological understanding of the two groups which will be invaluable to the industrial psychologist.

• RATINGS STUDIED

This study is based on the ratings made on 100 men who were candidates for leadman[1] jobs in 14 different depart-

* From *Journal of Applied Psychology* [Rating by Subordinates], Vol. 37, no. 5, October 1953, pp. 347–351. Copyright 1953 by the American Psychological Association. Reprinted by permission.

[1] At North American Aviation, Inc., a leadman directs a group of five to ten men. The job is covered by union contract.

ments of the manufacturing division of a major aircraft company. The ratings were made as a regular phase of the company's supervisory selection program in which each candidate is evaluated on the basis of his work experience, education, work record, and scores on mental ability, shop math, and job knowledge tests, in addition to the ratings. Ratings are made by two supervisors, representing two levels of supervision over the candidate, and by three co-workers who work closely with the candidate but who are not eligible to be candidates for the leadman job. The ratings analyzed here are the ratings made by two members of supervision and two of three co-workers (selected at random) for each of the 100 candidates. A total of 68 different assistant foremen and foremen made the supervisory ratings. The exact number of co-workers participating cannot be reported since these rating forms were not signed, but the number was probably between 150 and 175. A worker ordinarily rated only one worker for any one job opening and rarely did a job opening occur in the same group during the period studied.

The two rating forms used were the "behavior sample" type in which five gradations from very poor to outstanding were described for each characteristic. The form used by the co-workers consisted of five factors; namely, job knowledge, job performance, cooperation, ability to train others, and suitability for promotion to leadman. The form used by supervisory personnel consisted of eight factors; namely, job knowledge, quality of work done, quantity of work done, cooperation, drive, observing rules, personal appearance and manner, and suitability for promotion to leadman. The raters were instructed to check the one statement for each factor which best described the candidate. The ratings were made independently. For purposes of this report, the five intervals have been assigned values of 1 through 5, from lowest to highest.

• STATISTICAL METHOD

The degree of relationship between the variables studied has been measured by the product moment coefficient of correlation. It was believed that the nature of the data justified the use of this technique because the series were more nearly continuous than discrete and more nearly quantitative than qualitative.

When a difference is described in the report as significant, that difference is so large that it could be expected by chance not more than once in 100 times ($P \leqq 0.01$).

• RESULTS

Relationship between ratings made by members of supervision and co-workers. The coefficients of correlation between the ratings made by one member of supervision and one co-worker for each candidate on items common to both rating scales are shown in Table 1. The single supervisory rating was chosen at random from the two ratings made and the single co-worker rating was chosen at random from the three ratings made. Supervisory ratings on quality of job performance and quantity of work done have been compared with the single rating on job performance given by co-workers.

All of the correlations are rather low,

Table 1

RELATIONSHIP BETWEEN RATINGS MADE BY MEMBERS OF SUPERVISION AND CO-WORKERS

ITEM RATED	COEFFICIENT OF CORRELATION
Job knowledge	.15
Job performance–Quality	.25
Cooperation	.29
Job performance–Quantity	.33
General fitness for promotion	.39

ranging from .15 to .39; however, only the lowest coefficient is not significantly greater than zero. There is greatest agreement on the over-all rating of general fitness for promotion. The data in Table 1 suggest that co-worker and supervisory ratings do not duplicate each other unnecessarily; and, *at least in this respect,* the consideration of both types of ratings in evaluating candidates for promotion seems justified.

The low degree of agreement between the ratings of supervisory personnel and co-workers indicates that many factors determining the ratings of the two groups are either not similar or are not receiving the same relative emphasis. Perhaps their standards of judgment, based on differences in scope and type of experience and present job status, account for the lack of agreement. Their ratings may be determined by observations of different samples of behavior of the men being rated. On the other hand, the discrepancies in the ratings found here may be accounted for, in part, by differences of opinion on what characteristics are desired in a leader of the work group. Research on worker and supervisor attitudes with regard to how work groups should be led has suggested that such differences exist (*1*).

The data reported here merely show that differences between the opinions of co-workers and members of supervision do exist; further research is necessary to identify the sources of these differences.

Relationship between ratings made by pairs of co-workers. The coefficients of correlation between ratings made by pairs of co-workers on the candidates are shown in Table 2. The coefficients indicate an agreement between pairs of co-workers which, although greater than zero, is moderately low to moderate.

With one exception, the correlations between ratings made by pairs of co-workers are higher than the correlations between co-workers and supervisory personnel. There is slightly less agreement among co-workers than between co-workers and supervisors on general fitness for promotion; however, the difference is not significant.

When ratings given for all items on the rating form are combined, the coefficient obtained is slightly higher (though not significantly so) than for any individual item. The coefficients in Table 2 are in line with those reported in most studies of supervisory merit ratings (*2, 3, 4*).

The greater agreement among co-workers than between co-workers and supervisors may reflect more similarity

Table 2

RELATIONSHIP BETWEEN RATINGS MADE BY PAIRS OF CO-WORKERS

ITEM RATED	COEFFICIENT OF CORRELATION
Cooperation	.34
General fitness for promotion	.34
Instruction ability	.41
Job performance	.41
Job knowledge	.43
Total of all items	.48

among the former than between the latter with respect to standards of judgment, behavior actually observed, and/or opinions on what characteristics are desired in a leader of the work group.

The fact that only moderate agreement is found indicates that the co-workers are far from being a homogeneous group with respect to attitudes toward their co-workers.

The comparison here may be interpreted as a measure of the reliability of the co-worker ratings. The moderately low to moderate reliability of the ratings indicates that such ratings should not be used as the sole basis for selection and that care must be taken in their interpretation. The relatively low reliability of co-worker ratings, as compared with reliability coefficients of other types of measures, should be considered in deciding on the weight of these ratings in the battery of measurements to be used in evaluating the candidates.

Relationship between ratings made by pairs of supervisory personnel. The coefficients of correlation between the ratings made on each candidate by two members of supervision are shown in Table 3.

Table 3

RELATIONSHIP BETWEEN RATINGS MADE BY PAIRS OF SUPERVISORS

ITEM RATED	COEFFICIENT OF CORRELATION
Observing rules	.56
Personal appearance	.61
Quality of work	.61
Job knowledge	.63
Drive	.65
Quantity of work	.66
Cooperation	.67
General fitness for promotion	.71
Total of all items	.66

The coefficients, ranging from .56 to .71, indicate a fairly high degree of agreement between the members of supervision in rating workers on all items included in the rating scale. The over-all rating, general fitness for promotion, showed the highest degree of agreement although none of the differences between the items are clearly significant. The fairly high correlations indicate that members of supervision tend to base their ratings on similar observations of the workers' performance and to judge the various characteristics according to similar standards.

All of the coefficients reported in Table 3 exceed those reported in the previous comparisons and suggest a greater degree of agreement among members of supervision than among co-workers and between co-workers and members of supervision.

If the relationship is interpreted as a measure of reliability, then the supervisory ratings have a fairly high degree of reliability. The greater consistency of the supervisory ratings as compared with co-worker ratings suggests that the former are more dependable.

Comparison of the distributions of ratings by members of supervision and co-workers. The distributions of the ratings by the 200 members of supervision and the 200 co-workers on the items common to both rating forms are shown in Table 4.

The ratings of supervisors tend to be more conservative than those of the co-workers. This is evident in a comparison of the proportions of ratings of the two groups which are in the highest interval in the rating scale (step 5). For every characteristic rated a smaller proportion of the supervisory ratings is in the top interval than is true of co-worker rat-

Table 4

DISTRIBUTIONS OF RATINGS BY SUPERVISORS AND CO-WORKERS

ITEM RATED AND RATER	NUMBER OF RATINGS IN INTERVAL 1	2	3	4	5	MEAN OF RATINGS	STANDARD DEVIATION
Job knowledge							
Supervisors	1	8	73	80	38	3.73	.83
Co-workers	1	8	55	63	73	4.00	.92
Job performance–Quantity[a]							
Supervisors	0	5	84	68	43	3.74	.82
Co-workers	1	6	44	76	73	4.07	.86
Job performance–Quality							
Supervisors	0	1	56	86	57	4.00	.76
Co-workers	1	6	44	76	73	4.07	.86
Cooperation							
Supervisors	0	8	90	44	58	3.76	.92
Co-workers	1	10	41	67	81	4.08	.94
General fitness for promotion							
Supervisors	3	35	61	60	41	3.50	1.05
Co-workers	3	16	50	65	66	3.87	1.01

[a] Supervisory ratings on quality of work done and quantity of work done are compared with co-worker ratings on job performance which included both quality and quantity.

ings. In only one instance is the difference small enough to be attributed to chance (for job performance-quality, $P = .10$).

The tendency of supervisors to give lower ratings than co-workers is shown also in a comparison of the means of the various items rated. In every instance the mean of the supervisory ratings is lower than the mean of the co-worker ratings. The differences are significant at the 1% level, or better, with the exception of job performance-quality, where $P = .19$.

Very few of the workers were rated in the lowest category by either supervisors or co-workers. Since there had been some prior selection of the men (they had been proposed for consideration by either members of supervision or of Industrial Relations), it was expected that seldom would a candidate be rated as very unsatisfactory in any factor. Although the frequencies in the second interval are higher than in the lowest interval, the second interval is used in fewer than 5% of the ratings except for the over-all rating. For the item, general fitness for promotion, approximately 18% of the ratings of supervisory personnel and about 8% of the ratings of co-workers are in the next to the lowest interval.

The interval with the highest total frequency is the third, or average, interval for members of supervision and the fifth, or top, interval for co-workers. In the case of supervisors, for three of the five factors shown, the modal interval is step three, and for the other two factors is the fourth interval. For co-workers, step five is the modal interval for three of the four different factors shown. Thus, another method of analyzing the data shows that members of supervision tend to give lower ratings than do co-workers.

Several explanations might be suggested for the relatively low ratings given by members of supervision as compared with co-workers. Perhaps the status of supervisory personnel results in more realistic, less personal ratings. Also, members of supervision have had more training in the use of the rating form since many of them attend meetings of the Supervisory Selection Board. Some of them had reviewed the rating forms when the forms were being constructed.

Comparison of the individual items on the rating forms. In a comparison of ratings assigned to the various items shown in Table 4, it appears that the distribution for the final over-all ratings on suitability for promotion differs from the distributions on the other factors of ratings by both supervisors and co-workers. For example, the mean of the ratings for this factor is significantly lower than the mean of the ratings assigned any of the other items. A greater proportion of the ratings on this factor are in the two lowest intervals (below average) than is true of any other factor; however, only in the case of the supervisory ratings are the differences clearly significant.

The differences between the standard deviations for the ratings given by the two groups of raters are not statistically significant. The greatest variation in ratings of both groups is found in the ratings on general fitness for promotion.

When the final item, suitability for promotion to leadman, is compared with the total of the ratings on all other items in the rating forms, the correlations obtained are .85 for supervisors and .85 for co-workers. The coefficients approximate the ones reported in previous studies in which the same type of comparison was made (*3, 4*).

• SUMMARY AND CONCLUSIONS

A group of 100 men who were candidates for promotion to leadman jobs in the manufacturing division of an aircraft company were rated by members of supervision and by co-workers. Comparisons were made between ratings given each candidate by: (1) a member of supervision and a co-worker; (2) two members of supervision; and (3) two co-workers. The following conclusions are based on the results of these comparisons:

1. There is a low, positive degree of relationship between the ratings given by supervisory personnel and co-workers.
2. There is a slightly higher degree of agreement between the ratings of pairs of co-workers than between the ratings of members of supervision and co-workers. The correlations obtained indicate a moderately low to moderate statistical reliability for the co-worker ratings.
3. There is a much higher degree of agreement among the ratings given by members of supervision than among ratings given by co-workers. The correlations obtained indicate a fairly high statistical reliability for the supervisory ratings.
4. Supervisory personnel tend to rate the men lower than do co-workers on all items common to the two rating forms as shown by consistently lower mean ratings, by lower modal intervals, and

by a larger proportion of candidates considered below average on general fitness for promotion.

5. Both members of supervision and co-workers tend to be somewhat more conservative when rating the candidates on the over-all item, general fitness for promotion to leadman, than when rating individual characteristics.

6. There is a very high degree of relationship between the total of ratings on all separate characteristics and the ratings given on the single item, general fitness for promotion.

REFERENCES

1. Fleishman, E. A. The measurement of leadership attitudes in industry. *J. appl. Psychol.*, 1953, 37, 153–158.
2. Ghiselli, E. E. The use of the Strong Vocational Interest Blank and the Pressey Senior Classification Test in the selection of casualty insurance agents. *J. appl. Psychol.*, 1942, 26, 793–799.
3. Stead, W. H., Shartle, C. L., et al. *Occupational counseling techniques.* New York: American Book, 1940, pp. 49–72.
4. Tiffin, J. *Industrial psychology.* Englewood Cliffs, N.J.: Prentice-Hall, Inc., 1952, pp. 345–346.
5. Williams, S. B., and Leavitt, H. J. Group opinion as a prediction of military leadership. *J. consult. Psychol.*, 1947, 11, 283–291.

A NEW TOOL FOR SUPERVISORY SELF-DEVELOPMENT*

P. W. Maloney

and J. R. Hinrichs

Each year, American industry spends millions of dollars on supervisory development training programs, most of which train supervisors in the basic principles and techniques of management, often by means of role playing. Valuable though this training is, it does not, in most cases, provide the supervisor with the personalized guidance and help necessary for his effective development. It is a training axiom that all development is self-development—a process that, in turn, depends upon the trainee's full awareness of his weak and strong points. If a supervisory development training program does not give the supervisor this self-knowledge, it will inevitably fail in its ultimate goal.

With the aim of overcoming this limitation, Esso Research and Engineering Company has, for the past two years, been supplying its technical supervisors with a personalized analysis, made not by management, but by their subordinates. The program, called "Rate Your Supervisor," provides each supervisor with a personal report showing both how his men rate him and, for comparison purposes, how supervisors have been rated as a group. The technique is planned as an individual aid to growth—in other words, the entire program is geared to self-development. Thus, the individual supervisor is the only person in the company who knows how he was rated; he interprets the report as he wishes and then changes his performance, looks for help, or takes any other action he sees fit.

Before the actual rating begins, a thorough explanation of the program is made to all participating employees. (New ones are excluded.) This preparation includes giving to everyone involved in the program a copy of the company-prepared booklet entitled "Manual for Supervisory Evaluation by Subordinates." In most instances, a half-hour group presentation is also made jointly to all participants by Employee Relations and the management of the participating division.

• THE RATING FORM

The rating form itself, which is reproduced in the accompanying exhibit, can be summarized as follows.

Personal Traits

On a six-point scale, from "fits very well" to "doesn't fit at all," the rater indicates whether his supervisor is "considerate," "receptive to new ideas," an "apple polisher," and so forth—37 items in all.

Results

Here, morale and productivity in the *group* are rated from "tops" to "below average" (four items).

Methods

On 26 items, the supervisor's techniques are rated on a four-point scale.

* From *Personnel,* July-August 1959, pp. 46–53. Copyright 1959 by the American Management Association, Inc. Reprinted by permission.

Comments

Most meaty of all are five open-end items asking for the supervisor's strengths and weaknesses and for suggestions regarding his improvement.

Thus, the rating form is a diagnostic tool from which the supervisor should be able to see, through the eyes of his subordinates, the areas where he is in good shape and those in which he needs improvement.

In addition to filling out a rating form for his own supervisor, each rater also fills one out for the man to whom his supervisor reports. Finally, to build up the sample, a form is filled out for any supervisor for whom the rater has performed a reasonable amount of work during the 12-month period preceding the evaluation.

After the rating forms are filled out, they are sent to Employee Relations, where an individual report is prepared for each supervisor by precoding the forms for IBM key punching and producing a machine-processed card from each one. The numbers from this machine run go into the standardized personal report. In addition to being given the percentage breakdown of his own ratings on each item, the supervisor also receives a percentage breakdown of the ratings on all supervisors at his level in the company as a whole, as well as in his own division. The comment part of the rating form is paraphrased and included with the machine tabulation in the personal report.

• ANONYMITY THE KEY

Aside from its emphasis on self-development, the most important factor in the design of "Rate Your Supervisor" is its stress on anonymity. Before the program was put into operation, it was recognized that a rater would be most frank in his evaluations if he knew that no one but his own supervisor would see the report and that his own identity as a rater would be kept anonymous. Thus, anonymity is insured through the following steps:

1. Each supervisor is assigned a number which the rater writes in on the evaluation form. Thus, neither the supervisor's nor rater's name appears on the form.
2. Employee Relations tabulates and prepares the personal report for each *number*, not knowing whom it represents. To protect the rater, any idiosyncrasies of expression in the comments are washed out in the paraphrasing. (The impact and exact meaning are, of course, preserved.) For even further rater protection, no supervisor gets a report unless he has been rated by at least four people.
3. The personal reports, which are placed in individually sealed envelopes with the appropriate number written on the outside, are sent to a secretary in the division who is the sole holder of the name-number code list. She then adds the proper name to the envelope, and the report is sent to its final destination—the rated supervisor.

• RESULTS OF THE PROGRAM

Now for the key question—has the program paid off? Here's what we found from an opinion survey of both raters and ratees:

25 per cent of the subordinates said they had seen lasting changes in their supervisors.

SUPERVISOR EVALUATION FORM
(FOR USE BY SUBORDINATES)

SERIAL NO. OF SUPERVISOR YOU ARE RATING ______

HOW LONG HAVE YOU WORKED FOR HIM? ______

DATE ______

WHAT IS YOUR OWN LEVEL?

___ NON-SUPERVISORY

___ GROUP HEAD

___ SECTION HEAD

___ ASSISTANT DIRECTOR

A. CHECK LIST ON PERSONAL TRAITS

How well does each of the following words or phrases fit this man?	FITS VERY WELL	FITS FAIRLY WELL		DOESN'T FIT VERY WELL		DOESN'T FIT AT ALL
	1	2	3	4	5	6
Good technical man	___	___	___	___	___	___
Tactful	___	___	___	___	___	___
Indecisive	___	___	___	___	___	___
Considerate	___	___	___	___	___	___
Unselfish	___	___	___	___	___	___
Good listener	___	___	___	___	___	___
Easygoing	___	___	___	___	___	___
Scared of higher authority	___	___	___	___	___	___
Apple polisher	___	___	___	___	___	___
Good at handling people	___	___	___	___	___	___
Inexperienced	___	___	___	___	___	___
Puts things off	___	___	___	___	___	___
Regular guy	___	___	___	___	___	___
Plays favorites	___	___	___	___	___	___
Has confidence in his men	___	___	___	___	___	___
Good technical background	___	___	___	___	___	___
Honest	___	___	___	___	___	___
Stubborn	___	___	___	___	___	___
Too conservative	___	___	___	___	___	___
Sets good example	___	___	___	___	___	___

"Rate Your Supervisor" Evaluation Form (Page 1)

A. CHECK LIST ON PERSONAL TRAITS

How well does each of the following words or phrases fit this man?	FITS VERY WELL 1	FITS FAIRLY WELL 2	3	DOESN'T FIT VERY WELL 4	5	DOESN'T FIT AT ALL 6
Immature	____	____	____	____	____	____
Helpful	____	____	____	____	____	____
Fair	____	____	____	____	____	____
Receptive to new ideas	____	____	____	____	____	____
Jumps to conclusions	____	____	____	____	____	____
Hard worker	____	____	____	____	____	____
Treats people like numbers	____	____	____	____	____	____
Not forceful enough	____	____	____	____	____	____
Doesn't know how to delegate	____	____	____	____	____	____
Overemphasizes petty details	____	____	____	____	____	____
Has the respect of his men	____	____	____	____	____	____
Technically competent	____	____	____	____	____	____
Lacks backbone	____	____	____	____	____	____
Aggressive	____	____	____	____	____	____
Does most of the talking	____	____	____	____	____	____
When you ask him a question, he gives you or gets you an answer	____	____	____	____	____	____
Wants his men to get ahead	____	____	____	____	____	____

B. CHECK LIST ON RESULTS

How would you rate the group(s) this man supervises:	"TOPS" 1	BETTER THAN MOST 2	ABOVE AVERAGE 3	AVERAGE 4	BELOW AVERAGE 5
On "esprit de corps" (team spirit)	____	____	____	____	____
On creativity	____	____	____	____	____
On importance of project assignment	____	____	____	____	____
On over-all performance	____	____	____	____	____

"Rate Your Supervisor" Evaluation Form (Page 2)

C. Check List on Job Methods

How satisfied are you with the way this man:	VERY DIS-SATISFIED 1	SOMEWHAT DIS-SATISFIED 2	REASON-ABLY SATISFIED 3	VERY SATISFIED 4
Assigns work projects and outlines what he wants done	____	____	____	____
Gives you room for individual initiative	____	____	____	____
Considers your personal wishes in making assignments	____	____	____	____
Listens to your ideas and suggestions and uses them	____	____	____	____
Trains and helps you do your job better	____	____	____	____
Keeps up to date on what you are doing	____	____	____	____
Lets you know when he has criticisms of your work	____	____	____	____
Lets you know when he thinks you have done a good job	____	____	____	____
Explains his criticisms and the changes he suggests	____	____	____	____
Gives you the technical help and advice you need	____	____	____	____
Lets you make the decisions you should make	____	____	____	____
Sees that your abilities are fully used	____	____	____	____
Lets you know what you need to do to get ahead	____	____	____	____
Admits his own errors	____	____	____	____

"Rate Your Supervisor" Evaluation Form (Page 3)

C. Check List on Job Methods—*Continued*

How satisfied are you with the way this man:	VERY DIS-SATISFIED 1	SOMEWHAT DIS-SATISFIED 2	REASON-ABLY SATISFIED 3	VERY SATISFIED 4
Stimulates you to do good work	______	______	______	______
Keeps you informed on matters affecting you and your work	______	______	______	______
Plans and organizes the work of his unit	______	______	______	______
Stands up for you, when necessary, to higher management	______	______	______	______
Has authority to make the decisions you feel he should make	______	______	______	______
Makes you feel you are working with, rather than for, him	______	______	______	______
Is willing to sit down and help you with technical problems	______	______	______	______
Is able to sell his ideas to higher management	______	______	______	______
Is able to give you competent technical help	______	______	______	______
Makes prompt decisions affecting the output of his group	______	______	______	______
Keeps work from piling up on his desk for clearance	______	______	______	______
Sticks with his decisions once they're made	______	______	______	______

"Rate Your Supervisor" Evaluation Form (Page 3 *continued*)

D. Summary Evaluation

1. Over-all, what kind of a job would you say this man is doing?
   What do you think of the results he gets? The methods he uses?

2. Do you like working for him?
   Why? Or, why not?

3. In what respects is he a good supervisor?

4. What are his main shortcomings?

5. What do you think he can do about these shortcomings?

"Rate Your Supervisor" Evaluation Form (Page 4)

88 per cent of the supervisors said they had tried to change after getting their reports.

75 per cent of the supervisors wanted a second run.

60 per cent of both supervisors and subordinates agreed that productivity had been favorably affected by the program.

Apparently, then, the ratings do provide the supervisors with some eye-opening insights into their performance. Indeed, in the opinion survey, 63 per cent of the supervisors said that some of their ratings were totally unexpected. In 88 per cent of these cases, at least some of the surprise ratings were unfavorable. Nevertheless, only 7 per cent of the supervisors felt that their ratings were not valid. In fact, most of them took their reports quite seriously. Only 3 per cent had read them casually, whereas 43 percent said they had studied them carefully on receipt. More than half have referred to their reports repeatedly, and a third have even gone so far as to discuss them with their own bosses.

The general interest taken in the program may be deduced from the fact that, though participation is completely voluntary, 70 per cent of the ratings which could have been expected have been turned in—over 2,000. Actually, though—as has been said—three-quarters of all supervisors wanted a rerun, among first-level supervisors the proportion ran as high as 94 per cent. Even among the members of higher management (the program stopped just short of the VP level) two-thirds also asked for another round.

In view of such evidence, RYS will be rerun at Esso Research. At present, however, it is planned to make the personal reports even more valuable by adding more information. It is hoped, for instance, that factor analysis of the ratings will identify areas of supervisory performance as measured by RYS. Thus, a supervisor's personal report could contain a profile-type breakdown showing him how he stands in areas like communications, technical ability, or human relations, providing him with an even broader base for self-development.

EMPLOYEE SELF-APPRAISAL FOR IMPROVED PERFORMANCE*

William B. Hall

The problems we face in the banking business are similar to those of any service organization. The product we sell—service—is produced by our staff. Its quality is dependent on their attitude and actions. The degree of acceptance by the public is accurately measured in terms of growth and, more important, profits.

When we approached this subject three years ago, problems we would normally face were accentuated by two factors:

1. Our growth from December, 1932, to December, 1948—

   Employees: 235 to 1,025
   Customers: 82,000 to 344,000
   Deposits: $40,000,000 to $550,000,000

2. Loss of qualified personnel during World War II—many of whom did not return to us at the close of the war.

As a partial solution to these problems, we developed the program which I shall now describe.

• BACKGROUND

For the past three years we have had in effect at The Detroit Bank a revised and unusually comprehensive performance rating plan, one of the features of which is a self-appraisal by each employee to supplement supervisory ratings.

One of the considerations that led us to adopt the program was the need to establish a favorable "climate" for management and staff discussions on employee performance. Whether it is at home or in the office, most of us try to avoid unpleasant discussions. We search for reasons to avoid or postpone talking to people if it involves critical comment. Usually we wait until we have built up a head of steam to bolster our courage. The result is that what we say and the way we say it creates an unfavorable climate in which it is impossible to cultivate an understanding. Discussion of staff performance produces best results only if the interviewer and the one interviewed approach it with a comprehension of the basic reasons for it and minds open to accept suggestions and constructive criticism. The discussion must be a natural, periodic function of management and understood as such by both staff and supervisors.

Another consideration was the need for a continuing staff inventory. Our "merchandise" is the day-to-day performance of our staff. The quality of the merchandise is a direct reflection of the quality of the staff. If a merchant must continually review his inventory to improve its sales appeal, so must we in our business continually review our staff inventory toward improvement, promotion, reassignment, or release.

* From *Tools for Improved Personnel Relations*, New York, American Management Association, 1951, pp. 29–34. (Personnel series no. 140.)

Moreover, salary costs had increased considerably and there was every indication they would continue to do so. A successful operation demanded we obtain a greater yield for each dollar of salary cost, and we recognized that attaining this objective depended on human actions.

Another factor was the desirability of training management in staff direction and leadership. Those of us charged with personnel administration must give our management group a better understanding of the human factor in our business and, at the same time, train them to approach and solve human problems in a constructive manner.

Finally, there was the problem of the supervisory group, which of necessity has the primary responsibility of staff training. Reducing it to individual application, the question was raised as to what was being done with each employee to give him a better understanding of his work, his responsibilities, and his opportunities.

Could a program be developed that would include steps to insure meeting the foregoing problems? That was the assignment we were given approximately three years ago. In the analysis of our personnel policies and procedures, it seemed logical that the starting point should be merit rating.

Merit rating had been used in our bank for about 10 years. Included were a variety of ideas and forms, many copied from other banks and industries, but none designed to fit our particular needs. Examination of the ratings indicated in many cases there was no uniformity on the part of the raters. There was a tendency by some to rate in superlatives, while others were much more conservative. This in turn was reflected in the individual salaries paid and promotions. Ratings were prepared by the branch manager or department head only, and in many cases he was too far removed from the employee to be completely familiar with day-to-day performance. *The merit ratings were not reviewed with the employees in many instances although every form asked the question "Has this been discussed with the employee?" and in all cases the answer was affirmative.*

A study was made of the merit rating procedures followed by approximately 50 companies representing banks and industry. Out of this we selected a combination of ideas and added some of our own to form the program which, with some modifications, we have followed for about three years with definite benefit both to the staff and management.

• A FOUR-STEP PROGRAM

It is called our *Four-Step Program.* Included is an *Employee Self-Appraisal;* a *Two-Way Individual Management Appraisal* involving the department head or branch manager and immediate supervisor; a *Three-Way Interview* including the department head or branch manager, immediate supervisor and employee; and finally the *Panel Review,* with the executive vice president in charge of operations, the vice president of personnel administration, and the manager of the personnel department reviewing ratings with the branch manager or department head.

While designed for use in a bank with more than 1,000 employees, the program can be adapted for use in any size organization. *It is recommended, however, only if the complete procedure is fol-*

lowed. The elimination of any of the four steps will definitely limit the plan's value. Following is a more complete description of the procedures and their advantages.

Employee Self-Appraisal

Each employee completes an appraisal of himself, on a form provided for that purpose. Our experience has shown that staff members can and will do it accurately and will take pride in doing it well, *provided they are fully informed in advance of what it's all about.* Employee appraisals as a rule are remarkably correct. The best employees tend, modestly, to underrate themselves. Problem employees may overrate themselves.

The self-appraisal process lets people know what is expected of them, and the factors of measurement. It enables employees to give their opinions of their own performance, lets them indicate work preferences, and provides a medium for stating any grievances. It removes secrecy from management reviews; all employees know they are regularly rated, and this plan tells them how and why. Self-analysis encourages self-improvement and development, helps employees grow. Moreover, a record of performance is provided which can be used for employee protection in case of mistreatment by a supervisor.

Two-Way Management Appraisal

In this second step, the department or branch manager and the immediate supervisor independently prepare an appraisal on the employee. The two appraisals are then jointly reviewed to reconcile any major differences in the ratings, in preparation for the interview with the employee. Also, the manager selects the factors he will cover in the employee interview, and assigns the other factors to his assistant. This gives assurance that the assistant will have a part in the discussion and utilize his more intimate knowledge of work performance by the staff member. Factors assigned to the assistant usually include accuracy, quality, and quantity.

The dual appraisal promotes objective thinking about the employee, since it is necessary to substantiate all ratings. It helps to train the second man prior to his becoming a manager. The plan also encourages analysis of the staff training program, provides a method to tell whether it is effective, and leads to the development of special programs to suit individual employees.

Three-Way Interview

Under this third step an interview is arranged between the employee and the two management representatives. Each factor is discussed, and the method by which this is done will determine the success or failure of the interview. It must be constructive and factual, and include compliments for work well done as well as suggestions for work improvement where necessary.

This process provides increased recognition of the employee as an individual, and affords an ideal opportunity for a frank discussion with him on his performance. Since this discussion is preplanned, it is more objective and less emotional. The assistant is brought into the discussion, which provides for his training on conducting interviews, and indicates to employees that the assistant is a part of management. The three-way interview offers an excellent chance for supervisors to build good will with employees.

Panel Review

In this final step the department or branch manager reviews all three appraisals with representatives of the Operations, Personnel, and Personnel Administration Departments. During the panel review every available record affecting the employee is at hand. While the manager is discussing his appraisal, the panel members are reviewing the appraisals of his assistant and the employee, and rating the rater.

At the conclusion, the panel in cooperation with the manager establishes for the employee an over-all rating, ranging from one to seven. A rating of "one" indicates he should be promoted immediately and "seven" denotes he probably should be replaced. The ratings between these two extremes indicate grades of performance. The summary of these ratings constitutes the basis of our inventory which is used in considering promotions, transfers, and releases.

This panel review affords the best method we know to reach a final unbiased employee appraisal. It permits the funneling of all ratings through one body, and thereby makes for a greater uniformity of ratings. It makes possible a qualitative inventory of the entire staff, recording those qualified for promotion or additional assignments, eligible for transfer, or slated for replacement. Training needs are indicated, and a pattern is provided for training programs. A more equitable control of salary adjustments is made possible, and the plan also assists in making operational improvements. Top management has a better opportunity to judge the ability of supervisors to handle personnel problems. And the review helps management to know employees better, and to have a better understanding of their problems.

The first time this panel procedure was used, covering all the staff, reassignments were given to 21 employees receiving the bottom rating of seven, or unsatisfactory. Subsequent appraisals have rated all of these employees as satisfactory performers. This was a major salvage operation of people, representing a saving to the bank far in excess of any cost of the program. This experience has been repeated on almost every appraisal. Appraisals are now being held on a quarterly basis for employees whose anniversaries occur in the period.

• EXPLAINING THE EVALUATION PROCEDURE

Our performance evaluation procedure, particularly the first step involving employee self-appraisal, is a departure from the usual merit rating.

To be successful it must be understood. To be understood, the objectives must be carefully reviewed with the management group and the staff.

To accomplish this, we followed a definite pattern. First, of course, was its acceptance by our executive officers. Our recommendations covering the plan were completely reviewed by Charles H. Hewitt, Executive Vice President in charge of operations, who is directly charged with the responsibility of maintaining an adequate and qualified staff, and also with Joseph M. Dodge, President of our bank.

We next arranged meetings with our management group at which time the plan was described to them. Both Mr.

Dodge and Mr. Hewitt attended these meetings to support, advise, and counsel.

We recognized that one of the objections to the program on the part of the management group would be the time involved in completing the appraisals. However, we also realized that people will more readily accept and support programs which they have helped to prepare. So, we asked our branch managers and department heads to aid us in the preparation of the appraisal or merit rating form. *The primary value of any appraisal report is that it serves as a basis for constructive discussion between the employee and the supervisor.* The factors measured and the questions asked in the form itself should be selected with that thought in mind.

A merit or appraisal form should be tailor-made to fit the needs of the user. Our management group, the one which would do the rating, selected the factors to be included; the form thus became their own and this assured its acceptance. Definitions were provided for each factor selected so there would be a like understanding by all. At the time of rating, each factor selected must be supported with reasons for its selection, thus avoiding the check-off system and requiring constructive thinking on the part of each rater. The form also asks the employee to give a description of his job duties. This enables us to compare actual jobs assigned with the job description, and has been utilized many times in changing employee classifications. Also included in the form is the question, "What is the program for improvement of this employee?"

A separate form is used for rating supervisors. It includes factors not covered in general staff appraisals.

If the staff and the raters were sufficiently trained, a comparatively simple form could be used. It could be merely in question form without measuring specific factors—questions designed to indicate employee performance, potential, and training programs.

• TRAINING MANAGEMENT IN THE INTERVIEW PROCEDURE

Having arrived at the steps to be followed and the form to be used, and having sold them to the management and representative employees of the staff, the next problem was training management representatives in interview procedure. The three-way appraisal would be effective only if management representatives knew how to conduct an interview properly. In this phase of management training, we used an adaptation of the Massachusetts Institute of Technology "Role Playing Technique." The procedure is as familiar to us as the game of "Let's Pretend," which we played as children. Groups of management representatives met with us and typical interviews were held. A number of the management representatives took part in these staged interviews and the balance of the management group learned the procedure by analyzing, criticizing, and suggesting.

• EDUCATING EMPLOYEES IN APPRAISAL PROCEDURE

A letter was then prepared for the employee group describing the appraisal procedure, outlining the benefits to employees, and asking for their assistance. This letter was signed by President Dodge. Each of the departments and branches held a staff meeting at which time the letter was read, followed by a discussion and a complete review of the form to be used. Staff members were given ample opportunity to offer comments and were permitted to keep the forms and the letter. At subsequent meetings it was again discussed with them. They were informed they could retain their appraisals after discussion if they so desired.

In our research we had been told that employees would not want to rate themselves, and if they did, the appraisals would not be factual. Our experience has shown this to be completely wrong. That employees like to discuss their performance is indicated by the National Industrial Conference Board *Preview* of December 23, 1950, which said:

> How many employees, given an opportunity, wish to sit down with their supervisors to discuss themselves and their jobs? The Northwestern Mutual Life Insurance Company of Milwaukee, Wisconsin, wondered about the answer to this question as applied to its own organization. It studied the merit-rating reports covering a full calendar year. During this period, 828 employees were rated by their supervisors and, in accordance with the union agreement, were invited to talk things over. Only 38 employees declined the invitation extended to them by their supervisors!

• BENEFITS OF SELF-APPRAISAL

Our appraisal plan is admittedly time consuming. Benefits, however, far outweigh the effort expended. It has created a favorable climate for our conferences between the staff and the supervisors. It has given to our supervisors and employees a new understanding of their responsibilities and opportunities, and has improved the quality of their performance. It has also brought them closer to an understanding of management objectives. Two of the most fundamental human desires are for security and for an opportunity to improve one's status. This plan helps each employee to know where he stands, where is he strong or weak, and how he can improve. It has provided a basis for more effective salary adjustments and more considered selection of people for advancement, transfer, or release.

Most important, it has given management a better over-all understanding of the importance of the human relations phase of our business.

RATING SCALE CONTENT: III. RELATIONSHIPS BETWEEN SUPERVISORY- AND SELF-RATINGS*

J. W. Parker, E. K. Taylor, R. S. Barrett, and L. Martens

SUMMARY AND CONCLUSIONS

Four different ratings were completed on each of a group of clerical workers. Two of these were supervisory ratings. The third was a self-rating by the worker. The fourth was an estimate by the worker of his supervisor's ratings. Analysis of mean differences showed Self-ratings to be most lenient. Estimate-ratings were almost exactly halfway between Self- and Rater-ratings.

These data question the value of using self-ratings as a basis for performance review discussions between superiors and subordinates. An analysis of the intercorrelations among the scales for the several categories of ratings revealed rather striking differences between the ways in which superiors and workers viewed the relationship between personal and job traits.

Multiple correlational analysis indicated that the seven subscales accounted for a substantial portion of the variance of the Over-all rating of all categories of raters. More of this variance was accounted for by the subscales in the ratings rendered by the superiors than was the case in Self- or Estimate-ratings made by the workers. Practically all of the covariance of the Over-all scale could be accounted for by three subscales—Amount of work done, Quality of work done, and Conscientiousness.

INTRODUCTION

Analysis of the data collected for the project entitled "Influence of Rating Scale Construction Upon the Characteristics of Ratings Rendered," demonstrates some interesting differences between the ratings made by supervisory personnel and the ratings completed by the ratees themselves. The project was designed to study the effect of the amount of information on the scales given to the rater on the ratings rendered. The information supplied the rater varied from Format I which included only a trait name, Format II which had a trait definition only, Format III which had a trait name and scale-level descriptions, to Format IV which included both trait definition and scale-level descriptions. The reader is referred to the previous two articles in this series (*1, 2*) for the discussion of the effects of the four formats and the results obtained with the eight scales of the form. The results discussed in this article are those obtained with Format III. The relationships between supervisory- and

---

NOTE. This research was supported by the Office of Naval Research under Contract No. Nonr 2221(00) between ONR and the Personnel Research and Development Corporation.

* From *Personnel Psychology,* Vol. 12, no. 1, Spring 1959, pp. 49–63.

self-ratings were found to be consistent across the four formats. Since Format III was the best of the four formats on all of the various criterion measures used, it was felt that the presentation of results for the one format would be sufficient.

As discussed in Art. II (*2*), the eight scales of traits of the rating form can be divided into three categories. First, the Over-all rating—Scale 8—as its name implies was designed to provide a single comprehensive measure of the individual's effectiveness. The second type of scale is the person-oriented scale. The scales in this category are Scale 1—Ability to work with others, Scale 4—Leadership potential, and Scale 7—Conscientiousness. The third type is the job-oriented scale represented by Scale 2—Amount of work done, Scale 3—Quality of work done, Scale 5—Ability to do complicated jobs, and Scale 6—Ability to work with minimum supervision.

Throughout the discussion, reference will be made to the second and third types—the person-oriented scales and the job-oriented scales.

As a part of this project, in addition to obtaining ratings by first-level and second-level supervisors called "Raters" and "Endorsers," respectively, the ratees themselves were asked to complete ratings on how they would rate themselves on the various traits. This type of rating is known as "Self-rating." After the worker had rated himself, he was given an additional form and asked to estimate how he thought his supervisor had rated him on the various traits. This type of rating is known as the "Estimate-rating." Therefore, two types of ratings have been secured: supervisory ratings as measured by Rater-ratings and Endorser-ratings, and self-ratings as measured by Self-ratings and Estimate-ratings.

• LENIENCY

The tendency of raters to be generous in their recorded evaluations of subordinates' performance is too well documented to require further elaboration here. In spite of this rater-leniency, it was hypothesized that the ratees would afford themselves even higher ratings than those that they received from their superiors, and that their awareness that their bosses did not share their self-concept would be demonstrated in the fact that Estimate-ratings would fall somewhere between Self- and Supervisory-ratings.

In constructing the scales used in this project, it was expected that the mean rating would have a value of 8.0 on all scales. This is purely arbitrary. It might be found that, since the scales were not subjected to scaling techniques, the mean might have a value different from 8.0. However, for discussion purposes, this mean of 8.0 will be used as a point of departure.

Table 1 presents the means, scale-mean differences, and standard deviations for the eight scales for the supervisory- and self-ratings. Comparisons of the average mean ratings rendered by Rater-, Self-, and Estimate-ratings show that all were lenient. The average mean rating for Rater-ratings was .8 scale units above the expected mean of 8.0. The average mean rating for Self-ratings was 2.4 scale units above the expected mean, and the average mean rating for Estimate-ratings was 1.6 scale units above the expected mean. It is immediately evident that the Self-rating is much more lenient than either the Rater-rating or the Estimate-rating, being nearly one standard deviation unit away. As had been hypothe-

Table 1

MEANS, SCALE MEAN DIFFERENCES, AND STANDARD DEVIATIONS FOR SUPERVISORY- AND SELF-RATINGS (Format III, $N = 117$)

	MEANS			SCALE MEAN DIFFERENCES			STANDARD DEVIATIONS		
SCALE	RATER	SELF	ESTI-MATE	SELF-RATER	ESTI-RATER	SELF-ESTI.	RATER	SELF	ESTI-MATE
1. Ability to work with others	8.9	10.7	9.8	1.75	.88	.87	2.5	1.9	2.4
2. Amount of work done	9.4	10.5	9.8	1.04	.38	.66	2.7	2.3	2.0
3. Quality of work done	9.5	10.4	9.7	.94	.18	.76	2.4	1.8	1.9
4. Leadership potential	5.9	8.9	8.2	3.01	2.22	.79	3.0	2.4	2.4
5. Ability to do complicated jobs	8.5	10.4	9.3	1.87	.77	1.10	2.4	2.0	2.0
6. Ability to work with minimum supervision	9.2	11.6	10.2	2.44	1.04	1.40	2.9	2.4	2.3
7. Conscientiousness	8.9	10.4	9.7	1.47	.77	.70	2.8	1.9	2.3
8. Over-all performance	9.8	10.5	10.2	.69	.43	.26	2.6	1.8	2.0
Average–Total	8.8	10.4	9.6	1.65	.84	.82	–	–	–
Average–Personal scales	7.9	10.0	9.2	2.08	1.29	.79	–	–	–
Average–Job scales	9.2	10.7	9.8	1.57	.59	.98	–	–	–

sized, the workers have a relatively high opinion of themselves. Apparently, however, they have the idea that their supervisors will not think as highly of them as they think of themselves. This stereotyped conception of supervision operates on all of the eight scales, and varies from the smallest difference on Scale 8–Over-all performance–to the greatest variance in opinion on Scale 4–Leadership potential. Also interesting is the fact that the Estimate-rating was approximately half-way between the average mean rating for the Rater- and Self-ratings.

Turning to the individual scales, comparison was made between the Self-ratings and the Rater-ratings. The average scale-mean difference between Rater- and Self-ratings for the job oriented scales was 1.6 and the scale-mean difference for the person-oriented scales, 2.1.

Much of this difference can be accounted for by Scale 4–Leadership potential. While the mean on this scale was substantially lower for both supervisory-ratings (5.9) and self-ratings (8.9), the difference (3.0) was substantially greater for this than for any other scale. In Part II of this report, we addressed ourselves to consideration of ten possible reasons why ratings on this scale were so much less lenient than on any of the others. Self-ratings on "Leadership potential" were relatively almost as severe as were supervisors' ratings. The average clerk was described by his superior as belonging in the upper portion of a range whose midpoint is described as "Would have some success as a supervisor but could not lead a work unit as well as most." The word "most" is, of course, ambiguous in this context. If it were interpreted as referring to "most successful supervisors" by the Raters who might logically be expected to have such a frame of reference, their extensive use of this category is quite understandable.

Ratees, on the other hand, quite possibly interpreted the term as applying to "most other workers of my age, grade, and experience." If this were the case, they would logically be expected to spurn this rating category and concentrate on the less negative middle point which read "Appears to have neither good nor poor potential for a supervisor's job; would have average success in this capacity."

Also noteworthy with respect to this scale is the fact that the difference between Self- and Estimate-ratings was not greater than for the other scales. This would appear to indicate that the ratees were not at all sensitive to whatever it was that caused their superiors to rate them so much lower than they rated themselves on this scale.

The comparison between the Self-rating and the Estimate-rating demonstrated practically no difference in the scale-mean differences. The average scale-mean difference for job-oriented scales was 1.0 and the average scale-mean difference for person-oriented scales 0.8. We can conclude from these data that the greatest average difference occurs when supervisory- and self-ratings are compared. When comparing the two self-ratings, this difference does not hold up. It can be hypothesized from these figures that the employees are aware that their supervisors do not hold the same opinion of their job performances as they hold themselves. However, even though they are aware that there is a difference, they generally underestimate the magnitude of this difference.

To the extent that it is possible to generalize from these limited data, it would appear that for a large proportion of ratees, performance evaluation is a disappointing experience. There are several reports in the literature of situations in which personnel rate themselves and then compare these self-ratings with similar ratings by their superiors. In many such instances, it is reported that the subordinate is much harder on himself than his superior is in rating him. These data tend to refute such findings—and probably with good cause.

In the present study, supervisors' ratings were collected first. When the ratee groups were gathered, they were informed of this fact. They were asked to complete ratings of themselves with the assurance that they were only for experimental purposes and that they *would not be shown to their respective supervisors.* After they had completed their Self-ratings, new forms were passed out and they were asked to estimate how their respective supervisors had rated them. Again they were reassured that their Estimate-ratings would be treated confidentially.

Modesty—even false modesty—is a desirable characteristic in our culture. It may be hypothesized that in rendering self-ratings that will be reviewed by his superior, the average employee is "playing it safe." Consciously or otherwise, he rates himself much more harshly than his true self-evaluation would justify because

1. he knows that his superior has a lower opinion of him than he himself has;
2. it is impolite to appear immodest; and

3. by artificial self-deprecation, the subordinate is able to take a good deal of the sting out of any criticism his superior may intend to levy at him.

To the extent that these conjectures are valid, the use of self-ratings on a "for keeps" basis as a developmental tool may be both deceptive and defeating of their purpose.

CORRELATIONAL ANALYSIS

Table 2 presents the intercorrelations among the scales for the Rater-, Self-, and Estimate-ratings and, in addition, gives the mean z-transformed correlations for each of the levels of ratings.

Table 2

INTERCORRELATIONS AMONG SCALES FOR RATER-, SELF-, AND ESTIMATE-RATINGS
($N = 117$, Decimal points omitted)

CORRELATIONS BETWEEN SCALE NOS.	RATER-RATINGS	SELF-RATINGS	ESTIMATE-RATINGS
1–2	19	36	30
1–3	33	41	40
1–4	38	41	52
1–5	28	28	44
1–6	31	32	33
1–7	36	43	49
1–8	36	39	40
2–3	60	45	62
2–4	38	41	41
2–5	58	44	57
2–6	63	45	52
2–7	73	49	58
2–8	83	69	63
3–4	38	41	47
3–5	68	48	61
3–6	68	52	55
3–7	54	60	67
3–8	79	62	71
4–5	53	58	55
4–6	51	49	42
4–7	44	43	53
4–8	44	54	49
5–6	72	53	60
5–7	51	43	59
5–8	71	52	62
6–7	53	37	63
6–8	72	45	62
7–8	81	67	74
Mean r_z (omitting scale 8)	51	45	52

Comparison of the mean intercorrelations for the Self- and Estimate-ratings with the supervisory ratings shows that the Self-ratings average 6 correlation points lower than the Rater-ratings, and that the Estimate-ratings average 11 correlation points lower than the Rater-ratings.

As pointed out in Part I (*1*) of this report, the intercorrelations of the scales (particularly in Format III) were found to be somewhat lower than those which are ordinarily obtained in multi-trait graphic rating scales. In the self-ratings, the intercorrelations among the traits averaged lower than Rater-ratings (.45 vs. .51). Of the 21 correlations between pairs of traits (omitting the Over-all) there was one tie (1 vs. 5). In 11 comparisons, the rater correlations exceeded the self-rating correlations. In the remaining 9 comparisons, the intercorrelations of self-ratings exceeded those of supervisors' ratings.

Of the 10 instances in which intercorrelations of self-ratings equaled or exceeded those of supervisors' ratings, nine involved Traits 1—Ability to work with others—or 4—Leadership potential. Stated conversely, in *all* of the intercorrelations involving Trait 1, those of self-ratings equaled or exceeded the supervisors' ratings. With respect to Trait 4, this statement may be made for five of the seven intercorrelations involved. In the two exceptions (4 vs. 6 and 4 vs. 7) the differences are .02 and .01, respectively.

Examination of the correlations of the several traits with the Over-all shows a similar relationship to exist. For Traits 1 and 4, the correlations for the self-ratings exceed those of the supervisors by .03 and .10, respectively. For the other five scales, the correlation with the Over-all averages .18 higher for the supervisor than for the self-ratings.

These relationships give rise to some interesting speculations which may be summarized as follows:

1. Employees are at best only moderately more able than their superiors in making discriminations concerning their own behavior.

2. Superiors are inclined to base their generalized reaction to subordinates on production variables to a much larger extent than on "personal" factors. While the individual also stresses production, he gives more weight to the "personal" factor than do the supervisors.

3. In estimating an individual's over-all value to an organization, both stress production factors more than personal factors. Thus, there appears to be a recognition, at least in this population, of the importance of productivity. This suggests that there is possibly less discrepancy between the job concepts of superiors and subordinates than some writers on the topic may have led us to expect. It also questions the way in which the "people"-minded supervisors might be perceived by subordinates who are themselves "production"-minded.

That the differences that do exist are appreciated, in part at least, by the employees is evidenced by a comparison among the three columns in Table 2. While the trend is not as marked here as it is in the case of the means, the intercorrelations among the Estimate-ratings appear generally to be a compromise between those in the Rater-rating and those in the Self-rating column.

The correlations between the several classifications of ratings are provided in Table 3. Rater-Endorser ratings are included since these, having been taken as the best estimate of interrater reliability available, provide a basis for comparison. The most obvious though not surprising finding in these data is that the correlations between self- and supervisory-ratings are, in all instances,

Table 3

CORRELATIONS BETWEEN COMBINATIONS OF SUPERVISORY- AND SELF-RATINGS
(N = 117, Decimal points omitted)

SCALE	R-EN	R-S	R-ES	S-ES	$1\text{-}r^2_{SES}$
1. Ability to work with others	59	13	17	56	69
2. Amount of work done	74	53	55	66	56
3. Quality of work done	72	37	43	64	59
4. Leadership potential	52	19	28	58	66
5. Ability to do complicated jobs	67	28	42	46	79
6. Ability to work with minimum supervision	67	30	32	44	81
7. Conscientiousness	61	41	50	60	64
8. Over-all performance	77	35	48	64	59
Mean r_z	67	33	40	58	–

substantially lower than the reliabilities of the scales involved. The least agreement occurs in the two most "personal" scales, 1 and 4. These, it should be noted, are also the least reliable scales. With an N of 117, a one-tailed test of significance requires a value of .22 to be certain at the 1% level of confidence that the relationship exceeds zero. Neither of these correlations (scales 1 and 4) attain this level. The Rater-Self correlations for all of the other traits exceed it by a comfortable margin.

The highest Rater-Self correlation is only .53 (Amount of work done) and the correlation between the Over-all only .35. Clearly, then, there are some rather extensive disagreements between self-concepts and those of superiors. This is not merely a matter of the leniency of self-raters, since adding a constant to each superior's rating would not alter these relationships.

These low correlations could have resulted from any one or a combination of several factors:

1. Workers lack insight into their strength and weaknesses.
2. Supervisors are unable or unwilling to recognize merit in their subordinates.
3. Supervisors are insensitive or indifferent to weaknesses on the part of their subordinates.
4. Supervisors rate to a large degree on the basis of personal bias.
5. Supervisors have a tendency toward being harsh or lenient without reference to any established standards.

That the workers have some appreciation of the direction in which and the extent to which self-ratings will differ from supervisors' rating is evidenced by the fact that all of the correlations between Rater- and Estimate-ratings are higher than the correlations between Rater- and Self-ratings. That this appreciation is not very great is demonstrated by the fact that the average improvement is approximately seven correlation points and for none of the traits do the Rater-Estimate correlations come within ten points of the reliability.

For only one trait does the correlation between Self-ratings and Estimate-ratings exceed the reliability (Leadership potential). For two others, it comes quite close (Ability to work with others and Conscientiousness). These, it may be noted, are the "personal" traits. The magnitude of these correlations (granting certain assumptions) may be taken as an index of the rater's confidence in his superior's competence as a rater. If self-ratings were sincere (and we assume them to be) and confidence were complete, we would expect Self- and Estimate-ratings to correlate unity. We may take the column headed $1 - r_{SEs}^{2}$ as the raters' estimate of the superiors' variance of rating error.

The fact that the Rater-Self correlations are all lower than the Rater-Estimate correlations shows that the workers had more confidence that their superiors would rate them as they rated themselves than the data justify. Employees, however, are aware that they will not be rated as they think they should be and they are unable to predict their superiors' rating behavior at all well.

Thus, it may be concluded, that while both groups indicate that the seven subscales account for a substantial proportion of their over-all value to the organization, this is, however, much more true of the supervisors than of the workers themselves. The latter say, in effect, that 31% of their value to the organization is attributable to factors other than the seven that were considered in this study. The data collected offer no suggestions with reference to what these may be.

It may also be noted that in estimating the ratings rendered, the employees expected their superiors to consider factors not incorporated in the subscales to a much greater degree than the superiors actually did. It is not, of course, implied that these are conscious reactions on the part of the workers. Rather they are inferences based upon the obtained correlational relationship between the subscales and the Over-all scale for the several categories of ratings.

Further analysis of the data consisted of computing the coefficients between the first seven scales and Scale 8—Over-all performance. These results are presented in Table 4. The Rater and Endorser multiple correlations were very close; .94 and .92, respectively. Also very close were the Self and Estimate multiple *R*'s; .83 and .82, respectively. The Rater *R* of .94 accounts for 88% of the variance of the Over-all while the Self *R* of .83 accounts for only 69% of the variance. While both of these multiple correlations are high, the 11 correlation point difference indicates that for the Rater, the seven traits predict the "Over-all performance" scale to a greater degree than they do for the Self-ratings.

The weights for the seven scales are also presented in Table 4. These weights have been corrected for each of the rater-levels by dividing the obtained beta's by the sum of the beta's for that rater-level. This correction enables comparisons to be made between the various rater-levels. Examination of the β' weights, indicating the relative contribution of each scale toward the Over-all, showed that certain scales have small β' weights consistent across Rater- and Self-ratings. This is true for Scale 1—Ability to work with others, Scale 5—Ability to do complicated jobs, and to some extent, Scale 4—Leadership potential. The largest consistent contributors are Scale 2—Amount of work done, Scale 3—Quality of work done, and Scale 7—Conscientiousness. The first two of the scales are job-oriented scales. The third job-oriented scale, Scale 5—Ability to do complicated jobs—has a rather consistent low contribution as indicated by the β' weights in Table 4.

Scale 1—Ability to work with others—consistently contributes very little to the prediction of the Over-all performance ratings. Examination of the intercorrela-

Table 4

MULTIPLE CORRELATION (R) BETWEEN SCALES 1 THROUGH 7 WITH SCALE 8; WITH β'-WEIGHTS[a] FOR EACH SCALE
(Decimal points omitted)

SCALE	β'-WEIGHTS			
	RATER	ENDORSER	SELF	ESTIMATE
1. Ability to work with others	04	–04	–03	01
2. Amount of work done	27	27	38	15
3. Quality of work done	27	36	20	26
4. Leadership potential	–05	–04	17	03
5. Ability to do complicated jobs	12	05	06	09
6. Ability to work with minimum supervision	06	19	–04	12
7. Conscientiousness	29	21	27	34
Multiple R	94	92	83	82
R^2 (Scales 1–7 with 8)	88	85	69	67

[a] β'-weights are relative, i.e., each β has been divided by $\Sigma\beta_i$ ($i = 1$–7) for each Rater level, in order to facilitate comparisons between levels.

tions indicates that this scale correlates low with the Over-all rating. Scale 2—Quantity of work done—makes a considerable contribution in supervisory-ratings and even more so in the self-ratings. However, its contribution drops off in predicting the estimate of the Over-all rating. This would indicate that the workers did not feel that their supervisors placed as much emphasis on the quantity of work done as the workers believed they would. The indications are, however, that the supervisors did attach importance to quantity of work accomplished but they did not communicate this fact to their subordinates, although the workers assigned it greater importance than they thought their superiors would, or in fact, did.

Scale 3—Quality of work done—is also a consistent contributor to the prediction of the Over-all rating. The supervisors and subordinates agreed on its importance. The downward communication of the supervisors' opinion of the importance of this trait was good, as indicated by the closeness of the β' weights for Rater- and Estimate-ratings. The endorsers felt that it was even more important than did either the rater or the ratees. Workers themselves felt that quality was not quite so important.

Scale 4—Leadership potential—has a slight negative contribution for supervisory ratings. For the Estimate-ratings, it is slightly positive, but neither of these is of sufficient magnitude to merit consideration. The Self-rating has this trait contributing a fair amount of weight. All but the Self-rating has Scale 4 correlating moderately with Scale 8 (Over-all). It is apparent that the workers were aware of the supervisors' attitude toward this trait; this attitude being that of expecting subordinates to do what they were told without asking questions. Subordinates who were looked upon as trouble-makers were the ones who, perhaps, questioned some of their assignments and were, therefore, not seen as good, over-all workers by their supervisors. It might also be pointed out that "Leadership potential" is the only trait on which the supervisors consistently rated their subordinates below average.

Scale 5—Ability to do complicated jobs—does not contribute much for any level of rating. The Rater placed a moderate emphasis on this scale. This trait or scale was probably seen as somewhat of an intelligence trait. Probably the routine nature of the work of the Finance Office made this characteristic of little consequence for all but a few of the non-supervisory positions.

Scale 6—Ability to work with minimum supervision—has a small contribution in the Rater-ratings with the Estimate-rating contribution somewhat higher. This would indicate that the supervisors gave workers the impression that this trait was somewhat more important than it was. Perhaps this was due to the supervisors' giving the impression to their subordinates that they did not wish to be bothered by questions, yet, when the supervisors completed their ratings, they gave only small consideration to how much the subordinates came to them with questions. Again, the repetitive nature of the organization's work might reduce the importance of this factor as a predictor of over-all value.

Scale 7—Conscientiousness—has a consistently high β' weight for all levels of ratings. While there is some small variation, all are high enough to indicate that all levels of raters, both supervisory and self, agreed on the contribution of the conscientiousness trait to the Over-all performance rating. While it had been intended that this trait or scale be a "personal" rather than a "job-oriented" characteristic, its description in behavioral terms seems to make it much more a matter of consistency of effort and applicability than of "conscientiousness," as more broadly conceived.

It is particularly of interest to note that the relative weights of Traits 2 and 7 switch emphasis as we shift from Self-ratings to Estimate-ratings. What the workers appear to be saying in providing these data is: "The most important factor contributing to my value is the amount of work I turn out. But my supervisor is not nearly so interested in this as he is in my keeping my nose to the grindstone and keeping busy."

Nor do the employees appear to be seriously in error. Supervisors assign practically equal weight to "Amount of work done," "Quality of work done," and "Conscientiousness." In their self-ratings, workers assign a greater weight to "Quantity" and a lesser one to "Quality" but about the same to "Conscientiousness."

Actually, these three scales do almost as good a job of predicting the Over-all as do the optimum combination for all seven scales. These, then, are the factors that all parties consider to be important in determining their value to the organization.

REFERENCES

1. Barrett, R. S., Taylor, E. K., Parker, J. W., and Martens, W. L. Rating scale content: I. Scale information and supervisory ratings. *Personnel Psychol.*, 1958, 11, 333–346.
2. Taylor, E. K., Barrett, R. S., Parker, J. W., and Martens, W. L. Rating scale content: II. Effect of rating on individual scales. *Personnel Psychol.*, 1958, 11, 519–533.

D. Feedback of Appraisal Information

THE COMMUNICATION OF MERIT RATINGS: A PHILOSOPHY AND A METHOD

BERNARD J. COVNER

COUNSELING EXECUTIVES AFTER MERIT RATING OR EVALUATION: A PROJECT IN EXECUTIVE DEVELOPMENT

EARL G. PLANTY AND CARLOS E. EFFERSON

EVALUATING AN APPRAISAL AND FEEDBACK TRAINING PROGRAM

C. G. MOON AND THEODORE HARITON

THREE TYPES OF APPRAISAL INTERVIEW

NORMAN R. F. MAIER

The universal desire to know how well we are doing and what others think of us makes it inevitable that the organization experience pressures from individuals for information about how they have been rated. The problems of interpersonal relations which bulk so large in the communication of this information have been referred to earlier, notably in the McGregor article, "An Uneasy Look at Performance Appraisal," in Part One. The readings presented here discuss ways of feeding back to the individual information about his performance, with chief reliance placed upon the supervisor as the means of communication. McGregor's criticisms might profitably be reread along with the articles in this section.

FURTHER READING

Leavitt, Harold J., *Managerial Psychology*. Chicago, University of Chicago Press, 1958. 335 pp.

Maier, Norman R. F., *The Appraisal Interview: Objectives, Methods, and Skills*. New York, John Wiley & Sons, Inc., 1958. 246 pp.

THE COMMUNICATION OF MERIT RATINGS

A Philosophy and a Method*

Bernard J. Covner

More and more companies are using merit rating as a personnel administration tool, primarily to allocate wage and salary increases and to determine fitness for promotion and transfer. Hundreds of articles and several books have been written about it, and it probably has more euphemistic aliases (performance rating, performance evaluation, service rating, progress rating, etc.) than any other personnel technique.

The focus of attention in merit rating has been upon evaluation of individual performance; communication of the evaluation to the person involved has, in comparison, received exceedingly scant attention. This is evident both in the literature on merit rating and in company practice. Habbe's 1948 survey of merit-rating practices showed that only half the companies using merit rating made a practice of reporting the results to their personnel.[1] Further, as will be shown later in more detail, when companies do report the results, they frequently fail to take advantage of what is already known about effective communication procedures.

It is no accident that managements have given less attention to the communication of merit-rating findings than to merit rating itself. The reasons are many. A prominent one is that merit-rating procedures leave much to be desired and are a constant source of argument. Another is the fear that "a powerful and dangerous tool will be put in the hands of foremen and supervisors."

Logically, one would expect there to be a trend toward the communication of merit ratings, as this would be consistent with the very pronounced postwar emphasis upon better supervision and improved human relations in industry. Benjamin's 1952 survey[2] showed, however, that essentially the same percentage of plans provide for communication of results as of plans covered in Habbe's earlier study, or perhaps an even lower proportion. If this evidence is truly representative of companies in general, what does it suggest about the highly advertised postwar trend toward improved human relations in industry? Does it mean that many published statements about improved supervision are window-dressing? Or does it merely indicate that improvements have not as yet carried over to merit-rating programs?

The fact that Habbe found half of the companies with merit-rating programs providing also for communication of ratings suggests that some companies consider communication desirable. There are stronger reasons, however, than that "other companies are doing it."

For improvement to occur, the rated employee must sooner or later know about the quality of his performance. This is so simple a fact that it is amazing, though not incomprehensible, that

[1] Stephen Habbe, "Personnel Practices in Factory and Office" (Revised), *Studies in Personnel Policy No. 88,* National Industrial Conference Board, 1948.

[2] Roland Benjamin, Jr., "A Survey of 130 Merit-Rating Plans," *Personnel,* Vol. XXIX, No. 3 (November, 1952).

it is so frequently overlooked. To inform a person about his performance is to apply one of the best known and most successful learning principles—knowledge of results.

Knowledge of results is important even in cases where improvement in performance is not an issue. Employees need to feel that their performance is approved by others, particularly their superiors. Approval by implication—that is, by the absence of comment unless something has been done incorrectly—is not sufficient. Failure of supervisors to comment on satisfactory behavior frequently causes employees' performances to deteriorate or their development to be impeded.

How is it best to provide for communication of merit ratings? Merely to decide to "do it" is not enough. In the writer's opinion, few companies whose policies provide for the communication of ratings achieve the results they expected, because communication is a more complex activity than is generally understood. As the term is used in this article, it is a multi-direction, multi-person activity having three objectives: understanding of the points made, acceptance of these points, and constructive action.

• DYNAMICS OF THE RATING INTERVIEW

Success in merit-rating communication depends upon certain characteristics of ratees, which may be called "person-centered," and of companies, which may be called "management-centered."

Person-Centered Characteristics

The understanding and acceptance of points made by either ratee or rater are influenced considerably by several overlapping personality factors. Often the critical issue is not the points themselves, such as "room for improvement in letter writing" or "need for keeping me better informed." Instead, difficulty may stem from the way the points are perceived and reacted to.

Level of Aspiration. Perceptions of and reaction to points made in employee ratings are influenced considerably by the individual's desires, technically called his "level of aspiration." Consequently, the ease with which he understands and accepts evaluations of his behavior depends upon his aspiration—"to just get by," "to do as well as most," "to be the best in the group," etc.

A professional worker received an "outstanding" over-all rating. He soon learned that many of his co-workers received similar ratings. He became disgruntled, saying that his rating wasn't high enough to satisfy him, and that it implied that he "was no better than the next guy." From this time on, he became increasingly critical of the company's management.

Concept of Self. A closely related person-centered characteristic is the picture that an individual has developed over an extended period about the kind of person he is, technically called the "concept of self." To take a few common, somewhat oversimplified examples, a person may see himself as a leader, a "big shot," a genius, a "guy who gets things done," just an average "Joe," someone who doesn't let others push him around, etc. People tend to react negatively to experiences which are inconsistent with or threatening to their concept of self. For example:

A regional manager criticized a subordinate for doing too many things at once. The subordinate rejected this point vehemently, stressing that just the opposite was true and that he prided himself on "well-organized activity" and "always finishing whatever he started." (In actual fact, the superior was right, and the subordinate's claims about his characteristic behavior were also correct. The reasons for the inadequate performance in this particular instance were somewhat complex.)

A factory manager criticized his production supervisor for not requisitioning new help in time to be ready for manufacturing a new line of products. The supervisor replied that the manager had not notified him about the decision to produce the new line and that, as a matter of fact, he would have been even more unprepared if he had not accidentally "gotten wind" of the decision from a friend in another department. The manager immediately became enraged (which was characteristic of him when even the slightest error on his part was pointed out) and shouted that it was the supervisor's duty to know what was going on, and that he should not expect his superiors to pamper him.

Resistance and Defensiveness. The extent to which an individual is willing to accept unfavorable comments from others and the extent to which he gets along with others and adjusts to life in general are closely connected. Resistance and defensiveness are characteristic of many forms of maladjustment. Common examples of this type of behavior are displays of stony silence or the injection of counter-arguments which completely reject the suggestions of others.

The general manager of a large retail store reports about his secretary as follows:

> Talking to Nora does no good at all. She won't admit any mistake, no matter how small. Even when I catch her red-handed she pulls some completely far-fetched excuse out of the air. She is so defensive that if you told her it was raining outside she'd say it wasn't her fault.

These overlapping characteristics—level of aspiration, concept of self, resistance and defensiveness—apply to *both* parties in a communication situation. Each must listen carefully and patiently to the other. When one party sees that the other is unwilling to listen, chances are that he will either "clam up" or start arguing and thereby kill or delay the prospect of constructive action.

Company-Centered Characteristics

Now let us look at some characteristics of companies which affect the success of merit-rating communication. These characteristics have been noted by the writer while working on rating programs.

Foggy Objectives. Often objectives are no more precise than "to tell them how they stand." This objective may mean different things to different people. The result is that often such important goals as improved performance, continuation of good performance, planning, acquisition of important information, diagnosis of inadequate performance, etc. are not aspired to, tooled up for, or achieved.

Lack of Job Clarification. This shortcoming is seen in the common situation where a supervisor tells a subordinate that he should be doing something more efficiently, and the worker says he did not realize what he was supposed to be doing that something in the first place. Or the issue has arisen because a ratee has been doing something that he should not be doing at all. For example:

> *Plant Manager:* Harry, you check too often with me to make sure that you're doing the right thing.

Supervisor: Well, Sam, I know what you mean, but there's a reason for it. In the first place, on previous jobs I've been blasted by the boss for not checking with him constantly. Since I'm still relatively new here, and you never did tell me what to do and what not to do, I decided to play safe. I prefer to assume responsibility, and would have asked you for it. But I figured that you were biding your time to see how I panned out. I also felt that if I directly asked you for more responsibility, you'd think that I was trying to take over the place from the very start.

It should be obvious from this illustration that a communication session can help to clear up misconceptions. This function is important, and will probably always be necessary. But it is still more efficient for the employee to know from the start what is expected of him.

Lack of Training and Development Programs for Ratees. Many of the points made in a rating discussion require more than mere mention for constructive action to result. It is often necessary to integrate them carefully and to set up a specific program designed to do something about them. It is also important to demonstrate the value of improvement to the ratee in terms of the possibility of salary increases, better assignments, promotion, etc.

Rating Plan Defects. A very common defect of rating forms is that they are not designed with communication in mind. Such terms as average, initiative, aggressiveness, etc., even if precisely defined on forms (as they are frequently not) are likely to mean different things to different people. Not many supervisors can be expected to remember to define these terms when discussing them, or to have adequate skill for making their meanings clear. Descriptions of concrete behavior instead of abstract terminology make the job easier.

A more subtle issue is involved in the fact that the importance of certain aspects of behavior which are frequently rated is questionable. For example, the Standard Oil Company (New Jersey) and its affiliates asked supervisors to prepare descriptions of behavior characteristic of their best and worst subordinates. When individual descriptions were correlated with over-all evaluations of job performance, some of them were found to be non-differentiating. That is, certain descriptions were found to apply equally well to both low- and high-rated personnel.[3]

This finding raises the question of whether there is not much needless concern over certain aspects of job performance. Lateness and absenteeism, for example, are matters of serious concern on assembly line operations. But in some circumstances they are relatively unimportant. For example, a technical writer was frequently late for and absent from work. Yet on his assignment such behavior didn't matter. Besides, the quality and quantity of his work were far superior to his co-workers'.

Another issue is the accuracy of ratings. Just as it is important to rate a person on the *right* things, it is also vital that ratings be truly representative of a person's performance. Many studies have demonstrated that there is good reason for suspecting the accuracy of merit ratings. Factors contributing to inaccuracy include rater bias, form defects, failure to train raters adequately, and the use of subjective ratings where objective records are available.

[3] *Made to Measure,* Employee Relations Department, Standard Oil Company (New Jersey), 1951.

Another factor affecting rating accuracy is knowledge by the rater that ratings will be communicated. Whether such knowledge increases or decreases rating accuracy, however, appears to depend upon the situation and the persons involved. In a "to be communicated" rating program, raters tend to take their training and carry out their ratings more seriously. Logically, the communication requirement makes it necessary for the rater to be able to justify his statements *both* to his superiors and to his ratees. But whether the over-all situation results in more or less "generous" ratings is not clear.

Dr. Greydon Worbois, of the Detroit Edison Company, suggests that pressures on the rater are the key influence. He states: "If the rater has found 'generous' ratings easier to talk over with the ratee and has never felt any pressure against overly generous ratings, his ratings may vary from those of another rater who is subject to different pressures."

"Forced-choice" ratings, which have been used extensively by Standard Oil Company (New Jersey) and affiliates, are superior to those obtained by the conventional graphic methods, in the sense that the importance of the behavior aspects being rated is not known, and that ratings can't be slanted. When first introduced, they were considered more difficult to prepare and lacking in information that raters could communicate easily. According to Dr. Edwin Henry of Standard Oil, however, overall time in preparing scales is at the present time no longer than that required in preparing a graphic scale that works properly. He also states that recent developments and modifications now provide raters with information that can be communicated easily.

All in all, while merit-rating techniques are by no means perfect, progress is being made in improving them, and they are certainly not worthless. Further, many aspects of a person's work, such as productivity, attendance, nature of assignment, policies, etc., are matters of objective fact which do not require a rating, and are important subjects for communications.

DEFECTS OF WAGE AND SALARY ADMINISTRATION. Such defects include: complete absence of systematic plans for determining starting rates and increases, failure to obtain employee understanding of plans that are essentially sound, plans which are systematic but considered unfair, abuses of good plans, and "below par" wage and salary schedules.

MISCELLANEOUS SUPERVISORY DEFECTS. Attempts of a rater to "be nice" during an interview, when he has a reputation for being just the opposite, are either regarded with suspicion or are soon counter-acted by instances in which the rater acts the way he usually does. A closely related shortcoming is the failure of ratees to have faith in the judgment and basic fairness of raters. If, for example, a supervisor gives someone a rating that is considered far out of line by the majority of an employee group, the memebrs of the group are not well inclined to accept either their own ratings or the rating program as a whole.

FAILURE TO TRAIN RATERS IN COMMUNICATION TECHNIQUES. Some companies do a fair job of training raters in performance rating, but feel that almost any rater can handle the communication part without special training. The writer's experience indicates that this viewpoint is very unsound.

These company-centered characteristics which influence the success with which merit ratings are communicated undoubtedly affect the success of other personnel administration techniques as well. They illustrate the influence of over-all situations on the success of any management action. This point is all too often neglected in managements' attempts to short-cut thorough diagnosis and to find gimmicks or "packages" that will provide quick cures for their troubles.

COUNSELING EXECUTIVES AFTER MERIT RATING OR EVALUATION

A Project in Executive Development*

Earl G. Planty and Carlos E. Efferson

Only recently has science been invited to help in the human relations aspects of business. The scientific method is well established as the base of waste and quality control, market analysis, time and methods activities, and a host of other business functions. In human relations in business, however, we are belatedly making a beginning at the planned and organized approach that is fundamental to science.

The scientific approach in evaluating, counseling, and developing men has been delayed because of its necessary complexity and the specialized psychological terminology used in most scientific discussions of the subject. A large part of what is known in the field of human understanding and counseling is still in the college seminars and books of the professors. While this knowledge, however valuable it may be, remained in this obscure form we were unable to put it to work in the practical and ever-moving world in which business operates.

Because of the previous scarcity of simple and practical techniques and terminology, executives responsible for evaluation, counseling, and the development of other management members have understandably tended to avoid a planned approach and have let chance take its course. But there are now a few principles and techniques of *counseling for improvement* which can be expressed in practical terms and which make counseling after evaluation a profitable investment for business executives. Most of this report describes simple techniques which can be applied in an orderly, deliberate, and scientific manner to such counseling.

Before examining the techniques, we might outline four assumptions or principles upon which success depends.

• FUNDAMENTAL ASSUMPTIONS

One of the principles that must guide us is the old truism that we do not see ourselves as others do. In counseling after evaluations, we must proceed as though it is very unlikely that a subordinate will evaluate himself and all parts of his work as his superior does. We must accept it as completely natural that a man who appears to us to be good in personal relations might think himself a miserable failure in this function. We should also expect that the reverse may be true, and, in either case, we should not label the man "maladjusted" or "weak" but, rather, "human."

* From *Personnel,* March 1951, pp. 384–396.

We should expect to find people who, *in our eyes,* are not contributing enough, but who *themselves* think they are contributing more than their share. We must not be at all surprised to find men with insatiable ambition for executive positions whom we look upon as mediocre. We must not be surprised if we find here and there a man who expects a promotion when we thought he knew he was not doing his job satisfactorily.

Because these things are so, we must counsel regularly with our people for it is most unlikely that *our* evaluation of their work matches *theirs.* Now, as simple as this principle seems and as long as it has been recognized in our literature and in our own personal relationships, most of us in business do not use it in our day-to-day operations. Instead, most of us let our executives and supervisors roll along unaware of their failures or their successes, of their mediocrity or their brilliance. Thus we miss the greatest possible opportunity for strengthening the weak and making stronger those who are already successful. Some of us rationalize that if our subordinates are "good" men they will make an objective judgment of their own progress and personality. Others believe that "no news is good news" and think that their subordinates will also accept this negative sort of approval.

There are other important principles underlying counseling which find their roots in the blindness of man to himself. One of them is that we must counsel slowly and carefully, using the "feel" approach, recognizing that insight into one's own behavior comes slowly, sometimes not at all, and hardly ever completely. We must recognize that we ourselves may have as many false definitions as does the man with whom we are talking, and that it is impossible to recognize and allow for our own biases completely. Even when we are certain of the direction in which we want to lead the subordinate, we must remember that it may take him many interviews to see in himself what we see in him; we must lead the man into only as much self-criticism and suggestion at one time as his personality can absorb without disintegrating effects.

We must ever remember that the purpose of counseling is more one of development than of discipline. The approach must be positive, and our outlook on this score will go far to determine our success or failure. When the subordinate sees that the purpose of counseling is for his own good, one of the major obstacles to mutual understanding is overcome. He will see that our purpose is to help him if we keep in mind that people need to hear about their good points as well as the weak points, and if we make clear our intention to use his strengths and reward him for them while we simultaneously help him discover and overcome his weaknesses.

Of course, one of the most fundamental assumptions upon which we must proceed is the belief that most people can, if properly assisted, change their attitudes and behavior for the good. Contrary to the belief of many, success or failure is not born in a man, but comes in part as a result of the use to which he puts his talents and the way he is helped to develop them, however limited or liberally endowed he may be. Performance counseling, in addition to letting the subordinate know where he stands, helps by providing encouragement and assistance while improvement is taking place. The foregoing has attempted to explain a few assumptions regarding counseling for improvement. The remainder of this article will deal with specific counseling suggestions that were worked out and applied in Johnson & Johnson.

The practical suggestions below grew out of several conferences with the personnel directors of Johnson & Johnson and affiliated companies. The ideas and recommendations presented in these conferences were edited, organized in writing as below and used in executive development meetings. They were used with executives who had been studying the steps involved in the Executive Audit. The ideas were mimeographed, passed out and discussed in the meetings but not until all executives had (1) participated in a general conference-style discussion on counseling after evaluation and (2) participated in some role-playing where such counseling was demonstrated. The suggestions were then used in the executive development meetings to stimulate further discussion, bring up points that had been previously raised, and to serve as a summary to the whole learning unit.

• PRACTICAL SUGGESTIONS

Definition

We are referring to the interview and counseling which follow evaluation. In some cases, this counseling will be clear and direct; in other cases, it may be subtle and non-directive. In some cases a meeting will be called specifically for counseling. In other cases a less formal, more casual approach will be made.

Purposes of Counseling Following Evaluation

A. *Getting the subordinate to do a better job* through making clear your standards of performance. Remember that you too have peculiar traits and expectancies. Here is a chance for the subordinate to learn your preferences in quality, quantity, and methods of work and to understand your reasons for these standards.

B. *Giving the employee a clear picture of how he is doing,* with emphasis upon strengths as well as weaknesses—showing how well he meets your standards. We assume that much trouble results in business and industry from subordinates whose self rating is sharply at variance with their superior's evaluation.

C. *Discussing together plans for improvement* and projects for better utility of the subordinate's strengths.

D. *Building strong, personal relationships* between superior and subordinate in which both are willing to talk frankly about the job, how it is being done, what improvement is possible, and how it can be obtained—improving human-to-human understanding so that closer, stronger relationships exist.

E. *Eliminating or reducing anxiety,* tension, and uncertainty which may exist where individuals do not have the advantages of planned counsel.

Preparing for the Interview

A. Assuming that the rating has been done and that some brief time has passed between the evaluation and the interview, it is well to do a little reviewing before meeting with the subordinate.

1. Restudy the job of the man to be counseled and what it takes to do it.

2. Think about the man, his personality, record, experience, and training. Have his personnel file available.

3. Also review in your mind how you rated him in the light of his job requirements.

(a) Review and weigh the factors which entered into your evaluation.

(b) Review *why* you rated him as you did.

(c) Bring to mind specific facts or illustrations from his job performance to substantiate your opinions.

B. Determine what you want to accomplish in the interview and prepare a plan of discussion for doing so. You might wish to accomplish some of the following:

1. Leave the man with more *will to work* than he previously had.

2. Send him away with as much knowledge of his *specific strengths* and *weaknesses* as his personality can take.

3. Leave him with a specific or general *statement of his over-all effectiveness:* Example, "Adding it all up, John, we feel that you are an asset (or a distinct asset) to the company, and we hope you stay on with us for years," or, "John, I think your work as office manager compares so favorably with other similar work in the company that we should soon begin to look for new opportunities for you," or, "Your performance is not adequately meeting the needs of the position and suggested improvement is expected."

4. Work out with the subordinate a few specific steps that both of you are to undertake for his betterment. This might include your giving him a special assignment in a field where he thinks he is weak, assigning him to a committee or to a training program, etc.

C. After the first meeting has been held and cooperative relations established, some executives like to inform the subordinate of the time and subject of the meeting so that he can anticipate the discussion and be better prepared psychologically for it.

D. Plan to meet in private, and without interruptions.

E. If being done for the first time, anticipate some curiosity, tension, or anxiety in the individual. Prepare to reduce it.

F. Decide in advance how to use whatever rating form, narrative description, or questionnaire you have recorded your data upon. In some instances the rating form itself is used as a guide in the interview. The supervisor may, in such a case, show the employee his rating sheet and discuss it with him. However, there are certain disadvantages in this approach:

1. The form may come to be the principal issue of the interview. Discussion may center on the language of the rating form, the weighing of factors, or the definition of degrees.

2. The older executive may be so resistant to a written record that he also resists any corrective efforts. He may feel that he is condemned unalterably because of the record.

3. The employee may be so concerned with the end rating, the alphabetical or numerical score, that he never hears the constructive suggestions of the interview. (Some feel, in the light of the

above, that the form should never be shown. Whether or not he sees the form, the subordinate should eventually know how he has been evaluated.)

G. Visualize how you might lead into your points, indirectly at first.

Manner for the Interview (Acceptance depends heavily upon this)

A. Create the impression that you have time for the interview and that you consider it highly important.

B. Throughout the interview, place primary interest upon development and growth for the individual. The executive must see that the individual feels that the activity is a constructive, cooperative one. Minimize evaluation, rating, recording of evidence. Avoid implications that the meeting is or could be used for disciplinary purposes.

C. Create the impression that your evaluation or opinion is not unalterable and permanent. Let it be known that you realize men are dynamic and ever changing, and that your opinions, too, are open to change.

D. Be open-minded to the opinions and facts presented by the one being counseled—be prepared to change your estimation in the light of additional or new evidence. Be willing to learn about him.

E. Don't dominate or cross examine. Avoid argument. Listen. Listen attentively as well as politely. Listen to sift the important points from the detail, to separate facts from opinions, to identify information and know when it is presented as such and when it is used to persuade and influence toward the teller's own objectives.

F. Remember that the subordinate must do most of the talking at some points in the interview: in bringing his opinions and feelings to the surface and to your attention; in getting a better understanding of himself; and in making plans for self-improvement.

The Interview

A. Setting the stage for and beginning the interview.

1. Pick the right time, day and place. Counsel should not occur close in time to a disciplinary action or an argument. Pick a time when the relationship is strongest, when you are in a good mood, and have reason to believe the subordinote feels likewise.

2. At the outset relieve tension to make the man feel at ease and receptive.

(a) Get the man to talking.

(b) Then explain the objectives of evaluation; point out that everybody is involved; invite the man to raise questions and introduce his own problems; give him a feeling of security. Say that your interest is in helping him with his job or his future.

B. Techniques

1. Tell the good things first. Show appreciation of past successes.

2. Talk generally about the man's status at the outset.

3. Some executives ask the man to evaluate himself as a starter.

4. Get away from past failures as quickly as you can. Get the discussion into prevention of future failures, into plans for success. Build upon strengths.

5. In almost every instance allow for "face saving." Explain that you once failed similarly. If you are dealing with a first offense or a very good man, you may share some of the blame. With re-

peated offenders, however, you will need to be sterner.

6. You, however, should guide the interview. Invite the subordinate back from detours, escapes, fruitless conversation.

7. *Just how directly the subordinate should be told or led to see (a) his strengths and weaknesses and (b) the over-all quality of his performance, depends upon the levels in the organization which are being worked with, personal traits of the individuals involved, the subordinate's degree of success or failure on his job, the counselor's objective, etc. How direct to be must be determined in each individual case. Remember, however, that improvement is most rapid where an employee learns from counseling to understand himself, and where he himself makes judgments about his abilities. The skillful executive* leads *the employee to better evaluations of himself. He does not make them up for him. It is what the subordinate sees for himself and accepts that he does something about.*

8. Some specific suggestions for handling various reactions to the counseling are given below. It is true that typing like this is not completely realistic since some reactions will fall in more than one category. Allowing for this, however, good results have followed from use of these suggestions.

(a) *The man accepts your evaluation and indicates a willingness to improve.*

(1) With the average successful executive the reaction described above will be the ordinary one, occurring more often than all the other reactions mentioned hereinafter.

(2) The subordinate may express genuine surprise at some parts of your evaluation of him and his work, but his response will be positive and friendly rather than defensive or antagonistic, for most subordinates—particularly in the executive and supervisor levels – admire their superiors, respect their opinions, and want to please them.

(3) When the subordinate is told that his work is satisfactory, and when plans for self-improvement and growth are invited or suggested, the response is usually highly enthusiastic. There is no greater motivating force for an employee than for his superior to lay plans with him for improvement and security in his present position or for eventual advancement in the organization.

(4) The average person when being counseled about his work is likely to ask for elaboration of any constructive criticisms. This gives the counselor a chance to talk over the full story, although it appears to the counseled that the information is in response to his own request.

(5) We can look for most people to try to improve immediately after counseling and we can expect them to come back with evidence of their improvement, asking for further suggestions and help.

(6) The normal subordinate can be expected to accept his full share of responsibility for failure in departmental operations. In fact, particularly at the middle and higher levels of management, people tend to feel more responsibility for operations than their functions prescribe and they are usually quite ready to work on cooperative plans for improvement.

(7) We can expect frank and honest counseling to gain for the superior a reputation among his subordinates as being a "square-shooter." This can be of great help in efficient and cooperative performance of normal day-to-day operations.

(8) The subordinate is very likely to feel that an evaluation of his performance comes to him somewhat as a personal favor from his superior. All kinds of relations are likely to be closer and smoother where the superior has shown a genuine interest in letting a subordinate know his strengths and weaknesses and has helped him with the latter. An alert executive does not shut off other close personal relations which a subordinate is likely to invite following a good evaluation.

(9) Even successful people need frequent reassurance that their work is satisfactory. Some of your best men may appear somewhat over-eager for this reassurance.

(b) *The man can't agree with your evaluation or the constructive criticism; has evidence to show your evaluation in some respects is not accurate; disagrees constructively and unemotionally.*

(1) Don't try too hard to get agreement the first time, or even the first few times counseling is undertaken. Let your first job be to state your position; getting acceptance of your point of view may take more time.

(2) His disagreement with you may come from his own personal make-up, his experience on the job, and other factors which are entirely within him and which it will be difficult for you to understand at the outset.

(3) Be prepared to expect some disagreement based upon the difference in your personality and role within the company and his. Such disagreement should not handicap regular communications between you. No one of us completely agrees with any of the persons with whom we cooperate daily. *Full* agreement is impossible and unnecessary. It is impossible to expect people to have the identical motivation, values, definitions, outlooks, and so forth.

(4) Listen carefully to find out why the man does not agree. Check the reliability of your own facts and of his criticisms. Prepare yourself for future discussions with addi-

tional evidence about the man's performance.

(5) Say that you will look into this matter and give him every benefit of the facts. At the same time raise any questions which you have about the reliability of his own information. Send him away to think over his own position while you do the same with yours.

(6) Realize that experienced men who have done a great deal of evaluation and counseling agree that they frequently learn from those they are evaluating. Many experienced executives know that they have some time or other been given false steers and colored information, and they are happy to receive any additional facts which may improve their judgments.

(7) Be willing to change your evaluations in the light of more evidence. Evaluations are not static things. Just as men change constantly so should opinions about them.

(c) *The man agrees completely and almost too easily. You suspect he does not understand or is reserving his objections.*

(1) Get him to state the condition as you stated it to him. (Example: "Joe, I've been talking a lot here and I may have gone too fast; why don't you review for me what I've said?")

(2) In this case be sure that his agreement is fundamental, that it is not a device for complimenting the counselor, and thereby avoiding emphasis upon his need to improve. Some people use a device of easy agreement when criticized. In accepting easily like this, they seem to think there will be less stern insistence upon their taking some direct and immediate steps for improvement.

(3) Emphasize what is to be done about change, improvement, or development. Get the man who appears to have accepted your evaluation to commit himself strongly about doing something regarding it. Outline how you plan to follow-up on his plans for improvement. This check-up may be the very help he needs.

(d) *The man is too eager for promotion or financial reward.*

(1) If the subordinate uses your favorable evaluation of him to insist upon immediate financial reward, you may remind him that a man has to perform in a highly successful fashion for some period of time on any job before thinking of advancement.

(2) Outline the promotional route which he may expect to follow. Discuss in general or specific terms when you think he may be ready for advancement, and following readiness how long it has taken men in similar positions to find an opportunity.

(3) His insistence on promotion or salary increase in return

for a good rating may reveal his desire to see some tangible evidence of the success which you have told him he he enjoys. Be sure that you have made full use of intangible rewards—assignment to committees working on difficult problems on higher levels; release from routine operations to attend conferences, training schools, etc.; minor improvements in office facilities, secretarial services, and personal attention in a variety of ways.

(4) If too many of your men insist upon overly rapid rewards, perhaps you are stressing opportunity, promotion, and advancement too much. We should evaluate people *first* to improve their performance on their present job and only secondarily to prepare for promotion. Present success in the full meaning of the word must precede promotion. Put your emphasis upon it. People can and should be motivated to outstanding performance on their own job before there is promise of advancement.

(5) Review your salary schedules and rate of promotion to assure yourself that the man has been treated fairly.

(6) The man may not deserve advancement. It is the purpose of your counseling to get him to see this. Do not be surprised if you do not accomplish it at the first meeting.

(7) Wives are sometimes responsible for husbands' impatience. Your counseling may have to include her, too.

(8) If your salary schedules are adequate, over-frequent requests for pay increases may indicate that you are not providing enough intangible rewards. The subordinate may be compensating for their lack in demanding excessive financial returns in their place.

(e) *The man avoids blame, which is manifestly his, shifts the criticism to others—to his own subordinates, to associates on his own level, to you, or to company policy.*

(1) At the outset, listen to him rather than halting his recital. To do the latter might merely send him somewhere else with his complaints.

(2) Speak and act so as to create the impression that you are impartial and fair-minded and want him to take only that responsibility which is his. Above all, guard that his irrational conduct does not upset and annoy you; at any rate, do not let your words or actions convey your distress if you feel it.

(3) Try to find why he blames others. What inadequacy does he have that makes it impossible for him to accept justifiable blame?

(4) Then ask yourself how you

can help him to feel successful enough so that he will not need to use such an escape or excuse to provide for his requirements. Find out what taste of success you will have to help him achieve so that he will not find it necessary to deny *all* blame.

(5) Directly or indirectly compliment him for his willingness to assume responsibility where you find any evidence that he has done so. Let him realize that acceptance of blame, when accompanied with determination to improve, will not be a disadvantage to him.

(6) Watch carefully from meeting to meeting with him to see whether he grows in willingness to assume responsibility for his failures.

(7) Following a few sessions handled in this way, determine whether his blame-avoidance is basic in his personality and requires psychological counsel, or whether it is based on factors in his environment which you can help him to recognize and improve upon.

(8) Sometimes it helps to put the man in closer contact with the individuals or groups he is criticizing. Assign him to committees, give him special projects, find other ways to throw him into closer association with capable people whose abilities he underestimates.

(f) *The man wants to quit. He is a good man and you would like to keep him.*

(1) Find out why he wishes to leave. He may not be too clear on this himself. Perhaps the emotional release he gets in reviewing his reasons will satisfy him. If his reason for leaving is based on some failure which you recognize within the organization, take some prompt action to correct it. If this comes as a surprise, it may mean that the executive has failed to keep close enough relations with the subordinate.

(2) Do not be afraid to assure him of your respect for his ability. Some men talk of leaving only because they are not sure they are wanted in their present jobs. Remember, too, that success is not enough of itself to reassure a man. He must hear from *you* that you consider him successful. Too many executives feel that "He should know he's doing all right unless I tell him different."

(3) If the man is accepting temporary advancement with some other company in place of an ultimately better future with you, outline the growth possibilities in his present position. Make sure he sees all the inducements which you have to offer.

(4) If he has a better offer elsewhere and you truly wish to

retain him, look carefully at your own rewards, tangible and intangible. Can they be increased, now or in the future?

(5) Steer the conversation so that the man does not commit himself definitely to leaving and so that he does not make statements so harsh that he will feel that all confidence in him has been lost by his management.

(g) *The man loses his temper. Becomes emotional, angry, or abusive.*

(1) Listen.

(2) Don't argue. Don't show disapproval.

(3) Be sure to let the man know that his loss of temper or emotional behavior is not a permanent black mark against him. It is very important that you let him leave realizing that you still have a friendly feeling toward him. Next time you meet him be especially cordial.

(4) Call him back a few days later. If he is still in the same mood, listen, don't argue. Call him back once more.

(5) If there is no improvement you must soon state your case.

(h) *The man seems determined to argue. Denies most of your facts, evidence and opinions.*

(1) Let him talk freely. While he is talking try to find out what it is basically that is bothering him. Since all behavior has some reason for being, listen carefully. Try to find the cause of his resistance.

(2) Thank him for calling his point of view to your attention. Say that you will look into it and talk with him later.

(3) Avoid being drawn into an argument which may arouse emotions that might block or seriously delay an understanding.

(4) But don't retreat. Be sure he understands your point of view and your insistence upon it. Do this tactfully, moderately, without arguing.

(5) Close the interview tactfully. Try it again when he may be in a better mood, or when you have taken whatever constructive action is possible about the fundamental cause of his resistance. He may be completely cooperative and understanding in the next interview.

(i) *The man is surly, not cooperative, resentful, or just passive and unresponsive.*

(1) Try to figure out why he acts this way. Is it normal for him? Is he giving careful attention to what you say? Is it self-protection? Does he fear to reveal his own attitude, or something in his job?

(2) Don't be afraid of a certain amount of silence. Give him ample time to think and respond.

(3) Watch carefully for any sparkle of interest in what

you are saying. Try to get him to talk about anything you have said that seems to strike even a small response. Ask his opinions about things important to him: "What do you think about so and so?" or "What would you do in this case . . .?"

(4) Reassure him early in the interview. Talk about as many of the complimentary things as you can at the outset.

(5) He may think that you think he is worse than he really is.

(6) Don't push or try to persuade too much at one sitting. He may change his attitude by the next sitting, or you may learn more about why he is as he is.

(7) He may resist the whole idea of evaluations and counseling following them. Go over your reasons again. Show how he can profit from knowing where he stands and from laying plans for improvement. Long-service men sometimes see no merit in evaluations. Anticipate some of this and explain the reasons for the scientific evaluations. Ask the man's objections.

(8) He may feel that you are trying to change habits within him which exist of his own personal choice. He may resist your discussing what he thinks are personal matters and none of your affair. He may not realize that certain habits (courteousness, personal appearance, punctuality, modesty, for example) relate closely to success on the job. Show him how this is so.

(j) *The man is obviously nervous and sensitive.*

(1) Apparently you have not put him at ease. Talk about the things he knows best, both before and during the interview, and feel most free about—the new home he is building, a good idea he recently submitted, his service on the school board, etc.

(2) If he is not participating, try to get him to do so; make it a two-way communication.

(3) Explain the purpose and constructive values that may come from evaluations and counseling.

(4) Don't talk about him—instead, talk about his work or his job. Begin by referring to actual work situations in which he has done well—a new system he installed, a quality improvement, a report he prepared.

(k) *You have nearly given up the idea of improvement of the man. This may be the last or next to the last interview before he leaves. You are now thinking more of separating him pleasantly with good public relations and with constructive help for him in his future employment than you are of improving him so that he may stay on.*

(1) Talk frankly and directly about his leaving. It will be some shock to him at first,

but getting him to face the facts realistically will make his remaining days much easier and will minimize his future employment troubles.

(2) If there is evidence that he is not perfectly clear about his failures, review them. Ask him to recall your previous conversations, your recommendations for improvement and what he thinks he has done about it. If possible, get him to state what he had been told previously about past failures.

(3) Review assets in the man which may make him valuable in some other company. Talk about these places and how he can get contacts with them.

(4) Tell him just what kind of work you will recommend him for. Give him the proper names in the organization to use as references.

(5) Refer the man to the proper sources in the organization which will help him prepare resumes, register with agencies, or otherwise look for employment.

(6) Some like to review "the second chance." Discuss what he has learned from the failures, what he intends to do differently.

(7) Leave your mind open as to the possibility that the man may still change for the good.

C. Closing the Interview

1. Review the points made in the interview and encourage the subordinate to summarize them or put them in his own words.

2. Always reassure the man of interest in his progress and indicate willingness to take up the discussion again at any time.

3. You should close when you have made clear whatever points you intended to cover, when the younger or junior executive has had ample time to review his problems and release any emotional tensions that exist, when plans of action have been cooperatively developed, and when you and the subordinate are at a natural stopping point. It is particularly good to close when both of you have a feeling of satisfaction about the results obtained.

Evaluation and Follow-up

A. Following the interview, many executives like to make a few notes before the facts brought out and the plans developed are forgotten.

B. Some plan to follow-up the interview by a visit—stopping by the man's office or calling him into theirs on some detail or other—wherein the subordinate has opportunity to get any additional help he may require.

C. In the interim between interviews, keep careful, but unobtrusive, watch over the man's progress or lack of it. Early in the next interview review what the subordinate has done toward the recommended self-understanding or improvement and how effective his efforts have been.

• CONCLUSION

The scientific, objective approach to improving executive performance seems so simple and practical, including only three steps:

1. Setting performance standards.

2. Rating, measuring, judging—as objectively as possible—how close a particular executive comes to the standards. Learning where the man exceeds requirements, where he meets them, and where he misses them.

3. Counseling with the subordinate regarding the findings of step two above.

There is no magic or mystery to these steps. They are simple, straightforward, practical. In a great many cases the first two steps are undertaken and completed, more or less objectively and fully. But how rarely is the third step undertaken—with what timidity, anxiety, and reluctance is it approached. The list of excuses for procrastination in counseling is long:

The man being counseled will react badly he may argue; he may be upset and made insecure; or he may get a conceited notion of his own importance.

The man will reveal the content of his counseling, particularly that part which is complimentary and thus provoke jealousy in the group.

Executives don't have time for counseling. The men really know where they stand from hints and suggestions given them.

Lower level executives are not skillful enough to counsel with their subordinates.

Rarely, if ever, has the truest objection to counseling come out: Executives do not know how to begin what appears to be a complex, difficult job and possibly an unnecessary one for them. Instead of talking frankly with their subordinates about performance and development, they have spent thousands of dollars for executive talent scouts, psychologists, executive evaluations, and development programs. This investment is made to avoid the analysis of strengths and weaknesses and follow-up counseling which only a man's superior is ideally equipped to do.

The writers believe that use of the content of this paper in conferences, role-playing, and even lectures can go far toward removing top level reluctance toward tackling this fundamental need in executive development.

What successful development can there be until both the superior and the subordinate recognize specifically the candidates' strengths and weaknesses *and cooperatively lay plans for growth and improvement?*

EVALUATING AN APPRAISAL AND FEEDBACK TRAINING PROGRAM*

C. G. Moon and Theodore Hariton

Much has already been written about the need for and the difficulty of measuring the value of training and development programs in industry. Yet remarkably few evaluation studies have been reported, considering the numerous programs now under way. Our contention is that evaluations of these programs should be undertaken. The problems encountered in conducting evaluation studies are by no means insurmountable, and the results more than compensate for the effort required.

This article will describe a study to determine the effectiveness of a personnel development program installed in the Engineering Section of a department of the General Electric Company in 1956.

The study is a good example of the type of research venture which can be carried out in industrial and business settings. Admittedly, neither the experimental design nor the measuring instrument was very elaborate. Nevertheless, the fact that significant and meaningful findings can be obtained under these conditions may encourage other companies to undertake evaluation studies of their programs.

In the fall of 1955, a department-wide appraisal system was adopted by all sections including the Engineering Section. The plan involved a write-up of each position cast in the form of job factors for which the employee was held accountable, and also a list of personality traits on which he was rated.

In the spring of 1956, the Engineering Section embarked on a more extensive appraisal and personnel development program. Its two main features were: (1) a revised performance appraisal system and (2) a training program designed to equip line managerial personnel to use appraisal information in helping their subordinates develop themselves.

The performance appraisal plan used the field review technique of obtaining appraisal information. Each manager was interviewed by a member of Engineering Administration (a staff unit) who had received appropriate training in the procedures. Following a special outline form to insure that no relevant material was omitted, the staff specialist questioned the manager about the work performance and personal characteristics of his immediate subordinate.

Although the line manager made the actual appraisal, he was guided by the staff specialist, who served as a catalyst in the process. Rather than interjecting any of his own opinions, the specialist questioned and probed for evidence concerning the subordinate's particular strengths or weaknesses. Since he had responsibility for taking all the notes and attending to the various details, the manager was free to concentrate on thinking through and describing the job perform-

---

* From *Personnel,* Vol. 35, no. 3, November–December 1958, pp. 36–41. Copyright 1958 by the American Management Association, Inc. Reprinted by permission.

ance and underlying behavior of his subordinate.

The word picture of the employee which emerged gave a more dynamic and integrated description of the whole man than had been secured from the previous appraisal method. The specialist wrote up the material in summary form, and submitted it to the manager who was free to make any necessary modifications. At all times it was emphasized that the *manager* was the one who was doing the appraising.

The appraisal took place at two levels: (1) the job-performance level in which the man's job accomplishments and his methods of operation were carefully evaluated, and (2) the deeper, more analytical level in which the man himself was considered in terms of his abilities, training and experience, motivation, personality, and character.

ADVANTAGES OF THE METHOD

As in other companies where this method was used, it soon became apparent that it had considerable merit above and beyond the gathering of appraisal data. In the course of participating in the field review interviews, each manager gained a better understanding of the evaluation process and how to evaluate objectively and critically. He also gained insight into how well he knew the man's work and the man himself. In addition, the use of a staff specialist fostered greater consistency among the managers as to the areas of work covered, as well as more uniformity of rating standards. The active participation of the specialist also insured that the job got done. Moreover, the approach was flexible enough so that the same basic appraisal form could be used for a variety of managerial, administrative, and technical positions.

An additional procedure was also adopted—before the appraisal interview the subordinate filled out a Personal Review form on which he indicated his likes and dislikes on the job, accomplishments and development needs, future goals and plans, and so forth. This step proved helpful to the subordinate in getting him to think analytically about himself, and also alerted the manager to areas which might be difficult during the appraisal discussion.

All managerial, administrative, and technical employees in the Engineering Section were appraised and completed the Personal Review form.

TRAINING IN FEEDBACK PROCEDURES

Once the relevant information was available, the next step was to equip the managers with the understanding and skills needed to "feed back" the appraisal in a manner designed to stimulate the growth and development of their subordinates.

A training program was set up and conducted for approximately 50 managers in the Engineering Section. To facilitate group discussion and active participation, they were divided into four groups, each of which was given 30 hours of instruction spread over two weeks of half-day sessions.

The sessions covered guiding the subordinate in formulating plans for self-improvement. Ways of helping him to achieve greater personal and on-the-job efficiency were studied and included day-to-day coaching, job enlargement and rotation, appropriate training courses, and participation in professional and civic organizations.

The program not only covered essential *principles* but also provided practice in the necessary interviewing *skills*. Each participant practiced the recommended procedures in realistic role-playing sessions under close observation of his colleagues and the trainers. In subsequent discussions his performance was evaluated so that he gained a greater awareness of the interpersonal dynamics in the interview situation. These "post-mortems" also emphasized areas for further improvement, as well as the strong points upon which he could build.

The initial sessions were devoted to the essential principles and techniques, and the later ones to guided practice. Additional material was introduced during discussions of the practice interviews; as the participants gained in understanding and skill, they were taught various ways to handle problem employees. Thus, besides learning the general principles of coaching and improving their feed-back skills, they gained new understanding of the psychology of the individual and learned practical techniques for handling subordinates in a variety of situations. For future reference each trainee received a manual describing the program.

In the spring of 1958, two years after the adoption of the new appraisal and training program, a decision was made to attempt to evaluate its effectiveness. It was felt that the opinions of the subordinates about changes in the managers' attitudes and behavior would provide a better measure than what the managers themselves thought about the benefits of the program. Thus, the core of the study was a questionnaire designed to obtain the subordinates' views about changes in their managers' atti-

Table 1

THE MANAGERS' VIEWS OF CHANGES IN THEMSELVES

As a result of the new appraisal and feed-back programs which have been going on for the past two years:

	YES %	NO %	? %
1. Do you have a better understanding of the way in which your subordinates do their jobs?	59	34	7
2. Do you find it easier to appraise the job performance of your subordinates?	97	3	—
3. Do you have a better understanding of your subordinates as people?	56	31	13
4. Do you find it easier to talk with your subordinates about job problems?	75	22	3
5. Do your subordinates discuss more of their job problems with you?	34	41	25
6. Do you have a better understanding of your superiors?	59	22	19
7. Do you have a clearer picture of your own strong points?	59	34	7
8. Do you have a clearer picture of your own development needs?	56	31	13
9. Do you find it easier to lead your subordinates in following given courses of action?	72	15	13
10. Do you have better working relationships with your associates in other units?	38	47	15

tudes and behavior since the program. Nevertheless, it was felt that the opinions of the managers would add to the picture. Accordingly, an additional questionnaire survey was conducted among the managers. The results of this survey will be summarized first.

Of approximately 50 managers who participated in the training, 32 returned questionnaires. Employees who had taken the training but were no longer managers were not included. The questionnaire and results appear in Table 1. A "yes" answer indicates a change for the better, a question mark indicates some degree of uncertainty, and a "no" indicates no change from previous conditions.

The responses indicate that almost all the managers felt the appraisal and training programs made it easier to appraise the job performance of their subordinates. A substantial majority also found it easier to talk to them about job problems, and to lead them in following given courses of action. On the other hand, many managers did not feel that their subordinates discussed more of their job problems with them or that their working relationships with their associates in other units had been greatly improved.

In sum, if the criterion of judgments of the managers about their own behavior and what they got out of the programs were used, the over-all results are highly positive.

• WHAT THE SUBORDINATES THOUGHT

Now let us consider what the subordinates thought about the effects of the program on the managers. A questionnaire was filled out by 66 subordinates selected at random from the Engineering Section. In addition, it was also filled out by a control group composed of 67 subordinates from the Manufacturing Section. While the two sections were comparable in size and were under the same general department manager, the Manufacturing Section had a different appraisal plan and had *not* received specialized and extensive training in feedback techniques.

It should be mentioned that until spring, 1956, there had been less appraisal work done in the Manufacturing Section than in the Engineering Section. However, since that time, the Manufacturing appraisal plan had been implemented so that appraisals were made more frequently than before and the system was said to be well received. Consequently, it was expected that the responses of the Manufacturing subordinates would indicate some improvement in their managers' behavior.

The questionnaire asked the respondents to compare present conditions with what they were two years ago. (Only those who had had the same manager for at least the past two years were included in the sample.) Thus, in the absence of pretraining measurements, it provided an indication of change which was independent of any previous measure. The questions were constructed to get at some of the basic objectives of the program, with emphasis on the person-to-person relationship between the employee and his manager, rather than on the subordinate's opinions of his manager's administrative and technical talents.

The administration of the questionnaire and the analysis of the results was done by the department's Communication and Training group. The questionnaire and results are shown in Table 2.

Table 2

THE SUBORDINATES' VIEWS OF CHANGES IN THEIR MANAGERS

Compared to two years ago:	ENGINEERING			MANUFACTURING		
	YES %	NO %	? %	YES %	NO %	? %
1. Does your manager have a better understanding of how you perform your job?	73	15	12	67	13	19
2. Does he have a better understanding of you as an individual?	74	9	17	60	19	21
3. Does he better indicate recognition of your good work?	58	33	9	34	48	18
4. Does he better utilize your particular skills?	51	32	17	51	36	13
5. Do you have a better picture of what he expects of you in terms of job performance?	56	32	12	73	21	6
6. Do you have a better picture of how you stand with him over-all?	46	36	18	37	51	12
7. Does he discuss your job performance with you more frequently?	30	67	3	24	75	1
8. Do you have a greater opportunity to present your side of a story during those discussions?	61	24	15	40	39	21
9. Does he take a greater personal interest in you and your future?	46	24	30	30	39	31
10. Does he make a greater effort to help you develop yourself?	46	32	22	36	40	24

As may be seen, of the 10 areas covered, eight showed a greater positive change for the Engineering than for the Manufacturing managers. In general, the Engineering employees were considerably more conscious of improvement in their managers' attempts to keep them informed on job performance and to assist them in their self-development. The four areas of greatest relative improvement for the Engineering group over the Manufacturing group were: (1) manager has better understanding of subordinate as an individual; (2) manager better indicates recognition of good work; (3) manager gives subordinate greater opportunity to present his side of a story during discussions; and (4) manager takes greater personal interest in subordinate and his future.

On the question, "Does he better utilize your particular skills?" the responses were the same for both groups. The Manufacturing managers received a higher rating on only one question, "Do you have a better picture of what he expects of you in terms of job performance?" This may have been due to the fact that manufacturing jobs are more easily defined and the results easier to visualize. One write-in which seemed to shed some light on the higher rating of the Manufacturing managers on this question was, "The only real concern he (the manager) has is with my production performance and with the manufacturing loss report."

In both groups, the area of least improvement was the frequency of job-performance discussions. This was somewhat disappointing, particularly in the Engineering group, for during the training sessions there was considerable emphasis on the need for giving day-to-day recognition of good work and suggestions for improvement instead of waiting for a year-end discussion. It was evident that still further work is necessary in this area.

• CONCLUSIONS

Although undoubtedly there were other factors which were not examined in the study, the results definitely imply that the appraisal and training program had a positive impact on the Engineering managers and their subordinates. While there was general improvement in both the Manufacturing and the Engineering Sections, there was a significantly greater gain in Engineering—a gain that clearly seems to have been the result of the appraisal and training program.

The findings suggest areas for further improvement in both the Engineering and Manufacturing Sections and can be used as benchmarks against which to measure the success of future programs. While definite progress has been made in appraising performance and in communicating appraisal data to subordinates, it was evident that more emphasis should be directed toward the action follow-up with the subordinate on a day-to-day basis.

THREE TYPES OF APPRAISAL INTERVIEW*

Norman R. F. Maier

One of the most common procedures in company executive-development programs is the appraisal of a man's performance, followed by an interview in connection with the appraisal. This procedure may be set up in various ways but it is always adapted to the line organization and always requires the holding of interviews.

The skill of the interviewer is an important factor in the success of this plan and is a general managerial requisite, since appraisal interviews are conducted by supervisors at all levels. Unless skillfully conducted, however, such an interview may be an unpleasant experience for both parties and cause the interviewee to resist improving on the job. Fortunately, an interview that is satisfactory to the interviewer is likely to satisfy the interviewee as well and hence can be a constructive experience for both.

While it goes without saying that two interviewers may differ in skill, it is equally true that two *skilled* interviewers may practice quite different methods. It also follows that, while each method requires its own specific skills, more can be accomplished with the superior method even when skills are equal.

This differentiation between skill and method is important because the goal of the interview determines which method should be used to achieve it; and once we have clarified the goal in any activity, the problem of developing the necessary skills is greatly simplified. If, for example, in driving a golf ball, we are aiming at direction rather than distance, the skill we are concerned with is the orientation of the body while swinging rather than force of stroke.

Unlike our somewhat simplified example, however, appraisal interviews may have various and sometimes conflicting objectives. Among them we may note: (a) to let subordinates know where they stand; (b) to recognize their good work; (c) to point out how and where they can improve; (d) to develop them on their present job; (e) to develop and train them for higher jobs; (f) to let them know how they may progress in the company; (g) to serve as a record for assessing the department or unit as a whole, showing where each person fits into the larger picture; and (h) to warn some employees that they must do better. It is frequently supposed that several or all of these objectives may be achieved by a single interview, but this is not the case.

Conflicting Objectives

The differences between these objectives, however slight, will affect the whole course of the interview. For example, "letting an employee know where he stands" suggests a fairly comprehensive report, while an interview for the

* From *Personnel*, March-April 1958, pp. 27–40. Condensed from *The Appraisal Interview*, by Norman R. F. Maier, Copyright 1958 by John Wiley & Sons, Inc. Reprinted by permission of the publisher and of the American Management Association.

purpose of recognizing an employee's good work can be much more selective in content.

When the interview serves as a warning, some companies require the employee to sign an appraisal form. This precludes his saying at a later time that he was not told his work was unsatisfactory. However, the requirement of a signature is inconsistent with goals other than warning.

A discrepancy between the goals of the interviewer and the interviewee may also cause difficulties. For example, in praising a very superior employee who has many virtues and few faults, the interviewer may make a minor criticism or pass over something as merely "satisfactory." However, the employee may regard this as unfavorable and feel crushed by any suggestion that he should improve.

On the other hand, a supervisor may treat a weak subordinate with kid gloves to avoid hurting his feelings. Thus he may call the employee's best point "quite satisfactory" although in reality it is only about average, and praise him highly for effort. The employee may emerge from the interview feeling relieved and perhaps more secure than he should, considering his limited prospects.

This article will describe three types of appraisal interviews, each with a specific and slightly different objective. The differences are important in determining the skills required and, to a great extent, actually call for different skills from the interviewer's repertoire. A unique interaction characterizes each method, so that the three differ in kind rather than in degree. The three methods may be described as *Tell and Sell, Tell and Listen,* and *Problem Solving.*

• THE TELL AND SELL METHOD

The initial aim of the *Tell and Sell* method is to communicate the employee's evaluation to him as accurately as possible. The fairness of the evaluation is assumed and the supervisor seeks (a) to let the employee know how he is doing; (b) to gain his acceptance of the evaluation; and finally (c) to get him to follow the plan outlined for his improvement. These three goals seem, at first glance, to be consistent with each other and in some circumstances, they undoubtedly are so.

If it is assumed that people desire to correct faults, that the superior's judgment is acceptable to the subordinate and that he is able to change in the direction specified, then the desired aims can be achieved. However, it is not unusual for subordinates to regard their supervisors' expectations as unreasonable, their criticisms unjustified, and the methods of work they suggest inefficient. It is also unrealistic to expect a person to improve merely because he wants to. He may strive to make wise decisions, be patient, get along with people, conduct conferences effectively, and stand up under strain, but such behavior may not be subject to his voluntary control.

While improvement in such things as getting to work on time, turning in honest expense accounts, and working hard is usually considered a matter of volition, here, too, more than a wish may be necessary. Frequently, the problem is one of adjustment rather than motivation. Emotional maladjustment requires therapy, and improper attempts to make improvements may aggravate rather than correct the condition.

For purposes of this discussion it will be assumed that extreme cases are the exception and that the interviewer is going to deal with management people who are able to take criticism.

The Necessary Skills

Considerable skills are necessary for success in the *Tell and Sell* type of interview. They include the ability to persuade the employee to change in the prescribed manner and this requires knowing how to use the incentives that motivate him and sometimes developing new ones. The salesman must know his customer and the selling of an evaluation makes the same demands on a supervisor.

The method becomes especially difficult if the interviewer encounters resistance. Since he usually sees himself in the role of doing something for the employee's good, any failure to appreciate this gesture places him on the defensive. Thus the situation may become strained or deteriorate into obvious hostility.

However, the employee usually senses his supervisor's increased aggression before it is too apparent, and consequently refrains from questioning the evaluation. The passive resistance and verbal agreement that follow are often taken as acceptance of the evaluation by the interviewer. When the employee retreats from discussion, the supervisor may feel more obliged to talk and may end up lecturing or preaching.

Defensive feelings, whether expressed or covered up, are a natural reaction of the employer to this type of interview. The supervisor is cast in the role of a judge, while the employee wants to make as good a showing as possible and tries to conceal any weaknesses. As the supervisor can never know all the circumstances and provocations, his criticism is apt to seem unjust.

Once the subordinate questions his superior's evaluation, a face-saving situation is created. Unless the interviewer is very patient or something happens to break the chain of events, the conflict will become more acute. Since the superior usually has some power at his disposal, the subordinate invariably learns to give in. Subordinates often develop a degree of insensitivity to criticism on these occasions. The general viewpoint in the organization may be, "everybody gets criticized during appraisal interviews, so you just take it with a grain of salt." Some interviewers attempt to comfort their subordinates by telling how they, too, are evaluated and criticized.

Although the *Tell and Sell* interview may be unpleasant for both parties, this does not prove that it lacks merit. Correction usually is unpleasant, and almost everyone can recall discarding faults because of criticism that once was painful. Certainly, faulty behavior can be inhibited or replaced by having someone point out a better way. The crucial issue is finding the most effective approach. Both motivation and training are essential to change.

When a man lacks the skill or knowledge to do his job in the way his superior desires, the problem is one of training or transfer. If an employee is worthy of development on his present job, the interviewer should clarify the job demands and indicate where and how the employee can acquire the desired knowledge or skills.

Motivation to Change

The fact that people often want to do a job effectively may be sufficient motivation to adopt the correct methods and habits. The desire for the boss's approval may also provide motivation.

However, sometimes an employee has his own views about a job or does not wish to reveal his lack of ability to change. If he has "bad" habits or is negligent in certain respects, he may resist change because the undesirable behavior is attractive to him. In such instances, new motivation is necessary. One way is to make the old behavior unattractive by punishment and threats of discharge. This is similar to removing an undesirable growth by surgery. The *operative* approach is unpleasant for the employee because he must either give up the behavior he likes or suffer the consequences.

Another way is to make an alternate response attractive by rewarding it. This *substitution* method is usually more pleasant and effective than the operative, not only because punishment is unnecessary but also because an alternative is supplied. Thus a child's emotional disturbance is reduced if a broken toy is replaced by another, and a smoker will find it somewhat easier to give up cigarettes if he substitutes gum. However, something pleasant (a reward) must be added in order to make the choice attractive and voluntary.

Both methods require that an external motivating factor be added to one of the alternatives; a negative incentive (punishment) must be connected with the undesirable behavior or a positive incentive (reward) with the acceptable alternative. This form of motivation is *extrinsic* to the activity, in contrast with *intrinsic* motivation in which the activity itself is satisfying. When extrinsic motivation is used, the new behavior is not accepted for its own sake, but for other reasons.

Both the type of motivation used and the defensive attitudes aroused limit the effectiveness of the *Tell and Sell* method. Frequently the subordinate accepts the evaluation or says he does in order to get out of the interview situation. But the fact remains that a selling method permits only two courses of action: continue as before vs. change to the superior's plan. However, plans for improving a work situation and ways to deal with a behavior problem can seldom be reduced to two possibilities.

Advantages and Limitations

A plan may be effective in one situation while it fails in another. The *Tell and Sell* method has its greatest potential with young and new employees, who are inexperienced and insecure and want the assurance of an authority figure. They are likely to respect the superior not only because of his position but also because of his greater knowledge and experience. Similar reactions usually occur in employees who are new on an assignment.

Individual differences also play a part in reactions to the *Tell and Sell* method. Persons who are easy-going, uncritical, somewhat unimaginative and ready to accept authoritarian leadership are most able to profit from it.

From the company's viewpoint the method is efficient, providing it works. Presenting an evaluation takes less time than discussing it and if the employee accepts the presentation, a fairly complete interview can be held in about 15 minutes. However, if the appraisal is resisted, considerable time may be required to achieve the potential gains of this method.

Although the *Tell and Sell* method may produce positive results under favorable conditions, it also may do more harm than good. When, for example, a subordinate thinks his appraisal is unfair, he may feel that his interests and the company's are no longer compatible. Loyalty depends on *mutual interests* and both the supervisor and the company may lose men's loyalties in the process of conducting appraisal interviews.

Again, if the interview is unpleasant, the day-to-day relationship between supervisor and subordinate may become strained and job satisfactions decreased for both.

However, the greatest risk occurs, particularly in appraising middle and top management, when the subordinate accepts the judgment of his superior and tries to please him instead of giving his best thinking to the job. Every language has a phrase for a "yes man" and no superior wants to develop one. Yet the *Tell and Sell* method is bound to encourage this type of subordinate for it assumes that the boss knows best—he is the father figure who dispenses rewards and punishments. Such an executive expects his men to want to please him and they soon learn what he expects of them, often competing with each other to gain his favors. Although the boss may ask his subordinates to make independent judgments and take initiative, the fact that he appraises and recommends motivates the weaker among them to find out what he wants and to do it his way. To forestall criticism, some even adopt the boss' manners and dress. Thus when this method works, it is likely to develop dependent, docile behavior, and when it fails, rebellious behavior may result. Needless to say, neither extreme is desirable.

Finally, what is the over-all effect on company philosophy and values? Organizations vary in the extent to which they are receptive to new methods and ideas. When evaluations are made from the top down, it is difficult for new ideas to enter, unless top personnel are recruited from outside the company. However, this may require overcoming resistance to changes down the line and is often impractical. Since the *Tell and Sell* type of interview makes no provision for upward communication, it tends to perpetuate existing values. Although changes may occur effectively when initiated from the top or when approved by the proper superiors, there is no means of stimulating new ideas. While both radicalism and conservatism with respect to change have unique values, each makes its contribution under different circumstances. Insofar as conservatism rather than change is desired, the *Tell and Sell* method is effective.

• THE TELL AND LISTEN METHOD

The *Tell and Listen* method of conducting an appraisal interview is often viewed with skepticism because the role of the interviewer seems somewhat unnatural and ambiguous with respect to authority. The goal here is to communicate the evaluation to the employee and then let him respond to it. The interviewer covers his strengths and weaknesses during the first part of the interview, postponing points of disagreement until later. The second part is devoted to thoroughly exploring the subordinate's feelings about the evaluation. Thus the superior, while still in the role of a judge, listens to objections without attempting to refute them. In fact, he encourages the employee to disagree because the objective is not only to communicate the appraisal but also to drain off any negative feelings it arouses. The cathartic value of the verbal expression of frustrated feelings is assumed.

The initial reactions are similar to those of the *Tell and Sell* method since both begin with a presentation of the evaluation. However, the methods differ radically as regards the way disagreement and resistance are handled. Instead of the interviewer dominating the discussion, he sits back and becomes a nondirective counselor[1] during the second part of the interview.

Skills of This Approach

The skills of this approach are (a) active *listening*—accepting and trying to understand the employee's attitudes and feelings; (b) making effective use of *pauses*—waiting patiently without embarrassment for the other person to talk; (c) *reflecting feelings*—responding to feelings to show understanding; and (d) *summarizing feelings*—to indicate progress, show understanding and emphasize certain points, as well as to end the interview. None of these skills implies that the interviewer either agrees or disagrees with the employee. Rather they suggest the possibility that the evaluation may be unjust and even incorrect, and that the employee should accept only ideas which may be helpful.

Since it is assumed at the outset that there are two sides to the appraisal, face-saving issues are not aggravated. As the superior doesn't expect the subordinate to agree, he feels no need to defend his evaluation. The unpleasant aspects of the interview are reduced for he has a method for dealing with the employee's defensive responses, and is better able to understand and respect his feelings. Consequently, he will be less inclined to avoid conducting appraisal interviews than the *Tell and Sell* interviewer, who may be over-anxious.

The motivating factors in the *Tell and Listen* interview are somewhat complex. Since fears of reprisals and of displeasing the superior are reduced, inadaptive defensive behavior fanned, in part, by these fears is less likely to occur. Thus the countermotivation known as *resistance to change* is lessened by the counseling process, but the tendency to change to avoid displeasing the boss is sacrificed. Which of these two opposing motivations is stronger will vary in individual instances.

There is also the positive motivation that comes from having a pleasant interview with the boss. Hostility is minimized and the subordinate feels accepted and important. These feelings are conducive to forming a constructive attitude toward growth. Thus a subordinate tends to want to please a supervisor he likes more than one he fears. When fear is dominant, a person, at best, shys away from wrongdoing, but does not extend himself to perform beyond the call of duty.

The motivations discussed so far are *extrinsic* in that they lie outside job activity and the work itself has not been

---

[1] C. R. Rogers, *Counseling and Psychotherapy*, Houghton Mifflin (1942), p. 450.

made more interesting. However, some increase in job interest is possible. Intrinsic motivation would occur if the interview resulted in (a) solving some job problems; (b) clarifying certain misunderstandings between supervisor and subordinate; or (c) solving a personal problem. These gains are most probable in instances where the employee's job performances are deficient. The interview might also result in improvements in the work climate—another element of job interest.

If the superior listened and *learned* from the interview, additional gains would be possible. The superior might modify job assignments and expectations, alter his evaluation, perceive the subordinate's job differently, or discover his own negligence in training and assisting. However it takes an exceptional interviewer to learn from the interview. Since the appraisal is made before the interview, most interviewers feel committed to uphold it.

Benefits of the Method

This method usually insures a good relationship between superior and subordinate during the interview. The employee is likely to leave with a positive attitude toward the supervisor, feeling that the interview has been worth while and that he is important to the company. The interview provides an opportunity for the superior to learn his subordinate's needs, although his impressions may be incorrect.

However, there is some risk that the interview may not achieve its first objective—letting the employee know where he stands. In addition, while the employee may gain new insights which may cause him to change, he is not likely to discover ways for improving job performance. Thus he may leave the interview with satisfaction but without a program for developing on his job.

The values promoted by the *Tell and Listen* interview are those of tolerance and respect for the individual. Thus the method tends to make supervisors employee- rather than production-minded, an attitude which generally stimulates higher morale.[2] However, while high morale and productivity frequently are related, there may be variations in productivity among groups that have equally high morale.

The greatest value of this method comes from the fact that the interviewer may profit from the interview. Change initiated from below may occur when a subordinate is able to influence his superior's views on how the job may be improved in (a) supervision, (b) work methods, (c) job assignments and (d) job expectations. Frequently, superiors once performed the jobs of the men they now supervise, and very often expect their subordinates to act just as they did. Since people differ and times as well as jobs change, this expectation, while understandable, is usually impractical. In any events, a superior's expectations, at best, tend to restrict initiative and inhibit improvements. Although some of this loss may be recouped by using suggestion boxes, it is important not to stifle new ideas by an appraisal program that was designed to develop employees. A supervisor who listens and learns may encourage upward communication in deed as well as in word. The belief that constructive forces for change may spring

---

[2] D. Katz, N. Maccoby, and N. C. Morse, *Productivity, Supervision and Morale in an Office Situation*, Institute for Social Research, University of Michigan (1950), p. 84.

from below can become an important part of organizational philosophy.

• THE PROBLEM-SOLVING APPROACH

The *Problem-Solving* method of appraisal interview has grown out of the author's recent studies of executive development. Of the three methods presented here it deviates the most from common-sense views. It takes the interviewer out of the role of judge and makes him a helper. Although the interviewer may want to help his subordinate, in the other two types of interview this is difficult because the process of appraising is inconsistent with that of helping. It may appear that the purpose of the interview is lost if the appraisal is not directly communicated to the subordinate. However, one must also recognize that the development of the employee often is the primary reason for conducting an appraisal interview and that *this* objective may be lost in the process of communicating the evaluation.

As has been said, appraisal interviews may serve a variety of purposes of which development is one. Although the two other methods discussed communicate the appraisal to the subordinate, they do not assure his understanding and acceptance. The *Problem-Solving* approach has no provision for communicating the appraisal, and indeed it may be unessential for this purpose. If the appraisal is required for other reasons, it may be desirable to delay making it until after the interview.

The goal of employee development immediately establishes a *mutual interest* between the interviewer and his subordinate. Both would like the employee to improve on the job and agree that the boss could assist him. When the subordinate accepts this help-giving role of his supervisor, he is more willing to describe his difficulties. However, when the boss passes judgment on his job performance, their interests conflict. On the one hand, the employee wants to impress his boss favorably and hide his weaknesses. The interviewer, on the other hand, wants to avoid being deceived and to discuss weaknesses. *Mutual interests* are present only so long as the employee's merits are being praised and end when the interviewer indicates that he is somewhat less than satisfied.

Since the objective is employee development, the interviewer cannot specify the area for improvement, because this would be making a judgment. He must limit his influence to stimulating thinking rather than supplying solutions, and be willing to consider all ideas on job improvement that the employee brings up. His function is to discover the subordinate's interests, respond to them, and help the employee examine himself and the job. He must forget his own viewpoint and try to see the job as the employee sees it. If the employee's ideas seem impractical, the interviewer should ask questions to learn more specifically what the employee has in mind. Often the ideas may seem difficult to accept because they are misunderstood or viewed from a different frame of reference. Communication may be faulty unless each person tries to understand the background, attitude, and experience of the other.

When the interviewer finds that a subordinate's thinking is naive, he must be willing to assume that a problem-solving discussion is the best way to stimulate growth and sophistication. If an employee can grow in this manner, he need not know that he has had weaknesses and faults. The process may be compared to the training of children. Telling a child that he is gawky and uncoordinated does not help him to become graceful and skilled. As a matter of fact, he will probably improve more if left to himself, instead of being exposed to extensive fault finding. However, people are often so concerned with the faults they observe that they find it difficult to suppress comments and advice. Thus a supervisor's knowledge and experience will not help his subordinate unless he knows how to share them constructively.

Exploring Solutions

Problem solving is characterized by the exploration of a variety of solutions. It is inhibited when a person feels threatened by an evaluation which directs attention to him rather than to the situation. When a person is placed in the spotlight he tries to hide his defects and to protect himself by defensive behavior. As long as he defends himself, he is not searching for new or better ways of performing. If an evaluation is very threatening, it may arouse hostile and stubborn reactions which further delay problem solving.

The *Problem-Solving* approach uses non-directive skills similar to those of the *Tell and Listen* method—listening, accepting, and responding to feelings. The interviewer should be especially alert to expressions of concern at the start of the interview. Such a remark as "Well, this is the day we get overhauled, I suppose," should be met with a statement like, "I daresay you think these interviews are rough on people in some ways." However, the objective of the *Problem-Solving* interview is to go beyond an interest in the subordinate's feelings to a discussion of the job. If the employee is not over-anxious, the interviewer can ask questions about the job at the beginning. While such questions are directive, they do not limit the views and feelings that can be expressed.

In some instances, the various job activities should be discussed and evaluated. Differences in perceptions of what the job is may account for some unfavorable points in the evaluation. Thus the interviewer might learn that the subordinate saw his job as "getting an assignment finished on time, regardless of the feelings of others" and that he had gained this mistaken impression from a previous reprimand. However, the differences should be passed over, serving merely to enlighten the interviewer about the need for better job descriptions, training, or communication. Once the job is analyzed in terms of the way it is done, some time can be spent discussing the ideal working conditions.

If mutual understanding of the job has been accomplished in previous interviews, the employee can be asked to review the year's progress and discuss his problems and satisfactions. The idea is to make the interview an opportunity to get the boss' ear.

As has been said, the superior should consider all the ideas presented. By restating them in somewhat different words, the interviewer may test his understanding, and show his interest in considering the changes suggested. He need not agree or disagree with the ideas in order to understand and consider acting upon them.

When the employee expresses numerous ideas, it may be wise to jot them down. Making such a record is an act of accepting without taking a stand for or against. The ideas can be evaluated later on and the best ones selected. In this way none are called poor; some just fail to survive.

Skillful Questioning Is Needed

Skillful questioning can stimulate a subordinate to evaluate his ideas and plans. The questions should not put him on the spot, but should indicate that the listener wants to get the complete story. The following may serve as examples of questions of this kind:

Can this plan of yours deal with an emergency situation, in case one should arise?

Would you have other people at your level participate in the plan?

What kinds of problems do you anticipate in a changing market?

Exploratory questions are effective in drawing a person out and making him think more clearly; they may also serve to direct analysis to areas that may have been overlooked.

The use of summaries and pauses, already touched upon in discussing the *Tell and Sell* method, is equally helpful in the *Problem-Solving* interview. Pauses, in fact, perform an additional function in the latter technique, since they allow the subordinate to explore and evaluate ideas without feeling the pressure of time. If a subordinate is free to analyze the job with the prospect of influencing improvements in it, he will be motivated to think constructively, in a mature and responsible way. The problem of gaining his acceptance of any changes is non-existent because he has suggested them.

The problem-solving approach motivates original thinking because it stimulates curiosity. Curiosity is a strong drive and as long as fear is not aroused, leads to exploratory behavior. For example, children will explore a free and secure environment but stop in the face of danger or threats of punishment. Problems offer opportunities to explore and their solutions lead to new experiences. Some *extrinsic* motivations such as gaining approval or avoiding failure may be present, but essentially the problem-solving activity has interest in itself. This *intrinsic* motivation is present in many things we like to do and is an important aspect of play. If it could be made a larger part of the job, then work would become more like play.

A re-examination of the job is bound to suggest some changes because certain aspects are usually more satisfactory than others.

There are four different ways of improving job satisfaction: (a) the job itself may be reorganized or enlarged; (b) the subordinate's perception of the job may be changed; (c) the superior's understanding of a man's problems may be increased so that he will relate differently to his subordinate, supply assistance in the form that is needed, or improve communications; and (d) the opportunity may be created to solve problems of a group nature involving relationships between the various subordinates who report to the interviewer.

Since job satisfaction may be approached in various ways, some improvements should be possible for the employee. If none come under discussion, the interviewer may ask questions to stimulate exploration of the various areas. Once different possibilities are examined, a selection can be made in terms of practicality and interest. If the goal is to improve things in some way that is in line with the employee's wishes, then there is good assurance that a change will occur.

However, in order to achieve improvement in the direction desired by the subordinate, the superior must sacrifice his right to determine the change. It may turn out that both will agree but in order to gain the change that the subordinate will accept, the interviewer must not attempt to impose his own views.

In the event that a subordinate does not express any ideas and fails to respond to the *Problem-Solving* approach, it may be assumed that this method has failed. However, the failure does not preclude the use of one of the other two methods.

Upward Communication

The *Problem-Solving* approach affords both the participants a highly favorable opportunity for learning and communicating. Training is usually considered a one-way process in which the superior gives his knowledge to the subordinate. The *Problem-Solving* approach, like the *Tell and Listen* method, stimulates upward communication. In addition, it creates a climate for high quality decisions and changes since it pools the thinking of two people who have supplementary experiences. Resistance to change is a common obstacle to progress but this approach removes sources of resistance and stimulates change.

The interviewer places *mutual interests* above personal interests, and respects the problem-solving ability of the subordinate. Exploring the job with an understanding superior stimulates new ideas and leads to increased job interest as well as a better use of the employee's talents.

The attitude of mutual respect cuts across barriers of rank, focusing attention on problems to be solved rather than on prerogatives or status and personality clashes. It assumes that change is essential to an organization and that participation in change is necessary for individual growth.

CAUSE AND EFFECT RELATIONS IN THREE TYPES OF APPRAISAL INTERVIEWS

Method	TELL AND SELL	TELL AND LISTEN	PROBLEM SOLVING
Role of Interviewer	JUDGE	JUDGE	HELPER
Objective	To communicate evaluation To persuade employee to improve	To communicate evaluation To release defensive feelings	To stimulate growth and development in employee
Assumptions	Employee desires to correct weaknesses if he knows them Any person can improve if he so chooses A superior is qualified to evaluate a subordinate	People will change if defensive feelings are removed	Growth can occur without correcting faults Discussing job problems leads to improved performance

CAUSE AND EFFECT RELATIONS IN THREE TYPES OF APPRAISAL INTERVIEWS

Method	TELL AND SELL	TELL AND LISTEN	PROBLEM SOLVING
Role of Interviewer	JUDGE	JUDGE	HELPER
Reactions	Defensive behavior suppressed Attempts to cover hostility	Defensive behavior expressed Employee feels accepted	Problem solving behavior
Skills	Salesmanship Patience	Listening and reflecting feelings Summarizing	Listening and reflecting feelings Reflecting ideas Using exploratory questions Summarizing
Attitude	People profit from criticism and appreciate help	One can respect the feelings of others if one understands them	Discussion develops new ideas and mutual interests
Motivation	Use of positive or negative incentives or both (Extrinsic in that motivation is added to the job itself)	Resistance to change reduced Positive incentive (Extrinsic and some intrinsic motivation)	Increased freedom Increased responsibility (Intrinsic motivation in that interest is inherent in the task)
Gains	Success most probable when employee respects interviewer	Develops favorable attitude to superior which increases probability of success	Almost assured of improvement in some respect
Risks	Loss of loyalty Inhibition of independent judgment Face-saving problems created	Need for change may not be developed	Employee may lack ideas Change may be other than what superior had in mind
Values	Perpetuates existing practices and values	Permits interviewer to change his views in the light of employee's responses Some upward communication	Both learn since experience and views are pooled Change is facilitated

This article has analyzed three methods of appraisal interviews and has shown that they produce different results. It has pointed out that the method is a function of the particular objective the interview is designed to serve; and has shown that interviewing skills must be related to the objective as well as the method. The manner in which skills and objectives vary with the interviewing method is shown in the accompanying chart.

The chart also emphasizes the psychological difference between the methods—in the attitudes they reveal and the motivations they develop. It is hoped that this analysis will assist interviewers in adopting the methods and skills that support their particular objectives.

As has been said, common sense is often misleading, and too many or opposing interviewing goals may make it impossible to achieve any of them.

E. Appraisal Using Performance Statistics

HOW TO APPRAISE EXECUTIVE PERFORMANCE: PLANNED PERFORMANCE

ARCH PATTON

PROFIT PERFORMANCE MEASUREMENT OF DIVISION MANAGERS

JOEL DEAN

STANDARDS OF PERFORMANCE

The Standard Oil Company (Ohio)—Products Pipeline

In recent years the strong desire to substitute quantitative measures for ratings as much as possible at the managerial level has generated some interesting ideas. The problems of measurement are considerable and are regarded by some as insuperable. The readings in this section represent some different approaches to quantitative appraisal of the manager's performance.

FURTHER READING

Ferguson, Leonard W., "The L.O.M.A. Merit Rating Scales," *Personnel Psychology*, Vol. 3, no. 2, Summer 1950, pp. 193–216.

Umemura, George M., *Measuring Salesmen's Performance*. New York, National Industrial Conference Board, 1956. (Studies in Business Policy, no. 79, p. 55.)

HOW TO APPRAISE EXECUTIVE PERFORMANCE: PLANNED PERFORMANCE*

Arch Patton

Essentially, this composite approach to appraisal is aimed at providing a sound basis for judging the relative performance of executives, expressed in terms of their individual responsibilities. It establishes annual targets for the individual that are implicit in the job he holds. And it provides for *judging* performance in terms of these targets rather than a purely mathematical measurement. In addition, it relates these individual targets to the short- and long-term goals of the enterprise. This means that each member of the management team is working toward the same agreed-on objectives of the company or division and will be judged by how well he performs these tasks.

• COMPANY GOALS

This approach is called by a variety of names: programed management, management by objective, or planned performance programing. But whatever the title, its users have a common objective: that individual performance be judged in terms of agreed-on tasks reflecting the goals of the business. The first step, therefore, involves the development of long- and short-range company goals. The longer-term objectives are useful in "stretching" executive thinking—in making managers think "bigger"—but are also valuable as a guide to the practicability of the forecast targets:

Let us assume, for instance, that a single-product manufacturer, after considerable study, sets a five-year goal of doubling his unit volume. As a result, he has decided how much must be added to current sales in the first, second, and later years to attain this goal. The practicability of these estimates, of course, needs to be checked against the ability of the company to manufacture, sell, and finance such increases in volume. It makes no sense, for example, to set goals beyond the company's ability to provide funds at reasonable cost, or to agree to sell more of a product than facilities can be expected to turn out.

Once it is decided that a 15% increase in company volume is a realistic target for the first year, the next step is to determine what must be accomplished by each functional group in order to attain such a goal. To do so necessitates a careful assessment of interfunctional relationships. For instance, perhaps it is possible for the sales department to develop 15% more business by a greater utilization of salesmen's time; but if this is accomplished, new facilities might be needed by manufacturing in order to meet this goal. (These new facilities, in turn, would obviously have to be considered in relation to the forecast needs of future years as well.)

On the other hand, production facilities might be adequate to attain the necessary volume, but the sales department might have to introduce a new line of products in

* From *Harvard Business Review,* January-February 1960, Vol. 38, no. 1, pp. 63–70.

order to reach this figure. If this occurs, of course, other functional areas are likely to be involved. In addition to changes that a new line might necessitate in the sales department, i.e., the introduction of a specialized sales force, the engineering department would be expected to design the new line, credit standards might have to be tightened or loosened, transportation costs or lead times might need alteration, and so on.

• FUNCTIONAL TASKS

Experience has shown that translating short-term company objectives into 12-month goals for individual functional executives is best done by setting up both quantitative and qualitative tasks to be accomplished during the period. In other words, executive responsibilities include (a) those that can be *measured,* such as sales, behind-schedule production, or credit losses, and (b) those that must be *judged,* made up of the intangibles that arise when an executive develops a new process, establishes a training program, improves the quality of engineering candidates, and the like.

The advantage of separating qualitative and quantitative tasks lies in the very human tendency among executives to "let the numbers decide." It appears to be much easier for a superior to point out shortcomings to a subordinate when he can blame such an unpleasant conclusion on the results of a quantitative evaluation. Explaining weaknesses that must be *judged* impressionistically, while frequently more important to the training process, causes greater discomfort to the superior. The separation of the two induces a deeper awareness of the importance of both elements.

Further, these tasks need to be set up for both line and staff positions—a process that has proved to be a serious stumbling block to performance appraisal programs. Trouble results largely from line-oriented senior executives finding it difficult to visualize the possibility of setting realistic targets for staff jobs. There appears to be an unfortunate tendency among some senior executives to write off the entire approach because of this blind spot where staff is concerned. Thus:

> Dislike of this approach frequently occurs when the responsibilities of staff functions are vague, and their contribution to the management process has not been adequately developed. The senior executive subconsciously questions the value of the staff function, yet has come to believe that "staff is a hallmark of modern management." He remembers the time, a few years ago, when his company had two vice presidents —sales and manufacturing. Today, there may be vice presidents for finance, engineering, personnel, administration, and so on, but the senior executive does not have the same "feel" for these jobs that he has for the line sales or manufacturing jobs with which he grew up.

This problem has been reduced, however, as top management more and more recognizes the need for spending as much *time* in establishing company and functional goals at the outset as it spends in appraising performance at the end of the year. This more thoughtful approach to task setting results in a better understanding of staff activities, as well as a more practical evaluation of the contributions that can be made in this area.

A number of techniques have been found helpful in cutting the problem down to size. If the tasks of the line organization are worked out first, for example, the process of thinking through the supporting goals of the staff func-

Table 1

PLANNED PERFORMANCE TARGETS FOR DIVISION MANAGER

ANNUAL TARGET PLANS

List of major accomplishments needed this year to meet corporation, division, or department goals.

QUANTITATIVE TARGETS

Objectives for the year ahead that can be appraised in terms of *how much;* for example, "increase return on investment from 12% to 15%."

1. Increase billings by 17%, maintaining a 50%-30%-20% product mix in Departments A, B, and C.
2. Increase over-all profits (BT) by 35%.
3. Increase asset turnover from 1.3 times a year to 1.5 times.
4. Increase return on total asets from 18% to 21%.
5. Increase inventory turnover from 6.1 to 5.8 months.
6. Expand market share from 21% to 24%.

QUALITATIVE TARGETS

Objectives that can best be appraised in terms of *how well;* for example, "improve technical appraisal program," or "make more effective use of budgetary control."

1. Develop a new line of motors for introduction in 1961. Complete engineering phase, start production engineering.
2. Develop a more effective basis for testing candidates for supervisory positions, with particular reference to individual aptitudes for specific positions.
3. Increase the number of promotable executives by better training methods, including the introduction of job rotation and the establishment of a special assignment program designed to broaden the skills of outstanding men.
4. Start weekly department head meetings as a training and information medium.

Table 2

PLANNED PERFORMANCE TARGETS FOR DIRECTOR OF PERSONNEL

ANNUAL TARGET PLANS

List of major accomplishments needed this year to meet corporation, division, or department goals.

QUANTITATIVE TARGETS

Objectives for the year ahead that can be appraised in terms of *how much;* for example, "increase return on investment from 12% to 15%."

1. Reduce clerical costs of operating the employment function (recruiting and screening applicants) 60%.
2. Reduce cafeteria operating loss 3%.
3. Increase the typing pool from 25 to 30 employees.
4. Reduce the number of secretaries in headquarters staff by 15.

QUALITATIVE TARGETS

Objectives that can best be appraised in terms of *how well;* for example, "improve technical appraisal program," or "make more effective use of budgetary control."

1. Develop a safety training program for the operating divisions.
2. Simplify and reduce the number of clerical salary classifications.
3. Complete the management inventory.
4. Develop an approach to executive performance appraisal that will improve bonus plan administration.
5. Speed up new employee indoctrination procedure (estimated target—one hour).
6. Develop a program to provide the negotiating group with information that anticipates union demands more accurately.
7. Work with the manufacturing function to eliminate "assistants" to general foremen and plant superintendents within five years.

Table 3

PLANNED PERFORMANCE TARGETS FOR DIRECTOR OF MANUFACTURING

ANNUAL TARGET PLANS

List of major accomplishments needed this year to meet corporation, division, or department goals.

QUANTITATIVE TARGETS

Objectives for the year ahead that can be appraised in terms of *how much;* for example, "increase return on investment from 12% to 15%."

1. Cut lead time on component purchases from 120 to 100 days.
2. Reduce WDC to 70% in terms of present prices.
3. Manufacturing's phase of the cost reduction program for the division is one third of the $1,500,000 excess saving over last year.
4. Improve delivery schedule performance by 5 percentage points (to 83%).
5. Reduce spoilage ratio by 2% net from 1959 figure.
6. Improve net allowed hours ratio by 3%.

QUALITATIVE TARGETS

Objectives that can best be appraised in terms of *how well;* for example, "improve technical appraisal program," or "make more effective use of budgetary control."

1. Speed up the recognition and utilization of suggestions developed in the suggestion system.
2. Improve production planning on the assembly floor to reduce the need for stand-by stocks of sub-assemblies.
3. Restudy the manufacturing process now used for product "X" to reduce the direct labor needs.

tions is simplified. Similarly, there appears to be an advantage in setting up quantitative goals first and, subsequently, building the qualitative tasks on this foundation. One company has developed a master list of general goals for each functional area, some quantitative and some qualitative. While individual tasks will vary, of course, from year to year, these general goals have been found to be worth keeping in mind.

Examples of annual tasks developed as a basis for appraising the performance of a division head, a personnel executive, and a manufacturing executive are shown in Tables 1, 2, and 3. The tasks in these examples are obviously fewer than would be the case in real life, but they are adequate to show the kind of tasks that can be used as a basis for appraising the performance of top line and staff executives.

• LOWER-LEVEL TEMPO

The annual tasks established for the key functions naturally set the tempo for executives below the top functional level. The goals of subordinates are necessarily tied in with the targets set up for the boss. However, some confusion has crept into the picture at this point. There are those who regard goal setting as the job of the subordinate, with the supervisor merely helping the subordinate relate his own tasks "to the realities of the organization," as one commentator put it. The great advantage of this method, in the eyes of its supporters, is psychological. The executive sets his own tasks; hence paces his own development.

My experience indicates that it is unrealistic to expect middle-management executives to be broad-gauged enough to set their own tasks. They do not fully comprehend the goals that have been established for their boss by top management in order to maintain integration between functions. Further, there is little evidence that lower-echelon executives (those without full functional responsibility) are likely to set personal targets that fully "stretch" their capabilities. The political environment in most companies is such that it is very important for executives to "hit the target" they have agreed on. Since "stretched" goals are more difficult to attain, the incentive to play it safe is frequently overwhelming.

This does not mean that lower-level executives should not have an important voice in their job targets. The record indicates they should. But since their tasks are keyed directly to the goals of the functional executive, the latter must determine the targets of a subordinate, virtually in self-protection. Indeed, many of the tasks of the top functional executive are delegated directly to the subordinate:

For example, when a chief engineer has responsibility for reducing the number of motor frames in the product line, he almost certainly delegates this particular chore to someone on his staff.

When the top manufacturing executive is charged with cutting 20% off the lead time in component purchases, this too will be passed along if he is a good executive.

Thus, the tasks of this lower-level group are much like those of their superiors. The main difference is in the number of special, short-term assignments that do not appear in any job description because they change so rapidly.

• JUDGING PERFORMANCE

With job targets set up for top and middle-management executives, the next step involves determining where each executive's performance of agreed-on tasks falls in the spectrum from outstanding to poor.

Companies doing the best job of appraising the performance of their executives appear to have a number of points in common. For one thing, most of them have incentive bonus plans. The existence of this constant prod to developing better appraisal techniques seems to pay off in good results. Perhaps this reflects top management's willingness to spend more time on something involving a lot of money.

Another common attribute of such companies is top management's recognition that the most important aspect of the entire appraisal process lies in the identification of outstanding and poor performers. Many appraisal programs bog down because of the time spent trying to identify minuscule differences in performance among the middle 60% to 70% of the executive group whose performance approximates the average! As a result of the effort spent in this direction, the 30% to 40% of the executives who are either outstanding or poor performers receive inadequate attention. Naturally, this becomes a critically important roadblock to success if the appraisal program includes an unwieldy number of executives.

In this connection, a technique so simple that it hardly seems worth mentioning has proved of considerable value. The outstanding performer and the poorest performer are first identified; then, in pairs, the second most outstanding and the second poorest are determined; and so on in pairs until it becomes difficult to distinguish between the performance of individual executives. Thus, a sense of proportion and reality is built into what otherwise tends to be a swampy morass.

One of the most difficult problems in judging performance lies in the values to be assigned line versus staff contributions. A few companies have developed an approach that appears helpful and sounds practical. While its use seems to be limited to those with incentive plans, there is no apparent need for such a limitation. This approach involves appraising the performance of fully profit-responsible executives (such as division managers) first, line executives (sales and manufacturing) second, and staff executives only after tentative values have been set for the profit-responsible and line executives. In other words, the performance of staff executives is "slotted" around already established relationships among the line executives.

The technique makes sense. The performance of the fully profit-responsible executive can be measured with a good deal of accuracy, by means of share-of-market, return-on-investment comparisons, and the like. Yardsticks for appraising sales and manufacturing executives are also good. However, measures of the staff executive's performance still leave much to be desired, and the evaluation of his performance should benefit from being tied in to the more tangible landmarks used for line executives.

The risk, of course, is that staff executives will be "slotted" on a position-in-the-hierarchy basis, or, in other words, judged by their position on the organization chart rather than by their performance. But a hardheaded judgment of the relative value of the tasks agreed upon, as well as a careful assessment of performance, will go a long way toward protecting against this risk.

• ACTION NEEDED

Having determined where individual performance falls in the continuum from outstanding to poor, it is necessary to do something about these findings. One of the recurring problems in appraisal programs is that lower-echelon executives come to believe "nothing happens" as a result of the admittedly time-consuming appraisal effort.

An obvious first step is to see that the individual knows what is thought of his performance, and why. Since management's judgment of his performance is based on results racked up in the attainment of specific tasks, the individual's weaknesses and strengths are clearly delineated, and the supervising executive can discuss reasonably concrete "hits and misses" with the subordinate. This overcomes the natural reluctance among executives to criticize purely personal traits in their subordinates. Further, it focuses attention on specific opportunities for improvement. The planned performance approach, therefore, provides a basis for self-development on the part of the individual, as well as an assessment of "how he is doing."

For performance appraisal to be firmly rooted in a company's way of life it should play a key role in promotions, merit increases, and bonus payments. The outsider reviewing corporate administration practices all too frequently finds top performers, as measured by the appraisal program, doing no better than the average performer where bonuses, merit increases, and promotions are concerned. It may not make sense, but the rationalizations are plentiful. For instance, a top performer will be passed over for a merit increase "because his bonus was boosted this year"; or his bonus will be held unchanged despite outstanding performance "because he recently received a merit increase."

The point is this: if performance appraisal is worthwhile, it should provide the backbone for executive personnel administration.

• EARLY PROBLEMS

To date at least, only a handful of companies have seriously attempted to set up such a programed approach to performance appraisal. Because most of these pioneering efforts were started in the past few years, it is too early to look for success stories. However, the top executives of companies that have tackled task planning are almost uniformly enthusiastic with results achieved so far. The principal accomplishment, in their view, is the establishment of a task-oriented way of life. Job objectives are more clearly defined and, therefore, better coordinated. Individual executives know what is expected of them and can target their activities more effectively. Last but certainly not least, the annual review of "hits and misses" between superior and subordinate becomes more realistic and more productive of improved future performance.

Needless to say, there have been problems. It is significant, however, that the major problem areas follow a reasonably consistent pattern from company to company. For example:

(1) The detailed probing of individual job responsibilities essential to this approach takes a great deal of time and necessitates some highly creative thinking. Since executives are human, many of them tend to resist both the effort and the thought processes that are involved. For this reason, it is essential that the chief executive be solidly behind the project. If, for instance, executives come to suspect that their own bonuses may suffer from any neglect of the necessary time and thought requirements, so much the better.

(2) Another common problem of successful performance programing is the need for a competent and creative "control function." Executives who are to be rewarded or penalized, in part at least, on results developed by the budgeting and accounting function should have great confidence in the control techniques used, as well as the skill and honesty of this group. It is relatively simple to devise yardsticks, but the objectivity and courage of the top control executives must be respected at all levels if these measures are to be effective. Executives need to have faith that tasks set for the various functions are equally difficult, and that figures are not going to be juggled to protect someone's favorite.

The judgment of individual performance in terms of agreed-on tasks (such as those in Tables 1, 2, and 3) requires maturity of a high order at the top level. One of the great advantages of the approach is the coordination of effort that results from its thoughtful, orderly task-setting process. If top management is overly arbitrary in its judgments, understandable problems develop. The chief executive who looks only to the results, without a careful weighing of the difficulties encountered in the accomplishments, is storing up future trouble.

(3) The planned performance approach also necessitates a personnel staff of unusual competence. This group necessarily plays a key role in advising top

management when an imbalance occurs between functions. Several appraisal programs have suffered because the top personnel executives were unwilling or unable to convince top management of developing problem areas. In one instance, the personnel executive knew that the annual tasks set for one functional group were consistently more difficult to attain than were those of other groups. As a result this group had lost about 25% in bonus income over a four-year period. Top management became aware of the problem only after several promising young executives quit, and a subsequent study disclosed the source of the trouble.

Since this approach to performance appraisal is most effective when confined to executives who importantly influence company profits, many personnel executives find themselves dealing with new and complex problems when an executive appraisal program is adopted. As one personnel vice president put it, "I used to spend 95% of my time on problems dealing directly or indirectly with moves having union overtones. Now, more than half my time is spent on the recruitment, development, organization, and motivation of executives!"

Many personnel executives have found it difficult to effect a change-over. Thus, top management faces a serious handicap, since a strong, capable personnel group is a major ingredient in a successful appraisal program.

(4) The "cutoff point" of executives to be included in the appraisal program has proved to be another problem area. If too many are included, the programing task becomes monumental. The most effective course appears to involve starting off with a relatively limited group of key executives whose profit impact is unmistakable, and adding levels of executives to the program as its usefulness "proves out." The temptation to include too many, however, is almost overwhelming and needs to be consciously restrained.

Results to date indicate that the programed approach to performance appraisal is not for the laissez-faire management. It is a new way of life—and as difficult as it is rewarding.

• CONCLUSION

The planned performance approach provides several important advantages over earlier attempts at executive appraisal:

- The long- and short-term objectives of the enterprise become an integral part of the performance appraisal process.
- The job responsibilities of executives provide the basis for setting individual targets. As a result of the necessity for thinking through the interrelationships between job activities, there is a more effective targeting of individual effort.
- The outstanding and poor performers receive primary attention, spotlighting those eligible for promotion or merit increases and those requiring training or elimination.
- Personality plays a less important part in the final evaluation of performance, for the focus is on what a man does rather than what is thought of him. Thus, subjective criteria are replaced by objective ones.
- Mathematics is put in its proper role, providing guidelines rather than final decisions.

Companies using this appraisal approach believe its greatest contribution stems from the disciplines it imposes on the management process. Planned performance forces a company:

- To think hard about its objectives and review them constantly.
- To study the responsibilities involved in individual positions and determine their relative importance to the business.
- To set practical work tasks for individuals and hold them accountable for their attainment.
- To take whatever action is called for by the information presented to it, in order to build a more effective management team.

In a sense, therefore, such a program involves a down-to-earth executive development program. Since people learn by doing, on-the-job training has great advantages over the more formal executive development programs that bloomed in profusion after the war.

The planned performance approach requires an enormous investment of top management's time in its early years. Since it usually involves a more disciplined way of life in the management process, it needs strong support from the chief executive and those directly under him. Because of the great time demands involved, companies have found it advantageous to limit the number of positions included in the program to those having a clearly recognizable impact on profits.

The approach also requires unusually skilled and resourceful control, market, and economic research functions. Because quantitative yardsticks play a major role in establishing targets and judging performance, they must be demonstrably good or executive belief in the fairness of the process will be undermined. It should be recorded, however, that the performance of executives is subject to constant scrutiny, for decisions bearing on promotions, merit increases, and bonuses are being made by top management almost daily. The question is whether the planned performance approach is worth the time and the effort that are needed to make it effective.

Companies that have worked hardest to develop their skill in this area believe it to be a major improvement over earlier efforts. And the fact that these concerns are pacesetters in industry implies that the competitive pressure exerted by their success with this new management tool will force an ever-widening circle of companies to think in similar terms about executive performance appraisal.

PROFIT PERFORMANCE MEASUREMENT OF DIVISION MANAGERS*

Joel Dean

• REQUIREMENTS FOR PROFIT CENTER PERFORMANCE MEASUREMENT

To make a profit center system achieve these desired results of stimulating and measuring executive performance, it is necessary to:

A. Mark off profit centers correctly

B. Establish economically sound intracompany transfer prices and business arrangements

C. Measure the contribution profits of the profit center correctly

D. Determine realistic standards of contribution profit performance

E. Establish incentives in the form of executive compensation and nonmonetary rewards that will induce profit center managers to do what will be best for the corporation as a whole.

Profit Center Boundaries

The problem of marking off profit center boundaries has two aspects: (1) Segregating service functions from profit centers, (2) defining the scope of each profit center.

Service centers comprise staff activities which cannot be satisfactorily measured in terms of profit performance. Profit centers and service centers shade into one another so that each company's solution needs to be different. The contribution of a service center to company profitability may be great but is hard to isolate and measure definitively.

The problem of gearing staff service to profit performance is partly solved by pulverizing staff services and distributing among profit centers, where the activity must be justified economically.

Some services could be sold on a profit center basis but institutional arrangements would be too complicated and burdensome, e.g., engineering. Some services might not be used enough or in the right way if made a profit center, e.g., legal department or economics department.

The second problem is to define the scope of each profit center. A profit center is defined as a semiautonomous group of facilities and functions chosen so that profit performance can be the main guide to evaluation of divisional performance and the main guide by which the division manager makes his critical decisions.

Decisions involve economic choices among mutually exclusive courses of action. Each decision requires balancing of various kinds of costs and revenues. The company's interest lies not in maximizing a particular kind of revenue or minimizing a particular kind of cost in isolation, but in maximizing difference between all revenues and all costs. Hence the scope for profit performance meas-

* From *The Controller*, September 1957. Copyright 1957 by the Controllers Institute of America. Reprinted by permission.

urement should be a major guide in marking off profit center boundaries.

The details of divisional boundaries and institutional arrangements are important. Failures and frustrations of decentralization are often traceable to bad boundaries and rules. Boundary lines determine how well a particular profit center functions in the corporation's interests, i.e., minimize conflicts of interest. Good boundaries make the profit performance of the division manager more meaningful, produce better incentives, supervision and development guides.

Four economic tests can be applied in marking off profit centers: (1) operational independence, (2) access to sources and markets, (3) separable costs and revenues, and (4) managerial intent.

OPERATIONAL INDEPENDENCE. Unless a division has a large measure of independence it will have inadequate scope to reach decisions on a profit-oriented basis and hence delegation will be defeated. The division manager needs discretion over buying, production, scheduling, inventories, product-mix and pricing. This discretion should be exercised under broad rules of the game established centrally.

ACCESS TO SOURCES AND MARKETS. Independent access to sources and markets is essential if make-or-buy decisions are to be made correctly. It is also essential for make-or-sell decisions, i.e., choice between selling a product at an early stage of the process or later (e.g., cured vs. uncured hams).

Access to outside sources and markets is most useful if outside markets are highly flexible in the long run, i.e., capable of either supplying or absorbing the company's needs without extreme price disturbances. Markets which appear too imperfect in the short run frequently are not over a period of months or years, e.g., major components of an automobile.

SEPARABLE COSTS AND REVENUES. Profit centers should be marked off so as to minimize the necessity for cost and revenue allocations, since these are necessarily arbitrary and contentious.

Contribution profits of the division can be defined so as to exclude central and other costs outside the profit center manager's control. But when these controllable profits are too small a part of the total a profit center does no good.

MANAGERIAL INTENT. No division's contribution can be measured solely by its profits but this must be a good measure of performance if the division is to be a profit center.

Top management must be resolved to abide by the behavior and performance and the impersonal guidance of the price system which this measure of divisional performance implies.

Economic Transfer Prices

A second underlying requisite of effective profit center controls is competitive intracompany transfer prices negotiated in arm's length bargaining by profit center managers.

Transfer pricing must preserve profit-making autonomy of the division manager so that his divisional profit performance will coincide with the interests of the company. Small differences in unit price of transfer products make big differences in division profits and executive bonuses.

Conflicts of interests can be held at a minimum by transfers at marginal cost, but this prevents meaningful division profit performance and undercuts the main gains of profit center control.

Competitive negotiated transfer prices can be obtained by applying three simple principles:

(a) Buyers and sellers completely free to deal outside or inside the company.
(b) Prices determined by negotiation between buyers and sellers with a minimum of arbitration.
(c) Negotiators have access to data on alternative sources and markets and have facilities for using the markets.

Measurement of Profit Contribution

A third requirement is good measurement of the profit contribution of the division. Performance measurement of profit center management must be geared to the multiple and overlapping goals of the corporation.

PERFORMANCE AREAS. Key performance areas can be grouped and labeled in various ways. One pattern is:

1. *Current Profitability,* the dominant measurement will be discussed later.
2. *Growth* is usually conceived as sales growth, either absolutely or relatively to the industry. Frequently it is best measured in terms of market share. In whatever way it is measured, growth usually requires the development of a market franchise. This is generally achieved at the expense of some short-run profits. But presumably, it contributes to more distant points and hence it is a part of the picture of the management's profit performance.
3. *Progress* has many dimensions. Three important ones are

(a) Investment in ideas. Research is at the expense of short-run profits, designed for long-run survival.
(b) Modernity and acceptability of the product. Sometimes this, too, causes short-run profit sacrifice.
(c) Productivity. This can be indicated by output per man hour and rate of return on facilities investments.

4. *Executive Development:* investment in people for future profits.

The last three factors, growth, progress and people, though measurable in their components, are hard to weight and reconcile with current profitability. The key question is whether the right amount of near profits were sacrificed in attaining these various determinants of distant profits. The answer requires high-level judgment and technical familiarity with the kinds of investment in market franchise, in ideas, in facilities, and in people that are entailed.

Measurement of the current profitability of a division entails three kinds of considerations:

1. The concept of profits
2. The form in which that profit concept will be used
3. The measurement of profits.

PROFIT CONCEPTS. As to the concept of profit there are three choices:

(a) Book net profits
(b) Real net profits
(c) Contribution profits

Book net profits tie into the stockholder reports, have a surface acceptability and are not very fudgible. But they embroil executives in fruitless debates about allocation of corporate overheads over which they have no control and raise moot questions about capital consumption costs of plant acquisitions at widely differing price levels.

Real net profits may settle the latter questions (inflation and depreciation) but do not settle problems of allocation of overhead beyond the division manager's control.

Contribution profits have fewer of these drawbacks being confined to costs and revenues over which the profit center manager has control.

Form of Profits. As to the form in which any of these three profit concepts may be expressed, there are three choices:

1. As dollar amounts
2. As percentage of sales
3. As a rate-of-return on investment

All three forms are useful in measuring different aspects of executive performance. For best results each needs to be compared with a suitable bogey.

1. Contribution profit dollars aid economic decision-making by focussing division management energies on dollars of added profit.

2. Contribution profits as a per cent of sales facilitate comparison with past performance and with comparable outside companies. Standing alone and without a bogey this performance measure is misleading.

3. Contribution profits as a return on investment provides the most important guide to top management in evaluation of profit center performance.

Measurement of Profits. Technical problems of profit-performance measurement are in practice less formidable than they appear to many newcomers.

A moderately good approximation to contribution profits can be drawn from most accounting systems with few adjustments given correct profit center demarcation and transfer prices. Isolating the book value of investment used by the division is always possible with some rough approximations.

Determination of the economic value of the book investment can be done quite cheaply with a tolerable degree of accuracy, once the concept is accepted. Current assets have book values and real values generally close enough together. Other assets can be adjusted to replacement value or disposal value by sampling and index numbers with adequate accuracy. If the concept of economic investment rather than book investment is unacceptable the defect is not fatal, particularly when the company has grown fast so that most of its assets are at recent price levels.

Standards of Profit Performance

Standards of profit performance, our fourth requirement, is a big, complex subject. In this analysis we can only mention four thoughts.

1. Measurement of profit performance of division managers achieves in itself many of the benefits of decentralization. Indeed a good case can be made for not attempting to formalize the standards of profit performance. Instead, leave this to the informal judgment of top management, which must in any event tailor the standard to the individual division and take many dimensions of longer-term profit performance into account, e.g., growth, progress and executive development.

2. Lack of standards should not hold up decentralization: rough standards can be used first and refined later.

3. Historical perspective is essential in developing performance standards; backcasting of comparable performance measurements will be needed.

4. Par for the profit center course should also take account of economic climate and competitive conditions in the industry. Sometimes this can be done roughly by comparison with the earnings of independent firms of approximately the same product line.

Incentive Compensation

The final requirement for effective profit center operation is incentives which will power the profit center manager to maximize his division's contribution profits now and in the future. The following basic considerations should underly the development of a balanced plan for incentive compensation of the managers of profit center divisions:

1. Objective measurements of profit performance are in themselves incentives to the kind of man who makes a good division manager. But profit center control will be most effective if powered with incentive compensation which is geared dominantly to the contribution profits of the division.

2. Incentive compensation should fit the organizational environment and personality of the profit center management: (a) independence, (b) economic sophistication and (c) minimal concern about bureaucratic politics. This means it should be geared to his division's performance.

3. Since incentives are a reward for extraordinary performance the base salary should approximate a competitive level and the ceiling or target bonus should be 40 to 50 per cent of this salary though it is hard to find a principle to justify any ceiling.

4. The company's total incentive compensation fund should be based on a maximum percentage of corporate net income which may each year be put into the fund after deducting compensation for capital—a symbol of good faith to the stockholders. (Example, General Motors 12% of net income after deducting 5% of net capital.)

5. The amount of incentive compensation for any profit center manager should be determined by group judgment preferably at the board level based on multiple measurements of profit performance, compared when feasible with objectively determined standards.

6. Whether the payment should be in cash, in deferred compensation or in stock options ought to be tailored to the financial personality of the manager rather than determined by uniform formula.

STANDARDS OF PERFORMANCE*

The Standard Oil Company (Ohio)—Products Pipeline

Tri-State Division Area Supervisor

[Example of a set of standards developed through consultation between the incumbent in the position, those holding similar jobs, and the incumbent's immediate superior. This set of standards is almost entirely quantitative.]

Safety

Performance is satisfactory when—

a. Frequency of serious injuries is less than 10.0 per million man-hours.

b. Frequency of lost time injuries is less than 4.0 per million man-hours.

c. Frequency of vehicle accidents is less than .35 per hundred thousand miles.

Personnel Administration

Performance is satisfactory when—

a. Hours paid for, not worked (excluding vacations) are less than 15 per 1,000 man-hours.

b. Overtime hours are less than 4 per cent of scheduled hours.

Maintenance

Performance is satisfactory when—

a. Pipeline maintenance labor cost is less than $150 per year per mile of pipe maintained.

b. Pipeline maintenance material is less than $140 per mile of pipe maintained.

c. Total pipeline maintenance cost is less than $315 per year per mile of pipe maintained.

d. Cost of pump and engine maintenance labor is less than $125 per year per pump unit maintained.

e. Cost of pump and engine repair material is less than $220 per year per pump unit maintained.

f. Total cost of pump and engine maintenance is less than $335 per pump unit maintained.

g. Pipeline maintenance is performed by no more than 4.25 maintenance employees per 100 miles of pipe maintained.

h. Pump and engine maintenance is performed by no more than 1.75 mechanics per 100 pump units maintained.

i. Cost of pump and engine repair material does not exceed $10,000 per year per mechanic.

j. Corrosion leaks do not exceed 35 per year per 100 miles of pipe operated.

k. Accidental damage to pipelines does not exceed 4 incidents per 100 miles of pipe operated.

l. Unrecovered barrels per leak are less than 75 per cent of initial loss.

m. Oil damage is less than 50 cents per barrel spilled.

n. Warehouse turnover (except pipe) is greater than 200 per cent per year.

Operations

Performance is satisfactory when—

a. Gaugers required to run 1,000 barrels per day are less than .90.

* From *Setting Standards for Executive Performance,* by John W. Enell and George H. Haas, New York, American Management Association, 1960, (Research Study 42, pp. 20–21).

b. Tickets written by one gauger per month are in excess of 174.

c. Cost of gauging supplies is less than $300 per year per gauger.

d. Cost of gathering pump station supplies is less than $20 per year per pump unit.

e. Cost of fuel burned in gathering units is less than $3.75 per 1,000 barrels gathered.

f. Operating overtime hours are less than 2.5 per cent of scheduled hours worked.

g. Run ticket errors are less than .40 per cent of tickets written.

h. Barrels spilled per leak are less than 35.

i. Oil damage per leak is less than $20.

j. Total oil loss is less than .08 per cent of total barrels handled.

Communications

Performance is satisfactory when—

a. The supervisor visits each gauging district and each pump station at least once each month.

b. Training sessions are held for each classification once each month.

c. All employee meetings of any type are scheduled at least three weeks in advance with written agenda for each meeting.

d. Area staff meetings are held at least every two weeks.

General Administration

Exact statements have not been worked out in this area as yet, but they will be based on proper administration of accounting procedure and records; purchasing procedure and records; engineering procedure and records; crude-oil purchasing and records.

Public Relations

Performance is satisfactory when—

a. At least two planned visits per year are made to operating offices of other pipeline companies in the area.

b. At least one visit per year is made with municipal officials in the area.

c. At least one presentation is made each year to local schools.

d. At least two stories pertaining to SOHIO are carried by local newspapers each year.

PART THREE •

APPRAISAL IN PERSPECTIVE

The readings in this volume reflect the research findings and the experience of many men and organizations. They are a small but important fraction of a constantly growing body of literature. The readings in Parts One and Two dealt with the general nature of appraisal, certain pervasive problems and issues connected with its use, and details of appraisal techniques. Part Four consists of case studies of appraisal programs in various company settings.

At this point, the editors present their own summary and evaluation of appraisal in order to explore some of the questions growing out of the readings and cases, and to integrate the information we have acquired from many researchers and managers.

First, consider the framework within which appraisal activity takes place. Formal appraisal activity began centuries ago. Emperors of the Wei Dynasty (221–265 A.D.) were aided by an "Imperial Rater," who appraised the performance of the members of the official family; at a later date, Ignatius Loyola established a procedure for formally rating members of the Jesuit society. Since then, performance appraisal has come through many phases of development, related to the needs of succeeding eras and varying situations.

In the United States, formal appraisal of performance was probably first introduced by government service administrators. The newly established New York City Civil Service introduced a rating plan in 1883. Even earlier—in the 1850's—rating forms were used in federal government offices. School administrators began using rating plans for appraising teachers at least as early as 1896, but American business did not get around to attempting a systematic appraisal of performance until shortly before World War I. However, the executive and the student of today must evaluate performance in terms of the social and organizational characteristics of the world in which he lives. Hence, we consider first those aspects of the modern environment against which the techniques and philosophies of performance appraisal must be judged.

THE FRAMEWORK FOR EVALUATION

The contemporary manager must cope with a world characterized by rapid change. Every area of managerial responsibility has this dynamic aspect. Performance appraisal is no exception. The reasons why men find it necessary to appraise other men remain as compelling today as ever, but factors conditioning their relationships with one another have been changing.

Labor Market Changes

Certain labor market changes are affecting organizations. At least four trends are important:

1. The occupational structure of the labor force in the United States has been shifting. The long-term movement out of agricultural employment has accelerated since World War II. Within the last decade a relative decline in the manufacturing sector has developed. However, the percentage of the labor force employed in the service industries and in government has been growing rapidly. In addition, there has been a significant change in the mix of skills. The most pronounced change has been the decline in the number of blue-collar workers and the increase in that of white-collar workers and professionals.
2. Closely related to changes in the occupational structure of the labor force is the rapid development of "automation." A special case of the long-continuing replacement of human labor by machine power, automation involves the use of increasingly sophisticated machines—machines having the power to direct themselves to a great extent, to evaluate their own output, and to correct their performance. Automation, as it is popularly conceived, first appeared on the factory floor. There is growing evidence today that it will appear in many other places in the organization. As the latest marvel—the electronic computer—is applied to a widening range of administrative problems, managers may expect to find significant changes in their own jobs and in the organization structure within which they work.
3. The long-term trend toward increasing the size of the organization continues. While automation and other forces have made it possible for industrial organizations to increase output without adding to the human complement, the effects of these forces are likely to be felt rather unevenly. Perhaps the average number of employees per firm in the manufacturing sector of private business may increase only slowly, but in the service sector of private business and in government, the average size of organization complement will undoubtedly continue to grow.
4. A trend important in the last three decades has been the growth of unionization of the work force. This trend appears at the moment to have lost some of its force as the occupational structure has shifted. Perhaps growth may cease. On the other hand, many of the factors which seem to have been associated historically with unionization of the blue-collar worker appear to be developing in the white-collar labor area. Thus, the trend may reappear with vigor.

Changes in Organization

Paralleling the four trends just discussed, certain internal characteristics of private and public organizations have also been changing over the last several decades:

1. The long-term increase in staff activities continues. The initial development of the staff concept is generally credited to the military, but it got its real start in American business seventy or eighty years ago with the contributions of the Scientific Management school. Since that time the growth in administrative staff has continued unabated in all kinds of American organizations, and is developing today within those countries which have "imported" American concepts of management.

2. The growth in staff is one aspect of a pervasive and continuous trend toward increasing specialization in the roles of members of organizations of all kinds. Of course, the size of an enterprise limits the amount of specialization that can exist. But as enterprise has grown, so have the opportunities for further specialization of members of the organization. In fact, one of the important economic gains from increasing size is the opportunity for further specialization. The trend toward increasing specialization is of long standing. However, the prodigious growth in the stock of man's knowledge, following the development of the scientific method in the eighteenth century, has, since then, sharply accelerated specialization of work roles in organizations.

3. In the United States, the "philosophy of management" has changed in recent years. Dominance of the Scientific Management school during the early part of the twentieth century, with its emphasis upon measurement, systematic behavior, and formal bureaucratic organization, was replaced in the 1930's and 1940's to some extent with the philosophy of "human relations." The human relations philosophy, with its interest in the social aspects of work activity and in the presumably inhibiting effects of formal authority, for awhile became almost a creed for the personnel managers. Today, growing management interest in the computer and in quantitative decision techniques seems to be swinging managerial interest once more back toward concern with measurement and systematic control.

Implications for Performance Appraisal

One implication for performance appraisal is that, in the immediate future, both the kinds of work roles in American business and the kinds of workers being evaluated in these roles are likely to change rapidly. In recent years managerial interest has already begun to shift from problems of evaluation of the performance of hourly workers (both blue collar and white collar) to the appraisal of men and women in management jobs. Factory automation, growing union control over work rules, and expansion of staff activities, all are responsible for this changing interest.

The increasing size of organizations (in terms of the numbers employed) presages more complex job structures. Performance measurement is always most difficult in large-scale activities, where the relationship of individual effort to group output becomes quite remote and difficult to trace. In those sectors of the economy where organizations are continually growing larger, managers must make special efforts to seek better ways of assessing performance.

Attention has recently been focused upon the problems of evaluating physical scientists in the business environment. Now, with the rapid application of the computer and quantitative techniques to management operating problems, new and important contributions will be made by new kinds of highly skilled professionals. New problems of performance appraisal, demanding new solutions, may well appear. It is reasonable to expect that this new technology of information will shake up traditional organizational relationships and ways of thinking. The techniques involved place great emphasis on analysis of information flow and upon integration of information for many purposes and many functions in the business. No operation of the business fails to be affected; no practice of management appears immune from re-examination.

It is not hard to see how performance appraisal may be affected. Information relating to operations inside the organization almost always concerns joint output of men and machines. Evaluation of such information inevitably involves appraisal of individual contributions. Just as the accountant is already having to develop new ways of assessing over-all organizational performance, so the personnel executive may soon have to consider new ways of assessing the performance of men, simply because he has new sources and new kinds of information for doing this. Hopefully, through the application of information technology, we may find some way of reducing those difficult problems, discussed in the readings, which are created by the close interpersonal relationships of those who perform and those who must appraise this performance.

In sum, the changes taking place currently in the managerial world may soon require that new ways be devised for dealing with old problems. In the near future, appraisal may be done much differently than it is today. In the face of potential change it is useful to summarize the current state of the art.

• USING PERFORMANCE APPRAISAL: SUMMARY, EVALUATION, AND SUGGESTIONS

Appraisal of human performance in an organization directly involves personal relationships among people in that organization. It also requires understanding of certain technical problems of measurement. Both these areas and their interrelation are summarized here.

Woven into this summary are the editors' judgments concerning what problems are most important, what we actually have learned about appraisal, and what we still need to learn.

Organization Goals, Organization Structure, and Performance Appraisal

Performance appraisal is an unavoidable part of organization activity. Every cooperative group must assess the contributions being made by individual members in light of the rewards being paid to them. This process appears to be essential to the survival of any group; in fact, it is one of the fundamental processes noted by anthropologists in all societies.

In modern organization terminology, performance appraisal is required for effective functioning of a compensation system, and is necessary for intelligent allocation of individuals to jobs in the organization. In recent years, organizational concern for development of the individual has been emphasized. Here, performance appraisal is also vital. In the allocation function many kinds of information are used, of course. In particular, the use of psychological tests has been common. But the overwhelming appeal of performance data to those who must make job assignment decisions assures an important role for performance appraisal.

Performance appraisal can be thought of as a feedback system. The answer to the question "What should the individual's reward be?" is, over the long run, determined by feedback of information as to how he has performed. Likewise, the question as to where the individual would best fit in the organization still seems best answered by the feedback of information as to what his patterns of performance have been. Efforts to aid the individual to perform better (development) are also guided by information as to his current and past performance. We can add an important fourth feedback function for performance appraisal. Many organizational activities are undertaken on a trial basis. To evaluate certain of these activities, managers need information on individual performance. An example is personnel selection. The effectiveness of the selection procedure must be appraised against some criterion. Performance ratings are almost invariably the criterion used.

Performance appraisal, systematic or otherwise, is unavoidable. Modern organizations seek data on individual performance to validate decisions made in distributing compensation, in allocating people to jobs, in selecting new members, and in advising individuals on ways of improving their own performances.

Are there gains from making performance appraisal systematic? Even granting that appraisal of individual performance is an inevitable and universal aspect of group activity, one might question the practice of devoting organization resources to the elaborate systems for accomplishing it, such as those discussed by the authors quoted in this book. Yet most organizations continue to attempt to develop appraisal systems. What gains do they anticipate?

The most commonly cited gain is the attainment of objectivity in judgments that otherwise would not exist. So far, it appears that this has been more a hope than an achievement. Judgments gain visibility—are written down and collected—but do not necessarily thereby become more objective. However, until judgments are written down and made systematic, it is difficult to make them objective by any external means. Furthermore, simply writing down judgments effects a transfer of memory. The organization has on file somewhere a record of successive judgments of performance. The alternative is to leave this record locked up in the heads of individuals. Human memory is notoriously unreliable. Thus, perhaps the greatest single step toward objectivity in the area of performance appraisal is the recording of judgments.

Another goal in systematizing appraisal is to gain comparability of the judgments made by different people. Large organizations, organized bureaucratically, have always faced the uncomfortable situation of having to assign people to jobs (the important ones as well as the less important) on the basis of secondhand information. Perhaps five candidates presently in the organization are being considered for promotion to a significant job. Often, no one has ever seen all five perform. Or, at least, no one has seen them all perform in the same role recently. The familiar problem of having to evaluate the judge as well as the judgments then enters the picture. Appraisal experts have long sought, through some scaling technique, to achieve comparability of reported information. While this goal has been achieved only in limited degree, it is true that unless appraisal is systematized, the problem is apt to be overlooked.

Validation of selection and of other organizational activities necessitates some systematic collection of judgments. For this purpose judgments must be made at a specific point in time (usually at successive points in time) and in particular places by specific individuals. They have to be written down and in some way scaled. Clearly, system must be imposed.

Finally, systematic appraisal permits an organization to assess its ability to appraise people. Organizations seek always to evaluate their own procedures. To evaluate the effectiveness with which appraisals are being made, it becomes necessary to systematize the appraisal process. Since the payoff on judgments very often occurs long after the judgments are made, the quality of appraisals cannot effectively be assessed unless the appraisals are systematically recorded and later subjected to analysis. An example of such analysis is reported in the case of the D Company (see Part Four).

As important as assessing the quality of judgments is the need for the organization to maintain some sort of control over the decisions based upon appraisals. They should conform, by and large, to the judgments made. But research evidence indicates that often they do not. It becomes possible to determine how well decisions conform to judgments of performance if these judgments are systematically recorded. In the area of performance appraisal, as in so many other areas of management, systems become the handmaiden of control.

Some trends are apparent in purposes for which performance appraisal is utilized in organizations. Perhaps most prominent has been the trend away from tightly controlling wages and salaries with a merit-rating plan. There are several reasons for this trend. One important reason has been the growth of unions, with their strong dislike of supervisory discretion over rewards and their strong support of seniority as a substitute control. Behind this reason lie some other factors. One is the failure of rating experts to achieve their announced goal of making judgments completely objective in the sense of getting the judge to divorce his opinions from consideration of the probable effects these opinions will have when others learn of them. In addition, supervisors, with very few exceptions, find it difficult to make distinctions among individuals except at extremes of the performance range. Furthermore, appraisal usually occurs in a close and continuing work relationship in which efficient and impersonal evaluation of individuals by others who work with them is most difficult to obtain.

However, systematic appraisals are usually retained in the wage and salary area, if they have been used there at all. While they may not be absolutely controlling, such appraisals become "one thing to be considered." They become a framework which gives continuity and control to wage and salary decisions.

While formal appraisal today plays a smaller role in wage and salary admin-

Table 1

SURVEY RESULTS: USE OF FORMAL RATING IN BUSINESS FIRMS

YEAR	NUMBER OF COMPANIES IN SURVEY	QUESTION: Do you formally appraise rank and file employees? PERCENTAGE OF COMPANIES RESPONDING:		QUESTION: Do you formally appraise managers and executives? PERCENTAGE OF COMPANIES RESPONDING:		PERCENTAGE OF RESPONDING COMPANIES ANSWERING "YES" ON APPRAISAL OF RANK AND FILE EMPLOYEES	PERCENTAGE OF RESPONDING COMPANIES ANSWERING "YES" ON APPRAISAL OF MANAGERS AND EXECUTIVES
		YES	NO	YES	NO		
1930	195	[a]	[a]	[a]	[a]	[a]	[a]
1940	231	52.5	2.6	19.9	23.8	*95.3*	*45.6*
1947	325	42.2	9.9	20.9	27.0	*80.8*	*43.7*
1953	628	54.6	15.9	32.3	35.8	*77.5*	*47.5*
1957	852	57.3	17.2	42.1	30.8	*77.0*	*58.0*

[a] Available evidence shows only that 41% of responding companies used rating scales.

Sources: Adapted from W. D. Scott, R. C. Clothier, S. B. Mathewson, and W. R. Spriegel, *Personnel Management* (New York, McGraw-Hill Book Co., Inc., 2d ed., 1931; 3d ed., 1941; 4th ed., 1948) and Scott, Clothier, and Spriegel, *Personnel Management* (New York, McGraw-Hill Book Co., Inc., 1954).

istration, its use in "development" has received a great deal of attention lately. At the same time the trend has been away from formal appraisal of blue-collar workers and toward more systematic appraisal of white-collar workers and managers. This latter trend is illustrated in the last two columns of Table 1. The table summarizes the responses to two questions about the use of performance appraisal, gathered in five surveys of company personnel practices over a period of twenty-seven years.

These trends are related. "Development" has flourished where it presumably makes some difference. Managers and potential managers are considered important enough to justify collecting careful judgments of their performance to guide them in improving their performance in the future. Not so with blue-collar workers. It was all right to make systematic evaluations of the latter group as long as pay decisions could be geared to them, but development is apparently no longer regarded as important at this level. This seems to indicate that staff managers, at least, believe a blue-collar worker will probably remain a blue-collar worker all his life.

The blue-collar segment of the work force is shrinking, of course. Perhaps it is only logical to expect a decline in interest in the application of personnel management techniques to this work group and a growing interest in the white-collar group.

A few major problems and issues have dominated the attention of experts for many years. Much of this attention has been directed toward the problem of making "objective" judgments in an organizational setting. Readings in the present volume, as well as a number of references in the bibliographies, report research showing the influence of the length of acquaintance; of specific role relationships in terms of job content, authority, and other dimensions of variations in personality of the rater; of the influence of one man's judgment on that of another; as well as the effect of a number of other factors on the appraisals made in an organization. It has been the tendency of some people in management to react to such evidence by concluding that "systematic" performance appraisal is impossible. In their view, ratings are subject to so many influences that they are better not made at all. Actually, these influences are present whenever judgments are being made. Research findings simply reveal that appraisal is more complex than had previously been thought. The case for systematizing appraisal is strengthened, not weakened, the more we learn of such things. Given the knowledge that the work of careful researchers provides, managers should work with increasing interest at systematic appraisal. They should ask their own expert staff personnel to put this research knowledge to use in making the performance appraisal information system a better one all the time.

An issue which has come to the front in recent years raises ethical questions. It is best stated in the McGregor reading ("An Uneasy Look at Performance Appraisal") in this volume. He questions whether any man should be expected to sit in judgment of another man, at least for purposes of controlling the other man's rewards. Expressing judgments in order to help the other improve himself is acceptable and compatible with our cultural norms, runs this argument, but unilateral judgment which controls punishment and reward is abhorrent to the good manager. It is hard to deny that Americans tend to dislike the exercise of personal authority over themselves. Their political and social history shows a continuous effort to control and limit such authority. In the microcosm of the firm, the same issue can arise. On the other hand, the economic goals of the organization must be served if it is to survive competitively. Government and military organizations have their counterpart survival goals. How, then, are we willing to use authority in these units?

One answer has been the development of the labor unions. At the blue-collar level the union has challenged and in most cases restrained the application of authority in the particular form of unilateral appraisal of performance. At the managerial level, which is the level that interests McGregor, unions do not exist, nor does any identifiable substitute.

At this point, the issue has been clearly raised with few opinions expressed. One writer suggests the necessity for a change in attitude; the other, for a change in organizational arrangements. It is an interesting and important issue that needs further examination.

• TECHNICAL PROBLEMS AND LIMITATIONS OF PERFORMANCE APPRAISAL

Scaling problems have monopolized the attention of most researchers in the area of performance appraisal. The earliest rating plans in modern times utilized a brief essay appraisal, or, occasionally, word check lists from which the rater selected appropriate adjectives. Such appraisals lacked precision and were difficult to cross-compare. The search for other scaling techniques continued. There was no sort of explicit standard against which judgments were made, so that the reliability of the information was poor. However, these early devices had some advantages. Supervisors found them easy and natural to use, and usually cooperated in maintaining continuous appraisal records.

The graphic rating scale was the result of the intense interest and activity in psychometrics that developed during World War I. It was easy to use and moved toward more systematic scaling of judgments. Recent research indicates that the reliability of such a scale, after brief use of it, may be better than had been thought. One of the reasons for its early rejection by rating experts was that ratings tended to pile up on the favorable end of the scale.

Efforts to overcome this distribution skewness resulted in the forced-distribution technique. This technique was based upon the assumption that performance in a given group should be distributed normally, or nearly so, and required the rater to so distribute his ratings. Raters strongly resisted this procedure on the logical ground that any work group which had been screened through selection procedures would tend to show skewed performance results. Consequently, the forced-distribution technique was never widely used. One contribution of the technique, however, was the fact that an explicit standard was introduced into the judgment process. The standard was the group mean of individual performances (in theory), and each person was appraised in terms of his deviation from this mean.

Ranking techniques developed interperson comparison to a much finer point. The paired-comparison techniques and other ranking devices gave clear answers to the standing of individuals in given groups. Unfortunately, intergroup comparisons are not dealt with, so that the top-ranked men in different groups cannot be directly compared. The one exception to this is the officer rating scale of World War I, which, in theory at least, provided a bridge between various organizational units.

The scaling techniques just described, representing the state of the art about twenty years ago, left many technicians dissatisfied. One point of dissatisfaction lay in the fact that most of these scales called for appraisal in terms of traits or personal qualities. It was thought that semantic problems introduced a high degree of unreliability into appraisal information. Another point of dissatisfaction grew out of the commonly observed fact that raters tended to anticipate the actions that would be triggered by their ratings, and consequently, modified ratings to yield the outcomes they wanted. Human beings, in other words, behaved as human beings.

The forced-choice performance report was offered as an answer to both objections to earlier scaling methods. Described elsewhere in this volume, this technique concentrated on behavior reporting, concealing from the reporter (the rater) the significance of the behavior-descriptive phrases that he chose. However, this secrecy tended to arouse rater resentment. Often, it appeared, final ratings resulted which the rater was convinced were erroneous. This confirmed the suspicions of those who argued that ratings always have been influenced by anticipations of subsequent action and that they are therefore unreliable. It has been difficult to devise a test of the validity of these suspicions. Using a normal distribution of ratings as a criterion, as was done by the D Company (Part Four), is questionable.

Although the forced-choice technique has been seriously criticized recently, it continues to attract researchers and administrators. But its invulnerability to manipulation by the rater also makes its mistakes very difficult to handle. Where, for one reason or another, clearly erroneous judgments result (these highly visible errors necessarily occurring at the extremes of the range of performance in a group), there seems to be no way of correcting them without calling the whole system into question.

The last major development in scaling appraisals of performance has been the critical-incident technique. Focusing upon the reporting of behavior incidents, it attempts to obviate immediate appraisal of the individual. The input data are relatively unambiguous behavior incidents. While behavior incidents may be overlooked by a supervisor, those that are recorded are available for scrutiny by all. Conversion of such reports into an over-all appraisal is then rather mechanistic. The economics of using the critical-incident technique in an organization have not been explored. The experience of the G Company (Part Four) indicates that the cost of using such a technique at the nonmanagerial level is disproportionately high.

Both the critical-incident and the forced-choice techniques deal, with some success, with major technical weaknesses of earlier scaling methods. At the same time new problems are created by their use. It is safe to predict that these two techniques will continue to be the subject of study and analysis by administrators and social science researchers.

Who should rate? The question of who should be responsible for judging the performance of others has occupied the interest of rating experts for years. Actually two questions are involved: Who has the best information about the individual being judged? Who is apt to make the most objective judgment, given this information?

It would seem, logically, that the individual working closest to the person being judged would have the best information on performance. This often would be one of the individual's coworkers. But seldom do we see an organization asking for and heeding judgment of an individual's peer. The immediate superior is accepted as the best qualified judge, probably because he is presumed to know more about the over-all goals of the organization than the individual who stands in a peer relationship to another. Consequently, optimal observation of an individual's activity may be sacrificed in order to gain a rater who presumably has better knowledge of organizational needs. In some organizations, for example, the U.S. Army, this logic is carried a step further, using an additional rater one level higher in the hierarchy, who validates basic ratings made by immediate superiors.

The use of a third party in the appraisal process has appealed to some managers. The field review method uses a visitor who questions, and listens, as the rater makes an evaluation of another. This takes time and costs money, but seems to help to depersonalize the judgment process to some extent, at the same time making it explicit and deliberate.

The use of groups to evaluate individuals has been hotly debated. It is an expensive procedure and therefore has been little used at the nonmanagerial level except as it has been institutionalized in the activities of the union. At the managerial level, especially at the highest ranks, such group judgment is common. However, many are uneasy over the fact that a judgment rendered by a group turns out to be no one person's responsibility. Once again we gain some insight into the constant awareness of and concern with the close tie—the inevitable tie—between the act of judgment and its organizational consequences. If the group cannot be held responsible for the judgment it makes, why is group judgment used as often as it is in organizations?

One reason is that additional observers, at least up to some point, contribute additional information. With better information, a better judgment is possible. However, if the judgments are made in the presence of other group members, information is also lost. Dissenting opinions often are not heard because individuals who are not absolutely certain of their judgments (and these might even be the best judges), are sometimes reluctant to disagree with a majority of others. Group pooling and discussion of information, with privately rendered individual judgments, might optimize the use of group appraisal.

The use of appraisals by subordinates as a basis for decisions about an individual has not been taken seriously in hierarchical organizations. The morale survey is a popular technique for collecting judgments about those in authority, but such information is deliberately *not* focused upon individuals. Anonymity is a prime requisite. Such surveys are really appraisals of the organization rather than of specific individuals in it.

• ALTERNATIVES TO RATING

Industrial labor unions have almost invariably resisted any formal appraisal system in which the worker's superior makes the judgments. Unions object, of course, not to the formalizing of the boss's judgment, but to the fact that the judgment—which then controls the worker's rate of pay, his right to be employed, and his right to specific jobs—is unilateral and beyond challenge. What the union offers, in lieu of an appraisal system, is seniority. The arguments made by unions, and almost always resisted by managements, are that the superior's judgment is biased, does not reflect true performance by the worker, is subject to faulty memory, and is influenced by whimsical personal likes and dislikes. It is a repetition of the whole list of misgivings that everyone has about human judgment.

But not all the union arguments are simply negative reaction to using unilateral supervisory appraisals. It is argued, positively, that seniority is correlated with job knowledge, general wisdom, and good judgment. Managers are likely to argue that it is correlated negatively with motivation, that a system of seniority simply provides sinecures for those who are fortunate enough to have arrived early. Nevertheless, managers themselves place substantial value on seniority in a number of ways. One should work one's way up the hierarchy of jobs to acquire the knowledge, maturity, and understanding necessary to holding a higher ranking job, they will argue. Likewise, the willingness of the individual to stay with the organization (loyalty) to acquire the seniority necessary to make him eligible for more important jobs is felt by many in management to be something that should be rewarded. Fringe benefits such as vacations and pensions very often are scaled to the number of years of service of the individual.

The universal recognition accorded seniority has its roots in the ancient cultural deference to age. Though Americans are less inclined to be deferential to the aged than those in other cultures, they find seniority to be a useful social rule. "First come, first served" is a rule we all like to see honored. The queue efficiently solves dozens of daily problems of precedence that might otherwise produce conflict.

However, one frequently sees in daily life evidence of conflict between seniority and the socially useful contributions of individuals. We all realize that the queue cannot become a universal principle of social organization. Those responsible for the management of organizations have always had to face the necessity for compromising seniority in some intelligent and acceptable fashion. How this is best done seems not to have been solved on any general basis.

Seniority appeals because of its qualities of objectivity and precision. The use of individual judgment, subject always to challenge and controversy, is avoided. One group judgment, namely, that the first to arrive shall take precedence, is made once and for all. Thereafter, all that is necessary is to determine who in fact arrived first. Why could not precision and objectivity be achieved through performance measures other than seniority? The fact is that other measures have been used for many years. The use of performance records in conjunction with individual incentive plans on the nonmanagerial level has been common in American business for seventy or eighty years.

Unfortunately, while no one questions the precision of output records, an acceptable method for establishing performance standards is another matter. The battle over incentive plans is a classic in American industrial relations. The fight centers on who is going to set the standard, who is going to decide when, in what direction, and how much it can change. This sounds familiar. We are, in a way, right back to the problem of who shall rate whom, and what influence the rating shall have over the welfare of the individual rated.

At the nonmanagerial level, performance records have had the further weakness of being highly localized. They have been peculiar to the particular role or job that the worker fills, usually measuring physical output. When one attempts to predict, on the basis of performance in his present job, the probable performance of the individual in another job, judgment problems arise once again. What are job differences? Will motivation remain the same? The performance record is clean, precise—and it is there. It provides information apt to be superior in all respects to the offhand judgment, the unreliable memory of the supervisor. But if performance appraisal has been made systematic and a matter of record, it can very well be a superior way to make promotion decisions. The extremely narrow focus of performance records at the nonmanagerial level is their greatest limitation.

At the managerial level in private business, profit measures of performance have been experimented with in the last two decades. The theory is admirable: The firm exists to make a profit, managers control the firm, the measure of effectiveness of their control is the level (and growth) of profits, the best measure of a manager is his profit contribution. There is no reason, of course, why this argument should not be applied to all persons in the firm. The general belief has been, however, that the effect of the activities of those in nonmanagerial ranks on profits is too remote to measure. It turns out that problems of measurement, even for top-level managers, are acute. Broad economic measures of profit contribution are not feasible. A more limited measure becomes necessary. This immediately creates some of the limitations associated with the performance records used on nonmanagerial workers. For divisional vice-presidents the measure has considerable meaning. For people below this level the measure is only an approximation. Nevertheless, it is a managerial appraisal device which should continue to be studied and tried because of its close tie to the basic goals of the business firm.

Seniority and performance records have been discussed because of some discernible trends within the last few decades with reference to both of them. At the lowest levels in the organization in unionized firms, substitution of seniority for performance appraisal and formal ratings has been almost complete. The use of performance records is today confined (at these levels) almost entirely to automatic systems where output measures are tied directly to incentive earnings.

In the nonunionized sector, which includes almost all white-collar workers, whether employed in private or public enterprise, performance rating has continued to be an important management tool. However, where performance measures have been developed in this sector, the tendency has been to replace ratings with some sort of performance record data, especially for pay purposes, even though there is no direct incentive arrangement. When promotion and transfer decisions pend, direct appraisal once again is necessary.

Until the period following World War II, systematic appraisal of the performance of managers was done on a rather small scale in American business. At the present time some sort of regular appraisal is characteristic of most large American corporations. Rating of top personnel in the military and in the government has existed for a long time and continues. The substitution of profit performance measurement at the top levels of the private enterprise has received considerable attention in the last ten years and may be presumed to be spreading.

In summary, there has been a trend toward substitution of seniority at the very lowest levels and of performance records at the very highest levels for the regular rating procedures. This has been especially true in American business firms, particularly in those which are unionized. For the remainder of those employed in large organizations, whether private or public, regular and systematic performance appraisal remains a common feature of the management techniques used.

• SUGGESTIONS FOR EFFECTIVE USE OF PERFORMANCE APPRAISAL

From the study of a number of merit rating installations, particularly those discussed in the case studies in Part Four, come some conclusions regarding the conditions under which a performance appraisal system functions most effectively:

The appraisal technique must be matched with the objectives sought. It is easier to cite a mismatch than to specify exactly what is best in a given situation. The X Department of the D Company (Part Four) illustrates an extreme case of a poorly adapted technique. The forced-choice report is almost impossible to use for counseling and guidance purposes. Yet counseling was one of the major objectives of appraisal in that particular department. If, in another instance, one were interested in trying to validate selection techniques, it would be foolish to try to use an open-end essay rating. The simple ranking or some other scaling method yielding a quantitative answer would be the obvious choice.

Appraisal should be treated as an integral part of organization activity. One of the serious errors that seems to have been made by staff experts working with appraisal techniques is that of insisting that supervisors attempt to appraise an individual with no regard for the consequences of the appraisal. It seems, in fact, impossible to divorce the process of appraisal from the consequences attached to it. There seems to be little question that the rater will invariably see to it that the appraisal he makes officially results in the personnel action that he thinks appropriate. This simply indicates that he has previously made his private judgment. Appraisal is just this sort of continuous, largely unconscious process. There appears to be no way of breaking this process into independent pieces, no matter how logically such pieces might be defined.

Managers might more sensibly seek to control the appraisal process through keeping supervisory actions and decisions consistent with judgments made earlier. Often in the organization, appraisals are made, recorded, filed, and forgotten. Subsequent decisions which involve discriminating among individuals are then made without reference to previous recorded evaluations. Without some way of holding an individual accountable for judgments which he has expressed, he is apt to be careless in making such judgments. Furthermore, the system which requires the judgments eventually becomes a nuisance and dies. Some control feature must be built into any appraisal plan.

For nonmanagerial personnel, at least, a good control might be a seniority rule. The iron law of seniority would take away from the supervisor discretion over promotions and pay increases unless he has consistently built the case for making an exception to seniority. Discriminations on which everyone is apt to agree (that is, those having the greatest objectivity) will identify people who lie at the extremes of performance—either the very good or the very poor. This minority group of cases comprises those which are most important to identify and, at the same time, those on which greatest agreement is likely. These extremes the supervisor must identify. He must be willing then, also, to have them given special treatment—early promotion and accelerated compensation increases or, conversely, demotion, discharge, or some other action. For all others the economical rule then becomes, let seniority govern.

Under such rules the rater might take his job seriously, being spared from making innumerable discriminations which are impossible to defend, and, at the same time, being made to live with those discriminations he chooses to make.

Appraisal should be an economical activity. Many appraisal systems have failed simply because staff people responsible for planning the systems have become engrossed in trying to achieve technical perfection. In other situations, where experts have been more realistic about technical achievements, there have been many failures because not enough attention was given to the costs versus possible gains from formalized activity of this kind.

One way of looking at the appraisal process is that it is a technique for getting information about people for purposes having economic value to the organization. The importance of these purposes varies, not only among organizations, but also from time to time. Some omnibus system, then, is not likely to be economic more than a small part of the time that it is supposed to be in operation. It was argued above that the best and most effective appraisal systems are careful to match the technique to the purpose for which it is used. The point here is a little different, however. It is more than making a technically sound match. It is a matter also of matching the value of the information with the cost of getting it.

Unfortunately, in addition to the usual problems of measurement of any business costs, there are complications present in performance appraisal, due to the fact that organizational cost and personal cost are not necessarily congruent and equivalent at all times. As every rating expert knows, the most difficult thing to bring off in a performance appraisal system is to get the average supervisor or executive to take the time and expend the effort to d
of appraising those under
recording this for others in
tion to use. It is not easy to attach a penalty or reward to the supervisor's doing, or failing to do, the kind of job the staff expects in a formal appraisal system. In effect, the organization is not willing to pay for the information it ostensibly needs. The thoughtful personnel executive must ask himself what need exists for appraisal information, how much it is worth, and what the organization can then offer the appropriate individual to induce him to provide it.

Too often when it becomes evident that technical perfection cannot be achieved and that those who are supposed to supply appraisal information are treating the job with indifference, the whole business is given up as a bad show. This implies that information about the performance of individuals is either worthless or freely available. Experience indicates that either assumption is dangerous. Good men get lost in organizations, even in organizations that are not too large. The frailty of human memory is familiar to us all. The variation in individual judgment of the same event also is common experience to us. The consequences of haphazard judgment in staffing an organization are too obvious to allow an intelligent executive to dismiss the appraisal problem casually. The conclusion follows that performance appraisal must be treated as an important planning task, and one in which the costs and contributions of relevant information must be carefully assessed.

The best systems emphasize the development of performance standards and base appraisal upon achievement and efforts toward achievement. Except for a very few persons in an organization, most individuals will necessarily be appraised in somewhat subjective fashion. At best, this subjective appraisal will be reduced to a minimum through careful consideration of performance data. These data are useful, of course, only when they have some sort of standards established with which to interpret them.

Despite the continuing effort to appraise an individual directly in terms of performance data, there remain always some aspects of an individual's job which cannot be quantified. In such areas we cannot tell an individual we expect this or that amount of output. At best, we can say we expect more of this or less of that, and consider what the individual says regarding the feasibility of these demands. Such two-way communication is most profitable if it focuses directly on relevant bits of job behavior. The great promise of the critical-incident technique is that it may facilitate such discussion. Concentration on specific job-related activities and forms of behavior is the best substitute for quantitative performance standards where the latter cannot be formulated.

• FUTURE RESEARCH

Many field studies and laboratory experiments with small groups have been done in recent years, testing a number of variables related to performance appraisal. A number of these studies are cited in this volume. These studies have not been done on a coordinated basis, although each provides some useful information. What is needed is analysis of the interaction of these variables in a field situation to tell us which are more, and which less, important in the organizational setting within which appraisal takes place.

Military organizations, government departments, and large business corporations provide promising opportunities for such study. They permit control of important environmental variables related to organization policies, job content, and personnel selection criteria. At the same time they provide multiple, small administrative units and the opportunity for experimental variation.

Such studies, ideally, would be "longitudinal"—extending through time for sufficient periods to learn something about organizational adaptation. Occasionally the opportunity arises to do historical comparisons within organizations and thus gain much of the advantage of the longitudinal study. Imagination is required in such a study to get the design one might otherwise fashion deliberately. Above all, a large organization is required.

The small, tightly controlled, studies characteristic of recent years will still be useful—especially if replicated, where the cost of doing so is not too great.

The company case studies which have flooded the literature for years can, on occasion, provide some interesting ideas for testing. As behavioral scientists continue to infiltrate nonacademic organizations, we may expect them to provide well-thought-out analyses of specific organizational experience. Above all, we should expect them to begin the coordinated and careful research which performance appraisal has so far lacked.

PART FOUR • CASE REPORTS AND ORGANIZATION STUDIES

Because appraisal of individual performance is an essential and continuous activity in an organization, it affects and is affected by almost every other aspect of the organization. Perhaps the best way to gain some insight into the complexity thus created is to look at appraisal in action, through the eyes either of those in the organization who are using it or of outside observers.

Part Four is made up of a series of reports and analyses of both kinds. Considered together with Parts One and Two, it should help the reader come to his own conclusions concerning the proper role of formalized appraisal in an organization. The editors presented their summary and conclusions in Part Three.

All the cases are drawn from business. However, the public administrator and the military staff officer should find that the administrative problems of the business executive in this area are much like his own.

A. Appraisal Practices in Eight Companies: Description and Evaluation

APPRAISAL AS A MANAGEMENT TOOL

THOMAS L. WHISLER

The studies in this section represent the analysis and evaluation of eight companies by one observer. His interest was in learning what efforts the companies were making to appraise performance of individuals, how these activities were viewed by those in the company, and how well appraisal was done.

The companies range in size from 300 to 40,000 employees. Two are nonunion, four are unionized, and two partially unionized. Six are manufacturing firms; one, a utility; one, a retailer. Five are located in a metropolitan area; three are in smaller towns.

After the individual companies are analyzed, a summary of the study is presented in the form of general observations, notes about some common shortcomings, and suggestions for improving appraisal.

APPRAISAL AS A MANAGEMENT TOOL*

Thomas L. Whisler

THE A COMPANY—A SMALL METALS MANUFACTURING COMPANY (RURAL LOCATION)

Description of the Company

The A Company is a small manufacturing concern located in a Midwestern community of 2500 people in an agricultural area. Total personnel numbers slightly over three hundred.

The company had its start around the turn of the century, when the founder put into production a personal invention. Its growth from there on was due largely to the highly successful sales and promotional activities of the founder. Internal management was mainly a one-man show, with the founder keeping things running without benefit of formal organization or procedures. His retirement to board chairmanship in 1940 elevated his son to the presidency. The son, and present president, has professional engineering training and is a devotee of systems in all phases of management. On the face, the company appears to be ridiculously "overorganized," in terms of its size. This is attributed, by those in the management ranks, to the urgent need for organization at the time of the incumbent president's election and to the president's belief in the efficacy of modern management techniques in an enterprise, regardless of its size.

Most of the management personnel of the company are under forty-five. Youth tends to be coupled with an appreciable length of service (fourteen years on the average), reflecting a fairly consistent policy of internal promotion in filling managerial positions. Seventy-five percent of those in managerial jobs at present formerly held nonmanagerial jobs within the company. The president, in his reaction against one-man management, has been insistent upon decentralization of authority down the line. He has demanded that higher management personnel "keep on top of their jobs" through proper organization and delegation of authority rather than through constant supervision. He seems to have gained acceptance and fairly vigorous exploitation of the systems, techniques and procedures which he regards as indispensable to proper management. Executives and supervisors, in general, are aggressive, self-confident, and apparently quite competent. They give evidence, in conversation, of strong loyalty to the president and to his philosophy.

The company has a contract with an industrial union. Ninety-eight percent of the nonmanagerial workers are members. Only one grievance has ever gone to arbitration, and no official grievance has been entered since 1950. There has never been a strike.

Contract negotiation is the responsibility of the industrial relations division. With the one exception to be noted later,

* Adapted from *Merit Rating: A Management Tool,* unpublished Ph.D. Dissertation, University of Chicago, 1953.

the contract is quite short, general, and conventional in content. Management "prerogatives" with regard to work force administration, job content, and performance standards are preserved nearly intact.

The industrial relations division, consisting of five people, administers a personnel program which includes all the "latest" personnel procedures and techniques except a counseling program.

Performance Appraisal in the A Company

Employees are merit rated only after they have completed the ninety-day probationary period which each of them must serve before he is given permanent status on the payroll. The length of the rating period for each employee is determined initially by the interval between "merit" increases in pay. In the case of factory employees these intervals are four months in length. For office employees the intervals are six months. Merit ratings are made sixty days prior to the date at which the employee becomes eligible for a pay increase. When the employee reaches the top of the rate range for his job (after three and a half years in the office; two years in the factory), ratings are made from there on every six months.

The "merit increase" has a special meaning in this company. All jobs have been evaluated and rate or salary ranges established for each job class. Steps within the ranges have been created with fixed time intervals at which the employee may be advanced to the next higher step. *The presumption is made that the employee is eligible for the increase unless there is definite evidence to the contrary.* Denial of an increase must be accompanied by a letter to the employee fully stating the reasons for the action. Company officials insist that this procedure by no means results in "automatic" increases. Examination of personnel files reveals an occasional denial of an increase. The basis of such denials is almost inevitably failure of the employee to reach standard output.

The current rating procedure was preceded by a variety of the "free-written" rating. During the time this latter system was in use, each foreman, utilizing a personal notebook, was required to make a statement every month concerning the performance of each employee. This method was abandoned because the transcription process was unwieldy and because the method provided no assurance that the foreman would make ratings at the prescribed time.

The merit rating form lists eleven factors upon which employees are to be rated. The factors are traits except for two, "quality of work" and "speed-accuracy." Ratings are made on a five-category rating scale. It is stated on the form that use of the rating in considering promotions, transfers, and terminations is optional with the supervisor. Raters are encouraged to write comments on the reverse side of the rating form. Some do this when they make what they believe to be "unusual" ratings. Two foremen faithfully write comments on their rating sheets.

Each employee is rated by his immediate supervisor. This supervisor signs the rating and passes it to his superior who, in turn, signs it. The forms are then returned to the personnel office and filed. The person rated is not shown his rating, although this is not prohibited.[1] Most supervisors are doubtful of the idea of showing ratings to those rated. The employment manager felt that there might be advantages to so doing but indicated that this was a matter which the personnel people needed to think through further before making any moves in that direction. This matter aside, no formal effort is made to use the periodic rating as a communications or counseling device through the supervisor's discussing the employee's performance with him at the time the rating is made.[2]

Movement of employees in the job structure frequently results in the use of a formalized evaluation device other than merit rating. This device is the efficiency report, applicable to the factory only. The bulk of the jobs in this area carry standard rates. From production and payroll records, efficiency figures (in terms of percent of standard) are computed monthly for each employee. These data are summarized and copies are kept by manufacturing department heads and the factory manager. When transfers, etc., are being considered, these records are frequently consulted.

The procedure used in transfer and promotion is affected by a provision in the union contract which allows any (covered) employee to signify in writing his desire to be considered for particular jobs in the company outside his present department, should a vacancy occur. In event of a vacancy a list of interested persons is prepared. All on the list are given consideration before hiring from outside, those presently employed in the particular department being given first consideration. This contract provision is spelled out in detail in an otherwise brief and general contract. Its inclusion is attributed by the original union president (now a supervisor) to the failure of foremen in earlier years to bring up for consideration for a vacant job men under them whose qualifications would have merited their being considered. This former president emphasized that top management made an effort to learn of qualified persons within the plant, but inquiries were directed to first-level supervisors who, for various reasons, occasionally failed to nominate obviously qualified men.

In addition to efficiency reports, another formal evaluation device exists. During the employee's ninety-day probationary period (this period is six months long in the case of certain executive and professional personnel), "rating slips" are issued. Two-week and eight-week "check-ups" are made on factory personnel, each calling for a general over-all rating of the man. These ratings are signed by the immediate supervisor only. At the expiration of the probationary period, a free-written recommendation must be made as to whether the employee should be placed in a permanent status. The procedure for office personnel is the same except that the two-week check-up is eliminated.

The formal employee evaluation de-

[1] One foreman experimented with showing the men the ratings given to them. He found that the men noted the numerical ratings they received, compared notes with others, and then demanded an explanation of variations. He avoided this embarrassment thereafter by keeping the ratings secret.

[2] The engineering supervisor, faced with the prospect of reprimanding a man for poor performance, asks the man to rate himself. This rating is compared with the supervisor's rating as a basis for discussion.

vices utilized in the company can be summarized:

1. Merit ratings
2. "Check-ups" (probationary period)
3. Efficiency records

One other record which may appear in the employee's personal file irregularly is the "reprimand slip," which is issued by the employee's supervisor whenever a working rule is violated. Rule violations may lead to layoff or discharge, a published formula being used to determine this action. In any event reprimand slips remain in the individual's file.

An Evaluation of Performance Appraisal in the A Company

Performance appraisal in this company is accomplished by use of both merit ratings and performance records. The merit rating program consists of two parts:

1. The periodic ratings (merit ratings), which have little relevance to or significance for administrative decisions.
2. Special ratings made at the time of administrative decisions, which are in most cases controlling in these decisions. These ratings are limited to decisions with respect to conferring permanent status upon a new employee.

In the present scheme the periodic ratings represent virtually nothing but waste motion. This indictment is based upon the fact that there is no evidence that the ratings are utilized in management decisions and actions:

1. In wage administration, except for the fact that the wage increase schedule establishes the rating intervals, the periodic merit ratings are not in any way connected with rates of pay or changes in rates of pay. All those who rate others admit that they have never consulted an individual's previous ratings when a wage administration decision arises.[3]

2. Decisions relating to transfers and promotions are made jointly by a representative of the industrial relations department and the supervisors concerned. The complete files on the personnel being considered for a move are examined. Rating forms are briefly examined for evidence of "unusual" (other than average) ratings in making these decisions. "Unusual" ratings scarcely ever exist. Most raters stick close to the "average" column. Those who rate higher than average are regarded as having unusually liberal standards, for which allowance must be made. Written ratings carry little weight, however. The verbal opinions of the supervisors and staff personnel, in conference, are controlling. One foreman indicates that although he and his supervisor invariably consult the ratings of a candidate for transfer into the department, he does not believe ratings to be particularly meaningful or useful. This foreman believes this to be due to the fact that others are not as careful in making ratings as he is. In

---

[3] However, the factory manager cites an instance in which a subordinate rated a secretary below average, forwarding the form for signature together with reasons for the low rating. A subsequent merit increase for the secretary was approved by the subordinate. The factory manager made this action a matter of reprimand when he learned that the raise in pay had been recommended simply because the secretary had promised to improve performance. This incident seems to be an unusual one in that the rater called special attention to his rating, thus "tagging" it in the memory of the man who reviewed the rating. It should be noted that the factory manager seems to be more interested than most of the managerial group in ratings and their use.

general the efficiency record, attendance record, and reprimand records are deemed to be the most useful supplements to the supervisor's verbal opinion in making decisions in the area of work force administration.[4]

Other evidence that the periodic merit ratings are of little value was gleaned from examination of the records of three hundred former employees. Ten cases were found where, for reasons of inadequate performance, pay increases were denied or discharges effected and where the previous rating sheet indicated that the employee was average or better in all respects. Several cases were found where ratings were poor and no commensurate administrative action was taken. In only one or two cases were ratings and subsequent actions correlated. A few cases of similar nature were found with respect to the special rating made during the probationary period. The possibility of rather rapid change in individual performance cannot be completely discounted. The cases, however, are in accord with the thesis that the periodic ratings have little effect upon administrative decisions.

Only one person is able to cite an instance in which merit rating was positively utilized. This foreman was required to demote one of two men and chose a man whose seniority exceeded the other's. The second man protested violently up the line. The foreman thereupon took this man to the industrial relations office, pulled out a number of merit ratings on the two workers, and showed that his decision was justified by the differences in the ratings over a period of time. The worker accepted this evidence as justification, according to the foreman.[5]

The attitude of those doing the rating toward the rating system is, in the main, one of indifference and lack of conviction as to its usefulness. A few are strongly opposed to it and a few believe it to be good for various reasons. All, regardless of general attitude, believe the merit rating form to be inadequate and in need of revision.

The president explains the apparent uselessness of merit rating as an example of instituting a technique for certain purposes and retaining it when the circumstances requiring its use no longer exist. He indicates that merit rating was instituted during a period (the New Deal era) in which management actions with respect to workers were constantly subject to challenge and criticism. The reaction of management was to attempt to record all reasons for action as a means of justifying those actions. Merit rating was instituted as a part of this reaction. This sort of justification is no longer necessary, in the president's opinion, but the technique has remained largely because of management inertia.

It is difficult to assign a definite reason for the continuance of periodic merit ratings in this company. It appears that

[4] The light regard with which raters view one another's written ratings apparently does not indicate lack of faith in the judgment of these raters. In the case of two factory division superintendents, each is convinced that the other recommends for transfer into his division only those employees under the other's supervision who are "culls" and "no-goods." It is an example of absolute faith in the consistency of another's judgment.

[5] Another foreman believes that the ratings are potentially useful in that, if it were ever necessary for him to discharge a man, the ratings would serve to buttress the case upon which he rested his decision. The fact is that nonmanagerial employees are virtually never discharged after the probationary period except for violation of working rules.

in the thinking of those in the top management levels, realization that the present rating system leaves much to be desired is coupled with the belief that rating should be done because of certain rather intangible benefits. The prime benefit is believed to be that of forcing supervisors to analyze their subordinates regularly. (There is no evidence of any interest in attempting to test this belief.) A secondary benefit is believed to be that of having written ratings serve as a potential "clincher" in justifying administrative decisions in event that they are protested.

The prime reason for the failure to make more positive use of the periodic ratings appears to be the problem of variations in rating standards of the various supervisors. None of those concerned with the rating program see any way of achieving comparability between ratings of various supervisors other than by rough adjustment made on the basis of knowledge gained from acquaintance with the supervisors. This variation in rating standards is regarded by most of the supervisors as a fatal defect.

Possibly another reason for failure to make more use of merit ratings lies in the small size of the company. Supervisors emphasize the widespread personal acquaintance they have with individuals in all departments in the company. To a certain extent this may explain the apathy toward attempting to improve the existing merit rating system, which is evident in discussion of the matter with most managerial personnel.

It should again be noted that a series of performance records and special rating devices function to get the evaluation job done. The fact that no great need to improve or change merit rating is felt constitutes some evidence that the evaluation job is performed adequately with the aid of these devices.

THE B COMPANY— • A SMALL CONTINUOUS PROCESS PLANT

Description of the Company

The B Company engages in manufacturing in a Midwestern town of eleven thousand population. Plant and headquarters office personnel currently number between fifteen and sixteen hundred. (The company also has a number of subsidiaries throughout the Western Hemisphere.) Many of the nearly twelve hundred factory employees are extra-shift personnel, since the manufacturing process demands continuous operation.

The company was founded early in this century by an enterprising man who recognized the raw-material potentialities of the area for manufacturing of this type. As in the case of the A Company, management was for many years largely a one-man show. In the B Company, however, relatives of the founder began to fill managerial jobs. The founder's son was eventually made president, although he apparently had little desire or aptitude for the job. The founder's personal and family friends also found a haven in the company. At the conclusion of World War II many former supervisors who had been in service were rehired despite the fact that their jobs meanwhile had been filled. The result of all this was an extremely top-heavy organization. A management consultant was called in. On his recommendation, an extensive revision was made in the organization to rectify these earlier errors. One major organizational change was made by hiring an executive of one of the country's largest corporations to replace the founder's son as president.

A policy of promotion from the ranks has always been followed quite rigidly. Of the one hundred and fifty managerial personnel of all ranks in the home plant operation, all but eight have at one time held nonsupervisory jobs in the company.

The management consultant who recommended organization changes also devised and installed various systems including standard costs, job evaluation, merit rating, and production control. A reaction against consultants and systems occurred two years after this consultant's departure. The reasons for this were various. The case of merit rating is illustrative and will be discussed later.

This company is nonunion. Its major competitors, including another plant in the same industry and in the same town, are organized.

Performance Appraisal in the B Company

Merit rating made its debut in this company as part of a "package" designed by the management consultant. The other part of this package was a job evaluation plan. This latter plan yielded labor grades, which encompassed all jobs, and wage rate ranges for each labor grade. Merit rating was expected to determine, within the relevant rate range, a wage rate for each worker. This plan was applied to factory workers only.

To perform this wage administration function a "forced-distribution" merit rating plan was developed.[6] A rating scale on five traits yielded a point total. The totals were expected to average within three points of fifty (on a scale of one hundred) in every department of ten or more employees. The personnel department was expected to analyze each supervisor's ratings to see that this control was maintained. A rating of fifty or less entitled the worker to the minimum of the rate range. Fixed wage increments over the minimum were keyed to merit rating point ranges above fifty. In this fashion each worker's rate was determined directly from the total number of points he received on his rating sheet.

The plan was designed solely by the consultant. Every supervisor attended a single-session training conference on use of the plan. The training was conducted by the consultant. In addition each supervisor was given a manual of procedure to aid him in making ratings. The plan was used approximately a year and abandoned as a complete failure. The personnel manager ascribes the failure of the plan to three factors:

1. Failure to include supervisors in construction of the plan.
2. Insufficient rater training, resulting in a large amount of correction of ratings.
3. No provision for downward revision of rates. (The significance of this point will become clear in the discussion of the current wage plan.) The rating plan was quite time consuming. The personnel manager estimates that many of the supervisors spent twelve to fourteen hours making ratings (semiannually).

Supervisory opposition to the original merit rating plan became so strong that the personnel division experimented with alternative rating forms. By having supervisors rate their subordinates on various rating forms and comparing the

[6] The distribution was '"forced" in this case only to the extent that ratings had to average around the mid-point.

results, the conclusion was reached that simple ranking achieved as good results as did more complicated rating schemes. Results were appraised in terms of usefulness for wage administration. The original rating plan was abandoned. A semiannual wage review was substituted.

In the first wage review each supervisor ranked his men, and wage rates (within the established range) were assigned on the basis of these rankings. The principle was established that wage rates in a given labor grade in a department must be assigned in such fashion that the average wage rate equals (or closely approximates) the mid-point of the rate range. After the first review, ranking was no longer done. In all subsequent reviews, rate averages have been examined. If in any case the average is below the mid-point of the range, the foreman may recommend, for individuals he believes merit them, wage increases sufficient to raise the average to the mid-point of the range if he so wishes.

The wage scheme just described is a matter of great controversy in this company and has many interesting implications. Two points are relevant to this study. First, the basic principle of a (crude) forced-distribution was carried over into the wage plan from the abandoned merit rating plan. Second, the concept of wage increases, but no wage decreases—a concept which presumably helped make the merit rating plan unworkable—is also incorporated into the wage plan. The fact that no ranking has taken place since the first wage review indicates that no one seriously considers the possibility of reducing a rate. A number of the foremen were specifically asked about the feasibility of lowering rates. The unanimous answer was that it could not be done.

As a result of introducing this wage plan into the factory, merit rating of factory employees is no longer performed. Yet the most objectionable features of the former merit rating plan have been retained. The supervisors insist that the notion that a group of people must differ appreciably in performance and that these differences must be distributed about an average is not verified by their experience in supervision. Furthermore, given the reluctance to reduce rates, the system makes no provision for changes in individuals. Many of the supervisors point out that examination of the rates earned by a group of workers in a particular labor grade frequently is not likely to give a true picture of the relative merits of these workers. Other supervisors are uncertain as to whether the rate structure properly reflects the relative performance of individuals. In short, supervisors either become accustomed to a rate structure out of harmony with their opinions of worker merit or no longer bother to think about the matter of worker performance carefully.

Promotions in the factory usually occur within departments. As long as the promotions are from one nonsupervisory job to another, the foreman is given complete discretion. Where promotion to a first-level supervisory job is in order, the decision is made in a conference between foremen of departments in which it is believed there are workers with supervisory potentialities, and higher production officials. Occasionally a member of the industrial relations department sits in these conferences. Promotion offers an opportunity to move a man holding a top rate out of a labor grade, thus permitting others to receive rate increases. Those receiving promotions are not always those currently receiving top rates in their labor grade. Sometimes promotion constitutes the means of rewarding a good worker who cannot receive an increase in his present job because of the wage formula. Supervisors seem to be properly concerned with picking a man for promotion who appears to be best fitted for the vacant job, but the effect of such a move on the rate average is always a consideration. Promoting a man whose rate is below the mid-point of the rate range has serious consequences.

The following groups of employees are formally rated in the company:

A. Managerial and supervisory personnel below the second level (from the top)

B. All office workers, including professional personnel

C. Trainees – persons being formally trained for skilled jobs in the factory

None of these groups is subjected to the wage formula applied to factory workers. Trainees have a pay plan providing for regular periodic increases. The rating form used for trainees provides for recommendation that the rate of pay increases be accelerated if merited. The presumption is that the training period would be correspondingly shortened.[7] Office and supervisory jobs carry salary ranges, but assignment of salary rates to individuals within these ranges is left to the discretion of the superior.

Both the salaried employee and trainee rating forms use a rating scale. The trainee form provides for rating six factors on a five-part scale. The salaried employee form contains five factors classified as "results" and ten factors classified as "causes." This scale has nine parts. The point total on "results" is expected to be nearly equal to the point total on "causes." (The rationale of this provision remains a secret of the consultant who designed the form.) The salaried employee form provides for supplementary comments and recommendations (with respect to possible transfer, etc., and to supervisory potentialities). Lately added to this form is a question as to whether the rating has been discussed with the employee, and when.

The Purposes of Performance Appraisal in the B Company

Formal rating of hourly rated employees in this company no longer exists, except for trainees. The objective of rating trainees is to assure that those not making adequate progress are removed from the program.

Rating of office and supervisory personnel is performed semiannually and ratings are filed in the individual's personnel file. Ratings do not control the individual's pay or promotions in any fashion. There is no evidence that recommendations with respect to pay changes or promotions (recommendations initiated by office supervisors) are ever compared with ratings.[8] Actually, the current president of the company

[7] One foreman mentioned the strong incentive to push trainees along fast, an incentive that arises out of the factory wage plan. As soon as the trainee is promoted to regular employee status, his pay rate becomes the minimum of the rate range and is figured into the rate averages. This has the effect of lowering the average and permitting pay increases. Trainees are in training for skilled jobs where turnover is lowest and where the rigid pay formula causes the most dissatisfaction. Thus there is strong reason to move the trainee along as fast as possible.

[8] One exception to this statement is the assistant controller's contention that he at one time occasionally checked pay change recommendations submitted by supervisors under him against the merit ratings they had submitted in the previous rating period. Apparently he no longer bothers to do this. He further stated that he occasionally examines the ratings of individuals outside his department who are under consideration for promotion into the department.

discourages the idea of a scheduled wage review for office employees with increases in pay following from these reviews. He has encouraged supervisors to watch for instances of exceptionally good performance on the part of an employee and to reward the employee promptly for such performance by a pay increase. The supervisor is expected to make clear to the employee the reason for the pay increase. Promotions are a matter of conference, much as they are in the factory.

The industrial relations division has recently decided to emphasize performance appraisal as a communications device. To that end, when the most recent issue of rating forms was distributed to supervisors, a note was attached describing the value of discussing ratings with subordinates. Some supervisors have made a regular practice of discussing ratings with subordinates in the past. The industrial relations director hopes to extend this practice to other departments.

Attitudes toward Performance Appraisal

Line supervisors in this company are, in general, puzzled as to the purpose of performance or merit rating. Many are uncertain as to the ultimate disposition of the rating sheets and as to their importance in terms of the individual employee's progress in the company. That is, most supervisors express ignorance of what "they" do with the ratings once the sheets "go over there" (to the industrial relations department).

Some supervisors state that they believe the chief value of merit rating to be its use as a communications device. Only a few of these have actually discussed ratings with subordinates. The few that have done so regard this discussion as vital to a good job of supervision. They believe that periodic rating assures the employee of regular information as to his standing in the opinion of his boss and gives him a chance to get "grievances" and misunderstandings discussed. The chief engineer believes that the interest engineering personnel exhibit in discussing their ratings with their superiors stems from the engineer's analytical turn of mind. The purchasing agent suggests that periodic rating offers the supervisor a chance for a corrective interview without subjecting the employee to humiliation of being called in by the boss, in front of fellow employees, for a special conference.

Factory supervisors, at the lower levels, are indifferent toward rating. They can think of no use for it, particularly in the case of piece-rate workers. Some have forgotten what merit rating is, confusing the name with job evaluation. None of this is surprising, since rating was completely abandoned in the factory three or four years ago. The production-control superintendent has several interesting comments on rating in the factory. He believes that it is unfeasible at the worker-foreman level. He argues that discussing a man's worth with him in terms of traits is meaningless to the ordinary worker. The worker needs to have examples of behavior cited in justification of his rating.[9] The superintendent further believes that foremen lack the educational and intellectual background to rate men properly in terms of traits, and that foremen are unduly influenced

[9] Here, of course, this superintendent is thinking of rating in terms of the company's current rating forms. He is also thinking of rating as a communications device. He is strongly in favor of the present factory wage administration plan.

by the most recent behavior incidents of the workers.[10] He thinks that merit rating is good, however, because it forces the supervisor to think carefully of those under him.

All personnel presently performing rating are disturbed by the differences in raters' standards. Many regard this as a failure of the merit rating plan, feeling that if the plan worked properly workers in different departments could be compared in making promotion and pay decisions. Most supervisors doubt that a plan could be devised which would obviate the problem of variation in rating standards.

One office manager rejects the communications idea completely. He believes the community to be too small for a superior to give an employee an idea of how he is rated. As he puts it, "One must live with those he rates." He conceives the chief virtue of merit rating in the company at present to be its use as written evidence for justifying merit increases.

An Evaluation of Performance Appraisal in the B Company

The bulk of factory workers terminating employment in this company have in the past been given an exit interview. Some disappeared before they could be interviewed. Occasionally some were overlooked. The interview form is a good one, containing cross-check questions. The factory employment manager, who has apparently received little encouragement in continued use of the interview, completes it only infrequently at the present time. An examination of 209 interviews made in 1947 disclosed only seventy-nine cases where the foreman's recommendation as to re-employment was noted. A spot check of fifteen or twenty of the interviews on which this information was not shown indicated that in nearly half of these latter cases no recommendation had been made on the termination slip, which is completed by the foreman. Where recommendations had been made, most were against rehiring.

Of the seventy-nine cases where a recommendation concerning rehiring was noted, twenty cases were found where the employee quit and the foreman recommended not re-employing. In all but seven of these cases the employee quit within the probationary period (two months after hiring). In seven cases tenure on the job ran from a year upward. Several of these latter cases illustrate an egregious disregard for previous evaluation decisions. One employee worked two years, then quit. The recommendation was made not to rehire because of high absenteeism. The employee was rehired on the same job two months later. After working nine months he again quit. Again the foreman recommended not rehiring because the employee was "not a very good workman" and had a poor absenteeism record. Two months later the man was again hired on the same job. After working two months he again quit. Again the recommendation was not to rehire because the individual showed no interest in his

[10] Compare this with the president's belief that for pay purposes recent performance is most significant, at least if the performance is unusually good. Note also that this would appear to be an argument in favor of keeping appraisal records through time to afford a sounder basis for promotion decisions. The superintendent believes that the influence of recent events can be offset by having several informed persons share in evaluation of promotion candidates. This belief is shared by others in the manufacturing division.

work. He has not been rehired. Another employee quit, or was discharged, ten times in nine years. He was repeatedly rehired in the same department and his termination recommendations invariably were not to rehire. A similar case showed six quits and discharges in five years, and another, four terminations in five years. In three cases employees quit after working eleven to fifteen months. The foreman in each case recommended not rehiring because the individual was undependable or his work was unsatisfactory. All this appears to indicate careless and indifferent evaluation on the part of certain of the factory supervisors. The worst cases are concentrated in two departments. This is the kind of evidence that might logically be used in evaluation of supervisors. It is not evident that any use is made of exit interview data for this purpose.

In the office area no exit interview is conducted, but a termination rating and a rehire recommendation are made. A sample of 250 files on persons who have left the company within the past ten years was examined. Four cases were found where persons were discharged less than a year after receiving a merit increase. In one case discharge followed three months after receiving a merit increase. In two cases employees resigned within two months after receiving a merit increase. In both cases the recommendation was made not to rehire. In one of these cases the termination rating was very low. Another file disclosed that a clerk typist was laid off and rated average or above in all respects. The supervisor said not to rehire: the employee was too slow. (This employee was rated average on quantity of work.) A comptometer operator received poor merit ratings but was kept on the job for two years. She resigned and the supervisor recommended not to rehire. Again, in the office area, there is some evidence of carelessness in evaluation and of failure to take the action which should follow from the evaluation that is made.

In terms of personnel practices, particularly in the area of employee evaluation, there is appreciable room for improvement in this company. This opinion, based upon the limited evidence cited and anecdotes contributed at various times by members of the company, is shared by many of these same members. The feeling seems to be "we must go somewhere, although we are not sure just where." The factory organization is in greatest need of improvement with respect to employee evaluation. It is here where no merit rating is done.

• THE C COMPANY—A LARGE MANUFACTURING COMPANY

Description of the Company

The company has nationwide operations but this case is confined to one metropolitan-area plant which employs more than 23,000 people, a majority of whom are members of an independent union. The company enjoys a dominant position in its industry and is a subsidiary of a company in an equivalent position of strength.

The managerial staff numbers between two and three thousand. The personnel and industrial relations staff (managerial and nonmanagerial) number close to one thousand. One personnel group handles all work force adjustment procedures in an elaborate systematic manner. In fact, all procedure in personnel matters in this company is highly systematized.

Performance Appraisal in the C Company

Systematic performance appraisal was inaugurated in 1924. The rating scale technique, popular at the time, was used, with individuals being rated on various traits and behavior items. The purposes of rating were to aid supervisors to study their personnel, to ascertain training needs, and to provide an estimate of the supply of potential supervisors available.

In 1938 the rating plan was changed to a two-factor forced-distribution scheme. The factors were over-all job ability and supervisory potentiality. The change was made as a result of an elaborate statistical study, showing that the traits on the original scale overlapped. A second reason for the change was to reduce the time necessary to complete ratings.

In 1939 the forced-distribution system was supplemented by a ranking system, the supervisor being given a choice of methods to use. Later the five-category forced-distribution was changed to a five-category rating in which the categories carried percentage equivalents (from 60 percent to 100 percent) and were defined in terms of job requirements (e.g., "Satisfactory, meets job requirements," "Reasonably satisfactory, inadequate in some respects.").

In 1947 a shift was made to the rank-order method for rating all employees except those who were on jobs on which they could not be compared with others. The latter were rated on the five-category plan.[11] Increased attention was devoted to establishing homogeneous rating groups in order to make the rank-order rating more meaningful. As a result of supervisory complaints that rank-order failed to indicate the general caliber of the persons in a rating group, "double rating" was instituted a year later. Under this arrangement employees (except those in unique jobs) are rated both against others (rank-order) and against the job (the five categories). Since then a change in the definition of the categories has been made. Terminology emphasizing job requirements has since been abandoned and substitution of the words "below average," "average," etc., has been made. Allegedly, this change was made at the request of raters who found the earlier terminology indefinite and confusing.

Wherever possible the individual is rated by superiors in the two levels above him. A minimum of two ratings is sought and these ratings are averaged to yield a composite rating. All non-supervisory employees are rated, as are supervisors at the two lowest levels.

Several other ratings aside from the annual rating procedure just described are made at special times. Upon termination the employee is rated by his supervisor with respect to performance, ability, conduct, and attendance. Upon layoff the individual is rated *A*, *B* or *C* to indicate the order of preference in rehiring. "Service write-ups" are made on the employee on the second, fifth, tenth, fifteenth, twentieth, etc., anniversaries of his hiring date. These write-ups,

[11] This applies to the job ability factor. In all cases since 1938, employees have been rated on supervisory potential in terms of three categories.

involving a special interview between the individuals and a member of the managerial group (or higher ranking member where the individual is a manager) include a five-category rating on individual traits, a free-written appraisal, and recording of numerous personal data already in possession of the personnel department. As length of service increases, the rank of the person conducting the interview is correspondingly increased. The interview also includes presentation of a service badge.

Uses of Performance Appraisal

As stated in the appraisal manual, performance rating is to serve as a control mechanism. All recommended personnel actions are to be assessed in light of prior ratings. This does not mean that actions inconsistent with ratings are not tolerated. Length of service tends to be dominant in all decisions. Range of experience and physical limitations are of importance in promotions and transfers. Control is to be achieved by noting inconsistencies between ratings and actions or ratings and other factors, and determining the reasons for these inconsistencies. Responsibility for effective control thereby must rest upon persons other than those making the ratings. This responsibility is enforced by an elaborate system of approvals and counter-approvals necessary to effecting a personnel action. A large number of forms with numerous copies are involved in each action.

Nothing else is expected from performance appraisal. A company committee assigned to study merit rating in other companies concluded, in a 1950 report, that other objectives, particularly wage administration and communication, are of little value in this company. They based their conclusion with respect to wage administration on a speech by a professor who indicated that his research showed that tying wages to ratings in the government service resulted in a loss of production. As for communication (or counseling) the committee concluded that "employee development" is always present in the thinking of company supervision, and such use of appraisal is unnecessary.

The service write-up has a general communication function where the employee is encouraged to express all his gripes, ambitions, etc. It is also used as a vehicle for formal recognition of length of service.

An Evaluation of Performance Appraisal in the C Company

As a record designed to guide (a more accurate expression of actual purpose than "control") personnel decisions, the appraisal system yields clear answers, thanks to the rank-order device. An important innovation was the inauguration of "double rating" with its concept of man-to-job rating. The rank-order method necessitates grouping people so that all in the group are on the same or very similar jobs. The resultant multitude of small groups, each with its "number-one" man, leaves unsolved the problem of just how good these people are. As a solution the "man-to-job" rating was reinstituted.

It is difficult to assess the degree to which "control" is achieved in this system. Probably, some control is obtained simply by virtue of the hierarchy of approvals necessary to each personnel action. In addition there is a considerable amount of rotation of supervisors in different jobs (at least at lower levels). Under such conditions a supervisor may become a victim of his own poor ratings if he receives, as transfers, persons he erroneously rated high previously, when such high ratings are responsible in large measure for the transfers.

But the rating plan is overshadowed by the vast placement organization. A placement analyst exists for every thousand employees (or less). These analysts receive regular lists of vacancies in the company and suggest candidates from the group with which they work. From these candidates a selection is made by placement supervisors and, if line approval is obtained, a transfer is effected. The placement organization has complete authority to decide if vacancies will be filled from within or from the outside. Line supervisors can only choose from the candidates offered. The placement director argues that the placement analysts are extremely well informed through observation as to the performance of personnel assigned to them. Their observations serve as a check on supervisory ratings and at the same time their recommendations are partially based upon the ratings. The company may have succeeded in replicating, in part, the situation in a small company where everyone knows everyone else.

Seniority reigns supreme in the C Company. The burden of justification lies upon the one who would take action of a discriminative nature with respect to employees when discrimination is based upon anything other than length of service. This is a practice, apparently, of long standing. Coupled with this is a company policy of promotion from within. As one result, all of the several thousand present managerial personnel have been promoted from nonsupervisory jobs in the company, except two.[12]

However, two escapes from the seniority cage do exist. One is the possibility of taking action not in accordance with length of service where there is very strong evidence to support such action.[13] The other is complete managerial freedom to rehire those previously laid off without respect to length of service. At these points, of course, proper evaluation is crucial. Documentary evidence of the quality of evaluation was not available. However, layoff is governed by length of service except for outstanding individuals. An informal arrangement between company and union allows about 10 percent of layoffs to be made in violation of seniority.

Demotion or discharge for poor performance is virtually nonexistent, particularly in management ranks. One company official cites the case of a subordinate who does extremely poor work although he has shown himself capable of doing better. This person has over thirty years service and is virtually untouchable. This same official pointed out that, in his own case, providing he appears on the job regularly "and does not set fire to the building," his job is secure until he reaches retirement age. A considerable area in which employee evaluation is usually necessary tends to be eliminated under these conditions.

---

[12] One of these was brought in only after various company supervisors had successively been placed in charge of a high-accident, low-output department with no success. The department is now described as one of the best in the company.

[13] The placement director regards merit ratings as furnishing strong "talking points" in this respect.

This company seems to do an excellent job of evaluation within the narrow limits established by the pervasive seniority policy. But this excellence is achieved at what appears to be an extremely high cost in terms of time, money, and personnel.

• THE D COMPANY—A UTILITY

Description of the Company

This utility company services a wide area, although its main offices are in an urban location. Consequently, its organization structure shows a geographical departmentation at the vice-presidential level. Employment is over forty thousand.

Personnel administration is decentralized. Each department manager has a personnel staff performing the major personnel functions for his department. A general personnel staff, reporting to the vice-president of personnel, performs in an advisory and research capacity. The personnel staff, in total, numbers about four hundred. The manager of each department is permitted to proceed as he sees fit with respect to employee evaluation. The result is that six departments utilize formal appraisal systems while three do not. In each case a distinctive plan exists. Several of these plans are discussed here.

Performance Appraisal—W Department

The W Department employs 3000 people, mostly women, and is unionized. Virtually all jobs are clerical. All nonsupervisory employees and the lower four levels of supervision are formally rated. A rating is made of an individual only when action is to be taken with respect to promotion, discharge, pay changes, etc. The rating form contains a great deal of data not relevant to evaluation, permitting the form to be used for virtually all personnel purposes.

Ratings are usually made when pay increases are due. This is annually or biennially for supervisors and semiannually or annually for nonsupervisors. Rate ranges exist for all jobs. When the individual reaches the top of the rate range he is no longer rated regularly. Ratings are also made when a promotion decision is imminent and at any other time when the department head requests it.

A rating scale with four categories (excellent, good, fair, unsatisfactory) is used. The nonsupervisor is rated on five characteristics; the supervisor on eleven. The rater, always the immediate superior, is encouraged to write comments in a space provided. The ratings are examined and approved (or additions made) by the rater's supervisor, and in some cases by a still higher supervisor.

The personnel supervisor is of the opinion that ratings should be made at times other than when a pay increase is in order. The reason for rating only at the time of pay changes is to conserve time. The department head believes it to be unduly time consuming to have to seek the rating made previously on an individual when considering approval of a wage increase. This position makes some sense in the case of supervisors. However, nonsupervisors receive pay increases almost automatically. For a supervisor to deny an increase, he must secure approval of his superiors at each of the two levels above him, presenting a complete case for the denial. The easy (and usual) way out is to "recommend" the increase. Under these conditions the necessity for examining a rating is not evident. The personnel supervisor says that scarcely anyone ever receives an unsatisfactory rating. Supervisors are expected to explain any rating below "good."

The personnel supervisor indicates that he regards the chief value of rating to be its use as a foundation for a counseling interview with the employee. In the case of supervisors the ratings are to serve as guides in making promotion decisions.

In addition to ratings, careful record is kept of attendance, tardiness, and "contacts." These contacts are interviews between supervisor and subordinate made when employee performance merits reprimand or approbation. These records are extremely important when formal grievances arise. The union dismisses ratings as meaningless.

Promotions, other things being equal, are governed by length of service, according to the contract. The union carefully watches all promotion decisions. Formal grievances have recently been averaging twenty to thirty annually. Those grievances concerning pay or promotion average about half of the total. One recent grievance was that of a woman who twice failed to be promoted although she had greater seniority than those promoted. The company's case, eventually accepted by the union, was buttressed by performance data, which, interestingly, showed the woman to be extremely incompetent. Although she clearly should have been removed from the job, she was not. This reflects a general reluctance in the company to discharge. This reluctance is defended on the ground that the company's selection procedures are highly effective and that inadequate performance, therefore, is likely to reflect supervisory failure to motivate. No doubt a disinclination to incur union displeasure is also a factor—in this department, at least.

Performance rating seems of little effectiveness at the nonsupervisory level in this department because of the dominance of seniority backed by a strong union. With ratings made only at the time of automatic wage increases, it is perhaps not surprising to find an example such as the one provided by the grievance cited.

Appraisals of supervisors are perhaps more meaningful. The chief limitation apparent is the extreme brevity of the rating scale and the indefinite nature of the descriptions of rating categories ("good," "fair," etc.).

A measure of control is achieved by requiring two or three levels of supervision to approve the ratings. However, tying ratings directly to administrative decisions appears to eliminate the chief opportunity for control-checking decisions against ratings made at other times.

Performance Appraisal—X Department

Two hundred fifty persons work in the X Department, which performs the engineering function. Forty-five are supervisors. For appraisal purposes three groups are distinguished: engineers, supervisors, and nonsupervisory personnel other than engineers. At the present time all except supervisors are rated, although a supervisor rating plan is being considered.

Nonengineers are rated annually (twice during the first year of employment) on a scale of five degrees (undefined) on twelve "job performance and personal qualities." Various written comments are called for with respect to promotional possibilities, plans for improving performance, and the employee's reaction to discussion of his performance with his supervisor.

Engineers are rated annually (twice during the first year of employment) on a forced-choice performance report, consisting of twenty-nine groups of five statements. In each group of five, three statements are positive and two negative. This form has very recently superseded one containing twenty-five groups of four statements. The revision was necessary, according to the personnel supervisor, because raters were beginning to learn how to "rig" the results. This was deduced from observing that certain raters' ratings were consistently higher than those of other raters. Additional comments similar to those on the nonengineering form are called for on this report.

The proposed supervisor rating form, now being tested, contains fifty statements expressing desirable behavior characteristics. The rater is required to check one of five squares following each statement to indicate the degree to which the statement applies to the supervisor being rated.

The primary reason for formal appraisal, according to the personnel supervisor, is to assure that the supervisor discusses the employee's performance with him to point out areas for improvement. Also, it is hoped that regular formal evaluation will aid in discovering the "deadwood" before seniority makes elimination difficult. Wage and promotion recommendations are checked against ratings by the personnel supervisor. In this way a degree of control is effected.

The nonengineering and the supervisor rating forms are vague in defining both degrees on the scale and characteristics to be rated. They seem to be usable for the purpose of communication, however. The engineer's forced-choice report is another matter. It has been necessary to provide the supervisor with an alphabetically ordered list of all statements in the report to facilitate discussion with the engineer. This list permits him to keep a record of the statements he marked in filling out the report. Taken out of context, however, the statements appear bald, oversimplified, indefensible. Short of showing the engineer the actual rating, there would seem to be no way of getting across precisely the supervisor's opinions. Considering the fact that some of these statements have a low discriminative index,[14] the usefulness of this form for "development" interviews seems extremely dubious.

Appraisal, inaugurated some years ago for the purpose of determining training needs, is now directed mainly toward informing the employee of his strong and weak points. At best, the devices used are not particularly pointed toward this objective. The forced-choice report appears to be completely out of place.

Performance Appraisal—Y Department

The Y Department employs over seven thousand people, of whom one thousand are supervisors. The nonsupervisory force is unionized, several unions being represented. The lower three levels of supervision are appraised on one rating form and the nonsupervisors on another. In both cases a trait rating scale is used. The chief objective of rating in this department is to assess the volume

[14] Defined in the section on the forced-choice report.

of potential supervisors and to identify as early as possible those who will probably fail to achieve a satisfactory level of performance in the company.

Rating of both supervisors and nonsupervisors is done on a committee basis. The committee typically will consist of the immediate supervisor, his superior (who will include his staff personnel assistant), and other supervisors in a position to rate the performance of those persons being considered. The opinion of the group is assessed and resolved. The immediate supervisor records the group judgment. When the committee has completed initial rating of a nonsupervisory group, those individuals considered to be outstanding are again rated by the same committee on a special form. This form is much more detailed and is used in an effort to get clearer insight into all aspects of the individual who is alleged to be an outstanding man.

Both forms contain a section in which planned action with respect to low ratings is to be indicated. The ratings are made annually and, after each rating, it is expected that the supervisor will review the individual's performance with him.

The committee technique is utilized in an effort to gain more complete information as a basis for rating and to arrive at a pooled judgment without necessity for post-rating reconciliation of differences in raters' interpretations of the rating form. Various other benefits accruing from this technique are cited:

1. The supervisory staff gains better acquaintance with all personnel being discussed.

2. The supervisor is called to account for deficiencies in his subordinates.

3. Closer control of personnel actions is likely to be attained because the unit supervisor who has to approve recommendations from below has been party to discussion of the individual under consideration.

Rating is apparently carried out with dispatch. The personnel supervisor estimates that a four-hour session will usually suffice to rate thirty to forty people. The tendency is to quickly dispose of those performing about as expected and to pass to more extensive consideration of those who are outstandingly good or inadequate. This, of course, is exactly in line with the objective sought in rating.

The committee rating technique, resulting in a group judgment, minimizes the possibility of any one supervisor's being able to take actions not in line with ratings without being caught up by others. In addition it is likely that ratings representing the judgments of a group of supervisors are more likely to be respected—and hence consulted—than the ratings of an individual supervisor.

Appraisal technique and purpose seem well matched in this department. Improvement might be effected by reducing the number of descriptive phrases on the rating scale. The present potpourri is evidently confusing to raters, for rating forms which have been filled out frequently show phrases crossed out. The personnel supervisor believes this to be a minor matter, not interfering with the basic goal of distinguishing the mine-run employees from the inadequate and the outstanding.

Performance Appraisal—Z Department

This department employs 1000 women and 375 men. Nonsupervisory employees are unionized. Only male employees are formally rated. The personnel supervisor believes that outstanding female employees are obvious to the supervisors in the offices in which they work. Such outstanding women are sought for office supervision, the only supervisory job open to them. In contrast with the male employees who are dispersed over a wide geographical area, women are seldom transferred from the community in which they lived when they entered employment.

The objective of performance appraisal in this department is to assess, at the earliest possible time, the supervisory potentialities of male employees. Nonsupervisory jobs are regarded as training posts for future supervisors. The personnel supervisor visualizes the great personnel problem of this department to be that of developing a continuing adequate supply of good supervisors. Rating is to function as a technique for identifying potential supervisors and appraising their development.

To achieve this objective, an appraisal plan of considerable complexity is used. Two separate devices are used alternately each six months. One is the annual "personnel review." This has two parts. One is a rating scale on ten personal characteristics. The other is a list of the supervisory and nonsupervisory positions in the department followed by columns headed "Now," "Next Year," and "Ultimate." The supervisor is required to enter check marks in appropriate fashion. He is also asked to indicate the action to be taken with respect to the persons rated, both for the current time and the coming year. These actions are:

1. Promotion within the department
2. Lateral move in the department
3. Continue in present position
4. Transfer to other department

Finally the rater is required to make a written explanation of the action he has recommended.

The second device used is the annual progress report. Fourteen questions regarding various aspects of job performance must be answered in free-written form. Both over-all performance and prospects for advancement are rated on a four-part scale. In addition a rank-order rating is made. The rater must also make a free-written rating of his general impression of the person being rated. The progress report and the personnel review together include virtually every variety of rating device except the forced-choice technique. The personnel supervisor estimates that the individual's progress report alone takes several hours to complete.

Each of these rating forms, after being completed by the immediate supervisor, is examined and countersigned by supervisors at the next two higher levels. From there the forms are forwarded to the departmental personnel supervisor who examines and retains them. The personnel supervisor maintains an inventory of potential supervisors for every supervisory and staff position in the department. All recommended personnel actions are checked against the ratings which have been submitted. Inconsistencies must be justified by the rater. Progress reports are checked against the personnel reviews for consistency. All ratings made on these forms with respect to promotion possibilities of an individual are checked against the statements offered in justification of these ratings. In consequence a high degree of control is attained.

The personnel supervisor remains dissatisfied with the current rating plan. He believes it falls short of adequately revealing precisely why particular ratings and recommendations are made. In an effort to get specific behavior data justifying ratings, experiments are being conducted with a "field review" technique.

Various aspects of the individual's job performance are discussed in an interview between the supervisor and a personnel interviewer. The interviewer asks for the supervisor's rating on components of job performance and then questions the supervisor closely in an effort to seek substantiating data and information. All such information is recorded by the interviewer along with the rating. Experience to date indicates that as much as a full day is necessary to complete an interview on a single individual. The personnel supervisor, who is hopeful that this technique will eventually become standard practice, believes the importance of the objective justifies even this great expenditure of time.

Performance appraisal is taken very seriously in this department. The department's function (sales) and its geographic dispersion undoubtedly play some part in the matter. Hiring is usually done in the small local communities where the jobs are located. Under such conditions, communication of information about individual performance and potential is difficult, but extremely important. This may explain the tremendous expenditure of time on appraisal activity. As in other departments of this company, all personnel are completely trained within the company.

Purpose and technique are well adapted in this appraisal plan. Perhaps the apparently uneconomic expenditure of time is justifiable. Evaluation of supervisory potential is a difficult task and is done here under difficult conditions.

Performance Appraisal— College Trainees

The company regularly recruits college graduates, who are placed in a five-year training program. The program is supervised by a member of the general personnel staff. The trainees are expected to rise eventually to at least the third (from the bottom) level of management. During their period of training they are rated annually with that objective in mind.

The current rating form is simple, requiring a rating of work performance as either *A*, *B*+, *B*, or *C*, with *B* representing average performance. The supervisor is required to state reasons for his rating, to indicate what training has been given during the rating period and what further training is needed. He is further asked to estimate the trainee's capacity to reach the supervisory level mentioned and to indicate the latest date at which the trainee's progress has been discussed with him, together with the trainee's reaction to the discussion.

In thirty years of operation of this training program nearly 1400 college graduates have passed through it. A survey of those who entered this program twenty-five years or more ago shows that 130 have reached the supervisory level anticipated while 70 have failed to reach it. Those who attain this level do so, on the average fifteen to seventeen years after being hired.

Each time a "progress report" is submitted, the college training supervisor examines it for evidence of doubt with respect to the trainee's potentialities. When a *C*-grade man is discovered, a conference between the training supervisor and the line supervisor frequently occurs. The result frequently is simply to "worry" about the individual. As elsewhere in the company, there is reluctance to take positive action except where an egregious error has been made in selection. In practice, a rating of *C* is not given by the supervisor until he is ready to recommend a discharge of the trainee.

This appraisal plan could be improved

by requiring the supervisor to be more specific with reference to the evidence upon which he bases his decisions, as is done in the Z Department. The investment in selection and training of these college graduates would seem to justify a more careful appraisal system.

An Evaluation of Performance Appraisal in the D Company

The men's employment office maintains files on former male employees who have left the company. One hundred of these files were selected and examined. The cases selected were from among those persons who had terminated employment since 1949 and who had had at least two years of service. Two cases of dismissal were found in which no specific reason for the action was given. Three cases were found which illustrate the reluctance to take action when judgment indicates action should be taken—a weakness not only of this company, but of other companies as well. The outstanding example is that of a draftsman, dismissed after twenty-eight years on the payroll. During his last eight years he was absent 64 percent of the time (about 1800 days). His absences were absurd; e.g., 248 days with a cold and 150 days with athlete's foot. The company paid him over $14,000 in sickness disability benefits during his tenure. At length he was dismissed with a termination payment of over $7,000. As far back as 1934 performance appraisals indicated that he was "slow" and "very limited in ability." Thus, evaluation was not at fault. The other two cases were much less spectacular, but illustrate the same point.

In the interest of seeing how well those filling out progress reports on college trainees were able to predict the future success of these trainees, some data on this matter were obtained with the help of the training supervisor. This supervisor has found that the average length of time required for trainees to make the third rung up the managerial ladder—the level they are expected to attain—is fifteen to seventeen years. It was possible to identify the various ex-trainees and their current positions in the company. On a number of these ex-trainees merit ratings made years earlier were available. Two groups of ex-trainees in three departments were identified. A group of eighteen were classed as above average. These people had reached the third level sooner than average or had gone higher than that level in seventeen years. A group of seventeen were classed as below average. These people had required longer than average time to reach the third level or had not reached it after seventeen years.

The progress report form varied through time but nearly always called for a letter rating and some sort of estimate of the individual's supervisory potentialities. A summary was made of the letter ratings (*A*, *B*+, *B*, no rating) of each group and the estimate of supervisory potentiality (yes, no, uncertain, no comment). Of those classed as above average, eight were rated *A*, seven were rated *B*+, and three rated *B*. Fifteen of this group were judged to be potential supervisors. On two people the raters were uncertain. Of those classed as below average, two were rated *A*, six were rated *B*+, and three rated *B*. Eight were judged to be potential supervisors; four were judged not to be. On two people the raters were uncertain and on four they simply made no comment. These progress reports were dated as early as 1924 and as late as 1947. Hence the judgments were made over a period of twenty-three years.

The raters predicted rather well. They were more successful in picking the exceptionally able than in identifying the mediocre or poor. As can be seen, the rating *B*+, unless read together with the specific estimate of supervisory potentiality, has little meaning. The training supervisor believes that a general reluctance to give "poor" ratings accounts for the less effective prediction with respect to those in the below average group. It is interesting to note that, in this sample, supervisors rating trainees in the W Department predicted almost perfectly. This department performs the accounting task in the company.

In summary, evaluation as such appears to be performed well. The reluctance to act in accordance with judgment in many cases results in failure to exploit the value of this judgment for proper performance of the management task. Awareness of this weakness exists and there is evidence of attempts in some departments of the company to overcome it.

• THE E COMPANY—A SMALL METALS MANUFACTURING PLANT (URBAN LOCATION)

Description of the Company

The plant employs approximately 1200 people of whom about 100 are supervisory and staff personnel. Although other facilities of the company are engaged in mass-production of metal stampings, this plant produces machined precision metal products. As a result most jobs in the factory have a fairly high skill content.

The company is nonunion, having survived a representation election rather recently. Members of management state that employees are encouraged to bring complaints up the line individually as far as they wish and that employees avail themselves of this opportunity regularly.

The E Company has no official performance appraisal program. (It is included in the cases for that very reason.) A former rating plan was abandoned at the beginning of World War II. At that time a job evaluation program was inaugurated. It consumed so much time and effort that rating died from neglect. In lieu of the usual description of an appraisal plan, brief description will be made of the procedures involved in making those personnel decisions where appraisal is frequently used.

In wage administration, all jobs are evaluated and rate ranges established for each job class. The individual's rate of pay and rate of movement through the range is left to the discretion of line supervision. Some control is exerted by the personnel division, however. Constant watch is maintained over departmental rate averages. If the average begins to rise above the middle of the rate range, the wage administrator advises a higher level of line management —that the department is "getting out of line." Presumably the department is then brought into line. Some jobs are paid on an incentive basis. These jobs also have rate ranges on the base rate. Changes in the base rate do not affect direct earnings, but do influence vacation pay and other fringe items.

Promotions, transfers, etc., are also left to the discretion of line supervisors, with decision-making power given to second-line supervisors when nonsupervisory personnel are being moved, and to third (from the top) level managers, or higher, when supervisory personnel are involved. It is official company policy to place prime emphasis on ability and performance in making such work-force adjustments. But, by admission, seniority tends to receive strong consideration in all cases—and in some cases "too much." Promotions at the nonsupervisory level are mostly from one skill level to another on the same job. Seldom, except at their own request, are employees moved from one job to another.

It is the belief of the personnel department officials that an appraisal system would be of little use to the company in performing the wage administration and work-force adjustment functions. Their argument is that the line supervisor's judgment in no way becomes better because it is placed on a printed form. Therefore, rating could contribute nothing. They further argue that any "control" features of a rating system are not necessary because of the small number of personnel and consequent wide acquaintance of supervisors with the performance of nonsupervisory personnel. Also present is the attitude that inasmuch as things are going very well, there is little to be gained and perhaps much to be lost by introducing a new practice. The assistant personnel director is of the opinion that the communications or counseling use of performance appraisal has value, but believes its introduction of rating for this purpose should be deferred until some "old-line" foremen currently in the company have been replaced by more "modern" foremen who would accept and use the technique.

In the course of interviewing several line supervisors the discovery was made that the shop supervisor (in charge of approximately five hundred people in the shop) has, on his own initiative, instituted some practices that resemble merit rating. He has drawn up a list of the characteristics of a good supervisor. At regular periods he holds a conference of the supervisors under him, at which time these supervisors submit names of employees deemed to possess, currently or potentially, those characteristics on the list. Following a discussion of those whose names are submitted, a group is selected for training in all phases of shop work. These individuals are then drawn upon to fill supervisory vacancies. (They are also used as a "flying squadron" to relieve bottlenecks.) In addition to this practice all foremen are required, when submitting recommendations for wage increases, to forward a written statement explaining why the increase is recommended. These statements are expected to cover quantity of production, scrap record, attendance, time at the machine, and safety practices of the individual worker. These notes are held in file for a short while and then discarded. The purpose in establishing these formalities is to restore to the first-line supervisors some basic personnel authority and responsibility which over the years had been usurped by those above them, and at the same time to provide some instruments of guidance and control with respect to personnel decisions in the areas of wages, training, and promotion. Several company officials emphasized the need for returning more authority and responsibility in personnel matters to first-line supervision. The shop supervisor who has initiated the practices mentioned believes that some sort of "tool" must be created to aid foremen in fulfilling these responsibilities and to assure those above that they are being properly fulfilled. The tool he has established is nothing more or less than a homemade performance appraisal scheme.

It seems reasonable to conclude that, at least in certain parts of this company, there is need for an appraisal plan, despite the convictions of personnel officials to the contrary.

An Evaluation of Employee Appraisal in the E Company

In some respects the E Company is comparable with the B Company. They have approximately the same number of employees and both are nonunion firms in highly unionized industries. Neither has a formal rating plan for factory personnel, who constitute the large majority of the employees. The B Company, with a high turnover rate, preoccupied with a rigid wage formula and suffering from recent organizational upheaval, seems to be doing a mediocre job of evaluation. The E Company is apparently doing a considerably better job.

Turnover currently averages two and one-half percent per month. The bulk of the turnover is concentrated in the night-shift group of employees. The rate is low and reflects favorably upon the company. As always, however, it must be regarded as a resultant of the complex that makes up "the job" in the company.

A sample of 125 files of persons who had left the company was examined. The record of promotions and merit increases was compared with reasons for termination and termination ratings. These ratings, made by the immediate supervisor, cover "competency" and "conduct." A choice of "good," "fair," or "poor" may be made in rating. The sample covered several cases of promotion to minor supervisory jobs. There was no clear evidence of mistakes in promotion, at least in terms of promoting individuals incapable of handling the job. Two non-supervisory employees quit because they believed their wages were not being increased rapidly enough. Management-initiated terminations occasionally showed people being laid off for lack of work who were rated "good." This is explained as being a case of having to choose someone from a group in which everyone performs well.

Only two questionable cases were found in the sample. In one a draftsman had received four merit increases and one promotion in his four years of employment. When he resigned his termination rating was "fair" with the recommendation not to rehire. His last merit increase occurred seven months prior to his resignation. In another case an accounting machine operator, after a short period of employment, resigned. She received the highest termination rating (good) but the supervisor recommended not rehiring her, with no reason given.

There is no strong evidence that evaluation of employees has not, in the past, been performed competently. In the opinion of the shop supervisor a tendency to base wage and promotion decisions on length of service has developed through the years. The cases cited might be consistent with that belief. He is taking the steps described previously to halt this tendency. He indicates that some complaints have arisen where decisions have been made which have run counter to length of service. So far he has been successful in satisfying those complaining. His method is to ask the foreman to give to the man who is aggrieved a detailed explanation of the reasons for his decision. The shop supervisor regards his requirement that foremen make written justification of wage recommendations as valuable in preparing them for problems of this sort.

• THE F COMPANY—A SMALL, HIGHLY MECHANIZED PLANT

Description of the Company

The F Company is a small food-manufacturing concern located in a large city. Employment fluctuates seasonally, with a maximum of approximately five hundred employees. The majority of these employees work on production-line jobs. Because of the highly mechanized nature of the manufacturing process, the skill content of many production jobs is quite low. Fifteen minutes is sufficient training time for many jobs. Most production jobs are machine-paced and carry a fixed hourly rate. A few jobs are paid on a piecework basis, with a fixed base rate. A small group of maintenance and repair men fill jobs of considerable skill content. The latter jobs have a rate range, as do office jobs.

Employees are represented by an independent union, with the exception of a few boiler-room personnel who are members of an international union.

The company provides a pension plan, group insurance, and cafeteria service.

Performance Appraisal in the F Company

This company formerly used a "progress report" on all employees, which was a periodic rating plan of the familiar rating scale variety. It fell into disuse following World War II, from lack of managerial interest.

Currently, formal appraisal is used in only limited fashion. A rating plan was devised by the general maintenance foreman and is an instrument of wage administration applied only to maintenance personnel. The objective of rating is to establish the individual worker's pay within the rate range.

The rating form has some original features. Each job is listed, together with a series of numbers which refer to specific major duties of the job. A fraction of the total rate range has been assigned to each of these duties. This fraction is equal to the estimated fraction of total working time which the worker must spend on the particular duty. A percentage rating (100 percent maximum) is assigned to each duty by the rater as an estimate of the worker's performance with respect to that duty. The percentages are multiplied by the rate-range fractions and the results summed. This yields the increment which will be added to the base rate to determine the worker's rate of pay.

This form, designed and initiated by the maintenance foreman, is used to rate maintenance personnel at least every six months, but no more often than every three months. Following completion of the rating, the supervisor discusses it with the employee, indicating the resultant wage. The wage recommendation is then submitted for approval by the factory superintendent and the personnel director.

A less formal scheme is used for promotions and transfers in the factory. At least once a year a survey of the work force is made in which the workers are asked to indicate to which jobs, if any, they are interested in moving. A summary, by jobs requested, is prepared. Where the individual's request can not possibly be considered, he is notified as to the reason (physical limitations, lack of educational background, etc.), and his name is removed from the list. The remainder on the list are rated in rank-order of eligibility by the plant manager upon the advice of various supervisors who know the individuals listed. Eligibility is based first upon estimated ability. Where ability is roughly equal, eligibility is based upon length of service. The ratings are then submitted to the union and differences of opinion reconciled. The lists are then published. The personnel director urges individuals to submit their names in those cases where he believes these individuals to be superior to any who have voluntarily placed their names on the lists. When a vacancy occurs, the number one man moves into it.

New employees are rated on a check list form at the end of thirty, sixty, and ninety days. The items rated are attendance, tardiness, cleanliness, job performance, probable future performance, and ability to get along with others. The rater is asked also to indicate what he has done to correct the employee's faults and what further action is necessary.

Office personnel are subject to none of the rating procedures discussed. The office manager handles all personnel matters as he sees fit, subject to control by the personnel director only on matters of keeping rates within the established ranges and within the requirements of governmental stabilization programs.

An Evaluation of Performance Appraisal in the F Company

The rating technique used by the maintenance department is exceptionally good in one respect. The rating form is built exactly to suit the purpose of rating. The form yields a rate, which is precisely what is sought. Furthermore the form, by its design, forces consideration of performance in terms of actual job duties. This tends to minimize consideration of irrelevant factors.

Possible weak points in the form are the vagueness in meaning of percentage ratings and the failure to consider separately the degree to which the employee cooperates with others. It is true that many maintenance tasks are performed in comparative isolation, but not infrequently the maintenance man must deal with supervisors and workers in other departments. It is likely that the factor of cooperation tends to be taken into consideration to some extent when performance of the various duties is rated.

Occasionally the employee challenges the rating and consequent rate increase (or lack of). In such situations the maintenance foreman requests the employee to assign himself a rating on each of the job duties. With few exceptions he has found that the employee rates himself lower than the supervisor does. The union occasionally protests variations in the amount by which individuals' rates are increased, and increases which place rates out of harmony with length of service. Management, insisting upon consideration of performance, has asked union officials to devise a better plan. To date the request has been refused, but protests continue. If a more aggressive union (perhaps an affiliated union) were present in the plant or if a "run" of decisions contravening length of service were made (such decisions are apparently infrequent), the plan might fail. The percentage ratings seem nearly impossible to defend. Likely, the plan survives at present largely on the strength of the feature of rating performance of specific job duties.

The appraisal plan used in promotions and transfers appears to be well adapted to a small organzation. Again, as in the case of the maintenance rating system, purpose and method appear well adapted. The system exploits the cross-checks on judgment possible in a small organization. The personnel director, as much as his staff role permits, acts as a single rater, seeking out and consolidating rating information. The union usually accepts management judgment in this area except, of course, when that judgment seriously violates seniority.

The appraisal of new employees is more casual. While elements of performance most observable in the early months of employment are emphasized, supervisors are not required to make a definite recommendation (with reasons) with respect to continued employment of the individual.

On the whole this company seems to have done a good job of establishing appraisal systems, using them only where there are conditions warranting their use and tailoring them reasonably well to these conditions. The office force is conspicuously neglected. The strong personality and dominant organizational position of the office manager has placed the office force out of reach of the general personnel practices.

The company's evaluation problem is rather simple in comparison with many companies. Evaluation for wage administration purposes is simplified by virtue of the machine-paced nature of many jobs. In the factory rate-range jobs most employees on the higher rated jobs have reached the top of the range. The maintenance foreman admits that length of service tends to be given strong consideration in recommending wage increases.

The influence of seniority in management policy is strong. Reluctance to take action against an employee with a number of years in the company is present, as it is in many companies. Reputedly, a few long-service employees have openly boasted that they cannot be discharged. The problem of early identification of poor employees is recognized by the personnel director as a serious one. There seems to be some hesitancy on the part of lower level supervisors to act against a long-service employee because of possible reversal of the action by the top level of management.

A form known as a "personnel report" is available to supervisors as a means of recording unusual incidents in daily personnel supervision. The individual supervisor has discretion as to what he shall record. The report is frequently used, however. The bulk of the reports seems to be made on incidents which necessitate reprimand, although instances of commendatory behavior are in evidence, as well as notations on items other than performance, e.g., shift rotation arrangements. As noted in other companies in this study, these reports are valuable as justification for management decisions. The maintenance foreman relates a case of their use. He was asked to pick four men for layoff in a period of force reduction. The personnel director asked why he had chosen these men, several of whom were not junior in length of service. The foreman's answer was that they were poor workers and had created trouble. The personnel director challenged this on the grounds that the foreman had said nothing about this before and that the union would not accept the foreman's word. The foreman thereupon produced carbon copies of a series of personnel reports he had submitted on these men, covering incidents of poor behavior. The originals were found in the personnel files. The decision was then accepted. This case illustrates the value of these reports and, incidentally, some poor personnel management. The current personnel director (who was not involved in the case) believes these reports to be extremely valuable. He indicates that he is contemplating taking some action to encourage more extensive use of them, as well as considering methods of using them for general evaluation purposes.

• THE G COMPANY—THE CRITICAL-INCIDENT TECHNIQUE IN THE FACTORY

Description of the Company

The G Company, a manufacturing enterprise, is located in a Midwestern town of 42,000 population. The company is a division of a nationwide corporation, but enjoys a considerable degree of autonomy. Total employment is more than fourteen thousand. The company is organized into a number of separate shops and, hence, job skills are quite similar in the different departments.

The company deals with a strong industrial union. The personnel program includes a pension plan, group insurance, and disability benefits. These benefits are standard throughout the parent company.

Performance Appraisal in the G Company

Until two years ago the company had utilized various rating scale and check list merit rating systems. These were judged to be highly unsatisfactory, largely because supervisory actions and decisions seemed to bear little discernible relation to rating submitted. During the period in which these systems were used, a "safety card" was maintained on each employee. The card was to be used to record incidents of violation of safety rules or examples of good safety practice. Supervisors began to use these cards to record incidents of all sorts which necessitated reprimand and, presumably, those which warranted commendation. These notes were found to be useful in justifying management decisions, with respect to work-force adjustment and wages, which were challenged by the union. The ratings, on the other hand, were found to be of little value in this regard. Part of this was due to the inconsistency of ratings. More important, however, was the fact that after the union dismissed the ratings as being simply "recorded bias" and the management representatives asserted that they represented a fair appraisal of the employees' performance, the argument reached a stalemate. The recorded incidents made a stronger case than the ratings.

Several years ago a group of researchers developed and installed a rating system using the critical-incident record technique. This was one of the early installations of this technique in a private company. The plan applies to 13,000 nonsupervisory employees, both in the office and in the factory. At present supervisor-employee discussions of the critical-incident records are scheduled every six months. The records are maintained from the first day the employee works. Three times during the ninety-day probationary period the records are examined by personnel officials.

The critical-incident technique was initially installed for the purposes of determining those eligible for promotion, providing a basis for merit increases (where rate ranges existed) and assuring that the supervisor regularly discussed the employee's performance with him. This last purpose is now regarded as the most important one, according to the personnel supervisors in the company. Although not listed as an official purpose, it is clear that the plan is also used to provide data for reinforcing management decisions in the event that they are challenged. Those in the personnel department also plan to use the records to validate an elaborate testing program currently used in selection.

At the present time the company is investigating the possibility of developing a similar appraisal technique for supervisory personnel. These personnel are currently rated on a device employing a rating scale and free-written answers to questions concerning promotion potentiality, training needs, etc.

An Evaluation of Performance Appraisal in the G Company

Evaluation of performance appraisal in this company is nearly equivalent to evaluation of the critical-incident technique, as such. All other procedures—termination ratings, probationary employee ratings, etc.—have been replaced by this single plan.

It is clear that this technique, to be properly done, requires a great deal of the supervisor's time. Since the problem of finding the time is left to the supervisor, the question arises as to how much time the supervisor actually gives to it. The personnel department sampled 1,100 records to find the number of incidents recorded on employees over a six-month period. Some departments averaged as low as one-half item (good or bad) per employee, while one averaged around seventeen. This difference can reflect a number of things. It is possible that it reflects accurately a difference in employee behavior as among these departments. It may reflect a difference in supervisor interest and effort. Personnel officials know that some supervisors are not too strongly convinced of the worth of the plan, while others are quite enthusiastic. According to one foreman, most supervisors, their day already full of making reports and handling problems of supervision, cannot do as good a job as they would like in keeping the record.

Some pressure is brought to bear on the individual supervisor to make him give sufficient time to maintenance of the record. Statistical summations of departmental differences, such as that previously cited, are sent to plant superintendents. Many of these superintendents, in turn, call their foremen together to discuss the results. It is alleged that these superintendents frequently, while visiting the different departments in their respective plants, ask for the record book and look it over. The employee is given a small handbook explaining the rating procedure. He is told that his foreman *will* record incidents of performance, and he is encouraged to ask to see the record when he wishes. Foremen can expect, when they make recommendations for promotion, discharge, or disciplinary action, that the plant superintendent or, in some cases, the personnel department will examine the record as a check on this recommendation. In addition to these pressures, some degree of positive motivation to make adequate use of the plan probably derives from the fact that the company foremen were utilized in building the plan.

Although the bulk of the foremen appear to be reasonably faithful in maintenance of the report, admittedly a number of them fail to review the record regularly with the employee, every six months as they are supposed to. This again is largely a matter of finding time. One department foreman who, with two assistants, supervises 170 men, finds it necessary to take over the direct supervision duties of his assistants for a day or two at a time to permit them to carry out this interviewing. He has found that, if the incident is discussed with the employee at the time it occurs and is recorded, considerable time is saved at the regular review session. Some foremen apparently make this "on-the-spot" discussion but do not consistently perform the six-months review. If neither is done, the stated prime purpose of this plan—to keep the employee informed as to the specific things he is doing poorly and doing well—is not achieved.

This plan has never been used for wage administration purposes. All except about one thousand of the production employees are on jobs carrying fixed rates. The remainder are on rate-range jobs. No serious attempt has been made to set up merit increases based upon the record, for the simple reason that in a large number of cases those employees currently at the top of the rate range do not have the best records.

The records are maintained on file in the offices of the plant superintendents. Discretion as to the use of these records in matters of discipline (usually layoff for poor performance or violation of rules), promotions, and discharges is thus largely left to these superintendents. The employment director indicates that these men are inclined to check all personnel decisions against the records. A recent instance occurred when it was necessary to promote someone to a foreman's position. An employee was recommended by a general foreman (who supervises several departments). The recommendation was rejected by the plant superintendent when he found that this employee's record contained no "good" incidents. This sort of control action conceivably could result in future manipulation of ratings by means of padding the record with "good" items. However, it may also motivate a foreman to spend more time getting relevant information on the record.

The union officially refuses to recognize this appraisal plan. This, of course, is the standard union position with respect to any management rating device. Personnel officials indicate that "unofficially" the union shows considerable respect for the record. This means that where the record shows that, on balance, there is substantial difference in the performance of two individuals, union officials are not inclined to "push" a grievance very far. Grievances inevitably involve decisions that violate length of service. In several cases the union has made the record part of its brief. In these cases it has been able to show that the senior man, who was not promoted, had a better record than the man promoted. These, of course, were cases of foreman error, and the company conceded. The union, in introducing this record as evidence, is, in effect, giving partial recognition to the worth of the plan.

The common tendency to rate the job as well as the man seems to be minimized by the critical-incident technique. Whereas in most traditional rating plans relying upon the use of words such as "average," etc., there is a strong tendency to rate those in high-skill jobs average or better and those in low-skill jobs lower than average. This tendency is less evident in the G Company plan. From the sample of 1,100 records previously mentioned, a summation was made, by departments and plants, of the percentages of employees who had received only blue (good) entries, only red (bad) entries, and no entries. Two of the nonproduction departments show wide divergence in the general level of skill content in jobs. The maintenance department has a preponderance of high skills; the production control department a preponderance of low skills. The sample showed that 55 percent of the maintenance employees received only blue entries, 9 percent red entries, and 27 percent no entries. In the production control department 63 percent received only blue entries, 3 percent red entries, and 21 percent no entries. A summary of entries for the whole company, classified by general skill levels, shows that there is a tendency to make more entries, both red and blue, on employees in high-skill jobs than on those in low-skill jobs. This may reflect a greater opportunity for variation in performance in high-skill jobs; or it may simply reflect a more conscientious reporting job by supervisors of these jobs; or simply that with fewer people to appraise, the supervisor gives each more attention.

Performance appraisal seems to be carried out with more enthusiasm and earnest effort in the G Company than in most other companies included in these cases. Possibly some of this stems from the novelty of participating in the development and installation of a new appraisal technique. To some extent objectives have been altered to conform with the nature of the rating device. The value of the incident record for substantiating management decisions accounts for much of its appeal to line supervision. This type of rating device provides many opportunities to make cross-checks on rating effectiveness. Few of these opportunities are currently being exploited although management personnel indicate that they are aware of their existence and that they plan to make use of them.

Managerial decisions with respect to work-force adjustment are subject to formal grievance procedure, as are decisions involving discipline. Work-force adjustment grievances stem from interpretation of a clause in the contract (negotiated by the parent corporation) which states: "In the advancement of employees to higher paid jobs when ability, merit, and capacity are equal, employees with the longest seniority will be given preference." Those who formerly performed a job satisfactorily and whose tenure on the job exceeds their subsequent layoff time make up a pool of men who must be returned, in order of seniority, to the jobs before others can be considered. Aside from this "pool" group, merit is always considered with respect to promotion. Of 4,838 promotions made in a recent two and one-half year period, approximately 10 percent were made from the seniority "pool."

Grievances in the area of discipline dropped during the first two years that the critical-incident technique was in operation. Over the same time period grievances relating to promotion decisions were reduced 60 percent. These figures undoubtedly reflect improvement in the management job of evaluation. As a result of the 4,838 promotions mentioned previously, 101 formal grievances have been written. Of this number, two decisions have been reversed and two are as yet not settled. Thus, about 2 percent of promotion decisions are formally protested. While no norms exist upon which to evaluate this figure, it seems unlikely that it could be appreciably reduced unless all decisions were based upon length of service. The employment director has no statistical data on the matter, but estimates that about 50 percent of promotions do not correspond with seniority order.

• THE H COMPANY—A LARGE RETAILING COMPANY

Description of the Company

The H Company operates department stores in a metropolitan area. Employment totals 12,000, of whom 2000 are sales personnel and 1000 are supervisors.

Personnel management is partially decentralized. Program development, recruiting and screening, transfer and promotion, and wage administration are centralized. Record maintenance, training, and routine administration are decentralized under division personnel managers.

Some personnel are unionized. Clerical and sales personnel are not, although some organizing activity has been directed toward them in recent years.

Performance Appraisal in the H Company

Appraisal was initiated on a company-wide basis in 1942. Some departments had been using rating plans prior to this time. The wage administrator states that personnel in those departments which had no formal plan were complaining that they were being overlooked in the competition for promotions and wage increases. Partially because of these complaints and partially to standardize the appraisal system, company-wide rating was instituted.

Rating, performed semiannually on all nonsupervisory personnel, is utilized basically as a guide to work-force adjustment and wage-administration decisions. The plan, known as the "employee performance review," is also made a vehicle of supervisor training. In the formal training program for supervisors the review is given the role of a major tool for the supervisor to use in building good relations with his subordinates and in guiding him to be an effective supervisor. The review form is offered to him as a check-list type work sheet to aid him in organizing his thinking with respect to what performance is expected of his subordinates, how they are measuring up to expectations, and what his task is with respect to motivating improved performance. The relationship of the performance review to such things as work simplification is spelled out. In this particular case the items of originality and initiative, adaptability and cooperation are deemed relevant.

The rating form has three parts: (1) an over-all rating, (2) ratings on quantity and quality of work, (3) ratings on traits. Ratings on (3) and (2) are expected to furnish a guide to the rating on (1). Alternative ratings are: (1) standard, (2) above (below) standard, (3) far above (below) standard. Great effort is made, in training and in the supervisor's rating manual, to establish the concept of "standard" as meaning the standard of performance expected on the job. "Standard" and "average" are carefully contrasted to aid the rater in avoiding the common tendency to confuse the two. Ratings are reviewed by higher line supervisors and the job and salary standards division. Supervisors are expected to rate only those traits which are required in the employee's job.

At one time rating sheets were scored mathematically by applying various patterns of trait weights in accordance with the corresponding weights applied to such traits as job requirements in the job evaluation plan. This scoring is no longer done, the over-all rating constituting the guide to action. The scoring procedure was abandoned after it was discovered that the final adjective rating derived from scoring differed from the over-all rating assigned by the supervisor in only three out of 20,000 ratings studied.

In making consistent application of the concept of performance appraisal as a tool of supervisory training, continuous study has been made of supervisors' action versus supervisors' ratings. Where discrepancies become apparent, this is brought to the attention of the supervisor's superior and, at the same time, additional training is planned for that particular supervisor. However, the supervisor is not called to account in specific terms for his inconsistencies.

Whenever possible, performance data are entered on the rating sheet. These data, on quantity and quality of work, include the average of the particular employee's performance and the average of the group's performance. Internal checks—performance data against ratings, and sections of the rating form against one another—are made.

An Evaluation of Performance Appraisal in the H Company

This appraisal plan shows every indication of being well thought out. In addition, it is positively used. Control procedures are maintained in the plan by virtue of continuous audit of ratings and personnel actions. The unusual notion of using the rating procedure as a training tool gives meaning to these control procedures and tends to assure that the procedures are being used.

The success of the plan clearly depends upon the continued application of the training program. Apparently, this has recently failed. The reason for failure is the decentralization of the training function. This decentralization occurred as a result of reducing staff (because of adverse business conditions) and involved placing training responsibilities on those whose duties already occupied their full time. The staff reduction also reduced the amount of auditing possible. The result is that control is being lost. Some supervisors are doing a slipshod rating job and even failing to rate at the required time.

Discussion of ratings with employees, at one time actively promoted, is no longer emphasized. It is believed that, inasmuch as adequate training of supervisors in the technique of such discussion is no longer possible, more harm than good is likely to result from such discussions.

The last audit data were gathered three years ago. These data had been gathered at the end of every rating period since the inception of the plan. Ratings were compared with wages, years on the job, recommendations for personnel action, and job grades. The wage-rating relationship was roughly in line, with the bulk of the out-of-line wages being too high in terms of ratings. Ratings and recommendations were generally consistent, the two most common out-of-line tendencies being to recommend retaining in the present job those far above standard and to recommend wage increases for those below standard. In one division ratings were compared with job grades. No tendency to "rate the job" was apparent.

Sales clerks, on whom performance records are maintained, are also rated. The records show little correlation between ratings and average earnings in those sections where sales personnel are paid on a commission basis. This is explained by the wage administrator as reflective of the company's policy of placing great emphasis upon exceptional sales clerk tact and courtesy as part of the "prestige product" they are marketing. Ability to sell and courtesy apparently are not too closely related. Cooperation with other sales personnel is also rated. Frequently, high-earning sales people are uncooperative. Perhaps the incentive program is tending to overemphasize certain kinds of behavior at the expense of other equally desirable kinds. This, of course, makes effective evaluation nearly impossible.

Personnel officials have come to the conclusion that in the absence of a continuing training program, such as formerly existed, a modification of the appraisal form will be necessary for use on sales personnel. This conclusion has been reached as a result of complaints from sales supervisors about the present form and as a result of the indifferent job of rating being done by some of these same supervisors. It is believed that the form should be redesigned so as to rate certain behavior characteristics important in selling, rather than the present trait characteristics. Merchandising personnel, it is argued, are temperamentally inclined to think more in terms of behavior than in terms of traits.

The conclusion has also been reached that a supervisor rating form very similar in nature to the one used on nonsupervisory personnel is not satisfactory. The wage administrator believes that better evaluation of supervisors will result not from an improved form but from careful use of performance record data relevant to the department which the supervisor heads. She bases her judgment on the belief that to a great extent it is impossible to establish definitive job requirements in behavioral terms against which to rate supervisors. She is cognizant of the difficulties involved in establishing an evaluation system based on performance data, but regards it as a necessary long-range objective—a belief which she says is shared by many of the management group.

A considerable amount of intelligent effort has been, and is continuing to be, devoted to problems of evaluation of employee performance in this company. At present, budgetary difficulties are weakening the effectiveness of the rating plan. But the personnel organization is endeavoring to offset this to some extent by the form revision discussed earlier. The wage administrator believes the economy measures to be unwise in this case. She indicates that all control procedures—auditing, analysis, training—can be performed (and were performed) by one person at an "intermediate" staff level. This appears to be a rather small cost for the effective operation of a good merit rating plan covering more than 11,000 persons.

It is interesting to note that in this

company, as in most others studied, incident records are kept. These are records made by the supervisor of cases of poor performance necessitating reprimand and special corrective action. Their chief use is as defensive evidence in case of union challenge of management action.

SUMMARY OF THE STUDY

Presented here are observations about common features in these cases, comments on prevalent weaknesses observed, and a brief list of suggestions for doing a more effective job of appraisal-suggestions stimulated by this study.

General Observations

1. Staff people generally recognize that various needs are to be served by a performance appraisal plan, at least when the plan is in the design stage. In practice, however, the rating plan is generally used for one or two purposes only, although these purposes may change over time.

2. Rating plans are rarely incorporated directly into wage and salary systems—formal ratings being something "to be considered." On the other hand, "counseling" or communication of appraisal information is perhaps the most commonly cited purpose of an appraisal system, even where no appraisal interviews are actually held.

3. A surprising number of companies keep some official record of behavior incidents involving employees at the nonmanagerial level. Even though these incidents usually are not translated directly into ratings, they are regarded as quite important, particularly when it is necessary to defend some unpopular action. One would expect on the basis of this evidence that the critical-incident rating technique would have a widespread intuitive appeal.

4. Management, in union as well as nonunion companies, relies primarily upon seniority in making decisions about wage rates, promotions, layoffs, and other personnel actions. The notion of rewarding merit is never forgotten, but it appears that one of the handiest measures of merit turns out to be seniority.

5. The performance appraisal plans which appear to be most effective are those which require the most time and money. In some cases (for example, where the forced-choice report is used), the great expenditure of time is in planning and developing the technique. In others, much effort goes into devising and enforcing controls. In the case where the critical-incident technique is used, the cost is high in planners' time, in raters' time, and in the time of those who maintain control over the system.

Common Shortcomings of Performance Appraisal

1. Failure to discover and use an effective control procedure. Appraisals are so often made, recorded, filed, and forgotten. Subsequently, decisions involving discrimination among individuals are made, apparently without reference to the periodic evaluations previously made. Not everyone agrees that a man should be held accountable for judgments he has expressed, but where he is not, he is apt to be careless in making the judgments. The best job seems to be done by that company which insists upon correspondence between word and deed.

2. Failure to establish clearly defined standards against which individuals are to be rated. Most people are acutely aware that they never know for sure what is expected of them in the work situation. Most men who have supervised others know that it is enormously difficult, if not impossible, to spell out completely the requirements of their subordinates' jobs. So it is not surprising that we find once again what so many have noted—that no matter how elaborate a formal plan may be, it is usually vague or silent about performance standards.

3. The attempt to get unnecessarily and impossibly fine discriminations in judgments about individuals. It appears that rating specialists are inclined to overestimate the ability of supervisors to make fine distinctions and to underestimate the cost of making such judgments "stick."

Suggestions for Improvement in Performance Appraisal

1. Develop appraisal standards directly from performance standards required on the job. Although it is rarely possible to state precisely all the behavior standards expected on the job, job analysis and position analysis are common enough in modern business that it should be possible to develop rather explicit and objective norms of this sort.

2. Rating should be made as much as possible in terms of observed behavior on the job. Most individuals will demand, "What did I do that has led to this judgment on your part?" This need to know is understandable. How else does one modify one's behavior rationally?

3. A control feature must be built into any appraisal plan, or else it is likely to become first a nuisance, and then abandoned. For nonmanagerial personnel, at least, the best control is seniority. The iron law of seniority should take away from the boss his discretion over promotions and pay increases, unless he has consistently built a case with his ratings. In other words, by shifting the burden of proof, it may be possible to make raters take the appraisal job seriously.

4. Rating alternatives should probably be limited to three. Assuming standards based upon job requirements, the ratings might be, say: (1) meets job requirements, (2) fails to meet job requirements, (3) exceeds job requirements. Were behavior elements introduced, the ratings would become more specific, e.g., "in terms of *X* (kind of behavior) meets requirements of the job." Ratings outside the central zone might require supporting incidents (the critical-incident technique), but the average rating would not. On the other hand, where the individual engages in average expected behavior, seniority might be allowed to govern. Such a simplified rating structure with a built-in control could make appraisal a serious matter and at the same time one which does not make excessive time demands.

These suggestions are perhaps most appropriate for rating of nonmanagerial personnel. A number of other readings in this volume, such as those by McGregor, Whisler, and Kellogg (Part One-B-3), and by Richards (Part Four-C), contain additional suggestions for appraisal of managers.

B. A Study of a Cooperative Rating Plan

THE JOINT EMPLOYEE RATING PLAN OF THE P. J. RITTER COMPANY AND LOCAL 56, MEAT AND CANNERY WORKERS UNION, AFL

JOHN J. PEARCE, JR., AND D. N. DERTOUZOS

So often appraisal of worker performance is a major source of controversy between union and management. Here is an unusual case—where the two parties succeeded, for a while at least, in cooperating on this task.

THE JOINT EMPLOYEE RATING PLAN OF THE P. J. RITTER COMPANY AND LOCAL 56, MEAT AND CANNERY WORKERS UNION, AFL

John J. Pearce, Jr., and D. N. Dertouzos

• INTRODUCTION

The evaluation of individual employees is an ever-present problem in industry. This problem is not merely one of measuring productive output; it also involves an understanding of the morale, potentialities and all-around performance of the worker. It becomes more crucial with the advent of unionization of the plant and the signing of a formal collective bargaining agreement because management's authority to evaluate employees may then be subject to challenge.

One of the chief aims of unions is to protect the rights of the employees. To realize its objectives, the union seeks security for itself and its membership through a contract with management. The worker receives job protection through a negotiated seniority clause and the application of seniority to layoff, recall, and transfer clauses of the contract.

Management is in business to make a profit. To realize its objectives, management seeks an efficient work force and flexibility in its operations and policies in order that costs may be reduced and profits increased. Management, therefore, wants merit and ability to be recognized in such matters as layoff, recall, transfers, and wage rate increases, in order to protect (as well as increase) efficiency of operation.

A satisfied work force and a profitable company are common interests for they fulfill the desires of both parties. Disagreements arise, however, when there is no yardstick by which employees may be evaluated. When is ability equal? Who deserves an in-range wage rate increase? These, among others, are the practical, every-day problems that unions and managements face.

Their common interest in the evaluation of employees is recognized by the Management of the P. J. Ritter Company and the leaders of Local 56, Meat and Cannery Workers Union, A.F.L. To meet the problem, they have established a Joint Employee Rating Plan.

There is evidence that the parties are making progress through their co-operative approach. It is important to note that the parties believe in the success of the Plan. According to William H. Ritter, Jr., President of the P. J. Ritter Company:

> Production is our business and worker grievances or other dissatisfactions interfere with production. It is not enough to be pleased that we have never had a work stoppage of any kind—we must strive to

Source: Institute of Management and Labor Relations, New Brunswick, N. J., Rutgers University, 1951. (Case Studies of Co-operation Between Labor and Management, no. 2.)

create a relationship conducive to high efficiency and quality. A basic foundation is the atmosphere of mutual trust and sincerity of motive that has been built up over the years.

A second need is to accentuate the positive—to search for areas of agreement and of mutual benefit—and to play them for all they are worth in developing ways and means for presettling the most frequently recurring types of disagreement. Our Joint Employee Rating Plan is a step in this direction, and while far from perfect, it seems to be the best system to date for merit, in-range and seniority upgradings. In effecting these "designs for living" with our employees and their Union, the phrase "Management Prerogatives" has never been used. Maybe we have surrendered some prerogatives, but if we did, I feel sure that the *quid pro quo* was worth it.

From the Union's viewpoint, Leon B. Schachter, President of Local 56, stated:

One of the most important factors contributing to the success of the Employee Rating Plan is an attitude of mutual respect for and confidence in each other's actions on the part of the top leadership of both the Management and the Union.

I should like to point out that this respect and confidence grew from the confidence which the rank and file members of the Union have in the Employee Rating Plan. They have realized that the rating is a joint process between their immediate foreman and their immediate steward, and that it is their foreman and steward who provide the yardstick to the Labor-Management Committee when they take up the question regarding upgrading of an individual worker.

Secondly, I should like to point out that the individual worker's knowledge of the Plan has stimulated his interest, not only in his improvement on the job but also in the Union which is handling his welfare on a day-to-day basis. Thus, I believe we have given an incentive to the unskilled labor group in the same way as an incentive exists for the semi-skilled who seeks to become skilled or for the Mechanic B who seeks to become Mechanic A. He knows that his own ability and willingness to improve his job performance will upgrade him and, as a result, increase his wages.

Finally, I believe that the whole Plan points out how much can be done through labor-management co-operation with a sincere approach to the improvement of work standards for the group and improved operations for the Company.

We have been able to engage in such co-operation only because we feel secure as organizations and recognize the right of each other to exist.

Upgrading has been systematically handled so that complaints over wage rate inequities have been minimized. Although records were not kept before the installation of the Plan, both parties agree that their approach has substantially reduced the number of complaints regarding in-range wage rate increases.

Furthermore, the parties feel that the ratings have given them guideposts in choosing their course of action when settling cases dealing with layoff, recall, and similar problems of contract interpretation.

Finally, the parties have never taken a case involving such matters to arbitration. They have established a method which helps them to resolve disagreements consistent with the terms of their contract.

This record has not been achieved easily. The parties have spent many hours in discussion and many compromises have been worked out. They have established a method of solving their problems but they have found no easy answers to the many difficulties which certainly will face them in the future. This fact must be borne in mind in any attempt to apply the findings of this study to other bargaining situations.

• BACKGROUND

No single aspect of the relationship between management and labor in a plant remains isolated from and unaffected by the other parts of this relationship and the state of the industry in general. In order to understand the Joint Employee Rating Plan at the P. J. Ritter Company, it is essential to know something about the framework in which it operates.

The Industry

The canning, preserving and freezing of fresh fruits and vegetables is carried on in an industry which is highly mechanized and subject to extreme seasonal fluctuations in production and employment. In general, the season begins in May, reaches its peak in September, and gradually tapers off so that by mid-November employment and production are both comparatively low. Within the various "seasons," (*e.g.*, asparagus, tomatoes), the weather plays an important part in determining how much food will be processed and how many workers shall be employed.

The industry has grown considerably since the turn of the century. In the 48-year period from 1899 to 1947, according to statistics in the *Census of Manufactures, 1947,* prepared by the Bureau of Census, U. S. Department of Commerce, the "canning, preserving and freezing" industry has expanded tremendously in terms of value added by manufacture. In 1899, the value added by manufacture for the industry was $33,667,000, as compared with $916,621,000 for 1947. In terms of the number of establishments in the industry, the figure was 2,570 in 1899, while in 1947, it was 3,826. Furthermore, the average number of production and related workers employed per year in 1899 was 57,012, while in 1947, the figure stood at 181,004. A rough indication of the growth and increased mechanization of the industry can be seen from the fact that it took only a little over three times as many workers, employed in approximately one and one-half times as many plants, to produce over 25 times the value added by manufacture in 1947, as compared with 1899.

Small establishments, in terms of the number of employees, are characteristic of the "canning and preserving, except fish" industry—under which classification in the canning, preserving and freezing industry the Ritter Company is placed. As reported in the *Census of Manufactures, 1947,* there were 2,265 establishments in this branch of the canning industry employing a total of 135,974 employees. A breakdown of these figures shows the following distribution:

NUMBER OF ESTABLISHMENTS	AVERAGE NUMBER OF EMPLOYEES
250	1–4
295	5–9
482	10–19
607	20–49
319	50–99
215	100–249
70	250–499
27	500–and over

Thus, 86% of the establishments had less than 100 employees in the year 1947. In contrast to this, however, on the basis of *Census of Manufactures, 1947,* data for this industry, the 1,953 establishments employing under 100 persons accounted for only a little over one-fourth (29%) of the value added by manufacture in 1947.

World War II brought about an increase in productive capacity in both large and small canneries. In addition, as a result of government demand, new canneries were opened. For example, in the "canning and preserving, except fish" industry in 1939, there were 1,899 establishments, as compared with 2,265 in 1947, an increase of 19%.

The increased competition in the postwar period resulting from this increased capacity, in addition to mounting inventories and consumer resistance, led to a general, but not severe, recession in the industry in 1946. By November of 1948, a price war had begun in catsup which lasted through 1949. As a result, some canneries went out of business or were taken over by the larger companies which weathered the storm. In 1951, the general business climate appeared to be favorable, as compared with the ups and downs experienced in the early postwar adjustment period.

Turning to New Jersey's position in the canning industry, according to the *Census of Manufactures, 1947,* the State had 42 establishments engaged in "canning and preserving, except fish," in 1947. The following figures show the distribution of these canneries according to size, based on the number of employees:

NUMBER OF ESTABLISHMENTS	AVERAGE NUMBER OF EMPLOYEES
19	1–19
18	20–99
5	100–and over

New Jersey, therefore, follows rather closely the national pattern in terms of size of establishments with 88% (37) of the companies employing under 100 persons as compared to the national figure of 86%.

The 42 New Jersey establishments accounted for $53,409,000 of the $609,939,000 total value added by manufacture by this industry in 1947, or approximately nine percent. This amount was surpassed only by California which had a total value added by manufacture of $161,191,000 or approximately 26% of the national total. These figures give some indication of the importance of New Jersey in providing the nation with its canned fruits and vegetables.

The southern portion of New Jersey contains most of the canneries in the State. Furthermore, the town of Bridgeton (population approximately 20,000) and the outlying districts is the center of this concentration. One of the main reasons for the concentration of canneries in this area of the State is nearness to the farms. Aside from canneries and summer resorts, the main occupation in southern New Jersey is farming and a good percentage of the acreage goes into tomatoes and asparagus.

New Jersey is usually considered to be the center of the industry in the east, Indiana and Illinois in the mid-west, and California in the west. In the South Atlantic States, situated around Maryland, there are many canneries and, in 1947, they contributed the fourth largest total value added by manufacture in the "canning and preserving, except fish" industry.

The Ritter Company's main competitors are located in Maryland, New York, Delaware and to some extent, Indiana. Although Ritter's wage rates are in line with those paid by the canners in southern New Jersey, nevertheless the Company must continue to process high quality foods to meet the competition from New York and the South Atlantic States where wages are lower.

The Company

Historical Development. In 1854, Phillip J. Ritter established the business in Philadelphia, Pennsylvania. The Company's first products were the foods originated by Mrs. Ritter. In due time the fine quality of Ritter foods became known and the Company grew. On July 8, 1882, the Company was incorporated in Pennsylvania as the Phillip J. Ritter Conserve Company. Some time later the name was changed to the P. J. Ritter Company.

Up until 1915, the Company had one plant in Philadelphia. In the years between 1915 and 1918, other plants were established at Newark, Delaware; Bristol, Pennsylvania; Owensboro, Kentucky; Ellendale, Delaware; and Bridgeton, New Jersey. These were the first branch plants, although Phillip Ritter conducted a business in California in the early 1890's to supply fruits for his preserves. It was in 1892 that he and Robert Hickmott packed the first asparagus to be canned in California.

Around the turn of the century and the early 1900's, the Ritter Company packed many separate items. By 1915, however, the Company had re-evaluated its whole operation and market opportunities and was packing only two items —catsup and pork and beans. It was in 1917 that William H. Ritter, Sr., who became the second President of the Company in 1915, located the Company's manufacturing operations at its present site in Bridgeton, New Jersey. By 1929, all of the Company's manufacturing operations were located in Bridgeton.

With the entry of the United States into World War I there was a marked increase in government demand for canned goods. During this period, mainly as a result of government orders, Ritter's sales volume quadrupled and remained at that level until 1920. In the early twenties prices fell and a recession set in. The Ritter Company was hit hard but it managed to weather the storm. In the middle and late twenties there was a gradual growth in volume and a few additional products were added to Ritter's line of goods. The Company was making its way back when its progress was retarded by the depression of 1930–1933. Again, the Company withstood the blow and from 1935 on there was a gradual growth in volume of sales.

In 1937, William H. Ritter, Jr., the present President of the Company, was chosen to lead the firm. During the late thirties, under the new President's leadership, the Company continued its growth in terms of volume of sales and number of employees. With the advent of World War II, this growth was greatly accelerated.

In the war period (1941–1945) the government purchased substantial percentages of the Company's seasonal production. During this period the Company installed dehydration equipment and all of the output from this type of production went to the government. By the end of 1945, as government purchases of Ritter products tapered off, the Company retained its increased volume (excepting dehydrated products), which has averaged about three times as much as it was in the late thirties.

In 1946, the postwar recession hit the

industry and a period of readjustment was upon the Ritter Company. Fortunately for the Company and most of the employees, there was no drastic curtailment of production. The Company continued a three-shift production schedule into the spring of 1947, long after other plants in southern New Jersey had shut down. Also, diversification proved successful during this period; the soft spots hit the various lines of canned goods at different times. For example, the asparagus market took a big drop in 1946, resulting in a large reduction in Ritter's 1947 asparagus pack; meanwhile, the pack in other lines remained relatively stable. Then, in early 1948, the pepper market situation resulted in a small pepper pack. This was followed by the loss of a substantial amount of volume in catsup as a result of the price war which started in November of 1948 and lasted through the spring and summer of 1949. The period from 1946 to 1950, therefore, was one of gradual adjustment rather than radical change for the Ritter Company.

In general, the war and postwar years have been marked by relatively high levels of employment for the regular employees at Ritter. The Company has adopted a policy of "steady jobs." While this was costly and required a large investment in plant, equipment and inventory, it has paid off in terms of reduced turnover, retention of experienced employees and assurance of larger and steadier incomes for the work force.

To accomplish this, the Company added new seasonal pack items, such as blueberries and pumpkin pie, thus filling in and lengthening its seasonal operation while shortening the nonseasonal periods. For the latter period, long range planning of production, packing for stock instead of following sales needs and spreading of the work, all helped to flatten out the seasonal curve of employment characteristic of this industry.

THE PRESENT. In its 95 years of operation, the ownership and management of the Company have continued to be under the close control of the Ritter family.

The Company is considered to be a fairly large establishment in relation to the other canners in the industry. In 1947, when Ritter's total employment force was approximately 500 wage and salaried personnel, only 1 per cent of the 2,265 canning establishments in the "canning and preserving, except fish" industry had more than 500 employees. During the peak season, in one week, there have been as many as 1,000 employees on the Company's payroll.

For many years the Company has processed high quality canned goods. Its most important products at present are tomato catsup, pork and beans, asparagus, and chili sauce relish. Other tomato products, such as tomato puree and tomato juice, are produced in quantity.

As late as 1940, the Company's main pack was tomatoes during the six to eight-week season in August and September. Other than this, the regular employees had work only when the plant opened sporadically during the remainder of the year to pack special items. At present, as a result of experience gained during the war and through the efforts of the Company to stabilize operations and offer greater employment opportunities to the regular work force, the Company packs many items on a schedule which gives about seven months of almost unbroken employment to most of the regular work force. In

Table 1

SCHEDULE OF OPERATIONS—P. J. RITTER COMPANY
Fiscal Year, 1950–1951[a]

SEASON	DURATION		NUMBER OF PRODUCTION AND RELATED WORKERS[b] REGULAR	SEASONAL	TOTAL
Asparagus	May	1950	298	179	477
	June	1950	337	339	676
Blueberries	July[c]	1950	259	82	341
Red Tomatoes	August	1950	279	140	419
	September	1950	323	489	812
Relish and Peppers	October	1950	321	245	566
	November	1950	206	41	247
General Nonseasonal	December	1950	186	3	189
Production[d]	January	1951	191	0	191
	February	1951	174	0	174
	March	1951	186	0	186
	April	1950	208	3	211

[a] Company's fiscal year ends March 31.
[b] Average number of production and related workers on payroll during month. The figures include warehouse employees.
[c] Many regular employees taking paid vacations while others employed in this operation.
[d] Plant operates intermittently from mid-December to May to pack special items.

the fiscal year 1950–1951, for example, the schedule of operations was as shown in Table 1.

In 1950, there were 320 workers on the seniority list covered by the Union contract with Local 56. These workers on the seniority list are considered as "regular" employees by the parties. In addition, 47 warehouse employees belonged to a local of the Teamsters Union. During 1950, 183 production and warehouse employees were on the payroll for at least 34 weeks. In the canning industry, this is considered to be a steady job.

The workers who make up the work force are all union members in good standing in accordance with the union shop provision of the contract. Seasonal workers hold temporary Union membership and only pay dues for the weeks in which they are employed. These seasonal workers are recruited from many diverse locations. Many of them are housewives from Bridgeton and surrounding communities. Others come from Philadelphia and nearby towns in Pennsylvania and Delaware. At times, during the tomato season, people from Florida, Tennessee, Arkansas and West Virginia are added to the work force, with the understanding that they will return to their permanent residence as soon as the season is over. The Company bears the expense of transporting them to and from Bridgeton and also provides housing facilities for women, at modest cost, on Company property. It also maintains facilities for housing men which are located about three miles from town and serviced by a Company bus.

As previously mentioned, the Management at Ritter is interested in providing steady employment for the regular work force in the plant. The Company's research department is continually experimenting with new lines of canned goods. In 1948, the Company purchased a firm which manufactured dog food. This has added an additional six to eight weeks of nonseasonal employment for the regular employees. Considering the fluctuating nature of the industry and the competition faced, the Ritter Company has made notable advances in providing steady jobs for a number of its employees.

Management Organization and Administration. The President directs the Company's activities with the advice and assistance of a Management Board and an Operations Committee. The former is headed by Paul J. Ritter, Executive Vice-President and General Manager, and consists of the Production and Engineering Vice-President, Purchasing and Custom Packing Director, Sales Manager and the Comptroller. This Board meets frequently, conducting the day-to-day activities of the Company and makes recommendations on policy matters to the Board of Directors. The Operations Committee, in addition to the above officials, is composed of the Company Secretary, Director of Employee Relations, Director of Agricultural Relations and the Assistant Treasurer. Excepting the President and Executive Vice-President, all top level management positions are filled by individuals who are not members of the Ritter family and who worked up through the ranks.

The Employee Relations Director, Earl L. McCormick, started with the Company as a factory label boy 22 years ago. The Production and Engineering Vice-President, Alfred H. Funke, Jr., began service with the Company 21 years ago as an electrician. That is the pattern. It is the expressed policy of the Company to promote from within as an incentive for its employees.

The administration of the Company's activities is well-balanced. The Operations Committee is composed of the executive member of each of the various departments embracing every phase of the Company business. Each of these executives has the authority and responsibility of developing the program for his phase of the Company's activities. The chairmanship of this Committee is rotated among its members.

Since the Management organization is comparatively small, as in most canneries, and the individuals have known each other for long periods of time, internal communications at the top level appear to have been good. During the busy season of the year the Operations Committee meets frequently to discuss matters of importance to the Company. During contract negotiations, which are held during the off-season, a subcommittee of the Operations Committee represents Management and is composed of the President, Executive Vice-President, Production Vice-President, and the Director of Employee Relations. Also present at most contract negotiations is the Production Superintendent.

This arrangement is conducive to orderly and prompt action on the part of Management during negotiations. During the 1950 negotiations with the Union, for example, the Management Committee made proposals and counter proposals that were binding and not subject to further approval. Although the Union did not always like the proposals, they knew what Management's position was on any given subject at each stage of the negotiations. Furthermore, the Management officials, during the usual "recesses," are in a position to iron out whatever differences of opinion they might have.

The Director of Employee Relations serves in an advisory capacity. He reports to the Executive Vice-President but, in addition, as is the case with the other top level executives, he also takes many matters directly to the President. Although it could lead to confusion, top Management believes that the flexibility of communications at the higher levels is a definite asset to the Ritter Company.

The prompt action of top Management has paid dividends in its relations with the Union. The leaders of Local 56 believe that, although the parties have their differences at Ritter, labor-management relations, in general, would be much better if all managements were as sincere and business-like as the Management of the Ritter Company.

The Union

Historical Development. The Meat and Cannery Workers Union, Local 56, was chartered by the Amalgamated Meat Cutters and Butcher Workmen of North America, AFL, on February 14, 1941. The Constitution of Local 56 states that it has jurisdiction over "all workers employed in the meat, food processing, farm, poultry, and fish industries . . ." The Union, however, has concentrated its organizing activities in the retail meat (meat cutters and butcher workmen of retail stores) and cannery fields.

Geographically, the Union's jurisdiction in the retail meat field covers the southern half of New Jersey. The original officers of Local 56 and the nucleus of its retail meat workers were recruited from Local 195, Amalgamated Meat Cutters and Butcher Workmen of North America, of Philadelphia. Although there were some small meat cutters' locals in southern New Jersey in 1940, a majority of the organized meat cutters were affiliated with the Philadelphia organization whose jurisdiction not only included the metropolitan area but also ran over into Camden and extended as far north as Trenton. In order to solve the administrative problems resulting from the extent of its geographic jurisdiction across state lines, the officers of Local 195 petitioned its International to charter a new local whose jurisdiction in the retail meat field would cover the southern half of New Jersey.

Prior to the organization of Local 56, the American Federation of Labor decided to begin an organizing campaign in the canning industry. With the exception of the West Coast, the Amalgamated Meat Cutters and Butcher Workmen of North America received jurisdiction over the industry. When Local 56 was chartered it received jurisdiction over the canning industry in New Jersey.

The membership of Local 56 grew rapidly. From a total membership of 400 (including seasonal workers) in 1941, it grew to approximately 10,000 (including seasonal workers) in 1950. In the retail meat field it has organized many small independent stores along with the large chain stores. In 1951, it had organized approximately 1,000 meat cutters and butcher workmen. In addition, it had organized approximately 4,000 regular cannery workers and approximately 4,000 seasonal employees. It had contracts with 142 employers throughout the state.

It would have been difficult for the leadership of Local 56 to build a large, stable organization if they had not found a solution to a problem which hindered organizing activities in the canning industry in southern New Jersey prior to

1940. This problem centered around the conflict in interests between those more regularly employed and those less regularly employed in establishments which operate during nonseasonal periods. As a result of past hiring practices under open shop conditions, the more regularly employed worker felt that those less regularly employed were a threat to his job. Although the unemployed are a constant threat to the job security of the employed, this threat is obviously greater in a seasonal industry.

The less regularly employed, on the other hand, were not assured of seasonal employment. Having secured employment for one season, they never knew if they would be rehired the following year.

In organizing canning establishments, the Union had to choose between organizing a small group of regularly employed workers during the off-season when the number to be organized for collective bargaining purposes was least, but when the employees were not, in the judgment of the Union, as likely to protest against management's policies; or, it could organize during the season when productive activity was high and labor was scarce, but when the Union had to obtain a larger number of employees for collective bargaining purposes.

The officers of the Union decided to organize the canning establishments during the off-season. They felt that if the Union was to survive it had to be built around a nucleus of skilled workers who were fairly regularly employed.

In order to attract the loyalty of the regularly employed worker, the Union appealed to his main interest—job security. For example, under the first contract with the P. J. Ritter Company, the regular employees (those on the seniority list) received preference over the seasonal worker in terms of wage rates and hours of work. In the 1950 agreement, the regular employees were guaranteed 45 hours of work per week before seasonal employees could be hired; and, in the event that work became slack, it was provided that there would be an equal division of work among all the regular employees in each department until the average work-week was reduced to 40 hours. After this layoffs were to be made according to seniority. The contract also provided that a qualified regular employee could not be replaced by a seasonal worker and that a regular employee could not receive a lower wage rate than a seasonal worker unless the seasonal worker was assigned to a specialized job.

The Union is also the bargaining agent for the seasonal worker and therefore controls the terms of his employment. Furthermore, the seasonal employee who has demonstrated skill and ability is frequently assured of being recalled year after year.

The Present. The leadership of Local 56 has been and continues to be concerned with another major problem—differential basic wage rates between seasonal and regular employees. In many of the canning establishments in southern New Jersey, the hourly wage rate of the regular employee exceeds that of the seasonal worker, the amount depending upon the classification—skilled or unskilled—of the seasonal worker. The problem is further complicated, from the Union's point of view, by the fact that regular and seasonal employees may be working side by side on the same job.

Management, in most instances, justifies this differential by noting that temporary workers are, on the whole, less skilled and experienced than are the regular workers. Furthermore, management contends that the seasonal employee, as a result of the nature of his employment, does not have as great an interest in his work as does the regular employee. The seasonal employee works during the season and is not usually employed during the winter.

Although the Union believes that the differences in ability and interest justify a wage-rate differential, it contends that the differential was too large. It feels that the jobs assigned to regular and seasonal labor do not require any great difference in degree of skill.

The leadership of Local 56 has not relaxed its efforts to narrow the wage-rate gap. Whenever the contract is renewed with the Ritter Company, for example, its officers always ask for an across-the-board wage-rate increase in an attempt to increase the wage rates of seasonal employees percentage-wise as compared to the regular workers. In most instances, however, it is forced to scale down its demands for the seasonal employee. The Union's bargaining committee, which usually consists of regular employees, naturally is most interested in the welfare of the regular employees. This Committee did not originally realize the seriousness of the threat to the Union's internal stability posed by the large wage-rate differential between regular and seasonal employees.

The Union leadership has attempted, through workers' education, to teach the regular membership to understand their role as Union members and the problems confronting the organization. They feel that, as a result, those elected to the bargaining committee now recognize the factors that tend to threaten their security. The wage-rate differential has been narrowed, and the leadership is convinced that the time devoted to educational purposes has paid dividends.

The Union has also attacked the problem of wage-rate differentials by increasing the size of the seniority list (regular Union members), thereby increasing the number of regular employees available for employment who, according to the contract, must be employed before seasonal workers are hired. Furthermore, the Union feels that it has received considerable aid from the Ritter Management through its attempts to provide steady jobs the year around. As a result of both of these factors, the seasonal work force of the Ritter Company has decreased relative to the number of regular employees.

Union Organization and Administration. Local 56, because of the success of its organizing activities in the retail meat and cannery fields, and the extent of its geographic jurisdiction, has become a large, complex organization. Its structure is in many respects similar to that of an international union.

The Union is divided into "districts" and "groups," each of which performs the functions usually associated with a local union. A district, for example, represents the organized meat cutters and butcher workmen of the retail shops within a geographic area, such as Atlantic City and environs. Groups, on the other hand, represent the organized employees of a cannery. The organized employees affiliated with Local 56 at the P. J. Ritter Company, for example, are known as the "Ritter Group."

Furthermore, each group and district is a bargaining unit within itself. The Ritter Group negotiates its own contract with the Company and elects its department stewards and Chief Steward, who handle the day-to-day relationships with the help of the Assistant Business Agent. Each group and district also holds monthly membership meetings which are devoted to discussing the special problems of that bargaining unit.

In general, the groups and districts are urged to run their own affairs. The top officials of Local 56, however, usually enter the local scene through the weekly inspection visits of at least one of its eight paid agents, to settle grievances that have gone to the last stages of the grievance procedure, and during contract negotiations. During contract negotiations, for example, the Ritter Group elects a bargaining committee, usually the stewards, and instructs it to make certain demands. The nature of the demands relating to wage rates and working conditions is, of course, greatly influenced by the opinions of the leadership of Local 56. The Group, however, reserves the right to ratify or reject the agreement.

Although the top officers of Local 56 act as spokesmen for the Ritter Group during negotiations, they must often rely upon the stewards for specific information. Thus, the stewards play an active and important role in the negotiations.

Another factor which makes the resemblance between Local 56 and an international union apparent is the fact that the Local holds a general membership meeting, or convention, every January. The agenda consist of Executive Board and committee reports in addition to discussions of the general problems of the Union. The officers and trustees are also nominated and elected by the membership of the entire Union for three-year terms.

The administration of the activities of Local 56 appears to be democratic. First, the districts and the groups, for the most part, conduct their own affairs under the leadership of the Business Agents and Chief Stewards. At the P. J. Ritter Company, for example, the Chief Steward has become the natural leader of the Group. Management has a good deal of respect for his opinions and for the suggestions of the other stewards for improving the relationship between the parties.

Furthermore, each group and district elects a Grievance Board consisting of five members for a one-year term. These Boards are empowered to hear and determine all charges against any member within the unit and may impose a penalty if the member is found guilty. The Union's Constitution also provides for an appeal procedure to the Executive Board of the Local and to the International, the Amalgamated Meat Cutters and Butcher Workmen of North America.

In addition, the Executive Board, which oversees the activities of Local 56, includes representatives of the various groups and districts and is therefore cognizant of any problems which might be unique to any one of these units. For example, the Executive Board consists of the elected officers and the Trustees of Local 56, along with the Executive Board members elected by the groups and districts. Each group, or cannery, of 100 to 500 members is entitled to one Group Executive Board member; each group of 500 or more members is entitled to two Group Executive Board members. Each district, on the other hand, is entitled to one District Executive Board member. These representatives are elected by their respective groups or districts for three-year terms.

Finally, Local 56 is autonomous in its relationships with the International. Although the International often recommends certain policies to its locals in regard to collective bargaining demands with national meat packing and canning firms, the locals retain the right to make their own independent demands.

Because of the size of Local 56, the elected officers, especially the President, Leon B. Schachter and the Vice-President, Elmer J. Hewitt, have many duties and responsibilities. They must take part in all of the contract negotiations of all the groups and districts in addition to negotiating all grievances which have reached the last stages of the grievance procedure.

A situation such as this could very easily delay the solution of grievances. The officers recognize this danger and have taken certain measures to combat it. There are now six full-time paid agents in addition to the President and the Vice-President operating out of staffed offices located in Trenton, Atlantic City, Hoboken, Camden and Bridgeton. These agents assist the President in handling the day-to-day affairs of the Union.

In addition, the stewards are urged to assume the responsibility of settling minor grievances before they grow into important disagreements. For example, at the Ritter Company the stewards are encouraged to take an active part in the meetings of the Labor-Management Committee. The Union also places great reliance upon the Chief Steward and the Business Agent in handling the day-to-day relationships with the Company.

As another example of their reliance on the leaders of the Ritter Group, the top officers of the Local have encouraged their participation in the Employee-Rating Plan, which is the subject of this study, for it was felt that this Plan would reduce the number of grievances resulting from requests for in-range wage rate increases.

General Union-Management Relationships

Although the Management and the Union continue to have their differences, there is evidence which indicates that the relationship is one which contains a healthy degree of mutual trust and co-operation. During negotiations Management has frequently indicated that it understands the problems of the Union. The Union, likewise, has indicated that it understands the Management's problems and has shown a willingness to co-operate in solving them.

This co-operative spirit is not confined to the bargaining table. The Labor-Management Committee, which will be described later, is another medium through which co-operative activity is expressed. All problems relating to wages, working conditions, recreation, and so on, are discussed and all possible means are employed to arrive at mutually satisfactory agreements.

The fact that Local 56 has agreed to establish a labor-management committee and an employee rating plan with the P. J. Ritter Company is indicative of the high opinion held by the officers of the Union for the Management's employee relations policies. The Union feels that the Management is sincere in its attempts to improve the relationship through constant consultation.

This co-operative approach also manifests itself in athletics and recreation. Ritter's Rod & Gun Club boasts a membership representing top management, the supervisory and foreman force, stewards and rank-and-file employees. The Club is building a hunting and fishing lodge for its membership with the members providing the labor and the funds. In addition, the parties co-sponsor bowling and baseball teams which represent the Company in the community's industrial leagues. An annual sports banquet is held at which time trophies are given for outstanding individual and team performances.

Furthermore, the parties jointly conduct the activities of their own "Community Fund," "Blood Bank" and "Christmas Club." There is no Community Chest in Bridgeton; consequently, the "Community Fund" administers the distribution of funds donated by the employees and the Company to all community agencies.

There are further indications that Management is not competing with the Union for the loyalty of the employees. For example, the employee handbook, *A Good Place to Work,* is frank and honest in attributing credit to the Union for some of the benefits provided by the Company. On the other hand, the Union feels that the Labor-Management Committee may be used, consciously or unsciously, as a means of channelling the workers' loyalty toward the Company rather than keeping an even balance.

In 1948 and 1949, when the canning industry was experiencing a recession, there were indications that the harmonious relationship, which had existed since 1941, was partially disrupted. The Management felt that the Union had changed its tactics and was making things more difficult for it to meet the Union's demands at negotiation time. The Union, on the other hand, felt that it could not forego wage increases necessary to the realization of what it considered to be a "living wage" for its members. It was during this period that the Union had taken strike-votes and was prepared, on two occasions, to go out on strike. Just prior to the 1950 negotiations, with the improvement in the economic conditions of the industry, the tensions eased and the parties were able to survive the temporary disruptions without serious repercussions.

In spite of these events, it appears that the relationship between the parties has passed through the stage of "organization" and is now in the "bargaining" or "co-operative" stage, depending upon the issue confronting them in their day-to-day relations. Both parties agree that difficult problems remain to be solved but that the relationship has been relatively constructive and harmonious during the ten-year period. They are hopeful that they will continue to be able to iron out their difficulties without resorting to economic warfare.

Bargaining Relations

The leaders of both the Management and the Union have sufficient authority to carry on a consistent policy in their bargaining relationships. As previously mentioned, the Employee Relations Director has direct communication with the Executive Vice-President and the President of the Company. The Vice-President of the Union reports directly to the President of the Union. In addition, the Employee Relations Director and both the Assistant Business Agent and the Chief Steward are held responsible for the day-to-day administration of the collective bargaining agreement.

TERMS OF AGREEMENT. The first agreement between the Company and the

Union was signed on May 21, 1941. There was no open conflict during the early stages of organization. When approached by the Union organizer, the Management agreed to negotiate if the Union could prove to its satifaction that it represented a majority of the employees. This required only a show of Union membership cards. The Union met the requirement and it was felt by Management that the Union was there to stay. No attempts were made to forestall formal collective bargaining relations and in the first contract the union shop was accepted by the Management. In an election held in 1948, to conform with the provisions of the Taft-Hartley Act, over 95% of the employees who voted favored continuation of the union shop.

During the entire period of formal bargaining relationships the parties have had an agreement not to resort to the strike or lock-out during the period of the agreement unless either party refused to arbitrate or did not comply with any decision of a board of arbitration as provided for in the contract.

According to the Union, the regular employees at Ritter enjoy comparatively good wages in relation to workers in the industry as a whole. In 1951, the basic wage-rate range of $0.96 to $1.10½ per hour for regular male labor and $0.89 to $1.01½ per hour for regular female labor was in line with those paid by other canners in the area under contract with Local 56. Since 1941, when the Union was first recognized and a contract was signed, average weekly earnings (including seasonal employees) have risen from $18.68 to $48.04 in 1950, an increase of 157%. Furthermore, average hourly earnings (including seasonal employees) have risen from $0.42 in 1941 to $1.07 in 1950, a 155% increase.

"Fringe" benefits at Ritter appear to be fairly liberal as compared with general practice in the industry. Employees covered by the contract get three paid holidays—New Year's Day, Thanksgiving Day, and Christmas Day; Memorial Day, Independence Day, and Labor Day are nonpaid holidays, but all employees receive time and one-half for all hours worked on these three days. Employees are also entitled to leave of absence for good cause.

On the matter of vacations, a worker must have been on the payroll for at least 34 weeks during the calendar year last preceding the vacation period to be eligible for vacation pay. In 1950, 183 production and warehouse employees were on the payroll for at least 34 weeks, thus making them eligible for a paid vacation in 1951.

There are other fringe benefits which the workers enjoy although they do not appear in the Union agreement. In the 1950 contract negotiations, the Union was not successful in having the group life insurance and group hospitalization plans incorporated in the agreement. They did, however, gain broader coverage under these plans and were successful in having them written up as supplemental agreements, not to be considered as part of the contract. This written supplemental agreement formalized a "gentleman's agreement" in existence for a number of years. The Union did gain an additional fringe benefit in the form of group medical-surgical insurance.

The Company was the first in the canning industry to provide free group life insurance for its employees. The group life insurance plan now in effect covers all factory employes who meet certain requirements and is paid for by the Company. The policy starts at $1,500 and increases $100 each year to a maximum of $2,000. To be covered in any given year, an employee must have been on the payroll 34 weeks of the last preceding year or his policy is dropped.

The hospitalization and medical-surgical plans are also fully underwritten by the Company with provision made for the employee to cover his dependents on a contributory basis if he so desires. Coverage under these plans is also governed by the "34 weeks" provision in the insurance plan.

In addition to these benefits, in the 1950 negotiations the Union asked that the existing informal pension plan, with improvements, be incorporated in the contract. The request was not granted by Management and the Union did not force the issue since their main goals were an increase in wages, broader coverage under the hospitalization plan, medical-surgical insurance and a written agreement concerning group life insurance. The pension plan does not cover all the regular production employees. It was started in 1947 on a noncontributory basis when a few retired production employees were given modest monthly incomes to supplement their social security benefits. In 1948, other hourly rated employees received similar payments. There is no fund set aside for these pensions; the Management determines who shall receive them on the basis of need. In early 1951, there were eight retired employees receiving pensions all of whom were formerly hourly rated production workers.

Other benefits such as cafeteria service at reduced prices, ten minute rest periods in the morning and afternoon, and small noninterest bearing loans for emergencies are provided for the employees.

In general, bargaining, especially on wage matters and fringe benefits, is influenced by area practice. The spread between the higher and lower wage rates in the area is not very great, Ritter's being near the top. There is no consistent leader in the area; the Union usually attempts to strike a good bargain with one canner and have the others follow. In 1948 and 1950, Ritter was the "leader" in the area.

Administration of Agreement. The 1950–1953 agreement between the parties, as with previous contracts, provides for arbitration of any and all disputes relating to the determination of rights and obligations conferred or created by the agreement which cannot be adjusted by the parties through the preceding steps of the grievance procedure.

The grievance procedure, as outlined in the Union contract, has six steps starting with the foreman and steward, and ending in arbitration. In actual practice every grievance does not go through all of the successive stages. In fact, most cases go straight to the Labor-Management Committee, which is technically the third step. Usually, however, in an effort to settle grievances at the lowest possible level, both the Management and the Union push cases back down when they feel that the stewards and foremen can solve the problem.

There have been isolated cases of seemingly unnecessary delay but the available records show, and the Union stated, that Management is prompt in taking action on most grievances. In some cases where a substantial amount of money or an important principle is involved, the delay may be longer. On the other side of the ledger, Company officials felt that, in general, the Union pressed only legitimate grievances.

In spite of the breadth of the arbitration clause, in the ten years of collective bargaining relationships, only one issue has been taken to arbitration. The issue was a wage reopening in 1949, as provided for in the 1948–1950 agreement. Since that time the parties have redoubled their efforts to avoid arbitration since neither of them was satisfied with the outcome. This record would seem to indicate that the parties have accepted the principles of collective bargaining and are sincere in their determination to solve their own problems on an equitable basis.

Another fact which supports this conclusion is that there have never been any work stoppages due to labor disputes during the ten-year relationship. Although the Union has taken a strike vote on two occasions, the parties were able to settle their differences themselves on one occasion, and they submitted the dispute to arbitration on the other. Thus the parties, to date, have not resorted to the test of economic strength in resolving their differences.

The Labor-Management Committee

Composition. In essence, the activities of the Labor-Management Committee are predicated upon the belief that a constructive relationship can best be promoted by periodic, open discussions of union-management problems and a quick and equitable solution of grievances.

The effect of this belief upon the function of the Committee has been to expand its activities into all areas of cooperative endeavor. Furthermore, this increase in the Committee's activities has been accompanied by an increase in its membership; the parties found that more personnel were required if the Committee was to fulfill its responsibilities effectively.

The Labor-Management Committee grew out of the weekly meetings of the Chief Steward, the Union Agent, and the Employee Relations Director. Prior to 1946, these three individuals met every week to discuss pressing problems and other matters affecting the relationship between the Management and the Union. Two problems arose, however, which made it necessary for the Union to urge all of its five stewards to attend the meetings. First, there was a tendency under the old procedure for the stewards to shirk their responsibilities by passing their problems on to the Chief Steward. The Union believed that the stewards would more effectively assume their duties if they attended the meetings. Furthermore, the Union felt that the Chief Steward could not be expected to know all of the problems of the various departments. Therefore, in 1946, the Union decided that all of the stewards should attend the meetings. This became particularly important after the installation of the Employee Rating Plan late in 1945.

More recently, the Management decided that the supervisory personnel did not take an active interest in the Committee with the result that some problems it could have solved went to the last steps of the grievance procedure. As a result, the Management urged its Maintenance Superintendent, Production Superintendent and Industrial Engineer to attend the meetings. Also present at all meetings is the Assistant Employee Relations Director. The Company officials feel that the new arrangement has increased the Committee's effectiveness.

Meetings. Meetings of the Labor-Management Committee are held every Friday, except for an occasional break during the peak season when the urgency of production may require a cancellation. The meetings are usually held in the Personnel Office.

The conduct of the meetings is very informal. The Committee has not chosen a chairman or secretary. The duties usually associated with these officers, however, have been assumed by the Employee Relations Director.

The meetings of the Committee are not closed. In fact, it welcomes participation in its discussions from top Management and Union officials. The meetings last for one or two hours, and the interest of those present is evidently maintained. All of the members apparently feel free to participate in the discussion and are frequently called upon to report any grievances or problems which they feel should be brought to the attention of the other members.

Matters for discussion are not limited to the Employee Rating Plan nor to the administration of the other joint activities of the parties. The Committee devotes most of its time to discussing grievances and methods of eliminating health and safety hazards. Frequently, the Committee also discusses means of improving the efficiency of operation.

It is to be noted that the Union representatives on the Committee are paid for all of the time spent in meetings, even when this involves the payment of overtime for hours spent beyond their regularly scheduled hours of work.

Communications. The meetings of the Labor-Management Committee also serve an important purpose other than that of providing an opportunity for the lower echelons of the Management and the Union to discuss problems of mutual interest. These meetings are used to circulate information whether it originates from the top or from the bottom of the organization. Top Management has not only solicited suggestions from the Committee but has also relied upon it to forward information to the employees. The Committee is also constantly informed of the progress of grievances which have gone to the last steps of the grievance procedure.

Top officials of the Company and the Union are also provided with copies of the notes taken at the meetings so that they are aware of current problems and suggestions. A copy of these notes is also routed to all supervisors. It should be noted, however, that because these notes are not a complete stenographic record of the discussions that take place, the Union does not consider them as formal minutes of the meetings. Much more time is taken in these discussions than is indicated by the record.

• HISTORY OF EMPLOYEE EVALUATION AT RITTER

Before Union Cooperation

The employees of the P. J. Ritter Company, in the case of most workers before unionization, did not have any formal job protection through seniority before 1941, when Local 56 signed its first contract with the Company. It was true at the Ritter Company, however, that some of the skilled workers (such as maintenance men, cooks, retort operators) were considered part of the regular work force and hence had some guarantee of fairly steady employment. Nevertheless, according to the stewards, the employees objected to what they considered to be the arbitrary nature of hiring and firing, promotions and transfers and granting in-range wage rate increases; such complaints were common in all industries before unionization.

After the organization of the employees at Ritter by Local 56, some method was needed to systematize the conduct of daily affairs between the Management and the Union. The first contract contained a grievance procedure but the stewards and foremen were not prepared for their new roles. Some interim procedure was needed to fill the gap in order to expedite the processing of grievances without undue delay. This was accomplished through periodic meetings of the Employee Relations Director, the Chief Steward and a paid Union Agent. By 1943, these meetings were held weekly, usually on Friday, and the written record begins on July 9, 1943.

One of the main problems facing the parties in administering their agreement centered around the wage rate clause. The first contract, as with all succeeding agreements, contained wage-rate ranges for all job classifications within the plant. There was nothing and still is nothing in the contract which states how in-range wage rate increases (upgrading) shall be made. The big question was: What determines when a worker is entitled to upgrading? The Employee Relations Director stated that many times the Union was justified in claiming that the foremen allowed personal reasons to affect their decisions.

A second problem, concerning the "layoff" clause in the contract, posed administrative problems. It stated in part (and remains the same): "If the number of regular employees is to be reduced, all shop stewards, committeemen, and working foremen and those who have been longest in the service of the Company by plant or departments, shall in such order be the last laid off, *providing that such practice shall not affect the efficiency of operation*" (italics ours). This clause immediately poses the question: What does efficiency of operation mean in terms of Worker A versus Worker B on the job? Is the worker who does a "normal" day's work the person for the job?

A third problem was the administration of that section of the "transfers" clause dealing with promotions. It reads: "Promotion to jobs coming within this agreement shall be based on ability and seniority; where ability is equal, seniority shall prevail." In the early days of the relationship, Management alone did not determine ability; this was a matter for bargaining. Again there were no yardsticks. This led to complaints about Management favoritism on the one hand and Union interference with the flexibility of operations on the other.

These are some of the problems which faced the parties in their day-to-day handling of the familiar problem of "merit versus seniority."

According to the Employee Relations Director, not long after the advent of the Union, the Management began to consider the installation of a unilateral merit-rating plan. The Company officials wanted some control over these problems and they were seeking a means to have the foremen and supervisors rely on some form of "objective" data when solving them with the Union. After considerable thought and investigation, the Management decided to discuss this problem with the officials of the Union.

Union Co-operation Starts

SEMIFORMAL CO-OPERATION. In 1943, the President and the Employee Relations Director of the Company, and the President and Vice-President of the Union met to discuss the problem and develop a merit-rating plan. The Company officials took the initiative for they were seeking some method whereby they could control the wage rate structure and minimize the number of grievances pertaining to it, in addition to getting some flexibility in the operation of the contract clauses governing layoffs and transfers. They felt that seniority was being followed so strictly that efficiency of operation was being seriously reduced. The Union agreed that something had to be done but they were concerned, at the beginning, only with minimizing the number of grievances resulting from individual recommendations for upgrading. The Union would rather have had a single wage rate structure; but since they had "inherited" the wage rate ranges, and because the Company wanted to retain them as an incentive to the employees, the Union agreed to help solve the problem.

The plan as it was set up did not materially change the procedure for awarding in-range wage rate increases, nor did it set up any guideposts for judging ability in applying the contract clauses dealing with layoff and transfers. The unwritten agreement set up the following procedure. In the case of upgrading, the steward who thought that an individual's request for an increase was legitimate was to take the matter up with the Chief Steward. The Chief Steward then was to bring the recommendation to the attention of the Employee Relations Director at their weekly meeting. If an agreement was not reached, the case entered the grievance procedure. If an agreement was reached, the recommendation for an increase was forwarded to the Plant Manager for final Management approval. The Employee Relations Director usually checked with the employee's foreman to see if the latter felt that the employee was entitled to the increase. The Plant Manager did the same. This did not bar the supervisory personnel from recommending increases but it did channel the employees' requests through the Union and the weekly Labor-Management Committee meeting. A general, over-all picture was thus available concerning the rate structure.

This procedure did not meet the needs of the parties in solving the wage problem. The record shows that in some cases it was seniority ("service") that was used to justify an in-range wage rate increase. In others it was "merit." On occasions, the "Company found the Union recommendations warranted." The parties again found themselves involved in the old arguments which they had tried to eliminate. What constituted a warranted or unwarranted request for an increase? What factors entitled a worker to an increase on merit? Since automatic progression within wage rate ranges was not employed, both parties were continually faced with these and similar questions.

With regard to layoffs, recall and promotions, the parties continued to follow seniority with few exceptions. Where seniority was jumped, the Management had to prove to the Union's satisfaction that such action was necessary so as not to impede the efficiency of operation of the plant. The plan had not alleviated this problem.

Neither the Management nor the Union was satisfied with this arrangement. According to the Union, the procedure did not have any effect on the number of grievances resulting from recommendations for upgrading. It was during this period that Management again seriously considered the installation of a plan which would merit-rate employees on the basis of some predetermined factors.

In the contract negotiations of 1945, the Union asked for four meetings a year at which time both parties would present a list of workers considered to be eligible for in-range wage rate increases.

Soon thereafter, the Management offered to put in writing the practice which was already being followed in granting such increases. This practice which Management offered to put in writing was described as follows: "Reclassifications (upgradings) shall be reviewed at the weekly meetings of the Personnel Manager and the Chief Steward and their joint recommendations shall be forwarded for approval. The basis for reclassification shall be *merit rating* (italics ours). Notification of approved reclassifications shall be made to employees by approval form adopted by Company and Union at negotiations of June 28, 1945. Copies of each reclassification notice shall be forwarded to Company and Union Headquarters."

No definite action was taken on this proposal and the parties still had not devised a method of rating the employees. The term *merit rating* meant, at that time, merely discussing an employee's work and employment record to see if he merited upgrading. The parties recognized the gap which needed to be filled.

The President of the Company gave full authority to the Employee Relations Director to devise a plan to meet this need. The latter studied the problem and after much thought he was convinced that the best plan would be one in which the Union participated.

FORMALIZED CO-OPERATION. During the summer of 1945, the Employee Relations Director drew up a proposed program and met with Union officials to set up a new employee evaluation system. Since there were no specific written job descriptions available and values were not assigned to the skill and other factors pertaining to each job, both parties agreed that the employee ratings should not pertain to job performance alone. Furthermore, and more important, one employee during the year might be employed in as many as three or four different job classifications. This, coupled with the fact that jobs were not described and the factors entering into the job were not valued, led the parties away from setting up a merit rating plan in the usual sense of the term.

The Union agreed to participate in the Plan on the following three conditions: (1) The factors listed on the draft rating sheet prepared by the Management should be revised since they were too technical. (2) The Plan was not to be incorporated in the contract or as a written "supplement" thereto. (3) The Plan was to be tried on an experimental basis. Either party could request that it be dropped at any time. The Company agreed to these conditions and the Plan, with the revisions made in the rating factors, was ready to be installed. It was named "The Employee Rating Plan."

On September 21, 1945, the Chief Steward and the Employee Relations Director held their regularly scheduled meeting. Under new business, the following entry was recorded:

> Mr. Hewitt, Business Agent of Local 56, will be present next week at the meeting of Union stewards at which time the new employee rating system will be explained.

There is no mention made of the foremen being informed of the details of the Plan. According to the Employee Relations Director, however, the foremen were told of the objectives and mechanics of the Plan and their part in it. The Plan was installed and the first ratings were posted for the month of October, 1945.

• THE EMPLOYEE EVALUATION PROGRAM AT PRESENT

Before turning to a detailed description of the Joint Employee Rating Plan, it would be well to describe briefly the evaluation procedure for seasonal employees and foremen, although this is not formally part of the Joint Employee Rating Plan.

Independent Employee Evaluation

SEASONAL EMPLOYEES. Joint rating of employees by the foremen and stewards applies only to the regular employees at Ritter, the term "regular" meaning those employees on the seniority list. Seasonal employees (temporary union workers who are not on the seniority list) are rated by the foremen for Management's use at the end of the season for which they were hired. In their case, the following example outlines the procedure under which they are evaluated. Worker A is hired for the tomato season. When this season ends and his employment terminated, his foreman gives him an A, B, or C rating. The foreman does not use the standard employee rating form. He bases his rating on such factors as absenteeism, attitude, production record and any other factors which he feels will give an indication of the employee's value to the Company. This rating is then posted on his employment record card. The rating determines *only* whether or not he will be rehired during the next tomato season or during some other season (*e.g.*, asparagus) on a job where his services can be utilized.

The rating is also used *at times* as one factor in determining whether or not the seasonal employee shall be classified as a "skilled" seasonal worker and receive five cents per hour more (under the 1950–1953 agreement) than an "unskilled" seasonal worker. This reclassification of the seasonal worker is done by the Labor-Management Committee, composed of Union and Management representatives, thirty days after the date of employment as provided for in the contract. The Union officials do not put much weight on the foreman's rating of seasonal employees since the stewards do not participate in the evaluation. The parties have come to call the process "merit rating"—the Management and Union decide whether or not the employee merits an increase.

FOREMEN. One sentence of the contract clause on "layoffs" reads as follows:

. . . Recognizing the fluctuation and seasonal character of the Company business operations with its resultant needs for seasonal and temporary foremen and for other specialized workers not normally eligible for Union membership, and in order to encourage Company upgrading (reclassification) of regular Union members from within, the Union agrees that temporary assignment of any employee in a supervisory capacity shall be considered as a period of unbroken employment and that upon the termination of such assignment said employee shall be reinstated to his former job without loss of seniority provided he has remained in good standing with the Union . . .

All foremen, whether or not they are temporary, are also rated every month. This rating is made by the superintendent on the "Supervisors Rating Report." This rating then becomes part of the employees' permanent employment record. It is used *at times* to determine whether or not an employee who has served as a temporary foreman shall do so again. However, the Union does not recognize these ratings as a factor in determining promotion, layoff, and so on, when the employee goes back in the ranks because it has not participated in evaluating him as a foreman. All the working foremen at Ritter belong to and are in good standing with Local 56.

The Joint Employee Rating Plan

Informal Nature of Program. Procedure-wise the Employee Rating Plan has been formalized but contractually it has not. In other words, the parties have not put the Plan in writing. It is not in the union contract nor has any constitution been written stating the purpose and objectives of the Plan. There are only two sources of written references to the program. One source is the record of the Labor-Management Committee meetings. The other appears as a paragraph in the Company's *Foreman's Manual* under section V titled, "The Employee Relations Department." The paragraph reads:

Employee Ratings are used as a basis for recording worker performance and may be used for promotion or complaint. Regular employees are rated each month and the foreman will be supplied with an individual form for rating each of his employees. Ratings should be jointly made by the foreman and shop steward who can freely discuss each worker as ratings are made. Where differences of opinion occur between the foreman or shop steward as to the rating of an individual a mid-point may be used. All rating forms must be signed by both supervisor and steward before they will be posted as a permanent record.

The fact that the purposes, organization and working rules of the Joint Employee Rating Plan have not been written up in detail has led to some problems concerning the application of employee rating. It has, however, had the advantage of keeping the Plan flexible.

Location of Authority. The final authority on promotion, upgrading, layoff and recall is in the hands of top Management. The stewards may recommend upgrading based on an employee's rating, and often do, but the Vice-President in charge of Production must give the final Company approval before it becomes effective. The Union, of course, reserves the right to challenge Management's decisions through the grievance procedure.

The Employee Rating Plan has tended, however, to make an important change in the way Management's authority is

TOTAL POINTS ________

Confidential—Return to Personnel Dept.

EMPLOYEE'S NAME ________________

No. ________ Month Rated Date ________________

DEPARTMENT ________________

PRESENT POSITION ________________

EMPLOYEE RATED BY ________________ (Supervisor) (Steward)

APPROVED BY ________________ (Superintendent)

P. J. RITTER COMPANY

EMPLOYEE RATING REPORT

To be filled out jointly by Supervisor and Shop Steward and Checked by Superintendent.

INSTRUCTIONS — READ CAREFULLY

Each employee's ability and fitness in his PRESENT occupation or for promotion may be appraised with a reasonable degree of accuracy and uniformity, through this rating report. The rating requires the appraisal of an employee in terms of his ACTUAL PERFORMANCE. It is essential, therefore, that snap judgment be replaced by careful analysis. Please follow these instructions carefully:

1. Use your own independent judgment.
2. Disregard your general impression of the employee and concentrate on one factor at a time.
3. Study carefully the definitions given for each factor and the specifications for each degree.
4. When rating an employee, call to mind instances that are typical of his work and way of acting. Do not be influenced by UNUSUAL CASES which are not typical.
5. Make your rating with the utmost care and thought; be sure that it represents a fair and square opinion. DO NOT ALLOW YOUR PERSONAL FEEL.NGS TO GOVERN YOUR RATING.
6. After you have rated the employee on all ten factors, write under the heading "General Comments," any additional information about the employee which you feel has not been covered by the rating report, but which is essential to a fair appraisal.
7. Read all five specifications for Factor No. 1. After you have determined which specification most nearly fits the employee, place a check (√) at the proper point. Continue until you have rated the employee on all ten factors.
8. Complete this report by the 15th day of each month and return it to your superintendent.

Place a check (√) at point along line which you consider nearest accurate rating.

1. Is Employee interested in his job? Does he want to "get ahead"? Does he like his work well enough to do it well? Is he "around when needed"?
   5 Interested — 4 Average — 3 Mild Interest — 2 Indifferent — 1 Lacks Interest

2. Has the Employee a satisfactory knowledge of his job? Does he know what he is doing? Why he is doing it? Does he plan his work? Handle his tools well?
   10 Thorough Knowledge — 8 Knows his job well — 6 Average — 4 Poor — 2 Unsatisfactory

3. Is the quality of his work satisfactory? Does he dot his "i's" and cross his "t's"? Is he conscientious? Does his work reflect interest in the Company? Is his work done *right*?
   10 Superior — 8 Excellent — 6 Satisfactory — 4 Poor — 2 Unsatisfactory

4. Does the Employee cooperate with his fellow workers for the welfare of all? Does he allow personalities to affect his work? Is he just with his subordinates, and honest with his supervisors? Does he carry out instructions thoroughly and cheerfully?
   10 Always — 8 Usually — 6 Average — 4 Seldom — 2 Unsatisfactory

5. Does the Employee show good judgment? Does he watch what he is doing? Think about it? Make good decisions under pressure? Does he say, "I never thought of that!"?
   10 Superior — 8 Excellent — 6 Average — 4 Poor — 2 Unsatisfactory

6. Is the Employee progressive? Is he alert to better ways of doing his job? Does he make suggestions? Is he a clock-watcher? Is he interested in his own and the Company's future?
   10 Superior — 8 Excellent — 6 Average — 4 Poor — 2 Unsatisfactory

7. Is the Employee reliable in his work? Can he be trusted with responsibility? To do a job without constant supervision? When he has finished a job do you have to have it done over again?
   10 Thoroughly Dependable — 8 Needs Little Supervision — 6 Requires Average Supervision — 4 Needs Close Supervision — 2 Unreliable

8. Does he show any personality weaknesses (temper, temperament, moral qualities) which might affect his efficiency? Get angry easily? Fight? Drink on the job? Resent direction and proper supervision? Go off half-cocked? Talk too much?
   10 None — 8 Slight — 6 Normal — 4 Considerably — 2 Definitely

9. Is the Employee's health satisfactory? Does he take days off for illness? Is he at work on time? Does he complain about any illness or injury?
   5 Excellent — 4 Normal — 3 Periodically — 2 Frequently Ill — 1 Chronic

10. Does the Employee give an honest day's work? Is he a "self-starter"? Does he exceed his cafeteria rest periods? Does he loiter or loaf? Does he *look* for work to do? Is he doing what he is supposed to do when he is supposed to do it?
   20 Always — 15 Usually — 10 Average — 5 Loafs Frequently — 0 No

If any serious defects have been noted on this record, or any listing is below average, have you brought the matter to the attention of the Employee? Explain what action has been taken.

Fig. 1. Employee rating form.

exercised concerning in-range wage rate increases. The supervisors and superintendents no longer have the authority to recommend in-range wage rate increases for employees within the bargaining unit without review by the Labor-Management Committee. In cases where increases have been recommended and not felt to be warranted by the Union an adjustment has been made.

RATING PROCEDURE. Briefly, the rating procedure in use may be summarized as follows. On the first working day of each month, the Employee Relations Office pulls all the time cards from the rack. Employee rating forms (see Figure 1) are then forwarded to the foremen who signed the cards. Upon receipt of the forms, each foreman rates every employee for whom he has a rating sheet. He signs the forms, adding any additional comments he cares to make about particular workers on the back of their forms, and then sends them to the departmental steward.

The steward then reviews the ratings of the employees in his department. If he feels that the workers in his department have been justly evaluated, he signs the forms. (He may also make additional comments on the reverse side of the sheet.) If there is any individual rating with which he disagrees, he discusses the matter with the foreman to try to reach a compromise. If they cannot agree, they meet with the superintendent and attempt to settle the matter. If no agreement is reached at this point, no rating is posted for the individual employee in question for that month. The superintendent must also sign all forms containing ratings agreed to by the steward and foreman before such ratings become official.

Department stewards are jointly rated by the Chief Steward and the Production Superintendent. The Chief Steward is jointly rated by his departmental foreman and the Production Superintendent.

The ratings which are agreed to are then sent to the personnel office before the 15th of the month where they are filed. These ratings become a part of the employee's permanent employment record along with other items such as grievance record, attendance record, and seniority. The employees are not informed of their ratings but may, at any time, see their own record. The only people with access to the ratings of all employees are the stewards, foremen and other official Management and Union personnel.

FUNCTION OF THE LABOR-MANAGEMENT COMMITTEE. The Labor-Management Committee plays an important function in the operation of the Employee Rating Plan. It performs an essential role in determining how employee ratings are used. It is also continually seeking solutions to those problems which hinder the effective operation of the Plan, one of the most important being securing the participation and interest of the foremen.

Securing Participation and Interest of Foremen. It is generally agreed that if the Employee Rating Plan is to facilitate the disposition of requests for in-range wage rate increases, the stewards and the foremen must have a personal interest and participation in the operation of the Plan. Since the crucial step in the rating procedure is the joint evaluation of the employee by his foreman and steward, it is at this stage of joint activity that the sincere interest and participation of the parties must be secured in so far as the Employee Rating Plan is concerned.

There are at least two important factors which may hamper the effective operation of the Plan at this primary step in the procedure—undue delay in rating the employees and inability of the parties to compromise when ratings are disputed. Both of these problems have frequently arisen and it was not until recently that attempts were made to find and eliminate the real causes.

From all indications, the stewards have a sincere interest in the Plan. First, the Plan minimizes the number of disputes arising from frequent requests for in-range wage rate increases. Furthermore, it affords some quantitative measure, though inadequate, of the work efficiency of each employee. It therefore enables the steward to arrive at a better judgment of the validity of requests for in-range wage rate increases. Consequently, the steward is better able to meet his responsibilities to the membership.

It appears, however, that some of the foremen do not have the same interest in the Plan as do the stewards. Frequent notations in the record of the Committee's meetings make reference to undue delay on the part of some of the foremen in rating employees. In addition, the stewards frequently complain that some of the foremen are not willing to compromise disputed ratings. (The Management, on the other hand, feels that the stewards are guilty, at times, of taking an uncompromising position on individual ratings.) Furthermore, the foremen have made frequent complaints that the Plan involves too much time and paper work.

According to the Employee Relations Director, this lack of interest on the part of some of the foremen is part of a larger problem that has not been recognized, until recently, by the Management. On the whole, they have not been given a real opportunity to assume those responsibilities usually associated with their position. For example, the record seems to indicate that most of the grievances go directly to the Labor-Management Committee thereby by-passing the first step in the grievance procedure which involves the foremen.

In addition, the foremen are not properly informed of the terms of the collective bargaining contract in spite of the fact that they receive printed copies of the agreement. The stewards, on the other hand, are usually members of the Union's bargaining committee and are therefore acquainted with the letter and spirit of the contract.

Furthermore, the foremen are not members of the Labor-Management Committee. While the Committee has assumed the responsibility of administering all of the joint activities of the Company and the Union, the foremen do not have this means of contributing to the relationship.

Finally, the stewards have been the beneficiaries of a valuable educational experience as a result of their participation on the Committee. The foremen, however, have not had the opportunity to receive this education. In addition, the Union leadership has recognized the value of workers' education and meets regularly with the stewards to discuss current problems. The Management, on the other hand, has only recently recognized the value of informing the foremen of its policies and of the more valuable contribution the foremen could make to the relationship if properly trained.

In January, 1951, the Employee Relations Director began a series of discussion meetings with the foremen as a means of solving the general problem of the lack of foreman participation. Also present at these meetings is the Vice-President in charge of Production and, on occasions, other members of top Management.

The foremen are divided into four nine-man discussion groups, each group meeting for an hour every other week. The Employee Relations Director plans to discuss with them such topics as the contract, plant safety and health, human relations, handling grievances, social security, employee rating, and so on, and thereby acquaint the foremen with Company policies and provide them with the opportunity to participate in the making of these policies. The stewards expressed the belief that these meetings would result in a closer foreman-steward relationship.

Determining the Use of Employee Ratings. When the Employee Rating Plan was instituted on an experimental basis by the Management and the Union, the intent of the parties was that it would be used to facilitate the disposition of requests for in-range wage rate increases on an equitable basis, thereby minimizing the number of disputes arising as a result of these requests. Since the officers of the Company and the Union have not formulated a written policy which can be employed by the Labor-Management Committee as a guidepost to determine how the employee ratings are to be used, the Committee is guided only by the broad policy of the parties' original intent. Consequently, the use of employee ratings is determined by precedent. General principles have evolved; the application of these principles is left to the circumstances of the particular case.

In general, employee ratings play a major role in determining whether or not individual in-range wage rate increases are granted. A better-than-average rating is a necessary, and in many instances a sufficient, condition for granting such increases. (It should be remembered that every employee has the right to appeal his rating and the decisions of the Labor-Management Committee to the Group's Grievance Board.)

The rules established by precedent governing the use of ratings in settling grievances, however, are nebulous. There are many factors *including employee ratings* which are taken into consideration by the Committee. The value given to the rating factor varies with the circumstances of the particular problem.

USE OF EMPLOYEE RATINGS. *Upgrading.* The monthly ratings are used primarily for upgrading within wage rate ranges. In the case of a recommendation for upgrading for one individual, the most recent rating is compared with the plant average for the same month; in addition, the *three* most recent ratings of the individual are compared to see what his progress has been.

The usual procedure in making group increases is to compare individual ratings against the plant average. The following case was taken from the record of the Labor-Management Committee for April 26, 1946, and it appears to be the procedure now utilized:

> The matter of upgrading the female Union members who have been working on Union minimum rates was discussed, and it was recommended (by the Union members on the Labor-Management Committee) that all Union women who were on active payroll as of March 13, when the contract was signed, and who are receiving minimum rates shall be reviewed individually and

such female employees as have individual ratings of 70 or more shall be recommended for an increase to the top of the range.

Two weeks later the record read:

A review of the number of female Union members who are receiving minimum rates was continued. The average employee rating for the factory is 74.6% and it was agreed that a person should at least reach the average before moving him to the top of the range. It was pointed out by the Company that more than 75% of the total female Union workers were now receiving the top hourly rate. The Union recommended that all female workers now receiving minimum pay and who had attained a rating equal to or above average should be moved to the top of the range . . .

The determination of *when* an employee or group of employees is to be upgraded is flexible. There are no periodic reviews of the ratings for the purpose of upgrading; rather the recommendations for upgrading are made when an individual's rating record shows improvement. It should be mentioned that in the higher skilled jobs (*e.g.*, maintenance men, cooks) it appears that the rating needed for upgrading is higher than in the lower job classifications.

Most important, however, is the fact that to date, in determining when (not how much) upgrading is recommended, employee rating is the controlling factor. Prior to the November, 1950, wage reopening, the first in-range wage rate increase in the less skilled job classifications, where the spread between the minimum and maximum of range was not very great, was usually to the maximum. (In the past, the employees and Union counted on increasing the ranges at the annual wage reopening for additional increases in hourly rates.) In the 1950 wage reopening, the spread between the minimum and maximum hourly rates, for most job classifications, was increased. As a result, there are usually two or three upgradings before the maximum of range is reached in all but a few job classifications.

Warning. The rating of an individual employee, to the extent that an accurate appraisal has been made, reflects his fitness (improvement, lack of improvement, slipping) on the job. With respect to warnings, the employee's rating serves two main purposes. First, it is used to increase the interest of the below-average employee in qualifying for better rates of pay by improving his efficiency. For example, at the request of the Union, "a list of those workers who are under average (in their rating) was given to the stewards who will confer with them regarding their individual ratings in an effort to increase plant efficiency and to encourage these employees to try to qualify for better jobs and pay rates." In such instances, the Plan is used as an incentive to better individual effort. References of this type appear frequently in the records of the Labor-Management Committee.

Second, since employee rating usually reflects violation of plant rules, it is used to induce the employees to abide by these rules. It is also used as one factor in giving the employee an official warning that, if disobeyed, may lead to discharge. The following case illustrates this point:

A complaint was registered against Worker A. Supervisor B reports irregular attendance, especially on pay days. Supervisor B also complained that Worker A reports on the job with strong alcoholic breath. He has received warnings from Supervisor B. Individual rating of Worker A is 51 (plant average is 76). The departmental steward is familiar with the case and will give Worker A a final warning.

Layoff. At the conclusion of seasonal operations, layoffs among the regular employees are usually made according to seniority. In some cases, especially in the more skilled jobs, employee rating is used as one factor in jumping seniority It is the usual procedure at the time of layoffs to notify the Union of those individuals to be laid off and the reasons for doing so. The following case illustrates the fact that the Union has been willing to agree to jump seniority when it is convinced that ratings and other factors warrant it:

Because of the conclusion of seasonal operations it is necessary to lay off nine mechanics. The Maintenance Department Supervisor submitted the following names for layoff on Saturday next:

Worker A–Millwright. Worker A has not measured up to expectation and his rating is considerably below the departmental average. It was pointed out by the Committee that this layoff meant jumping seniority but the departmental steward said he believed the layoff justified in the interest of departmental efficiency. Committee approved.

Worker B–Millwright. The Committee questions this layoff as it would mean retaining Worker C, a new employee, who held only a fractional rating advantage over Worker B. The Committee authorized Steward A to investigate with Maintenance Department Supervisor before this layoff was approved.

Worker D–Pipefitter. Worker D is the lowest pipefitter from standpoint of seniority and his rating, though satisfactory, is below other pipefitters in the department. Worker D will be called back should there be a need for a pipefitter in the future. Committee approved.

Worker E–Carpenter. From the standpoint of seniority and employee rating, Worker E's layoff is justified under the circumstances. Call-back will be issued when necessary. Committee approved.

Worker F–Carpenter. New man, employee rating only fair. Call-back will be discretionary with Maintenance Department Supervisor. Committee approved.

Worker G–Maintenance Laborer. Maintenance prefers to retain Worker H despite the fact that Worker G has greater seniority. Worker H is an exceptional worker with an employee rating of 97, Worker G is below average. Committee approved.

In the case of Worker B, the matter was disposed of the following week. The records of the Labor-Management Committee read:

Maintenance Superintendent was called before the Committee to present his reasons for wanting to jump seniority in the case of Worker B. Maintenance Superintendent said he had recommended a layoff for Worker B as he did not feel that this mechanic was doing his work as well as he should. Chief Steward and departmental steward said they had discussed the matter with Worker B, who claimed that the Maintenance Supervisor had never once complained to him about his work. He said in fact that the Maintenance Supervisor had told him that he was getting on all right in response to a direct question to the Supervisor asking him how he was doing. The Committee voted to retain Worker B as the employee ratings over the past year did not bear out the Supervisor's charges against him. Worker B has been employed by the Company for six years and there has never been a complaint about his work.

Thus, in the case of layoffs, employee rating has, at times, played a part in determining who shall be laid off. This, however, does not occur frequently.

Recall. On the matter of call-backs, employee ratings do not play an important part. In this case the Union also receives a list of workers to be recalled. The main tests used in this case are seniority and demonstrated ability to do the job. Thus, a person with less seniority may be recalled before others with greater seniority on a job if the others have never done the job before or have failed to demonstrate their ability during previous trials on the job.

The records of the Labor-Management Committee frequently record Union protests about re-hiring out of order of seniority. In a case involving asparagus packers, however, the Union recognized the need for giving additional weight to employee rating and skill in a situation where manual dexterity is important.

Promotions. Employee rating enters into the matter of promotion only indirectly. The parties do not consider employee rating to be an exact measurement of a worker's ability to do a particular job. The Management and Union still rely on other means to judge a particular worker's job ability as compared to others with equal or more seniority. Although the Union officials would rather follow strict seniority in all cases, they have subscribed to the policy of the best man for the job when there is a clear-cut case of differences in demonstrated ability between candidates for skilled jobs and little difference in their seniority.

Many promotions are only temporarily made for a particular "season." The following example indicates the type of problem faced in such a situation:

> The Union complained that Worker A had been assigned to the position of cook 2nd class, a job paying a special rate of ——— per hour. Worker B had been holding this job for the past three years without ever having had a complaint lodged against him. The employee rating of the two workers covering the past 4 months indicates a 70.2 rating for Worker B; an 82.7 rating for Worker A. Worker B was employed in May, 1945, and Worker A was employed in February, 1946. The Company said that Supervisor C had been contacted by the Director of Employee Relations and had stated that he had assigned the job to Worker A because he believed that Worker A was the better worker, and that it had been known that Worker B had a habit of being tardy for work. The Union said they questioned whether Worker B was habitually tardy for work. Under the circumstances the Union said that the retention of Worker B as cook 2nd class would not in any way affect the efficiency of operations and that they did not believe bumping Worker B from his job in favor of Worker A was justified. The Union said that they subscribed to the policy of the best man for the job but did not feel that the Company had fully established a justifiable reason in this case. The matter will be reviewed.

This problem was settled the following month as follows:

> The case of Workers A & B has been disposed of when it was agreed to move Worker B to the top of the finisher operator range. The Union agreed that at present Worker B *did not have qualifications* (italics ours) to be developed into a first class cook and for that reason Worker A was permitted to serve as cook 2nd class although having less seniority.

In this case, employee rating did not play an important part. However, a review of the ratings of the two workers gave some indication of their qualifications and was at least a *starting point* in the evaluation of the worker. There are few cases of this nature, but the parties are beginning to establish a framework within which they can arrive at mutually agreeable decisions.

• ANALYSIS AND CONCLUSIONS

Place of Joint Employee Rating Plan in Employee Evaluation

It is evident that the joint rating of employees by the foremen and stewards is only one part of employee evaluation at the Ritter Company. It applies only to the regular hourly rated production employees and it is the determining factor only in the matter of upgrading within established wage-rate ranges.

Neither the seasonal employees nor the foremen are rated under the Joint Employee Rating Plan. It was noted, however, that the Union does play a part in determining when seasonal employees are reclassified from unskilled to skilled seasonal laborers.

Employee Rating, moreover, is only one of the factors that is considered in solving problems of promotion, layoff, warning and recall. An employee's rating is given more weight when the difference in seniority between two workers is negligible. Even in such cases, however, other factors usually play a more important part in the final analysis.

The results of joint rating of the employees still do not play a decisive role in solving all of the problems concerning merit versus seniority. It has helped and will probably continue to help the parties reach mutually agreeable solutions in resolving some of these problems.

Advantages of the Plan

The Joint Employee Rating Plan has helped the parties solve some of their problems, although it is difficult to evaluate its success in quantitative terms. A few of the advantages of the cooperative activity deserve mention.

1. The program has provided for a systematic and periodic review of the regular production employees by the foremen and stewards. The parties no longer have to trust their memories when discussing how particular employees were applying themselves to their jobs in the past. Through joint rating of all regular production employees every month, the Company and the Union have established a fairly orderly method of evaluating the work force.
2. This systematic review provides the basis for a relatively consistent method of granting in-range wage rate increases. Employee rating has given the parties a guidepost to use in the determination of when in-range wage rate increases are to be granted. This has proved to be particularly useful in cases where group increases are requested.
3. The Plan provides an incentive to the employees to improve their knowledge of their job, their attendance record, their production record, and so on, in order that they may obtain better monthly ratings and qualify for better hourly rates of pay and promotions.
4. Finally, the Plan brings the stewards and foremen together to work on a problem which affords them the opportunity of constructive participation in arriving at some understanding of the morale, progress and abilities of the workers in their departments. This pro-

vides a valuable "training-ground" for the stewards and foremen to help them solve problems which might arise in the future.

Unsolved Problems

There are a number of problems which remain to be solved in the administration and application of the Employee Rating Plan. It is important to note, and it is a healthy sign, that these weaknesses are recognized and that the parties are working to correct them. Some of the more important of these problems are the following:

1. One of the most pressing problems is the lack of participation by the foremen in the Labor-Management Committee meetings. The foremen rate the employees but they do not have the opportunity of discussing with the stewards, superintendents and the Employee Relations Director, assembled in a group, the use of employee ratings and the administration of the Plan. In other words, they are not on the "inside" and, therefore, receive most of their information secondhand. To meet this problem, the Company has recently instituted weekly meetings for the foremen at which time the employee rating system and the other matters discussed at the Labor-Management Committee meetings are analyzed.

2. Closely related to this same problem is the fact that there have been unnecessary delays in the rating procedure. Some foremen have been as much as two months behind in rating the employees in their department, although this does not happen very frequently. This makes accurate rating difficult and tends to alienate the stewards. To meet this problem, the Employee Relations Office now makes a weekly check to determine which departments have not turned in ratings. It is hoped that this procedure, coupled with the weekly foremen meetings, will help solve this problem.

3. The personal element enters as a problem in administering the Plan. The stewards complain that some foremen are "uncompromising" in their ratings. The fact that the stewards play an important part in the collective bargaining machinery also tends to affect the objectivity of the ratings. Additional training in employee rating for foremen and stewards may provide a partial answer to this problem.

4. Another problem facing the parties is that some employees may be rated for one month on the basis of one day's work in a department. Thus far, no solution has been found to meet this difficulty. Fortunately, it does not happen very often, yet it may be unfair to some employees. Recently a disagreement developed on this matter and it was decided that no ratings would be posted for the month in question for the three employees involved.

5. In terms of the over-all program, the fact that no clear-cut decision has been made as to the application of employee rating has led to differences of opinion. It is evident that both parties agree that employee rating is the determining factor in granting in-range wage rate increases. But as far as promotion, warning, layoff and recall are concerned, there is still no clearly understood weight attached to employee rating. It is considered as *one* factor but the record indicates that in some individual cases it plays a more important part than in others. The Union, in most

instances, wants to follow strict seniority in layoff and recall. The same holds true for promotions but with less force. The Company, on the other hand, is desirous of more flexibility in administering these clauses of the contract. The parties have not yet resolved this problem although the Company has been considering changes in the Plan. Herein lies a potential area of disagreement for there are indications that the Union may not be willing to agree to radical changes in the program as it is presently set up.

Although the parties have made some progress, they still have not completely solved the problem of seniority versus merit in administering their contract. That they have made some progress through their Employee Rating Plan is evident. Those familiar with the process of collective bargaining will realize that they have gone further towards a solution of this problem than many other companies and unions.

Factors Contributing to Success

There are certain underlying factors which appear to have been especially important in contributing to the success of the Joint Employee Rating Plan at the P. J. Ritter Company. These factors in several cases are peculiar to the bargaining relationship at Ritter. It would, therefore, be unrealistic to expect that this particular Plan, in all its details, would work successfully in any other bargaining relationship. These factors may be summarized as follows:

1. The Employee Rating Plan was installed in a generally favorable environment of labor-management relations. The relationships between the Management and Union started without the bitterness that often accompanies the "organizational" stage of collective bargaining. Almost from the beginning, the parties were co-operating on the solution to some of the problems which they faced. It should be noted that the relationship has been improved, in turn, by the Employee Rating Plan. The fact that it has minimized the number of grievances resulting from requests for in-range wage rate increases and has given the parties a guidepost in solving problems dealing with promotion, warning, layoff, and recall has served to eliminate difficulties which otherwise might have disturbed the good relations of the parties. Consequently, the Plan is partly the cause, as well as the result, of the generally good relationships.

2. The general economic conditions during the period of collective bargaining relationships have been good. Except for the two-year postwar recession in the canning industry, demand for the Company's products has been sustained at a reasonably high level. Consequently, the parties have been better able to satisfy their basic objectives, an improving standard of living for the rank-and-file and profitable operations for the Company. Furthermore, this favorable economic background has enabled the Company to lessen the seasonal fluctuations characteristic of the industry through its "steady jobs" program. It is to the credit of the Management and the Union that, in spite of the difficulties encountered during the postwar recession in the industry, the area of disagreement was confined to the general wage issue and did not run over into the areas of co-operative endeavor.

3. Perhaps the most important factor is that both parties appear to enjoy a feeling of security as organizations. They

both recognize the right of the other to exist since each party realizes its dependence upon the other. The Management has not attempted to break the Union or compete with the Union for the undivided loyalty of the employees. Both parties seem to realize that the employees can be loyal to both organizations. The granting of the union shop in the first contract was concrete evidence to the Union that it would not have to fight for its existence. On the other hand, the Union's willingness to help Management solve many of its problems was very tangible evidence to Management that it was dealing with a responsible Union.

4. There appears to be no confusion as to the location of authority. It is generally understood that top Management is finally responsible for making decisions within the limits imposed by the collective bargaining agreement. The Union, of course, reserves the right to challenge Management's decisions through the grievance procedure. The fact that the Company officials consult with the Union before executing measures involving layoff, recall, warning, and promotion has probably meant that the chance of conflict over the location of authority has been greatly reduced. The Management, however, still runs the business.

5. The parties have not become involved in bitter arguments over the maintenance and respect for their "prerogatives." Although approval from top Management must be secured before recommendations for upgrading become final, the record reveals only one instance in which top Management did not approve a recommendation by the Labor-Management Committee. The Union, on the other hand, is willing to depart from strict seniority although there is no agreement that employee rating is the controlling factor.

6. Employee ratings have been applied, for the most part, to upgrading, one of the least controversial problems dealt with under the Plan. This has been partly the result of the realization on the part of both parties that the ratings determined through the established employee rating procedure are inadequate as a *final* measure of individual efficiency.

7. In general, recommendations for upgrading are acted upon promptly. A large majority of the requests are immediately approved when they come before the Committee. Final approval from top Management usually is forthcoming within one week. Also, problems concerned with layoff, recall, and so on, are handled promptly to avoid undue delay in these matters. In all cases when Committee opinion is divided as to the merits of a recommendation, disposition is delayed until the matter is investigated by the department supervisor and steward. In such cases, the problem is usually resolved within one or, at most, two weeks.

8. Participation in the Plan begins at the grass roots level. The foremen and stewards jointly rate the employees at the first and crucial step in the rating procedure. Thus, the employees are evaluated by those who are best acquainted with their capabilities. In addition, the stewards actively participate in the administration and application of the Employee Rating Plan through the Labor-Management Committee. This participation by the Union's shop leaders has contributed a good deal towards the maintenance of the Union's interest in and satisfaction with the Plan.

9. Finally, one of the most important

factors contributing to the success of the Employee Rating Plan is an attitude of mutual respect for and confidence in each other's actions on the part of the top leadership of both parties. Although the top officials of the Company and Union have had disagreements, they have been resolved partly because of the ability of each to look at specific problems not only in the light of their own objectives and beliefs, but also from the point of view of the other party. Furthermore, this attitude is not confined to the leaders of the Management and the Union. It has permeated the lower levels of supervision and union leadership to the extent that co-operation on employee rating is possible.

C. Case Reports on the Evaluation of Managerial Personnel

APPRAISING THE PERFORMANCE OF MANAGEMENT PERSONNEL: A CASE STUDY

M. S. KELLOGG

MANAGEMENT INVENTORY AND DEVELOPMENT: A CASE STUDY

VIRGIL K. ROWLAND

AN APPRAISAL PLAN FOR USE IN MANAGEMENT SELECTION

WELLINGTON POWELL

A NEW CONCEPT OF PERFORMANCE APPRAISAL

KENNETH E. RICHARDS

Interest in formal appraisal of managers has been strong in recent years. Consequently, we have included three cases of appraisal of managerial performance and one of the evaluation of nonmanagers for prospective advancement to managerial status.

These concluding case studies give us a look at appraisal through the eyes of managers who have developed plans, tried them out, and reflected intelligently upon their experiences.

FURTHER READING

Collins, R. S., and A. Winn, "Making Merit Rating More Objective: A Case Study," *Personnel,* September 1951, Vol. 28, no. 2, pp. 154–161.

Finn, Robert H., "Is Your Appraisal Program Really Necessary?" *Personnel,* Vol. 37, no. 1, January–February 1960, pp. 16–25.

Plantation Pipe Line's formal appraisal program, how they made a thorough and impartial study of it, and what they found out.

Ohmann, O. A., *Executive Appraisal and Counseling.* Ann Arbor, Bureau of Industrial Relations, University of Michigan, January 1956 (address on industrial relations), p. 17.

Randle, C. Wilson, and Willis H. Monroe, "Better Ways to Measure Executive Performance," *Management Methods,* Vol. 19, no. 4, January 1961, pp. 64–76.

Enell, John W., and George H. Haas, *Setting Standards for Executive Performance.* New York, American Management Association, 1960. (A.M.A. Research Study no. 42.)

APPRAISING THE PERFORMANCE OF MANAGEMENT PERSONNEL

A Case Study*

M. S. Kellogg

For the past four years, Russian schools have outstripped our own production of engineering graduates by 10,500 a year. This rather sobering statistic points to two conclusions. The first is that we must stimulate an increasing number of competent young men to choose engineering as a profession; and the second is that we must make the best use of the engineers we have.

This latter task is both a placement and a personnel development problem. We must use current skills to full advantage and at the same time try to develop greater technical competence and managerial ability. The development of engineering manpower is particularly important in an organization that has to meet the dual challenge of competition and expansion. This is why the Aircraft Gas Turbine Development Department of the General Electric Company has placed considerable emphasis on personnel development. One of the key features of our personnel development program is the periodic appraisal of the performance of our management personnel.

Few problems that confront industry are as challenging and rewarding as the difficult task of evaluating performance. Whether a company relies upon the "huddle and muddle" technique or measures performance through a formal program, it is constantly evaluating a man's abilities in relation to his present job and future growth possibilities. This is a day-to-day activity whether it is recognized as such or not. Thousands of man-hours are spent by industry annually in an effort to make formal rating techniques as sensitive and as precise as possible. Despite these continued efforts, subjective considerations are often major influencing factors in assessing individual performance. While it is not suggested that personal judgment should be eliminated in appraising men, the reliability and validity of personnel evaluation can undoubtedly be increased by sharper individual judgment and the encouragement of more critical thinking.

Most progressive businesses have some type of personnel evaluation program. Often the program is adopted after an intensive study of the organization's needs and their relationship to its immediate environment. This is as it should be, for the time and effort spent in formulating a made-to-measure program are a wise investment. This article describes our experience in evolving a made-to-measure program for appraising the performance of management (predominantly engineering) personnel.

* From *Personnel,* Vol. 31, no. 5, March 1955, pp. 442–445. Copyright 1955 by the American Management Association. Reprinted by permission.

• THE EARLIER SYSTEM

To understand the progress we have made, an outline of the system we used before January, 1954, may be helpful.

Our old personnel evaluation system was based on two different trait-rating forms. The first, used for all professional and supervisory personnel, listed 11 traits or personal characteristics, such as analytical ability, industry, judgment, initiative, leadership, and so forth. In evaluating the employee on each count, the rater could choose one of six ratings ranging from outstanding to unacceptable. The rating form was also designed to give information on the employee's value in his present work and his capacity for future growth. Raters were encouraged to discuss the rating with employees, but there were rather frequent instances when this was not done.

The second trait-rating form was used primarily for salary administration. This form listed six of the same traits as appeared on the first form and provided similar choices which were used to establish a numerical index of performance. Since the information was confidential, the engineer usually did not know what his numerical index was.

We decided to change the dual trait-rating system described above because we found it unsatisfactory in the following respects:

1. The two ratings did not have to be made simultaneously and seldom were. There was often a lack of agreement between the rating a supervisor made on a "confidential" basis and the one he discussed with the employee. This frequently made it difficult to explain to an employee why he did not get a raise after he had been told that his performance was good.

2. Supervisors found it difficult to differentiate between such terms as "initiative" and "leadership." It was also difficult to get common understanding of specific traits.

3. Since ratings were not always discussed, many employees never knew where they stood.

4. The difficulty of the job was not a major determining factor in fixing compensation. Consequently, two engineers carrying out similar duties at the same level of performance were sometimes paid different salaries because of the emphasis placed on technical experience.

5. To be effective, any personnel development program must possess a reasonably objective measure of an employee's on-the-job performance and a realistic estimate of his growth potential. Our merit-rating plan was not sufficiently critical in these areas.

We believed that our trait-rating plan could be improved upon in all these respects. However, before considering the merits of alternative measurement techniques we began by clearly defining our objectives.

• OBJECTIVES OF THE NEW PLAN

Our objectives were determined by our two-fold aim of fostering our employees' personal development and providing a guide to their equitable compensation. Accordingly, we decided that our plan should incorporate the following basic features:

1. *Require supervisors to consider, at regular intervals, the relative strengths*

and weaknesses of each subordinate and to measure the effectiveness of his performance in relation to his assigned responsibilities.

This objective is fundamental to the adoption of a formal periodic performance appraisal plan. While evaluation of performance is a continuous activity, which is independent of a formal program, there are many advantages to formalizing supervisory judgments and making them a matter of record. Both the administration of merit increases and personnel development activities are without factual foundation if no evaluation program exists. Before effective coaching or counseling can be done, it is necessary to define the areas of strength and weakness and to select those which can be modified by the ratee. This presupposes the critical evaluation of personnel through the medium of a formal appraisal program. In common with industry as a whole, therefore, our decision was not whether to appraise but, rather, how to appraise most effectively.

2. *Provide the opportunity for periodic discussion of performance, (a) to let the employee know where he stood, and (b) to improve on-the-job performance.*

This aimed at overcoming one of the basic deficiencies of our old rating system—the fact that it did not assure that every employee knew where he stood. We felt that, to be truly effective, a personnel measurement plan must provide for discussion of performance between the supervisor and the employee. Most of the personnel development benefits to be gained from an effective appraisal program are dependent upon frank and full discussion between supervisor and employee. In this way, the employee learns what is expected of him, how far he measures up to the requirements of his job, and what he must do in order to advance. This provides a basis for self-appraisal and spurs him on to improved performance and self-development. It also makes for better and closer working relationships because of the opportunity to air misunderstandings and misgivings, as well as the coaching and counseling to improve on-the-job performance which generally result from such discussions.

3. *Serve as a guide to supervisors in observing and evaluating employee performance for the purpose of salary adjustment, and place responsibility for merit increases closer to the immediate supervisor.*

There is a significant change of emphasis here. In view of our experience with the earlier trait-rating form, we wanted to relate performance and merit increases more closely; but we also wanted to place more responsibility for recommending merit increases in the hands of the immediate supervisor. Hence, we departed from a system that aimed at measuring general ability and potential to one that placed more emphasis on how well a specific job is performed.

4. *Provide supervisors with information that would be helpful in the promotion, transfer, or discharge of personnel, and that would serve as a measure of an employee's performance over a period of time.*

To be of real value, an appraisal system must provide accurate data, not only as a help in making decisions involving promotions, transfers, or discharges, but also to throw light upon organizational weaknesses and deficiencies. While the trait-rating form provided some valuable information, and has therefore become a useful part of the record of employees with longer service, we felt that it could be improved upon in a number of respects.

5. *Encourage the rater and ratee to consider together and formulate plans helpful to individual improvement.*

This was adopted to stimulate individual development. Our personnel development program is founded on the basic premise that development is primarily the responsibility of the individual. Our efforts are therefore directed toward: (a) helping the individual do his present job better, and (b) giving him the opportunity to acquire new skills that will fit him for positions of greater technical and managerial responsibility.

To achieve these aims, the employee must not only be willing to help himself, but must also recognize that some improvement is necessary. This is why we felt it important that the employee should evaluate his own performance and set his own objectives. Since every supervisor is responsible for the development of his men, we felt that he should share in this task.

6. *Assist supervisors and employee relations personnel to identify personal development and training needs.*

This objective reflects the importance of slanting personnel development and training programs to individual needs. We recognize that learning by doing is more important and more effective than learning by study and formal education; but we do not minimize the importance of courses to increase technical knowledge and managerial ability. Consequently, we sought to incorporate into our plan an accurate means of identifying the employee's individual needs for training and development.

After considerable study, we finally decided that the "responsibility appraisal method" would best meet the objectives of our new personnel measurement plan. In putting this method into effect, we had the assistance of a consultant.

• THE EXISTING ORGANIZATION AND "CLIMATE"

To appreciate the magnitude of the problems that confronted us, it is necessary to know something of the organization of the Aircraft Gas Turbine Division of the General Electric Company. This division is composed of five departments, one of which—the Aircraft Gas Turbine Development Department—assumed responsibility for the preliminary work before the performance appraisal plan was established on a divisional basis. Of the 2,400 management personnel of the Aircraft Gas Turbine Division, roughly 400 were employees of the Aircraft Gas Turbine Development Department. However, while the following account of the plan's initiation applies more specifically to the Aircraft Gas Turbine Development Department, the same general procedure was followed in the rest of the division.

In passing, it should be emphasized that a fundamental requirement for the success of a performance appraisal plan is an organizational climate in which management is both able and willing to provide good performance information and to make wise use of it. (This is also one of the best measures of a plan's effectiveness.) The top management of the Aircraft Gas Turbine Division was fully aware of the need for an appraisal plan that would measure performance more accurately, because the company's proposed new salary plan depended upon a systematic method of appraisal to provide a basis for establishing merit increases.

A pilot study was launched to test the rating plan and procedures, and the experience gained from it helped us to make further refinements in the plan.

• INITIATION OF THE PLAN

Following the pilot study, the appraisal plan was initiated on a divisional basis. Our first step was to inaugurate a series of two-hour training and orientation sessions for raters, explaining the philosophy underlying the performance appraisal plan. In the training sessions, appraisal techniques were thoroughly discussed, and attractively illustrated booklets entitled "How to Appraise the Performance of Management Personnel" were distributed. At the close of the sessions, rating forms were handed out for completion and target dates were set for their return.

The forms were returned to designated Employee Relations personnel in each department, who acted as a central control to enable the General Managers to guard against rater errors. It was thus easy to identify raters who were either too lenient or too critical, or who were disposed to rate centrally. Chats with these raters proved beneficial in stimulating critical evaluations. The accompanying graph shows how the Aircraft Gas Turbine Development Department fared in the distribution of ratings.

The letters in the graph refer to the

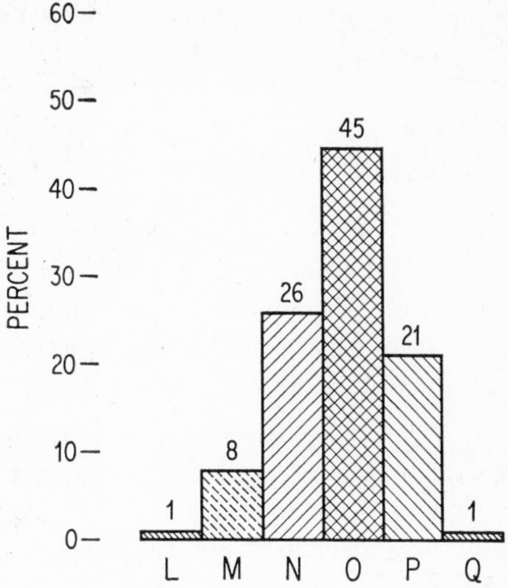

rating scale which is part of the overall evaluation summary on the performance appraisal form. These are defined as follows:

L – Fails to meet requirements.
M – Meets minimum requirements.
N – With a few exceptions meets normal requirements.
O – Without exception meets normal requirements.
P – Exceeds normal requirements.
Q – Far exceeds normal requirements.

On the initial "go-around" of the new plan, discussions of performance were deferred until the appraisals were approved and a short training course could be conducted. Two-hour training sessions for raters were held, pointing out the most effective way to conduct performance discussions. As a further aid to raters a discussion check list was distributed as well as copies of a booklet giving hints on how to improve discussions of performance with management personnel.

The discussion of performance and the preparation of a long-range individual improvement plan concluded the appraisal cycle.

• FEATURES OF THE PLAN

Before enumerating the conclusions we reached from our first year's experience with the performance appraisal plan, it is appropriate to consider the answers to the following basic questions:

1. *Who is appraised?* The new appraisal plan is used for all management personnel. This includes engineers, supervisors, specialists, and administrative staff.

2. *When is the appraisal made?* When the new performance appraisal plan was installed, all appraisals were scheduled for the same time period and it was initially planned to schedule subsequent annual appraisals in the same way. Special appraisals were provided for, should the growth and pace of the individual warrant them. In the event of a transfer before the close of the normal appraisal period, provision was also made for an appraisal before the employee took up his new duties.

3. *What is appraised?* Demonstrated performance of the items listed in the "responsibility summary."

4. *What is the responsibility summary?* The responsibility summary consists of the ten to fifteen responsibilities which are most important for fulfilling the job. By way of illustration, three of the Performance Appraisal Administrator's responsibility summary statements follow:

The performance of the Performance Appraisal Administrator is measured by:

(a) The quality of the performance appraisal plan, forms, and booklets as measured by the degree of uniformity of interpretation by raters, usefulness of appraisal information obtained and acceptance of recommended changes in the plan by supervision, as appraised by supervisory judgment.

(b) The degree to which established schedules for appraising performance are maintained as appraised by supervisory judgment.

(c) The quality of instruction provided in appraisal and discussion courses as measured by the extent to which such training is reflected in the quality of class members' appraisals and discussions before and after the course and the reaction of individuals trained as appraised by supervisory judgment.

Each specific responsibility is numerically weighted to reflect the relative importance the immediate supervisor attaches to it. The numerical weights distributed throughout the responsibility statements total 100. The summary provides the basis for evaluating each person's accomplishments in relation to the most important features of his position and insures a distinctive appraisal sheet for each position, but not necessarily for each person rated.

5. *Who prepares the responsibility summary?* The responsibility summary is jointly prepared at three levels: by the person to be appraised, his supervisor, and the latter's immediate superior. It is developed for the most part by the person to be appraised. For this purpose he is provided with a copy of his job description and a Responsibility Summary Preparation Check List (Figure 1).

The immediate supervisor looks over the responsibility summary with the employee, weighs the statements and approves or alters it as appropriate; in turn, his superior reviews and exercises final approval of its content and weighing.

RESPONSIBILITY SUMMARY PREPARATION
CHECK LIST
(for the person to be rated)

__________Read your position analysis.

__________List the 10–15 most important responsibilities of your position based on your position analysis. These may be specific items under any Factor in the position analysis or a combination of two or more items that make up a major responsibility.

__________Begin each with an action verb.

__________Avoid overlap.

__________Place more important items nearer the top of the list.

__________Submit to your supervisor no later than__________
____

__________(Suggestion) Mentally rate yourself.

Fig. 1. Responsibility summary preparation check list.

(The reverse of this form, the Responsibility Summary Work Sheet, consists of a blank sheet, ruled off for completion in accordance with the instructions shown above.)

6. *Who makes the appraisal?* The immediate supervisor is the primary rater but he may ask one or more supplementary raters to help him. The appraisal form used by the primary rater is shown in Figure 2. The supplementary rating form is similar to the one used by the primary rater except that it has a different title and color. The primary rater has final responsibility for preparing the performance appraisal, subject to the review and approval of his superior. Therefore, he has the option of accepting, modifying, or rejecting the comments of the supplementary raters. The latter are selected from management personnel, at approximately the same level as the primary rater, who have knowledge of the ratee's performance.

7. *How is the appraisal made?* The appraisal is made by evaluating employee performance against the specific statements of the responsibility summary. Raters are encouraged to request employees to submit evidence of accomplishments at periodic intervals. This gives a factual basis for the rater and assures the employee that his achievements are fully considered. The rater considers the ratee's performance and records the objective basis or critical incidents that support his choice of one out of six alternative points on a performance scale ranging from "fails to

Code	Name of Person Rated
	Position
Date person assumed present position	Department, Section & Building

MANAGEMENT PERFORMANCE APPRAISAL
AIRCRAFT GAS TURBINE DIVISION
GENERAL ELECTRIC CO.

Typed name and signature of Supervisor	Date Appraisal Completed
Reviewer	Date Reviewed
Signature of Primary Rater (Indicates discussion of results has been completed)	Date Discussed

PURPOSE

To provide an appraisal of the over-all effectiveness of this individual as a member of management, since the last rating, based on his supervisor's and two supplementary raters' analyses of his *performance of assigned responsibilities.*

RATING CATEGORIES

These refer to effectiveness in executing responsibilities.

Fails to meet the minimum requirements of the position.
Meets minimum requirements of the position
Meets normal expectations in fulfilling position requirements. *with few exceptions*
without exceptions
Exceeds normal expectations in fulfilling position requirements
Far exceeds normal expectations in fulfilling position quirements

Fig. 2. The responsibility summary *(page 1).*

(Page 2 of this form consists of a blank sheet ruled off for completion by the raters.)

	Not observed	Fails to meet requirements	Meets minimum requirements	With few exceptions – meets normal requirements	Without exceptions – meets normal requirements	Exceeds normal requirements	Far exceeds normal requirements	Weight of each item expressed in points (Total = 100)	REMARKS WHICH SUPPORT EACH APPRAISAL
1									
2									
3									
4									
5									
6									
7									
8									
9									
10									
11									
12									
13									
14									
15									
									OVER-ALL SUMMARY APPRAISAL

COMMENTS WHICH SUPPORT OVER-ALL SUMMARY APPRAISAL

Fig. 2. The responsibility summary *(page 3).*

Describe the strengths which the employee has demonstrated in performing his present assignment. (Add strengths which are not brought out on previous pages.)

____

____

____

____

Describe any needed improvement indicated by the performance of the employee. (Add needs not brought out on previous pages.)

____

____

____

____

What is required to achieve this improvement?

____

____

____

____

What has the long range performance record of this individual been? For example: remarkable progress upward, ups and downs, poorer recent performance, relatively little change. Do you expect the trend to continue?

____

____

____

Indicate specific recommendations for development action.

Action	*By Whom*	*When*

Fig. 2. The responsibility summary *(page 4)*.

meet requirements" to "far exceeds normal requirements." The appraisal form shows the points on the scale and how the evidence supporting the appraisal is recorded. It will be noted that provision is made for an over-all evaluation. Though this is often an average of the individual ratings on specific responsibilities, it need not be. For instance, a man might be rated as "fails to meet requirements" on one or two responsibilities because priority for other projects or factors beyond his control prevented him from doing his best in these particular instances. The over-all evaluation is not mathematically determined and therefore need not necessarily be lowered because of such ratings.

8. *What is the personal improvement plan?* The personal improvement plan is one of the most valuable products of the performance appraisal discussion. This enables the supervisor and the subordinate to discuss the latter's relative strengths and weaknesses and determine a course of action to help him fulfill the requirements of his job and prepare him for greater responsibilities. On the form used for this purpose, the rater can comment on the ratee's reaction to the discussion. The discussion itself is particularly fruitful if the employee is encouraged to appraise his own performance before the supervisor makes his appraisal and the personal improvement plan has been jointly formulated. A copy of the personal improvement plan, but without the rater's comments on the ratee's reaction, is given to the subordinate.

The personal improvement plan can perhaps be better understood through specific examples. Two typical plans for young engineers, showing the raters' comments on the discussions, are reproduced here.

Major Strengths

1. Excellent technical ability shown on titanium project.
2. High degree of initiative, enthusiasm and aggressiveness.
3. Ability to grasp a technical problem and work out details.
4. Demonstrated ability to improve and develop equipment, as dictated by the needs of the over-all titanium program.

Major Improvement Needed

1. Distinguish between important and less important, particularly in written expression.
2. Broader knowledge of the melting and casting practices employed in ferrous and high temperature alloys.

Action to Be Taken

1. Effective Presentation of Ideas and Technical Writing courses.
2. Brief special work assignment to increase technical knowledge.

By Whom:	*When:*
Ratee	Fall—1954
Rater	Within 6 months

Discussion revealed that:

Ratee's trouble with reporting was not with organization or expression but rather with selecting that which was pertinent to report in a given situation. Ratee indicated his opportunities for reporting have been restricted largely to a different type of report. Since he had not had the chance to prepare specific detailed technical reports, he tended to overburden his summary reports with detail. He was encouraged to prepare a few detailed reports on the results of his melting studies in the near future while working to eliminate this detail from the summary report. He was pleased with the prospects of a temporary duty assignment to learn more of melting and casting practices since he recognized his weakness in this area.

* * *

Major Strengths

1. Has warm and friendly personality.
2. Has ability to evaluate critically technical problems and pursue a logical course of action.
3. Is very forceful and highly motivated.
4. Has keen sense of responsibility.

Major Improvement Needed

1. More theoretical familiarity with technical aspects of gas turbines.
2. Must become better acquainted with state of the art and development work in progress both internal and external to AGT.

Action to Be Taken

1. Take Gas Turbine Fundamentals course.
2. Investigate other positions within Department containing increased technical content for subsequent reassignment.
3. Participate actively in engineering societies and collaborate with senior engineer on a paper if possible. Read religiously progress reports and proceedings of the design boards.

By Whom:	*When:*
Ratee	September, 1954
Employee Relations	About October, 1954
Ratee	Continuing

Discussion revealed that:

He felt that I had not been critical enough; I agreed I had been lenient because of his newness in AGT. He stated that he thought he was capable of doing quite a bit more than he has accomplished to date and was going to strive to do so.

He was very pleased that I had listed warm and friendly personality as one of his strong points since he had been working on this factor as a result of previous criticism.

As will be seen, the personal improvement plan is a valuable means of ascertaining what is needed for self-development. Following analysis of these plans on a departmental basis, we have established a course in the basic elements of flight dynamics, as well as courses in technical writing and air design. To stimulate active participation in technical societies, we have held a "Technical Societies Week" and regularly provide information on forthcoming meetings. Many other aspects of our personnel development program have likewise been stimulated by the information obtained from personal improvement plans.

• CONCLUSIONS

Our past year's experience has led us to conclude that certain modifications in the performance appraisal plan are desirable. A research study which evaluated such factors as acceptance of the plan, the use and quality of the data obtained, and procedural aspects proved helpful in singling out certain merits and defects. The conclusions we have reached are summarized below:

1. The performance appraisal plan provides supervisors with an orderly and systematic method of recording their considered judgment of the effectiveness with which an employee performs the duties that have been assigned to him.

2. The information obtained provides a useful tool for personnel development and a guide for the equitable administration of merit increases.

3. The plan does not provide sufficient information about the employee's potential for future advancement. While considerable information can be derived by

inference, it would appear that the questions about promotability on the back page of the appraisal form should be revised to elicit specific data on this score.

4. Our experience suggests that a system of staggered yearly appraisals is better than department-wide appraisals held annually over a short period. We are therefore adopting an individually scheduled appraisal plan to apportion the workload on supervision throughout the year and meet the objections of some supervisors who felt that rating all employees simultaneously created too much of a burden. Further, this system emphasizes that appraisal is a continuous and individual process, not an annual mass affair; it also points up the fundamental thesis that performance "pays off." The plan also provides for a salary review at the same time, thus enabling the supervisor to include the question of compensation in the performance discussion.

5. It was found that the rating scale on our appraisal form caused some confusion to supervisors, owing to the fact that there was no established median rating among the alternative choices on the rating scale. While each supervisor has a concept of "average," this concept is not necessarily the same for all supervisors. For instance, some supervisors thought that "With few exceptions—meets normal requirements" was an average rating whereas others took the view that this was expressed by "Without exception—meets normal requirements." Accordingly, we are considering changing the latter rating to "Meets normal requirements" and the former to "Exceeds minimum, below normal," and propose to establish "Meets normal requirements" as average.

6. The value of the personal improvement plan may be improved by emphasizing to supervisors the importance of their role in helping to formulate realistic and worthwhile objectives. To promote this end we intend to offer a course in "How to Discuss Performance Appraisals with Management Personnel" which will make use of role-playing and lectures to increase skill and knowledge in this area.

7. A real hazard to the integrity of the performance appraisal plan comes from the fact that the over-all evaluation is used as a guide to compensation. Because supervisors may let this factor influence their rating judgment, there is a danger that some appraisals may not be truly critical. It is necessary, therefore, to continually impress supervisors with the vital importance of making critical appraisals. Consequently, the Performance Appraisal Administrator has an important function to perform in reviewing appraisals and discussing them with supervisors.

• REACTIONS OF PERSONNEL

An attitude survey conducted in May, 1954, showed that 91 per cent of management personnel in the Aircraft Gas Turbine Development Department liked the periodic performance appraisal and the accompanying discussions. Random interview samples since that date show that this same feeling still prevails. We are particularly encouraged by the frequently expressed sentiment that the new performance appraisal plan provides a fair and just means of evaluating performance and assuring equitable rewards. We feel the same way.

While we are satisfied with our progress to date and the results achieved by the performance appraisal plan, the comments summarized above reflect our view that considerable improvement can still be made both in the quality of appraisals and in the measurement technique. Though the responsibility summary provides a good point of departure it can undoubtedly be improved upon by establishing more objective standards of performance and better indices of success. We intend to work toward this end.

MANAGEMENT INVENTORY AND DEVELOPMENT

A Case Study*

Virgil K. Rowland

This case account is concerned with the program of Management Inventory and Development in effect in the Accounting Departments of The Detroit Edison Company. Due to the nature of the subject, statistics are purposely omitted. It is clear, however, that the program has produced many tangible and intangible results; it has been well accepted and has proved useful to all levels of management.

The procedure is only one of the several available methods for arriving at a Management Inventory and Development plan, but it has been an effective one for us. Further, it should be borne in mind that the outlines of the program, as presented here, represent only the skeleton, upon which may be placed such additional techniques as position specification, promotion tables and other related tools of management.

As a means of describing the field of coverage of the program, I should like to point out the types of positions covered by the term, "management personnel." For purposes of discussion, management personnel are all persons on the management team, from first-line supervisors (those directly in charge of a group of employees) through all higher levels of supervision, up to and including corporate officers.

It is possible for a company, or a section of a company, to have a physical inventory of its management personnel which will pinpoint such factors as present capacity, potential strength, and development needs in the organization. Some of the important objectives of such a program are: improved executive and supervisory performance; increased reserve strength; better communications—both vertical and horizontal; greater operating efficiency; and higher morale.

The entire program is composed of four parts: Appraisal, Review, Discussion and Development. Each part is of equal importance in the complete program which we call Management Inventory and Development.

In order to have an inventory, it is necessary to make an appraisal of each member of the management group. This applies to all levels of the management team.

• THE APPRAISAL

The purpose of the appraisal is to determine the present work competence of the individual through group discussion and agreement by those who have the facts, and to design a plan for developing him.

The appraisal, which is actually a "summary appraisal," is usually made by at least four persons, all from a higher management level than the person being appraised. This number may be varied because of differences in organizational structures. The appraisal is made by their sitting down together and talking

* From *Personnel,* Vol. 28, no. 1, July 1951, pp. 12–22.

SUMMARY APPRAISAL

MANAGEMENT INVENTORY AND DEVELOPMENT
GE FORM AG 19 1-50

DATE February 1, 1950

NAME Alfred B. Cantrell POSITION Methods Coordinator

DEPARTMENT Collection Department LOCATION Service Building

AGE 45 COMPANY SERVICE 20 years YEARS ON PRESENT JOB 6

This Summary Appraisal is a narrative description developed from a detailed analysis of the employe's work.

PERFORMANCE

RESULTS (What has this individual accomplished in measurable results since his last appraisal? Consider quantity, quality, cost and time element of work. Be specific. Give facts and figures wherever possible.)

Mr. Cantrell originates new ideas and works them out to logical conclusions. Does the same on specific assignments given him. Submits well-organized reports, but occasionally omits some detail. His creative thinking has resulted in short cuts in routine and machine operations. (Example: Putting stock record cards in machine backwards to eliminate a reversing operation later.) Has the cooperation of all persons in the department as evidenced by a testimonial given him at a recent supervisors' meeting. Still shows some evidence of irritating people--impatient with them because they do not grasp ideas as readily as he thinks they should.

METHODS (How does this person go about getting his job done? How does he work with and through people? Be specific.)

Constantly searches for problems and their solutions in this and other related departments. Goes out of his way to assist others in solving their problems. When helping others he is inclined to perform the job himself rather than to have them do it. Supervisors have a tendency to lean on him because he is willing to shoulder their responsibilities. He keeps himself informed of new developments in the mechanical accounting field. He executes his duties promptly and plans his work well.

Fig. 1. Summary appraisal sheet.

about his work, the results he gets, his methods, his personal qualifications—in short, all pertinent factors about him and his work. The chairman of the appraisal group is usually the man's immediate superior.

To guide the appraisal, the facts brought out in the discussion are recorded under appropriate headings on the Summary Appraisal Sheet which lists the following: Performance (results and methods), Personal Qualifications, Po-

PERSONAL QUALIFICATIONS

List only outstanding qualifications either above or below average

GENERAL Has an excellent knowledge of mechanical accounting equipment and the over-all routines of this department. Has recently shown outstanding initiative. Occasionally jumps to conclusions because he is sometimes carried away by his enthusiasm before he thinks the problem through. However, he readily sees and admits his error in judgment. Has a slight hearing defect. Has recently shown improvement in general attitude. He has had a nearly perfect attendance record for 1949, missing only three days because of illness.

STRONGEST SINGLE QUALIFICATION Extending himself beyond normal requirements.

MOST NOTICEABLE WEAKNESS Hesitancy in delegating detail.

POTENTIAL

What is the next step ahead for this individual and does he have further potential beyond next step? If so, outline.

Mr. Cantrell could discharge the responsibilities of the Assistant Department Head position in Collection and Customers Accounting Departments. Preliminary training and development in personnel matters will be necessary because he has never served in a supervisory capacity.

ACTION

[X] **LEAVE ON PRESENT JOB** Continue to encourage Mr. Cantrell to delegate detail. Give him as much training and experience in supervisory matters as possible.

(Recommend action for improvement such as Training, Change of attitude, Change in pay, Encouragement, etc.)

[ ] PUT ON PROBATION ________ UNTIL WHAT DATE? ________

[ ] **REPLACE** [ ] PROMOTE

[ ] DEMOTE TO ________ [ ] TERMINATE [ ] TRANSFER TO JOB OF SAME CLASSIFICATION

WHEN SHOULD RECOMMENDED ACTION BE TAKEN? ________

CHECK THE CURRENT STATUS OF THIS INDIVIDUAL

[ ] IMMEDIATELY PROMOTABLE [ ] SATISFACTORY PLUS [ ] DECISION DEFERRED BECAUSE NEW

[x] PROMOTABLE [ ] SATISFACTORY [ ] QUESTIONABLE

[ ] UNSATISFACTORY [ ] UNSATISFACTORY—ACTION DATE SET

APPRAISAL MADE BY

NAME	TITLE
Louis [illegible]	Supervisor, Collection Department
Joseph B. [illegible]	Asst. Supervisor, Collection Dept.
Henry C. Bush	Supervisor, Cust. Accounting Dept.
[illegible] O'Berry	Supervisor, Meter Reading Dept.

The performance and personal qualification sections of this report have been discussed with the employe by

NAME [illegible] DATE 2/24/40

Fig. 2. Summary appraisal sheet (continued).

tential, Action, Current Status, Signature and Date of Discussion. (See Figures 1 and 2.) The discussion itself may be quite disorganized; but one member of the group, acting as secretary, can sort or classify the different statements under the appropriate headings. When the discussion seems to have reached an end, as far as the introduction of new factors is concerned, the notes can be reviewed, rearranged where necessary, and classified more carefully. However, the secretary must be sure that all members of the group agree with the final wording.

The technique of the appraisal is simple; there are no set rules to be followed. It consists merely of discussing the individual's effectiveness in an informal, conversational way. The discussion is carried on in the same spontaneous way that a group of business men would discuss an engineering development or a sales program.

On factors where records are available, such as cost reports, employee turnover data, production records, etc., statements about these factors can be verified and examples cited.

The final editing and re-stating of the factors discussed should be the result of the *unanimous agreement of all members* of the Appraisal Group. No statements should be included unless complete agreement is reached.

Only one copy of this information on a summary appraisal sheet should be available in the organization and all members of the appraisal group should sign this copy.

I should like to cite a few examples of the different kinds of appraisal factors which can be discussed and finally written in narrative form in the appraisal as we work our way through this procedure. One may question, at this time, the exactness of classification—whether a statement should be listed as a Result or Method or Personal Qualification. The examples here cited are actual and were agreed to while the appraisers were very new at this formalized sort of approach. It seemed better to let errors in classification occur at this time, rather than to make the procedure overly complicated. These techniques could be and were sharpened as subsequent appraisals were made. Thus the examples cited are the original attempts of management people making an earnest effort to be realistic and honest in appraising members of their team.

Appraising Performance

In talking about the *Performance* of an individual, the first thing to consider is the Results he has obtained. The question, "What has this individual accomplished in measurable results?" should supply the answer. In this field the quantity, quality, cost, time element of work done; customer, employee and union relations; safety and any other measurable qualities known to the group will usually be discussed. These results should be specific and should be borne out by the various operating reports and cost figures maintained in the organization and by any other evaluation means available in the organization. The final statement of the performance of the individual should be in narrative form, pointing out the various factors brought out in the discussion; for example, see the comments under the heading Results in Figure 1.

A second subject to be considered under the general heading of Performance is Methods. How does this person go about getting his job done? How does he work with and through other people? His methods can be evaluated by answering such questions as: What kind of records does he keep? How does he follow through on activities? How does he delegate responsibility? How does he organize his work? How does he develop his people? What are his work attributes? For example, see the comments under the heading Methods in Figure 1.

Appraising Personal Qualifications

What *Personal Qualifications* does this individual have that are pertinent to his job? What do you think of first when you think of this individual? In discussing Personal Qualifications, only factors which are particularly noticeable are used.

Following the general discussion of the Personal Qualifications, the Strongest Single Qualification and the Most Noticeable Weakness are determined. This necessitates a thorough analysis of the man's personal qualifications, and often brings out additional important factors previously overlooked.

An example of these factors is seen in the second half of the Summary Appraisal Sheet, shown as Figure 2.

Appraising Potential

In speaking of Potential it is important to know what is the next step ahead for this individual and whether he has further potential beyond that step. It must be specific, in terms of positions which are now in existence. It is important to consider all jobs in the company for which this individual may be qualified. In addition, it must be decided at this point whether further training or experience is needed before the potential can be realized.

Examples of appraisals of Potential range from statements such as "he can be promoted immediately to such and such a position" through all degrees of training to "we see no advancement possible for this person in the immediately foreseeable future."

Action

Having established the qualifications of the person being appraised, it is only natural that the Action to be taken as a result of this appraisal should be indicated. This means deciding whether the person will be left on his present job or what other action needs to be taken, such as place him on probation, replace him by promotion, demotion, transfer or termination. It is highly important at this stage that we be right, realistic and reasonable.

Further, this Action section requires the group to state specifically certain remedial or development steps to be recommended or taken to help the individual improve, both on his present job and for future consideration for promotions. I shall not at this time repeat the many different actions which can be used to accomplish the desired growth and improvement. Every management is well aware of the multitude of activities and techniques available, both in-company and out-of-company. It is enough to say that this Action section serves as a means to tailor-make a development procedure for the individual.

All this information can be condensed and recorded on the two sides of a single sheet of paper, known, as has been previously stated, as the Summary Appraisal. In addition to a few personal facts, the entire first page is used to record *Performance,* subdivided into Results and Methods (Figure 1). The reverse page is used to record *Personal Qualifications,* which is subdivided into General, Strongest Single Qualification and Most Noticeable Weakness, Potential, Action (including recommended development, training or any contemplated change), Current Status; and Appraisers' Signatures (Figure 2).

Current Status

The Current Status of the individual is his status on his present assignment. This section is included on the Summary Appraisal as a device to facilitate management discussions of the results of the appraisals. There are eight different degrees of status. Each one is carefully defined so that the exact meaning is understood by anyone using these terms. Each degree is assigned a color code for use later in preparing an organization chart. This chart enables management to see at a glance the condition of its team. It is most important that current status be looked upon by the appraisers as highly temporary. Status can change in one day and often does.

The definitions for the degrees of status follow:

Immediately Promotable: The individual can fill immediately a specific job at a higher management level without need for any further training.

Promotable: The individual can fill a specific job at a higher management level with further training. Such training may be accomplished within a stated time interval, such as six months, one or two years.

Satisfactory Plus: The individual is supplying what can reasonably be expected on his present job and could accept additional responsibilities and authorities within his present management level.

Satisfactory: The individual is supplying what can reasonably be expected on his present job, but you do not see him going beyond his present management level in the immediately foreseeable future.

Decision Deferred Because New: The individual has not been on his present assignment long enough (less than one year) to determine whether or not he is performing his present job in a completely satisfactory manner.

Questionable: The individual's performance on his present assignment is not completely satisfactory.

Unsatisfactory: The individual's performance is not acceptable on his present job. He may be able to improve his performance with further help and encouragement. In other words, we are not giving up on him.

Unsatisfactory—Action Date Set: The individual's performance is not acceptable and his personal qualifications are such that he will not be able to improve this performance. You are setting the date when you expect to have made the necessary changes.

At this stage, a complete appraisal has been made of the individual, but there are three additional steps necessary to complete the plan of Management Inventory and Development. The whole picture, it will be recalled, entails Appraisal, Review, Discussion and Development. The next step in the Management Inventory and Development procedure, therefore, is the Review.

• THE REVIEW

The purpose of the Review is to give higher management an account of the department head's stewardship and to point out the performance of his supervisors. The review emphasizes the importance top management attaches to the appraisals. It permits the evaluation of the department head's skill in appraising supervisors in his own organization. It improves communication and operating efficiency. The Review is the key to the success of the whole program.

The Review Board

The Review Board is composed of the highest management persons in the organizational unit and always includes the immediate superior of the department head whose appraisals are to be reviewed. The board may consist of three, four, or even five members.

Review Technique

When the department head appears before the Review Board, he brings with him the Department Appraisal Book which contains the Summary Appraisals, the Personal Data and Service Records, and Position Descriptions for all members of his management staff.

The Personal Data and Service Record is a concise statement of the service record of the individual, including his pay rate.

The Position Description describes his duties and responsibilities on his present job in a minimum sort of way. This is for use of the Review Board and is not the description used in establishing a grade for the position.

In addition to the Department Appraisal Book, the department head will have a large color-coded organization chart set up according to the Current Status of the persons appraised. This is for use in the Review Board Meeting.

In the meeting this book is given to the Chairman of the Review Board and is available to any member of the Board during the Review sessions.

The Review technique requires the department head to *tell* the appraisals to the Review Board while they refer to the written appraisals. Members of the Review Board may question the department head about the Results, Methods, Personal Qualifications, Potential, Action, established routines and possible improvements in efficiency. These questions enable them to discover whether the department head has presented a true appraisal of the person under discussion and also point out any weaknesses in the department head's handling of the appraisal technique. The Review Board neither accepts nor rejects the appraisals, for such is not the purpose of the meeting. The members of the Review Board may make recommendations about organization changes, means of improving supervision, changes in policies, methods, work schedules, or means of strengthening future appraisals. The Review Board closes its activity with a short, general analysis of the department head's stewardship.

Results of the review sessions are a closer understanding between the department head and his superiors; a keener appreciation of what they want and think; and a more complete picture of the department's operation for upper management.

Department Head's Appraisal

To insure full use of the entire Management Inventory and Development procedure, the department head himself is appraised after his Review has been completed. This appraisal is usually made by the Review Board now sitting as an Appraisal Group. On occasion other higher management persons are called in to assist.

The technique is basically the same as for the supervisory appraisals. Any variations, however, may be due to the higher responsibilities of his position, for he is supervising supervisors and foremen instead of production employees. In addition, his own appearance before his Review Board gives the Appraisal Group many good leads for consideration when they are making his appraisal. Additional factors to be considered are organization strength, his ability effectively to appraise his own supervisors, self-confidence, attitude and receptiveness to suggestions.

• THE DISCUSSIONS

Discussion is the third step in our four-step process of Appraisal, Review, Discussion, and Development. This phase of Management Inventory and Development is essential if the people who have been appraised are to receive the benefits of their appraisal. Its purpose is to tell the supervisor how he has been appraised. This telling is done by his superior and requires that he be told what is expected of him and how well he is fulfilling these expectations. Further, it permits the supervisor to question the appraisal and to air his own feelings. In this connection, management is in a position to point out to the supervisor that his appraisal is the result of the joint opinion of four or more persons and that the appraisal has been agreed to by the Review Board.

In handling the discussion, the higher supervisor should clearly state the purpose of the appraisal procedure. He should emphasize the fact that the statements made are the unanimous thinking of the Appraisal Group. He should tell the individual who appraised him. How much of the appraisal is revealed to the individual can best be answered by asking yourself the question, 'What do you want to do to the man?' Do you want to discourage him or do you want to raise expectations that cannot be fulfilled? Neither do you tell the man his prospects for promotion, even though they may be indicated in the appraisal. Both time and events can cause such statements to become impossible of fulfillment. It is a safe rule, when talking about a man's potential, to discuss with him how much better he could be doing on his present job. The amount of the appraisal which should be revealed depends largely on the supervisor being appraised and his ability to "take it."

• DEVELOPMENT

The final phase of Management Inventory and Development is that of Development. Its purpose is to help the person improve his job performance, his progress in the company, and his human relations skills. This development may be of a type that can be accomplished on the job or it may require outside activity on the part of the person appraised. It may be of two kinds—that started in the Discussion and the long-range managerial kind.

In order to keep Development need in the foreground, frequent reference to appraisals is essential to the department head. He must take action and recommend needed development to the individual, assist him with counsel and discuss his progress. In fact, he should use his Appraisal Sheet as a working record, setting down opinions, attitudes, reactions and results which arise in the Discussion. This is not a "one-shot" program. It requires continuing thought and effort if it is to be effective.

Long-range managerial development requires planning. It may consist of helping the individual to improve his job performance, make more progress in the company, increase his human relations skills, and acquire a broader outlook on the company's activities. Some of these objectives may be accomplished by assignment to other work groups in his own department, loans or transfers to other departments, granting of memberships in recognized professional organizations, special technical assignments, and enrollment in established training programs. In any event, these are steps which management can take to help develop those members of the management team who need further development, as distinct from the things the person must do for himself.

Those development procedures, which by their nature must be undertaken by the individual, should be called to his attention; for example, it can be recommended that he take certain courses in specialized subjects needed in his occupation, such as public speaking, report writing, letter writing, etc.

• OTHER OBJECTIVES

In addition to the objectives set forth at the opening of this article, there are three general groups of objectives which can be met through this method: (1) those of top management of the company; (2) those of middle management; and (3) those of the person being appraised (regardless of his own management level).

The program of Management Inventory and Development requires those above the first-line supervisors to make appraisals of their subordinates, present their findings in the review sessions, discuss the appraisals with the persons appraised, and formulate and promote the Development needs of those reporting to them. It thus makes them better management men. This program also provides the higher management levels with a bird's-eye view of the executive ability of all management groups.

Objectives of Top Management

The objectives of top management cover all the above, but in many cases the degree of importance varies. Top management of necessity becomes better informed about all levels reporting to it and all supervisors are better informed on a variety of subjects.

In a sense the performance of middle management in its appraisals of lower management is a revealing thing to top management. It is conceivable that top management may discover in a review that the appraisal conducted by middle management either put the wrong emphasis on factors of performance, overemphasized unimportant factors, or was improperly conducted for some other reason.

The measurement of employee and supervisory morale becomes more useful to top management as a result of appraisals.

Even more important than this, the inventory of management talent as appraised within a committee, department or division is revealed; and it is here that top management can see with a reasonable degree of assurance what it has in the way of promotable material.

Cost figures are bound to be favorably affected when the performance of each supervisor is improved.

When the appraisal technique is properly administered, vertical and horizontal communication is greatly improved, since the individual at all levels is made aware of his own status and of management's interest in his development.

Again from the standpoint of top management, the organization as a whole may be viewed with an eye to strengthening weak or faulty areas, or even redesigning the organization to overcome existing difficulties which have been brought to light by this technique.

Reserve strength or lack of it becomes apparent as soon as the entire organizational group has been appraised.

The development of those reporting to any management man not only strengthens the persons being developed, but also creates a stronger relationship between the various levels participating in the development program.

Objectives of Middle Management

The basic objective of middle management is three-fold: (1) a more efficiently run department or division; (2) the improvement of the appraised person's performance on his present job and the consequent improvement in individual morale; and (3) development of the appraised person's promotional possibilities and the resulting favorable impression on the superior's own performance.

What second-line supervisor doesn't have his own opinions of the supervisors who report to him, both as to their present job performance and promotability? Yet, time after time, a good appraisal has either caused him completely to revise his long-held opinions or better still to find concrete reasons to back them up. In either case a firmer ground for the discussion with the person appraised is always found.

The very act of talking things over with the person appraised improves communication and enhances the person's feeling of individuality. It indicates the personal interest of the superior in those reporting to him and reduces the feeling, all too prevalent in modern industry, of being a "cog in the machine."

Appraisal from top management naturally follows when improved performance occurs. Middle management can only gain this by improving its own and its staff's performance.

Objectives of Person Appraised

From the standpoint of the person appraised, his future in the company is at stake. Thus the appraisers have an important duty to furnish the individual appraised with an understanding of his status with regard to his present position and to his chances for promotion. They must point out to the appraised what his best points are and which characteristics he needs to develop if he is to be considered for a higher-level position. They must also point out weaknesses which he must recognize as barriers to his progress if not corrected. To indicate or convey clearly these factors to the person appraised, a careful choice of words is essential in describing the individual appraised.

Further, because the person being evaluated will know what his appraisal is, and who his appraisers were, it is even more important in the interests of harmonious relations and productive work that a complete and honest appraisal be made.

Unless the person appraised can honestly benefit from his appraisal, the appraisers have failed in their most important duty. "Honestly benefit" does not necessarily mean immediate promotion. It is conceivable that he may honestly benefit from a reversal or demotion, or perhaps even from actual dismissal. It is important that we analyze "honestly benefit" carefully from the individual's long-range viewpoint. It is possible that the course of his future company history may be changed by one of his appraisals.

It is in the Discussion that the appraised person is made to feel that the entire program is keyed to improving all members of management. His immediate goals are enumerated so that he can sense their accomplishment.

Through the Management Inventory and Development program he actually becomes a part of the management team and participates in the team play. His sights are raised; he has assistance for solving his problems; his future in the company assumes new importance.

• RESULTS

Results of such a program are of two types: (1) results achieved or evident immediately; and (2) those which will be achieved over a longer period of time.

Perhaps the most important single widespread result is in the modified attitude evident in almost all the persons appraised. While it is too early to forecast the degree of change in the intangible morale factor, it is apparent that certain individuals are beginning to feel that the future for them may not be as dark as they had feared. The mere fact that more than one person is doing the appraising has encouraged them to feel that they now may be able to get out from under the figurative thumb that has held them down in the past. Whether or not such feelings were justified by the facts, their elimination represents an improvement.

Another single result in many instances—and it, too, most certainly ties in with the morale factor—is the fact that for the first time some systematic plan has been in effect for telling supervisors "how they're doing." The appraisal procedure behind such discussions has given them added weight and support.

A number of operational results also have been noted. For example, it became clear that there was no justification for having a given group of employees do a specific kind of work. It was then possible to consider a reclassification of work and the elimination of certain unnecessary procedures.

As one executive summed it up, "This procedure brings out the damnedest things—things that one never suspects, such as deafness affecting work, need for simple surgical operations, petty prejudices, unhappy relationships and awkward operational procedures."

Finally, it should be noted that, on the second round of appraisals, the most noticeable weakness, as mentioned in the first appraisal, was in almost every case completely corrected or eliminated—and always improved.

• CONCLUSION

In times when many companies are reaching the age limits set for the retirements of those who helped develop the organization, replacements are of prime importance for the continuation of well-established business policies and relationships. The current national emergency, with its resultant drain on corporate brains and displacement of young executives points even more importantly to the need for a planned method for taking a management inventory and accomplishing sound management development. The more or less "permanent crisis" stage which we appear to have reached in industrial relations, from both labor and government activities as they affect management, behooves us to keep our house in order and to be ready for further changes and emergencies.

One final word: This entire case study has highlighted only the objectives, techniques and results of our program. It should be looked upon as an example of only *one* way in which management inventory and development can be accomplished. The operation of such a plan must certainly be tailored to the needs of any given company and certainly should not be attempted without benefit of considerable study and planning.

The persons appraised, the appraisers, the various levels of management in the Accounting Departments of The Detroit Edison Company feel that this is a step forward in an important area of management responsibility. It is hoped that the future use of this plan will bring many additional benefits to all parties concerned.

AN APPRAISAL PLAN FOR USE IN MANAGEMENT SELECTION*

Wellington Powell

In companies where high management is ultimately drawn from the craft level, careful attention must be paid to basic selection processes for bringing people into craft jobs. These processes must be selective enough, and rigid enough, to assure the company's having not only people with adequate abilities for its craft jobs but, among these people, a sufficient number with potential to meet the requirements of the jobs and opportunities which will open higher up.

The foreman, or first-line supervisor, is encouraged to look for supervisory qualifications in his subordinates. His boss includes in his day-to-day and week-to-week contacts with him many detailed discussions about each craftsman, and one of the purposes of these talks will be to unearth potential management candidates and to bring the foreman into his full share of responsibility for selecting and developing them.

Continuously initiated, the discussions may take the shape of comprehensive reviews of a man or they may be specific, pointed inquiries about certain aspects of his qualifications. Such questions as these will come up time and again:

1. Does he understand his work?
2. Does he show evidence of being able to plan his work well—especially when he comes up against situations or jobs which are more than ordinarily complicated and drawn out?
3. Does he do a good-quality job, and does he do it at a high level of productivity?
4. When he comes up against a new situation that needs some explaining, does he ask intelligent questions? And is he quick to grasp the new, necessary information?
5. Is he a self-starter with initiative that is tempered by good judgment? Is he a steady worker?
6. Does he get along well with others and does he have the ability to work as a team member?
7. Is he reliable?

And, as the more experienced workers develop, they will have more and more opportunity to take on complicated jobs, break in new people, perhaps act as supervisors for temporary periods. Such experience will then form a background against which further questions are discussed between the foreman and his boss:

1. Does he show the ability to accept responsibility?
2. Can he command the respect of the men with whom he is associated?
3. When he has the opportunity to play some role with supervisory aspects, does he show a sense of being able to assign part of the job, in proper proportions, to others?
4. What kind of tight situations has the man been in, and how did he handle himself?
5. If the man is assigned to a job that is

---

* From *Selection of Management Personnel*, by M. J. Dooher and E. Marting, Editors. (New York, American Management Association, 1957) pp. 518–528. Copyright 1957 by the American Management Association, Inc. Reprinted by permission.

complicated and extended, can he give you a good estimate of how it's going to shape up fairly early in the game?

6. Is the man tactful?
7. Does he show evidence of being able to give intelligent, measured consideration to a problem? Or, by natural habit, is he inclined to impulsive decisions?
8. Does he create a feeling of confidence?
9. Does he have the ability to tackle tough assignments without evidences of worry or tension?

Regardless of the types or complexities of individual promotion plans, this kind of continuous questioning and probing, though seemingly unscientific, gives the most effective basic information on which final decisions on promotions can rest. Not to be overlooked is the obvious advantage which such discussions are bound to develop in connection with focusing attention on the training and development a man requires—either as a craftsman or as a potential supervisor.

But eventually, in any training and development program, the point is reached where a specific choice must be made among several candidates for promotion. At that point quantitative evaluations of some sort must be arrived at in order to form a judgment of the relative merits of the several candidates under consideration. The appraisal system whose development will be traced in the following pages has been found very useful for this purpose. Think of it as a mechanism, if you will, for organizing the kind of information which should be continuously developed through day-to-day observing, questioning, and probing by all supervision. There is no magic about the plan itself, since it can't give results that are one whit better than the value of the information which goes into it.

• DEVELOPMENT OF RATING FACTORS

In developing this plan, the New York Telephone Company took three groups of first-line management people. Relative proficiencies were established by trained observers through comprehensive discussions with the second- and third-line levels of supervision involved. The resulting judgments were then checked against all the accepted departmental ratings of performance. There was general agreement that the first group was most proficient, the second average, and the third group least proficient. Also, as an entirely independent enterprise, and after considerable study, 12 characteristics descriptive of management ability were developed for rating purposes. By use of the forced-choice method, a rating ranging from "1" for low proficiency to "4" for high proficiency was introduced. To illustrate, under "judgment," the appraisal was made as follows:

1	2
Has often had difficulty in distinguishing between important and unimportant things.	Has some sense of relative importance of things but has often needed some guidance.
3	**4**
Generally has good sense of relative importance of things. At times has been "off the beam" but not seriously.	Has excellent sense of proportion as illustrated by handling of situations.

These ratings were applied to the three groups of first-line supervisors mentioned. Totaling up the scores and plotting them against the known estimates of proficiency produced a fairly good fit. Scores in the low third agreed with a low proficiency rating 89 per cent of the time. None of the more proficient group was included in this scoring range. Scores in the middle third agreed with an average rating 75 per cent of the time. Of the remaining 25 per cent, 19 per cent were less proficient and only 6 per cent were in the more proficient group. Scores in the top third agreed with a more proficient rating 66 per cent of the time. Of the remaining 34 per cent, 28 per cent were in the average group and only 6 per cent were in the less proficient group.

It was then reasoned that, if these 12 management characteristics appeared in a greater degree in the most proficient supervisors, these traits should be looked for in the consideration of future management appointments. Briefly, the 12 management abilities, broken down under four headings, were as follows:

1. *Proficiency in Handling Administrative Matters:*
   a. Alertness.
   b. Judgment.
   c. Insistence on quality in details and techniques.
2. *Proficiency in Handling Personnel:*
   a. Obtaining cooperation of force.
   b. Training subordinates.
   c. Ability to recognize differences in individuals.
3. *Cooperation with Higher Supervision:*
   a. Understanding instructions.
   b. Meeting service objectives.
   c. Interest in production objectives.
4. *Personal Characteristics and Data:*
   a. Tenacity.
   b. Confidence in self.
   c. Energy and drive.

Note that there are certain customary measurements which are not included in this list—among them health, honesty, attendance, and ability to do a craft job. These are all quite factual; and, if the candidate were not satisfactory with respect to them, he would more than likely be eliminated as a candidate for promotion and, in some circumstances, as an employee.

• PITFALLS AND LIMITATIONS

Here we have on paper a rating plan for use in selecting management personnel. How, then, to apply it? First of all, it should be said that this may be a dangerous tool and that there are pitfalls which lie in the way of its use.

One of the questions which arises is this: How uniform is the judgment involved? Assume, for example, that we want to appoint an installation foreman in the Plant Department, which installs and maintains telephone equipment. Such a foreman has direct supervision of possibly eight craftsmen who visit customers' premises to install telephones. In an average plant district, there are perhaps 120 installers and 16 foremen, who report to supervising foremen who, in turn, report to a district plant superintendent, thus giving three levels of management supervision in that district.

If a rating form is handed to a particular foreman without considerable background discussion, will he rate down from the best man in his group although the best man may be only average? Has the foreman always the ability to rate his men? Remember, in the case study, we did have some "least proficient supervisors." How does a foreman rate a craftsman on training subordinates or on obtaining the cooperation of the force when the craftsman has no subordinates? How do we measure the variations in judgment between different foremen, supervising foremen, and district superintendents? These are all weak points in the plan.

However, it would be wholly unrealistic to expect any rating plan to reduce to arithmetic, without potential errors, such complex and relatively intangible qualities as leadership, personality, psychology, intelligence, and drive. To repeat—management views this plan as a tool to better organize the collective judgments of the several levels of management involved in making promotions. Its limitations are recognized and supplemented. Above all, an effort is made to have the highest possible quality of information fed into it through the development of such information on the day-to-day basis of good supervision. Within this kind of framework, it has been useful and, in management's opinion, effective.

• JOB OF SUPERVISION

The New York Telephone Company, as has been said, fosters the concept that the promotion and development of people is the job of all supervision. To get down to cases and cite an illustration of how this works in practice—let us consider the typical plant division, employing 2,000 to 2,500 craft and clerical people. It has four or five districts, and each district has—among others—the responsibility for installation discussed earlier. The division superintendent knows from force studies that in the coming year he will probably need five new installation foremen. He has 500 craftsmen from whom to choose.

The team that chooses these foremen consists of the division superintendent, the district superintendent, the supervising foreman, and the foreman. First, the district superintendent has the continuing responsibility of securing uniformity of appraisal in the other three lines of organization. This is a day-to-day development process supplemented by planned, periodic discussion. The foremen then make periodic ratings of their men to the best of their ability. In many instances, point scores are not insisted upon as long as a thought process is followed which will dig out the top people.

When knowledge is lacking, a definite program is laid out by the foreman or supervising foreman to develop an evaluation. Depending on circumstances, such a program might include temporary assignment as a foreman, special training work, and the job of breaking in a new installer who is not trained sufficiently to be on his own. The manner in which an installer reports his completed work to the clerical force, how he handles verbal requests in the field from telephone people other than his foreman, how he cooperates with other maintenance people with whom he has to deal—all give indications of the degree to which certain desirable management qualifications are possessed or not possessed by the individual craftsman.

Once the best prospects have been shaken out, transfers in craft work are planned so that cross-judgment can be secured. Generally speaking, all candidates for the foreman level within a whole division are considered for each opening. Experience has established that this is a broad enough base, and to extend it would involve unrewarded effort. Thanks to day-by-day development effort, and discussion up and down and across supervisory lines, it is expected that two or more candidates will be available for each job vacancy. All foremen whose men are under consideration are of course informed of the reasons for the final choice.

• YOUTH OR EXPERIENCE?

It may be interesting to review briefly some of the management "cobwebs" that are encountered in this job of creating and perpetuating management. Take the experience factor, for example. There have been cases where craftsmen and supervisory candidates for further promotion have been 30 years in the business—and still the recommendation reads: "With another two years' experience So-and-So will be ripe for promotion." Surely we are looking for experience, but we must keep our aim focused on the basic abilities that go into leadership, such as planning and the ability to follow through in an organized manner to the immediate objectives.

Conversely, there is sometimes a misplaced accent on youth. We may be misled into transferring a man so fast that he does not learn any job. And, regardless of the age factor, every supervisor should have been in one craft long enough to know it well.

Age considerations, to a great extent, depend on the requirements of the business. (The telephone industry is, of course, closely linked to the dynamic pattern of our national economy; therefore, it has had periods of expansion and contraction, periods of rapid and slow opportunities for advancement.) Analysis of supervisory composition by age groups may indicate the wisdom of considering appointments over a fairly broad age range. For example, assume that you have had a definite 10-year gap in appointments to management. In most businesses, it is highly desirable, in the interests of continuity, to have a well-balanced age distribution in order to avoid abrupt changes due to large blocks of terminations within short periods—with the attendant dilution of experience caused by the necessary appointments to management. Under these circumstances isn't it practical to fill in the gap from both ends of the age bracket so as, eventually, to attain a more or less uniform volume of experience loss? Certainly, it's a factor to keep in mind.

Within broad limits, we need be concerned with no magic cutoff point in the age of a man so far as his eligibility to become a supervisor is concerned. Some men are old at 35, and some are young at 60. The real basic question is: Has the man got what it takes? If he has it, and if his appointment would fit the needs of the business, don't pay too much attention to his calendar age.

• THE FEAR OF RISK

Another "cobweb" entails what is really a management fault: the fear of risk. Fear that the man won't make good and that his failure will reflect unfavorably on his old boss. Fear that a delegation of authority or the education of his own people will detract from his own security and place in the sun. The action of higher supervision will largely determine the extent and continuation of this fear. If the man in question is an otherwise good supervisor, it can be corrected.

There is also a fear of employee reaction which may lead to the abandoning of objective sights and doing the expedient thing—appointing, for example, the most popular man or the oldest man. If you are appointing one man out of a group of eight, human nature being what it is, one man is happy; seven other men, in varying degrees, are disappointed. This, however, is a condition of business operations. Expedient appointments, if they do not also meet the requirements that have been discussed, will, in the long run, be the source of greater and more far-reaching discontent. Generally, employees are fair; they recognize over a given period, just as quickly as management, the assets and the liabilities of a new boss.

Moreover, we are seeking in this entire process of management selection and development to develop a responsibility for the whole enterprise, an urge for attaining higher goals, a self-reliance and a stimulation of creative thought about the job. How can we accomplish these things unless we are prepared to take risks both in appointments to management and in the after-development of management people?

• WHEN A MISTAKE HAS BEEN MADE

One of the more difficult situations related to the appointment of new management people is the treatment of those who do not make the grade. Craftsmen recognize a good boss as soon as management, but they also may recognize a poor boss even sooner. We can't shut our eyes to the fact that this presents a serious problem. First, we must think of the man's future, his personal fortunes, his own peace of mind. There is no more unsatisfactory experience in business than to see a man beyond his depth, tormented by fear and indecision. Second, we must think of the effect on the corporate business, and, third, of the effect on the working lives of those whom the man is supposed to lead. And we are dealing not only with the immediate effect, but also with the continued cumulative effect through the 20 to 40 years that the supervisor might normally continue to serve.

We have done our best not to make a mistake, but one has been made. What do we do? First, we must ask ourselves whether we have done what we should and can do as management to develop the man as a good member of the management team. This is a serious obligation of the business as a whole. If we have exhausted the possibilities for satisfactorily developing the man, should we not ask ourselves if there is not a nonmanagement job which he could fill in an entirely satisfactory manner? Would he be satisfied in that job not only now but five years from now? What can be done to condition the man's thinking?

The fair handling of such cases is a real test of management's skill, fairness, and humaneness. The answer is not to be found by drifting into a situation unsatisfactory to all interests involved.

• AS YOU GO UP THE LINE

Another question that may have some bearing on first-line appointments is the level at which you are making appointments. Do you look at all appointments as future presidents, or are you simply appointing foremen? The human being is not always predictable. Some of us reach maturity and stability earlier, others later. Some of us even lose stability. A happy or unhappy home life, outside interests—many factors outside the business can start or stop the inner growth of ambition, creative ability, courage, and imagination that leads to higher management. So why make the final bet on the first heat of the long race?

This discussion has dealt primarily with the selection of first-line supervisors because, in New York Telephone's experience, their selection presents the greatest problem and also the greatest opportunity. The same principle obtains for most other levels of supervision, although, as you go up the line, there is perhaps less reason for a rating system and greater emphasis on personal exchange of appraisals by a selection team.

The candidate at a higher level has established a record of management, whereas in the crafts you have no such specific record. And in any business, as the higher levels of supervision inevitably become more general and less specific, there is less need for detailed craft and technique skills and more for general business judgment. But how does general management become well-rounded? And how do you develop the ability to grasp a whole problem and not merely a part of it? Just as the barrier between craft and first-line supervision must be breached, so must the barrier between departments. For the interests of all must be served; and, although cross-promotion between departments has its element of risk, it is one way of arriving at the breadth of understanding required of true management.

• EFFECT OF EMPLOYEE ATTITUDE

Finally, it is both wise and necessary to consider selection for promotion against the broad background of employee attitude. The New York Telephone Company has found that, to a very considerable degree, the attitude of people toward the business is a measure of how well they feel that the business meets their needs and expectations—and there are few things that touch the individual more personally and more deeply than promotions. Where attitude is good, generally more has been done to let individuals know how they are doing; more has been done to help them understand the procedures and thinking underlying promotions; more has been done to make selection plans work through such steps as careful training of appraisers.

It has also been found that good attitude seems to be closely related to effective supervisory training. And not just formal training courses. Much more important is the effect of the day-to-day discussion and thinking carried on between each supervisor and his boss, since—as stated—a not inconsiderable part of these discussions is necessarily concerned with the development of people and the selection and training of candidates for promotion.

The company finds, too, that good attitude is related to the degree that higher management is well known to lower management—how closely higher management is in close contact with field conditions. There is no more effective way of establishing close liaison than through such conferences and discussions as must be held at all levels in order to carry out the selection processes that have been described.

Where attitude is good, supervisors have clearly delegated authority. Their recommendations on such matters as promotions are given serious weight—and, if they are not accepted, careful explanations are given to enable the supervisors to understand why particular decisions were made. Thus they feel satisfied that they have an adequate say in promotions.

The relative success we have in meeting our selection objective—of getting the management abilities we are seeking—will be reflected in even greater measure in the attitude of our employee body. We must do such a good over-all job of appraisal and selection that the promotion of the one man out of ten won't cost us the value of the other nine. They're the ones on whom we rely to get the job done!

A NEW CONCEPT OF PERFORMANCE APPRAISAL*

Kenneth E. Richards

Performance appraisal is a major subject of controversy in management circles. While business leaders see the need for appraisal systems, they are frequently disappointed in them. This article presents a new concept of performance appraisal, one that has been developed at United Air Lines following three years of study. This article suggests that personnel appraisal is capable of being used successfully as a supervisory tool. While most other firms use personnel appraisal for salary administration, promotion, or internal control, United's program specifically limits its use in these areas. We believe assisting the employee to maintain satisfactory performance on his *present* job is a worthwhile objective in itself and have other programs for administering salaries and appraising potential.

Also, it is apparent that further research should be conducted into what actually takes place during and following an appraisal interview. Studies reported in this article suggest that a great many supervisors and executives have quite erroneous notions concerning the motivations and attitudes of employees toward these interviews and of the changes in behavior and other benefits which may result from them.

Mixed feelings concerning performance appraisal have been expressed frequently in publications directed to management—such as the *Harvard Business Review,* American Management Association's *Personnel,* and the *Journal of Business.*

In the *Harvard Business Review* Douglas McGregor says: "Of course, managers cannot escape making judgments about subordinates. Without such evaluations, salary and promotion policies cannot be administered sensibly." But, in his conclusion he condemns the conventional performance appraisal because "it places the manager in the untenable position of judging the personal worth of his subordinates and of acting on these judgments."[1]

In *Personnel*[2] researchers from the University of Minnesota report that 12 of the 22 firms studied expressed dissatisfaction with their present systems of management appraisal.

This is not a controversy of recent origin. Thomas L. Whisler says that "this combination of interest and dissatisfaction exists despite the fact that for four decades many competent people have seriously studied the whole problem of rating and have endeavored to develop answers to what seem to be the major difficulties involved."[3]

Whisler believes "the chief impediment to making performance appraisal

* From *Journal of Business,* Vol. 32, no. 3, July 1959, pp. 229–243.

[1] Douglas McGregor, "An Uneasy Look at Performance Appraisal," *Harvard Business Review,* May-June, 1957.

[2] Thomas A. Mahoney, Wallace Dohman, and Thomas Jerdee, University of Minnesota's Industrial Relations Center Management Development Laboratory, "Applying Yardsticks to Management," *Personnel,* May, 1957.

[3] Thomas L. Whisler, School of Business, University of Chicago, "A Realistic Role for Merit Rating," *Journal of Business,* Vol. XXVIII, No. 1 (January, 1955).

into a workable and usable aid to management lies in the traditional notion that a rating plan is basically a measuring stick." The reaction of those who do the rating under this concept is one of opposition. To Whisler, the rating specialists appear to have a standard reaction to this behavior on the part of raters. "They either come fighting back with a scheme which has more statistical horsepower or surrender on the ground the time is not right for installing a rating plan." Whisler's solution is to make the appraisal a "tool of control" instead of a "measuring stick."

McGregor sees the underlying cause of the problem as something "dangerously close to a violation of the integrity of the personality. Managers are uncomfortable when they are put in the position of 'playing God.' The respect we hold for the inherent value of the individual leaves us distressed when we must take the responsibility for judging the personal worth of a fellow man."

His solution is to have the subordinate make his own appraisal of his progress toward his performance goals and bring it in for discussion with his superior.

Various aspects of performance appraisal have been studied at United Air Lines over a three-year period in order to evaluate and revise its Personnel Evaluation Program. These studies support the general criticisms noted above with respect to performance appraisal as a tool of management control. However, it was found that performance appraisal had much value as a tool of immediate supervisory control.

In our studies particular attention was given to personnel scores or grades obtained with the traditional graphic scale method. One item on the non-management form is shown below. A total of seven factors were rated on this form. There was also a management form with provision for twelve factors.

QUALITY OF WORK: Disregard volume. Consider accuracy, neatness, thoroughness. Did employee turn out work which met acceptable standards?

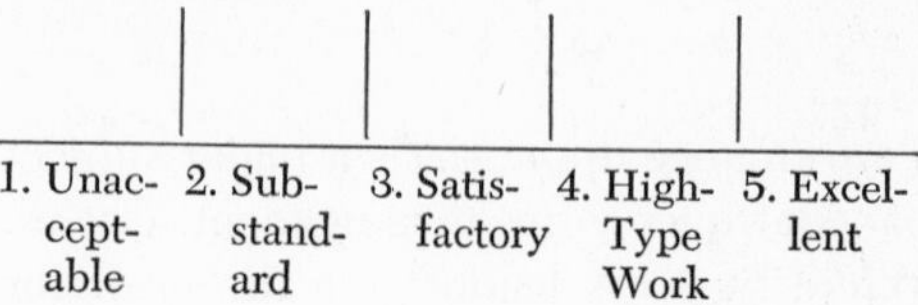

The scale was arranged so that a rating of "3" was considered "satisfactory" for each factor, and space was provided for comments under each of them. The ratings for all the factors were summarized on a profile that appeared on the first page of the form.

A number of studies indicated that these forms resulted in ratings which were largely concentrated in two middle values, in the creation of employee ill-will, and in inconsistent and probably invalid scores. Some details are given in the following section.

1. *"Everyone" gets 3's and 4's.*—A review of employee files showed little discrimination between ratings because of the central tendency on the part of supervisors to award only 3's and 4's. This same tendency was found to exist for additional ratings obtained confidentially for study purposes as shown in the accompanying tabluation.

	PROFILE SCORES				
	1	2	3	4	5
Confidential ratings for study purposes	0	9	202	145	8
Ratings in file for same people (364 ratings on 52 employees)	0	1	205	150	8

This similarity of ratings existed in spite of the fact that approximately one-third the people in this study were those that supervisors wanted "fewer like" or "no more like."

Comments made by supervisors indicated the danger of using "low" (2) ratings. They caused trouble for the evaluating supervisor because his own supervisor and the personnel office checked up on him to "see what action he had taken to get performance up to the satisfactory level."

Similar feelings existed about a "high" (5) rating. Supervisors say that even if employees deserve them, it might be necessary to lower them the next time, and giving a lower rating is just about as bad as giving a cut in pay. "It's better to keep most ratings in the 3 or 4 area."

2. *"2's" make people mad.*—A case arose during the study which illustrates what happens when supervisors *do* give a 2 rating. A few months previous to the trial run the supervisor gave this employee the customary 3's and 4's. But he was not satisfied with all aspects of her work because he said: "We also discussed her attitude during recent months. She was told while we gave her a 3 we felt that a better attitude should be expected of an employee with her seniority than has been evidenced recently."

During the study the supervisor had an opportunity to prepare an evaluation which would not become a part of the personnel file. He gave her two 2 ratings, one on quantity of work and one on attitude, with these comments: "She should show more spunk in getting her work accomplished. She should also make it more evident that she takes an interest in her work. Absences from work because of illness are somewhat above average and it would be well that she make a greater effort to restrict such absences. She felt the evaluation was unfair, but after considerable discussion she agreed there is room for improvement."

The form provides a space for employee comments. When she had received all 3's and 4's, she merely signed the report but made no comments. The 2 ratings stimulated the following comments: "If there wasn't an interest in my work, I certainly wouldn't have stayed on the same job for 7 years. It is true I accomplish more work when the other worker is absent. Part of this is due to the fact that many a time I did not go out on my pass, working longer than I should. But no one can keep up that pace. As far as restricting my absences, I would be very happy to because it runs into money I can't afford. It's not very pleasant working in an office that's too cold because the radiators are turned off. There are times when the heat comes through the ceiling vents, then the windows are opened. It's not very pleasant or healthy to have cold air blowing on you and that to the best of my knowledge is largely the cause of the absences I've had."

Many comments can be made on this, but they will be limited to the point that a low score is likely to raise the employee's defenses and widen the differences between the supervisor and the employee. While the supervisor indicated that she admitted there was room for improvement, we see no evidence in the employee's comments that she agreed that she could do any better work. As a matter of fact, all her comments were to the effect that she could not do any more or any better.

3. *Profile scores are invalid.*—In an-

AVERAGE PEP PROFILE SCORES OF EMPLOYEES BY FACTOR

	QUALITY	QUANTITY	DEPEND-ABILITY	CONTACT	ATTI-TUDE	INITIA-TIVE	JUDGMENT
High-ranked group	3.4	3.2	3.2	3.6	3.6	3.4	3.2
Low-ranked group	3.6	3.2	3.0	3.4	3.4	3.8	3.2

other study a supervisor was asked to rank his employees in order according to job performance. He reported that those who ranked at the top were considerably better employees than those who ranked at the bottom of the group. A review of the profile scores in the personnel files are shown in the accompanying tabulation. We see that those in the higher-ranked group did not receive any higher profiles than those in the lower-ranked group. As a matter of fact, the lower-ranked employees tended to receive higher ratings in quality of work and in initiative.

The "halo effect"—the tendency to rate people we like high and those we do not like so well low—is a common criticism of rating plans. One of our studies enabled us to demonstrate the "halo effect" in operation. In this case the supervisor evaluated three people in his group—one he wanted "more like," one he was willing to have "some like," and the other he wanted "fewer like." In each case he indicated that the individual "never observes the lunch and rest period time limits." But, on the evaluation form for the individual he wanted "more like," he had an asterisk and a footnote which said: "He can't due to the crowded conditions in the cafeteria, but he tries." For the individual he was willing to have "some like," he said: "He can't but it's no reflection on him." There was no indication that this individual tried. For the individual he wanted "fewer like," who was also checked as "never observing the time limits," there was no asterisk and no footnote. Here we seem to have degrees of the "halo effect" related to the supervisor's over-all opinion of the individual.

WHY APPRAISAL SYSTEMS • ARE DISAPPOINTING TO MANAGEMENT

Appraisal systems are disappointing to management for the following reasons: grades or scores are likely to be invalid because everyone gets basically the same scores; the scores are distorted when they have to be discussed with employees; they can widen the differences between people who have to work together; and they reflect bias. These are rating difficulties which are basically the result of human tendencies, and limitations and attempts to overcome them with a system or a form are likely to end in frustration.

There are other difficulties which arise when the ratings are used in connection with other activities. A review of some of these indicates that performance-appraisal programs have been placed under stresses they are not capable of withstanding. Let us look at a few activities often associated with performance appraisals.

Salary administration.—When salary administration is tied to performance appraisal, supervisors frequently use the ratings to justify salary increases. In doing this, they are likely to emphasize an employee's strong points. When trying to improve job performance, however, they may have to call attention to weak points. Expecting a performance-appraisal program to achieve many objectives, when some of them are contradictory to each other, weakens its ability to achieve any of the objectives well.

Promotions to other jobs.—It has been long known that the best workers do not necessarily make the best supervisors or managers. One often sees a good worker promoted to a supervisory position, but he continues to perform in the same old way and does the work himself. While he may *say* he was chosen because of his ability to handle people, he has little knowledge or understanding of human behavior or of what motivates people. The fact that hundreds of "human-relations" courses are being conducted in industry testifies to this common situation.

The same is true of promotions from one level of management to another. Robert N. McMurry expressed it this way:

> It is important to distinguish the qualities needed by the top executives from those typical of successful middle-management executives generally. The magnitude of the difference between the two levels of leadership is not always appreciated by students; hence the assumption that the transition from one level to the other is easy and that success in the upper echelons of middle management automatically qualifies the incumbent for promotion. . . . It is primarily because there is so little general awareness of the real difference between the unique constellation of special qualities required for the success as an entrepreneur-manager and the more pedestrian and vocational qualifications of middle management—that so many errors are made in choosing chief executives.
>
> Even within the ranks of middle management itself, no clear appreciation exists of the differences between the requirements of staff and line positions. . . . Hence it is possible for an individual to make an outstanding record as a staff man without possessing any administrative talents whatsoever. In spite of this, promotions are not infrequently made from staff to line activities and even to top management solely on the basis of the candidate's technical competence supplemented of course by the customary attributes of the faithful employee.[4]

Potential.—Some programs have a rating on potential. Certainly we would all like to be assured by our supervisors that we have the potential to reach our personal level of aspiration. However, an individual who is told he has the potential for a higher level job has some expectations of receiving it. *But is he also told there are 50 other people in the company with the same potential?* Telling an individual he has the potential is like picking the winner of a race before all the entries are known. The appraisal of potential is beyond the scope of performance appraisals. More and more companies are relying upon specialists to assess the potential of their manpower.

Securing appraisals on a standard basis.—A great deal of time and effort is being given to training supervisors to evaluate on a standard basis. But can this be done? Will an aggressive, gregarious supervisor and a quiet, reserved supervisor both see a given individual in the same light? This can be further illustrated in a typical business situation. A successful department head, with a successful staff, retires and is replaced

[4] Robert N. McMurry, "Man Hunt for Top Executives," *Harvard Business Review*, January-February, 1954.

by an equally successful department head. The new man inherits the staff of the former department head—will he see them in the same way the original leader did? Before long changes will begin. They might start when the new department head brings his secretary with him (although the secretary of the former department head is highly competent). After a while this man will be changed and that man brought in, and within a relatively short time the entire staff changes.

Why is there uneasiness when a new manager takes over? Each individual involved is wondering how he will be viewed by the new boss. Finally, could any appraisal system be devised which would produce a standard rating of General MacArthur by President Eisenhower and former President Truman? Appraisals are likely to be nothing more or nothing less than a reflection of the relationships existing between the people involved.

WHY HAVE EVALUATIONS?

With this imposing array of weaknesses and limitations, what is the value of an appraisal program? We do not see it as a control tool, or a tool for use in salary administration, or for handling promotions. The new concept is that the performance appraisal is a *supervisory* tool—not a management tool. The major activity of all employees is the work they perform on a day-to-day basis. They are not always being considered for salary increases or for promotion to another job. These are important but special events which occur once or twice a year or even less. But everyone is constantly participating in a supervisory-employee relationship, and this does apply to everyone. Even the president has a relationship with the chairman of the board or with the board of directors. From the vice-president on down, every employee in industry has a supervisor. Studies continually indicate the importance of effective supervisory-employee relationships—it is here that leadership begins. Despite misgivings of one kind or another, supervisors and employees still are interested in having a performance-appraisal program. Employees want regular opportunities for discussions of a personal nature with their boss. In one of our studies supervisors and employees alike responded to a questionnaire which included the item: "What are the reasons why United should have or should not have a Personnel Evaluation Program?" Not one of the seventy supervisors and employees who participated in this study gave a reason for *not* having such a program! The following are some typical comments:

A Personnel Evaluation Program in a company the size of UAL is a good sound program. With the number of employees that there are under each manager, there is little time during the period of a year when the supervisory people are able to talk over to any great length the employee's job performance. With the program we have, we can be assured that we will, at least once a year, be enlightened as to what is the thought of our present performance and what is expected of us in the future.

There should be an evaluation program. It helps the employee and supervisor to discuss and iron out any small problems. During the discussions many things can be cleared up and you feel that you are not interrupting the supervisor when he might be busy on some other work.

Most of the supervisor-employee contacts involve getting the work out and also involve the things that are on the supervisor's mind. Is it not appropriate to spend *an hour or two hours a year* to give the employee an opportunity to discuss the things that are going on in his mind? This concept of performance appraisal appears to be quite different from the usual one in industry. In a recent survey of merit-rating programs, Prentice-Hall, Incorporated, found that only 9.4 per cent of the companies saw their program as proving a counseling and interview opportunity, and only 4.7 per cent believed that a principal advantage was to create better supervisory-employee relationships. In United's program, however, these objectives are major ones.

An individual assigned to develop a performance-appraisal program for his company can find a considerable number of articles on the subject. He can obtain specific information about systems built around rating scales, the forced-choice method, or the critical-incident technique—to name a few. As Whisler indicated, rating specialists tend to come fighting back with new schemes which have more statistical horsepower. But there is little in the literature which attempts to describe what really goes on between the participants in a performance appraisal. Apparently there is little research in the appraisal area which would help us understand *why* the problems involved in developing a completely satisfactory program have not been solved.

Research conducted along these lines in United Air Lines gives some insight into what is going on between the participants, and it points up the need for more research in this entire field. It is known that behavior is influenced and controlled by both conscious and unconscious[5] components. Tests, such as the Rorshach and the Thematic Apperception Test, known as "projectives," have been in use for a number of years to gain access to attitudes at the unconscious level. But it is only within recent years that these same methods have been applied in business. Now the businessman is becoming increasingly aware of the influence of the unconscious factors, particularly through motivation studies in market research.

Exhibit 1

REPRESENTATIVE ITEMS FROM THE PEP SURVEY

	AGREE	DISAGREE
Once a supervisor has given the employee a fair evaluation of his work it is easy to get him to change by suggesting areas where he can improve	----------	----------
Most employees are anxious to get their supervisor's evaluation so they can improve their performance on the job.	----------	----------
Telling an employee what he is doing wrong and how he can correct it is the most effective way of getting him to change.	----------	----------

We have used two different methods to measure the attitudes of supervisors toward performance appraisal. One of

[5] The term "unconscious" is viewed differently by different schools of thought in the field of psychology. For our purposes here, we are using the definition given in Collier's *Encyclopedia* (XIX, 16): "we will call a process 'unconscious' when we have to assume that it was active *at a certain time* although *at that time we* knew nothing about it."

these is the PEP Survey—a traditional type questionnaire which requires agree-disagree responses to thirty-seven specific items about the Personnel Evaluation Program (Exhibit 1). It was developed to measure the conscious attitudes toward personnel evaluation. The other, a projective device called the PEP Situation Survey, consists of four pictures related to personnel evaluation, with the respondent required to write a short story about each picture (Exhibit 2, Figs. 1–4). The PEP Situation Survey pictures were designed to tap some of the attitudes and feelings at a deeper, unconscious level. The analysis of the stories brings out attitudes and feelings which differ considerably from those revealed by the traditional approach!

It is believed that until we are aware of the differences in conscious and unconscious feelings about performance appraisal, industry is likely to find the development of a satisfactory program quite frustrating. And, unless evaluating supervisors and managers have an understanding and awareness of the deeper implications of performance appraisal, they cannot be fully effective in using such a program.

We will compare the responses to a few of the items from the PEP Survey with the stories written about the pictures in the PEP Situation Survey. In both cases the responses are from forty-seven supervisors and managers from various departments in United Air Lines. Each picture appeared on a separate piece of paper with room for the story. The following instructions were read:

> We'd like to get your reactions to these pictures about the Personnel Evaluation Program. You are to write a brief story about each picture, describing the thoughts and feelings that are involved.
>
> If you wish you may give the people in the pictures a name and a job classification. Tell what each person in the picture is thinking, feeling and saying. In concluding your stories, tell the outcome or results of the meeting.
>
> You'll have about five minutes for each story. However, if you're not quite finished at the end of five minutes you'll be given a little more time to complete your thoughts. If you finish before five minutes are up wait until the rest of the group has finished so we'll be able to read the instructions for each picture together.

The first picture (Fig. 1) was designed to obtain the thoughts and feelings of an individual about to be evaluated. Picture No. 2 (Fig. 2) was to bring out the thoughts and feelings of both participants in an evaluation review meeting—the supervisor and the employee. Pictures Nos. 3 and 4 (Figs. 3 and 4) were identical except the instructions varied. In Picture No. 3 (Fig. 3) the employee improved as a result of the meeting, and in Picture No. 4 (Fig. 4) he did not improve. This was done to try to obtain more information as to why some meetings result in improvement on the part of the employee and some do not.

It is, of course, possible to analyze stories of this type for a number of different purposes or factors related to evaluation. For the purposes of this article we will limit the information to a few areas. Space does not permit us to reproduce the 4 stories written by each of the 47 participants at the beginning of the course and the 4 stories they wrote about the same pictures at the end of the course—a total of 376 stories. The before-training stories about Picture No. 1 (Fig. 1) will be summarized, but to give more of an idea about the kind of story obtained from pictures of this type, here are three stories in their complete form

Exhibit 2

PEP Situation Survey Pictures

Fig. 1.—In this picture the individual is about to enter his supervisor's office for his annual PEP review. You are to write a story about this picture which describes the thoughts and feelings that are involved.

Fig. 2.—In this picture the employee feels he is doing a good job. The supervisor also thinks the employee is doing a good job except for a few areas where he would like to see improvement. Write your story telling what each person is thinking, feeling, and saying and the outcome or results of the meeting.

Fig. 3.—In this picture the supervisor and the employee have completed the PEP review meeting and both seem to be pleased with the results. The supervisor is pleased because he feels the employee is definitely going to improve. The employee does improve! Now, write your story, telling what went on during the meeting and the kind of improvement he made.

Fig. 4.—In this picture the situation is the same—except the employee does *not* improve! Now, write your story, telling what went on during the meeting and the kind of improvement the supervisor had expected.

Table 1

FEELINGS INDICATED	EXPLANATION OF FEELINGS	MENTION OF PLANS TO IMPROVE
1. Glad	Try not to see as grade card but opportunty to improve	May be opportunity to improve
2. Pleased, but nervous, tense	Pleased to get supervisor's opinion, nervous, tense, because of unknown	Will help him know what supervisor expects
3. Uncertainty	Will supervisor recognize good work or just criticize?	No plans to improve
4. Apprehensive and tense	Because supervisor's evaluation will reflect future with the company	No plans indicated, but PEP could help if handled with tact
5. Confident	Perhaps already knows results; pleasant supervisor-employee relationship	No plans to improve
6. Looking forward to meeting	Will learn performance firsthand from supervisor	Program helpful to correct faults
7. Confident, eager	Chances PEP more than satisfactory; can discuss future with company	No plans to improve
8. Anticipation, concern	Wonders if supervisor conscious of things he feels he has been lacking	No plans to improve
9. Uncertainty	Knows doing good job, but does the boss recognize it?	No plans to improve
10. Looking forward to meeting	Knows boss anxious to help him	Plans to improve with supervisor's counsel
11. Apprehensive, uncertain, awed	Not sure his boss will report his work objectively	No plans to improve
12. Uncertainty	Wonders if he will get a good report	No plans to improve
13. Insecurity and apprehension	Until he finds out "which way the wind blows"	No plans to improve
14. "Undoubtedly" concerned	Wonders what supervisor thinks	No plans to improve
15. Defensive	Where will I be downgraded?	No plans to improve
16. Hopeful	Hopes boss will discuss good points and those needing attention	Plans to become an "even better" employee
17. "Does not dread" meeting	Wonders what will happen, but not treated badly the last time	No plans to improve
18. Anxious	To see what supervisor thinks—has he noticed good work, helping others?	No plans to improve—wants to mention a few things on mind
19. Uncertainty	Wonders if work good enough for new job—has done everything to qualify	No plans to improve—feels already proven self
20. Uncertainty	Will good work be noted as well as errors?	No plans to improve
21. Anxious	Hopes boss feeling well when he writes PEP. Hopes recognition of how hard he's tried	No plans to improve
22. Defensive	Wonders what this is all about	No plans to improve
23. Confident	Read report in advance—knows what he's going to say	No plans to improve
24. Hopeful	Hopes he's made progress and can move into a higher job	No plans to improve
25. Anxious	Will boss recognize good work and show tolerance?	No plans to improve
26. Confident	Feels he's done a good job	No plans to improve

Table 1—Continued

FEELINGS INDICATED	EXPLANATION OF FEELINGS	MENTION OF PLANS TO IMPROVE
27. Reflective	Wants encouragement and direction	Wants advice to improve
28. Defensive	Let's get this over with. I don't agree with some items on report	No plans to improve—this is a waste of time
29. Defensive	Improvement of past not recognized, no chance to express my feelings	No plans to improve
30. Defensive	How can boss evaluate me when our contacts are so limited?	No plans to improve
31. Defensive	Next in line due to seniority—demands boss give specific examples where substandard	No plans to improve
32. Welcomes opportunity	Knows supervisor interested in seeing him advance when ready	Plans to improve
33. Anxious	What will boss say? Hope he's fair	No plans to improve—face it and get it over with
34. Anxious	What's in store for me? Will I get credit? Am I in line for raise?	No plans to improve
35. Confident	Knows doing good job and sure boss will tell him so	Plans to improve—wants to know shortcomings
36. Anxious	What will boss say? Will he remember boner I made last January?	No plans to improve
37. Hurt	In his estimation, lack of recognition	No plans to improve
38. Confident, comfortable	Chance to have good work confirmed and to discuss his future	Plans to improve—to do "even better"
39. Uncertainty	Does supervisor see finer qualities?	No plans to improve
40. Apprehensive	Will what the boss thinks coincide with his own thoughts?	No plans to improve
41. Somewhat tense, but looking forward to meeting	No explanation for feelings given	No plans to improve
42. Uncertainty	What does the boss think?	Plans to improve—hopes boss has good suggestions
43. Uncertainty	What will boss say? Will he compliment, bawl me out, or try to help me?	Plans to improve—"takes two to make a team"
44. Anxious	Wish I knew mood he's in—will he rake me over the coals?	No plans to improve
45. Uncertainty	Will boss see good work or just the boner I made last month?	No plans to improve
46. Defensive	No credit given for correcting past complaints—just stereotyped phrases	No plans to improve
47. Uncertainty	Will rating be higher than last year? Hope improved and that comments are in my favor	No plans to improve

about Picture No. 1 (Fig. 1): What are the thoughts and feelings of an individual about to enter his supervisor's office for his annual PEP review?

1. I'm glad to have this opportunity to sit down with the boss and talk about myself and my efforts with the company. I'm going to try and not consider this PEP as just some sort of "report card" kind of discussion but an opportunity to improve my job and my opportunities with the company.

2. A feeling of uncertainty exists—a year's work accomplishments will be reviewed. Will the supervisor recognize those good qualities or will he criticize me for that mistake I made yesterday? Will he honestly and constructively criticize?

3. I wonder where I'm going to be downgraded. I have plenty of material to refute anything my supervisor will say. I doubt if he is qualified to give me an evaluation on certain aspects of my work. He never knows about some of the better things which are done because I do not tell him while I do discuss my problems with him perhaps too freely.

Here we see different types of feelings expressed about performance appraisal. The individual in the first story is glad for the opportunity, the second individual is apprehensive, and the third individual is defensive—prepared to refute the supervisor's evaluation of his work. How do the attitudes and feelings about performance appraisal revealed in the picture stories compare with those indicated by the responses to the questionnaire?

One of the unique differences our studies have brought out involves the question of what is the central motivation of the appraisal review *to the employee himself*. Most supervisors agreed with the statement in the questionnaire that employees were anxious to get their supervisor's evaluation *in order to improve their performance*. If this is a realistic picture of the central motivation of performance appraisal to the employee, we would expect the theme of self-improvement or plans for changing job behavior to occur frequently in the stories. The stories to Picture No. 1 (Fig. 1) are summarized and reviewed in Tables 1 and 2, with this purpose in mind: To what extent does the theme of self-improvement, or plans for changing, occur?

The unconscious attitudes and feelings about performance appraisal as revealed by the pictures were directly opposite to the conscious attitudes as indicated by the responses to the questionnaire item which was stated as follows:

	YES	NO
Most employees are anxious to get their supervisor's evaluation so they can improve their performance on the job	36	11
Plan to improve job performance indicated in the stories	11	36

Most of the employees in the stories were not anxious to get their evaluation so they could improve their performance —the majority were either anxious or defensive owing to a need for recognition and reassurance by the supervisor that their performance is already more than just satisfactory. Typical comments: "I know I've been doing good but does my boss know it?" "Has he noticed I've been coming early and staying late and how much I help others?" Whether or not any improvement is going to occur as a result of an appraisal review, the analysis shows that other, stronger feelings are more likely to be present and dominant in the appraisal situation.

It is also interesting to note that plans

Table 2

TABULATION OF FEELINGS RELATED TO EVALUATION AND PLANS TO IMPROVE

	NUMBER	PLANS TO IMPROVE YES	PLANS TO IMPROVE NO
Non-Anxious Feelings:			
Glad, pleased, hopeful	4	3	1
Confident	7	2	5
Looking forward to meeting	4	3	1
Reflective	1	1	----
Subtotal	16	9	7
Anxious Feelings:			
Apprehensive, insecure, anxious	13	----	13
Uncertainty	10	2	8
Hurt	1	----	1
Subtotal	24	2	22
Defensive Feelings:	7	----	7
Grand total	47	11	36

for improvement were noted in 50 per cent of the cases where non-anxious feelings were involved, in only 8 per cent of the cases where anxiety was involved, and in none of the cases where the individual was outright defensive. We are not saying that employees are not interested in improving their jobs in terms of obtaining a position with higher status and pay. This was mentioned a number of times in the stories. But there is a difference! Here they are saying that they want an improvement in their situation—not in themselves.

The stories written about the other three pictures in the PEP Situation Survey enable us to investigate additional aspects of performance appraisal. A number of these stories are quoted directly in the balance of this article to illustrate United's program and the rationale behind it.

Two items in the PEP Survey questionnaire tap supervisory attitudes about the ease of bringing about improvement in the employee's performance. About half the supervisors indicated in the PEP Survey that once a supervisor had made a fair evaluation, it was easy to get the employee to change and that telling an employee what he is doing wrong and how he can correct it is the most effective way of getting him to change.

The stories indicate, however, that it is not so easy to bring about change in other people. First, what is a "fair" evaluation of the employee's work—the supervisor's concept of how the employee is doing, or the employee's concept? Many evaluation plans call for a review of the supervisor's evaluation by a higher-level supervisor. Now the employee is outnumbered, with more strength added to the supervisor's power position in the relationship; but how does he *really* feel about it? Considerable research, with the possible use of methods illustrated here, is needed prior to adding procedural steps such as this in an appraisal system.

Supervisors indicated in the stories that while the individual may appear to be accepting the suggestions, he is not really doing so. Here are illustrations of this:

I think the boss is right in some areas and splitting hairs in others.

The supervisor is concerned about pointing out weak areas in such a manner as not to affect his attitude.

And this complete story:

SUPERVISOR: You need to improve your vocabulary in your job as a salesman. Good use of the English language is important as hell.

EMPLOYEE (*to himself*): What does he think, I speak better English than he does.

He's always "cussin." (*Aloud*): Yes sir, I understand what you mean—I am now involved in some self-training on using good grammar.

SUPERVISOR: That's fine, the next thing we got to take up. . . .

EMPLOYEE (*to himself*): Wow! (*Aloud*): Yes sir.

The stories are useful in getting additional insights into other phases of performance appraisal. For example, a fairly common suggestion to those who are to review the results with employees is to use the "sandwich method," that is, to start off with a compliment, then bring up a point needing improvement and continue to "sandwich in" the suggestions with the compliments. What are the reactions to these techniques?

1. The employee is thinking that the supervisor is giving him a good build-up for any criticism.

2. SUPERVISOR (*to himself*): I'll start with some of his good points. Perhaps in the conversation I can get him to bring up his weak areas. If not, I'll bring them up.

EMPLOYEE (*to himself*): The supervisor is trying for something. I don't like his paternalistic attitude. If he has something on his mind [why doesn't he] say it and leave psychology out of it.

3. From the smile on the employee's face he is evidently being complimented on the good points of his job. There are some areas of improvement to be made and the employee may be knocked off his high throne shortly.

There is a tendency in programs to come up with a list of "suggested techniques." The principles behind them may be very sound, and they may work very well for those who have knowledge and experience in their use. But stated as "techniques," they are likely to be oversimplifications with their real values lost to those looking for a quick way or a simple solution to the problems of supervisory-employee relationships. We learned very early in life to sense when we were being manipulated and to react accordingly. Most people can spot a "technique" a mile away, and it is apparent here that employees conditioned to the "sandwich method" are likely to react accordingly. This does not mean that supervisors cannot talk about both strong points and weak points during a performance review:

1. Exchange of ideas was done constructively and specific instances discussed where the supervisor felt improvement was necessary. Employee can understand exactly why the supervisor feels as he does, and the supervisor can get the picture of why the employee reacted the way he did to this set of circumstances. Common ground is established between both men, so that discussion on the job about improvement can be made with just a few words and both know the extent of improvement or otherwise.

2. The meeting was conducted with proper emphasis on strong points and points of needed improvement. The supervisor created an atmosphere of sincere and helpful interest. He had constructive ideas for the benefit and development of the employee, but of equal importance, he secured the acceptance of these ideas.

No "techniques" are at work here. There is an exchange of ideas—participation on the part of the employee too—mutual understanding of each other's point of view—a man-to-man relationship—on equal footing, with no emphasis on the power position of the supervisor. There is an atmosphere of sincere and helpful interest, with constructive ideas for the benefit and development of the employee. This latter point is important—*for the benefit and development of the employee.*

Evidently the supervisor did a good job of communicating this feeling because he secured the acceptance of these ideas.

PRINCIPLES BEHIND • UNITED'S PERSONNEL EVALUATION PROGRAM

The United Air Lines program is based upon a rationale of human behavior, the purpose of which is to give supervisors some understanding and insight into why people behave like people. Giving advice and directions frequently do not result in change because people act the way they do for specific reasons, some of which follow:

Self-concept

Each person has a picture of himself that has been built up for years. It consists of the individual's understanding of himself and the reasons he believes he behaves and feels as he does. These are at the conscious level. Now, if someone were to tell him that his ideas about himself are all wrong, he simply would not be able to accept it or believe it. We see evidence of the importance of the self-concept in such stories as these:

Employee (*to himself*): How did he ever get the impression I don't have good relations with other departments? (*To the supervisor*): I don't understand why you feel I don't get along with other departments. I've got lots of friends in those groups.

Supervisor (*to himself*): Looks like I didn't get that one across. I don't want to embarrass him by telling him point blank how he's been antagonizing the supervisors in "X" department. How in the world am I going to get it across?

When the individual's self-concept is similar to the supervisor's concept, progress toward improvement or change can be made, as seen in this story:

As a whole we reached the same conclusions. He let me express myself. He was very fair and did not put me on a spot. The manner in which he let me find my faults and express myself so it was not embarrassing to either of us was appreciated.

When the individual's self-concept differs, we find resistance or defensiveness:

The supervisor stated that the employee was unco-operative with others and cited examples. The employee, feeling he was a normal person, did not consider his attitude to be anything more than normal aggressiveness and did not attempt to change his general manner.

Defense Mechanisms

When a person's self-concept, or picture of himself, is threatened, he tends to build up a defense for himself. The important thing for the supervisor to remember about defense mechanisms is that an individual is not likely to change when he is in the process of defending the status quo. When his energies are being used to man his defensive system, they are not available for growth and change.

Motivation

This term is used to describe the needs within an individual that drive him to act. Hunger, thirst, etc., are physiological drives, but we are primarily concerned with psychological needs, such as economic need, need for recognition, need for security, need to excel, need to serve, and need for group acceptance—to name some of them. Fulfilment of these needs is vital to each individual. A supervisory appraisal may be seen as an obstacle to satisfy an individual's needs and raise his defenses to hinder or actually block change.

Understanding Change

Most people, and Americans in particular, believe that change is something they look forward to. But a man who was responsible for a great deal of change in our lives knew better. He was the late Charles F. Kettering, famous electrical engineer, inventor, and manufacturer. Among his many inventions were an automobile starting, lighting, and ignition system and a cheap power plant for farm lighting. He contributed to the development of Duco pyroxylin lacquer, the diesel engine, crankcase ventilator, ethyl gasoline, the electric refrigerator, and other inventions. The following is quoted from a radio interview conducted with Mr. Kettering by Len O'Connor, NBC newsman.[6]

MR. O'CONNOR: Looking at the world now, do you think it would be better if science had not been so rapid across the last three or four decades?

MR. KETTERING: No, the only reason that science has caused trouble is that people don't want to move.

MR. O'CONNOR: I don't follow you.

MR. KETTERING: They want to sit still and when you try to get them to move they think that's trouble. To get people to change their minds about a thing is the most difficult thing in the world. To do anything new—I don't care how simple it is—is the most difficult thing in the world to do. People don't want to be disturbed.

MR. O'CONNOR: But they're living in an age now where they have to be.

MR. KETTERING: Well, that's just their hard luck. You see, you hear people talk about the good old days and things like that. Well now, the only reason for this is that you can be a resident in space but you've got to be a transient in time. But people try to be a resident in time so they want to fix a date from which everything is reckoned. Well, now, the thing that upsets is tomorrow. They want to live in history and we're looking back into history and backing into the future and that's where we have so much trouble. If we would just look around and plan for the future a little more instead of getting so excited about what we used to do we'd be a lot better off.

Having supervisors understand these four points about human behavior—(1) the self-concept, (2) defense mechanisms, (3) motivation, and (4) the factors involved in change—is very important in the operation of a successful performance-appraisal program.

• THE PROGRAM IN ACTION

In United's program the supervisor prepares a narrative report.[7] All grades and scores have been eliminated, since it was found that many people are only interested in them as a symbol of a passing grade and seem to lose interest

[6] Permission to quote from this interview was granted by Mr. O'Connor, who interviewed Mr. Kettering over Chicago radio station WMAQ on October 10, 1957.

[7] There are four different types of report forms—a standard form for most jobs, a form for staff and professional jobs, a form for supervisory jobs, and one for administrative positions. Each is accompanied with a worksheet designed to stimulate the supervisor's thinking prior to writing the report. More details about the forms or procedures for their use will not be included here. Suffice it to say they are similar in appearance to many other appraisal forms, the difference being in the concept of their use.

in further discussion of their work. Supervisors are trained to write their reports in a way which will promote rather than eliminate discussion—a difficult thing to do but still important. Once a supervisor completes a report, he reviews it with *his* supervisor. This is to make certain it is complete, accurate, and representative of the employee's over-all performance during the period and that it will promote increased understanding and assist in motivating the employee. In addition, the review provides an opportunity for the supervisor to prepare for the review meeting with the employee.

We have seen that passing judgment may result in the employee marshalling his defenses in such a manner as to make improvement difficult or perhaps impossible. Change is most likely to come from the employee when he has an opportunity to express his thoughts and opinions in an understanding atmosphere—one in which the supervisor actively listens and reflects the employee's thoughts and feelings so the individual is better able to see himself. The active listener steers clear of attempts to force changes in others. He leaves the responsibility for the change with the individual.

Direct counseling can be effective too —*if the proper conditions exist.* For example, a new employee is more likely to accept suggestions because he is not expected to know everything about the work, or an individual who indicates an awareness of his shortcomings may be receptive to the suggestions. In addition, some *highly motivated individuals* desirous of pleasing their supervisors at all times may accept suggestions, painful though they may be.

United's program of training tries to develop supervisors to the point where they are sensitive to the possibilities of change. In this way they learn when a direct suggestion will be acted upon and when it will be more profitable to listen and let the individual discover the need for change himself.

However, as the supervisor is a representative of management in the supervisory-employee relationship, and as his opinions have a most important bearing on the employee's work life, he must accept the responsibility for performance appraisal.

This new concept has been in operation for two years. As with other changes, a change of concept in this area is not easy to make—and it takes time. Its general acceptance thus far is excellent, although there is still much more to be done in developing complete understanding and skill in using the program.

THE AUTHORS

A. G. BAYROFF, HELEN R. HAGGERTY, and E. A. RUNDQUIST made their study of the "Validity of Ratings as Related to Rating Techniques and Conditions" at the Personnel Research Branch, Adjutant General's Office, U. S. Department of the Army. Dr. Bayroff is chief of induction and recruitment research, and Dr. Haggerty is research psychologist, at the Personnel Research Branch. Since 1959, Dr. Rundquist has been with the System Development Corporation, Santa Monica, California.

JAMES R. BERKSHIRE and RICHARD W. HIGHLAND prepared their study of forced-choice rating while at the Human Resources Research Center, Chanute Air Force Base, Illinois. Mr. Berkshire is now assistant head of the Department of Psychology, U. S. Naval School of Aviation Medicine, Pensacola, Florida. Dr. Highland is engineering psychologist at Hughes Aircraft Company, Los Angeles.

GEORGE E. BROWN, JR. and ALLAN F. LARSON wrote "Current Trends in Appraisal and Development" for *Personnel* when both were with the Los Angeles City Department of Water and Power. Mr. Larson is now principal job analyst with the Department; Mr. Brown is a California State Assemblyman, representing the forty-fifth district of Los Angeles County.

BERNARD J. COVNER, formerly assistant vice-president of Dunlap and Associates, Inc., is now director of the Man-Management Center, Stamford, Connecticut.

LEE W. COZAN, research psychologist with the U. S. Department of Commerce, was with the U. S. Department of Health, Education and Welfare when his article summarizing studies of the forced-choice rating method was written.

JOEL DEAN, president of Joel Dean Associates, Inc., is an economist and management consultant. He is also professor of business economics at Columbia University and author of a widely used text, *Managerial Economics.*

JOHN C. FLANAGAN and ROBERT K. BURNS developed the employee performance record for use of the Delco-Remy division of the General Motors Corporation, and it has been adopted by other divisions of G. M. Dr. Flanagan is director of research at the American Institute for Research, Pittsburgh. Dr. Burns is executive officer of the Industrial Relations Center and professor of business and social science at the University of Chicago.

EDWIN E. GHISELLI and CLARENCE W. BROWN are co-authors of the book *Personnel and Industrial Psychology,* from which the section "Ranking Methods" is presented here. Both are in the Department of Psychology at the University of California, Berkeley.

STEPHEN HABBE is with the Division of Personnel Administration of the National Industrial Conference Board. His work with the Board has included many surveys and reports concerning appraisal.

William B. Hall is senior vice-president of The Detroit Bank and Trust Company.

E. P. Hollander, now associate professor at the School of International Service, The American University, was at Carnegie Institute of Technology when he prepared his comprehensive study of buddy ratings.

Verne Kallejian, Paula Brown, and Irving R. Weschler were members of the Human Relations Research Group of the Institute of Industrial Relations, University of California, Los Angeles, when their study was written. It is one of several projects carried on by this group for the U. S. Office of Naval Research. Dr. Kallejian, a psychologist, is now in private practice in Los Angeles. Dr. Weschler is now associate professor of personnel management and industrial relations at the Graduate School of Business Administration, University of California in Los Angeles. Dr. Brown is in the Department of Anthropology and Sociology at The Australian National University, Canberra.

Arthur W. Kornhauser is professor of psychology at Wayne State University in Detroit. His article "What are Rating Scales Good For?" is one of the classics on appraisal from the personnel literature.

Marion S. Kellogg is manager of individual development service at General Electric Company. "Appraising the Performance of Management Personnel" is a case study reported to the AMA in 1955. "New Angles in Appraisal" is a previously unpublished speech presented at an AMA Personnel Conference in 1961.

C. H. Lawsche, N. C. Kephart, and E. J. McCormick, authors of an article on the paired comparison technique, are all at Purdue University. Dr. Lawsche is professor of industrial psychology and dean of university extension; Dr. Kephart is professor of psychology; Dr. McCormick is professor of psychology and a member of the Occupational Research Center. (See also under Joseph Tiffin.)

Douglas McGregor, formerly president of Antioch College, is professor of management at Massachusetts Institute of Technology. He is the author of *The Human Side of Enterprise*, 1961, a statement of modern organization theory; and of many articles in professional and management journals, among them the selection presented here.

Norman R. F. Maier is professor of psychology at the University of Michigan. He is the author of several works in the personnel and training fields, including *Psychology in Industry*, a text now in its second edition; *The Appraisal Interview*, 1958; and *Supervisory and Executive Development*, 1957.

P. W. Maloney and J. R. Hinrichs are with the Esso Research and Engineering Company, Linden, New Jersey. Mr. Maloney is assistant manager of employee relations, and Mr. Hinrichs is personnel assistant.

James Burt Miner, who died in 1943, was on the faculty of the Carnegie Institute of Technology.

C. G. Moon and Theodore Hariton describe an appraisal program in the engineering section of a department of the General Electric Company. Mr. Moon is with General Electric; Mr. Hariton is director of the industrial division of the Psychological Corporation.

James W. Parker, Erwin K. Taylor, Richard S. Barrett, and Leon Martens prepared their article as part of a series on rating scale content when all were with the Personnel Research and Development Corporation, Cleveland. Mr. Parker is now assistant head of the Personnel Assessment Branch, U. S. Naval Medical Research Laboratory, U. S. Naval Submarine Base, New London, Connecticut. Mr. Taylor is president of the Personnel Research and Development Corporation. Mr. Barrett is associate professor of management engineering and psychology at New York University. Mr. Martens is deceased.

Donald G. Paterson is emeritus professor of psychology of the University of Minnesota. Before joining the faculty there in 1921, Dr. Paterson was personnel research technician at the Scott Co., Philadelphia. In addition to his work on rating, he is noted for many contributions in the fields of aptitude testing and readability.

Arch Patton, of McKinsey & Company, Management Consultants, is a specialist on executive compensation and appraisal of executive performance.

John J. Pearce, Jr., and D. N. Dertouzos prepared their study of the Ritter Company joint rating plan as staff members of the Institute of Management and Labor Relations, Rutgers University. Mr. Pearce is now a mediator with the New Jersey State Board of Mediation; Mr. Dertouzos is assistant professor at the School of Business Administration, Rider College, Trenton, New Jersey.

Earl G. Planty and Carlos E. Efferson prepared their article on "Counseling Executives After Merit Rating or Evaluation" when both were in New Brunswick, New Jersey. Mr. Planty was with Johnson and Johnson as executive counselor and is now professor of management at the University of Illinois. Mr. Efferson was staff training director of the Chicopee Manufacturing Corporation and is now manager of organization planning, Kaiser Aluminum and Chemical Corp., Oakland, California.

Wellington Powell is vice president of the American Telephone and Telegraph Company.

Kenneth E. Richards is personnel research manager of United Air Lines, Inc.

Marion W. Richardson is with the firm of Richardson, Bellows, Henry & Company, Inc., consultants, New York.

Virgil K. Rowland, assistant to the president of the Detroit Edison Company, New York, has contributed many articles to management publications. His book, *Improving Managerial Performance,* was published in 1958.

Thomas Arthur Ryan is professor of psychology at Cornell University. He is the author of *Work and Effort,* published in 1947, and of *Principles of Industrial Psychology,* published in 1954.

Donald Sisson was assistant chief of the Personnel Research Section of the Adjutant General's Office, U. S. Army, when he wrote his article describing the

Army's forced-choice rating plan, developed during World War II. He is now deceased.

AARON J. SPECTOR conducted his study of "Influences on Merit Ratings" while a member of the faculty at the University of Massachusetts. Subsequently he joined the staff of the Officer Education Research Laboratory, Maxwell Air Force Base; then became head of the Morale and Motivation Research Branch, U. S. Navy Personnel Research Field Activity. Since 1959 Dr. Spector has been vice president of National Analysts, Inc., Philadelphia.

DORIS SPRINGER is now human factors specialist with the System Development Corporation, Santa Monica, California. Her article on "Rating of Candidates for Promotion by Co-workers and Supervisors" is based on her previous work at North American Aviation, Inc.

RONALD TAFT, of the University of Western Australia, Nedlands, received his M.A. from Columbia University and returned to this country in 1949-1950 to obtain his doctorate at the University of California, Berkeley. His extensive review of the literature on "The Ability to Judge People" was prepared, in part, during his stay at the University of California.

ERWIN K. TAYLOR and ROY HASTMAN prepared their study on "Relation of Format and Administration to the Characteristics of Graphic Rating Scales" under a U. S. Office of Naval Research contract with Western Reserve University, where Dr. Hastman was a research associate in Psychological Research Services. Dr. Taylor is president of Personnel Research and Development Corporation, Cleveland; Dr. Hastman is now executive and technical placement specialist at General Electric Company, Flight Propulsion Division, Cincinnati, Ohio.

JOSEPH TIFFIN and ERNEST J. MCCORMICK, co-authors of "Industrial Merit Rating," are both with the Occupational Research Center, Purdue University. The first reading in this book is taken from their well-known text, *Industrial Psychology,* now in its fourth edition. A portion of Dr. Tiffin's chapter in *Rating Employee and Supervisory Performance* (published by the American Management Association), is also included in this book. Dr. McCormick's second contribution is an article, with C. H. Lawsche and N. C. Kephart, on the paired comparison technique.

GUY W. WADSWORTH, JR., is president of the Southern Counties Gas Company of California. His interest in appraisal stems from his earlier work in test development and personnel administration.

ROBERT J. WHERRY, co-author with Erwin K. Taylor of "A Study of Leniency in Two Rating Systems" is professor of psychology at Ohio State University.

THOMAS L. WHISLER is associate professor in the Graduate School of Business, the University of Chicago.

DEAN K. WHITLA and JOHN E. TIRRELL, of Harvard University, studied rating of flight mechanics by various levels of supervisors under an Air Force contract. Dr. Whitla is now director of the Office of Tests, Harvard University; Dr. Tirrell is general secretary of the Alumni Association of the University of Michigan.

ALVIN ZANDER and JOHN GYR prepared their study "Changing Attitudes Toward a Merit Rating System" at the Research Center for Group Dynamics, University of Michigan. Dr. Zander is a professor at the University of Michigan and has served as director of the Research Center for Group Dynamics. Mr. Gyr spent two years at the University of Colorado and is now a research associate at the Mental Health Research Institute, University of Michigan.

INDEX OF NAMES

INDEX OF SUBJECTS